THE DICTIONARY OF CRIMINAL JUSTICE

Sixth Edition

George E. Rush
California State University, Long Beach

With Summaries of Supreme Court Cases Affecting Criminal Justice

Judy Hails
California State University, Long Beach

Dushkin/McGraw-Hill

A Division of The **McGraw-Hill** Companies

Dushkin/McGraw-Hill

*A Division of The **McGraw·Hill** Companies*

Cover © 2003 PhotoDisc, Inc.
Cover Design   *Lara M. Johnson*

Library of Congress Catalog Card Number: 99-74549

ISBN 0-07-295112-5

Printed in the United States of America

10 9 8 7 6 5 4 3 2 1

http://www.mhhe.com

CONTENTS

To my family—my children, Susan and Michael, and their families

ABOUT THE AUTHOR

George E. Rush, after retiring from the United States Air Force (Security Police, MSGT), received his B.S. and M.S. degrees in criminology from California State University, Long Beach, and his Ph.D. in government from Claremont Graduate School. He is a professor at California State University at Long Beach, in the Department of Criminal Justice, and serves as the editor-in-chief for the *Journal of Contemporary Criminal Justice*. He is a member of the California Peace Officers Associations' Standards and Ethics Committee; past director of the Center for Criminal Justice Research and Training; served two years as the chairman of the Public Safety Committee, City of La Mirada, CA; and is a reserve officer with the Los Alamitos Police Department. Dr. Rush is also a founding member of Death Penalty Focus, a California-based abolitionist movement, and hoods memberships on the American Society of Criminology, the Academy of Criminal Justice Sciences, and the Western Society of Criminology. He is the author of *Malfunction* and co-author with Paul M. Whisenand of *Police Supervision: Back to the Basics*, and *Police Supervision: The Fifteen Responsibilities*. His research and writing have been published in numerous academic and professional journals.

PREFACE

The criminal justice student, researcher, or practitioner continually encounters certain words, names, personalities, court cases, events, phrases, and terms that by their selective nature have somewhat special meaning.

The Dictionary of Criminal Justice is intended to compile in one reference volume information that could otherwise be found only by tediously searching through a myriad of interdisciplinary literature—for the study of criminal justice and its process crosses, blends, and overlaps several disciplines.

As a result, this book satisfies a long-recognized need. This ready-reference volume will enable the instructor as well as the student, practitioner, and layperson to quickly pinpoint the object of a search. The scope goes far beyond conventional coverage, as political, psychological, historical, sociological, economic, statistical, and organizational aspects are included.

This dictionary is a comprehensive attempt to cover terms associated with the wide spectrum of law enforcement, courts, probation, parole, and corrections and cites information and information sources particular to each area.

To reduce the overall length, cross-references have been minimized by listing most multiple-word entries under their first word. In some cases, it is necessary to look under the more important word to find the desired entry.

This edition contains, for the first time, a compilation of Web sites that will lead the reader to key statistics, research, and resources that expand the scope of this book, and organizations of interest to law enforcement and criminal justice professionals and students.

Simply stated, *The Dictionary of Criminal Justice, Sixth Edition*, defines the terms commonly used in the broad, interdisciplinary field of criminal justice.

ACKNOWLEDGMENTS

The author is indebted to the following individuals who contributed their time, effort, and expertise in the several editions of *The Dictionary of Criminal Justice:*

My colleague Judith (Judy) Kaci, L. .M., Department of Criminal Justice CSULG, who compiled all legal cases cited in this dictionary, and my other supporting faculty members: Drs. Paul M. Whisenand, A.C. Germann (Emeritus), Ronald Vogel, Dean Champion, and Harvey Morley, Professional assistance was provided by: Leo E. Pert (retired Chief of Police, Irvine, CA); Chief Mike McCrary and members of the Los Alamitos Police Department; SEARCH Group; NIJ Reference Service; John Mattingly, Los Angeles Police Department; City Manager Oliver (Lee) Drummond, Sanger, CA; Hilton C. Hayes, MO; Marvin DeRose, WA; Rober Carter, Ph.D., U.S. Military Academy, West Point; Capt. James Nunn, San Bernardino County Sheriff's Department, G. Thomas Gichoff, D.Crm., San Diego State University, who provided a wealth of information, data, and charts; Catherine Leonard, who diligently and professionally edited the fourth and fifth editions; and finally, my mentor, Albert J. Lilly (USAF-ret). Special thanks goes to Bob Weaver, of Veritech Publishing Services, for his help in editing the Sixth Edition.

THE DICTIONARY OF CRIMINAL JUSTICE

Sixth Edition

With
Summaries of
Supreme Court
Cases
Affecting
Criminal Justice

Part I

THE
DICTIONARY
OF
CRIMINAL
JUSTICE

A

abandonment. (1) The relinquishment of a claim or privilege. (2) In marine law, the relinquishment, by the insured to the underwriters, of what may remain of the property insured.

abate. To do away with; annul; remit. To become void.

abatement. A legal process designed to rid properties of nuisances that occur in the course of narcotic and/or vice activity. In order for a property to be abated, the illegal activity must be prolonged and continuous. If the owner is uncooperative, the abatement procedures require an extensive investigation followed by civil court proceedings. Abatement documentation involves: (1) Case Summary (provides basic description of the problem); (2) Property Owner Information; (3) Property Information (legal description); (4) Photos; (5) Arrest Reports; and (6) Officer Summary. *See also* nuisance

ABA transit numbers. A numerical code developed by the American Bankers' Association (ABA) to route checks to the bank of origin. The code, which is printed in the upper right-hand corner, identifies the city or state of the bank the check was drawn against, the name of the bank, and the Federal Reserve Bank district. The code key is held by the ABA.

abduction. (1) The taking of a female, a man's wife, a child, or a ward, without his or her consent or consent of parents or guardian, by fraud, persuasion, or open violence. (2) Unlawfully taking away any maid, widow, or wife contrary to her will. In common law, a taking for money and a marriage or defilement are essential to the completion of the offense. *See also* seduction

abeyance. A state of suspension; being undetermined; in expectation.

ab inconvenient (Lat., lit. "from inconvenience or hardship"). A term applied in cases where, because of inconvenience or practical impossibility, the prosecution can't establish a fact which is part of its case.

ab initio (Lat., lit. "from the beginning"). The first act or the beginning of a state or condition. (A void marriage is of no effect *ab initio*.)

abjuration. The renunciation under oath of one's citizenship or some other right or privilege.

abnormal psychology. The specialized field that studies behavioral disorders such as mental illness and mental retardation. Abnormal psychologists search for causes, explain behavioral disorders, and provide principles to guide prevention and treatment.

abnormal sex. A generic term for all criminalized or devalued sexual behaviors except adultery and fornication.

abolitionists. Term now applied to those who oppose capital punishment. Public opposition to the death penalty is said to have originated with Dr. Benjamin Rush, a Philadelphia physician and reformer, signer of the Declaration of Independence, opponent of alcohol and tobacco use, and champion of psychiatry.

abortion and birth control laws. A century ago, the dissemination of birth control information was prohibited by the Comstock Law of 1873. Through the efforts of pioneers like Margaret Sanger, however, such dissemination by physicians was legalized in 1937. In 1965 the Supreme Court, in *Griswold v. Connecticut*, declared laws regulating birth control unconstitutional on the grounds that they infringed the right to marital privacy. Demand for abortion had risen in the 1960s with evidence that rubella (German measles) and drugs like thalidomide could cause fetal deformities. Decisions as to whether an abortion was legal—that is, necessary to preserve the mother's life—were being made by boards of doctors. In 1962 the American Law Institute (ALI) recommended, in its proposal for a Model Penal Code, that abortion be permitted (a) when the mother's mental or physical health was in jeopardy, (b) when there

1

was significant risk of fetal deformity, and (c) in cases of rape or incest. In 1967 the American Medical Association reversed its opposition to abortion and supported the ALI recommendation. The same year, Colorado became the first state to liberalize its abortion laws according to the new guidelines, and several other states followed—sometimes with slight variations from the ALI model. Controversy over abortion often centers on whether a fetus, before the 20th week of pregnancy, is a living human being, as the Roman Catholic Church asserts it is. Since 1869, Church leaders have stated the belief that life begins at the moment of conception. Feminist and other pressure groups argue for a woman's right to control her own body. There are no abortion laws that force a woman to undergo abortion against her will. Restrictive abortion laws have been challenged in the federal courts. It has been contended that the right to have an abortion is protected by the Ninth Amendment, since at the time this amendment was adopted in 1791, women enjoyed such a liberty under common law. This view was upheld in 1973 in a landmark Supreme Court decision, *Roe v. Wade*, which ruled that abortion could be barred only during the last 10 weeks of pregnancy. In 1990 Connecticut became the first state to give women the legal right to abortion in a law intended to stand even if the Supreme Court should reverse its 1973 decision. The most recent challenge to *Roe v. Wade* was *Planned Parenthood of Southeastern Pennsylvania v. Casey* in 1992. In June 1994, the federal Freedom of Access to Clinic Entrances Act was passed in an attempt to prevent harassment of women entering health clinics known to provide abortion services. The first person to be charged, tried, and convicted under this law was former Presbyterian minister Paul Hill, in Pensacola, FL, on October 13, 1994.

Selected Supreme Court decisions on abortion:

1973: *Roe v. Wade.* Legalized abortion during the first six months of pregnancy.

1976: *Planned Parenthood of Central Missouri v. Danforth.* Invalidated require-ment that a married woman obtain consent from her husband or a minor from one parent.

1981: *H. L. v. Matheson.* Upheld law requiring doctors to notify parents of minors seeking abortions.

1983: *City of Akron v. Akron Center for Reproductive Health.* Struck down requirements for preabortion counseling, parental consent, and waiting period.

1986: *Thornburgh v. American Counsel of Obstetricians and Gynecologists.* Struck down requirements for preabortion counseling.

1989: *Webster v. Reproductive Health Services.* Upheld law restricting use of public facilities and funds for abortions.

1991: *Rust v. Sullivan.* Barred federally funded family planning clinics from providing information about abortion.

1992: *Planned Parenthood v. Casey.* The Court upheld Pennsylvania law: (a) doctors must counsel women on risks of abortion and alternatives; (b) 24-hour waiting period; (c) a minor must get one parent's consent or judge's approval; (d) doctors must keep detailed records of abortions and the reason for performing late-term abortions. This decision overturned the provision that a married woman must notify her husband of her intent to obtain an abortion.

abrogate. To annul by authority or by a later enactment; abolish, repeal.

ABSCAM. This term is a contraction from "Arab scam" referring to a 1980 FBI undercover investigation into political corruption involving several members of the U.S. Congress and a number of state and local political figures. Agents posing as wealthy Arab businessmen offered bribes to several members of Congress in exchange for political favors. The resulting exchanges were secretly videotaped and used to secure the conviction of one senator and six members of the House of Representatives, three of whom resigned to avoid expulsion, while three were defeated in their reelection bids prior to their court convictions.

abscond. To leave one's usual residence or to conceal oneself, usually in order to avoid legal proceedings.

Academy, American Police (APA). Founded in 1977. Publishes *Crime Investigator Bulletin* (quarterly). Address: Lock Box 15350, Chevy Chase, MD 20815.

Academy of Criminal Justice Sciences (ACJS). Founded in 1963. Address: 7319 Hanover Parkway, Suite C, Greenbelt, MD 20770. Tel: (301) 446-6300 (800) 757-2257. Web: www.acjs.org.

accelerant. A substance that increases the speed of a reaction; for example, a flammable liquid used by an arsonist.

access control. The control of pedestrian and vehicular traffic through entrances and exits of a protected area or premises.

accessory. A person who helps a criminal either before or after a crime is committed, but who is not present during the crime.

accessory after the fact. Anyone who, after a felony has been committed, knowingly harbors or conceals the felon, or helps him or her avoid arrest, trial, conviction, or punishment.

accessory before the fact. One who helps another to commit a crime but is absent when the crime is committed.

accident investigation (AI). Includes search for physical evidence; taking measurements and photographs, interviews, sketching/diagrams. The goals of AI are to determine the causes of traffic collisions, which can include human behavior, mechanical failure, or environmental factors.

accomplice. One who knowingly and voluntarily aids another in committing a criminal offense.

accountability. The state of being responsible and punishable for a criminal act; this responsibility is reduced or abolished in some cases because of age, mental defect, or other reasons.

Accreditation for Corrections, Commission on. Founded in 1974 as a private, non-profit organization to improve the administration and operation of correctional agencies through the implementation of an accreditation program. The commission revises standards in conjunction with the American Correctional Association (ACA). Address: 4380 Forbes Boulevard, Lanham, MD 20706-4322; telephone (800) ACA-JOIN.

Accreditation for Law Enforcement Agencies, Inc., Commission on. Provides assistance to agencies in the accreditation process. Address: 4242 B Chain Bridge Rd., Fairfax, VA 22030; telephone (800) 368-3757.

accuracy of firearms. The accuracy of firearms depends on many factors. The barrel must be as nearly perfect as mechanical skill can make it. It must be of uniform size of bore its entire length, and the grooves of the rifling must be of uniform width and depth throughout, with no defects. The fit of the bullet is next in importance: it must be of correct diameter, hardness, density, lubrication, etc. The powder charge must be exactly the same for any given cartridge, and the same lot of powder must be used. The primers must have a uniform amount of priming composition.

accusation. Accusations of guilt may be made by complaints or affidavits, and sworn to by injured persons or by police officers, especially in minor offenses. Accusations of felonies are made by indictments found by grand juries or by information filed by prosecuting attorneys, generally following preliminary examinations in magistrates' courts.

accusation, modes of. A person charged with a crime may be prosecuted following (a) an indictment or a presentment upon oath by a grand jury; (b) a coroner's inquisition in cases of homicide (where authorized by law); (c) information proffered by the proper prosecuting officer without the intervention of a grand jury; and (d) a complaint or information given under oath by a private person.

accusatorial system. A system of administering criminal justice law, like those of the

United States and Canada, that is based on the assumption that justice and truth can best be attained through a process that resembles a contest between opposing parties—the accused, or defendant, and the accuser, or plaintiff, who can be either an individual or a government.

accusatory stage. The part of a police investigation that is carried out once suspects have been identified.

accused. The defendant in a criminal case; a prisoner.

accused persons, rights of. As stated in the Sixth Amendment, the right to a speedy and public trial by impartial jury in the state where the crime was committed; the right to be informed of the nature and cause of the accusation; the right to confront witnesses in court (cross-examination); the right to subpoena witnesses in favor of the accused; and the right to counsel. Although the Sixth Amendment originally applied only to federal courts, Supreme Court decisions interpreting the due process clause of the Fourteenth Amendment have found that most of these restrictions also apply to state courts. The Sixth Amendment evolved from the early colonists' grievance against George II that the benefit of trial by jury was withheld from many of them. The Supreme Court has clarified most of the provisions of the Amendment. In 1968, for instance, the Court ruled that states must provide a jury trial in criminal cases. Although this right is provided by the Sixth Amendment, it does not include the constitutional right for trial without a jury. A defendant may waive his right to a jury trial in favor of being tried by a judge, but the government and the judge must consent to the waiver.

The demand for a speedy and public trial stemmed from the Old World's secret inquisitions and long questioning. Thus far, there is no common definition of a "speedy" trial, and some defendants wait more than a year before being brought to trial. The due process clause requires public trials in the state courts and establishes the right to subpoena witnesses to appear and testify, even if they are unwilling.

The requirement that the trial be held where the crime was committed was included because the colonists were transported to England for trial. So far, the Supreme Court has not extended this Fourteenth Amendment clause to the states.

The right to counsel stems from the colonists' experience with English common law, under which the accused had to rely on the judge for counsel. In 1963, this right to counsel was also applied to the states. Decisions in 1964 and 1966 stated that, if a person is too poor to hire counsel, it must be provided for him, and that the right to counsel extends to the time before the trial.

ACLU. *See* American Civil Liberties Union

acquit. To absolve a person legally from an accusation of criminal guilt.

acquittal. A release or discharge (as from an accusation), especially by verdict of a jury.

action. A lawsuit; a proceeding taken in a court of law. A civil action is taken to enforce or protect the rights of an individual; a criminal action, to punish an offender.

ACTION. An independent federal agency established in 1971 to coordinate various voluntary service programs within the federal government, including Volunteers in Service to America (VISTA), working to aid impoverished communities, and the Peace Corps. ACTION also administers the Foster Grandparents Program, the Retired Senior Volunteers Program (RSVP), and the National Center for Service Learning. RSVP volunteers have augmented local law enforcement agencies in assuming many tasks, such as crime prevention and parking restriction enforcement. The central ACTION office in Washington, DC, directs domestic and overseas operations.

active intrusion sensor. A device that detects the presence of an intruder within its range. Examples are an ultrasonic motion detector, a radio-frequency motion detector, and a photoelectric alarm system. *See also* passive intrusion sensor

act of God. An inevitable event, one which occurs without human aid or intervention (e.g., hurricane, flood, or tornado) and thus, for which no one can be blamed. On this ground, carriers are released from liability for loss, and a person is in some cases discharged from covenant or contract.

acts of state legislatures. State legislatures, unlike Congress, have inherent power to declare acts criminal and to impose penalties for acts. Their power in these respects, however, is not absolute. Their enactments must adhere to all provisions of the U.S. Constitution, the state constitution, and valid acts of Congress.

acts of territorial legislatures. Territorial legislatures are created by Congress, and their powers are limited to those conferred upon them by that body. Their legislative power extends to all rightful subjects of legislation not inconsistent with the Constitution and laws of the United States.

ACT-UP (AIDS Coalition to Unleash Power). A radical group involved in civil disobedience to raise public awareness regarding inadequate government funding for AIDS research. Founded by Larry Kramer, who reportedly believes in anger and envisions a gay movement based on the Israeli guerrilla group Irgun. Kramer says of Irgun, "They started fires. They threw bombs. They kidnapped. They assassinated. They won."

actus reus (Lat.). The requirement that, for an act to be considered criminal, the individual must have committed an overt act that resulted in harm.

Adamsite. (Diphenylaminechlorarsine chloride, DM). This war gas (also a mob- and riot-control gas) has a rapid rate of action. Only about 1 minute is required for temporary incapacitation. It causes the same symptoms as dishenychloroarsine (DA), but the long-term effects develop more slowly. Also called a "sternutator" or "sneeze gas," and can cause vomiting and diarrhea. It was developed at the end of World War II by Roger Adams, an American.

addict. One who habitually uses drugs, especially morphine or heroin, to the extent that cessation of such use causes severe physical or psychological trauma or both.

addiction. (From Lat. verb *addicere*, to bind a person to something). Socially, this term refers to compulsive use or pursuit of a substance, e.g., alcohol, or activity, e.g., gambling, despite adverse consequences. Pharmacologically, addiction has three components: tolerance, the need for progressively higher doses of a substance to produce the desired effect; dependence, the need to maintain a certain dosage or level in order to avoid withdrawal symptoms; and compulsion, or a powerful craving for the substance or activity. The World Health Organization (WHO) defined addiction in this way in 1957 but by 1965 had replaced the term in favor of "drug dependence."

ad hoc committee. A committee established for the purpose of investigating or otherwise handling a specific matter. Generally an ad hoc committee is created as a temporary subcommittee of a standing committee. Both houses of Congress establish numerous such committees, one of which was the original Committee on Un-American Activities.

ad hominem (Lat., lit. "to the man"). An argument against an opponent personally instead of against the substance of the argument.

adjective law. That part of law prescribing the method or procedure for carrying out the rights and obligations of persons. Includes the code of procedure, e.g., the manner of executing a warrant of arrest, extradition proceedings, the presenting of an indictment, and appeal procedure. Conversely, "substantive law" defines the rights of persons which the courts are bound to administer and protect.

adjournment. Termination of a session or hearing; postponement to some other time or place.

adjudge. To rule upon judicially; to grant through a judicial process.

adjudication. The process of judicial settlement; the settlement itself.

adjudication withheld. A court decision, made at any point after filing of a criminal complaint, to continue court proceedings but stop short of pronouncing judgment. The usual purpose of such a decision is to avoid the undesirable effects of conviction, which can include both unnecessary harm to the offender and unnecessary expense or harm to the public interest. "Withholding adjudication" places the subject in a status where the court retains jurisdiction but will not reopen proceedings unless the person violates a condition of behavior.

adjudicatory hearing. In juvenile justice usage, the fact-finding process wherein the juvenile court determines whether or not there is sufficient evidence to sustain the allegations in a petition. An adjudicatory hearing occurs after a juvenile petition has been filed and after a detention hearing, if one is necessary. If the petition is not sustained, no further formal court action is taken. If it is sustained, the next step is a disposition hearing to determine the most appropriate treatment or care for the juvenile. These last two stages of judicial activity concerning juveniles are often combined in a single hearing, referred to as a "bifurcated hearing," meaning a process that encompasses both adjudication of the case and disposition of the person.

administration of criminal justice. Comprises the following subjects: criminal procedure, police organization and administration, prosecution, accusation, the defense of accused persons, the organization of courts, pleadings, arraignment and trial, evidence, judgment and sentence, appeals, probation, parole, pardon, penology and prison administration, juvenile courts, special procedures for crime prevention, and laws designed to change social and industrial conditions in order to prevent crime.

administrative courts. (1) Specialized courts in western Europe that are organized in a separate hierarchy, that apply administrative law, and that have jurisdiction over all cases in which the government or officers of the government are concerned. Generally, administrative courts have a reputation for fairness in protecting the interests of citizens, for rendering speedy justice, for invalidating administrative orders which lack proper statutory authority, and for granting compensation for injuries suffered at the hands of officers or employees of the government. (2) Those courts not created under Article II of the U.S. Constitution and that are usually called legislative courts.

administrative judge. A judicial officer who supervises administrative functions and performs administrative tasks for a given court, sometimes in addition to performing regular judicial functions. Typical duties of administrative judges are (a) assigning cases to other judicial officers within a court; (b) setting court policy on procedure; and (c) performing other tasks of an administrative nature, such as those concerned with personnel and budgets.

administrative law. *See* law, administrative

administrative services. The specialized bureau in a traditionally organized police department responsible for community relations, planning and development, code enforcement, personnel recruitment and training, and disciplinary review.

administrator (m), administratix (f). One to whom letters of administration have been granted by a court and who administers an estate.

admiralty. The court dealing with maritime questions; the branch of law administered by such courts.

admiralty jurisdiction. The authority to try cases arising under maritime law. It is concerned with (a) wartime captures, collisions, piracy, lesser crimes, and torts on the high seas, navigable lakes, and rivers; and (b) with contracts for shipments of goods, insurance, and wages of seamen. It is not concerned with crimes and other incidents committed on board ships in port. Original jurisdiction in admiralty cases is exercised by federal district courts acting as admiralty courts.

admiralty law. Maritime law dealing with ships and the sea, including events and transactions, both civil and criminal, occurring at or involving the sea. Although now administered by national courts and affected by municipal law, the legal principles of admiralty law, being a composite of customs of the sea and maritime nations, antedate even Roman law and transcend national borders.

admissible. Capable of being admitted; in a trial, such evidence as the judge allows to be introduced into the proceeding.

admission. (1) A voluntary statement or acknowledgment, made by a party, that is admissible in court as evidence against that party. (2) The act by which attorneys and counselors become officers of a court and are licensed to practice law. The requirements for admission to the bar vary greatly in different states.

adolescence. The age between puberty (14 for males, 12 for females) and majority.

Adult Education Act (1964). A law providing federal funds for schooling to remedy deficiencies in communication, computational, or social skills that substantially limit adults' employment opportunities.

Adult Internal Management System (AIMS). Also known as the Quay system, AIMS is a process for evaluating inmates' behavior during their entry into the prison system and incarceration. An analysis includes five factors or dimensions of behavior.

adultery. Voluntary sexual intercourse between a married person and a partner other than his or her spouse. Most societies have had customs or laws relating to adultery. Some have treated it as a private wrong to be handled by the families concerned; others have made adultery a crime subject to severe penalties, even death. Today, adultery is still a crime in many parts of the United States, although the law is rarely enforced. Adultery is grounds for civil divorce in all states.

ad valorem tax. Tax on a percentage of an item's value, such as sales taxes or real estate taxes.

adversary proceeding. A legal proceeding involving contesting or opposing parties.

adversary system. The Anglo-American system for resolving both civil and criminal disputes. It is characterized by a contest between the initiating party, called the plaintiff in civil proceedings and the prosecutor (representing the state) in criminal proceedings, and the responding party, called the defendant. The case is presided over by a judge, who adjudicates and renders final judgment for one party or the other. The judge sometimes has the aid of a jury for finding disputed facts, acts on the basis of the evidence presented by the parties in oper court, and makes a decision in light of the applicable law. *See also* inquisitorial system; party-dominated process

advertising, legal. The American Bar Association (ABA) traditionally prohibited lawyers from advertising, but in June 1977 the Supreme Court ruled that lawyers may advertise their services and customary fees for those services. The Court held that a ban on advertising was a violation of the free speech guarantees of the First Amendment. The ABA then adopted a code of guidelines for advertising for ABA members.

advocate. The attorney who speaks or writes in support of a client's cause.

affiance. To assure by a pledge, such as a mutual promise or agreement between a man and a woman that they will marry.

affiant. A person who creates and signs an affidavit.

affidavit. Written statement made under oath usually before a notary public or other authorized person.

affirmance. A pronouncement by a higher court that the case in question was rightly decided by the lower court from which the case was appealed.

affirmation. Positive declaration or assertion that the witness will tell the truth; not made under oath.

affirmative action. A general term for statutes and procedures designed to redress wrongs committed against minority groups in hiring and promotion practices. The Office of Federal Contract Compliance Programs (OFCCP) requires that all federal contractors make a positive effort to employ women and minority group members in numbers corresponding to the demographics of the available labor force. There appear to be conflicts between Title VII of the Civil Rights Act and the OFCCP standards for affirmative action programs.

affray. A fight involving two or more persons in some public place, and which disturbs the peace. An affray differs from a riot in that it is not considered premeditated.

aftercare. The status or program membership of a juvenile who has been committed to a treatment or confinement facility, conditionally released from the facility, and placed in a supervisory and/or treatment program.

agar composition. A substance used to create molds of evidence in criminal cases, such as footprints. More elastic than plaster when set, it is sufficiently resilient to pick up more complex impressions. "Alginates" also have the advantage of being usable cold without losing their elasticity.

age. With children under the age of 14, it must be shown that they have the capacity to understand that certain acts are wrong. In common law, children under the age of 7 were incapable of committing a crime.

agent. A person employed to act for another (the principal) in dealing with third parties. Principals are generally bound and liable for (other than criminal) acts by their agents.

agent provocateur. (1) An unofficial police agent who associates with politically disaffected groups or persons suspected of crime to win their confidence or encourage them to resist authority and commit illegal acts, and who subsequently informs on them. (2) An undercover individual hired by one nation to encourage disaffected elements of another nation's citizenry to commit acts of sabotage, sedition, or treason.

age of consent. The youngest age at which a female may consent to sexual intercourse without her partner's being liable to a rape charge. In most states it is 18.

age of maximum criminality. That age, when judging from criminal statistics, a person is most likely to get into conflict with the criminal law. In the case of serious offenses against property (robbery, burglary, and larceny), that age seems to be 16 to 20 years; a slightly older age group leads in offenses against the person. Offenses against public order are most common in the third decade of life. Generally speaking, crime rates decline somewhat after the age of 20, and very rapidly after the age of 40.

agglutinin. Antibody substance in the blood that causes a clumping of blood cells or bacteria in liquid suspension. This property is used (e.g., in a crime laboratory) in blood typing.

aggravated assault. Unlawful, intentional causing of serious bodily injury with or without a deadly weapon; unlawful, intentional attempting or threatening of serious bodily injury or death with a deadly or dangerous weapon.

aggravating circumstances. Circumstances relating to the commission of a crime which cause its gravity to be greater than that of the average instance of the given type of offense. Examples: the causing of serious bodily injury, the use of a deadly or dangerous weapon, or the accidental or intentional commission of one crime in the course of committing another crime or as a means to commit another crime.

aggravation. (1) Any action or circumstance which increases the magnitude of a crime or its penalties. (2) Any action or circumstance which intensifies the seriousness of a dispute and makes its solution more difficult.

aggression. The attempt by one state to impair another state's political sovereignty or territorial integrity by forcible means devoid of moral or legal justification. Aggression remains one of the most challenging areas of study because of the elusiveness of an adequate definition of the term. Some researchers have applied it to any act that inflicts pain or suffering on another individual; others feel that a proper definition must include some notion of intent to do harm. Still others use a situational definition, so that what might be described as aggression in one context might not be considered as such in others.

agnomen. A nickname or additional name

aid and abet. To assist in the commission of a crime through words, acts, presence, or other encouragement and support.

AIDS (acquired immune deficiency syndrome). Fatal disease caused by a virus known as the human immunodeficiency virus (HIV), which infects and destroys certain white blood cells, undermining the body's ability to resist infection. A person can be infected with HIV for years without developing symptoms of AIDS, and can transmit the virus in the absence of symptoms. Victims do not die from AIDS itself, but from "opportunistic infections" such as pneumonia, malignancies, and a type of skin cancer. AIDS is transmitted via exposure to contaminated blood, semen, and vaginal secretions; it occurs primarily through sexual intercourse, needle-sharing by intravenous drug users, and blood transfusions. By 2002, 886,575 cases of AIDS among Americans had been reported to the Centers for Disease Control, with 40,000 new cases predicted for each year. The Connecticut Correctional Institution at Somers has the services of a thanatologist to address the needs of terminally ill inmates infected with AIDS. *See also* assault; thanatology

Aid to Incarcerated Mothers. Founded in 1980. Serves women inmates' needs throughout Massachusetts, providing counseling on parenting and substance abuse, weekly visits with children, and advocacy. Address: 32 Rutland Street, 4th Floor, Boston, MA 02108; telephone (617) 536-0058.

Airport Security Council (ASC). Founded in 1968, the ASC is responsible for the development and administration of air cargo loss-prevention (e.g., theft-prevention) programs for airlines that utilize the three New York/New Jersey metropolitan airports. Headquartered at 570 Elmont Road, Elmont, NY 11003.

alarm, class A. A fire protection specification that requires alarm operation even in the event of a single break or ground fault in the signal line.

alarm, class B. A fire protection specification that requires the detection of an alarm, a single break, or a ground fault in a signal line. A break or ground fault causes further alarms to go undetected.

alarm station. (1) A manually activated device installed at a fixed location to transmit an alarm signal in response to an emergency, such as a concealed holdup button in a bank teller's cage. (2) A well-marked emergency control unit, installed in fixed locations usually accessible to the public and used to summon help in emergencies. The control unit contains either a manually activated switch or a telephone connected to fire or police headquarters or a telephone answering service.

alarm system. An assembly of equipment and devices designed and arranged to signal the presence of a situation urgently requiring attention, such as an unauthorized entry.

Albastone. A commercially prepared material for casting footprints and similar indentations and used by some investigators instead of plaster of Paris.

Alcatraz. A 12-acre rock island in the middle of the San Francisco harbor, discovered by the Spanish land expedition of Portola in 1769 and named *Isla de Alcatraces* (island of the pelicans), since it was white with pelicans and guano. The island was the site of the first lighthouse on the West Coast, and of the first army garrison. When it had been refitted as a maximum-security prison, James Johnson served as the first warden from 1934 to 1948, followed by Edwin Swope (1948–1955), Paul Madigan (1955–1961), and Olin Blackwell (1961–1963), who was the last warden. Alcatraz accepted only high-risk prisoners from other federal prisons. Upon its closing, inmates were sent to the federal prison in Marion, IL.

Alcoholics Anonymous (AA). A voluntary fellowship, founded in 1935 by New York stockbroker Bill Wilson and surgeon Bob Smith from Akron, OH. Concerned solely with the personal recovery and continued sobriety of the alcoholic members who turn to the organization for help. AA does not engage in research or medical or psychiatric treatment, nor does it endorse causes or affiliate with other groups. AA is self-supporting through its own membership and declines contributions from all outside sources. Although AA may cooperate with other organizations concerned with problems of alcohol abuse, and its members often take part in outside endeavors related to alcoholism research or treatment, the members preserve personal anonymity in the public information media. AA has been the major influence in gaining acceptance of the disease concept of alcoholism. The aim of AA members is to help each other maintain their sobriety and to share their recovery experience freely with anyone who may have an alcohol problem. The AA program consists basically of Twelve Suggested Steps designed for personal recovery from alcoholism. Several hundred thousand alcoholic people have achieved sobriety in this way, but members recognize that their program is not always effective with all alcoholic persons and that some individuals may require professional counseling or treatment. The General Service Board of Alcoholics Anonymous publishes the monthly *AA Grapevine* and other materials. Alcoholics Anonymous also runs Alateen and AlAnon for families of alcoholics.

Alcohol Information Library, National Clearinghouse for. Founded in 1972 by the U.S. Department of Health and Human Services, National Institute on Alcohol Abuse and Alcoholism. Provides a collection of alcohol-related information and publishes *Alcohol Research and Health* (quarterly). Address: 6000 Executive Blvd., Willco Building, Bethesda, MD 20892-7003.

alcoholism. The chronic, progressive, treatable disease of alcohol dependency or addiction, victims of which tend to relapse.

Alford plea. Term for the technique of refusing to admit guilt while expressing unwillingness to risk a federal court trial.

algolagnia. Sexual satisfaction derived from the anticipation or actual infliction of pain or suffering; it is a type of sadomasochism.

alias dictus (Lat.). In its common use, this term is contracted to "alias" and means "otherwise called."

alibi. A type of defense in a criminal prosecution that proves the accused could not have committed the crime with which he or she is charged, since evidence offered shows the accused was in another place at the time the crime was committed.

alien. Noncitizen, resident or transient, who owes allegiance to a foreign government. Aliens are subject to the laws of their country of residence. In the United States, resident aliens can be drafted and own property, but have no voting rights.

alienate. To transfer property or a right to another.

alienation. A sense of estrangement or separation of individuals from community or society; a lack of cohesion with the surrounding environment, people, and social institutions, or estrangement of a married couple.

Alien Documentation, Identification, and Telecommunications (ADIT). The computer system operated by the Immigration and Naturalization Service.

alimony. The allowance made by court order to an individual for support from his or her spouse in a divorce case. When the award is made while the divorce suit is pending and it includes money for support as well as for legal fees incurred in the suit, it is called "alimony *pendete lite.*"

allegation. An assertion of what a party to an action expects to prove in court.

allege. (1) To assert; to set forth. (2) To plead.

Allen charge. Term for instructions given by a judge to a jury that is having difficulty reaching a decision. Such instructions are prohibited in some states.

alley. Any highway with a roadway no more than 25 feet wide that is used primarily for access to the rear or side entrances of abutting property; a narrow highway in a city or a narrow access road in a suburban or rural area.

allocution. A prisoner's answer (which is recorded in the trial proceedings) to the court's query as to whether or not judgment should be pronounced against the prisoner if he or she is convicted.

alpha (code). A set of authorized words standing for the letters of the alphabet, used in transmitting messages when a possibility of a misunderstanding exists. It supersedes the old ABLE code. The following are authorized code words: Alpha, Bravo, Charlie, Delta, Echo, Foxtrot, Gold, Hotel, India, Juliet, Kilo, Lima, Mike, November, Oscar, Papa, Quebec, Romeo, Sierra, Tango, Uniform, Victor, Whisky, X-ray, Yankee, and Zulu. *See also* Code, International

Alston Wilkes Society. Founded in 1962 and named for the late Rev. Eli Alston Wilkes, Jr., the Methodist minister who founded it, this private correctional services agency assists prison inmates, their families, and those being released. Publishes a quarterly newsletter. Has different locations in South Carolina, with the state office at 3519 Medical Drive, Columbia, SC 29203-6517.

altercation. A fracas, fight, fuss, or noisy quarrel. *See also* affray; riot

alternative writ. A writ granted on ex parte affidavits and requiring the person to do a certain thing or show cause why he or she should not be compelled to do so. *See also ex parte*

altruism. Helping behavior that occurs at some cost to the helper. Altruism is usually motivated intrinsically, not by observable rewards or threats of punishment, and is therefore characterized by an unselfish motive.

Alveolar Air Breath Alcohol System. Trade name of a device to test the breath to ascertain a blood-alcohol ratio.

AMA. *See* American Medical Association

amateur radio. *See* American Radio Relay League

ambisexual. another term for bisexual.

amentia. In medical jurisprudence, insanity or idiocy.

amercement. The act of punishing by an exactment, assessment, or deprivation. A pecuniary penalty in the nature of a fine.

American Academy for Professional Law Enforcement. Founded in 1973, the Academy focuses on education and development programs in the areas of law enforcement professional and ethical standards. Its membership consists of practitioners, educators, planners, and research personnel. Headquartered at 444 W. 56th Street, Suite 2312, New York, NY 10019.

American Academy of Judicial Education. Organized by the American Judges Association, its objective is to provide educational programs and services to state court judges. The academy presents 18 national programs annually in addition to assisting the 50 states, U.S. territories, and Puerto Rico in presenting in-state judicial education seminars and conferences. Publishes *Recent U.S. Supreme Court Decisions* (annually). Address: 539 Woodward Building, 1426 H Street, NW, Washington, DC 20005.

American Association of Probation and Parole. Provides technical assistance and information regarding probation and parole systems and related court-ordered treatment programs, including community supervision. Address: Council of State Governments, Ironworks Pike, P.O. Box 11910, Lexington, KY 40578.

American Association of Wardens and Superintendents. A national group of correctional administrators, which can provide information, surveys, consultation, and assistance when requested. Publishes the *Grapevine* (quarterly). Address: P.O. Box 100, Jean, NV 89019.

American Bar Association (ABA). A professional association, comprising attorneys who have been admitted to the bar in any of the 50 states, and a registered lobby. The organization's basic objectives are to advance the science of jurisprudence, ensure the fair administration of justice and uniformity of legislation throughout the country, and maintain the standards of the profession. Through its committees, the ABA provides information, research, and technical assistance on various issues including substance abuse, crime and violence prevention, and children's needs. The Special Committee on the Drug Crisis, for example, provides technical assistance on drug courts and linkages to local bar associations. Address: 740 15th Street, N.W., Washington, DC 20005-1019.

American Bar Foundation (ABF). Founded in 1952, the ABF is a research entity affiliated with the ABA. Address: 750 N. Lake Shore Drive, Chicago, IL 60611.

American Civil Liberties Union (ACLU). Founded in 1920 with the purpose of defending the individual's rights as guaranteed by the Constitution. Toward this end, the group's primary activities are direct involvement in test cases, organized opposition to legislation considered unconstitutional, and public protests. Among the many prominent cases in which the ACLU has participated is the Sacco-Vanzetti trial. The ACLU played a vital role in decisions citing the unconstitutionality of prayer in public schools, state-administered loyalty oaths for teachers, and illegal police search and seizure. In recent years the organization has been involved in the fight for civil rights. Privately sponsored, the ACLU has a membership of nearly 150,000, with offices in 45 states. Vital to its successful operation are 2,000 lawyers who represent the ACLU without fee in over 300 cities. Headquartered at 125 Broad Street, 18th Floor, New York, NY 10004.

American common law. Similar in most respects to English common law. Insofar, however, as English common law is inapplicable to our conditions and surroundings, it is not a part of our common law. The Supreme Court of the United States has decided, however, that English statutes that were enacted before the emigration of our ancestors, which were in force at that time, and which are applicable to our conditions and surroundings, do constitute a part of our common law. The common law of many states is expressly defined by each state's legislature; in some states there are no criminal offenses except those expressly declared by statute. In the absence of evidence to the contrary, the courts of any state presume that the common law prevails in other states. Federal courts have no common law jurisdiction in criminal cases.

American Correctional Association (ACA). Originally formed in 1870 as the National Prison Association, the organization changed its name to ACA at the Congress of Corrections held in Philadelphia. Address: 4380 Forbes Boulevard, Lanham, MD 20706.

American Criminal Justice Association–Lambda Alpha Epsilon (ACJA-LAE). Founded in 1937. Publishes *Journal of the American Justice Association* (semiannually). Address: P.O. Box 61047, Sacramento, CA 95860.

American District Telegraph Company. A company operating nationally in the burglar alarm field. It uses various protective devices in businesses and homes to detect unauthorized entry into their premises and activate alarms.

American Federation of Labor (AFL). Organized and founded by Samuel Gompers in 1886 as a labor union, the AFL represented the members of skilled trades who did not want to be associated with the Knights of Labor. In 1955, the union merged with the Congress of Industrial Organizations to form the AFL-CIO. *See also* Hoffa, James

American Federation of Labor and Congress of Industrial Organizations (AFL-CIO). Under the leadership of AFL vice president John L. Lewis, several industrial unions sought charters with the AFL. When the AFL ordered these groups to disband, they left the AFL and joined the CIO in 1938. Both organizations enjoyed success in the late 1930s and early 1940s. However, union power was curtailed in 1947 with the passage of the Taft-Hartley Act. This prompted the merger of the AFL and CIO in 1955. The only major unions not affiliated with the AFL-CIO are the United Mine Workers and the National Education Association.

The International Union of Police Associations (IUPA)(AFL-CIO), 1016 Duke St., Alexandria, VA 22314, has established locals throughout the United States and claims to represent over 200 law enforcement agencies. The Los Angeles County Professional Peace Officers Association (Local 612) is affiliated with IUPA and publishes *Star & Shield* (monthly).

American Federation of Police, Inc. Founded in 1966, the federation is an association of federal, state, county, local, and private security officers of all ranks; provides information and training services. Publishes the *Police Times* (monthly). Address: 1100 NE 125th Street, North Miami, FL 33161.

American Humane Association. Founded in 1876, its objectives are to provide information, advice, and training to prevent animal abuse and child abuse, and to promote better services for both groups. Address: 63 Inverness Drive East, Englewood, CO 80112.

American Indian Movement (AIM). An activist group of Native Americans founded in 1966 in Minneapolis with the purpose of changing the attitude of the U.S. Bureau of Indian Affairs toward Indians not living on reservations. Since its inception, AIM has expanded its activities throughout the Midwest and its interests to a broad range of concerns. It has been particularly active in Minneapolis, where its Indian Patrol, through surveillance of the police, proved discrimatory practices against Indian citizens.

On June 26, 1975, two FBI agents, Ronald Williams and Jack R. Coler, both in their late 20s, drove onto Indian land near Oglala, SD, a small village on the Pine Ridge Reservation. A shoot-out resulted in the deaths of both agents and a male Indian, leading to a 71-day blockade costing approximately $7 million. Of the four AIM members indicted for this civil disorder, one was released due to "weak evidence," and two others were acquitted in July 1976 for firing "in self-defense." The fourth man, Leonard Peltier, was extradited from Canada, tried in 1977, convicted on two counts of first-degree murder, and sentenced to consecutive life terms in federal prison.

American Institutes for Research. Founded in 1946, the institute examines various facets of the law enforcement and criminal justice systems, such as personnel training and selection and program administration. Address: 1000 Thomas Jefferson Street, NW, Washington, DC 20007-3835.

American Judicature Society. Founded in 1913, the purpose of the society is to promote the effective administration of justice. Publishes *Judicature* (monthly) and *AJS Update* (bimonthly). Address: The Opperman Center at Drake University, 2700 University Avenue, Des Moines, Iowa 50311.

American Justice Institute. Founded in 1959. Address: 349 Main Street, Laurel, Maryland 20707.

American Law Enforcement Officers Association. Founded in 1976, and comprising police officers of all ranks, all departments, full- and part-time, in the criminal justice system. It provides leadership and planning in cooperative programs among police, prosecutors, courts, corrections, and private security personnel. Publishes the *Police Times* (monthly). Address: 2000 P Street, NW, Room 615, Washington, DC 20036.

American Law Institute. A national association of prominent lawyers and legal scholars who voluntarily draft model laws, such as the Model Penal Code.

American Medical Association (AMA). A national organization composed of state and regional medical societies, the AMA represents the professional interests of the bulk of American physicians and seeks to establish standards for drugs and therapeutic devices and to influence legislation and opinion on health care matters. It sponsors the AMA Program to Improve Medical Care and Health Services in Correctional Institutions and provides liaison between administrators of correctional facilities and organized medicine. Publishes *Correctional Stethoscope* (bimonthly). Address: 515 N. State Steet, Chicago, IL 60610.

American Municipal Association. A federation of state leagues of municipalities, with headquarters in Chicago, IL, and Washington, DC. The local leagues provide consultant services on problems of municipal government, and some issue periodicals and other publications.

American Police Association (APA). A national, nonprofit professional organization for college-educated police officers. Address: 5200 Leeward Lane, Suite 102, Alexandria, VA 22315.

American Psychological Association (APA). A scientific and professional society of psychologists and educators founded in 1892.

"The purpose of the APA is to advance psychology as a science, as a profession, and as a means of promoting human welfare. It attempts to further these objectives by holding annual meetings, publishing psychological journals, and working toward improved standards for psychological training and service." Its members (about 48,000) include most of the professionally qualified psychologists in the United States. There are 53 affiliated state associations. Headquartered at 750 First Street, NE, Washington, DC 20002-4242.

American Radio Relay League. Organization for amateur radio operators, or "hams." Many have assisted police efforts during emergencies in which normal communications channels have been overtaxed or disabled. Headquarters: 225 Main Street, Newington, CT 06111.

American Society for Industrial Security. National organization of industrial security officers. Address: 1625 Prince Street, Alexandria, Virginia 22314-2818.

American Society of Criminology, The (ASC). Founded in Berkeley, CA, in 1941, the ASC is an interdisciplinary society that seeks to encourage scholarly, scientific, and practical exchange or cooperation among those engaged in the study of criminology. The society serves as a forum for the dissemination of criminological knowledge. Affiliated with the American Association for the Advancement of Science. Presents annual awards and sponsors student paper competitions. Publishes *Criminology: An Interdisciplinary Journal* (quarterly) and the *Criminologist* (10 times yearly). Address: Executive Administrator Sahara Hall, 1314 Kinnear Road, Suite 212, Columbus, OH 43212.

Americans for Effective Law Enforcement, Inc. (AELE). Founded in 1966, AELE provides research assistance in civil liability for law enforcement agencies and administrators. Publishes *Law Enforcement Legal Liability Reporter* (monthly); *Law Enforcement Legal Defense Manual* (bimonthly), *The Police Plaintiff* (quarterly), *Jail Administration Law Bulletin* (bimonthly), *Criminal Justice Impact* (quarterly), and *Fire and Police Personnel Report* (monthly). Address: 841 W. Touhy Avenue, Park Ridge, IL 60068-3351.

Americans with Disabilities Act, The (ADA). The U.S. Supreme Court's 1896 decision in *Plessy v. Ferguson* allowed the continuation of segregation and other discriminatory employment practices based not only on race, but also on age and disability. The Court reversed that decision and declared segregation to be inherently unequal treatment in *Brown v. Board of Education* in 1954. *Brown*, along with the Civil Rights Act of 1964 and the results of advocacy group activities, brought about the passage of the Rehabilitation Act of 1973, which specifically addressed disabled Americans for the first time but applied only to the employment practices of the federal government. The Air Carrier Access Act (1968) and the Fair Housing Amendments Act (1988) broadened legislation to include private-sector businesses. The ADA was signed into law on July 26, 1990, and included these definitions:

"Covered Entity" Under Title I: An employer, employment agency, labor organization, or joint labor-management committee.

Employers: Those engaged in an industry affecting commerce who have 15 or more employees for each working day in each of 20 or more calendar weeks in the current or preceding calendar year.

1. As of July 26, 1992, only employers with 25 or more employees are covered.
2. Beginning July 26, 1994, employers with 15 or more employees are covered.
3. The term "employer" does not include the United States, a wholly owned government corporation, an Indian tribe, or a bona fide private membership club that is exempt from taxation under section 501(c) of the Internal Revenue Code of 1986.

Individual with a Disability: An individual must satisfy at least one of the following: (1) Have a physical or mental impairment that substantially limits one or more of major life activities; or (2) Have a record of such an impairment; or (3) Be regarded as having such an impairment.

Physical or Mental Impairment: Any physiological disorder or condition; cosmetic disfigurement; anatomical loss that affects one or more of several body systems; mental illness or retardation; hearing, speech, and visual impairments; cancer or infection with HIV. An impairment does not include: eye or hair color; pregnancy; obesity that is not the result of a physiological disorder or impairment that is covered under the Act; environmental, cultural or economic disadvantages; nicotine addiction; psychoactive substance disorders resulting from current use of illegal drugs; temporary, nonchronic impairments, such as the flu or a broken limb; transvestism, and other sexual behavior disorders; compulsive gambling; kleptomania; pyromania; homosexuality; bisexuality; and advanced age in and of itself.

amicus curiae (Lat., lit. "friend of the court"). One who is permitted or invited by a court to participate in a legal proceeding but who is not a party to it. In cases involving civil and criminal rights where a question of general applicability is being decided, courts have increasingly allowed "amicus briefs," which give legal argument or facts. The practice can be of value in providing the court with a clear analysis of both the factors it should consider in making its decision and the possible implications of that decision.

amphetamine. Benzedrine sulfate, a synthetic (analog) drug that stimulates the central nervous system, causing local constriction of mucous membranes. The effects are similar to those of cocaine, with mental and physical hyperactivity, including increased breathing rate and rapid or irregular heartbeat, increased blood pressure, sweating, headache, dizziness, and blurred vision, tremors, insomnia, loss of appetite, abdominal cramps, nausea, and vomiting; diarrhea, or impotence. Can cause brain damage or death from stroke, high fever, or heart failure. Street names include meth, speed, and uppers. Ice is a crystallized form of methamphetamine that is smoked, with effects lasting up to 24 hours. Benzedrine sulfate can be taken orally (affecting the central nervous system within 30 minutes for up to 14 hours), inhaled as a white powder, or by injection when in solution (with immediate effects that last only 1–2 hours). Amphetamines are highly addictive, with tolerance developing within 2–4 weeks. causing users to increase the dosage. Withdrawal symptoms include depression, irritability, extreme fatigue, intense hunger, and disturbed sleep patterns. Amphetamines were first synthesized in 1887 and marketed under the name Benzedrine in 1932 as inhalants for use as nasal decongestants. *See also* ephedrine

anabolic steroids. Man-made derivatives of the male sex hormone testosterone, a natural substance responsible for the development of such secondary sexual characteristics as facial hair and deep voice. Testosterone also plays a major role in increased muscle size and strength. Long-term use of anabolic steroids can cause liver cancer, decreased sperm production, prostate enlargement, heart and kidney disease, sterility, and a host of other afflictions.

anal eroticism. Sexual behavior focusing on the anus, which may include oral/anal contact, insertion of the penis into the anus (sodomy), digital insertion into the anus, and sexual stimulation by anal odors. The additional term "analism" refers to a preoccupation with the anus as a focus of sexual stimulation.

anaphrodisiac. A chemical preparation intended to reduce or eliminate a male's sexual stimulation or erection.

anarchism. The political philosophy that equality and justice may be obtained only through the abolition of the state and its organs. It opposes capitalism and free enterprise. In the United States, anarchists exercised some influence in the trade union and radical political movements in the last third of the nineteenth century. Anarchists were accused of perpetrating the Haymarket affair in Chicago in 1886, leading to the arrest of seven anarchists and the ultimate execution of four of them. An anarchist assassinated President William McKinley in 1901. Sacco and Vanzetti, two anarchists, were arrested in 1921 and executed in 1927.

anarchist. One who proposes the violent overthrow of the govemment; one who advocates a lack of government.

anarchy, criminal. Advocacy of the overthrow of any authorized government or the assassination of any of its executive heads.

androgynous. A term referring to individuals who possess both male and female personality and/or sexual characteristics.

angel dust. *See* phencyclidine.

animal abuse. All 50 states have legislation relating to animal abuse; however, definitions vary from jurisdiction to jurisdiction. A common definition includes the following elements: "socially unacceptable behavior that intentionally causes unnecessary pain, suffering or distress to and/or death of an animal." *See* child abuse

annulment. The act, by competent authority, of canceling, making void, or depriving of all force, as a contract.

anomalies, physical. The physical signs that criminologist Cesare Lombroso held would identify a criminal. It was Lombroso's contention that criminals were born, not made, and that evidence of criminality could be seen in the peculiar shape of various body parts, particularly the head and face. Although the theory has been discredited, it has been revived in recent years by a small group of physical anthropologists. *See also* Lombroso, Cesare

anomalous plea. A court plea that is partly affirmative and partly negative.

anomie. A concept first formulated by sociologist Emile Durkheim to describe a state of normlessness in which social control of individual behavior has become ineffective. The concept is fundamental to Durkheim's whole sociology and provides the reference point for his critical analysis of the problems of modem society. The concept was later used by Robert Merton (American sociological theorist, 1910–) to describe the conflict between culturally instilled goals and socially approved means of attaining those goals. *See also* Genovese, Kitty

anonymity. In sociological theory, the conditions that occur when an individual is masked or not highly visible. Under normal conditions, people's antisocial impulses are held in check by fear of embarrassment or punishment. But one factor that can free individuals from these restraints and provide them with the opportunity to engage in nontypical behavior is anonymity. Thus many burglars work at night, bank robbers wear masks, and members of the Ku Klux Klan wear white sheets. In an experiment testing the effects of anonymity on aggression, it was found that girls whose identities were masked with hoods delivered more than twice as much shock to a "victim" as did girls whose identities were not masked. Individuals are thought to seek anonymity as a defense against hostile environments in which they fear punishment or retribution. *See also* deindividuation

anonymous groups. Patterned after Alcoholics Anonymous, the most notable self-help movement of its kind, and often involving a 12-step process of recovery along with reliance on fellow group members who have all experienced similar problems, usually addictions. Groups include Co-Dependents Anonymous, Compulsive Stutterers Anonymous, Debtors Anonymous, Drugs Anonymous, Gamblers Anonymous, HIV+ or HIVIES Anonymous, Incest Anonymous, Narcotics Anonymous, Nicotine Anonymous, Obsessive-Compulsives Anonymous, Overeaters Anonymous, Pill Addicts Anonymous, Sex Addicts or Sexaholics Anonymous, Workaholics Anonymous.

anorexia nervosa. An eating disorder characterized by the inability to take in sufficient nourishment, based primarily on the patient's misperception of herself (the malady is much more common in women than in men) as overweight. Has the highest fatality rate (20 percent) of all psychiatric disorders. *See also* bulimia nervosa

answer. A defense in writing to charges contained in a bill or complaint filed by the plaintiff against the defendant.

Antabuse therapy. A treatment for alcoholism using the drug disulfiram (Antabuse), a relatively inert chemical compound. It interferes with the metabolism of alcohol, resulting in a buildup of the toxin acetaldehyde in the blood. If an individual on Antabuse consumes alcohol, he or she experiences increased blood pressure, flushing of the skin, rapid breathing, and accelerated heart rate. If drinking continues, dizziness, nausea, and vomiting occur, eventually followed by a rapid fall in blood pressure, unconsciousness, and possibly death. Giving disulfiram is not in itself a sufficient therapeutic program. Many physicians, however, regard the drug as a useful tool to help patients overcome the urge to drink while pursuing psychological rehabilitative techniques, such as group therapy.

antecedent. Prior to; preceding.

anthropology. Science focused on the study of mankind and its development in relation to its physical, mental, and cultural history. It is a comprehensive science, touching upon such other disciplines as criminology, biology, physiology, psychology, comparative anatomy, and sociology. Specifically, anthropology may be considered the science of man's natural history in relation to his physical character, rather than the general science of man.

anthropometry. The study of the measurements of the human body for the purpose of comparison; also known as the Bertillon system. *See also* Bertillon method

anthropophagy. Cannabalism; human consumption of human flesh.

anti-lynch bills. Federal bills that, since the early 1920s, have attempted to provide the protection of the U.S. courts against lynching, a crime that still results in virtually no arrests, presentments, or court convictions. In 1922 the Dyer Anti-Lynch Bill was passed in the House but rejected by the Senate. Subsequent attempts at legislation have all failed, including 59 anti-lynch bills introduced in Congress in 1937 alone. This legislation has consistently been opposed on states' rights grounds. *See also* lynching

antipsychotic drugs. Prescription medications such as thorazine that are used to relieve or control, but not to cure, the symptoms of psychosis.

Antiracketeering Act. A law of Congress, passed on June 18, 1934, which made it a criminal offense to interfere with foreign or interstate commerce by violence, threats, coercion, or intimidation.

antitrust cases. Federal cases against large business conglomerates, or trusts. Prosecutions are conducted under the provisions of the Sherman Antitrust Act of 1890, which barred any joint action by business "in restraint of trade" and made it a criminal offense to attempt to monopolize interstate commerce. The act expressed the traditional American hostility to monopoly and "privilege." In 1914 President Woodrow Wilson introduced the Clayton Antitrust Act to strengthen the Sherman Act. A notable recent case was the U.S. Department of Justice's suit against the Bell System, leading to the separation of AT&T from its local telephone companies on January 1, 1984.

Apalachin Meeting. A meeting of high officials of the Cosa Nostra held at Apalachin, New York, in 1957. The meeting was interrupted by law enforcement officers who had obtained the identity of several persons in attendance.

apathy. Indifference. In an increasingly urban and impersonal society, apathy has become a problem of growing concern to social scientists. In 1964 at least 37 individuals watched the stabbing murder of 28-year-old Kitty Genovese in New York City; not one of them called for help during or after the stabbing. Anonymity and deindividuation play a large role in creating such a climate of indifference. A second factor contributing to indifference is perceived loss of control. As individuals perceive themselves to be less and less in charge of their own lives, their willingness to try to change things decreases. *See also* anonymity; deindividuation

aphrodisiac. A chemical substance that is alleged to stimulate sexual interest and/or capability.

apocrypha. Writings or statements of doubtful authorship or authenticity.

apparent danger. Used in reference to self-defense, to justify a killing as necessary for self-preservation. The danger must be presumable, or clear and manifest.

appeal. A proceeding found in many ancient legal codes, appeal in civil law was the removal of a case from a lower to a higher court for retrial as to both law and fact. Most appellate proceedings (appeals) are now governed by statute. The term in modern-day usage connotes any form of appellate review of errors of law rather than of fact, and distinguishes appellate review as a matter of right from appellate review as a matter of the appellate court's discretion (*certiorari*).

appeal bond. The bond posted by an individual who is appealing a case; the appellant guarantees to pay damages and costs if he or she fails to go forward with the appeal.

appeal case. A case, filed in a court having incidental or general appellate jurisdiction, to initiate review of a judgment or decision of a trial court, an administrative agency, or an intermediate appellate court.

appeal proceedings. The set of orderly steps by which a court considers the issues and makes a determination in the appeal case before it. The major steps in appeal proceedings are: (a) the appeal is initiated by the filing of a formal document in the court having appellate jurisdiction; (b) a record of the original proceedings (the court reporter's transcript) in the trial court is obtained by the appellate court; (c) briefs are filed in court by the opposing parties (appellant and respondent); (d) if there are to be oral arguments, a hearing is scheduled and the arguments heard; and (e) following completion of arguments or submission of briefs, the court deliberates, reviewing the record of the earlier proceedings and considering the allegations and arguments of the parties, and announces its decision in the case. This decision may be embodied in an opinion that also gives the reasons for the decision.

appearance. An individual's formal presentation of him- or herself in court, usually to present testimony in a lawsuit.

appellant. Relating to appeals; the individual who appeals, especially from a lower to a higher court.

appellate. Relating to or having jurisdiction to review appeals.

appellate court. A court that reviews cases originally tried and decided by lower courts. The appellate court acts without a jury and is primarily interested in correcting errors in procedure or in the interpretation of law by the lower court.

appellate judge. A judge in a court of appellate jurisdiction who primarily hears appeal cases and also conducts disciplinary or impeachment proceedings.

appellate jurisdiction. The authority of a superior court to review and modify the decisions of an inferior court.

appellee. The party in a lawsuit against whom an appeal is taken; the respondent.

appose. To examine an officer of a business firm for the purpose of reviewing the firm's accounts.

apprehend. To make an arrest on a charge of a crime.

approver. One who confesses a crime and at the same time accuses others to save him- or herself; such an individual is also said to become state's evidence.

appurtenance. A right (such as a right-of-way) attached to something else; an accessory or adjunct.

aquaeroticism. Sexual gratification from submerging the head and/or the entire body in water so as to produce a sensation of losing consciousness during orgasm.

arbitration. A process by which labor-management disputes may be resolved, using a third party to render a decision. Arbitration may deal with controversies arising in the determination of a new contract (interest arbitration) or with disagreements over the interpretation of an existing contract's provisions (grievance arbitration). More flexible and less expensive than court proceedings, arbitration is usually preferred by both labor and management. *See also* collective bargaining; conciliation; mediation

arbitrator. The person chosen by parties in a controversy to settle their differences; a private judge. Arbitrators are usually chosen from the American Arbitration Association, the Federal Mediation and Conciliation Service, or an agency of the federal, state, or city government.

archives. Records preserved as evidence; public papers and records.

area, delinquency. An area of a city marked by an unusually high delinquency rate compared to other areas of the city of similar size and population. Such areas are often located in zones of transition and are marked by industrial buildings, waterfronts, railroad yards, and deteriorated buildings.

area, metropolitan. A region including a large concentration of population together with the surrounding areas, where the daily economic and social life is predominantly influenced by the central city.

aristocracy. A high social class, especially one that is a nation's governing or ruling class.

armory. (1) A place or building where arms are stored or where drills and reviews are held. (2) Aboard ship, a compartment where small arms and light machine guns are stowed and serviced. (3) Formerly, a place or building where arms were manufactured.

arms, right to bear. A provision of the Second Amendment that prohibits Congress from interfering with the right of the people to arm themselves. Enacted at a time of strong popular distrust of standing mercenary armies and a fear of the creation of an overly powerful central government, the Second Amendment allowed the establishment of state militia free of congressional restraints. The amendment and the inherent power of the states to control firearms have bred considerable controversy over gun control.

arraign. To bring a person before a court to answer a charge.

arraignment. (1) Strictly, the hearing before a court having jurisdiction in a criminal case, in which the identity of the defendant is established, the defendant is informed of the charge(s) and of his or her rights, and the defendant is required to enter a plea. (2) In some usages, any appearance in court prior to trial in criminal proceedings.

arraignment and trial. The procedure according to which the defendant is brought into court, informed of his or her rights, and placed on trial, as well as the familiar routine of selecting a jury, making the opening statements, introducing evidence, arguing the case to the jury, instructing the jury, and receiving the verdict.

array. The group of persons summoned into court for jury duty; the order in which these people are ranked in the jury box.

arrest. The legal detainment of a person to answer for criminal charges or (infrequently at present) civil demands. Constitutional limitations prevent arrest or detention under false or assumed authority and harassment of persons without warrants properly issued. *See also habeas corpus*

arrest by officer without warrant, when lawful. A peace officer may, without a warrant, arrest a person when: (a) the person to be arrested has committed a felony or misdemeanor in the officer's presence (in the case of such arrest for a misdemeanor, the arrest shall be made immediately or on fresh pursuit); (b) the person to be arrested has committed a felony, although not in the officer's presence; (c) a felony has in fact been committed, and the officer has reasonable grounds to believe that the person to be arrested has committed it; or (d) the officer has reasonable grounds to believe that a felony has been or is being committed and reasonable grounds to believe that the person to be arrested has committed or is committing it.

arrest by private person, when lawful. A private person may make an arrest when (a) the person to be arrested has in the former's presence committed either a misdemeanor amounting to a breach of the peace or a felony, or (b) a felony has been in fact committed and the private citizen has reasonable grounds to believe that the person to be arrested has committed it.

arrestee dispositions. The class of law enforcement or prosecutorial actions which terinmate or provisionally suspend proceedings against an arrested person before a charge has been filed in court. Such actions, permanent or provisional, are: (a) police release—arrestee released after booking because of law enforcement agency decision not to request complaint; (b) complaint rejected—prosecutor declines to prosecute case on grounds such as insufficient evidence, lack of witnesses, or interests of justice (c) prosecution withheld—prosecutor suspends proceedings conditional upon behavior of arrestee with referral to probation or other criminal justice agency, or with referral to a noncriminal justice agency, or with no referral.

arrest rate. The number of arrests as a percentage of the crimes known to the police; also, the number of arrests as a percentage of a certain population group, such as the rate for males or for youths under the age of 16.

arrest record. A list of a person's arrests and charges made against him/her, usually in-

Arrest, Conviction, and Imprisonment Risk for Index Crimes: 1994						
	Arrest Risk[a]				Probability of Imprisonment	
Crime Type	Victimi-zations	Reported Crimes	Conviction Risk[b]	Imprisonment Risk (NJRP/BJS)[c]	Victimizations	Reported Crimes
Homicide	n/a	64.00	55.74	93.00	n/a	0.332
Rape	31.60	52.00	55.38	68.00	0.119	0.196
Robbery	11 .43	24.00	29.93	74.00	0.025	0.053
Aggravated Assault	25.31	56.00	11 .63	44.00	0.013	0.029
Violent Crime	21.39	45.26	18.99	61.84	0.025	0.053
Burglary	6.43	13.00	27.04	52.00	0.009	0.018
Auto Theft	12.22	14.00	9.78	41.00	0.005	0.006
Larceny	6.63	20.00	6.62	38.00	0.002	0.005
Property Crime	6.91	17.67	10.75	44.86	0.003	0.009
Total	**8.55**	**21.35**	**12.97**	**51.56**	**0.006**	**0.014**

[a]Crimes cleared by arrest per 100 crimes of this type.

[b]Number of felony convictions for this type of crime per 100 arrestees whose most serious arrest is for this type of crime.

[c]Number of felony defendants sent to prison for this type of crime per 100 felony convictions for this type of crime.

Source: National Judicial Reporting Program/Bureau of Justice Statistics.

cluding those dismissed or dropped and those of which he/she was found innocent. The arrest record also contains information on dispositions and sentences if there was adjudication of guilt. *See also* security and privacy

arrest register. The document containing a chronological record of all arrests made by members of a given law enforcement agency, each entry containing at a minimum the identity of the arrestee, the charges at time of arrest, and the date and time of arrest. This kind of record is also called an "arrest register book" or "initial entry record." In some agencies the information is entered directly into an electronic processing system. These records and arrest reports are key sources of statistical information. A "police blotter" is used in some jurisdictions to record arrests and other information about police activity. All these types of records, being chronological accounts of government activity, are usually open to public inspection. Jail registers or jail books are records of "bookings," that is, admissions of persons into detention facilities.

In some jurisdictions these may be the chief or only source of information about completed arrests.

arrest upon hue and cry. An old common law process of pursuing with horn and with voice all felons and individuals who have dangerously wounded others. The hue and cry could be raised by officers, private persons, or both. The officer and his or her assistants have the same powers, protection, and indemnity as if they were acting under a warrant.

arrest upon order of magistrate. When an offense is committed in the presence of a magistrate, he or she may, by an oral or written order, command any person to arrest the offender immediately, and may then proceed as though the offender had been brought before him or her on an arrest warrant.

arrest warrant. An official document signed by a judge or other authorized court official accusing an individual of a crime and authorizing law enforcement personnel to take that person into custody.

arson. The intentional or attempted damaging or destruction, by means of fire or explosion, of the property of another without the consent of the owner, or of one's own property or that of another with intent to defraud.

Arson Investigators, International Association of. Founded in 1949. Publishes *The Fire and Arson Investigator* (quarterly). Address: 25 Newton Street, P.O. Box 600, Marlboro, MA 01752.

arsonist. A person who deliberately starts a fire for the purpose of destroying life, property, or evidence, or for collecting insurance.

artifice. Trickery.

artificial. Having an existence presumed in law or on paper only, such as a corporation.

artificial presumption. A presumption that derives its force and effect from the law rather than from belief or actual events. Thus, a legal presumption that a person is dead after continued absence is an artificial presumption created by law. The period of absence varies from state to state, but the majority hold seven years as the mark.

Aryan Brotherhood. A group of white activists that originated in San Quentin Prison. These men form an elite Caucasian prison gang that exists throughout the Califomia prison system. They can be identified by the tattoo A.B.

asportation. Taking and carrying away. If a defendant, having taken possession of goods, has not moved them from their original location, the *asportation* necessary to constitute larceny is lacking.

assassination. (1) Murder of a public figure. A wide range of U.S. political officials—from presidents and cabinet members to local judges and tax collectors—have been targets of assassination attempts, as have other prominent public figures such as leaders of protest movements and candidates for office. Motives for assassination have included gaining revenge for a real or imagined wrong, earning fame or a reward, and removing a political enemy or group from office. Four presidents have been struck down. On April 14, 1865, our 16th president, Abraham Lincoln, was shot by Confederate sympathizer John Wilkes Booth in Ford's Theater in Washington, DC. On July 2, 1881, James A. Garfield, the 20th U.S. president, was shot by Charles Julius Guiteau, a religious fanatic. Garfield survived until September 19 of that year. On September 6, 1901, in Buffalo, NY, 25th president William McKinley was shot by Leon Czolgosz and died eight days later. On November 22, 1963, our 35th president, John F. Kennedy, was shot by Lee Harvey Oswald in Dallas, TX. Five other presidents (Jackson, both Roosevelts, Truman, and Reagan) escaped death by assassins. In 1965 it became a federal crime to kill, kidnap, or assault a president, vice president, presidentelect, or acting president. It had already been illegal to threaten the life of a president.

(2) Any murder in which the distinguishing feature is resort to treachery or stealth. The word *assassin* comes from the Arabic *hashshashin*—or hash eaters. The original assassins were followers of Hasan Al-Sabah, "The Old Man of the Mountains," a political and religious leader of eleventh-century Persia. They terrorized the Middle East for two centuries. The first recorded assassination attempt in the U.S. was in New York City in 1774, when a Tory attempted to murder George Washington by feeding him a stew made with tomatoes, which at the time were thought to be poisonous. An attempt was made on President Andrew Jackson's life on January 3, 1835, by Richard Lawrence, both of whose pistols misfired. John Schrank shot President Theodore Roosevelt on October 14, 1912; the president survived but carried the bullet in his body for the rest of his life. New York City mayor William J. Gaynor died on September 10, 1913, from a bullet wound inflicted three years earlier by James J. Gallager. On February 15, 1933, in Miami, Florida, Chicago mayor Anton Cermak was shot by Joseph Zangara, who had aimed at president-elect Franklin D. Roosevelt. On September 8, 1935, Dr. Carl A. Weiss shot Louisiana senator Huey P.

Long, who died two days later. President Harry Truman was assaulted on November 1, 1950, by two Puerto Rican nationalists at Blair House in Washington, DC, during which White House guard Leslie Coffelt was killed and two of his fellow guards were wounded trying to protect Truman, who was unhurt. On February 21, 1965, Malcolm X was shot and killed in New York City by three Black Muslims. On April 4, 1968, Martin Luther King was killed in Memphis, Tennessee, by James Earl Ray. On June 5, 1968, Senator Robert F. Kennedy, brother of the late president, was shot by Sirhan Sirhan in a Los Angeles hotel, dying the next day. On May 15, 1972, Alabama governor George C. Wallace was paralyzed with four bullets fired by Arthur Herman Bremer. On September 5, 1975, Lynette "Squeaky" Fromme aimed a gun at President Gerald Ford but was seized before she could fire. Sarah Jane Moore fired at President Ford in San Francisco on September 22 of that year, but she missed. On March 30, 1981, John W. Hinckley Jr. shot at President Ronald Reagan in Washington, DC, wounding him as well as James Brady and three others.

assault. Occurs when an individual, without lawful authority, places another person in fear of receiving, or actually delivers to that person, a battery (that is, touching with the possibility of physical harm or death). If performed with intent to kill or to inflict severe bodily injury, the act is called aggravated assault. In 1987, a Minnesota federal court upheld a defendant's conviction for assault with a deadly/dangerous weapon. The charge was based on the biting of two correctional officers by an inmate who was infected with AIDS (*U.S. v. Moore*), 669 F. Supp. 289 (D. Minn. 1987), aff'd., 846 F.2d 1163 (8th Cir. 1988).

assault weapon. Essentially a civilian, semi-automatic version of a military weapon. Features often used to characterize or differentiate assault weapons from "normal" rifles, pistols, and shotguns usually include folding stocks, bayonet mounts, detachable ammunition magazines, pistol grips (on rifles and shotguns), and the ability to attach flash suppressors or silencers to the barrel. There is no universal definition of an assault weapon, and both the U.S. Congress and the legislatures of six states (California, Connecticut, Hawaii, Maryland, Massachusetts, and New Jersey) have attempted to codify the definition by listing specific makes and models of weapons, along with a general description as outlined above. Assault weapons have been banned by the federal Violent Crime Control and Law Enforcement Act of September, 1994. Most statutes outlaw the manufacture, transfer, or possession of assault weapons after that date. However, possession of weapons possessed prior to the enactment of legislation is in many cases permitted so long as the weapon is not sold or transferred. In 1999, California had to enact legislation specifically exempting many pistols used in Olympic and international competition because of the general nature of the definition of an assault weapon found in California law.

assembly. The meeting of a number of persons in one place, for a common objective.

assignation house. A house of prostitution; brothel.

assigned counsel. An attorney in private practice who is appointed to represent an indigent defendant.

assigned counsel system. This method of providing legal defense for individuals accused of crimes exists in almost two-thirds of U.S. counties, particularly in smaller counties in which there are not enough cases to justify the cost of a salaried public defender. The system is funded primarily by local units of government; the states and the federal government generally provide only a small proportion of funds to operate indigent defense services. *See also* public defender's organization

assistance, writ of. A writ from the court of chancery, in aid of the execution of a legal judgment, to put the complainant into possession of lands adjudged to him or her. *See also* chancery procedure

assisting officer in making arrest. An officer authorized to make arrests may call upon private persons for assistance in doing so. This assistance by the public is generally referred to as *posse comitatus*, which means power of the county to command any male person over 18 years of age either to aid and assist in taking or arresting any person against whom a legal complaint may be lodged or to prevent breach of the peace or any criminal offense.

association, differential. The distribution of a person's associations in a manner different from those of other persons; generally stated as a hypothesis of criminal behavior, namely, that a person who develops criminal behavior differs from those who do not both in the quantity and quality of associations with criminal patterns and in his or her relative isolation from anticriminal patterns, and that differential association with these criminal and anticriminal patterns is therefore the cause of criminal behavior.

assumpsit. A suit based on the breach of a simple contract.

asylum state. The state in which a fugitive from justice from another state, which is demanding his or her return, is found.

atavism. A theory of criminal behavior, developed by Lombroso and other evolutionists in the post-Darwinian era. It postulates that criminality diminishes in the evolutionary development of humanity, and that its appearance as a biological predilection in some persons is a hereditary throwback on the evolutionary scale. *See also* Lombroso, Cesare

Atcherley system. *See modus operandi*

Atlanta serial murders. On July 28, 1979, Atlanta police found the bodies of Alfred James Evans, age 13, and Edward Hope Smith, age 14. Over the next 22 months Atlanta citizens were terrorized by the abductions and murders of 29 young blacks (27 males and two females). The FBI entered the case and in May 1981, after 29 nights of surveillance, stopped Wayne Bertram Williams near the James Jackson Parkway Bridge; 2 days later, a third victim's body was recovered from the Chattahoochee River 1½ miles from the bridge. A search warrant was issued for Williams's home, automobile, and person, and significant fiber evidence was collected linking him to a number of the victims. On February 26, 1982, Williams was convicted of two counts of murder in Fulton County Court, Georgia. *See also* serial murders

attachment. Taking into custody an individual being sought by the court, or seizing the property of an individual who has been asked to appear in court and has failed to do so.

attainder. The annihilation of all civil rights and privileges, which, in early English law, followed a condemnation for treason or felony. The person attained forfeited all property and lost all capacity to inherit or transmit property to his descendants; nor could he appear in court or claim the protection of law. A bill of attainder, which is prohibited by the U.S. Constitution, is a legislative condemnation without the formality of a judicial trial.

attaint. To convict of a crime; also, a writ to inquire whether a jury has given a false verdict.

attempt to commit a crime. An act done with intent to commit a crime and tending to, but falling short of, its commission. (1) The act must be such as would be closely connected with the completed crime. (2) There must be an apparent possibility to commit the crime in the manner proposed. (3) There must be a specific intent to commit the particular crime at the time of the act. (4) Voluntary abandonment of purpose after an act constituting an attempt is no defense. (5) Consent to the attempt will be a defense if it would be a defense were the crime completed, but not otherwise. All attempts to commit a crime, whether the crime be a felony or a misdemeanor, in common law or by statute, are misdemeanors in common law.

attestation. The act of verifying or affirming, orally or in writing, the genuineness or validity of some legal document, such as a will or an affidavit.

attorney. Lawyer, counsel, advocate; a person trained in the law, admitted to practice before the bar of a given jurisdiction, and authorized to advise, represent, and act for other persons in legal proceedings. He or she may represent private individuals, corporations, or the government. The *prosecuting* attorney acts on behalf of the government ("the people") in a criminal case. The *defense* attorney advises, represents, and acts for the defendant (or, in postconviction proceedings, the offender). *Retained counsel* is a defense attorney selected and compensated by the defendant or offender or by other private person(s). *Assigned counsel* is a defense attorney assigned by the court on a case-by-case basis to represent indigent defendants and offenders, compensated from public funds or not compensated at all. A *public defender* is a defense attorney regularly employed and compensated from public funds to represent indigent defendants and offenders. When a defendant acts as his or her own defense attorney, that person is said to be represented *pro se* or *in propria persona*.

attorney at law. An officer in a court of justice.

attorney general, state. The chief legal officer of a state, representing that state in civil and, under certain circumstances, criminal matters; furnishes legal advice to the governor and state departments.

Attorney General, United States. A member of the president's cabinet and head of the U.S. Department of Justice; appointed by the president as the chief legal officer of the federal government, representing the national government in civil and criminal matters; also gives legal advice to other federal agencies and the president. This post was created by the 1789 Judiciary Act.

attorney in fact. A private attorney; one who is authorized by his client to perform a particular service. One who exercises power of attorney. *See also* power of attorney

Attorney, United States. The chief law officer (federal) in the Federal Judicial District; represents the U.S. government in civil and criminal matters; acts under the direction of the U.S. Attorney General, who heads the U.S. Department of Justice. The U.S. Attorney usually has assistants, who aid in performing the duties of the office.

Auburn system. A prison system or procedure first created in Auburn (NY) State Prison in 1816. It demanded silence on the part of the inmates, who were assigned to individual cells at night and forced to work in silence during the day.

audita querela, writ of. A remedial writ that sets aside execution of a judgment because of some injustice performed by the party obtaining the judgment but which could not be pleaded at the time of the trial; an arrest of judgment.

Augustus, John. Founder of the probation system in the United States. In 1841 he became the first probation officer, with supervision over minor offenders.

authentic document. A document bearing a signature or seal attesting that it is genuine and official.

authoritarianism. (a) A type of government or (b) a type of individual personality. In the first sense, the term refers to rigidly hierarchical, undemocratic structures. In the second sense, it refers to a personality syndrome that finds comfort in such structures. A considerable body of evidence shows that the authoritarian personality is highly correlated with a mind that is closed to new ideas and subject to ethnic and racial prejudice and discrimination, chauvinistic nationalism, willingness to restrict civil rights and liberties, and punitiveness as a response to deviance.

authority. (1) The power or right conferred on a person by another to act on his or her behalf. (2) A public officer or body having certain powers of jurisdiction. (3) Constitutions, statutes, precedent cases, opinions of text writers, and other material cited in arguments.

autocracy. A government of a monarch or other absolute ruler who is not limited by law; a dictatorship.

autoerotic death. An accidental death, usually by strangling, in which the victim dies while attempting to achieve sexual gratification. The goal is to increase sexual pleasure by coming close to, but stopping just short of, death.

autoeroticism. Masturbation and other forms of sexual self-gratification.

automated data processing (ADP). Data processing performed by computer system(s). It functions by devices that: (1) use common storage for all or part of a program or data necessary for execution of the program, (2) execute user-written or user-designated programs, and (3) perform user-designated symbol manipulation, such as arithmetic operations, logic operations, or character-string programs that can modify themselves during their execution. Also called electronic data processing.

Automatic Data-Processing Intelligence Network (ADPRIN). In use by the U.S. Bureau of Customs to combat smuggling.

automatic fire. Continuous fire from an automatic weapon, lasting until the pressure on the trigger is released. Automatic fire differs from semiautomatic fire and single-shot fire, both of which require a separate trigger pull for each shot fired.

automatic weapon. Specifically, as used in reference to antiaircraft artillery, any weapon of 75mm or smaller.

automobile theft. The stealing of an automobile or motor vehicle. Under state law it is theft of a motor vehicle. Under federal law it is a violation to transport a vehicle, or cause it to be transported, from one state to another, knowing the vehicle has been stolen. CYMBALS is an acronym that assists the recall of basic motor vehicle descriptors: color, year, make, body style, and license serial number. *See also* vehicle identification number

Automobile Theft Bureau, National (NATB). Founded in 1912. NATB is a nonprofit organization supported by associated insurance companies to assist law enforcement in suppressing vehicle thefts, including heavy industrial and marine equipment; identifying vehicles or equipment bearing altered or obliterated identification numbers; and investigating organized theft rings and frauds. Address: 10330 South Roberts Road, 3A, Palos Hills, IL 60465. *See also* Motor Vehicle Theft Law Enforcement Act of 1984

automonosexual perversion. Sexual activities performed on or with one's own body, such as self-fellatio, self-abuse, or self-mutilation.

autonomy. The state of being self-governing or self-directing.

autopsy. Examination and dissection of a dead body to discover the cause of death.

auto theft deterrence. LOJACK Auto Recovery System, manufactured in Massachusetts, was introduced as a Department of Justice model program in Los Angeles County in June 1990, with 41 agencies participating.

Auto Theft Investigators, International Association of. Founded in 1931. Publishes *Training and Education* (quarterly). Address: 255 5. Vernon, Dearborn, MI 48124.

autrefois. (Fr., "convict or acquit"). A plea made by a defendant that he or she has previously been tried and convicted or acquitted of the same offense.

aversion therapy. A process attempting to treat/modify/control behavior either by accompanying the behavior with a disagreeable experience, such as physical pain, or by administering rewards. *See also* Antabuse therapy; behavior modification

Aviation Crime Prevention Institute. Founded in 1986. Address: 226 N. Nova road, Ormond Beach, FL 32174.

avowtry. Adultery.

axiom. In logic, a truth that is self-evident.

B

baby boom. In criminal justice, a demographic term referring to the large number of males born between 1945 and 1960, who reached their peak crime ages during the 1960s and 1970s.

badges and shields, law enforcement. The five-pointed pentacle is the symbol of the U.S. Marshal's Service. It is the star in the American flag, in the insignia of an army general, and on the Medal of Honor. In ancient eras, the pentacle was used by sorcerers and believed to impart magical powers. As late as the sixteenth century, soldiers wore pentacles around their necks in the belief they would be invulnerable to enemy missiles. Over time, the six-star shield emerged as the local badge of choice, simply because it is easy to manufacture.

bad-tendency test. A rule, enunciated by the Supreme Court in *Gitlow v. New York*, that a legislative body may suppress speech that tends to spread revolutionary doctrines, even though danger of resulting armed uprising or other violence is remote. *See also* dangerous tendency test.

bail. A form of pretrial release in which a defendant deposits 10 percent of the total amount of his or her bond with the court and receives a refund of 90 percent of the deposit if he or she appears in court at the appointed time. Also called the Illinois plan.

METHODS OF PRETRIAL RELEASE
Both financial bonds and alternative release options are used today

Financial Bond

Fully secured bail—The defendant posts the full amount of bail with the court.

Privately secured bail—A bondsman signs a promissory note to the court for the bail amount and charges the defendant a fee for the service (usually 10 percent of the bail amount). If the defendant fails to appear, the bondsman must pay the court the full amount. Frequently, the bondsman requires the defendant to post collateral in addition to the fee.

Deposit bail—The courts allow the defendant to deposit a percentage (usually 10 percent) of the full bail with the court. The full amount of the bail is required if the defendant fails to appear. The percentage bail is returned after disposition of the case, but the court often retains 1 percent for administrative costs.

Unsecured bail—The defendant pays no money to the court but is liable for the full amount of bail should he or she fail to appear.

Alternative Release Options

Release on recognizance (ROR)—The court releases the defendant on the promise that he or she will appear in court as required.

Conditional release—The court releases the defendant subject to his or her following specific conditions set by the court, such as attendance at drug treatment therapy or staying away from the complaining witness.

Third party custody—The defendant is released into the custody of an individual or agency that promises to assure his or her appearance in court. No monetary transactions are involved in this type of release.

Citation release—Arrestees are released pending their first court appearance on a written order issued by law enforcement personnel.

Source: Bureau of Justice Statistics.

bail bondsman. A person, usually licensed, whose business it is to effect releases on bail for persons charged with offenses and held in custody, by pledging to pay a sum of money if the defendant fails to appear in court as required. In law, a bail bondsman is also called a surety.

Bailey, F. Lee. (1933–). Attorney born in Waltham, MA. While in law school he organized and operated a detective agency. Bailey is a self-taught expert in electronic techniques used in criminal investigation and in polygraphy. It was as an authority on polygraphy that he was originally called into his first major case, that of Dr. Samuel Sheppard of Cleveland, who had been convicted in 1954, amid blaring publicity, of murdering his wife. Bailey helped to force a review of the trial by the Supreme Court, which ruled in 1966 that the pretrial publicity may have prejudiced the jury. In a retrial, completed in 1966, Bailey secured Sheppard's acquittal and thus became one of the country's leading trial lawyers. Employing tactics that bordered at times on the flamboyant, Bailey was occasionally censured formally for his trial conduct, but his method of tirelessly pursuing every possible line of investigation and legal action made him one of the most sought-after legal defenders in the country.

bailiff. An officer of the court. This office evolved from the Statute of Winchester in 1285, by which King Edward I tried to establish a uniform system of law enforcement in England. Original responsibilities were to keep persons under surveillance who were traveling town streets after dark, and to check on strangers. Currently is responsible for keeping order in the court and protecting the security of jury deliberations and court property.

bailiwick. The territorial jurisdiction of a sheriff or bailiff.

bail revocation. The court decision withdrawing a defendant's previously granted release on bail.

bail system. Developed by the early common law courts to secure the defendant's appearance in court at trial. Originally required in both civil and criminal cases, bail has come to be used primarily in criminal cases. In the bail system, the defendant is released to his or her surety, who undertakes to produce the defendant at trial, usually giving a bail bond to secure that obligation. The bail system also provides for a defendant's release on "recognizance," an obligation entered into in court to do some act, usually to appear at trial. The bail system has come under increasing attack as a violation of civil liberties and due process. With the bonds' nonrefundable cost being approximately 10 percent of the face amount, not uncommonly in excess of $50,000, the system has served to keep many defendants in jail pending trial, depriving them of their liberty before they have been found guilty of any crime. However, efforts at reform face the problem that this system has been more effective than most in ensuring the end for which it was designed: that the defendant appear at trial. Also know as the Illinois plan.

balance of sentence suspended. A type of sentencing disposition, consisting of a sentence to prison or jail that credits the defendant for time already spent in confinement awaiting adjudication and sentencing, suspends the execution of the time remaining to be served, and results in the defendant's release from confinement.

ballistics. The science or art that deals with the motion and impact of such projectiles as bullets, rockets, and bombs. Ballistics also involves the behavior, appearance, or modification of missiles or other vehicles acted upon by propellants, wind, gravity, temperature, or any other modifying substance, condition, or force.

banditry. Consistent and organized robbery and other forms of theft with violence; especially, such behavior when committed by persons who reside in mountainous or other sparsely populated regions.

banishment. The sending away of a criminal from his or her place of residence.

bank fraud. A scheme to (a) swindle a federally chartered or insured financial institution or (b) obtain any of the moneys, funds, credits, assets, securities, or other property owned by or under the custody or control of these institutions by means of false pretenses, representations, or promises. The term "federally chartered" or "insured financial" institution means any type of bank or financial institution organized or operating under the laws of the United States.

bank robbery, the first. Occurred Saturday, March 19, 1831, when two doors of the City Bank, on Wall Street, New York City, were opened by duplicate keys and the bank was robbed of $245,000. Edward Smith, an Englishman (alias Jones, alias James Smith, alias James Honeyman), was indicted by a grand jury and arraigned May 2, 1831, at the Court of General Sessions. On May 11, 1831, he was sentenced to five years at hard labor at Sing Sing. Over $185,000 was recovered.

bankruptcy. The financial status of a person when a court has determined that his or her property is to be administered by the court for the benefit of his or her creditors. Congress enacted statutes governing some aspects of bankruptcy that were in effect in the years 1800–1803, 1841–1843, 1867–1878, and since 1898. In the absence of federal law governing some aspect of bankruptcy, the states may legislate, providing they do not impair the obligation of a contract. At present a person may file a voluntary petition of bankruptcy, listing his or her assets and liabilities, or may be forced into bankruptcy on petition of his or her creditors. In either case, the individual's assets are disposed of by an officer appointed by the court, creditors are paid pro rata, and the individual is discharged from further obligation. In 1933 special provision was made by law to facilitate the reorganization of railroads and other corporations which might otherwise have been declared bankrupt. The three most common filings in Federal Bankruptcy Court are: *Chapter 7*, which allows businesses and individuals to keep some personal property and, in some instances, their home and automobile, but they must sell the rest of their property to pay off

at least part of what is owed; *Chapter 11*, which provides businesses with protection from creditors while they reorganize operations and establish a payment plan; and *Chapter 13*, which allows individuals protection from creditors and payment extensions of up to 5 years.

bankruptcy, criminal. An individual's fraudulent declaration of excessive indebtedness or insolvency in an effort to avoid partial or full payment of his or her debts.

Bank Secrecy Act. A law requiring, among other things, that financial institutions file Currency Transaction Reports (CTRs) on all cash transactions of more than $10,000. CTRs must be filed with the IRS within 15 days of the transaction, and the financial institution must keep copies of them for 5 years. The reports require specific information regarding customers' identities. In addition, a Currency and Monetary Instrument Report must be filed for cash or certain monetary instruments exceeding $10,000 in value that enter or leave the U.S. Multiple transactions in amounts less than $10,000, called "smurfing," is now also illegal (31 U.S.C. 5324).

bar. (1) The railing separating the judge, counsel, and jury from the general public. (2) The whole body of attorneys and counselors who have been admitted to practice in a court. *See also* bench

barbed wire. Commonly used to supplement prison fencing, barbed wire was first patented in 1867 in New York by William D. Hunt, but perfected and marketed in 1874 by J. F. Glidden of Illinois.

barbiturates. Drugs that can produce a state of depression of the central nervous system resembling normal sleep. In smaller doses these drugs are referred to as sedatives. In larger doses they are known as hypnotics and can produce anesthesia, coma, and even death. Barbiturates are made from barbituric acid, which was first synthesized in Germany in 1863 by Nobel Prize–winning chemist Adolph Baeyer. The first barbiturate was synthesized in 1882 but not marketed until 1902, when it was released under the name Veronal and known generically in the U.S. as barbital.

bargain, implicit. A sentencing practice by which the defendant pleads guilty and seeks the mercy of the court, with the implied understanding that he or she will receive a lighter sentence in this way than by pleading not guilty and demanding trial.

barratry. The criminal offenses of exciting groundless quarrels or lawsuits. (1) In criminal law, the offense of frequently provoking suits and quarrels, either at law or otherwise. (2) In maritime law, any willful and unlawful act by the master or crew of a ship that causes the owners to sustain injury.

BARS (behaviorally anchored rating scale). A method of evaluating an individual's job performance.

basic car plan. The assignment of one or two officers in a motor vehicle to permanently patrol a designated geographic area. The "basic car" officers are responsible for all activities reported in that area, and for interacting with the comunity in formal and informal meetings. Other patrol units serve as back-up or to handle calls as needed.

Bastille. (Fr., "small fortress"). La Bastille, the infamous prison of Paris, was destroyed by revolutionaries on July 14, 1789—a day celebrated in France ever since. A synonym for all prisons, especially those holding political prisoners.

Bates, Sanford. (1884–1972). First director of the U.S. Bureau of Prisons; LL.B, Northeastem University, 1906; served in Massachusetts State Legislature, 1912–1917; Commissioner of Penal Institutions in Boston, 1917–1929. Appointed Superintendent of Prisons, U.S. Department of Justice, in 1929, Bates prepared the legislation that established the Bureau of Prisons in 1930. Chairman of Federal Prison Industries, Inc., 1934–1972; Executive Director of the Boys Club of America; Parole Commissioner for New York State; New Jersey State Commissioner of Institutions and Industries.

bathroom phobia. Also known as toilet phobia, this is a fear of falling into a toilet or of being attacked, especially in the genitals, by creatures emerging from the toilet. This phobia is alleged to afflict males who are anal erotic.

baton. A law enforcement officer's night stick; often called a billy or billy stick. Batons are most frequently made of hardwood and come in lengths of 24 to 29 inches. The "side-handle" baton, 24 inches long with a short protruding handle, is a variation on the traditional baton. Some agencies are replacing the wooden baton with a spring-loaded telescoping metal baton, commonly referred to as an "ASP."

Battelle Law and Justice Center. Founded by the Battelle Memorial Institute in 1971. Program objectives are "information and referral and dissemination of research results. Areas of specialization include arson (for profit and juvenile, especially), and white-collar crime." Address: 4000 NE 41st Street, Seattle, WA 98105.

battered child syndrome. The physical and emotional effects of deliberate and continuous injury to children by adult brutality. The majority of victims are under three years of age. Most injury is caused by parents or custodians.

battered woman syndrome. The physical and emotional effects of deliberate and continuous beating of a female by her spouse or live-in partner. Wife abuse did not begin in the twentieth century. There are statements in Frankish common law which indicate that a man has the right to discipline his slaves, his children, and his wife. In some cultures it was not a crime to murder one's wife. Battered woman syndrome is so named because, in the opinion of some experts, the condition does not describe only the woman, but refers to a collection of characteristics that appear in both the man and the woman. Wife battering tends to be episodic, with sometimes long periods of relative peace between episodes. The battered woman syndrome is seen by some as an ailment of a marriage. It occurs less frequently among those who live together unmarried. In assessing the probability of battering in a particular household, any prior occurrence of domestic violence is the most common indicator. An additional 10 risk factors have been identified. In homes where two factors are found, the risk of battering is twice as high as in homes displaying no factors. Households exhibiting seven or more factors engage in 40 times more violence than those with none. Risk factors are:

- Male is unemployed.
- Male uses illicit drugs at least once a year.
- Partners have different religious backgrounds.
- Male witnessed his father striking his mother.
- Partners cohabit but are unmarried.
- If employed, male has blue-collar job.
- Male does not have a high school diploma.
- Male is between 18 and 30 years of age.
- One of the partners is violent toward children in the household.
- Total household income is below the poverty level.

In 2002, California enacted legislation that allows women convicted prior to 1992 to petition for a new trial in cases where evidence of battered woman syndrome was not allowed into evidence during their original trial.

battery. Any unlawful application or use of force upon an individual.

Baumes's laws. The restrictive penal legislation sponsored by a committee of the New York State Senate in 1926, of which Senator Caleb H. Baumes was chairman. These laws provided an increase in penalty with each successive offense and an automatic life sentence for the fourth offense, whether known at the time of conviction or discovered after sentencing. The term Baumes's laws has been widely applied to similar habitual-offender laws subsequently enacted in other states.

bayonet. An edged steel weapon with a tapered point, a blood groove, and a formed handle designed for attachment to the muzzle end of a rifle, shotgun, or the like. Bayonets were first introduced in Bayonne, France, in the seventeenth century, and the earlier forms were made to be fitted into the bore of a musket or rifle.

beam test. A microscopic examination of crushed marijuana as a means of accurately distinguishing it from similar-looking material.

Bean, Roy. (1825?–1903). An outlaw born in Mason County, KY, Bean worked at various jobs, sought gold in the West, and traded in Mexico. In 1847 he shot a man in a barroom brawl; several years later, he killed a Mexican army officer in a gun duel over a woman, after which he was hanged (but survived). Bean's career in frontier justice began in 1882, when he drifted across the Pecos River into West Texas, dispensing whiskey from a tent. The records of Pecos County, TX, document that Bean was appointed justice of the peace on August 2, 1882, by the County Commissioner's Court and that he fully qualified for the position by submitting a $1,000 bond. He held court sessions in his saloon, where he dispensed rough-and-ready justice and hung a sign designating himself "the law west of the Pecos." In 1896, after the number of votes cast for Bean proved to be in excess of the voting population, he was removed from the bench.

Beccaria, Marchese de (Cesare Bonesana). (1738–1794). Referred to as the "father of criminology," and one of the founders of the classical school of criminology. His major work, *An Essay on Crimes and Punishments*, became the manifesto of the liberal approach that led to major changes in European criminal laws. Besides denouncing torture and excessive use of the death penalty, he further argued that penalties should equal offenses and that certainty of penalties is more effective as a deterrent than severity. He also advocated the prevention of crime and rigid rules of criminal procedure.

bedlam. A popular name for an asylum for the mentally ill. The word originated as a contraction of St. Mary of Bethlehem, the name of a hospital in London. Used for mental patients as early as 1402, the institution was formally designated a "lunatic asylum" by King Henry VIII in 1547. Conditions in Bedlam were so terrible that the word became a general term for confusion and uproar.

behavioral model of crime. An approach in criminology which seeks to explain crime in terms of the individual pathology of the offender, the social pathology of the society, or a combination of the two.

Behavioral Research Institute. Founded in 1974, the Institute is a nonprofit organization "conducting basic evaluation in the areas of crime, delinquency, alcoholism, drug abuse, and related contemporary social problems." Address: 2305 Canyon Boulevard, Boulder, CO 80302.

behavior modification. A method of treatment of offenders, based on the belief that all behavior is learned and that socially acceptable behavior can be learned as a replacement for deviant behavior. There are two basic types of behavior modification: (a) classical conditioning, spawned by the Russian physiologist Ivan Petrovitch Pavlov in the 1920s, which has usually been associated with negative reinforcers, such as shock treatments and deprivation of privileges for undesirable behavior; and (b) operant conditioning, which is best exemplified in the research and writings of B. F. Skinner. The distinction between the two theories appears to be that classical conditioning seeks to modify basic emotional responses, while operant conditioning is used to teach individuals how to act or how to manage their emotions.

bench. The place where judges sit in court; the collective body of judges sitting as a court.

bench probation (bench parole). The process of allowing individuals on probation to remain at liberty in the community, with the sentencing judge as their only direct supervisor, on the basis of their pledge not to engage in any further illegal behavior.

bench trial. In this procedure, also called a court trial, no jury is present, and only a judge hears all evidence and determines the guilt or innocence of the defendant. Bench trials are held when the accused waives his or her right to a jury trial and requests or agrees to be defended only before a judge.

bench warrant. A document issued by a court, directing that a law enforcement officer bring before the court the person named therein, usually a person who has failed to obey a court order or a notice to appear.

benefit of clergy. A thirteenth-century practice that allowed members of the clergy to escape capital punishment and other severe sentences by transferring their cases to church courts, where they were routinely acquitted.

benzidine test. A preliminary chemical test for blood. If the test is negative, the presence of blood is eliminated. If it is positive, the stain may be blood, but the laboratory should conduct further tests to determine whether blood is definitely present.

bequeath. To give personal property by will.

Berkowitz, David. ("Son of Sam"). From July 1976 through most of 1977, Berkowitz terrorized more than 12 million residents of greater New York City. Born out of wedlock in 1953, as David Falco, Berkowitz was phobic as a child and psychotic as an adult. On Christmas Eve 1975, he committed his first act of violence by stabbing two women. Six months later he struck again, with a .44 caliber revolver, and by July 1977, he had fired his weapon a total of 32 times, killing six of his victims and wounding another seven. A special detective squad known as the Omega Group was formed to hunt down the ".44-caliber killer." On April 17, 1977, after killing two more victims, Berkowitz left a note in the street addressed to Joseph Borelli, a police detective assigned to supervise his capture. In it, Berkowitz remarked that he was not a woman-hater but a monster and wrote the sentence that would make him the centerpiece of thousands of headlines on the following day: "I am the Son of Sam." The Omega Group traced hundreds of leads each day and investigated a total of 3,167 suspects. Berkowitz was traced through a parking ticket and arrested on August 10, 1977. He readily admitted his guilt and was sentenced, on several counts of murder, attempted murder, assault, and possession of a deadly weapon, to a total of 365 years in prison. Berkowitz is in Attica Correctional Facility, a maximum-security prison in northern New York State. *See also* serial murders

Bertillon method of identification. A system of determining whether an individual under investigation is the same individual as one whose anthropometric measurements are on record. It was invented by Alphonse Bertillon when he was head of the Paris police department in 1883, and applied to the identification of criminals. It consisted of measuring certain parts of the body, standardizing forensic photography, noting peculiar markings, and classifying the data to make easy the location of thousands of records. His method, based on the unreliable observation that physical maturity fixes the skeletal dimensions for life, has been widely superseded by the fingerprint method.

best evidence rule. One coming into court must bring the best available original evidence to prove the questions involved in the case. If a written document is involved, it is the best evidence and must be produced, unless it is shown to have been lost or destroyed.

bestiality. Sexual intercourse between humans and animals. Bestiality occurs predominantly in rural areas and most commonly involves male adolescents and farm mammals.

beyond a reasonable doubt. A legal term used in relation to proof by evidence. In cases where the state (prosecution) uses direct evidence in whole or part as proof of the offense, such evidence must convince the jury, or the judge if no jury is used, of the guilt of the accused *beyond a reasonable doubt. See also* doubt, reasonable

bias. The theoretical or emotional preconceptions or prejudices of individuals or groups, which may lead to certain subjective interpretations that are radically different from objective reality.

bifurcated trial. A special two-part trial proceeding in which the issue of guilt is tried in the first step and, if a conviction results, the appropriate sentence or applicable sentencing statute is determined in the second step. The two steps of a bifurcated trial generally take place in separate hearings. Typical issues in the second step of a bifurcated trial are (a) what sentence to impose (e.g., for capital offense convictions, whether to impose the death penalty) and (b) what statute section should determine the convicted person's sentence (e.g., whether or not the convicted person meets the statutory definition of habitual criminal).

bifurcation. The dividing or forking of one line into two or more branches. A term used in describing fingerprint patterns. *See also* fingerprints

bigamy (or polygamy). (1) Unlawful contracting of marriage by a person who, at the time of the marriage, knows himself or herself already to be legally married. (2) A statutory and not a common law crime; involvement in two monogamous marriages at one time. In most states the second marriage is void, the partners are criminally liable, and any children of the second marriage are illegitimate.

big brother plan. A plan for reducing juvenile delinquency by securing the cooperation of recognized community leaders to act as "big brothers" to boys who appear before the juvenile court. The plan aims to organize the economic and social resources of the community to assist boys who need a helping hand and practical guidance in growing into self-respecting manhood. The service is entirely voluntary, and the success of the plan is almost impossible to determine, since adequate records are seldom maintained.

bill of attainder. A legislative act declaring an individual guilty, without trial, of a crime such as treason. The U.S. Constitution specifically forbids bills of attainder.

bill of exceptions. A written statement of objections made, or exceptions taken, by either side to the court's rulings or instructions during a trial. The statement becomes an integral part of the record when the case is appealed and is used by the appellate court in reaching its decision.

bill of exchange. A written order from one person to another, requiring the person to whom it is addressed to pay a certain sum on demand or at a fixed date.

bill of indictment. A document, usually prepared by a prosecutor, which charges a person with the commission of a crime and is submitted to a grand jury for its consideration. If the jury finds there are sufficient grounds to support the charge, it returns the document with the endorsement "true bill." If there are not sufficient grounds, the endorsement reads "not a true bill."

bill of pains and penalties. A legislative conviction similar to a bill of attainder, except that it imposes a penalty of less than death. It, too, is prohibited in the United States.

bill of particulars. An amplification of the proceedings, designed to make more specific the allegations made in the case.

bill of rights. A brief statement of certain fundamental rights and privileges that are guaranteed to the people against infringement by the government. The English Bill of Rights, from which some provisions of American bills of rights have been derived, is a statement of Parliament passed in 1689. The Virginia Bill of Rights, 1776, incorporated some common law principles. The first ten amendments to the Constitution of the United States, popularly called the Bill of Rights, were added to the Constitution in 1791, after state ratifying conventions had objected to the absence of such guarantees in the original document. They were originally limitations on the federal government only (*Barron v. Baltimore*). Beginning in 1925, many of the substantive provisions of the federal Bill of Rights have also become limitations on state governments by judicial interpretation. A bill of rights is nearly always the first article of a state constitution.

bill of sale. A written document transferring the rights and interest in certain personal property or chattels.

bind over. (1) The decision by a court of limited jurisdiction requiring that a person charged with a felony appear for trial on that charge in a court of general jurisdiction, as the result of a finding of probable cause at a preliminary hearing held in the limited jurisdiction court. The basic meaning of *bind over* is to send forward; the contrasting term, *remand*, means to send back. (2) To require by judicial authority that a person promise to appear for trial, appear in court as a witness, or keep the peace.

bio-assay. The estimation of the amount of potency of a drug or other physiologically active substance by its action on a suitable living organism.

biocriminology. A relatively new branch of criminology, developed in the past decade, that attempts to explain criminal behavior by referring to biological factors that predispose some individuals to commit criminal acts.

biological determinism. The theory that certain qualities inherent in an organism cause its behavior. In this view the substantive concerns of social science are eliminated or at least enormously subordinated. A number of theories of human development are biologically deterministic. Cesare Lombroso claimed that those who become criminal are degenerate and animalistic, with identifiable atavisms—regressive, apelike qualities. *See also* Lombroso, Cesare

biometry. A measuring or calculating of the probable duration of human life; the attempt to correlate the frequency of crime between parents and children or siblings. *See also* Goring, Charles

biosocial criminology. A contemporary resurgence of pre-sociological and nonsociological explanations of the sources of crime. According to these theories, the ultimate

THE BILL OF RIGHTS

First Amendment
Congress shall make no law respecting an establishment of religion, or prohibiting the free exercise thereof; or abridging the freedom of speech, or of the press; or the right of the people peaceably to assemble, and to petition the Government for a redress of grievances.

Second Amendment
A well regulated Militia, being necessary to the security of a free State, the right of the people to keep and bear Arms, shall not be infringed.

Third Amendment
No soldier shall, in time of peace be quartered in any house, without the consent of the Owner, nor in time of war, but in a manner to be prescribed by law.

Fourth Amendment
The right of the people to be secure in their persons, houses, papers, and effects, against unreasonable searches and seizures, shall not be violated, and no Warrants shall issue, but upon probable cause, supported by Oath or affirmation, and particularly describing the place to be searched, and the persons or things to be seized.

Fifth Amendment
No person shall be held to answer for a capital, or otherwise infamous crime, unless on a presentment or indictment of a Grand Jury, except in cases arising in the land or naval forces, or in the Militia, when in actual service in time of War or public danger; nor shall any person be subject for the same offence to be twice put in jeopardy of life or limb; nor shall be compelled in any criminal case to be a witness against himself, nor be deprived of life, liberty, or property, without due process of law; nor shall private property be taken for public use, without just compensation.

Sixth Amendment
In all criminal prosecutions, the accused shall enjoy the right to a speedy and public trial, by an impartial jury of the State and district wherein the crime shall have been committed, which district shall have been previously ascertained by law, and to be informed of the nature and cause of the accusation; to be confronted with the witnesses against him; to have compulsory process for obtaining witnesses in his favor, and to have the Assistance of Counsel for his defence.

Seventh Amendment
In Suits at common law, where the value in controversy shall exceed twenty dollars, the right of trial by jury shall be preserved, and no fact tried by a jury, shall be otherwise re-examined in any Court of the United States, than according to the rules of the common law.

Eighth Amendment
Excessive bail shall not be required nor excessive fines imposed, nor cruel and unusual punishments inflicted.

Ninth Amendment
The enumeration in the Constitution, of certain rights, shall not be construed to deny or disparage others retained by the people.

Tenth Amendment
The powers not delegated to the United States by the Constitution, nor prohibited by it to the States, are reserved to the States respectively, or to the people.

---

causes of criminal behavior are found in the physical and biological makeup of the individual offender.

bio-terrorism. A biological or chemical assault on persons or property. According to the Centers for Disease Control and Prevention (CDC), biological or "germ" warfare could include agents such as botulism, smallpox, anthrax, pneumonic plague, tularemia, and hemorrhagic fevers such as Ebola and Marburg. The CDC publishes the *Morbidity and Mortality Weekly Report*.

The National Laboratory Response network was formed in 1998 after the 1995 sarin gas attack in the Tokyo subways by the Aum Shinrikyo Supreme Truth cell. The network is a partnership among the CDC and Prevention in Atlanta, the Association of Public Health Laboratories, the FBI Laboratory's Hazardous Materials Response Unit and other federal agencies. *See* terrorism

bisexuality. Engaging in sexual acts with or being attracted both to members of the opposite sex (heterosexuality) and to members of the same sex (homosexuality). The capacity for bisexual behavior is now believed by many scientists to be inherent in all humans; according to this theory, heterosexual orientation is culturally, not biologically, determined. The term bisexuality is sometimes inaccurately used to mean having the characteristics of both sexes; it is therefore often confused with hermaphrodism.

Black Guerrilla Family. A prison gang formed at San Quentin by the late George Jackson. The BGF is estimated to number about 400 members within Califomia prisons and about 200 at liberty.

Members were initially characterized by prison officials as having tight internal discipline and a left-wing political ideology that held that blacks were essentially political prisoners. Authorities said the group, which had ties to the Black Panther Party and Symbionese Liberation Army in the mid-1970s, once had a political strategy that included plans to kidnap Department of Corrections officials. At least two murders in Los Angeles during 1985 have been linked to BGF attempts to move in on the cocaine trade.

Black Hand. An organization that obtains money by threats and violence committed against its victims. *See also* Mafia; organized crime

Black, Hugo (Lafayette). (1886–1971). An associate justice of the U.S. Supreme Court (1937–1971) who pursued a judicial career marked by the absolute defense of civil rights as they are literally defined in the Bill of Rights and the Constitution. Born in Alabama, he practiced law before his election to the Senate in 1924. As a senator he supported President Franklin D. Roosevelt's plan to add six justices to the Supreme Court, which became known as the "court packing" plan, and was appointed by Roosevelt to the Supreme Court in 1937. Black held that the First Amendment freedoms of speech, press, and religious liberty were "absolutes." His position resulted in occasional intellectual confrontations with those who held that individual rights should be weighed against the need for governmental authority.

Black Law Enforcement Executives, National Organization of (NOBLE). Founded in 1976. Publishes NOBLE Actions (quarterly). E-mail noble@noblenatl.org. Web site: http://www. noblenatl.org. Address: 4609 Pinecrest Office Park Dr., Suite F, Alexandria, VA 22312.

black-light stamps. A security measure in which visitors to any site have their hands stamped with ink that reflects ultraviolet light, which is then visible when a black-light device is shone on it.

blacklist. A list of the names and other identifying data about prominent union leaders, organizers, and members. Such a list was used before the 1930s by anti-union business firms in their attempts to avoid hiring pro-union people. The enactment of the Wagner Act has rendered the blacklist unworkable.

blackmail. The extortion of money from a person by threats of accusation or exposure. *See also* extortion

Black Muslims. The Black Muslim nationalist movement was founded in Detroit in 1930 by Wali Farad, who was succeeded by Elijah Muhammad with the help of Malcolm X. The Muslims, headquartered in Chicago, maintain their own schools, stores, farms, and a newspaper, *Muhammad Speaks*. They believe they are descendants of an ancient lost tribe of Muslims, and they adhere to some orthodox Islamic beliefs. Members are taught to shun white people. The group denounces lying, gluttony, drinking, and the use of narcotics. *See also* Malcolm X

Black Panther Party. Militant black organization. In October 1966, two black students from Merritt College in Oakland, CA, Bobby Seale and Huey P. Newton, purchased guns and drafted their 10-point self-defense program. In 1967 they opened their first storefront headquarters in Oakland. They called for complete equality for black people, including demands for black exemption from military service, the freeing of all imprisoned blacks, and the calling of all-black juries for blacks accused of crime.

Between 1968 and 1971 the Panthers (never more than 2,000 strong) established headquarters across the nation, claiming they were armed and would defend themselves if attacked. The police systematically harassed the Panthers, killing a score of them and jailing their leaders (including Seale and Newton, who were eventually exonerated). In 1972 the Panthers discontinued their armed-defense tactics and moved into black community-development programs. Seale ran for mayor of Oakland in 1973, and Newton was shot and killed in Oakland in 1989.

Blacks in Criminal Justice, National Association of. Founded in 1972. An association of criminal justice professionals concerned with the impact of criminal justice policies and practices on the minority community. Compiles statistics on minority involvement in the criminal justice field. Publishes *Local Criminal Justice Issues Newsletter* (bi-monthly); *NABCJ Minority Criminal Justice Personnel Directory* (annually). Address: N.C. Central University, P.O. Box 19788, Durham, NC 27707.

Blacks in Law Enforcement, Inc. (BLE). Founded in 1986. Publishes *Blacks in Law Enforcement*. Address: 256 E. McLemore Avenue, Memphis, TN 38106.

blood alcohol. A chemical test for determining the concentration of alcohol in the blood. The test refers to the weight of the alcohol measured in grams per 100 milliliters of blood, given in percentage figures. Also called blood alcohol concentration.

blood alcohol level (BAL). The measurement of breath, blood, or urine samples to determine intoxication. It is expressed in terms of the percentage of alcohol in a person's blood: a BAL of .10 percent means one part alcohol to 1,000 parts blood. The following list indicates general BAL effects:

- .02% Moderate drinkers feel some effect.
- .04% Most people begin to feel relaxed.
- .06% Judgment begins to be impaired. There appears to be less concern with

environment and difficulty making rational decisions.

- .08% Talkative, noisy, moody. Muscle coordination and driving skills are definitely impaired. In 34 states a driver is considered legally under the influence.
- .10% Reaction time and control have clearly deteriorated. In 16 states, a driver is considered legally under the influence.
- .12% Serious loss of judgment and coordination. Vomiting often occurs.
- .15% Staggering; slurred speech.
- .30% The person may lose consciousness.
- .40% Loss of consciousness and possible death.
- .45% Death.

"Drunk-driving suspects' homes can be entered without a warrant to get evidence of blood-alcohol content." In this Califomia appeals court ruling of March 1985, the court acknowledged a Supreme Court ruling against Wisconsin officers making such warrantless entries, but indicated that California's more serious view of drunk driving justifies warrantless entries in that state.

blood-borne pathogens. Disease-causing organisms, such as bacteria or viruses, that are carried by means of the circulatory system.

blood feud. A quarrel between families or clans. The feud between the families of Hatfield and McCoy is one of the more famous.

Bloodhound Association, National Police. Founded in 1962. Publishes *Nose News* (quarterly). Address: R.D. 1, Box 345, Allenwood, PA 17810.

bludgeon. A short stick with one thick, heavy, or loaded end, used as an offensive weapon; any clublike weapon.

blue-collar workers. A term used to designate employees who are not involved in supervision or administration of a business. The term originated when factory-floor workers wore blue collars and office personnel wore white collars. Blue collar does not imply a skill level. A skilled machinist and the janitor who sweeps the floor are both considered blue-collar workers.

blue laws. (1) A puritanical code regulating public and private morality in the theocratic New Haven, CT, colony during the seventeenth and eighteenth centuries. (2) All laws prohibiting athletic contests or the opening of stores and theaters on Sunday, race-track betting, or any similar activity usually regulated by individual conscience. Recently the Supreme Court, as a protection of religious freedom, has exempted businessmen who observe a Sabbath day other than Sunday from the obligation to obey Sunday-closing laws. In 1982 the Supreme Court overturned Vermont's blue laws, which had prohibited stores from opening on Sunday.

blue-ribbon jury. A petit jury selected for its special qualifications, either because the case is too complex for a regular jury or because some expert knowledge is required. Such juries existed from the earliest period of development of the common law and were common in London by the mid-fourteenth century. Because of the modern emphasis on impartial selection of jurors, blue-ribbon juries have fallen into disfavor. They were abolished in U.S. federal courts in 1968.

blue sky laws. Laws intended to prevent the sale of fraudulent securities. The term is attributed to a facetious remark made by a Kansas bank commissioner, who said that certain skillful promoters were able to "sell blocks of the blue sky" to gullible victims. The U.S. Supreme Court upheld the law on the ground that prevention of deception is within the competency of government. This law requires companies selling stock to file financial statements with state banking commissioners in all operating locations.

board of pardons. A state board, having various official names, that acts alone or with the governor in granting executive clemency to criminals or advises the governor in the exercise of that function.

board of parole. An eight-man board in the Department of Justice which grants or revokes all paroles of federal prisoners. If authorized by a court, the board determines the date of a convicted person's eligibility for parole.

board of review. An administrative appeals board which, after hearing evidence, determines whether an assessment, action, or decision of an officer was correct.

body types. Human physical structures or builds. Constitutional psychologist William Sheldon created a typology consisting of three categories, each of which he related to a characteristic temperament. The endomorph was flabby and easygoing, the skinny ectomorph was inclined to be introspective, and the mesomorph was restless and tended to translate impulse into action.

Bomb Data Center, National. Founded in 1970. Provides technical information and services to law enforcement agencies. Details may be obtained from the International Association of Chiefs of Police (IACP).

Bomb Technicians and Investigators, International Association of. Founded in Sacramento, CA, in March 1973. Publishes *The Detonator Magazine* (bimonthly). Address: IABIT, P.O. Box 160, Goldvein, VA 22720-0160.

bomb training school. The Department of Justice operates the Advanced Bomb Training School, Bureau of Alcohol, Tobacco & Firearms (ATF) Technical Branch, Building 20, FLETC, Glynco, GA 31524, for law enforcement specialists. Due to its length and specialized content, the ATF glossary of terms has not been included in this dictionary.

bona fide. In good faith; honestly, without fraud or unfair dealing; genuine.

bona fide occupational qualification (BFOQ). Any physical attribute and/or skill that an employer has proven is necessary for satisfactory performance of a particular job, as distinguished from characteristics that have sometimes been required, such as race, height, gender, property-owning status, or passing grades on tests, but that can't be shown to be related to job performance.

bond. A pledge of money or assets offered as bail by an accused person or his or her surety (bail bondsman) to secure temporary release from custody; forfeited if the conditions of bail are not fulfilled.

bondsman. An individual, bound by a contract, who is responsible for the performance of an act on behalf of another person.

boodle. Money accepted or paid for the use of political influence; bribe money. The term originated in New York City about 1883.

bookie. A person who operates a racing "book"; one who takes illegal bets on horse races.

booking. A law enforcement or correctional process that officially records an entry-into-detention after arrest; involves recording the identity of the arrestee, place, time, reason for arrest, and name of arresting authority.

bookmaking. The practice of receiving and recording bets made on the results of horse racing and other sporting events; often illegal.

boot camps. *See* shock incarceration

Booth, John Wilkes. Born near Bel Air, MD, in 1838, a son of Junius Brutus Booth and a brother of Edwin Booth. After the fall of Richmond and General Lee's surrender at Appomattox, Booth decided on assassination, enlisting one accomplice to murder Vice President Andrew Johnson and another to kill Secretary of State William H. Seward. On the evening of April 14, 1865, Booth ascended the stairway to the president's box at Ford's Theater and shot Abraham Lincoln in the head. He leaped to the stage, crying, "Sic semper tyrannis! The South is avenged!" and escaped through the rear of the theater. His accomplices were unsuccessful in their assassination attempts, although Seward was badly beaten. Booth was not located until April 26, when he was found hiding in a barn near Bowling Green, VA, and was either killed by his captors or died by his own hand.

bootlegging. Illegal manufacture, transportation, and/or sale of alcoholic beverages.

border. *See* U.S.–Mexico border

borstals. English institutions that are organized for the treatment of youthful offenders. Eleven in number, these institutions provide special care for the varying types of offenders. Of these, four of the borstals are walled, four are open, one is for boys who have broken parole (designated as "revokees"), and one is for especially difficult problem cases.

borstal system. Halfway houses in Europe. Devised there and used to reorient persons recently released from prisons or substance abuse treatment centers. *See also* halfway house

Boston Massacre. Name applied to the killing of five men and the wounding of others when British troops fired into a crowd of men and boys in Boston in 1770. The incident occurred as a result of the quartering of two regiments of troops in Boston, sent to protect British officials in executing the Customs Acts. John Adams acted as counsel for the British in the trial that followed. The British officer in command was acquitted of the charge of giving the order to fire. Two British soldiers were given light sentences for manslaughter.

Boston Police Strike. A strike of 75 percent of the Boston police force on September 9, 1919. The immediate cause was refusal by the police commissioner to recognize the policemen's union. Governor Calvin Coolidge was requested to intercede after the outbreak of the strike, but refused. Mayor Petes then brought in sections of the militia, which broke the strike. Coolidge followed this act by commanding the police commissioner to assume charge and calling out the entire state guard, after order had already been established. His often-quoted declaration that "there is no right to strike against the public safety by anybody, anywhere, anytime" projected him into the national limelight as a supporter of law and order. This led to his nomination for president by the Republican Party in 1920.

bounty. A reward or premium, usually offered as an inducement for some act.

bounty hunters. *See* thief-takers

bourgeoisie. In Marxist theory, the owners of the means of production; the ruling class in capitalist societies.

Bow Street Runners. A unit of the police force organized in the London, England, metropolitan area in the last half of the 1700s by John and Henry Fielding to prevent crime. This concept was developed into "the new science of preventive police." Some called this unit the first police detective squad, as its function was to arrive at the scene of the crime quickly and investigate the case.

brachioproticism. Also known as brachioprotic eroticism, this practice involves inserting one's hand into another's rectum for sexual pleasure.

brain death. A legal definition adopted by many states. Under it, an individual is dead when the brain and the brain stem cease all functioning. This definition of death became necessary once the medical profession developed the ability to maintain heart and lung functions by artificial means.

Brandeis, Louis Dembitz. (1856–1941). Served as associate justice of the Supreme Court from 1916, when he was appointed by President Woodrow Wilson, until 1939. Born in Louisville, KY, Brandeis was educated in public schools, in the severe academic discipline of Dresden, Germany, and at Harvard Law School. He gained recognition for his expertise in litigation in his private law practice in Boston. Brandeis disdained the traditional lawyer's brief, which was filled with narrow procedural points. Instead, he filled his legal presentations with social and economic arguments. "The Brandeis brief" became the label given to this type of argument. While he was a lawyer, he became an ardent Zionist. Once on the Court, Brandeis immediately became associated with Justice Oliver Wendell Holmes Jr., and his advocacy of judicial restraint. Brandeis believed that legislative regulations in the economic sphere were necessary, but he held that the judicial branch had to remain aloof from them. A thorough scholar, Brandeis filled his opinions with cross-references and footnotes.

Brandeis is also associated with Holmes in the formulation of the "clear and present danger" test of laws restricting speech and press, although, if anything, Brandeis was more emphatic in his defense of the First Amendment freedoms. Nonetheless, he is still generally associated with the tradition of judicial restraint. He consistently argued for a limited role in judicial decision making, and he was a dedicated defender of federalism.

breach of peace. A violation of the public tranquility and order. Such violations include blocking the sidewalk, fighting, cursing, spitting on the sidewalk, loitering, panhandling, and other types of disorderly behavior defined as illegal in various jurisdictions. Such offenses are crimes against the state.

breach of trust. Willful acts that use knowledge or power acquired through one's official position to gain unfair advantage in competitive situations or to achieve monetary or other gain. Many such acts are not regarded as crimes but are merely subject to ethical sanctions. To constitute a crime, there must be a breach of some official duty sufficient to justify the state's intervention. *See also* fiduciary; organized deception of the public

breaking. A forcible destroying, removing, or putting aside of something material that constitutes a part of a building and is relied on as security against intrusion; forcible entry of a building.

Breathalizer. A commercial device to test the breath of a suspected drinker and determine that person's blood-alcohol content.

breath-testing equipment. Equipment designed to test the breath to determine blood-alcohol level. There are several brands of such products. *See also* passive alcohol sensor

bribe. A price, reward, gift, or favor bestowed or promised with a view to perverting the judgment, or corrupting the conduct, of a judge, witness, or other individual.

bribery. The giving or offering of anything of value with intent unlawfully to influence persons in the discharge of their duties; the receiving or asking of anything of value with unlawful intent to be influenced.

briefs. Summaries of the law relating to a case, prepared by the attorneys for both parties and given to the judge.

Brink's Armored Car Service. Established in 1859 in Chicago, IL, by Washington Perry Brink.

British North America Act. Legislation passed by the Canadian Parliament in 1867 that created the structure of the Canadian criminal justice system.

broken window syndrome. A public safety theory that neighborhoods deteriorate rapidly if initial cases of vandalism, such as broken windows or graffiti, are ignored by law enforcement people and/or neighborhood residents. The premise is that police officers should take cases seriously and residents should repair damage promptly, since neglect indicates no one is concerned.

bug. (1) To plant a microphone or other sound sensor or to tap a communication line for the purpose of surreptitious listening or audio monitoring; loosely, to install a sensor in a specified location. (2) The microphone or other sensor used for the purpose of surreptitious listening.

buggery. *See* sodomy

bulimia nervosa. An eating disorder in which the patient engages in binge eating or gorging and then deliberately regurgitates the food and/or takes excessive laxatives to purge it from his or her system. The root of the word bulimia is "ox appetite."

bullet. A projectile made for firing in a rifle or pistol; the part of a cartridge, usually made of lead, that is discharged from a firearm.

Types of bullets include: (1) connelure—has grooves around it for a lubricant or for crimping; (2) flatpoint—has a flat nose ("wadcutter" is of this type); (3) hollowpoint—has hollow nose which causes the bullet to flatten or mushroom on impact; (4) metal-cased—has a jacket of metal covering the nose; (5) softpoint—has a metal case except for the nose, which is made of lead.

bunco game. Act or trick contrived to gain the confidence of a victim, who is then defrauded.

burden of proof. Duty of establishing the existence of fact in a trial.

bureaucratic model of legislation. The view that a society's laws are enacted as a result of power exerted by clearly identifiable bureaucratic organizations.

Bureau of Justice Assistance. Established in 1984 and authorized to provide block grants to assist state and local governments in carrying out programs to improve the criminal justice system, with special emphasis on violent crime and serious offenders. Located at Bureau of Justice Assistance, 810 Seventh Street NW, Fourth Floor, Washington, DC 20531.

Bureau of Justice Statistics. *See* National Institute of Justice

Bureau of Narcotics and Dangerous Drugs. Formed April 8, 1968, by a merger of the Bureau of Narcotics of the U.S. Treasury Department and the Bureau of Drug Abuse Control of the Department of Health, Education, and Welfare. Located at the U.S. Department of Justice, Washington, DC 20537. BNDD has regional offices and laboratories throughout the nation.

Burger, Warren Earl. (1907–1995). Fourteenth chief justice of the Supreme Court (1969–1986), appointed in 1969 by President Richard Nixon, who wanted a "law and order" jurist with "strict constructionist" views. Born in St. Paul, MN, Burger developed a successful law practice and also taught law. In 1953, he was appointed assistant attorney general by President Dwight Eisenhower and in 1956 was named to the U.S. Court of Appeals for the District of Columbia. He made a reputation as a conservative judge in a generally liberal appellate court. When appointed to the Supreme Court, Burger indicated that it was not the place for the type of liberal judicial reform practiced by the Warren Court. Several of his more notable contributions were to define obscenity legally, establish busing as a tool to end school segregation, force Nixon to release the Watergate tapes, lead the national celebrations of the Constitution's 200th anniversary in 1987 and the Bill of Rights' 200th anniversary in 1989, uphold affirmative action, and establish the right to abortion.

burglar alarm pad. A supporting frame laced with fine wire or a fragile panel with foil or fine wire, installed so as to cover an exterior opening in a building, such as a door or skylight. Entrance through the opening breaks the wire or foil and initiates an alarm signal.

Burglar and Fire Alarm Association, National. Founded in 1948. A clearinghouse for all materials related to the business of security alarm systems and services. Address: 8380 Colesville road, Suite 750, Silver Spring, MD 20910.

burglary. An early legal definition was trespassing and breaking and entering of the dwelling house of another in the nighttime with the intent to commit a felony. The term now means entry of any fixed structure, vehicle, or vessel used for regular residence, industry, or business, with or without force, with intent to commit a felony or larceny. Next to theft, burglary is the most frequent major crime and comprises more than one-quarter of the total FBI crime index. Burglary involves close to $1 billion in residential losses and $0.5 billion in nonresidential losses.

burglary, safe. The illegal entry of a safe. Several methods are used: "blowing"—using an explosive; "peeling"—peeling the safe back until entry is gained, usually by manipulating the locking device; "punching"—using a punch to force the locking mechanism; "ripping"—using a device working on the principle of a can opener and ripping open parts of the safe; "drilling"—drilling holes in the safe at pertinent points and either forcing the locking mechanism or actually gaining access to the inside chamber of the safe by reaching through the hole; and "burning"—gaining entry by using a flame-cutting torch or thermal burning bar.

burglary tools. Tools suitable for gaining illegal entry to a safe. Possession of such tools is illegal in many states, but the intent to use them to commit a crime must also be shown. The courts have held that it is immaterial that the tools might also be used for lawful purposes.

burnese. A powder high in cocaine content and used by many drug addicts.

burnout. The depletion of an individual's mental and physical resources, often due to excessive stress. Symptoms of burnout can include feelings of exhaustion, boredom, and impatience, as well as psychophysiological problems such as headaches, ulcers, and heart disease. Although it can occur in anyone, burnout appears to be more prevalent among caring professionals, such as counselors, social workers, doctors, police officers, and teachers. Treatment includes relaxation techniques, social support networks, variation of activities, and control of responsibilities. *See also* stress

burns (classification). . . . .

Type	Causes and Effects
First degree	Sunburn: steam. Reddening and peeling. Affects epidermis (top layer of skin). Heals within a week.
Second degree	Scalding: holding hot metal. Deeper burns causing blisters. Affects dermis (deep skin layer). Heals in two to three weeks.
Third degree	Fire. A full layer of skin is destroyed. Requires a doctor's care and grafting.
Circum-ferential	Any burns (often electrical) that completely encircle a limb or body region which can impair circulation or respiration; requires a doctor's care; fasciotomy (repair of connective tissues) is sometimes required.
Chemical	Acid, alkali. Can be neutralized with water (up to half an hour). Doctor's evaluation recommended.
Electrical	Destruction of muscles, nerves, circulatory system, and so on, below the skin. Doctor's evaluation and ECG monitoring required.

Burns International Security Services Inc.
Founded by William J. Burns in 1909; formerly called the Burns International Detective Agency.

Burns, William John. (1861–1932). Founder of Bums International Detective Agency and chief of the Federal Bureau of Investigation, Burns was born in Baltimore, MD. He served in the Secret Service and in the Department of the Interior. In 1909 with William P. Sheridan he formed the Burns and Sheridan Detective Agency, headquartered in Chicago. On March 11, 1910, Sheridan sold his interest to Burns, and the Burns National Detective Agency was born.

C

CA. Abbreviation for the federal Circuit Court of Appeals. The letters are followed by the designation for the circuit; that is, CA5 = Fifth Circuit and CADC = the District of Columbia Circuit Court.

cache. A hidden quantity of materials or items, often used in reference to weapons, as an arms cache.

cadaver. A corpse; dead body.

cadre. Trained and dedicated activists in an organization, forming its core and capable of training others.

Cain. An Old Testament farmer, son of Adam and Eve, known as world's first murderer for killing his brother Abel.

calendar. In criminal justice, a listing of pending cases and the date and place of the next step in their processing; a listing of all cases in any particular court for a given day.

caliber. A term that derives from the Latin *qua libra*, "what pound," first applied to the weight of a bullet and then to its diameter. The bore diameter is measured in hundredths of an inch. A .22 caliber gun has a barrel measuring 22/100 of an inch in diameter. This term is similar to gauge, used in shotguns, but caliber is measured differently. *See also* gauge

Calley, William L., Jr. On March 16, 1968, U.S. Army Lieutenant Calley and his platoon were helicoptered into My Lai, Vietnam, with orders to "clean the village out." They expected to find forces of the 48th Battalion of the Viet Cong but instead found several hundred civilians. The soldiers herded their captives to the center of the village, where Calley ordered them shot. By the end of the day, an estimated 567 civilians had been executed. Many soldiers refused to take part in the "My Lai Massacre," claiming the order was unlawful. On September 5, 1969, the day before Calley was scheduled to be discharged, he was accused of killing 109 Vietnamese civilians. He claimed innocence on the grounds that he was acting under orders. Calley was tried by a general court martial, convicted, and sentenced to life imprisonment. After several years under house arrest and confined to quarters, he was released and his life sentence commuted.

calumny. A false and malicious accusation of some offense or crime; slander; defamation.

Camarena, Enrique (Kiki). A DEA agent, Camarena in November 1984 assisted in a raid on a huge Mexican marijuana plantation owned by drug lord Rafael Caro Quintero. Camarena was kidnapped in Guadalajara in February 1985, tortured, and murdered. In December 1989 Caro Quintero and Ernesto Fonseca Carrillo, another drug kingpin, were convicted of Camarena's murder in Mexico City. In April 1990, Dr. Humberto Alvarez Macham, a third suspect in the murder, was abducted from Guadalajara and delivered to DEA agents in Texas.

Camorra. An underworld, secret, criminal organization that began in Naples, Italy, in 1830 and thrived until about 1922. While the Camorra was identified with the underworld of Neapolitan life, it also had contacts with civil, political, and religious authorities during its varied career. It represented a nineteenth-century version of an entrenched "racket" protected by civil and political authorities.

CAMP. The Campaign Against Marijuana Planting. Established in California in the early 1980s, this program has as its goal the eradication of marijuana planting in the state. Marijuana is typically planted in mid-April, late September, or early October. CAMP agents start their operations in late July or early August. In 2002, the program seized over 350,000 mature plants with an estimated street value of $1.4 billion. In 2003, more than 100,000 plants with a value of approximately $400 million were seized in the first 10 days of the program in the counties of Calaveras, Fresno, Mendocino, Tulare, Tuolumne, and Yolo. The program brings together officers from 70 local, state, and federal law enforcement agencies from throughout the state. Since its inception CAMP agents have eradicated more than 3 million marijuana plants with an estimated wholesale value of $12 billion.

Campaign for an Effective Crime Policy. This nonpartisan effort was launched in 1992 by criminal justice officials to encourage a less politicized, more informed debate about one of the nation's most difficult problems. The campaign's "A Call for a Rational Debate on Crime and Punishment" has been endorsed by more than 1,100 criminal justice professionals and elected officials in all 50 states and the District of Columbia. Address: 916 F St., NW, Suite 501, Washington, DC 20004.

Campus Law Enforcement Administrators, International Association of. Founded in 1958. Publishes *Campus Law Enforcement Journal* (bimonthly). Address: 342 N. Main Street, West Hartford, CT 06117-2507.

Campus Unrest, President's Commission on. A nine-member panel commissioned on June 13, 1970, to explore the causes of campus violence and recommend ways of peacefully resolving student grievances. The impetus for the commission, chaired by William Scranton, former Republican governor of Pennsylvania, was the shooting of students by National Guardsmen and police, respectively, at Kent State University in Ohio and Jackson State University in Mississippi in May 1970. On September 26, 1970, the commission issued separate reports on the two incidents, pointing to an "unparalleled crisis" on the nation's campuses. The studies saw the prolonged agonies of the Vietnam War and domestic economic instability as causes of student violence, which the commission vigorously condemned.

Canadian Association for the Prevention of Crime. Founded in 1919, the association and its provincial counterparts "work for crime prevention through public education, promoting a private citizen's voice in government policy and program development, providing a channel for the exchange of information and ideas, interdisciplinary study of specific issues, and consultation." Sponsors the biennial Canadian Congress for the Prevention of Crime and publishes the *Canadian Journal of Criminology* (quarterly). Address: 55 Parkdale Avenue, Ottawa, Ontario K1Y lES, Canada.

canine (K-9). Police, detection, or security dogs. Detector dogs and handlers are assigned by the Customs Service to international mail facilities, airports, cargo docks, terminals, and border ports. They screen mail, cargo, baggage, ships, aircraft, and vehicles. They are never used to search people. Customs uses a wide variety of dogs, many of which are recruited from animal shelters. Customs also accepts dogs donated by individual owners. Dogs may be available to the public when they retire (at age 9), if their handlers do not wish to keep them. Contact: Canine Training Center, Inspection and Control Division, Customs Service, Department of the Treasury, RR22, Box 7, Front Royal, VA 22630. *See also* Bloodhound Association, National Police; Canine Association, United States Police; Dog Association, North American Police Work

cannabis. The Indian hemp plant *cannabis sativa* that is the source of marijuana and hashish. It is a herbaceous annual growing wild in many parts of the world. Marijuana and hashish can have sedative, euphoric, or hallucinogenic effects. *See also* hashish; marijuana

cannabism. Poisoning with hemp or hashish.

canon. A standard or principle accepted as fundamentally true and in conformity with good usage and practice.

canon law. Church law, developed by the ecclesiastical courts of the twelveth and thirteenth centuries, with sources in Roman law. When the Roman Empire collapsed (A.D. 476), the popes found themselves acting as temporal rulers, and the influence of canon law grew rapidly. In 1140, Gratian, a Benedictine monk, made the first great codification of church law, assisted by professors of the University of Bologna. Church law has left its mark on the common law. In such

areas as crimes against morality involving adultery, incest, and sodomy, and in regulations concerning marriage and probate, the influence of the Church can be seen. Perjury and defamation were also once within the jurisdiction of the ecclesiastical courts. The element of guilt and criminal intent, together with the correctional theory of penitence, can be viewed as part of the overall impact of the Church on ethics and morality in the legal process.

canons of police ethics. Standards, principles, and policies governing the conduct of law enforcement officers. Adopted by the International Association of Chiefs of Police in 1957, the canons include the following articles: (a) primary responsibility of job; (b) limitations of authority; (c) duty to be familiar with the law and with the responsibility of self and other public officials; (d) utilization of proper means to gain proper ends; (e) cooperation with public officials in the discharge of their authorized duties; (f) private conduct; (g) conduct toward the public; (h) conduct in arresting and dealing with law violators; (i) gifts and favors; (j) presentation of evidence; and (k) attitudes toward profession.

capacitance alarm system. An alarm system in which a protected object is electrically connected to a capacitance sensor. The approach of an intruder causes sufficient change in capacitance to upset the balance of the system and trigger an alarm signal. Also called proximity alarm system.

capacity. In criminal justice, the legal ability of a person to commit a criminal act; the mental and physical ability to act with purpose and to be aware of the certain, probable, or possible results of one's conduct.

capias (Lat., lit. "that you take"). A generic name for writs (usually addressed to the sheriff), ordering the arrest of the individuals named in them.

capital offense. (1) A criminal offense punishable by death. (2) In some penal codes, an offense which may be punishable by death or by imprisonment for life.

capital punishment. *See* punishment, capital

capper. A person employed by an attorney to solicit business.

carbineer, carabiniere. A term derived from the French *carabinier*, or cavalry soldier armed with a carbine. In modern Italy a carabiniere is a policeman. Also spelled carabineer.

carbofuchsin. A chemical dye which, when mixed with a slow-drying glue, is applied on doorknobs, drawer handles, coins, or other objects. It immediately stains the hand and is difficult to wash away, rendering it useful in crime prevention and detection.

carbon monoxide poisoning. The result of inhaling the odorless, poisonous element contained in illuminating gases and in exhaust gases of motor vehicles or incompletely oxidized coal in a dampened furnace. The victim loses consciousness, the skin flushes, breathing is deep and noisy, and the pulse is full and rapid.

cardiopulmonary resuscitation (CPR). An emergency revival procedure involving chest compression to assist the heart and forcing air into the lungs by breathing into the unconscious victim's mouth, both techniques aimed at maintaining the flow of blood to the brain.

Cardozo, Benjamin Nathan. (1870–1938). Lawyer and jurist of distinction whose liberal but balanced judgments profoundly influenced the Supreme Court in its consideration of New Deal legislation. Born in New York City, Cardozo was educated at Columbia University and admitted to the bar in 1891. He was elected to the New York Supreme Court in 1913. Cardozo held that the intent of historical law, not its form, should guide justice. He believed the value of the Constitution lay in its intrinsic generality and that the function of the judiciary was to apply established principles to current trends.

career criminal. A person having a past record of multiple arrests or convictions for serious crimes or an unusually large number of arrests or convictions for crimes of varying degrees of seriousness. This term has a formal effect on allocating prosecutorial resources and setting priorities in case scheduling, in order that defendants and cases warranting special attention can be dealt with effectively and speedily. The definition varies, but generally describes offenders who:

- have an extensive record of arrests and convictions
- commit crimes over a long period of time
- commit crimes at a very high rate
- commit relatively serious crimes
- use crimes as their principal source of income
- specialize (or are especially expert) in a certain type of crime
- have some combination of these characteristics.

Such criminals are often described as chronic, habitual, repeat, serious, high-rate, or professional offenders.

career criminal, armed. A person who receives, possesses, or transports, in commerce or affecting commerce, any firearm and who has three previous convictions for robbery, burglary, or both.

Cargo Criminal Apprehension Teams (Cargo CATS). Comprised of county, state, and federal law enforcement officials, these groups conduct investigations to identify, apprehend, and prosecute cargo thieves. During 1995 in California, for example, CATS made 68 arrests and recovered stolen cargoes and equipment valued at $10,268,785. *See also* Operation Guatemalan Auto Theft Enforcement.

carjacking. The unauthorized seizure of a motor vehicle by the use of force, threats, or coercion. Two arrests in Philadelphia on November 13, 1992, were the nation's first under a new federal law. This 1992 legislation mandates a 15-year sentence for convicted carjackers and imposes an automatic life sentence if a victim is killed during the commission of the crime.

carnal abuse. A male's contact with a female's sexual organs with his genitals, but that does not involve penetration.

carnal knowledge. A general term for sexual activity, usually applied to males who engage in intercourse in a way that violates a law.

carotid choke hold. A controversial hold sometimes used by law enforcement officers to subdue violent subjects. Pressure is applied with the arm, a baton, or a flashlight to the carotid artery, located below the jaw at the side of the neck, which causes unconsciousness. The carotid is the principal artery of the neck, supplying blood to the head. Because this hold is potentially lethal, its use is banned in many jurisdictions.

Carrier's Case. A legal precedent of 1483 that changed the definition of larceny in England in a way that favored the interests of traders and merchants.

Carroll Doctrine. In *Carroll v. United States* (1925), petitioner George Carroll was convicted of transporting liquor for sale in violation of the federal prohibition law and the Eighteenth Amendment. The liquor, used as evidence, had been taken from his car by agents acting without a search warrant. But the Supreme Court sustained Carroll's conviction against his contention that the seizure violated his Fourth Amendment rights. Known as the Carroll Doctrine, the Court's decision maintained that an automobile or other vehicle may, upon probable cause, be searched without a warrant. In 1931, the Court upheld the search of a parked car as reasonable, since the police could not know when the suspect might move it. The Carroll Doctrine was reaffirmed in 1970, when the Supreme Court held that a warrantless search of an automobile that resulted in the seizure of weapons and other evidence, but that was conducted many hours after the arrests of the suspects, was lawful.

case. At the level of police or prosecutorial investigation, a set of circumstances under investigation involving one or more persons; at subsequent steps in criminal proceedings, either a charging document alleging the commission of one or more crimes or a single defendant charged with one or more crimes; in juvenile or correctional proceedings, a person who is the object of agency action.

case law. Judicial precedent generated as a byproduct of the decisions that courts have made to resolve unique disputes, as distinguished from statutes and constitutions. Case law concerns concrete facts; statutes and constitutions are written in the abstract.

caseload. (1) The total number of clients registered with a correctional agency or agent on a given date or during a specified period, often divided into active supervisory cases and inactive cases, thus distinguishing between clients with whom contact is regular and those with whom it is not. (2) The number of cases requiring judicial action at a certain time or acted upon in a court during a given period. A model court caseload statistical system has recently been developed by the National Court Statistics Project under Bureau of Justice Statistics sponsorship. The model was developed as part of the State Court Caseload Statistics Program, to encourage development of fully comparable cross-jurisdictional caseload data.

cast. (1) To mold; to take the impression of certain objects and markings by using a substance that will harden and retain its shape. Used in law enforcement to record in physical form such evidence as footprints in soil, tire impressions, tool marks, and so forth. Many casting materials are used, including plaster of Paris for casting impressions in soil and a material called moulage for detail work on a rigid surface. (2) The physical object or reproduction made by casting.

castration. The surgical removal of the testicles. In 1997 Texas became the first state to offer castration on a voluntary basis to repeat sex offenders. Castration drastically reduces a man's level of testosterone, a hormone that is associated with aggression.

castration, chemical. Through weekly injections of a synthetic female hormone called Depo-Provera, this criminal justice procedure is intended to suppress the sex drive of male offenders. The practice received its first statutory approval in California, effective January 1, 1997, for twice-convicted child molesters. At a judge's discretion, first offenders can also be treated with this method. Since the effect is temporary, injections continue until authorities determine they are no longer necessary.

catamite. A homosexual male prostitute or a kept male.

cause. The matter brought before a court for decision.

cause, challenge of jurors for. Each side in a trial—prosecution and defense—has the right, prescribed by law, to challenge prospective jurors (veniremen) for cause, such as prior convictions, unsound mind, kinship to one of the parties, bias or prejudice, and so forth. If the court agrees with the challenge, the prospective juror will not be allowed to serve.

caveat. A formal notice given by an interested party to a court or judge, warning against the performance of certain judicial acts.

caveat emptor (Lat., lit. "let the buyer beware"). A formula that, under certain legally qualified conditions, enables sellers to decline legal responsibility for the quality or quantity of their wares. It does not, however, apply to the question of the title of property.

CB Radio Patrol of American Federation of Police. Founded 1976. Publishes *Police Times* (bimonthly). Address: 3801 Biscayne Blvd., Miami, FL 33137.

cease-and-desist order. An order, issued by an administrative agency to an individual, firm, or corporation, requiring that a particular fiscal or business practice be discontinued, and remaining in effect until reversed by the court that decides the resulting lawsuit. The order is commonly used by agencies charged with the regulation of business, such as the Federal Trade Commission or a state public utilities or railway commission.

celerity. Speed or swiftness; in criminal justice it refers to the apprehension, trial, and punishment of an offender. The advocates of the concept of deterrence regard speed as a major factor in the effectiveness of punishment. *See also* deterrence

censorship. The act of suppressing or controlling books, plays, films, or other media content or the ideas, values, and beliefs held by certain groups, on the grounds that the contents or ideas are morally, politically, militarily, or otherwise objectionable. Such control may be imposed internally, by the groups producing the information, or externally by governments, regulatory bodies, or other organizations. Many legal codes of censorship represent the formal embodiment of customs or mores. Such codes may express the values of only one segment of a society, however, and thereby infringe the rights of other segments. Thus censorship remains a controversial topic.

censure. The formal resolution of a legislative, administrative, or other body to reprimand an administrative officer or one of its own members for specific conduct.

census tract. A relatively small, permanent, homogenous geographic area, having a population usually between 3,000 and 6,000, into which certain large cities (and sometimes their adjacent areas) have been subdivided for statistical and local administrative purposes; an area the size of a few city blocks. Many police departments have realigned their "beats," or reporting districts, to conform with census-tract boundaries, allowing for demographic crime analysis.

Center for Criminal Justice. Founded in 1969 at Harvard University, the center conducts studies and evaluations on selected aspects of the criminal justice system, concentrating on policy issues in juvenile justice, court management, and criminal sanctions. Publishes the *Annual Report of the Center for Criminal Justice*. Address:

1653 Massachusetts Avenue, Cambridge, MA 02138.

Center for Criminal Justice Training and Research. Connected with the College of Human Services, California State University at Long Beach, this is the college's research and postcertification training arm. Address: 1250 Bellflower Blvd., Long Beach, CA 90840.

Center for Law and Justice. Established by the University of Washington in 1976, it is the criminal justice research organization at the university. The major area of inquiry has been the prevention of juvenile delinquency. Address: Suite 505, 1107 45th Street, NW, Seattle, WA 98105.

Center for Research in Criminology. Founded by Indiana University of Pennsylvania in 1983. The goals of the center include the advancement of criminology and criminal justice as both a discipline and a system. The center actively participates in research and provides consultants for national, state, and local criminal justice agencies. Address: Department of Criminology, G-1 McElhaney Hall, 441 North Walk, Idiana, PA 15705.

Center for Studies in Criminal Justice (CSCJ). Founded in 1965. Address: University of Chicago Law School, 1111 E. 60th Street, Chicago, IL 60637.

Center for Substance Abuse Treatment. Federal organization that collaborates with private and public treatment providers to develop and support policies, approaches, and programs for individuals who abuse alcohol and other drugs. Address: Rm 12-105 Parklawn Building, 5600 Fishers Lane, Rockville, MD 20857.

Center for the Administration of Criminal Justice. Founded in 1967, the center "seeks to combine law and social science skills and develop demonstration programs and research activities to improve the system." Address: University of California at Davis, Davis, CA 95616.

Center for the Study of Crime, Delinquency, and Corrections. Founded in 1961 by the College of Human Resources, Southern Illinois University, the center is responsible for instruction and research in the field of criminal justice. The center provides teaching internships at Marion Penitentiary. Address: College of Human Resources, Southern Illinois University at Carbondale, Carbondale, IL 62901.

Center for the Study of Law and Society. Founded in 1961 by the University of California at Berkeley, the center is "where analysis of legal institutions and legal change is encouraged." Address: 2240 Piedmont Avenue, University of California, Berkeley, CA 94720-2150.

Center for Women's Policy Studies. Founder of the Resource Center on Family Violence in 1972, the center "gathers and disseminates information about 'domestic' violence. There is a particular focus on shelters, prosecution and police response, violence in military families, legislation, and programs for batterers." Publishes *Response to Violence in the Family* (quarterly journal). Address: 1211 Connecticut Avenue, NW, Suite 312, Washington, DC 20036.

Centers for Disease Control and Prevention (CDC). An agency of the U.S. Department of Health and Human Services with the mission of promoting health by preventing and controlling disease and disability, including that caused by violence. Based in Atlanta, Georgia, the CDC includes 11 centers, institutes, and offices providing health information, publications, data, software, training, funding grants, and other products.

Central Intelligence Agency (CIA). An agency, created by the National Security Act of 1947, that advises the National Security Council in matters concerning such intelligence activities of the government departments and agencies as relate to national security; correlates and evaluates intelligence relating to national security and provides for its dissemination; collects foreign intelligence (the collection of information within the U.S. is coordinated with the FBI); produces and disseminates foreign intelligence relating to the national security, including foreign political, economic, scientific, technical, military, geographic, and sociological intelligence; collects, produces, and disseminates intelligence on foreign aspects of narcotics production and trafficking; conducts counterintelligence activities outside the U.S. and coordinates similar activities by other agencies in the intelligence community; without assuming or performing any internal security function, conducts counterintelligence activities within the U.S., but only in coordination with the FBI; produces and disseminates counterintelligence studies and reports. Operates a Cartographic Automated Mapping Program and World Data Bank II (represents natural and manmade features of the world in a digital format). The CIA training school is located at Camp Peary near Williamsburg, VA (sometimes called "The Farm"). Address: CIA, Office of the Public Affairs, Washington, DC 20505.

central station alarm system. An alarm system or group of systems, the activities of which are transmitted to, recorded in, maintained by, and supervised from a central station. This differs from proprietary alarm systems in that the central station is owned and operated independently of the subscriber.

Centre of Criminology Library. Founded in 1963 by the University of Toronto, the centre is a comprehensive library devoted to criminology in all its aspects. The resources of this library are available to interested persons outside the university in any area of the administration of criminal justice. Located at the University of Toronto, Room 8001, 130 St. George Street, Toronto, Ontario M5S 1A5, Canada.

certificate plan. A system of legal aid in the province of Ontario, Canada, whereby an eligible defendant is issued a certificate that entitles him or her to choose any counsel, whose fee will be paid in whole or in part out of public funds.

certification. A process in which a lower court requests a higher court to decide certain questions in a given case, pending final decision by the lower court.

certified copy. A copy to which is added a certificate, with signature and official seal, of the public officer authorized to certify it.

certiorari (Lat., lit. "to be more fully informed"). (1) An original writ or action whereby a case is removed from a lower to a higher court for review. The record of the proceedings is then transmitted to the superior court. (2) A discretionary appellate jurisdiction that is invoked by a petition, which the appellate court may grant or deny; a dominant avenue to the Supreme Court. *See also* rule of four

chain gang. On May 10, 1995, the Limestone Prison facility in Alabama became the first American penal institution to use chain gangs in more than 30 years. Inmates are shackled at the ankle with three-pound leg irons and bound together by eight-foot lengths of chain. Arizona soon followed suit, although prisoners there are not shackled together. Instead, each prisoner's ankles are bound together, and 20-person work groups are monitored by three guards. After 49 years without them, Florida because the third state to use chain gangs, on November 21, 1995, at the South Florida Reception Center. In April 1996, the Alabama prison commissioner who had revived the gangs in his state, Ron Jones, was demoted by the governor to a warden's job after he proposed putting female prisoners in leg irons.

chain of command. A supervisory hierarchy; the levels of personnel from the top to the bottom. It is the route taken for formal communications. In theory, this system, adopted originally from the military, supports the principles of unity of command, span of control, and regulated communiation channels. In large organizations it is cumbersome and time-consuming and is usually rectified by decentralization.

chain of custody. A formal, written process recording the persons having custody of evidence from initial point of receipt/custody to final disposition. The record also reflects the dates and reasons evidence is transferred from one location or person to another.

challenge of jurors. Action, on the part of either side of a trial by jury, against the prospective jurors (veniremen) to prevent them from serving. There are two kinds: (a) peremptory—no reasons must be given for objecting to the prospective juror, but the number of peremptory challenges is limited by law, and (b) challenge for cause—the reason for objecting to someone as a juror must be given (such as prior conviction, kinship to parties, bias or prejudice), but no limit is placed on the number to be so challenged. *See also* cause, challenge of jurors for; peremptory challenge

chambers. The official private office or quarters of a judge; the office of the judge when he or she is not in the courtroom.

champerty. Participating in a lawsuit in the name of another person but at one's own expense, with the goal of receiving as compensation a certain share of the proceeds of the suit.

chancery procedure. Formerly the procedure in chancery courts where the king's representative (the chancellor) presided over cases involving certain persons, usually women or children, who were unable under existing laws to protect themselves. Today such a procedure has been adopted by juvenile courts in assuming the guardianship of delinquent children and a protective interest in their welfare.

change of venue. The movement of a case from the jurisdiction of one court to that of another that has the same subject-matter jurisdictional authority but is in a different geographic location. The most frequent reason for a change of venue is a judicial determination that an impartial jury cannot be found within a particular geographic jurisdiction, usually because of widely publicized prejudicial statements concerning the events that are the basis for the case.

Chaplains, International Conference of Police. An organization providing assistance to members of the ministry in law enforcement agencies. Address: PO Box 5590, Destin, FL 32540-5590; telephone: (850 654-9736.

character. Evidence of a person's character is admissible in the following cases: (a) the fact that the defendant has a good reputation for the trait of character involved in the crime charged may be shown, but the state cannot show that he or she has a bad character, unless that character is itself a fact in issue or evidence has been given that he or she has a good character; (b) the character of the deceased as a violent and dangerous person may be shown in prosecutions for homicide, on the question of whether the defendant acted in self-defense; the term "character" as used in the rules above means reputation as distinguished from disposition; (c) a witness may be impeached by proof of bad character for truth and veracity, and a witness who has been impeached may be rehabilitated to a degree by proof that his or her reputation for truth and veracity is good; and (d) in crimes where character is an element.

charge. An allegation that a specified person or group has committed a specific offense, which is recorded in a functional document, such as a record of an arrest, a complaint, an indictment, or a judgment of conviction.

charging document. A formal, written accusation submitted to a court, alleging that a specified person or group has committed one or more specific offenses.

Chase, Salmon Portland. (1803–1873). American statesman; U.S. senator from Ohio (1849–1855, 1861); antislavery leader; U.S. secretary of the treasury (1861–1864); responsible for national bank system (estab. 1863); Chief Justice of the Supreme Court 1864–1873). His dissenting opinion in the Slaughterhouse Cases subsequently became the accepted position of the courts as to the restrictive force of the Fourteenth Amendment. Presided fairly over the impeachment trial of President Andrew Johnson. Chase earnestly sought the presidency four times but was never nominated.

Chase, Samuel. (1741–1811). American Revolutionary patriot, signer of the Declaration of Independence, associate justice of the U.S. Supreme Court (1796–1811). Impeached in 1804 on charge of political partiality but was acquitted.

chattel. Item, article, or piece of personal property that can theoretically be transferred to another person.

chattel mortgage. A security for the payment of a debt on personal property.

cheating. A fraudulent, financial injury to another person by some token, device, or practice calculated to deceive.

cheating at common law. The fraudulent obtaining of another's property by means of some false symbol or token that, when not false, is commonly accepted by the public for what it purports to represent; if the value of what was obtained is below a certain amount, cheating is a misdemeanor; above that amount it is a felony.

cheating by false pretense. Not a crime at common law but generally made so by statute, this term means knowingly and designedly obtaining the property of another with intent to defraud. The pretense must be (a) a false representation as to some part of existing fact or circumstance and not a mere expression of opinion or a promise; (b) knowingly false; (c) made with intent to defraud; (d) in some cases calculated to defraud; and (e) believed by the cheated party so that he or she gives up the property.

check fraud. Issuing or passing a check, draft, or money order that is legal as a formal document and signed by the legal account holder, but with the foreknowledge that the bank or depository will refuse to honor it because of insufficient funds or a closed account.

CHEMTREC (Chemical Transportation Emergency Center). Operated by the Manufacturing Chemists Association. Information about hazardous chemicals involved in an accident may be obtained by dialing, toll free, (800) 424-9300. District of Columbia callers dial 483-7616.

Cherry Hill. Nickname of the Philadelphia prison opened in 1829 on the site of an old cherry orchard. This historic Eastern Penitentiary was designed as a solitary-confinement facility.

Chicago Area Project. Begun in the early 1930s by Clifford R. Shaw of the Chicago School of Sociology, this was an influential crime study. Researchers proceeded on the assumption that crime was high in particular urban areas because those neighborhoods lacked cohesiveness, with a subsequent lack of concern for the welfare of the children living there. The project's goal was to develop self-help concepts to enhance mutual responsibility, neighborliness, and neighborhood pride. The project drew the attention of juvenile workers throughout the country and was copied by numerous other cities, including New York and Minneapolis. In 1959 the Illinois Youth Commission used the model to establish programs throughout the state. By the mid-1970s, similar programs existed in many American communities.

Chicago Boys' Court. This court was established in 1914 as the first special court for minor boys, aged 17 through 20, who were over the age for juvenile court jurisdiction.

Chicago Law Enforcement Study Group. Founded in 1970, the group is sponsored by 20 "not-for-profit organizations, [and] is a private, not-for-profit research and advocacy agency specifically interested in police, courts, and corrections issues as they affect local communities." Located in Room 303, 109 North Dearborn, Chicago, IL 60602.

Chicago Seven, the. The group of David T. Dellinger, Thomas E. Hayden, Rennard C. Davis, Abbie Hoffman, Jerry C. Rubin, Lee Weiner, and John R. Froines, who were tried on the charge of crossing state lines to incite riots in 1968 (at the time of the Democratic National Convention). On February 18, 1970, the first five were found guilty. All seven and two of their attorneys were sentenced on contempt of court due to their actions during the trial.

chicanery. Stratagem; trickery; sharp practice.

chief justice (federal). The official head of a collegially organized court of justice. The Chief Justice of the Supreme Court of the United States presides over the hearing of cases and over meetings of justices for the purpose of reaching decisions; assigns the writing of opinions to different justices who voted with him or her in making up the majority decision in a case and also writes opinions; appoints members of the Court to consider revisions of the rules of procedure; performs other administrative duties; and presides over the Senate when the president or vice president is impeached. The following have held this office: John Jay, 1789–1795; John Rutledge, 1795–1796; Oliver Ellsworth, 1796-1800; John Marshall, 1801–1835; Roger B. Taney, 1835–1864; Salmon P. Chase, 1864–1873; Morrison R. Waite, 1874–1888; Melville W. Fuller, 1888–1910; Edward D. White, 1910–1921; William Howard Taft, 1921–1930; Charles E. Hughes, 1930–1941; Harlan F. Stone, 1941–1946; Fred M. Vinson, 1946–1953; Earl Warren, 1953–1968; Warren Burger, 1969–1986; and William Rehnquist, 1986–.

chief justice (state). The official head of the highest court of the state. The first woman to be appointed as state chief justice was Rose Elizabeth Bird of California in 1977.

chief of police. A law enforcement officer who is the appointed or elected head of a municipal police department, department of public safety, or special authority or district police unit. Chief of police usually refers to the head of a local, municipal police department, but the title is also used for the heads of agencies organized to serve other jurisdictions. Director or superintendent may be the title for the head of a public safety department or division. Commissioner usually refers to one of several persons sitting on a board or commission intended to direct police agency policy.

Chiefs of Police National Drug Task Force. An organization that provides education to help neighborhoods and communities overcome their drug problems. Activities and programs emphasize prevention, education, enforcement, and community involvement. Address: 1300 N St., NW, Washington, DC 20005.

child. A person under the age of puberty. In law, a person under the age of 7 years is usually not capable of committing crime, and a person from 12 to 14 is presumed to be incapable of crime unless it can be proved that person has sufficient mental capacity to know the wrongfulness of the act with which he or she is charged.

child abuse. As recently as the nineteenth century, American law regarded children solely as chattels belonging to the parents. Not until 1874 did abused children receive legal protection, and then only when the American Society for the Prevention of Cruelty to Animals argued in court that a child, Mary Ellen, was covered under laws barring the barbaric treatment of animals.

Child abuse is generally described as any act of commission or omission that endangers or impairs a child's physical or emotional health and development. The major forms are (a) physical, including neglect or lack of adequate supervision; (b) emotional, including deprivation; and (c) sexual. Child abusers are found among all socioeconomic, religious, and ethnic groups. The abuser is usually someone closely related to the child, such as a parent, stepparent, or other caretaker—seldom a total stranger—who engages in a repeated pattern of behavior. The number of child abuse cases reported in 1984 was over 1 million, and many experts believe that for every case brought to the attention of social welfare agencies, at least four go undetected. *See also* Childhelp USA/International; Child Abuse and Neglect Information, National Center for

Child Abuse and Neglect Information, National Center for (NCCAN). Founded in 1975 by the U.S. Department of Health and

Human Services, NCCAN is a clearinghouse that tracks state laws and case law regarding child welfare; collects Indian Tribal Codes on the same topic; collects and provides information on child maltreatment and child protective services in the U.S.; and publishes an annual summary of Child Protective Services. Address: Children's Bureau, P.O. Box 1182, Washington, DC 20013.

Childhelp USA/International. Founded in January 1984, Childhelp is "a charitable and humanitarian organization committed to the prevention—primary and secondary—of child abuse and neglect in the United States and worldwide through Childhelp International," which offers free publications such as *I Wasn't Too Young at Sixteen*, and *The Call That Came Too Late!* National headquarters are located at 15757 N. 78th Steet, Scottsdale, Arizona 85260; telephone: (480) 922-8212 or 1-800-4-A-CHILD® (1-800-422-4453) (The National Child Abuse Hotline).

child delinquency law, first state. Passed on April 28, 1909, by Colorado, this law defined as guilty "persons who shall encourage, cause or contribute to the delinquency or neglect of a child."

child molester. One who injures or has questionable sexual dealings with a child. The child molester who is a sexual deviate is termed a pedophile. The victim may be subject to rape, sodomy, indecent exposure, or murder. *See also* pedophilia

child neglect. Willful failure to provide for one's child (or ward) adequate food, clothing, shelter, education, or supervision. Such neglect frequently brings the child under protection of the juvenile court.

child support. Judicially mandated obligations owed by absent parents for the maintenance of minor children. The U.S. Department of Health and Human Services (DHHS) operates the Office of Child Support Enforcement to "provide leadership in the planning, development, management, and coordination of programs that require states to enforce support obligations owed by absent parents to their children by locating absent parents, establishing paternity when necessary, and obtaining child support." Address: 370 L'Enfant Promenade SW, Washington, DC 20447. For a free copy of *Handbook on Child Support Enforcement*, write: Child Support Handbook, Consumer Information Center, Pueblo, CO 81009.

children's courts. Special courts established to solve the unusual legal and judicial problems of juvenile delinquency. Although a considerable body of protective legislation for the administration of juvenile crime was enacted in the Jacksonian period, it was not until the late nineteenth century that special children's tribunals were created to handle such cases. It had come to be accepted that juvenile lawbreakers were to be considered apart from adult criminals and subject to the special guardianship and administration of children's courts. A system of jurisprudence developed that emphasized informal procedures, separate hearings, psychiatric care, and probation and parole provisions. The medical and psychological sciences have contributed much to the concepts of prevention, therapy, and penology.

Children's Defense Fund. A private agency that serves as an advocate for children's rights by researching the manner in which children are handled by social and justice agencies and by increasing public awareness about children's problems and needs.

child welfare boards. A panel of local citizens elected by a Swedish community, who have the responsibility of investigating and adjudicating matters involving juveniles; these boards are similar to the juvenile courts of other Western societies.

chose **in action**. (Fr. *chose*, lit., thing). An issue in action; the right to receive or recover a large debt or damages through action at law.

Christopher Commission Report. The 226-page report issued by a panel chaired by Warren Christopher, Secretary of State in the Clinton administration, to investigate the causes of the 1992 Los Angeles riots. Officially called the Independent Commission on the Los Angeles Police Department, the panel sought to examine all aspects of the law enforcement structure in LA that might cause or contribute to the use of excessive force. The report summary said, "The Report is unanimous. The [Rodney] King beating raised fundamental questions about the LAPD including:

- the apparent failure to control or discipline officers with repeated complaints of excessive force.
- concerns about the LAPD's 'culture' and officers' attitudes towards racial and other minorities.
- the difficulties the public encounters in attempting to make complaints against LAPD officers.
- the role of the LAPD leadership and civilian oversight authorities in addressing or contributing to these problems. These and related questions and concerns form the basis for the Commission's work." *See also* King, Rodney

chromatograph. An instrument used in a crime laboratory to analyze gaseous substances or compounds that can be readily converted into gases.

chromosomal aberration. Some scientific findings since 1961 have indicated that a number of males with an extra Y chromosome (XYY) have histories of violent and antisocial behavior. There were different points of view about this unique genotype until 1968, when news stories focused on three convicted murders who reportedly had this chromosomal defect. (One of them was later shown to be normal in this respect.) Many geneticists doubt that the available evidence establishes a cause-and-effect relationship between such defects and deviant behavior. *See also* XYY chromosomes.

Church of Satan. Founded on April 30, 1966 (Walpurgis Night), by Anton Szandor La Vey, who is the author of the 272-page *The Satanic Bible* (Avon Books, December 1969) and a former San Francisco police photographer and criminology student. The legally recognized church is focused in its Central Grotto (congregation) in San Francisco. The Temple Set was founded by Michael A. Aquino, who broke away from the Church of Satan in 1975. Aquino defines Set as another name for Satan, coming from the hieroglyphic Set-hen, the god's formal title.

CIA. *See* Central Intelligence Agency

circuit. A division of the state or county appointed for a judge to visit for the trial of cases.

circuit, class A. A type of four-wire alarm circuit used to detect an alarm or line fault. The circuit allows reporting of an alarm condition even when a trouble condition has occurred. Two conductors run from the alarm panel to the sensor, and two return. A single break does not prevent the reception of an alarm signal, but does cause a trouble condition.

circuit, class B. (1) A four-wire system in which two conductors travel from an alarm panel, connect with one or more alarm sensors, and return to the panel. One broken conductor prevents reception of an alarm signal from any point beyond the break, causing a trouble condition. (2) A two-wire system in which only one conductor travels from the panel to the sensors and back again. A single break prevents all alarm transmissions and causes a trouble condition at the panel.

circuit court. One of the lower constitutional courts created by the Judiciary Act of 1789. For a major portion of U.S. history, these courts were the principal trial courts in the federal judicial system, having jurisdiction over federal criminal offenses and diversity jurisdiction (between citizens of different states) where over $500 was in dispute. There was no intermediate appellate court, and appeals went directly to the Supreme Court. The circuit courts also had appellate jurisdiction over the district courts, but neither they nor any other federal court had general, original federal-question jurisdiction until 1875, when it was given to circuit courts by Congress. Before that, such questions were left to the state courts—with right of appeal to the Supreme Court. Because Congress did not provide for any circuit judges, the district judges came to preside over the circuit courts, and, with time, only the initiated knew which court was sitting. In 1891 Congress created the circuit courts of appeal, now called simply courts of appeal, to which the appellate jurisdiction of the circuit courts was given. The Judicial Code of 1911 abolished the circuit courts and gave their original jurisdiction to the district courts. There are 2 federal and 12 regional circuit courts of appeals: First Circuit in Boston covers Rhode Island, Massachusetts, Maine, New Hampshire, and Puerto Rico; Second Circuit in New York covers New York, Vermont, and Connecticut; Third Circuit in Philadelphia covers Pennsylvania, New Jersey, Delaware, and the Virgin Islands; Fourth Circuit in Richmond, Virginia, covers Virginia, North and South Carolina, West Virginia, and Maryland; Fifth Circuit in New Orleans covers Louisiana, Mississippi, and Texas; Sixth Circuit in Cincinnati covers Ohio, Kentucky, Michigan, and Tennessee; Seventh Circuit in Chicago covers Illinois, Indiana, and Wisconsin; Eighth Circuit in St. Louis covers Missouri, Arkansas, Iowa, Minnesota, Nebraska, and North and South Dakota; Ninth Circuit Courts in Seattle, Portland, San Francisco, Los Angeles, and Honolulu cover Washington, Oregon, Montana, Idaho, California, Nevada, Arizona, Alaska, Hawaii, Guam, and the Northern Mariana Islands; Tenth Circuit in Denver covers Kansas, New Mexico, Oklahoma, Utah, Wyoming, and Colorado; Eleventh Circuit in Atlanta covers Georgia, Alabama, and Florida. The District of Columbia Circuit covers the District of Columbia, and the Federal Circuit in Washington, D.C., has jurisdiction over the U.S. The U.S. Ninth Circuit of Appeals is the largest and busiest federal appeals court in the nation. It covers an area of almost 1.4 million square miles, about the size of India.

circumstantial evidence. Evidence from which a fact can be reasonably inferred, although not directly proven.

citation to appear. A written order, issued by a law enforcement officer, directing an alleged offender to appear in a specific court at a specified time to answer a criminal charge and not permitting forfeit of bail as an alternative to court appearance.

cite. (1) To summon. (2) To read or refer to (legal) authorities, in support of a position.

citizen complaints. Complaints by citizens against police officers should, ideally, be made a matter of record and promptly referred to the officers' immediate superiors. Complainants should be assured that an investigation and a report of the complaint will be made and that they will be informed as to the final disposition of the matter. The complaint dispositions will fall into one of four categories: (a) sustained, the act did occur; (b) not sustained, the act might have happened but cannot be proven; (c) exonerated, the act did occur, but the officer was justified; and (d) unfounded, the act never occurred.

Citizen Involvement, National Center for. Founded in 1979 by Volunteer, a resource for volunteer programs promoting the exchange of ideas and information among volunteer programs. Publishes *Voluntary Action and Volunteering* (quarterly); *Exchange Networks* (newsletter). Address: Suite 500, 1111 North 19th St., Arlington, VA 22209.

citizen's arrest. An arrest by a citizen who is not a law enforcement officer for a felony, without a warrant. A citizen is not authorized to make an arrest by means of a warrant. In some common-law states (if not changed by statute), an arrest for a breach of the peace committed in his or her presence can be made by a citizen.

city court. A court that tries people accused of violating municipal ordinances, and which has jurisdiction over minor civil or criminal cases or both.

civil. Distinguished from criminal. Pertaining to (a) a legal dispute that is noncriminal in nature; (b) the personal or private rights of an individual; or (c) legal action in court to enforce private or personal rights. (A suit for personal injury is a civil action.)

Civil Aviation Security Service. This agency maintains information and expertise on domestic and foreign aircraft hijacking, including bomb threats at airports and on carriers; compliance and enforcement of violations of regulations; prevented attempts, explosives and explosive devices found in airports and aircraft; worldwide criminal incidents involving civil aviation; information on number of people screened, number of weapons found, and weapon detection devices. Address: Civil Aviation Security Services (ACS 400), Federal Aviation Administration, Department of Transportation, 800 Independence Avenue, SW, Room 707, Washington, DC 20591.

civil commitment. The action of a judicial officer or administrative body ordering a person to be placed in an institution or program, usually one administered by a health service, for custody, treatment, or protection.

civil case. A judicial proceeding to enforce a private right or to obtain compensation for its violation; distinguished from a criminal case.

civil commotion. A serious and prolonged disturbance of the peace, but less severe than an insurrection.

civil/criminal courts. Civil courts are established for the adjudication of private wrongs. Criminal courts are charged with the administration of the criminal laws under which public offenders are tried.

civil death. Denial of an individual's right to vote, to hold public office, and to enter into contracts.

civil disabilities. Rights or privileges denied a person as a result of conviction or a guilty plea, in addition to or other than the imposed legal penalty.

civil disobedience. Nonviolent action, such as demonstrating or picketing, against a law, on the basis that the law is morally wrong or unjust, and acceptance of the penalty for disobeying it. In a sense, civil disobedience involves adherence to a higher law than the current written code when a conflict exists between the two. In using this technique, the demonstrator hopes to appeal to the conscience of the community by serving a seemingly unjust jail sentence. The term was used by Henry David Thoreau, in his famous 1849 essay "Civil Disobedience," to describe his refusal to pay taxes because of his objections to slavery and war. Civil disobedience was used by Mohandas K. Gandhi in his fight against British rule in India and also was employed effectively during the United States civil rights movement in the 1960s under the leadership of such men as Dr. Martin Luther King, Jr.

civil disorders. Cincinnati, April 9–11, 2001. This 3-day riot of looting, beatings and arson attacks in the downtown area started two days after a white officer shot an unarmed black male (Timothy Thomas, 19) felling arrest on foot.

Civil Disorders, National Advisory Commission on. Known as the Kerner Commission, established in 1968 to study the increasing number of civil disorders in the nation. Under the chairmanship of former Ohio governor Otto Kerner, the commission saw the nation as moving toward "two societies, separate and unequal." An attempt by vice chairman Mayor John V. Lindsay of New York and Senator Fred Harris of Oklahoma to reconvene the body for further study failed, but a follow-up report was issued in 1969 by the Urban Coalition and Urban America, Inc. The findings of the Kerner Commission related to those of the Eisenhower commission on the causes and prevention of violence and to the Scranton commission on campus unrest. All three panels saw the country becoming increasingly polarized as a result of the prolonged Vietnam War and the domestic inequalities inherent in a society that was described as racist, whether consciously or unconsciously. As a result of these reports, federal organizations such as the Minority Business Development Agency and ACTION were created to combat the divisiveness of American society.

civil disturbances. The most costly civil disturbances, or urban riots, in U.S. history, in terms of property damage, are as follows:
- Los Angeles, April 29–30, 1992. $775 million (53 dead; 2,383 injured)
- Miami, May 17–19, 1980. $65 million

- Los Angeles, August 11–17, 1965. $44 million
- Detroit, July 2–3, 1967. $42 million
- New York City, July 13–14, 1977. $28 million
- Washington, DC, April 4–9, 1968. $24 million
- Newark, NJ, July 12, 1967. $15 million
- Baltimore, April 6–9, 1968. $14 million
- Chicago, April 4–11, 1968. $13 million
- New York City, April 4–11, 1968. $4 million
- Pittsburgh, April 4–11, 1968. $2 million
- Cincinnati, April 9–11, 2001. This 3-day riot of looting, beatings, and arson attacks in the downtown area started two days after a white officer shot an unarmed black male (Timothy Thomas, 19) fleeing arrest on foot.

See also Civil Disorders, National Advisory Commission on; King, Rodney; McDuffle; Arthur; Overtown; urban riots

civilianization. The process in police departments of replacing sworn peace officers with civilians to handle such non–law enforcement functions as dispatch, parking, training, budget, and planning/forecasting. Civilianization is a relatively recent innovation, with the general ratio now being 30 percent civilians to 70 percent sworn peace officers. *See also* community service officer

Civilian Oversight of Law Enforcement, International Association for (IACOLE). A voluntary, nonprofit organization, IACOLE has members worldwide, is governed by a 12-member board of directors, and publishes a quarterly newsletter. Address: 1204 Wesley Ave., Evanston, IL 60202. *See also* civilian review boards

civilian review boards. Advisory groups of citizens from outside the police department who are responsible for investigating charges of misconduct by municipal employees, including police officers. Such oversight boards or commissions may be established by state law, municipal charter, charter amendment, referendum resulting in ordinance, ordinance, or police order. A few civilian review boards

have subpoena power, but most only conduct investigations and recommend disciplinary actions.

The idea of review boards was initially formally opposed by such vested-interest groups as the International Association of Chiefs of Police, the International Conference of Police Associations, and the Fraternal Order of Police. The first review board was established in Philadelphia in October 1958. New York City created its Civilian Complaint Review Board in July 1966. Within four months, the New York Patrolmen's Benevolent Association had persuaded voters to abolish the review board, and the Philadelphia board was similarly disbanded in 1967. Subsequently, however, questionable police practices created sufficient pressure to revive the civilian oversight movement.

Currently active civilian review boards include the New Orleans Office of Municipal Investigation (created in 1981) and boards in Los Angeles, San Francisco (1983), Albuquerque, Baltimore, Berkeley, Cincinnati, Cleveland, Dade County, FL, Dallas, Detroit, Flint, Hartford, Milwaukee, Minneapolis, New York City, Portland, San Diego, and Washington, DC. *See also* Civilian Oversight of Law Enforcement, International Association for; White Night

civil law. This term originally referred to the system of jurisprudence developed in the Roman Empire and now usually refers to the legal system descended from Roman law and prevailing in most of continental Europe. In this system of law, cases are decided *a priori*, applying highly abstract legal concepts known as codes. In this sense, civil law is opposed to common law. The Western world generally adheres to one or the other of these two legal systems. The term civil law is also used to distinguish the law of a political entity from international law and natural law, but municipal law is a more appropriate term in this context. In other contexts, civil law has been distinguished from criminal law, canon law, and admiralty law.

civil liability. A complaint filed in an appropriate court by an individual seeking to recover damages, which includes the reason for the suit (cause of causes) and the amount of damages sought. The right of civil or private redress stems from the common law of torts. It first appeared in U.S. federal law in Section 1 of the Civil Rights Act of 1871, which has now been codified as 42 U.S.C. 1983. *See also* vicarious liability

civil liberties. Basic individual rights guaranteed in the U.S. Bill of Rights. They include freedom of speech, religion, and the press; the right to trial by jury; protection against unreasonable searches and seizures; protection from being forced to testify against oneself in a criminal trial; and protection from being deprived of life, liberty, and property without due process of law. It was argued at the Constitutional Convention that the Bill of Rights (the first 10 amendments) were unnecessary because the federal government had no power whatsoever to abridge civil liberties. However, others at the Constitutional Convention, such as James Madison, favored the amendments in order to separate "the well-meaning from the designing opponents of the Constitution." During several periods in American history, there have been serious infringements of citizens' civil liberties. Examples are the Civil War, World War I, the notorious "Red Scare" Palmer raids of 1920, the treatment of Americans of Japanese descent during World War II, and racial prejudice. However, the Supreme Court has generally supported such liberties. Perhaps some of the most far-reaching civil liberties decisions were handed down during the Warren Court; these included several on school desegregation and the one-man-one-vote ruling. Civil liberties have been legislated by specific statutes, as in the Civil Rights Acts of the 1960s that outlawed discrimination in public accommodations, employment, and schools. Civil liberties are intended to guarantee equality of all individuals before the law. As set forth in the Bill of Rights, they are an embodiment of natural law principles. But the Bill of Rights also implies the responsibility of society to preserve individual liberties against infringement by the government and its agencies, while those very liberties

protect the mass media, political leaders, courts, and a vigilant public. Organizations such as the American Civil Liberties Union offer legal counsel in selected constitutional cases.

civil process. Official orders and documents issued by, or under the authority of, a court when handling civil matters such as summonses, subpoenas, injunctions, eviction orders, and so forth.

civil rights. Those liberties possessed by the individual as a member of the state, especially those guaranteed against encroachment by the government. In this latter sense, civil rights are enumerated in the bills of rights of federal and state constitutions and include both substantive rights, such as freedom of speech, press, assembly, or religion, and procedural rights, such as protection against unreasonable searches and seizures or against punishment without a fair trial. The most important civil right is embodied in those clauses in state and federal constitutions that prohibit government from depriving anyone of life, liberty, or property without due process of law. Twice found in the Constitution, such clauses impose limitations on the states as well as on Congress. Of somewhat less importance is the equal protection clause of the Fourteenth Amendment, which limits state action. By its interpretation of these clauses, the Supreme Court largely determines the scope of civil rights in America. Recently, interest in civil rights has been directed toward legislation by Congress and state legislatures to secure certain liberties of the individual against encroachment by other individuals and groups, and to prohibit such individuals and groups from discrimination on the basis of race, color, religion, or membership in labor unions.

On April 26, 1996, Len Davis, a former New Orleans policeman who in October 1994 ordered a woman murdered the day after she filed a brutality complaint against him, was given the death penalty by a federal jury. Davis is the first person sentenced to death in a civil rights case.

Civil Rights Acts (CRAs). Congress passed seven civil rights acts during Reconstruction to guarantee the rights of freed slaves and to implement the Thirteenth, Fourteenth, and Fifteenth Amendments to the Constitution. Despite this far-reaching egalitarian legislation, social and political equality remained far out of reach. Those provisions that were not declared unconstitutional in the next two decades by the Supreme Court were rendered ineffectual via narrow rulings handed down by judges responding to broad sentiment against legislating equality between the races.

The CRA of April 9, 1866, extended citizenship to anyone born in the United States and gave blacks full equality before the law. Debate over the constitutionality of this act ended in 1868 with the adoption of the Fourteenth Amendment.

The CRAs of April 21, 1866, and March 2, 1867, implemented the Thirteenth Amendment and are still on the books. The first sets punishment for kidnapping or delivering anyone into involuntary servitude or exporting blacks into slavery. The second prohibits the system of peonage—holding debtors or legal prisoners in servitude to their creditors or to persons who lease their services from the government.

The CRA of May 31, 1870, set out specific criminal sanctions for interfering with suffrage. Sections 3 and 4, however, were disallowed by the Supreme Court in 1903, while Section 16 was stricken in 1906.

The CRA of February 28, 1871, called for the appointment of two election supervisors and two deputy marshals to oversee congressional elections.

The CRA of April 20, 1872, stipulates that anyone using law or custom to deprive an individual of his rights, privileges, or land immunities secured by the Constitution or by federal law is guilty of a federal crime and liable for damages. Section 2, however, which imposed penalties for depriving any person of equal protection under the law, was declared unconstitutional in 1883 and 1887.

The CRA of March 1, 1875, declared that all persons are entitled to "the full and equal enjoyment of the accommodations, advantages, facilities and privileges of inns, public conveyances on land or water, theaters and other places of public amusement" and imposed penalties for violations. The act was nullified by the Civil Rights Cases of 1883.

The CRA of 1957 established the Civil Rights Commission, added an assistant attorney general to oversee the new Civil Rights Division within the Justice Department, and qualified all persons for jury duty in their home districts unless they were illiterate in English, had a criminal record, or were physically or mentally incapable. On May 4, 1961, civil rights workers sought to win enforcement of a 1958 Supreme Court ruling ordering the desegregation of bus stations and waiting rooms. Led by James Farmer and CORE (Congress of Racial Equality, founded by Farmer in 1942), two buses carrying 13 "freedom riders"—6 whites and 7 blacks—left Washington, DC, for New Orleans. In Alabama, one bus was firebombed and the demonstrators beaten. In 1962 James Meredith, a black student, attempting to enroll in the University of Mississippi at Oxford, prompted a clash between thousands of southern whites and a small force of federal marshals, which lasted for more than 15 hours and resulted in more than 70 casualties. Civil rights workers, both black and white, who were martyred in the early 1960s include Medgar Evers, the NAACP field secretary; white civil rights volunteer Viola Liuzzo, a Detroit housewife and mother who was shot by nightriders while ferrying marchers between Selma and Montgomery, Alabama; and James Chaney, Andrew Goodman, and Michael Schwerner, three young civil rights workers murdered by members of the Ku Klux Klan in Mississippi, with the connivance of local law enforcement officers.

The CRA of 1960 set penalties for obstructing a federal court order by threat of force and for illegally using and transporting explosives, required election officials to keep all records of federal elections for 22 months, and appointed persons residing in judicial districts to serve as district voting referees to take evidence and to report to the courts instances of voting discrimination.

The CRA of 1964 forbade discrimination on the basis of race, color, religion, national origin, employment, and sex. Most controversial was Title II, outlawing discrimination in public accommodations and providing for court action by the attorney general when a "pattern or practice" of resistance is evident. Other sections extended the duties and life of the Civil Rights Commission, specified the right to equality in employment opportunity, and set up the Equal Employment Opportunity Commission. This act encourages voluntary compliance, in line with the Fourteenth Amendment's "due process" clause, to avoid testing the constitutionality of older laws.

The CRA of 1968 provided protection for civil rights workers, forbade discrimination in most housing, and provided penalties for those who attempt to interfere with an individual's civil rights or who use interstate commerce for the purpose of organizing or furthering a riot.

Civil Rights, Commission on. An independent, bipartisan federal agency set up in 1957. The commission investigates complaints of interference with voting rights, studies and collects information on violations of the principle of equality before the law, serves as a national clearinghouse for civil rights information, and submits reports and recommendations to the president and Congress. The commission has no power of enforcement (*see* Civil Rights Enforcement) and sometimes clashes with the Department of Justice over forcing corrective action. Many of its recommendations were basic to the civil rights, voting rights, education, and economic opportunity legislation of the 1960s. The commission's 1970 report, *The Federal Civil Rights Enforcement Effort*, and its May 1971 follow-up report documented great delays in federal civil rights compliance and expressed "serious doubts about the degree of commitment of some federal agencies to take the steps necessary to assure equal rights for all."

Civil Rights Enforcement. Under the Department of Justice, the Civil Rights Division prosecutes actions under several criminal civil rights statutes, coordinates the civil rights enforcement efforts of the federal agencies whose programs are covered by Title VI of the 1964 CRA, and assists federal agencies in identifying and eliminating sexually discriminatory provisions in their policies and programs. Contact: Office of Federal Civil Rights Evaluation, Commission on Civil Rights, DOJ, 1121 Vermont Avenue, NW, Room 606, Washington, DC 20425.

Civil Rights Institute. Established in fall 1992 in Birmingham, AL, the institute is located at 520 16th St. North, telephone (205) 328-9696; admission is free. Of particular interest to scholars of criminal justice is the exhibit section "Movements," which includes a life-sized replica of a burned-out Greyhound bus and video footage of freedom riders, police officers wielding fire hoses against demonstrators, sit-ins, and packed jails.

Civil Rights of Institutionalized Persons Act (CRIPA). A federal law (42 U.S. Code 1997) that gives the Justice Department the authority to sue correctional facilities on behalf of inmates, to protect their civil rights, and encourages the development of inmate grievance procedures and programs.

Civil Rights—Special Litigation. An office under the Department of Justice that is responsible for protecting rights secured under Title VI of the CRA of 1964 requiring nondiscrimination against persons confined in state and local prisons and jails. Contact Civil Rights Division, DOJ, 10th & Constitution Avenue, NW, Room 7341, Washington, DC 20530.

civil service. The term applied to the body of employees working for a government. In the U.S., employees of business enterprises operated by federal, state, or local governments are included; elected officials, judges, and the military are excluded.

civil suit. Legal process before a court to recover property, maintain a right or privilege, or satisfy a claim. *See also* civil law; civil process

clandestine. Describing actions that are concealed or secret. *See also sub rosa*

class action. A legal effort made by one or more persons on behalf of themselves and all others similarly situated or injured. Although the process has existed for some time, class action has only become prominent in the last three decades. It has proven a very useful device for the enforcement of liabilities when the interest of any one person is too small to render a suit economically viable. A court will usually award lawyers' fees out of the aggregate judgment on behalf of the class.

classification of crimes. Crimes in common law are divided into treason, felonies, and misdemeanors. Some jurisdictions have a fourth classification of minor or petty offenses, less than misdemeanors, sometimes described either as those of which magistrates have had exclusive summary jurisdiction or as police regulations.

classifications of prisoners. The process, usually referred to as diagnostic classification, through which a new prisoner is classified according to educational, vocational, treatment, and security needs for proper placement in treatment programs.

Clayton Act (1914). Federal legislation enacted to exempt labor organizations and their legitimate concerted activities from the provisions of the Sherman Antitrust Act and to narrow the jurisdiction of the federal courts in labor disputes. *See also* antitrust cases

clearance. The step in police-level reporting in which a known occurrence of an offense is followed by an arrest or other decision that indicates a solved crime. In Uniform Crime Report (UCR) vocabulary, a known offense is "cleared" or "solved" when (a) a law enforcement agency has charged at least one person with the offense or (b) a suspect has been identified and located and an arrest is justified, but action is prevented by circumstances outside law enforcement control (e.g., the suspect is dead, the suspect is al-

ready in custody, or the victim of the offense has refused cooperation in prosecution).

Clearance rate is a related term defined as the number of offenses cleared, divided by the number of offenses known to police. Although a "clearance by arrest" or by "exceptional means" may have been recorded for UCR purposes, active investigation will continue, for example, where a crime has been cleared by the arrest of one suspect but a second suspect is still being sought. Conversely, the closing of a police case may or may not indicate a "clearance." Where, for example, investigation of all available leads has not resulted in the identification of a suspect, a case not cleared may be filed inactive or closed pending new information.

clear and present danger. A court test used in determining the limits of free expression guaranteed in the First Amendment. This yardstick was first formulated by Justice Oliver Wendell Holmes in the Supreme Court's 1919 decision in *Schenck v. United States*, in which Holmes said that speech could be punished if there were a serious and imminent danger that such speech would result in illegal action. The clear-and-present-danger test is applied in times of crisis. Other tests of the right to free expression include the more limiting dangerous-tendency test (of speech that has a tendency to bring about dangerous results), the preferred-position test (a more rigorous standard of review required because of the importance of the right of free speech), and the sliding-scale test (involving careful examination of the facts of each individual case). *See also* dangerous-tendency test

clemency. The doctrine under which executive or legislative action reduces the severity of or waives legal punishment of one or more individuals, or an individual is exempted from prosecution for certain actions. Grounds for clemency are such mitigating circumstances as postconviction evidence of a prisoner's innocence; a prisoner's dubious guilt, illness, reformation, services to the state, or turning state's evidence; reasons of the state such as the need to restore civil rights; and corrections of unduly severe sentences or injustices stemming from imperfections in penal law or the application of it. The chief forms of clemency are pardons (full and conditional), amnesties, commutations, reduced sentences, reprieves, and remissions of fines and forfeitures.

Clink. Originally a London prison that dominated the south bank of the Thames near London Bridge, where it was a well-known landmark in the days of Hogarth and Dickens. Not only a generic name for all prisons, but also for the brothels and the Southwark Fair depicted by Hogarth; now only its name survives at its site on Clink Street.

closed shop. A labor agreement by which an employer may hire only people who are continuing union members. The closed shop is now illegal under federal labor statutes.

CN. A lacrymator (tear-causing) chemical most commonly used in tear gas and in aerosol irritant projectors. The chemical name is chloroacetophenone.

Coast Guard jurisdiction. Commissioned, warrant, and petty officers of the Coast Guard are empowered to make inquiries, examinations, inspections, searches, seizures, and arrests upon the high seas and the navigable waters of the United States, its territories, and possessions. Such power does not apply to inland waters, except for the Great Lakes and its connecting waters.

cocaine. A drug that occurs naturally in the leaves of the coca plant, *Erythroxylon coca*, which is native to Colombia, Peru, and Bolivia. Neither physical dependence nor tolerance is known to result from prolonged use of cocaine, but psychological dependence may develop. Euphoric excitement is produced when cocaine is sniffed. Delusions and hallucinations are common with large doses. Cocaine was widely used as a local anesthetic but has been replaced by a synthetic, Novocaine. First purified by German chemist Albert Neimann in the nineteenth century, cocaine was used as a central nervous system stimulant, appetite suppressant, and local anesthetic. Freud recommended it as a cure for depression, alcoholism, and morphine addiction, and the general public made it a fashionable social pastime. A 1902 survey indicated that the nonprescription use of cocaine accounted for 92 percent of its total use in the United States. Until it was legally restricted in 1914, cocaine was regularly added to tonics and such beverages as Coca Cola. Medical acceptance of the drug declined as its detrimental effects became obvious and nonaddicting medications became available. An estimated 27 million Americans have tried or are current users of cocaine. However, current users (those who have taken the drug in the last month) declined by 71 percent between 1985 and 2001. Nevertheless, it is still the second-most popular illicit drug, after marijuana, among adolescents and young adults. Cocaine is a $35 billion industry, now exceeding coffee as Colombia's number-one export. Bolivia is the second-biggest producer of coca leaf in South America, behind Peru. The Bolivians cultivate between 25,000 and 40,000 metric tons of leaves each year, enough to produce 50 to 80 tons of cocaine.

cocaine, crack. The product created when powdered cocaine is dissolved in water, combined with baking soda, and heated until the water evaporates, leaving crack rocks. One lb. of powdered cocaine produces 0.9 lbs. of crack. It appears as small, colored rocks or chips that vary in size, shape, color, and consistency, but are usually yellowish or beige with a waxy look resembling that of soap chips.

code. (1) A body of law covering one general subject, established by the legislative authority of the state. (2) (in Roman-law countries) A systematic statement of the body of the law enacted or promulgated by the highest authority of the state, on which all judicial decisions must be based. (3) (in the United States) A private or official compilation of all permanent laws in force, consolidated and classified according to subject matter. Such compilations of national laws are the *Revised Statutes of the United States*, first enacted in 1874, and *A Code of the Laws of the United States*. Many

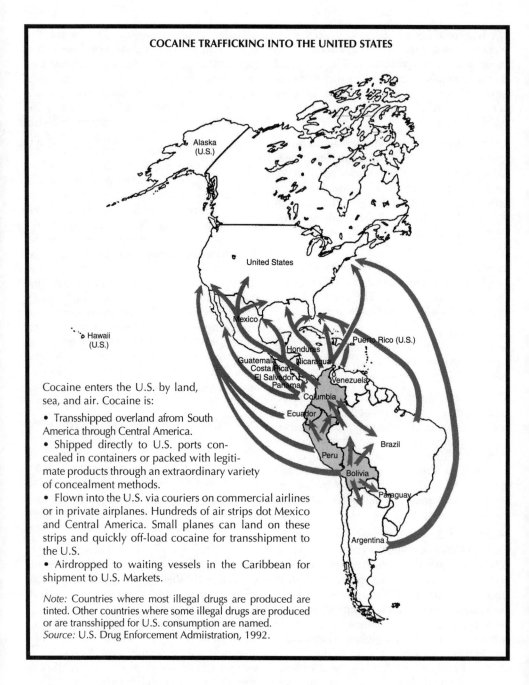

COCAINE TRAFFICKING INTO THE UNITED STATES

Cocaine enters the U.S. by land, sea, and air. Cocaine is:

• Transshipped overland afrom South America through Central America.
• Shipped directly to U.S. ports concealed in containers or packed with legitimate products through an extraordinary variety of concealment methods.
• Flown into the U.S. via couriers on commercial airlines or in private airplanes. Hundreds of air strips dot Mexico and Central America. Small planes can land on these strips and quickly off-load cocaine for transshipment to the U.S.
• Airdropped to waiting vessels in the Caribbean for shipment to U.S. Markets.

Note: Countries where most illegal drugs are produced are tinted. Other countries where some illegal drugs are produced or are transshipped for U.S. consumption are named.
Source: U.S. Drug Enforcement Admiistration, 1992.

states have published official codes of all laws in force, including the common law and statutes as judicially interpreted, which have been compiled by code commissions and enacted by the legislatures. American codes lack the permanence and authority of European codes because of the volume of new statutes and of judicial decisions, each of which, under common-law principles, constitutes a precedent for the decisions of later cases.

Code, International. A code of words used in law enforcement to clarify letters of the alphabet when spelling orally, as by telephone or radio. The code words are: A = Alpha, B = Bravo, C = Charlie, D = Delta, E = Echo, F = Foxtrot, G = Gold, H = Hotel, I = India, J = Juliette, K = Kilo, L = Lima, M = Mike, N = November, 0 = Oscar, P = Papa, Q = Quebec, R = Romeo, S = Sierra, T = Tango, U = Uniform, V = Victor, W = Whiskey, X = X-ray, Y = Yankee, Z = Zulu.

Code, Napoleonic. The codification of French private, substantive law prepared at the urging of Napoleon Bonaparte. It became widely accepted as a model among Latin peoples.

code of ethics. Written rules, regulations, and/or standards of conduct for members of groups engaged in given professions or occupations. The Law Enforcement Code of Ethics was first developed by the California Peace Officers' Association and the Peace Officers' Research Association of California in 1956 and adopted by the IACP at its 1957 conference. *See* box on pp. 66–67.

American Correctional Association Code of Ethics

The American Correctional Association expects of its members unfailing honesty, respect for the dignity and individuality of human beings, and a commitment to professional and compassionate service. To this end we subscribe to the following principles.

Relationships with clients/colleagues/ other professions/the public

Members will respect and protect the civil and legal rights of all clients. Members will serve each case with appropriate concern for the client's welfare and with no purpose of personal gain. Relationships with colleagues will be of such character to promote mutual respect within the profession and improvement of its quality of service. Statements crit-

ical of colleagues or their agencies will be made only as these are verifiable and constructive in purpose. Members will respect the importance of all elements of the criminal justice system and cultivate a professional cooperation with each segment. Subject to the clients' rights of privacy, members will respect the public's right to know, and will share information with the public with openness and candor. Members will respect and protect the right of the public to be safeguarded from criminal activity.

Professional conduct/practices

No member will use his official position to secure privileges or advantages for himself. No member will act in his official capacity in any matter in which he has personal interest that could in the least degree impair his objectivity. No member will use his official position to promote any partisan political purposes. No member will accept any gift or favor of a nature to imply an obligation that is inconsistent with the free and objective exercise of his professional responsibilities. In any public statement members will clearly distinguish between those that are personal views and those that are statements and positions on behalf of an agency. Each member will be diligent in his responsibility to record and make available for review any and all case information which could contribute to sound decisions affecting a client or the public safety. Each member will report without reservation any corrupt or unethical behavior which could affect either a client or the integrity of the organization. Members will not discriminate against any client, employee, or prospective employee on the basis of race, sex, creed, or national origin. Each member will maintain the integrity of private information; he will neither seek personal data beyond that needed to perform his responsibilities, nor reveal case information to anyone not having proper professional use for such. Any member who is responsible for agency personnel actions will make all appointments, promotions, or dismissals only on the basis of merit and not in furtherance of partisan political interests. (Adopted August 1975, at the 105th Congress of Correction)

LAW ENFORCEMENT CODE OF ETHICS

All law enforcement officers must be fully aware of the ethical responsibilities of their position and must strive constantly to live up to the highest possible standards of professional policing.

The International Association of Chiefs of Police believes it is important that police officers have clear advice and counsel available to assist them in performing their duties consistent with these standards, and has adopted the following ethical mandates as guidelines to meet these ends.

Primary Responsibilities of a Police Officer

A police officer acts as an official representative of government who is required and trusted to work within the law. The officer's powers and duties are conferred by statute. The fundamental duties of a police officer include serving the community; safeguarding lives and property; protecting the innocent; keeping the peace; and ensuring the rights of all to liberty, equality and justice.

Performance of the Duties of a Police Officer

A police officer shall perform all duties impartially, without favor or affection or ill will and without regard to status, sex, race, religion, political belief or aspiration. All citizens will be treated equally with courtesy, consideration and dignity.

Officers will never allow personal feelings, animosities or friendships to influence official conduct. Laws will be enforced appropriately and courteously and, in carrying out their responsibilities, officers will strive to obtain maximum cooperation from the public. They will conduct themselves in appearance and deportment in such a manner as to inspire confidence and respect for the position of public trust they hold.

Discretion

A police officer will use responsibly the discretion vested in the position and exercise it within the law. The principle of reasonableness will guide the officer's determinations and the officer will consider all surrounding circumstances in determining whether any legal action shall be taken.

Consistent and wise use of discretion, based on professional policing competence, will do much to preserve good relationships and retain the confidence of the public. There can be difficulty in choosing between conflicting courses of action. It is important to remember that a timely word of advice rather than arrest— which may be correct in appropriate circumstances—can be a more effective means of achieving a desired end.

Use of Force

A police officer will never employ unnecessary force or violence and will use only such force in the discharge of duty as is reasonable in all circumstances.

Force should be used only with the greatest restraint and only after discussion, negotiation and persuasion have been found to be inappropriate or ineffective. While the use of force is occasionally unavoidable, every police officer will refrain from applying the unnecessary infliction of pain or suffering and will never engage in cruel, degrading or inhuman treatment of any person.

Confidentiality

Whatever a police officer sees, hears or learns of, which is of a confidential nature, will be kept secret unless the performance of duty or legal provision requires otherwise. Members of the public have a right to security and privacy, and information obtained about them must not be improperly divulged.

(*continued*)

Integrity

A police officer will not engage in acts of corruption or bribery, nor will an officer condone such acts by other police officers.

The public demands that the integrity of police officers be above reproach. Police officers must, therefore, avoid any conduct that might compromise integrity and thus undercut the public confidence in a law enforcement agency. Officers will refuse to accept any gifts, presents, subscriptions, favors, gratuities or promises that could be interpreted as seeking to cause the officer to refrain from performing official responsibilities honestly and within the law. Police officers must not receive private or special advantage from their official status. Respect from the public cannot be bought; it can only be earned and cultivated.

Cooperation with Other Officers and Agencies

Police officers will cooperate with all legally authorized agencies and their representatives in the pursuit of justice.

An officer or agency may be one among many organizations that may provide law enforcement services to a jurisdiction. It is imperative that a police officer assist colleagues fully and completely with respect and consideration at all times.

Personal/Professional Capabilities

Police officers will be responsible for their own standard of professional performance and will take every reasonable opportunity to enhance and improve their level of knowledge and competence.

Through study and experience, a police officer can acquire the high level of knowledge and competence that is essential for the efficient and effective performance of duty. The acquisition of knowledge is a never-ending process of personal and professional development that should be pursued constantly.

Private Life

Police officers will behave in a manner that does not bring discredit to their agencies or themselves.

A police officer's character and conduct while off duty must always be exemplary, thus maintaining a position of respect in the community in which he or she lives and serves. The officer's personal behavior must be beyond reproach.

Adopted by the Executive Committee of the International Association of Chiefs of Police on October 17, 1989, during its 96th Annual Conference in Louisville, Kentucky to replace the 1957 code of ethics adopted at the 64th Annual IACP Conference.

The IACP gratefully acknowledges the assistance of Sir John C Hermon, former chief constable of the Royal Ulster Constabulaiy, who gave full license to the association to freely use the language and concepts presented in the RUC's "Professional Policing Ethics," Appendix 1 of the Chief Constable's Annual Report 1988, presented to the Police Authority for Northern Ireland, for the preparation of this code.

Lawyers' Code of Professional Responsibility

Canon 1

A lawyer should assist in maintaining the integrity and competence of the legal profession.

Canon 2

A lawyer should assist the legal profession in fulfilling its duty to make legal counsel available.

Canon 3

A lawyer should assist in preventing the unauthorized practice of law.

Canon 4

A lawyer should preserve the confidences and secrets of a client.

Canon 5

A lawyer should exercise independent professional judgment on behalf of a client.

Canon 6
A lawyer should represent a client competently.

Canon 7
A lawyer should represent a client zealously within the bounds of the law.

Canon 8
A lawyer should assist in improving the legal system.

Canon 9
A lawyer should avoid even the appearance of professional impropriety. (Adopted by the Supreme Court of the State of Ohio on October 5, 1970)

Code of Hammurabi. Babylonian laws of the twenty-second century B.C., generally regarded by historians as a moderate and humanitarian code for its period; one of the oldest codes of law.

codefendants. More than one person charged jointly for the same crime.

codeine. Methylmorphine, a sedative and pain-relieving agent found in opium, structurally related to morphine but less potent, and constituting approximately 0.5 percent of the opium extract.

Co-Dependents Anonymous. Self-help group for individuals who believe they have low self-esteem and are addicted to destructive relationships. Address: P.O. Box 33577, Phoenix, AZ 85067-3577.

codicil. Any provision appended to a will after its original preparation, which adds to, takes from, or alters its earlier content.

coercion. (1) The use of force to compel performance of an action. (2) The application of sanctions or the use of force by government to compel observance of law or public policy.

cognomen. A family name; a surname.

cohabitation. Living together as husband and wife, especially when not legally married. Legally, a couple must share a residence all or most of the time to be cohabiting; occasional intercourse does not constitute cohabitation. Cohabitation is still a misdemeanor in Florida, Michigan, Mississippi, North Carolina, North Dakota, Virginia, and West Virginia.

cohort. In statistics, a group of individuals having one or more statistical factors in common in a demographic study. The landmark study *Delinquency in a Birth Cohort*, authored in 1972 by Marvin Wolfgang and his associates at the University of Pennsylvania and replicated in 1985, is the single most important piece of criminal justice research in the last quarter-century and has become a major influence in crime control methods. The authors discovered that a small group of delinquents are responsible for a majority of all crimes and for about two-thirds of all violent crimes.

Cointelpro. An FBI counterintelligence program (1956–1971) that emphasized harassment of suspected subversives. The program was brought to light by the 1967 Freedom of Information Act.

cold blood. Term used to describe crimes committed in the absence of a fit of anger; homicide cases in which the murderer experienced no strong emotion or violent passion.

collateral consequence. Any penalty that may result from a guilty plea or a conviction, in addition to the preordered punishment. Examples include deportation, disenfranchisement, disbarment, or loss of license to practice certain professions.

collateral facts. Facts not directly connected with the matter in dispute.

collateral security. A bond or deposit in addition to the principal or original security.

collective bargaining. A process of setting wages, hours, and working conditions for employees by means of structured meetings involving affected employees, acting through their unions or associations, and their managers, or employers. The term thus includes both contract negotiation and ongoing administration of the provisions of existing labor contracts. Several states have enacted legislation enabling police unions or associations to "meet and confer, in good faith" with city or county officials regarding "wages and conditions of employment." All law enforcement personnel at virtually any rank have union/association representation. Since most law enforcement agencies bargain collectively, they have established memorandums of understanding to delineate the process of contract negotiation and define that issues will be decided through this process. *See also* arbitration; conciliation; mediation; public sector unions

collusion. An agreement between two or more persons to defraud a third person of his or her rights or to obtain an object forbidden by law.

colony, penal. A secluded area, generally a distant island outside a nation's borders, or occasionally a remote part of a nation, where criminals are sent upon conviction of crimes, usually those within special categories. In effect, sentence to a penal colony involves virtual banishment.

color of authority. An apparent prima facie right or authority; the presumption of authority, which justifies the actions of an officer and which is derived from a badge, certificate, or writ which is apparently legal.

Colt, Samuel. American inventor (1814–1862) famous for the invention of the six-shooter revolver, accepted by the U.S. Army in 1847 but first patented in 1836. The revolver was ideal for mounted warfare, and the Colt became the standard weapon on the Great Plains. Colt's revolver sometimes overshadows his great contribution to the technique of the mass production of large quantities of complex components.

Columbine Massacre. On April 20, 1999, in the Colorado Columbine High School, students Eric Harris and Dylan Klebold shot and killed twelve people. Both assailants committed suicide inside the school building.

comity. Courteous behavior: used primarily in the phrases judicial comity and comity of nations. Judicial comity refers to the principle that the courts of one state or jurisdiction should give full effect to the laws and judicial decisions of another state. Comity of nations refers to the recognition granted by one nation, out of courtesy or convenience, to the laws of another nation, even though such recognition is not required by international law.

command. In accordance with statutory requirements, a warrant must command an officer or officers to search for personal property, seize it, and create an inventory of the property. The warrant is void if it does not command the officer to present both property and inventory to the judge who issued the warrant, or to another other judge or court that has some official responsibility in the case.

commercial law. This branch of law embraces those statutes relating both to the rights of property and to the relations of persons engaged in commerce.

commission. (1) A warrant, usually issued by the chief executive, which confers the powers and privileges of an office upon a person newly appointed to it. (2) A body of three or more officials who collectively discharge the duties of an administrative agency.

commissioner. A member of certain independent federal agencies, certain state boards, a principal county board, or the governing board of a city under the commission form of government.

Commissioner of Deeds. An officer authorized to administer oaths in all cases where no special provision is made by law.

commission of inquiry. A board composed of members of the legislature, administrative officials, nonofficial members, or a combination of two or more of these groups, appointed to investigate and report on a particular problem.

commission on interstate cooperation. The first interstate commission to establish cooperative law enforcement procedures in U.S. history was the New Jersey Commission on Interstate Cooperation, created by a joint resolution passed on March 12, 1935. The commission was responsible for developing cooperation among states on various problems in the areas of crime control, motor vehicles, conflicting taxation, agriculture, and other matters.

commitment. The action of a judicial officer ordering that a person subject to judicial proceedings be placed in a particular kind of confinement or residential facility for a specific reason authorized by law; also the result of the action, that is, the individual's admission to the facility.

common law. In its broadest sense, the original English legal system that has been adopted, in varying degrees, by most English-speaking countries. It is a system of judge-made law, although its principles theoretically derive from general usage and immemorial custom, which the judge only applies. Common law is often called "unwritten law," even though one looks to printed reports of decided cases to deduce its principles. No comprehensive listing of its legal rules is available, unlike civil law's codes. Because the legal rules depend on the nuances of the particular situation, decisions on cases are reached by reasoning inductively, comparing the cases' facts with those of previously decided cases. Within this legal system, the term common law is used to distinguish both judge-made law from statutory law and the system of rigorously applied legal principles from the system of flexible, equitable remedies. After 900 years, the common law endures as a great collective achievement. Today the family of common law takes its place beside two other major families of law, the Romano-Germanic and the socialist. *See also* Common Law of England

Common Law of England. A type of law that emerged from the way the government of England was centralized and specialized after the Norman Conquest in 1066. In the course of unifying England, the Normans and their succesors were faced with the problem of gaining universal jurisdiction for the royal courts. This was by no means an easy task. The Anglo-Saxon courts were local in nature, and customs varied from shire to shire. Elements of canon, Roman, and Germanic law can be found in the common law, which gradually emerged from administrative efforts to centralize legal processes.

common-law marriage. A marriage in which the partners have simply accepted each other as husband and wife, with no license, formal ceremony, blood test, or official witnesses. The term derives from historical roots: when marriages were neither religious nor civil but were arranged between two families, they were part of the unwritten or common law. If a state does not have a law against common-law marriages, they are legal and involve all the obligations and rights of formal marriages.

Community Anti-Crime, National Center for. Founded in 1981, with the goal of training community members and criminal justice personnel in how to plan, develop, and implement crime prevention programs. Address: Norfolk State University, Norfolk, VA 23504.

Community Anti-Drug Coalitions of America. A membership and advocacy organization offering information and technical assistance for developing and implementing strategic plans and public policy initiatives. The organization is affiliated with the National Association of Drug Court Professionals. Address: 901 North Pitt Street, Suite 300, Alexandria, VA 22314.

community-based corrections. Includes any form of correctional treatment, such as halfway houses or parole, that deals with the offender within, as opposed to outside, society (in contrast with incarceration or institutionalization).

community-based policing. A style of local law enforcement emphasizing the idea that the public should play a more active and coordinated role in crime control and prevention. Imposes a police responsibility to devise new and innovative ways of associating the public with law enforcement and the maintenance of order. The four major elements are: (1) organize community-based crime prevention; (2) reorient patrol activities to emphasize nonemergency servicing; (3) increase accountability to local communities; and (4) decentralize command. *See also* community-oriented policing; neighborhood watch.

Community Effort to Combat Auto Theft (CECAT). A multiagency task force coordinated by the Los Angeles Police Department. In 1995 CECAT arrested 346 suspects and recovered 259 vehicles with an estimated value of $3.5 million. *See also* Operation Guatemalan Auto Theft Enforcement; vehicle theft.

community-oriented policing (COP). A continuing organizational philosophy, management style, and cooperative community strategy to enhance local crime prevention and control. COP is a form of policing oriented toward the public, or police forces' clients, and designed to provide communities with responsive, ethical, high-quality police service. COP involves a commitment to attitudinal change at all levels of local law enforcement and an on-going partnership among the police force, the local government, and the community.

COP law enforcement tactics might include foot patrols, storefront police stations, bilingual crime hotlines and prevention newsletters, open communication, external review boards, multiethnic recruitment, and cultural-awareness training for police officers. Although some communities interpret COP to include addressing the causes of crime, police forces generally do not have the resources to alleviate social pressures believed to cause crime. Community relations, team policing, and problem-oriented policing were all earlier methods leading up to COP. COP also shares many features with Total Quality Management (TQM).

The Community Policing Consortium (CPC) publishes *Community Policing Exchange*, a free bimonthly newsletter. Address: Publications Manager, CPC, 1726 M Street, NW, Suite 801, Washington, DC 20036. *See also* National

Center for Community Policing; total quality management

Community Policing Consortium (CPC). This initiative includes five leading U.S. policing organizations: the International Association of Chiefs of Police, the National Organization of Black Law Enforcement Executives, the National Sheriffs' Association, the Police Executive Research Forum, and the Police Foundation. CPC is funded by the U.S. Department of Justice, Bureau of Justice Assistance, and provides information and assistance to community-oriented policing efforts. Address: 1726 M Street NW, Suite 801, Washington, DC 20036.

community property. Property acquired during a marriage by either husband or wife or both, except property that is acquired separately by either spouse.

community relations. A concept involving local residents and police in a partnership to resolve mutual concerns. Generally, police-community relations (PCR) consist of public relations, community service, community participation, and crime prevention. PCR has much to do with attitudes, both those of the police toward themselves and the community and those of the community toward themselves and the police. Open communication, honesty, fairness, and equality are essential elements. Although some police departments have a special section/division under the chief of police to develop, implement, maintain, and evaluate such programs, ideally every member of a department should feel a part of such an effort.

Community Relations Service (CRS). An agency of the Department of Justice, CRS sees its primary duty as helping to resolve disputes over violations of antidiscrimination statutes. CRS may also assist in resolving other social or multiethnic problems.

community service dispositions. A correctional practice in which, in lieu of or in addition to time in jail or on probation, an offender must perform service to the community in the form of public works or volunteer activity at hospitals or other agencies or institutions.

community service officer. A nonsworn officer who handles nonemergency situations for a police department.

community standard. A phrase used by the U.S. Supreme Court in its 1973 *Miller* decision in defining material as pornographic and subject to criminal sanctions if patently offensive in a given geographic or local area. *See also* pornography.

commutation. A reduction of a sentence originally prescribed by a court.

commutation laws. *See* good-time

comparison microscope. A microscope with two objectives (the part nearest the object being viewed), each of which views a different object. Both images are magnified and brought into focus in a single or double eyepiece with prisms. This instrument is usually found in a crime laboratory and used to examine, among other things, markings on two bullets to determine if they were both fired from the same weapon.

competency. (1) Capability, such as power, jurisdiction, or the ability to serve as a witness; (2) evidence, written or otherwise, that is appropriate for presentation.

competent evidence. Any evidence declared admissible by law, or, more specifically, the type of evidence that the nature of a given case requires as proof.

complainantless crime. A type of crime that typically involves a "willing victim," such as gambling, drug use and addiction, or prostitution. One result of such victimless crimes is that no one complains to the police about the illegal activity. *See also* consensual transaction

complaint. (1) In general criminal justice usage, any accusation that a person has committed an offense, received by or originating from a law enforcement or prosecutorial agency or received by a court. (2) In judicial process usage, a formal document submitted to the court by a prosecutor, law enforcement officer, or other person, alleging that a specified person has committed a specified offense and requesting prosecution.

complicity. Any conduct, on the part of a person other than the chief actor in the commission of a crime, by which that person intentionally or knowingly serves to further the intent to commit the crime, aids in the commission of the crime, or assists the person who has committed the crime to avoid prosecution or escape from justice.

compounding a criminal offense. Unlawful agreement by a person to avoid or stop prosecution, or assistance in prosecution, in return for payment of money or anything else of value.

Comprehensive Crime Control Act of 1984. A major revision of Title 18 U.S. Code, the Omnibus Crime Control and Safe Streets Act of 1968, and of other federal statutes (codes) and acts containing definitions, penalties, and enforcement provisions related to crime control, such as the Labor Management Relations Act. The 1984 act established the United States Sentencing Commission, the Bail Reform Act, the Insanity Defense Reform Act, the Sentencing Reform Act, the Comprehensive Forfeiture Act, the Controlled Substances Penalties Amendments Act, the Justice Assistance Act, an Office of Juvenile Justice and Delinquency Prevention, the Missing Children Act, the National Narcotics Act, the Victims of Crime Act, the Trademark Counterfeiting Act, the Credit Card Fraud Act, the Armed Career Criminal Act, the Act for the Prevention and Punishment of the Crime of Hostage-Taking, the Counterfeit Access Device and Computer Fraud and Abuse Act, and the President's Emergency Food Assistance Act. For further information or copies of provisions, contact the Bureau of Justice Assistance, Department of Justice, 633 Indiana Avenue, NW, Washington, DC 20531.

compulsion. An abnormal urge to commit an act without the rational desire to do so. Compulsion is seen as an underlying, unconscious motive that the individual cannot control.

Compulsive Stutterers Anonymous. Self-help group. Address: P0. Box 1400, Park Ridge, IL 60068.

compurgation. A primitive form of defense against an accusation of crime, whereby the accused tried to establish innocence by bringing into court a sufficient number of persons who by oath testified to their belief in the innocence of the defendant. It is commonly assumed that the jury system evolved from this procedure.

Computer-Aided Dispatch (CAD). Electronic data processing that assists the human dispatcher by performing simple, repetitive tasks such as assigning case numbers and storing, retrieving, and displaying information. Data include the nature of complaints, the locations of calls for service, and the units and officers assigned. An interface using the Geobase system allows verification of the address of the call and provides a history of the location prior to the arrival of the officer.

computer crime. Any illegal act in which knowledge of computer technology is used to commit the offense. A popular name for crimes committed by use of a computer or crimes involving misuse or destruction of computer equipment or computerized information; sometimes theft committed by means of manipulation of a computerized financial transaction system or the use of computer services with intent to avoid payment. The special kinds of crimes that can be committed in relation to computer systems have rarely been codified in penal statutes; however, conventional theft provisions often do not adequately cover losses that can occur in relation to these systems. Electronically recorded information, for example, can be stolen without the loss of any tangible object. States have dealt with this problem by establishing a type of crime called "offenses against intellectual property," which includes crimes relating both to unauthorized modification of computer equipment or supplies and to unauthorized access to computers and computer sys-

tems. In recent years, criminals have used computers to pilfer trade secrets; appropriate personal credit histories; illegally purchase stereos, telephones, and other merchandise; change university grade records; sabotage the files of former employers; and manage criminal organizations specializing in stolen auto parts, illegal gambling, narcotics, and prostitution.

Between 1964 and 1973, some 64,000 fake insurance policies, involving $2 billion, were created on the computer of the Equity Funding Corporation. Stanley Mark Rifkin was arrested in Carlsbad, CA, by the FBI on November 6, 1978, and charged with defrauding a Los Angeles bank of $10.2 million by manipulation of a computer system. In June 1980 he was sentenced to 8 years. In May 1985 the Los Angeles Police Department established a computer fraud unit, one of the first such specialized details in the nation. The unit works closely with the electronic crime section of the Los Angeles County district attorney's office, which was established in 1979, the year the state legislature passed a computer trespassing law. In January 1990 Robert T. Morris became the first person convicted under the 1986 federal Computer Fraud and Abuse Act of breaking into a federal computer network and preventing authorized use of the system. Morris created a "worm" program while at Cornell University on November 2, 1988. The program immobilized an estimated 6,000 computers linked to the Internet research system, including some at military bases and universities. Morris was sentenced May 4, 1990, to three years probation, a $10,000 fine, and 400 hours of community service. Computer crime investigation training has been available since 1976 at the FBI Academy in Quantico, VA, and the Federal Law Enforcement Training Center in Glynco, GA. The FBI has formed the Computer Assistance Reaction Team to work with the academic, commercial, and government sectors on detecting and combating new "hacker" schemes that make computer networks vulnerable.

Internal computer crimes are alterations to programs that cause unauthorized functions within a computer system, while computer manipulation crimes involve changing data or creating records in a system for the advancement of another crime. Telecommunications crime involves illegal access to communications or the use of computer systems over telephone lines. A hacking program searches for valid access codes for a computer system by randomly generating and trying such codes. Viruses are computer-generated sets of instructions that not only perform unauthorized functions but also secretly attach themselves to other programs.

Computer Crime Information. The Bureau of Justice maintains the toll-free number (800) 851-3420 and offers publications such as *Electronic Fund Transfer Systems* and *Crime and Computer Security Techniques. Computer Security Handbook, the Practitioner's Bible* and *Computer Security, the Newsletter for Computer Professionals* are published by Computer Security Institute, 43 Boston Post Rd., Northborough, MA 01532. The *Handbook* contains a listing of computer security newsletters, magazines, and journals; computer security special interest groups; and associations with computer security subgroups.

Computer Emergency Response Team (CERT). Set up in 1988 by the U.S. Department of Defense and based at Pittsburgh's Carnegie Mellon University, CERT helps computer administrators close security breaches and notifies other networks of problems. In 1990 CERT handled 252 computer security cases. In the first half of 2003 that number had climbed to over 76,000.

Computer Protection Systems. Founded in 1980, CPS provides asset-protection and loss prevention advice and counsel to private industry, financial institutions, law enforcement agencies, attorneys, and certified public accountants. Publishes *Corporate Fraud Digest* and *Computer Security Digest* (newsletters). Address: Suite 4, 711 West Ann Arbor Trail, Plymouth, MI 48170.

Computer Security Institute. Founded in 1975, this organization publishes the *Computer Security Journal.* Address: 360 Church St., Northborough, MA 01532; telephone (617) 393-2600.

conciliation. A process that originated in French civil law—there is no such process in common law—and that requires disputing parties to appear before a judge, who tries to persuade them to settle their differences and thus avoid further court proceedings. A "pretrial conference" can be held at the court's discretion, but involving the lawyers rather than their clients, and for the purpose of simplifying, but not settling, the case. Conciliation is frequently used by U.S. courts in certain civil proceedings, such as labor disputes. In the context of labor disputes, it is generally an informal type of third-party intervention into collective bargaining over new contract terms, when the bargaining has broken down or threatens to do so. The conciliator attempts to bring the parties together and restore constructive dialog and bargaining. Conciliation is a voluntary and nonbinding process. If conciliation fails, mediation may be mandated for the disputing parties. *See also* arbitration; collective bargaining; mediation

conclusive evidence. That which is incontrovertible, either because the law does not permit it to be contradicted or because it is so strong and convincing as to overbear all proof to the contrary and establish the proposition in question beyond any reasonable doubt.

concubinage. Informal marriage; cohabitation.

concurrent. To operate or run at the same time. When used in reference to sentences imposed upon someone convicted of crime, it means the person serves all sentences simultaneously. If anyone should be sentenced on two charges and receive five-year sentences on each charge, to run concurrently, he or she has satisfied both after five years' imprisonment.

concurrent jurisdiction. A situation when more than one court is entitled to consider the same case, which often occurs in the United States because of its federal structure. The Constitution does not prohibit state courts from hearing suits involving federal questions, although Congress does so in specific instances such as national security cases and seditions. Article III of the Constitution grants federal courts jurisdiction where there is a diversity of citizenship. Where concurrent jurisdiction exists, a person can choose whether to begin the suit in state or federal court.

concurrent writs. Several writs running at the same time for the same purpose. Examples are writs in several locations for the arrest of a person whose whereabouts are unknown or writs to be served on several persons, such as codefendants.

condemn. (1) To find a person guilty or impose sentence on someone convicted of a crime; (2) to judge a property or facility unfit or unsafe; or (3) to set a property or facility apart for public use.

condemnation. (1) The judgment by which property seized for violation of revenue or other laws is declared forfeited to the state. (2) The determination of a court that a ship is unfit for service or was properly seized and held as a prize.

conditional pardon. Any pardon to which one or more conditions, or qualifications, are attached. conditional release. The release, by executive decision, from a federal or state correctional facility, of a prisoner who has not served his or her full sentence and whose freedom is contingent upon obeying specified rules of behavior.

conditions of criminality. To render a person criminally responsible for the commission of a common law crime, that person must (a) be of sufficient age, (b) have sufficient mental capacity, (c) act voluntarily, and (d) have criminal intent.

confabulation. The relating of events or experiences as though they actually occurred, when in fact they are imaginary, a trait sometimes found in psychopaths.

confession. A statement, usually recorded, by a person who admits violation of the law;

an admission of criminal activity. A confession must be given voluntarily, without force, threats, promises, or coercion being used by the officer receiving it. Under the Miranda ruling, persons being interviewed must be warned of their constitutional rights, and suspects must understand and waive such rights before any incriminating statements they make in response to questions can be admitted into evidence.

confidence game. A popular name for false representation to obtain money or any other thing of value, where deception is accomplished through the trust placed by the victim in the character of the offender. The term is not used in statutes. "Swindle" is sometimes used as a synonym for confidence game, but a distinction is often made. A swindle is an intentional false representation to obtain money or any other thing of value, whereas deception is accomplished through the victim's belief in the validity of some statement or object presented by the offender. Trust in a person, as opposed to belief in a statement or object, distinguishes a confidence game from a swindle.

confidential communications. Statements, made by one person to another when their relationship requires mutual truth and confidence, that the receiving person cannot be compelled to disclose (for example, the statements made by a husband to his wife or by a client to his or her attorney).

confinement. Physical restriction of a person to a clearly defined area, from which (a) he or she is lawfully forbidden to depart and (b) departure is usually constrained by architectural barriers and/or guards or other custodians.

confinement, congregate. A method of imprisonment characterizing the early jails of Europe and of the U.S. before the reforms introduced into the Walnut Street Jail of Philadelphia in 1790. Before these reforms, the prisoners were allowed to associate with each other day and night. Owing to serious abuses, the Walnut Street Jail began keeping more hardened inmates in separate cells without work, while allowing the others to live in dormitories and work together in common workshops. Later the term was applied to the Auburn, NY, system to contrast it with the Pennsylvania, or separate, system.

confinement, solitary. The most severe measure of prison discipline now used in most prisons, it involves placing the prisoner in a special cell with little light and usually providing only a board or the floor on which to sleep, a ration of bread and water; the prisoner is sometimes chained to restrict his movements. Such measures are becoming less common as prison discipline becomes better understood.

confiscation. Government seizure of private property without compensation to the owner. This is often a consequence of conviction for crime or participation in rebellion, or because possession of the property was contrary to law, or because it was being used for an unlawful purpose.

conflict model. A theory that views law as emerging from conflict between interest groups with differing degrees of power.

conflict model of legislation. The view that a society's laws represent the interests of its most powerful groups.

conflict of interest. In law enforcement, the situation that arises when an officer, in the discharge of his public duties, has to administer, decide, or vote on some matter in which he, or a member of his family, has a private financial interest. Anticipating such a situation, high public officials, upon being elected or appointed, sometimes divest themselves of stock or other forms of ownership in private companies or place their property in the hands of trustees. Very little legislation regulating conflict of interest has been enacted.

conflict of laws. Differing provisions of two or more laws, any or all of which can be interpreted to apply to a given case.

conflict resolution. Means by which individuals or groups with competing goals find ways of eliminating their disagreements. Conflicts can be resolved through war, negotiation, compromise, the finding of a common enemy, and so forth.

confrontation. A meeting arranged between a witness and an accused for such purposes as identification, or to determine what objections the accused has to the witness.

conjugal visitation. A program in which prison inmates and their spouses are permitted to spend time together in private quarters on prison grounds, during which they may engage in sexual relations. It has been promoted as a means of reducing homosexuality in prison, as well as of raising inmate morale and maintaining family ties.

connivance. (1) Guilty knowledge of, or assistance in, a crime. (2) Consent, express or implied, by one spouse to the adultery of the other.

conscience. Representing the internalization of the rules of society, conscience is experienced through feelings of anxiety and guilt that accompany anticipated or actual transgression. The two major theories of its origins are the psychoanalytic view and the behavioristic view. Self-regulation of behavior—particularly resisting temptation—is determined in large measure by conscience.

conscientious objector. One who, for reasons of conscience, refuses to participate in war or combat. In the U.S., the period since World War I has seen the progressive broadening of the term to include not only members of organized religions opposed to war, as was the case in 1917, but also anyone whose "religious training and belief" need not necessarily imply belief in a supreme being in the conventional sense. The courts have so far refused, however, to allow "selective conscientious objection," or objection to a particular war as immoral or unjust.

consecutive sentence. A sentence that is one of two or more sentences imposed simultaneously after conviction for more than one offense, and which is served in sequence with the other sentences; or, a new sentence for a new conviction, imposed upon a person already under sentence(s) for a previous offense(s), which increases the maximum time the offender may be confined or under supervision.

Consecutive sentences are served one after the other; concurrent sentences are served at the same time. A concurrent sentence is composed of two or more sentences being served at the same time and imposed at the same time after conviction for more than one offense; or, a new sentence imposed upon a person already under sentence(s) for a previous offense(s), to be served at the same time as one or more of the previous sentences.

consensual transaction. A mutually agreed-upon exchange of goods and services that often characterizes victimless or complainantless crimes such as drugs, gambling, or prostitution.

consensus model of legislation. The view that a society's laws are based on agreement among diverse groups about basic values. *See also* conflict model

consent decree. A judgment of a court that is agreed to by all parties involved in the litigation. Although it is not a judicial sentence, it is a solemn contract among the parties and, in effect, their admission that the decree is a just determination of their rights upon the real and proven facts of the case. Consent decrees are especially common in the U.S. prison system, as approximately 40 states are operating prisons under decrees regarding such prison conditions as overcrowding, unsatisfactory food, and uneven disciplinary procedures. *See also* decree, special master.

consent, implied. Consent that is not expressly given but that is inferred from actions or is prescribed by law. Several states have laws, for example, that provide that when the operator of a motor vehicle obtains a driver's license, he waives his right to object to an intoxication test if he should at a later date be charged with driving while intoxicated. This type of statute is generally referred to as an implied consent law.

consenting adult laws. In its 1986 *Bowers v. Hardwick* decision, the U.S. Supreme Court upheld the right of states to regulate adult consensual sexual behavior.

consent of the victim. Any voluntary agreement of a victim to an offending party's action that the victim knowingly gives. That a victim consented can be a criminal defense, provided that: (a) the victim was capable of giving consent; (b) the offense was "consentable" (murder and statutory rape are not considered consentable crimes); (c) consent was not obtained by fraud; and (d) the person giving consent had authority to do so.

consent search. Voluntary consent of the legal owner of premises or property for it to be searched. A person, place, or piece of property may be lawfully searched by an officer of the law if the owner gives his free and voluntary consent. However, owners may not always have the legal right of possession to all their property. For example, a hotel owner cannot consent to a search of a room currently occupied by a hotel guest. In that case, the guest, as the legal possessor of the room, must consent to a search.

conservative. A term used to describe a political or social position that holds that individuals act with free choice and based on free will, so that each person is seen to be responsible for his or her own actions or inactions. In the conservative view, crime is basically the result of moral failure rather than of political or social factors. This view emphasizes reactive punishment as a crime deterrent. Conservatives thus generally support more prisons, stiffer penalties, and the imposition of capital punishment.

consolateur. A manual or electric dildo, or penis-shaped tool used in erotic play.

consolidated laws. A compilation of all the laws of a state that are in force, arranged according to subject matter. *See also* code

conspiracy. A combination or agreement between two or more persons to commit an unlawful act, whether that act be the final object of the combination, or only a means to the final end, and whether that act be a crime, or an act hurtful to the public, a class of persons, or an individual. The offense is usually divided into three categories: (a) an act where the end to be attained is in itself a crime; (b) an act where the object is lawful, but the means by which it is to be attained are unlawful; (c) an act where the object is to do an injury to a third person or a group, even though if the wrong were inflicted by a single individual it would be a civil wrong rather than a crime. An overt act is generally necessary. Conspiracies are misdemeanors, unless made felonies by statute.

constitution. The fundamental law of a state, consisting of: (a) the basic political principles that ought to be followed in conducting the government; (b) the organization of government; (c) the vesting of powers in the principal officers and agencies; (d) the limitations on the extent of, and methods of exercising, these powers; and (e) the relationship between the government and the people who live under it. The constitution may be simply an uncollected body of legislative acts, judicial decisions, and political precedents and customs, like that of the United Kingdom. At the other extreme, a constitution may be a single document drafted and promulgated at a definite date by an authority of higher competence than that which makes ordinary laws, like constitutions in the United States. It may be endorsed by the courts as superior to statutes that conflict with it, as in the U.S. and a few other countries, or its preservation may be entrusted to the political authorities. In the latter case, which is still the usual one in Europe, a written constitution stands as a convenient standard by which the people may judge the conduct of their government and the degree of its respect for their liberties. Constitutions are sometimes classified as (a) written or unwritten, according to whether or not their written material is presented in consolidated and systematic form; or (b) as flexible or rigid, according to whether they can be amended by legislative enactment or require a more complicated procedure of proposal and ratification by different authorities. *See also* state constitutions

constitutional court. (1) A court created by or under a specific authorization of a constitution. (2) A court in the U.S. federal judicial system, established under Article III of the Constitution, whose judges are entitled to tenure during good behavior and to salaries that cannot be decreased. The U.S. Supreme Court of Appeals and district courts were created as constitutional courts, and the same rank was accorded by Congress in 1946 to the Court of Claims, the Court of Customs and Patent Appeals, and, in 1956, to the Customs Court, all three of which previously had been legislative courts.

constitutionalism. The doctrine that the power to govern should be limited by definite and enforceable principles of political organization and procedural regularity embodied in the fundamental law or custom, so that basic constitutional rights of individuals and groups will not be infringed.

constitutional law. The body of legal rules and principles, usually formulated in a written constitution, which define the nature and limits of governmental power, as well as the rights and duties of individuals in relation to the state and its governing organs, and which are interpreted and extended by courts of final jurisdiction exercising the power of judicial review.

constitutional rights. The rights of citizens as guaranteed by the United States Constitution. *See also* bill of rights

constructive contempt. A contempt, committed out of the presence of the court, which does not involve a failure to appear in court or other official judicial body as ordered by the court. *See also* contempt of court

consumer fraud. Deception of the public with respect to the cost, quality, purity, safety, durability, performance, effectiveness, dependability, availability, or adequacy of choice relating to goods or services offered or furnished and with respect to credit or other matters relating to terms of sales. Consumer fraud, like white-collar crime, is not amenable to strict definition. Its chief use is as a generic term, indicating the focus of crime prevention or law enforcement activities associated with consumer affairs agencies. Particular instances of consumer fraud are prosecuted as types of fraud designated in statutes under a variety of names.

consumer protection. Local, state, and federal laws and regulations governing various aspects of business. Examples of federal laws are the Sherman and Clayton Antitrust Acts, the Food and Drug Act, and the Truth in Lending Act. In addition, administrative laws and regulations are handed down by agencies such as the Federal Trade Commission and the Pure Food and Drug Administration, which are charged specifically with regulating commercial activities. Industry's efforts to protect consumers are exercised via trade associations, chambers of commerce, and better business bureaus through the adoption of codes of conduct and product standards. Consumer advocates study industry practices and product performance to determine abuses against which the consumer should be protected. Their chief weapon is carefully documented publicity that is adverse to a company or a product. Consumer movements are sometimes formalized: delegates meet and attempt to exert pressure for legislation to protect the consumer.

consumers' rights movement. Action begun by public groups and individuals in the 1960s and 1970s to secure standards of safety and honesty in the public marketplace. The movement in its current form was begun with the publication of Ralph Nader's *Unsafe at Any Speed* (1965), a critique of the Corvair automobile. The disclosures in Nader's report struck a spark, and the public began to demand legislation to protect their rights as consumers. Congress responded with such legislation as the Fair Packaging and Labeling Act of 1966, the Toy Safety Act of 1969, and the Poison Prevention Packaging Act of 1970. In 1972 the Consumer Product Safety Commission was created.

contact surveillance. The use of tracer preparations which will adhere to the hands,

other body areas, or clothing of a suspect when he or she comes in contact with it.

containment theory. Theory of criminality, especially juvenile delinquency, which postulates that delinquency and crime occur to the extent that a breakdown occurs in "inner" and "outer" constraining or restraining forces of society. Inner restraints consist of moral, religious, and ethical values, while outer restraints derive from family, educators, and other authority figures.

contemporaneous. Occurring at the same time as something else. In an arrest, it is something that happens at the time of the arrest or soon thereafter and is part of a continuous, uninterrupted lawful investigation.

contempt of Congress. The refusal to answer pertinent questions before a congressional committee when summoned. Contempt of Congress is a misdemeanor, punishable by a fine of at least $100 and imprisonment from 1 to 12 months. To cite a person for contempt, the committee concerned must introduce a resolution into the House or Senate. A simple majority is needed for approval, and, if approved, the matter is referred to a U.S. attorney for presentation to a grand jury and prosecution in a federal court. Contempt of Congress was first ruled a criminal offense in 1857.

contempt of court. Intentionally obstructing a court in the administration of justice, acting in a way calculated to lessen its authority or dignity, or failing to obey its lawful orders. The term applies to disobedience of a court order, disruptive acts, and the use of objectionable language in a courtroom. One need not be a party to an action pending before a court to be held in contempt.

Contempts are classified in two ways: civil or criminal and direct or constructive. Direct contempt is committed in the presence of the court; constructive contempt is committed elsewhere. Civil contempt is a failure to do something ordered for the benefit of one's adversary, while criminal contempt is a failure to act as ordered for the court's benefit.

continuance. Adjournment or postponement of a case or action before a court, either to a later date or indefinitely.

continuous crime. A crime consisting of continuous violations, such as possession of stolen property or carrying a concealed weapon. The statute of limitations does not begin to operate on such a crime until the person discontinues the acts constituting the violation.

contraband. Goods, the possession of which is illegal, especially smuggled goods.

contraband, possession in prison. Punishments are prescribed in Title 18, U.S. Code, for an inmate of a federal prison found to possess, or anyone who provides or attempts to provide an inmate with, (a) a firearm or destructive device; (b) any other weapon or object that may be used as a weapon or as a means of facilitating escape; (c) a narcotic drug as defined in the Controlled Substances Act; (d) a controlled substance other than a narcotic drug or alcoholic beverage; or (e) United States currency.

contract. A legally enforceable agreement between two or more parties, under the terms of which, for valid consideration, the parties agree to perform, or refrain from performing, some act.

contract law enforcement. A form of regional law enforcement in which small communities contract with their county or an adjacent city for police services. For example, the Los Angeles County Sheriff's Department provides police services to 39 incorporated cities within the county.

contract system. A system of employment of prison labor in which an employer contracts for the use of prisoners at or near the prison, which continues to provide inmates with food, clothing, and general supervision. The system began at the end of the eighteenth century and for a time was the most popular form of prison labor. Opposition of labor unions and private manufacturers and the abuses caused by unscrupulous prison officials led to the rapid decline of the system.

Less than one percent of all prisoners are now employed under this system. In spite of its drawbacks, no other system of prison labor has succeeded in providing such a large volume of work under disciplined conditions as the contract system. A return to it, however, is improbable.

contractual rights. Property or other rights secured under a contract. The courts afford protection for such rights, so that an injured party to a contract can sue for damages any other party to the contract who has failed to fulfill his or her covenanted obligations. Another legal remedy is a writ of specific performance, to secure the fulfillment of contractual rights. Contracts, and rights thereunder, are protected by the contract clause of the Constitution, as well as by its due process clauses against impairment by state legislatures, but contractual rights are safeguarded no more than other rights against the exercise of a state's prerogatives of eminent domain, taxation, and the police power.

contravention. (1) A process of social interaction, midway between competition and conflict, consisting of a wide range of activities, from mere withholding of cooperation to reproaching, disparaging, thwarting, betraying, or conniving against another, but always falling short of the use or the threat of violence. (2) In the French penal code, offenses are divided into crimes, delits, and contraventions in the order of their diminishing seriousness. This classification does not correspond exactly with that of the English common law—treason, felony, and misdemeanor. Under French law contraventions are violations of police regulations.

contributing to the delinquency of a minor. The offense committed by an adult who in any manner causes, encourages, or aids a juvenile to commit a crime or status offense. *See also* status offense

contributory negligence. An old common law rule that any lack of care on the part of an injured employee relieves the employer of liability for damages. It has been modified by statute in most states in favor of the rule of comparative negligence, by which the employer is relieved of responsibility only in proportion to the relative negligence of himself and the employee.

Controlled Substances Act. Title II of the Comprehensive Drug Abuse and Control Act of 1970. It brought together under one law most of the drug controls that had been created since the Harrison Act in 1914; categorized certain substances into five "schedules"; and defined the offenses and penalties associated with the illegal manufacturing, distributing, and dispensing of any drug in each schedule. The act was amended by the Comprehensive Crime Control Act of 1984, which redefined the schedules and provided penalties for distribution in or near schools. The act also established the Dangerous Drug Diversion Control Act of 1984. *See also* narcotic drugs

contumacious. Willfully disobedient to an order of a court.

conversion. In law, taking the property of another and using it for one's own benefit, or changing property from real property to personal, or the reverse.

conveyance. A written instrument transferring property, or title to property, from one person to another.

convict. (1) To find guilty. (2) A person found guilty of a crime or misdemeanor. (3) Any person confined to a state or federal prison under sentence of more than a year for the commission of crime. The term does not apply to persons confined in city and county jails.

convict code. A value system among prison inmates that is heavily influenced by the thieves' code, which includes these precepts: Do your own time, never snitch on another prisoner, maintain dignity and respect, help other convicts, leave the majority of other prisoners alone, and show no weakness.

conviction. The judgment of a court, based on the verdict of a jury or judicial officer or on the guilty or *nolo contendere* plea of a defendant, that the latter is guilty of the offense(s) with which he or she has been charged.

convict labor. Work performed by inmates of penal institutions, either under contract with private parties or directly for the state, the products of which were forbidden in interstate commerce by an act of Congress effective in 1934. *See also* contract system

Cooper, D. B. The man who boarded a Northwest Orient Airlines jet on November 24, 1971, and then hijacked it. After receiving $200,000 in ransom and a parachute, Cooper jumped from the jet over a rural area of Washington State. Expert meteorologists and skydivers indicated that when the skyjacker hit the freezing air at 200 miles per hour, his eyes would have been immediately blackened, his clothing torn off, his body thrown into a severe tumble, and that he would have been unable to open his parachute.

coprolalia. Medical term for using obscene language. Sudden overuse by an individual may be a symptom of mental illness, and compulsive use may occur involuntarily in victims of Gilles de la Tourette syndrome.

coprophagia. Sexual arousal or activity while watching others evacuate their bladders or bowels or being urinated on. Can also involve writing graffiti on bathroom walls.

coprophilia. Sexual arousal or activity involving speaking or hearing sexual or obscene language.

coprophobia. The fear of excreting or of excreta.

copulatio analis. Pederasty, or anal sodomy.

copycat syndrome. The tendency of individuals to commit antisocial or criminal acts that imitate those of others, either compulsively or to avoid detection. The so-called copycat effect is also thought to lead to multiple suicides in a given community after one individual has killed him- or herself. *See also* Werther effect

copyright. The 1976 United States Copyright Act declares that a work written, or fixed in some tangible form, is protected by statutory copyright. The term of copyright continues from the moment of creation in a fixed tangible manner for 50 years after the author's death. Unpublished works created before January 1, 1978, enjoy the same copyright as those created after this date. Formerly, works were copyrighted for terms of 28 years; therefore the Copyright Act stipulates that the work of a deceased author whose work was copyrighted after September 19, 1906, and was copyrighted again after September 19, 1962, or was in its final year of copyright protection in 1977, is automatically protected further so that the total length of copyright protection (including its renewal period) will not exceed 75 years. A copyright held by a living author, prior to January 1, 1978, in its first 28-year term must be renewed in its 27th year of copyright (unlike new works under the 1976 Copyright Act, which require no renewal), but its renewal term will be for 47 years, thus bringing the total copyright protection to 75 years. This renewal is not automatic but must be applied for. A work that has been copyrighted for its initial term and has not been renewed and has thus fallen into the public domain cannot be afforded any further copyright protection.

corneali complex. The incestuous desire of a mother for her son.

coroner. From the Latin *coronae*, or of the crown, an official who performs specified duties in investigating cases of death where there are questionable circumstances or where the deceased was unattended by a physician at the time of death. This office of coroner originated in England in the twelfth century and has been adopted in most of the United States. Usually there is one elected coroner in each county. In some states the coroner has been replaced by a medical examiner.

corporal punishment. Physical punishment. As of 1996, 23 states, including Arizona, Nevada, Texas, and Florida still permit corporal punishment, usually paddling, of public school students. By the twentieth century, state-sponsored flogging of criminals in the U.S. had become rare. The pillory, an upright wooden frame used to confine offenders and allow the public to pelt them, has been virtually extinct in the U.S. for more than 150 years. **1775:** John Adams's "Rules for the Regulation of the Navy," drawn up by the Constitutional Congress, authorized flogging on American warships, permitting up to 12 lashes to any enlisted man for such offenses as swearing or drunkenness. **1786:** Pennsylvania, setting the pace for penal reform, passed a new criminal code establishing a system of proportional prison time to replace capital and corporal punishment, the hallmarks of the English Code. **1839:** The pillory was abolished in the U.S. except in Delaware, which abolished it in 1905. **1840s:** Several state prisons experimented with the "shower bath," in which inmates were placed in a small closet, with their legs, arms, and necks confined in wooden stocks. They were then drenched with water for hours at a time. **1850:** The U.S. Senate abolished naval flogging. **1863:** The Emancipation Proclamation abolished slavery, under which blacks had often been flogged. **1867:** New Jersey became the first state to ban corporal punishment in schools. But local authorities defied the ban, which wasn't honored until the twentieth century. **1874:** The revised Articles of War banned flogging, branding, marking, or tattooing on the body of any serviceman. **1952:** The last legal flogging in the U.S. was held in Delaware, which did not abolish the practice completely until 1972. **1994:** West Virginia became the 27th state to ban corporal punishment in public schools.

corporate crime. Illegal act(s) committed by a corporate body or by executives and managers acting on behalf of a corporation. Such acts include consumer fraud, price fixing, and restraint of trade. *See also* white-collar crime

corpus delicti (Lat., lit, body of the crime). The facts constituting or proving a crime, composed of (a) the act and (b) the criminal agency producing it. In a homicide case, it must be shown that a human was killed and that the killing was done by another human being. A suicide or accidental death does not satisfy the proof of *corpus delicti*. Loosely, the term also means the victim's body in a murder case.

correctional agency. A federal, state, or local criminal or juvenile justice agency, under a single administrative authority, of which the principal functions are the intake, screening, supervision, custody, confinement, treatment, or presentencing or predisposition investigation of alleged or adjudicated adult offenders, youthful offenders, delinquents, or status offenders.

correctional client. A person, either prisoner or parolee, who has been convicted of a crime and sentenced to correctional treatment.

correctional day program. A publicly financed and operated, nonresidential educational or treatment program in which persons required by a judicial officer must participate.

Correctional Association, American. Founded in 1945, the group's goals are to increase the effectiveness, expertise, and skills of educators and administrators providing services to adult and juvenile students in correctional settings, and to improve the quality of educational programs and services. Address: 4380 Forbes boulevard, Lanham, Maryland 20706-4322; telephone: 1-800-ACA-JOIN.

correctional facility. A building or part thereof, set of buildings, or area enclosing a set of buildings or structures operated by a governmental agency for the physical custody, or custody and treatment, of persons sentenced or subject to criminal proceedings.

corrections. A generic term that includes all governmental agencies, facilities, programs, procedures, personnel, and techniques concerned with the intake, custody, confinement, supervision, treatment, or presentencing or predisposition investigation of alleged or adjudicated adult offenders, delinquents, or status offenders. *See also* National Institute of Corrections; status offense

Corrections Services of Canada. The agency of the Canadian federal government that has re-sponsibility for providing correctional services to all offenders sentenced to serve two or more years in a correctional institution.

corrections statistics, history of. In 1850 the federal government, in cooperation with the states as a part of the Seventh Decennial Census, initiated a count of prisoners in 32 states and the territories of Minnesota, New Mexico, Oregon, and Utah. Between 1850 and 1870, U.S. marshals administered the census of prisoners as part of a special schedule of social statistics. The 1880 report indicated there were 61 state prisoners per 100,000 residents. By 1890 Nevada had the highest per capita rate among the states, 203, and Wyoming had the lowest at 16; New York had 136 prisoners per 100,000, and California had 169.

In 1910 the introduction of the indeterminate sentence was described in prisoner statistics: 21 percent of state prisoners on January 1 had received such sentences. The 1923 report showed that more than half of the prison admissions were under indeterminate sentences, and observed that such sentences resulted in wide ranges between minimum and maximum sentences and disparities in setting release dates. In 1926 the Bureau of the Census began the annual collection of prisoner statistics, and that year's report described the goal of the collection of data: "to show the application of penal policies for various classes of offenders and in different parts of the country." That first annual report in 1926 provided information by jurisdiction on admissions, releases, sentences and time served, inmates under sentence of death, recidivism, and crowding.

In 1950 data collection was transferred from the Bureau of the Census to the Bureau of Prisons in the Department of Justice, and in 1971 to the predecessor agency of the Bureau of Justice Statistics (BJS), the National Criminal Justice Information and Statistics Service of the Law Enforcement Assistance Administration (LEAA). LEAA added the statistical series on local jails (1970), parole (1976), and probation (1979). In 1979 the first annual report on parole and probation appeared, published by BJS.

corrupt. (1) Evil, depraved; debased. (2) Taking bribes; dishonest. *See also* Operation Greylord

Corrupt Practices Acts. State and federal statutes aimed at eliminating campaign and election abuses. The basis of modern federal legislation is the act of 1925, the scope of which was widened in 1972.

corruption. In the broadest sense, any illegal act by a sworn peace officer, including all violations of fiduciary trust and the professional codes of conduct and ethics. Specific examples include taking bribes, selling favors, accepting gifts, and committing, aiding, or abetting criminal behavior.

corruption of blood. The legal consequence, under the old common law, of conviction of treason or felony, according to which the person so convicted could neither possess nor transmit by inheritance any property, rank, or title.

Council of State Governments. Founded in 1933, the council operates the States Information Center "to assist state officials with up-to-date research pertaining to problems within state government jurisdictions." Address: Iron Works Pike, Lexington, KY 40578.

counsel. Legal assistance from one trained in law; an attorney.

count. *See* charge

count, prisoner. (1) In published summary data, usually the number of inmates present in a given facility or facility system on a regular, specified day of the year, month, or quarter. (2) In management usage, the daily, weekly, or other periodic tally of inmates present in a particular facility.

counterfeiting. The manufacture or attempted manufacture of a copy or imitation of a negotiable instrument with value set by law or convention, or the possession of such a copy without authorization, with the intent to defraud by claiming the genuineness of the copy. In statutes, counterfeiting is included with the definition of forgery. Where a distinction is made, it rests on the fact that counterfeiting presupposes the prior existence of an officially issued item of value that provides a model for the perpetrator. Examples include currency, coins, postage stamps, ration stamps, food stamps (under the jurisdiction of the U.S. Department of Agriculture), bearer bonds, and so forth. This preexisting model is absent in a forgery.

counterfeiting, trademark. The Trademark Counterfeiting Act of 1984 provides that (a) whoever intentionally traffics or attempts to traffic in goods or services and knowingly uses a counterfeit mark on or in connection with such goods or services shall, if an individual, be fined not more than $250,000 or imprisoned not more than five years or both, and, if other than an individual, be fined not more than $1 million; and in the case of a second offense for an individual, be fined not more than $1 million or imprisoned not more than 15 years or both, and, if other than an individual, be fined not more than $5 million; and (b) upon a determination by a preponderance of the evidence that any articles in the possession of a defendant in a prosecution under this section bear counterfeit marks, the United States may obtain an order for the destruction of such articles. In a prosecution, the defendant shall have the burden of proof, by a preponderance of the evidence, of any such affirmative defense. The term *counterfeit mark* means a spurious mark—one that is identical with, or substantially indistinguishable from, a mark registered for those goods or services on the principal register in the U.S. Patent and Trademark Office and in use, whether or not the defendant knew such mark was so registered, and the use of which is likely to cause confusion, to cause mistake, or to deceive.

In addition, defendants are prosecuted under the Lanham Act, which provides for the registration and protection of trademarks used in commerce, carries out the provisions of certain international conventions, and has other purposes, as approved on July 5, 1946.

county. A geographical and political division of the state, in all states except Louisiana, where a county is termed a parish.

county court. A body, formerly composed of all the justices of the peace within a county, which was both the chief county administrative board and a court lower than the circuit court. At present it may have purely administrative or judicial functions or combinations of both, depending on the laws of particular states.

county judges—criminal court. A criminal court of general jurisdiction in Canada which sits without a jury to hear indictable offenses.

coup d'état. A sudden, forcible seizure of power by a political faction. Statisticians contend that Bolivia, since it became a sovereign country in 1825, has had 189 coups d'état.

court. Agency or unit of the judicial branch of government, authorized or established by statute or constitution and consisting of one or more judicial officers, which has the authority to decide upon cases, controversies in law, and disputed matters of fact brought before it. Court, judge, and bench are used interchangeably in many contexts; often the court means the judge or the judicial officer. The term includes: (a) trial court, of which the primary function is to hear and decide cases; (b) court of limited (special) jurisdiction, a trial court having original jurisdiction over only that subject matter specifically assigned to it by law (these courts go by such names as municipal court, justice court, magistrate court, family court, probate court, and traffic court); (c) court of general jurisdiction, a trial court having original jurisdiction over all subject matter not specifically assigned to a court of limited jurisdiction (these courts are frequently given jurisdiction over certain kinds of appeal matters and are usually called superior courts, district courts, or circuit courts); (d) appellate court, of which the primary function is to review the judgments of other courts and administrative agencies; (e) intermediate appellate court, of which the primary function is to review the judgments of trial courts and the decisions of administrative agencies and whose decisions are in turn usually reviewable by a higher appellate court in the same state; and (f) court of last resort, an appellate court having final jurisdiction over appeals within a given state.

court administrator. The official responsible for supervising and performing administrative tasks for a given court(s).

court, adolescent. An experimental court designed to deal with persons between the ages of 16 (when the jurisdiction of the juvenile court ends) and 18 or 21, when moral responsibility seems to have matured. Its procedure follows the same informal pattern as the juvenile court, and probation and other protective services are used extensively. Chicago and New York City have experimented with this type of court, but opinions differ as to its value.

court calendar. The court schedule; the list of events comprising the daily or weekly work of a court, including the assignment of the time and place for each hearing or other item of business or the list of matters which will be taken up in a given court term.

court, canonical. The ecclesiastical court of the Middle Ages, to which both criminal cases and those involving domestic and marital law were referred.

court clerk. An elected or appointed court officer responsible for maintaining the written records of the court and for supervising or performing the clerical tasks necessary for conducting judicial business; also, any employee of a court whose principal duty is to assist the court clerk.

court, criminal. A court where criminal, as opposed to civil, cases are tried.

court decision. In popular usage, any official determination made by a judicial officer; in special judicial usages, any of several specific kinds of determinations made by particular courts. A decision may be called a judgment, decree, finding, court order, or opinion.

Court Delay Reduction Program. A number of states have reduced both criminal and civil court delays through the exercise of rulemaking powers and statewide case reporting systems. The Portland (OR) Criminal Court has processed felony cases from arrest to trial in less than 60 days. A research team from the Whittier Justice Institute has drawn upon the Portland experience to identify seven principles or "critical factors" for successful, speedy criminal case processing. These factors were published in a report, *Arrest to Trial in 45 Days*. Additional study of court systems has confirmed those principles. Address for further information: Court Delay Reduction Program, Bureau of Justice Assistance, Office of Justice Programs, DOJ, 633 Indiana Avenue, NW, Washington, DC 20531.

court disposition. The judicial decision terminating proceedings in a case before judgment is reached; the judgment. The data representing the outcome of judicial proceedings and the manner in which it was reached.

court, domestic relations. A court having jurisdiction over cases involving strained relations, such as desertion and neglect, between husband and wife, as well as cases of juvenile delinquency. In the latter cases, parent-child relationships are recognized as being important in producing the delinquency and significant in working out any effective adjustment or treatment for the child. The general philosophy of such courts in dealing with delinquency is that the family is a unit and that the problem is frequently a familial rather than an individual one. Domestic relations courts exist only in our larger cities, where sufficient cases arise to warrant a separate court.

Court Employment Project. Founded in 1967, and called the Manhattan Court Employment Project until 1970. Its purpose is to provide counseling, education, employment, and legal and vocational services to young offenders (ages 14–21) involved with the New York City Criminal and Supreme Courts. Address: 346 Broadway, New York, NY 10013.

court house. The building at the county seat that houses the principal offices of county government and provides for courts.

court, inferior. A court of primary and/or limited jurisdiction that tries cases of a minor nature. It is generally not a court of record; that is, no record of its proceedings is made unless one is specifically requested by the parties. Inferior courts usually try misdemeanor cases and hold preliminary hearings or examinations. Also called lower courts, they also act as committing agencies for higher courts. Examples of inferior courts include justice of the peace, police courts, mayor's court, and municipal or city courts.

court, juvenile. A court dealing with youthful offenders or juvenile dependents and with adults who contribute to the delinquency of children. In most states the jurisdiction of such courts is limited to children under 16; a few have jurisdiction over those under 18, and California has jurisdiction over young persons under 21. In general, capital offenses of juveniles may be transferred to the regular criminal court, but juvenile delinquents are considered wards of the court and are presumed to be treated as children needing help rather than as guilty persons requiring punishment. Hearings are usually private and there is generally no trial, although a number of states paradoxically allow a trial if demanded by the child's parents or his or her "next friend."

court, magistrate's. In most cities, the lowest court of original jurisdiction in criminal cases. Suspects apprehended by the police are first arraigned in magistrate's court, where evidence is examined. If, in the mind of the magistrate, the evidence is sufficient, the suspect is bound over to the grand jury or some other specialized court, and bail is set to ensure the suspect's appearance at trial. If the offense is a minor one, such as violation of a city ordinance, the magistrate may have the power to make a judgment and set the penalty.

court-martial. A tribunal in each of the armed services, composed of officers and enlisted persons, that tries armed forces personnel or others accused of violating military law under the provisions of the Uniform Code of Military Justice. A general court-martial may try any offense; special and summary courts-martial have limited jurisdiction. In the American armed services, a court-martial verdict may, in some instances, be appealed to the U.S. Court of Military Appeals, which is composed of civilian judges, but not to the civil courts. The first U.S. court-martial was held on August 24, 1676, in Newport, RI. The first court-martial trial at which enlisted men were allowed to sit as members was convened on February 3, 1949, at Fort Bragg, NC, and consisted of four sergeants and five officers.

Court of Assizes. The highest court of original criminal jurisdiction in France and the only court in which a jury considers the case against the accused and assists in rendering a verdict.

court of chancery. A court of equity. Formerly existed in England and still exists in some U.S. states. *See also* equity jurisdiction

court of common pleas. A court of original jurisdiction for trials according to common law.

court of equity. A court that administers justice according to the principles of equity. *See also* court of chancery

court of errors and appeals. In New Jersey (and formerly in New York), the court of last resort.

court of general sessions. In certain states, a court of general original jurisdiction.

court of primary jurisdiction. A court that has authority to hear (try) cases at the point of origin.

Court of Queen's Bench. The highest court of general jurisdiction in Canada, which sits with a jury.

court of record. A court in which a complete and permanent record of all proceedings or specified types of proceedings are kept. Felony trial courts are courts of record. Trial proceedings are supposed to be recorded verbatim. The record, usually in the form of a stenotype or shorthand representation but sometimes stored on audiotape, is not necessarily transcribed. The court reporter may store such material in its original form, which will not be converted into a typed transcript unless the record pertaining to a case is requested.

Court of Star Chamber. An English court originally created to prevent the obstruction of justice in the lower courts. Its powers were expanded to an unreasonable degree, and it was finally abolished.

court order. A mandate, command, or direction issued by a judicial officer in the exercise of his or her judicial authority.

court-ordered release from prison. A provisional exit, by judicial authority and from a prison facility, of a prisoner who has not served his or her full sentence and whose freedom is conditional upon an appeal, a special writ, or other legal proceeding.

court packing. A term first used to describe President Franklin Roosevelt's plan to alter the composition of the Supreme Court. Roosevelt attempted to gain the authority to appoint up to six additional justices.

court probation. A criminal court requirement that a defendant or offender fulfill specified conditions or behavior in lieu of a jail sentence, but without being assigned to a probation agency's supervisory caseload.

court report. A social study of an individual offender containing recommendations for his or her treatment, assessment of family status and functioning, and plans for the future.

court reporter. A person present during judicial proceedings who records all testimony and other oral statements.

courtroom disruptions. Misconduct that disrupts the orderly proceedings of the court. The Supreme Court has ruled that a judge may take one or more of three steps to ensure orderly conduct in court: (a) warn the defendant (if he or she is disruptive) and then exclude him or her from the courtroom and proceed with the trial, (b) bind and gag the defendant and (c) cite him or her for contempt of court.

courts, federal. The courts established or provided for by Article III of the Constitution or established by Congress under its delegated powers. As defined by the Supreme Court, these include the constitutional courts—the Supreme Court, the Courts of

THE FEDERAL COURTS

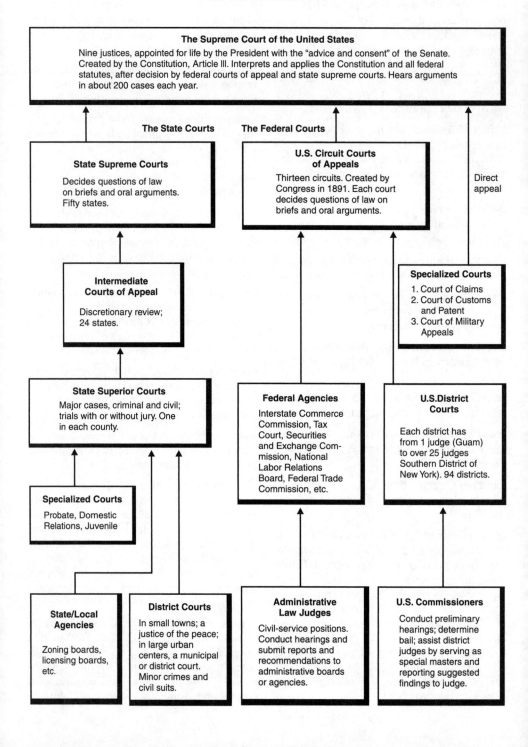

The Supreme Court of the United States
Nine justices, appointed for life by the President with the "advice and consent" of the Senate. Created by the Constitution, Article III. Interprets and applies the Constitution and all federal statutes, after decision by federal courts of appeal and state supreme courts. Hears arguments in about 200 cases each year.

The State Courts

The Federal Courts

State Supreme Courts
Decides questions of law on briefs and oral arguments. Fifty states.

U.S. Circuit Courts of Appeals
Thirteen circuits. Created by Congress in 1891. Each court decides questions of law on briefs and oral arguments.

Direct appeal

Intermediate Courts of Appeal
Discretionary review; 24 states.

Specialized Courts
1. Court of Claims
2. Court of Customs and Patent
3. Court of Military Appeals

State Superior Courts
Major cases, criminal and civil; trials with or without jury. One in each county.

Federal Agencies
Interstate Commerce Commission, Tax Court, Securities and Exchange Commission, National Labor Relations Board, Federal Trade Commission, etc.

U.S.District Courts
Each district has from 1 judge (Guam) to over 25 judges Southern District of New York). 94 districts.

Specialized Courts
Probate, Domestic Relations, Juvenile

State/Local Agencies
Zoning boards, licensing boards, etc.

District Courts
In small towns; a justice of the peace; in large urban centers, a municipal or district court. Minor crimes and civil suits.

Administrative Law Judges
Civil-service positions. Conduct hearings and submit reports and recommendations to administrative boards or agencies.

U.S. Commissioners
Conduct preliminary hearings; determine bail; assist district judges by serving as special masters and reporting suggested findings to judge.

Appeals, and district courts—as well as the special or legislative courts.

Courts of Appeals. One of the systems of appellate courts in the United States. Congress created courts of appeals because the Constitution itself created only one court, the Supreme Court. Nevertheless, courts of appeals are called constitutional courts because they exercise part of the judicial power of Article III of the Constitution. Courts of appeals have appellate jurisdiction over most administrative agencies and the final decisions of district courts, except in the few cases where there is a right of direct appeal to the Supreme Court. Appeal from district court decisions is a matter of right, as these courts do not have any original jurisdiction. Since the availability of Supreme Court review is limited, the courts of appeals function as courts of last resort in most instances. There are 13 courts of appeals, 1 for each judicial circuit and 1 federal, and cases there are heard before three judges.

court, specialized. A court which has jurisdiction over special types of criminal civil suits, such as a morals court, juvenile court, or appellate court.

courts, state. The various judicial systems in the 50 states, authorized under the Tenth Amendment of the Constitution and established by the state constitutions or state legislation. Three features are common to the organization of all state court systems. Each state has a high court of appeals (usually a Supreme Court); a level of courts of original and general jurisdiction commonly called district or county courts; and, at the bottom, a tier of justice of the peace courts, including municipal, police, and magistrate courts for the trial of minor civil and criminal cases. Some states have an additional group of intermediate courts of appeal. All states have various specialized courts for the administration of estates, wills, domestic relations and children's problems, juvenile delinquency, and small claims.

FEDERAL COURTS OF APPEALS

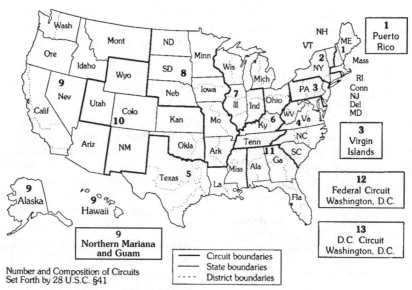

Source: Administrative Office of the United States Courts.

Most decisions by our 94 federal district courts are not appealed, but those that are usually go to one of the 13 federal courts of appeals. These courts of appeals may reverse the decision of a lower court if a judicial error has been made.

THE STATE COURTS

COURTS OF LAST RESORT
Supreme Court
Supreme Court of Appeals
Supreme Judicial Court
Court of Appeals

INTERMEDIATE APPELLATE COURTS
Appeals Court
Superior Court
Court of Criminal Appeals
Commonwealth Court

MAJOR TRIAL COURTS
Chancery Court
Circuit Court
District Court
Superior Court

COURTS OF LIMITED JURISDICTION
Probate Court
Magistrates Court
Municipal Court
Justice of the Peace Court
Police Court
Country Court
Justice Court

Court, Supreme. The court of last resort; the highest court found in the federal system and in each state.

Court, Tax. The federal forum in which a taxpayer may contest a tax deficiency (tax due) asserted by the Internal Revenue Service. The Tax Court hears only contests involving deficiencies. A taxpayer who feels he or she has overpaid may sue the government for a refund in either the Court of Claims or the district court, but not in the Tax Court.

covenant. A binding legal agreement or promise.

covert. (1) Hidden or secret, as opposed to overt. (2) Sheltered. (A covert woman is under the protection of her husband.)

coverture. The legal status of a married woman.

CPR (cardiopulmonary resuscitation). The reestablishment of heart and lung functions following cardiac arrest, cardiovascular collapse, electric shock, drowning, respiratory ar-

rest, or other causes; the manual basic life support provided until advance support is available; a combination of artificial respiration (rescue breathing) and artificial circulation (external cardiac compression.) ABCD is the acronym for basic CPR steps: Airway, Breathing, Circulation, and Definitive therapies.

Crank-Up Task Force. A California program created within the Department of Justice as part of the Clandestine Laboratory Enforcement Program with responsibility for establishing, conducting, supporting, and coordinating groups of state and local law enforcement agencies to investigate, seize, and clean up secret laboratories used to manufacture methamphetamine.

credit card fraud. The Credit Fraud Act of 1984 stipulates that whoever "(a) knowingly and with intent to defraud produces, uses, or traffics in one or more counterfeit access devices; (b) knowingly and with intent to defraud traffics in or uses one or more unauthorized access devices during any one-year period, and by such conduct obtains anything of value aggregating $1,000 or more during that period; (c) knowingly and with intent to defraud possesses 15 or more devices which are counterfeit or unauthorized access devices; or (d) knowingly, and with intent to defraud, produces, traffics in, has control or custody of, or possesses device-making equipment; shall, if the offense affects interstate or foreign commerce, be punished as provided by Title 18 of the U.S. Code" (as amended by the Comprehensive Crime Control Act of 1984).

Credit, Equal Opportunity Act. *See* Fair Housing and Equal Credit Opportunity

crime. An act committed or omitted in violation of a law forbidding or commanding it, for which the possible penalties upon conviction for an adult include incarceration, for which a corporation can be penalized by fine or forfeit, or for which a juvenile can be adjudged delinquent or transferred to criminal court for prosecution.

Crimes are defined as offenses against the state and are to be distinguished from violations of the civil law that involve harms done to individuals—such as torts—for which the state demands restitution rather than punishment. An antisocial act is not a crime unless it is prohibited by criminal law and coupled with a specified punishment. Criminal law generally requires proof of both *mens rea*, or a criminal intent or a wrongful purpose, and of the commission of an overt criminal act. Criminal law commonly classifies violations into (a) crimes against property, (b) crimes against the person, and (3) crimes against public safety and morals. *See also* Crime Index

crime analysis. A system using regularly collected information on reported crimes and criminal offenders for crime prevention, suppression, and the apprehension of criminal offenders. Crime analysis supports police operations particularly in strategic planning, manpower deployment, and investigation assistance.

Crime and Justice Foundation. Founded in 1878, the foundation "is a correctional reform agency that strives to bring about progressive changes in the administration of justice." The foundation provides direct assistance to develop and operate mediation and other programs, staff assistance on research projects and requests for information, and assistance in the use of criminal justice library publications.

crime, business. The Department of Commerce has published a number of reports and reference works on the subject of crime in business. Subjects include crime in retailing, the cost of crime, crime in service industries, and a bibliography on crime in business. Address: Office of Service Industries, 14th Street & Constitution Ave., NW, Washington, DC 20230

crime, capital. An offense where the punishment may be death, regardless of whether or not the death penalty is actually inflicted. It remains so even where juries are given the option of imposing life imprisonment instead of death as the penalty. Capital crimes are usually not bailable. The number of offenses regarded as capital has been sharply reduced in modern times. *See also* punishment, capital

Crime Clock. A term used in the FBI's Uniform Crime Report (UCR), published annually, which represents the ratio of crime to fixed time intervals. An example from the 1992 UCR is: "One murder [is committed in the U.S.] every 22 minutes." UCR readers are cautioned in the report that the Crime Clock should not be interpreted to imply any regularity in the commission of crimes. *See* the crime clock diagram for 1997 on page 92. *See also* Crime Index

crime commission model. Introduced by the President's Commission on Law Enforcement and the Administration of Justice, the Crime Commission Model applied the systems approach to the process of criminal justice. It provided a conceptual framework, and focused on the flow of cases between agencies. The main shortcoming is that it portrays a single justice system, handling all cases the same. *See* President's Crime Commission and wedding cake model

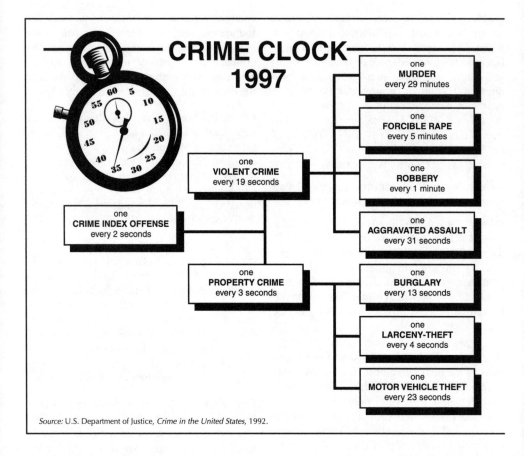

CRIME CLOCK 1997

one **VIOLENT CRIME** every 19 seconds	one **MURDER** every 29 minutes
	one **FORCIBLE RAPE** every 5 minutes
one **CRIME INDEX OFFENSE** every 2 seconds	one **ROBBERY** every 1 minute
	one **AGGRAVATED ASSAULT** every 31 seconds
one **PROPERTY CRIME** every 3 seconds	one **BURGLARY** every 13 seconds
	one **LARCENY-THEFT** every 4 seconds
	one **MOTOR VEHICLE THEFT** every 23 seconds

Source: U.S. Department of Justice, *Crime in the United States*, 1992.

crime, companionate. A crime committed jointly by two, or occasionally more than two, persons against a third party. Companionate crime, as differentiated from organized crime, is occasional and generally involves only one offense. Organized crime is consistent and habitual behavior. Companionate crime is also unlike such potentially illegal behavior as fornication or gambling in that it involves a victim, while fornication and gambling may be considered victimless offenses.

crime control model. A perspective on the criminal justice process based on the proposition that the most important function of criminal justice is the repression of crime. The book, *The Limits of the Criminal Sanction*, authored by Herbert L. Packer in 1975, fully develops this concept, contrasting it with the due process model. The crime control model is central to Packer's adversarial/conflict theory, in which the goal of crime control is the quick and efficient processing of those who violate the law. *See also* due process model

crime displacement. Term describing what happens when law enforcement or prevention efforts cause a particular criminal activity simply to shift to another location. For example, police will often crack down on prostitution in particular neighborhoods because of citizen complaints. The prostitutes then move their business to another location until enforcement has died down.

crime, etiology of. The study of the causes of criminal behavior by the case study or clinical method, usually proceeding from the study of individual cases. This method can be contrasted with the isolation of factors connected with crime in general, by statistical or observational methods, which is the study of general causes.

crime gradient. A concept adopted by some criminologists in the study of the ecological distribution of crime. It designates the profile of a curve based on the crime rates of consecutive geographic areas located along a straight line.

Crime Index. A set of numbers compiled by the Federal Bureau of Investigation that indicates the volume, fluctuation, and distribution of crimes reported to local law enforcement agencies, for the U.S. as a whole and for its geographical subdivisions, based on counts of reported occurrences of the FBI's annual Uniform Crime Report's index crimes. These index crimes are murder and nonnegligent manslaughter, forcible rape, robbery, aggravated assault, burglary, larceny theft, motor vehicle theft, and arson. All UCR Part I Offenses except negligent (involuntary) manslaughter are index crimes. Negligent manslaughter is the only Part I Offense lacking the feature of specific criminal intent. *See also* National Crime Victimization Survey.

In national UCRs, the crime rate is the number of Crime Index offenses known to police, per 100,000 population. In some state-level publications, crime rates are based on a different population unit, typically 1,000 persons.

crime insurance, federal. A government-subsidized risk pool allowing residents and business owners to purchase burglary and robbery insurance in cities where this coverage is difficult to obtain or not affordable in the private market.

crime, multiple causes of. As opposed to the concept of a single cause of crime, such as congenital predisposition, mental retardation, or poverty, the multiple-causes approach posits several or many factors operating cumulatively to produce crime.

crime of passion. An unpremeditated murder or assault committed under circumstances of great anger, jealousy, or other emotional stress.

crime of violence, mandatory penalty for use of a firearm in. The federal Felony-Murder Rule (as amended by the Comprehensive Crime Control Act of 1984) provides a mandatory penalty for the use of a firearm during a federal crime of violence. The rule states: "Whoever, during and in relation to any crime of violence, including a crime of violence which provides for an enhanced punishment if committed by the use of a deadly or dangerous weapon or device, for which he may be prosecuted in a court of the U.S., uses or carries a firearm, shall, in addition to the punishment provided for such crime of violence, be sentenced to imprisonment for five years. In the case of his second or subsequent conviction under this subsection, such person shall be sentenced to imprisonment for ten years. Notwithstanding any other provision of law, the court shall not place on probation or suspend the sentence of any person convicted of a violation of this subsection, nor shall the term of imprisonment imposed run concurrently with any other term of imprisonment, including that imposed for the crime of violence in which the firearm was used or carried. No person sentenced under this subsection shall be eligible for parole during the term of imprisonment imposed herein."

crime pact, first interstate. Effected between New York and New Jersey and signed September 16, 1833, in New York City, the agreement to cooperate in certain aspects of crime prevention and control was ratified by Congress on June 28, 1834.

crime prevention. A significant function in police work that aims to (a) increase public awareness of opportunistic criminal activity; (b) to provide the public with profiles of typical crime victims (in police parlance, (a) and (b) are tactics to "harden the target"); (c) provide mechanisms for rapid response to crimes in progress; (d) encourage citizens to mark their valuable property; (e) to promote the establishment of Neighborhood Watch programs. These tactics illustrate two basic strategies of crime prevention: opportunity reduction, or encouraging individuals to behave less vulnerably; and informal social controls, or encouraging groups of people to act cooperatively in protecting each other's persons and possessions.

Crime Prevention Council, National. Provides assistance in community crime and drug abuse prevention, including educational materials and comprehensive listings of local crime prevention programs. Its Crime Prevention Coalition publishes *The Catalyst* and reports the latest news of the coalition and crime prevention efforts. Address: 1000 Connecticut Avenue, NW, 13th Floor, Washington DC 20036.

crime prevention, special procedures for. A number of special legal procedures have been created to control crime that avoid the use of trial by jury. One is the abatement of nuisances, including houses of prostitution, illegal gambling parlors, and buildings used to manufacture liquor. A similar procedure involves confiscating stills, motor vehicles, and ships used to manufacture or transport liquor; and other instruments used illegally. *See also* forfeiture; Racketeer Influenced and Corrupt Organizations

crime score. A number assigned from an established scale, signifying the seriousness of a given offense with respect to the extent of personal injury or damage to property it caused.

crime statistics, U.S. A compilation based on law enforcement information furnished by nationwide local agencies. It is prepared and published annually by the FBI under the title *Crime in the United States J9XX.*

Crime Stoppers. The first Crime Stoppers program was established by an Albuquerque police officer in 1976. It offered cash (to overcome apathy) and anonymity (to overcome fear of retaliation) to any citizen willing to provide police with information on criminal conduct that could lead to conviction of the criminals. By 2003 there were more than 1158 local programs. Address: 620 Public Avenue, Beloit, WI 53511; telephone: (608) 363-5611.

crime, violent. (1) Any offense that has as an element the use, attempted use, or threatened use of physical force against the person or property of another. (2) Any other offense that is a felony and that, by its nature, involves a substantial threat of physical force against the person or property of another. *See also* racketeering

crimes against family members of federal officials. Such offenses are defined in federal law as follows: "Whoever attempts to, threatens to, or actually assaults, kidnaps, or murders a member of the immediate family of a U.S. official, a U.S. judge, a federal law enforcement officer, or an official whose killing would be a crime, with intent to impede, intimidate, interfere with, or retaliate against such an official while he is engaged in or on account of the performance of his official duties, shall be punished as provided. A threat shall be punished by a fine or not more than $5,000 or imprisonment for a term of not more than five years, or both, except that imprisonment for a threatened assault shall not exceed three years."

crimes against the state. Acts that are directed against the interests of the sovereignty rather than the individual. In the United States, few crimes are included in this category, and rarely is anyone prosecuted for an act against the government other than for disorderly conduct.

crimes without complaints. Another term for victimless crimes, or crimes that provide goods and/or services that are in demand but illegal, such as gambling, narcotics, and prostitution. The police themselves typically serve as complainants in such crimes, since citizens are usually not willing to accept this role.

criminal. Broadly, a person who has committed a crime; but legally and statistically, only a person who has been convicted of a crime. The attempt to limit the concept of "criminal" to persons who have committed serious crimes or those whose motives are distinctly evil involves value judgments that have no scientific basis and is therefore at odds with modern criminal justice.

criminal action. The accusation, trial, and punishment of a person charged with a public offense. Cases may be prosecuted by the state, either as a party itself or at the request of an individual to prevent a crime against his or her person or property.

criminal anthropology. A criminological theory of Cesare Lombroso, postulating that there are discernible and identifiable criminal types. *See also* anthropology; Lombroso, Cesare

Criminal Appeals Act. An act of Congress that allows the United States to appeal to the Supreme Court in a criminal case when a lower court, without having placed the defendant in jeopardy, has held that a federal statute is unconstitutional.

criminal biology. The scientific study of the relation of hereditary physical traits to criminal character, that is, to innate tendencies to commit crime in general or crimes of any particular type.

criminal case. A case initiated in a court by the filing of a charging document containing one or more criminal accusations against one or more identified persons.

criminal charge. A criminal accusation, through a written complaint, an indictment, or information, which is then acted upon by a prosecutor.

criminal conversation. Adultery; illegal sexual relations involving a married person and a partner other than his or her spouse.

criminal homicide. The causing of the death of another person without legal justification or excuse.

criminal identification. The recording of significant physical characteristics, especially fingerprints, of individual criminals for rapid and permanent identification.

criminal intent. The intent to commit an act, the results of which are a crime or violation of the law. There is general intent and specific intent. Some statutes require the existence of specific intent; some, only general intent. If no intent is set forth in the description of a particular crime by law, then the commission of the act is sufficient for charging, and intent need not be proven.

criminal justice. In the strictest sense, the criminal (penal) law, the law of criminal procedure, and that array of procedures and activities having to do with the enforcement of this body of law. The federal Crime Control Act of 1973 defines this term as part of a longer phrase: " 'Law enforcement and criminal justice' means any activity pertaining to crime prevention, control, or reduction or the enforcement of the criminal law, including, but not limited to, police efforts to prevent, control, or reduce crime or to apprehend criminals, activities of courts having criminal jurisdiction and related agencies (including prosecutorial and defender services), activities of corrections, probation, or parole authorities, and programs relating to the prevention, control, or reduction of juvenile delinquency or narcotic addiction."

criminal justice agency. Any court with criminal jurisdiction and any government agency or identifiable subunit that defends indigents or has as its principal duty(s) the performance of criminal justice functions (prevention, detection, and investigation of crime; the apprehension, detention, and prosecution of alleged offenders; the confinement or official correctional supervision of accused or convicted persons; or the administrative or technical support of these functions) as authorized and required by statute or executive order.

Criminal Justice Archive and Information Network. Established in 1978 by the U.S. Department of Justice, Bureau of Justice Statistics, CJAIN provides data concerning victimization, the criminal justice system, and juvenile delinquency. Publishes *Criminal Justice Data Directory*, and *Criminal Justice Archive and Information Network Newsletter*. Address: Inter-University Consortium for Political and Social Research, P.O. Box 1248, Ann Arbor, MI 48106.

Criminal Justice Association, National. Founded in 1971, this coordinating effort focuses on innovations in the criminal justice system. Publishes *Justice Alert* (periodical); *Justice Bulletin* (monthly). Address: 720 7th Street, NW, Third Floor, Washington, DC 20001-3716.

Criminal Justice Audiovisual Materials Directory. A source directory of materials for education, training, and orientation in the field of criminal justice; covers courts, police techniques and training, prevention, prisons and rehabilitation/corrections, and public education. These films and videotape recordings can be borrowed for educational and informational purposes. Address: The National Criminal Justice Research Service, 2277 Research Boulevard, Rockville, MD 20850.

Criminal Justice Center. Founded in 1965 by Sam Houston State University, the center is an educational agency designed to serve institutions and practitioners. Maintains a reference library (50,000 books, reports, and documents). The center also operates the National Employment Listing Service (NELS), established in 1976, which provides nationwide up-to-date information about available positions in criminal justice and social services. Publishes NELS Bulletin (monthly). Address: Criminal Justice Center, Sam Houston University, Huntsville, TX 77341.

Criminal Justice/National Council on Crime and Delinquency. Founded at Rutgers University in 1983; has extensive material in the John Cotton Dana Library. Address: Rutgers University, 185 University Avenue, Newark, NJ 07102.

Criminal Justice Reference and Information Center. Established by the University of Wisconsin Law School with emphasis on law enforcement, corrections, and juvenile justice. Maintains a special collection of the penal press (inmate newspapers), and statistical and annual reports from criminal justice agencies throughout the United States. Located in Madison, WI.

Criminal Justice Research Institute. Organization providing evaluative services and operations reviews and consultations. Address: 520 N. Delaware Ave., Suite 304, Philadelphia, PA 19123.

criminal law. A branch of law dealing with crimes and their punishments. A crime is an act considered an offense against public authority or a violation of a public duty. Crimes are usually classified as *mala in se*— immoral and wrong in themselves—or *mala prohibita*—illegal only because proscribed by statute. Crimes are also graded according to their gravity as felonies, misdemeanors, or offenses. Procedural rules relating to proof of crime and defining and prescribing penalties for crimes are referred to as criminal, or substantive criminal, law. Criminal law is both common and statutory, although the former aspect has been of decreasing importance in the United States.

criminally insane. The legal term for the state of mental derangement that accompanies or induces the commission of a crime and prevents the criminal from knowing the criminal nature of the act committed. The basic test of insanity is the knowledge of right and wrong; thus mental defect is often confused with mental deficiency. Greater interest in the mental processes of those who commit crimes led to a direct challenge of the traditional legal interpretations of insanity as a defense in criminal cases. *See also* Durham rule

criminal mischief (malicious mischief). Intentionally destroying or damaging, or attempting to destroy or damage, the property of another without his consent, usually by a means other than burning.

criminal offense. An offense against a state, including both crimes and misdemeanors. The term has been defined by statute as consisting of (a) a violation of a public law, in the commission of which there shall be a union or joint operation of act and intention, or criminal negligence, and (b) any offense, misde-

CRIMINAL JUSTICE

What is the sequence of events in the criminal justice system?

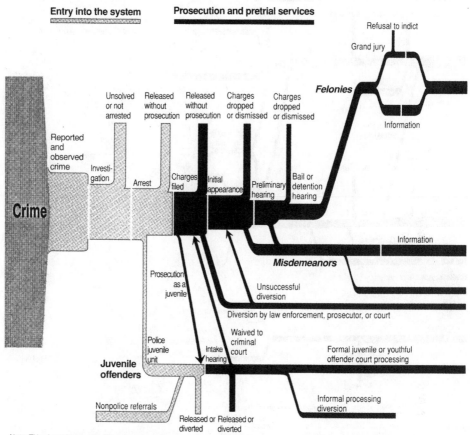

Note: This chart gives a simplified view of caseflow through the criminal justice system. Procedures vary among jurisdictions. The weights of the lines are not intended to show actual size of caseloads.

meanor, or felony, for which any punishment by imprisonment or fine or both may by law be inflicted.

criminal organization. The structure of relationships between persons and groups that makes the commission of crime possible and facilitates avoidance of the legal penalties. This structure may be loose, informal, and decentralized, or it may be explicitly institutionalized and centralized. Also, any group of persons who systematically devote them-

selves, as a collective unit, to the commission of crime. *See also* organized crime

criminal, pathological. A criminal who deviates from the mental norm. The following classification of such criminals is frequently used: mental defective or feeble-minded, psychotic or insane, and psychopathic. Psychopathic is the most difficult to define. It includes criminals who are neurotic or epileptic, and is often used to describe those who behave amorally, asocially, and irrespon-

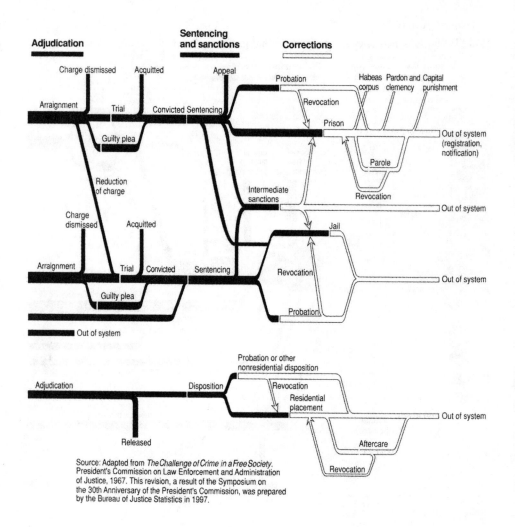

Adjudication | **Sentencing and sanctions** | **Corrections**

Charge dismissed — Acquitted — Appeal — Probation — Habeas corpus — Pardon and clemency — Capital punishment — Revocation — Prison — Out of system (registration, notification) — Parole — Revocation — Out of system — Jail — Revocation — Out of system — Probation — Out of system

Arraignment — Trial — Convicted — Sentencing — Guilty plea — Reduction of charge — Intermediate sanctions

Charge dismissed — Acquitted — Arraignment — Trial — Convicted — Sentencing — Guilty plea — Out of system

Adjudication — Disposition — Probation or other nonresidential disposition — Revocation — Residential placement — Out of system — Aftercare — Released — Revocation

Source: Adapted from *The Challenge of Crime in a Free Society*. President's Commission on Law Enforcement and Administration of Justice, 1967. This revision, a result of the Symposium on the 30th Anniversary of the President's Commission, was prepared by the Bureau of Justice Statistics in 1997.

sibly. A comparison of psychiatric reports on the psychopathy of criminals shows wide variations in the conclusions as to the proportion of criminals so characterized.

criminal procedure. The legal methods used in the apprehension, trial, prosecution, and sentencing of criminals.

criminal proceedings. The regular and orderly steps, as directed or authorized by statute or court of law, taken to determine whether an adult accused of a crime is guilty or not guilty.

criminal responsibility. Criminal liability for an offense. To be so liable, the person committing the act must do so of his or her own free will and volition, have the capacity to distinguish right from wrong, and have the ability to foresee the evil consequences of the act. The presence of these conditions constitutes responsibility and, hence, liability and punishability. On the other hand, certain circumstances may negate responsibility. These are principally: (a) Infancy. Under the common law, children under 7 years of age are not regarded as being responsible. A like presumption holds for children between 7 and 14 years of age unless evidence overcomes it. In most states, statutory provisions have given the juvenile courts jurisdiction over the criminal or delinquent acts of children beyond the age of 14, but for grave crimes, these courts may waive jurisdiction. (b) Insanity. This is interpreted by the courts to mean that a person is incapable of making moral distinctions between right and wrong or of knowing the evil consequences of his acts. (c) Intoxication. Ordinarily, intoxication provides no exemption from criminal liability, though it may reduce the degree of responsibility and, hence, lessen the severity of punishment. *See also* culpability

criminal saturation, law of. A theory developed by the Italian criminologist Enrico Fern, the gist of which was that each society has the number of criminals that the particular conditions in that society produce. "As a given volume of water at a definite temperature will dissolve a fixed quantity of chemical substance and not an atom more or less; so in a given social environment with definite individual and physical conditions, a fixed number of delicts, no more and no less, can be committed."

criminal statistics. The tabulated, numerical data found in the official reports of agencies that deal with the apprehension, prevention, and treatment of offenders of the criminal law. The unit of tabulation may be the case, the offender, or the offense. A common classification of criminal statistics distinguishes among police, judicial, and penal statistics. In the United States the term is generally inclusive; on the continent of Europe, it is ordinarily used to designate only the tabulations based on the characteristics of the offender, as distinguished from statistics of criminal justice, or penal institutions.

criminal syndicalism. A legal phrase of American law to describe the advocating of the unlawful destruction of property or an unlawful change in its ownership; a doctrine and practice attributed to the Industrial Workers of the World, a labor organization, and embodied in many state statutes aimed to curb such activities, adopted between 1917 and 1924.

criminal tendencies. Classifiable behavioral tendencies that, if not recognized or checked, may end in ultimate commission of a criminal act or acts; behavioral tendencies that under certain conditions can be expected to develop into a delinquent or criminal pattern; tendencies toward criminal behavior.

criminal tribes. Tribes with a culture that sanctions behavior toward nonmembers of the tribe that is prohibited by the laws of the state to which the tribe belongs.

criminal typologies. American criminologist Stephen Schafer's life-trend classification of criminals. According to Schafer, who authored *Introduction to Criminology* and *The Political Criminal* in the mid-1970s, types of criminals include abnormal, convictional, habitual, occasional, and professional.

criminal, white-collar. An employee or professional who violates the criminal law in the course of his/her occupational or professional activities. The state, insofar as it reacts against white-collar crimes, generally does so through bureaus and commissions rather than through the police and the criminal courts.

criminalist. A scientist trained to perform crime laboratory functions and relate the findings to criminal investigations.

criminalistics. The science of crime detection, involving the application of chemistry, physics, physiology, psychology, and other sciences.

Criminalistics Laboratory Information System. This computerized database is currently composed of a general Rifling Characteristics File that is used to identify the manufacturer and type of weapon that may have been used to fire a bullet or cartridge. Address: Laboratory Division, FBI, DOJ,

9th Street & Pennsylvania Avenue, NW, Washington, DC 20535.

criminate. To accuse of a crime.

criminogenic. Refers to those features of a culture that are believed to produce crime.

criminologist. One whose professional study encompasses all facets of crime, criminals, and the justice process or system. *See also* criminology

criminology. The study of crime and corrections and the operation of the system of criminal justice. Criminology had its origins in the Enlightenment of the eighteenth century, when such men as Cesare Beccaria and Jeremy Bentham explored ways of making criminal law a more just and humane instrument of the state. The nineteenth century saw the rise of the positivist school, which stressed the need for a scientific understanding of the causes of crime and its control. In the United States since 1900, criminology has been largely in the domain of the social sciences. *See also* Beccaria, Cesare

crisis intervention center. A service designed to give immediate help to people with serious emotional problems. Examples are suicide prevention centers and suicide hot lines.

crisis intervention units. Special programs for peace officers who frequently deal with domestic disturbances. These officers undergo extensive training in the study of psychology, body language, conflict resolution, and referral services.

critical stage. One or more points in the criminal justice process that are viewed by the court as crucial to the outcome of a case.

criticize. To make a statement of a critical nature concerning something or someone. It may be constructive or destructive criticism. The Circuit Court of Appeals, in Washington, DC, on June 19, 1970, ruled in the case of *Minard v. Mitchell* that officers have the constitutional right to criticize the operations of their departments and that no punitive action may be taken against them for it.

crony. A close friend, associate, or companion.

cronyism. The practice of favoring one's close friends, especially in political situations. This includes hiring, promotions, assignments, and cover-ups.

cross-examination. The questioning of a witness by the party opposed to the party that called the witness for direct examination.

cross-projection. A method of sketching the details of a room in which the walls and the ceiling are shown or drawn as if they were on the same plane as the floor. This method gives a clear understanding of a crime scene, especially if evidence is found on the walls or ceiling.

crosswalk. Any portion of a roadway distinctly indicated for pedestrian crossing by lines or other markings on the road surface.

Crowley, Aleister. Considered one of the most diabolical individuals who ever lived. He was born in 1875, the year of the death of Eliphas Levi, who wrote several books on occultism. Crowley believed he was a reincarnation of Levi. Many called Crowley the beast or the Antichrist. He was thought to have made human sacrifices. In 1898 he joined the OTO (Odro Templi Orientis) cult, also known as the Order of the Golden Dawn. He founded the Argenteum Astrum (Silver Star) in 1904. Crowley's most famous book was *Magick in Theory and Practice*, published in 1919. He died in 1947.

crown attorney. The term for a prosecutor in Canada.

cruel and unusual punishment. Prohibited by the Eighth Amendment to the Constitution, which states, "Excessive bail shall not be required, nor excessive fines imposed, nor cruel and unusual punishments inflicted." At the time of the original congressional debate over the Bill of Rights, some delegates objected that the provisions of the Eighth Amendment were vaguely defined; in practice, the courts have determined the amendment's applications and limitations. The Supreme Court has held that

Eighth Amendment guarantees apply to the states by the due process clause of the Fourteenth Amendment.

cryptographer. One who solves or deciphers cryptograms or decodes any secret communications.

CS. A chemical agent used as tear gas. Chemical name is orthochlorbenzalmalononitrile.

culpable (Lat., *culpa*, lit. "blame"). At fault or responsible, but not necessarily criminal.

culpability. (1) Blameworthiness; responsibility in some sense for an event or situation deserving of moral blame. (2) In Model Penal Code usage, a state of mind on the part of one who is committing an act that makes him or her potentially subject to prosecution for that act.

culprit. One who has violated the law but has not been convicted. He or she may still be sought for, or may have been legally charged with, the crime but not tried.

cults. Types of social or organizational groups formed to conduct ritual, magical, or religious practices, cults vary according to their membership, belief systems, and types of ritual practices. Neognostic groups believe in a sacred wisdom accessible only to a select few.

On November 18, 1978, the Rev. Jim Jones led 913 members, including 300 children, of his People's Temple in a murder-suicide ritual on his 300-acre Guyana compound after his followers had killed several visitors.

On May 13, 1985, 11 people were killed, including 4 children, and 250 were left homeless after a fire following an armed confrontation between police and members of a cult called MOVE in Philadelphia. *See also* SWAT.

On August 29, 1987, the bodies of 33 people linked to a religious cult in South Korea were found in a factory attic as the results of an apparent murder/suicide pact in the town of Yongin, about 50 miles south of Seoul.

On February 28, 1993, about 100 Bureau of Alcohol, Tobacco and Firearms (ATF) agents moved against the cult of Branch Davidian leader David Koresh at his 77-acre compound in Waco, TX. Four agents were killed and 16 others wounded in the 45-minute battle. Between March 1 and March 21, 18 children, 2 women, and 9 male cultists left the compound. On April 19 the compound was burned to the ground with 86 members, including 24 children, inside. There were 9 survivors. The ATF siege had lasted 51 days.

In October 1994, 53 members of an extremist sect known as the Order of the Solar Temple died in grisly murder/suicide rituals in France and Canada.

On March 20, 1995, poison gas in Tokyo, Japan's subway system killed 12 people and sickened 5,500 more in an attack linked to a cult known as the Aum Supreme Truth.

On December 23, 1995, the charred bodies of 16 cult members linked to the Order of the Solar Temple were found in a forest in southeastern France, dead as the result of an apparent murder/suicide.

On March 23, 1997, 5 followers of the Order of the Solar Temple died in an apparent group suicide in a small town near Quebec (City), Canada.

On March 26, 1997, in a mass suicide, 39 members of the Heaven's Gate cult were found dead in Rancho Sante Fe, near San Diego, CA. They had ingested pudding or applesauce laced with phenobarbitol and washed down with vodka.

cunnilingus. Oral contact with the female genitals.

curative statute. A law, retrospective in effect, which is designed to remedy some legal defect in previous transactions and to validate them.

curfew violation. The offense of being found in a public place after a specified hour of the evening, usually established in a local ordinance and applying only to persons under a specified age, but sometimes imposed on all residents during civil disturbances.

curtilage. The grounds inside a wall surrounding a house or building.

custodial care. The care afforded in institutions to socially or physically incompetent persons who need close supervision or assistance in performing basic tasks.

custodial officer. One charged with the keep, safety, and/or detention of persons in a prison, jail, or hospital.

custody. Legal or physical control of a person or thing; legal, supervisory, or physical responsibility for a person or thing.

custody, close. Constant supervision of a prisoner on the assumption that he or she will not only escape if the opportunity is offered, but will also make the opportunity.

custody, maximum. Care in the type of prison that provides the maximum security—high walls, tool-proof bars, numerous guards, rigid discipline, and so forth—for the most hardened prisoners.

custody, medium. Care for prisoners in an institution with a type of physical plant less strongly built and equipped than a maximum-custody facility and intended to house less hardened and dangerous criminals and to give them more freedom of movement and greater self-direction.

custody, minimum. Care of prisoners in an institution built, equipped, and guarded with the least possible restraint required to keep them safely and to allow the greatest possible freedom. Such an institution is exemplified by some of the prison camps and farms, reformatories, or honor dormitories within a prison facility.

custody, protective. Detention by the police of persons essential to the prosecution of justice, presumably in order to prevent reprisals against them by criminal elements for their part in furthering the investigation of a crime.

Customs and Patent Appeals, Court of. This specialized court was created by Congress and given appellate jurisdiction over decisions of the Customs Court, Patent Office, and Tariff Commission. Appeal through this court is available as a matter of right. There is no appeal from decisions of this court, but they may be reviewed by the Supreme Court on a writ of *certiorari*.

Customs Court. This court has exclusive jurisdiction to review decisions of customs collectors on questions affecting imports and import duties. Formerly called the Board of General Appraisers, the Court's name was changed by Congress in 1926, but no change was made in its functions, which are quasi-judicial and quite similar to those usually performed by an administrative agency. Its decisions can be appealed to the Court of Customs and Patent Appeals.

Czolgosz, Leon. The American anarchist (1873–1901) who shot and killed President William McKinley in Buffalo on September 6, 1901. He felt that the president was "an enemy of the good working class" and must be executed. He was adjudged and electrocuted in New York's Auburn Prison.

D

dactyloscopy. (1) Fingerprints as a means of identification. (2) The study of fingerprints and their use as a means of identification.

damages. Compensation that the law will award for injury done.

dangerous-tendency test. A court test used in determining the limits of free expression guaranteed in the First Amendment. In *Gitlow v. New York* (1925) the Supreme Court rejected Oliver Wendell Holmes's clear-and-present-danger test for interfering with freedom of speech, as enunciated in *Schenck v. United States* and *Abrams v. United States*, both 1919 decisions, in favor of a bad- or dangerous-tendency test. More limiting than the clear-and-present-danger test, the dangerous-tendency test makes punishable, by the government, those responsible for publications and speeches that, even though they create no immediate danger, have a "tendency" to bring about results dangerous to public safety—corrupting public morals, inciting to crime, or disturbing the public peace. In *Dennis v. United States*, a

1951 Supreme Court case involving the Communist Party in the United States, the Court attempted to reconcile the two tests by a yardstick measuring the gravity of an evil against the probability of its occurring.

DARE. Drug Abuse Resistance Education is a program, originated in 1984 by the Los Angeles Police Department, under which uniformed police officers visit elementary and middle school classrooms throughout the United States. The program offers weekly lessons intended to help students build self-esteem and resist peer pressure to use drugs.

darkness. Anytime from one-half hour after sunset to one-half hour before sunrise and any other time when visibility is not sufficient to render clearly discernible any person or vehicle on a road at a distance of 1,000 feet.

Darrow, Clarence (Seward). Celebrated defense attorney. Born in Kinsman, OH, in 1857, he studied law for one year at the University of Michigan and was admitted to the Ohio bar in 1878. His early career was as a law partner of Illinois governor John P. Altgeld. In 1894, however, his defense of Eugene V. Debs and the American Railway Union launched him on a vocation as defender of unpopular causes and minority rights. As a labor lawyer, he represented, among others, the coal miners in the anthracite strike of 1902 and William Haywood and other Wobblies for their alleged murder of a former Idaho governor. An ardent opponent of capital punishment, he secured life imprisonment for Richard Loeb and Nathan Leopold in the infamous thrill-slaying of a Chicago youth. In the Scopes trial of 1925, he engaged in a famous clash with William Jennings Bryan over the right of Tennessee to forbid the teaching of evolution in the public schools. The following year he defended 11 blacks accused of the murder of a Detroit Ku Klux Klansman. A lifelong Democrat, Darrow was chosen by Franklin D. Roosevelt in 1934 to head a commission to study the operations of the National Recovery Administration. He died in 1938.

data, class I. Computer data that require off-site storage of backup copies under secure vault conditions, providing for timely retrieval in case of operational information loss.

data, class II. Computer data that require off-site storage of backup copies under conditions that resist accidental damage, providing for timely retrieval in case of operational information loss.

data, class III. Computer data that require no off-site storage of backup copies because the data can be regenerated if needed at a cost less than the cost of off-site storage, or because loss of the data would cost less than off-site storage.

Data Encryption Standard (DES). Adopted by the U.S. National Bureau of Standards, DES is a complex nonlinear ciphering algorithm capable of high-speed operation in hardware applications. It is used for sensitive, but unclassified, data transmission, mostly within the federal system.

date rape drug. *See* gamma hydroxy butyrate

Daugherty, Harry M. (1860–1941). The U.S. attorney general from 1921 to 1924, Daugherty was accused of taking part in the scandal concerning the oil lands at Teapot Dome. The case was dismissed.

Davis, David. (1815–1886). Associate justice of the Supreme Court (1862–1877). His decision in *Ex parte Milligan* (1866), denouncing arbitrary military power, became a bulwark of civil liberty in the U.S. Davis helped manage Lincoln's campaign for presidency.

daytime. In law enforcement, the "rule of thumb" criterion for distinguishing daytime is that there is enough natural light to recognize a person's features at a distance of 10 yards. This becomes important in connection with searches where the law and the search warrant specify search during the daytime. Some courts adopt the so-called "burglary test" of the ability to recognize a person's features, holding that, when recognition is possible, a daytime warrant may be executed even though it is after sundown. Other courts, to set a clear and easily ascertainable period, limit the definition of daytime to the period between the rising and the setting of the sun; under this rule a service of a daytime warrant after sunset is invalid.

dead body. A corpse. The body of a human being deprived of life but not yet disintegrated. The legal definition of corpse covers all deceased human beings except stillborn infants.

dead letter. Term used to describe statutes that have become obsolete through long disuse.

deadly force. On March 27, 1985, in *Tennessee v. Garner,* the U.S. Supreme Court established guidelines for police use of deadly force, deciding that a Tennessee statute was unconstitutional insofar as it authorized the use of deadly force against fleeing suspects who are unarmed and pose no threat to the officer or third parties. As taking a life is considered a seizure subject to Fourth Amendment protections, any use of deadly force must be reasonable under the circumstances. The Court, like the Sixth Circuit, seemed to prefer the guidelines of the Model Penal Code, restricting the use of deadly force by the police to more serious felonies and situations. Many police agencies limit the use of deadly force to life-threatening situations only.

deadly weapon. An instrument designed to inflict serious bodily injury or death or capable of being used for such a purpose.

dead, presumed. *See* Enoch Arden law

death. Condition of being dead; permanent cessation of the functions of the vital organs. With the advent of vital-organ transplants by surgery, determining the definition of death has become a very controversial legal question.

death penalty. *See* punishment, capital

Death Penalty Focus of California. A group of legal, academic, medical, and religious professionals joined by victims and other concerned citizens opposing the death penalty. Address: 870 Market Street, Suite 859, Sanfancisco, CA 94102.

Death Penalty, National Coalition Against the (NCADP). An organization that provides resources and an information center to aid in the abolition of the death penalty, coordination of local efforts, and a united voice against executions. NCADP publishes *Lifelines*, a newsletter, *Organizing Against the Death Penalty: A Handbook*, and *The Abolitionist Directory*, providing up-to-date listings of national, regional, state, and local organizations working against the death penalty. Address: 920 Pennsylvania Avenue, SE, Washington, DC 20003.

Death Penalty, Oregon Coalition to Abolish the. Address: P.O. Box J61, Portland, OR 97207.

Death Penalty, Washington Coalition to Abolish the. Address: P.O. box 3045, Seattle, WA 98114-3045.

Death Row Support Project. A program of the Washington Coalition to Abolish the Death Penalty that matches volunteers with pen pals on death row.

Death Row, U.S.A. A monthly newsletter listing data under the following headings: Death Row Inmates, Disposition Since January 1, 1973; Jurisdictions with/without Capital Punishment Statutes; U.S. Supreme Court Capital Case Decided/Pending during current term; Execution Update; Race of Defendants Executed; Race of Victims; Victim-Defendant Racial Combinations; Executions by State; and a listing of all individuals on state death rows. In the fall 2002 edition the newsletter detailed the backgrounds of 3,704 prisoners then on Death Row. Published by NAACP Legal Defense and Educational Fund, Inc., Suite 1600, 99 Hudson Street, New York, NY 10013.

death warrant. A written order issued by the legally authorized executive official (usually the governor), setting the place and time for executing an individual sentenced to death by the court.

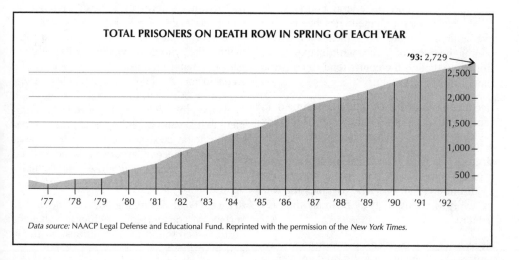

TOTAL PRISONERS ON DEATH ROW IN SPRING OF EACH YEAR

'93: 2,729

2,500
2,000
1,500
1,000
500

'77 '78 '79 '80 '81 '82 '83 '84 '85 '86 '87 '88 '89 '90 '91 '92

Data source: NAACP Legal Defense and Educational Fund. Reprinted with the permission of the *New York Times*.

Debs, Eugene V. American Socialist leader (1855–1926). Advocate of industrial unionism and a pacifist; imprisoned in 1895 for violating injunction in strike at Pullman, IL, and in 1918 under Espionage Act. Presidential candidate five times. Widely revered as martyr for his principles.

Debtors Anonymous. Self-help group. Address: General Service Office, P.O. Box 920888, Needham, MA 02492-0009.

decedent. One who has died, especially one recently dead.

deceptive advertising. Advertising that misleads the consumer in some material respect about a product offered for sale. This current legal definition, supplanting the earlier view that deceptive advertising is that which misleads the consumer in any particular, recognizes that, while some exaggeration or "puffing" of claims for a product is inevitable, the consumer is entitled to protection against substantial misstatement or intent to deceive. Deceptive advertising is prohibited by the Wheeler-Lea Act of 1938.

decision. A court order, decree, or judgment on a question of law or fact. It is distinguished from an opinion, which forms the basis of the decision.

decision tree concept, management. A graphic technique for assessing decision alternatives. Decisional alternatives are displayed in the form of a tree with nodes and branches. Each branch represents an alternative course of action/decision, leading to a node (event).

declaration. A statement.

declaration of intention. A necessary step in the procedure an alien follows to become an American citizen. In this step, he or she renounces allegiance to a native country and expresses the intention of becoming a citizen of the United States.

declarations of persons other than defendant. In court, such declarations cannot be proven unless they are (a) part of the *res gestae*; (b) admissible as dying declarations; (c) admissible as declarations by authority of the defendant; or (d) admissible as evidence given in a former proceeding.

declaratory judgment. A binding judicial declaration in a dispute over the rights of parties under a statute, contract, will, or other document, without further action to grant relief. It is not necessary to show either that any wrong has been done, as in action for damages, or that any is immediately threatened, as in injunction proceedings. In most states and territories, and in federal courts since 1934, declaratory judgment has been made available by statute as a means of ascertaining the rights of parties without expensive litigation, though the courts tend to construe these statutes narrowly.

declaratory statute. A statute designed to remove doubts as to the meaning of the law on some particular subject.

decoy. (1) One whose role is to lure someone into a situation where he or she may be the victim of a crime; one who assumes the role of diverting attention away from another. (2) To lure.

decree. A judgment of a court or admiralty, or of another agency or individual answering for most purposes to the judgment of a court of common law. A decree in equity is a sentence or order of the court, pronounced following a hearing and understanding of all the points at issue and determining the rights of all parties to the suit according to equity and good conscience. A decree is a declaration of a court that announces the legal consequences of the facts found.

decriminalization. The process of removing some form of conduct, previously defined as criminal, from the jurisdiction of criminal justice agencies. Several states have, for example, reduced criminal sanctions from a felony/misdemeanor to an infraction for the possession of small amounts (less than one ounce) of marijuana.

dedicated line. A telephone line connecting two points, such as a protected premises and a central station, for alarm signaling. Also called leased line, direct wire, and direct connect.

dedicated security mode. An automated data processing system, its peripherals, and remotes that are exclusively used and controlled by specific users or groups of users to process a particular type and category of sensitive material. System users must have a need-to-know for all material in the system.

deduction. A form of logical inference in which particular conclusions are drawn from general principles. The classic deductive argument is the syllogism, which consists of three parts—a major premise, a minor premise, and a conclusion. A well-known example of a syllogism is: All men are mortal; Socrates is a man; therefore, Socrates is mortal. An argument that is valid according to the rules of deductive logic need not be true in the factual sense. A deductive argument is considered sound only when the premises are factually true and the derived conclusions are valid.

deface. To disfigure, mar, or alter the face or surface of something; to obliterate, alter, or destroy such things as inscriptions, writings, and so forth.

de facto (Lat.). (1) Actually; in fact. (2) Pertaining to a condition of affairs that actually exists. *See also de jure*

defamation. Intentional causing, or attempting to cause, damage to the reputation of another by communicating false or distorted information about his or her actions, motives, or character. Defamation is not a criminal offense in all jurisdictions; it can, however, always be a cause of action in a civil suit.

defame. To make slanderous statements about someone; to maliciously publish or express to any person, other than the one defamed, anything which tends to expose (a) any person to hatred, contempt, or ridicule or (b) the memory of one deceased to such things; to injure the good name or reputation of another.

default. (1) Failure to appear in court at an appointed or particular time. (2) Failure to pay a debt or obligation when it is due.

defendant. A person formally accused of an offense(s) by the filing in court of a charging document.

defendant dispositions. The class of prosecutorial or judicial actions that terminate, or provisionally halt, proceedings regarding a given defendant in a criminal case after charges have been filed in court. Dispositions are: no true bill, *nolle prosequi*; dismissal; transfer to juvenile court; adjudication withheld (with referral to probation or other criminal justice agency, with referral to noncriminal-justice agency, or with no referral); incompetent to stand trial; civil commitment; acquittal; not guilty by reason of insanity; sentencing postponed; suspended sentence (unconditionally suspended sentence or conditionally suspended sentence); balance of sentence suspended or sentenced to time served; grant of probation (court probation or supervised probation); restitutional fine, forfeit, or court costs; residential commitment; jail commitment; and prison commitment (definite term, minimum-maximum term, life term, or death sentence).

defense. (1) The party (or his or her attorney) against whom a civil or criminal action in court is brought. Under the adversary system used in our courts, the two parties in a criminal action are the prosecution and the defense. (2) That which is offered or pleaded in denial of the charge against the accused. *See also* consent of the victim; duress; entrapment; insanity; justification; mistake of fact; mistake of law

defense attorney. The lawyer representing the defendant in a criminal action.

defense counsel. Counsel for the defendant; an attorney who represents and aids the defendant. The courts have held in recent years that a defendant has the right to counsel, either employed by the defendant or appointed by the court, to represent him or her at each critical stage of the prosecutive procedure, as guaranteed by the Sixth Amendment of the U.S. Constitution.

defense of accused person. It is a universal principle of criminal law in the United States that a person accused of crime is entitled to be advised by a lawyer and to be represented by one at his or her trial. In felony cases this principle is carried further, and in many states counsel is provided without cost for a defendant who is too poor to employ a lawyer. In most states, such counsel is appointed by the judge in the court where the defendant is standing trial. Some jurisdictions have an officer, known as a public defender, who represents needy defendants.

Defense Intelligence Agency. DIA produces and disseminates defense intelligence to satisfy the requirements of the Secretary of Defense, the Joint Chiefs of Staff, and major components of the Department of Defense. Address: DOD, The Pentagon, Washington, DC 20301.

Defense Investigative Service. DIS provides U.S. Department of Defense components and other government activities, when authorized, with a single, centrally directed, personnel-security investigative service. Address: DOD, Buzzard Point, 1900 Half Street, SW, Washington, DC 20324.

Defense Supply Agency File. An index of personnel cards maintained by the Defense Supply Agency. It details security clearance information on individuals employed by contractors engaged in classified work for the DOD and certain other federal agencies.

defensible space. (1) A theory suggesting that proper physical design of housing encourages residents to extend their social control from their homes and apartments into surrounding common areas. Residents change what had been perceived as semi-public or public territory into monitored private territory. Collective care and attention to the common areas results in a form of social control and discourages crime. (2) Protective devices such as guards, alarms, locks, lights, barriers, and animals, to discourage or thwart unauthorized entry, sometimes referred to as "hardening the target." *See also* broken window syndrome

deferred sentencing. A system, provided by law in some states, in which a person convicted of a crime may be placed on probation immediately following the conviction or after serving a term of imprisonment.

deficiency judgment. A creditor's claim against a debtor for that part of a judgment debt not satisfied by the sale of the mortgaged property. Example: A owes B $1,000 secured by a mortgage on property belonging to A. A defaults in payment of the debt. B obtains a judgment and forecloses, and the mortgaged property is sold according to law for $900. The difference—$100—is still owed by A and is covered by a deficiency judgment.

definite sentence. A sentence that includes a specific period of imprisonment.

definition of crime. An act injurious to the public, forbidden by law, and punishable by the state by fine, imprisonment, or both, through a judicial proceeding brought by the state.

defounding. The process of statistically lowering unsolved felonies to misdemeanors. *See also* unfounding

defraud. To cheat or deprive another.

degree. In criminal law, the ranking of crimes according to seriousness.

Dei gratia (Lat.). By the grace of God.

deindividuation. The process by which a person in a group loses responsibility as an identifiable individual. This loss can account for the uncharacteristically bold group actions of usually restrained individuals, as in mob behavior.

deinstitutionalization. In criminal justice, moving juveniles out of secure-care facilities, detention centers, or jails and into community-based programs or the community.

de jure. (1) By right, according to law. (2) Pertaining to a situation that is based on law, or right, or previous action. *See also de facto*

deliberately. Intentionally, "in cold blood."

deliberation. The action of a jury to determine the guilt or innocence, or the sentence, of a defendant.

delinquency. In many states and in the Canadian provinces, the laws define delinquency as "any act which, if committed by an adult, would be a crime." In its broadest sense, delinquency is defined as (a) juvenile actions or conduct in violation of criminal law; (b) juvenile status offenses (a variety of acts and behaviors that are not illegal if committed by adults); and (c) other juvenile misbehavior. The National Center for Juvenile Justice's study, *Juvenile Court Organization and Status Offenses: A Statutory Profile*, described the various state codifications of juvenile offenses.

delinquency law, first state. *See* child delinquency law, first state

delinquent. A person guilty of antisocial conduct that, generally speaking, is considered less serious than the type of misconduct designated as criminal. In American penology the term *delinquent* usually refers to the juvenile offender whose misconduct is an infraction of the law. Such conduct is generally considered less offensive than an adult's misconduct because of the child's immaturity and the unfortunate environmental circumstances that frequently occasion his or her behavior.

delinquent, defective. A delinquent who has some defect in his or her physical or mental faculties. Generally speaking, the term refers to delinquents who are feeble-minded or otherwise mentally incompetent and are hence incapable of assuming responsibility for their conduct.

delirium tremens. A psychotic reaction that occurs in chronic alcoholics, usually in people who are over 30 and have been drinking excessively for a number of years. The following symptoms may be observed: patients do not know where they are or what time it is and cannot recognize people; they have hallucinations, "see pink snakes" or rats and roaches, and feel great fear of these creatures; they readily believe that they see strange animals if it is suggested to them that they do; they show tremor (tremens) of the hands and mouth, sweats, and fever. The symptoms last for three to six days, after which the patient goes into a deep sleep. There is danger of death from heart failure or pneumonia.

delit. A grade of crime. American criminal law has followed the English common law in dividing crimes into treason, felonies, and misdemeanors. The Continental European Codes use a different, although roughly comparable, classification. In the French *Code Penal*, crimes are classified as *crimes* (felonies), *delits* (indictable misdemeanors), and *contraventions* (violations of police regulations). The Italian *Codice Penale* uses *delitti* for felonies and *contravenzioni* for misdemeanors. The German *Strafgesetzbuch* employs *verbrechen* (felonies), *vergehen* (the French *delits* and American misdemeanor), and *ubertretung* (violation of police regulations).

Delphi management technique. A methodology that pieces together various opinions to arrive at a consensus on the probability of a future event.

delusion. A false belief that persists in the face of evidence that it is irrational. Such beliefs are often symptoms of mental illness. A paranoid patient, for example, may have delusions of grandeur, being convinced that he or she is the Messiah or the secret power in the government. Also found in paranoid psychosis are delusions of persecution, such as an elaborately detailed belief that hidden enemies have been plotting against the patient for years. Delusions of extreme worthlessness, sin, and guilt are found in depressed patients. Many delusions center around sexual problems.

dementia. Mental deterioration, having symptoms of apathy, impairment of memory, confusion, and lowering of willpower and reasoning power.

demise. The transfer or conveyance of an estate to another.

democracy. A form of government in which the nation's (or state's) power resides in the people. If all the people participate directly, it is a pure democracy. If the people elect representatives to speak for them, as in the United States, it is a representative democracy.

demography. The statistical study of population size, composition, distribution, and patterns of change. *See also* census tract; Metropolitan Statistical Areas

demonstration. A group display of feelings and opinion, manifested by parades, meetings, exhibiting placards, shouting, speeches, sit-down actions, and so forth.

demonstrative evidence. Evidence that speaks for itself, such as real or physical evidence. Evidence that a jury can see and use in arriving at a conclusion without needing it explained. A gun in a murder case would be an example.

demur. To object or take exception.

demurrage. (1) Detention of a vessel or vehicle beyond the time allowed for loading or unloading. (2) Payment for such detention.

demurrer. Plea for the dismissal of a suit on the grounds that, even if true, the statements of the opposition are insufficient to sustain the claim.

de novo (Lat.). As new; anew; all over again. When an appellate court reviews a case of a lower court that is not a court of record, the case is heard *de novo*; that is, it is tried again in its entirety.

Department of Justice (DOJ). The legal department of the federal government, created by law on June 22, 1870, which expanded the office of the attorney general. The DOJ furnishes legal advice and opinions to the president and heads of other federal departments and represents the government in legal matters concerning taxes, lands, monopolies and trusts, immigration and naturalization, civil rights, internal security, and other civil and criminal proceedings. The department directs and supervises the work of the Federal Bureau of Investigation, the U.S. marshals and district attorneys, the federal penal institutions, the pardon attorney, and the Parole Board and conducts all suits in the Supreme Court in which the United States is a party. The Border Patrol Academy of the DOJ is located at Port Isabel, TX, also the site of the Port Isabel Detention Center of the Immigration and Naturalization Service. DOJ Web site is http://www.usdoj.gov/.

Department of the Treasury. A department of the federal government, created on September 2, 1789, which superintends and manages national finances and is especially charged with improvement of public revenues and public credit. It analyzes taxing policies, collects customs duties and internal revenue taxes, is responsible for borrowing, paying off, and refunding long- and short-term debts, continually studies the flow of lending, enforces export controls, registers and licenses vessels engaged in foreign and domestic commerce, administers the narcotics laws, coins money, prints paper money and postage and other stamps, suppresses counterfeiting and violations of the revenue laws, investigates thefts of government property, and, through its Secret Service division, protects the person of the president.

dependency. The state of being dependent for proper care upon the community instead of on one's family or guardians.

dependent child. A minor who has been judged and declared to be under the jurisdiction of the juvenile court.

deponent. (1) One who makes a deposition. (2) One who testifies or swears to the veracity of certain facts; an affiant.

deport. To banish; to return a person to the country from which he came.

deportation. Forcible removal of a person from his or her territory or country of residence. As a form of punishment, deportation appears in history from very ancient times. In the United States several laws concerning deportation have been enacted since the Alien Act (1798), later repealed, which gave the president power to deport any alien judged dangerous. Only aliens can be deported; American citizens cannot be expelled from the United States. Undesirable foreign-born citizens can be deported if they have previously been stripped of their U.S. citizenship. *See also* Immigration and Naturalization Service

deposition. Sworn testimony obtained outside, rather than in, court.

deputy. A substitute; a person duly authorized by an officer to exercise some or all of the officer's duties in his or her stead.

deputy sheriff. One appointed to act in the place and stead of the sheriff in his or her official duties. A general deputy or "under-sheriff" is one who, by virtue of his or her appointment, has authority to execute all the ordinary duties of the office of sheriff and who executes process without any special authority from his or her principal. A special deputy, who is an officer *pro hac vice*, is one appointed for a special occasion or service, such as keeping the peace when a riot or tumult is expected or in progress. He or she acts under a specific, and not a general, appointment and authority.

deringer; derringer. A small pocket pistol, originally made by Henry Deringer of Philadelphia, but copied by many others.

derivative evidence. Evidence obtained as the result of information gained through a previous act or statement, such as a search of premises that furnished leads on the basis of which the later evidence was found. The same would hold where a statement or confession is the basis for obtaining the derivative evidence. If the first acts are illegal, then the derivative evidence falls into "the fruit of the poisonous tree" category and is inadmissible. *See also* fruit of the poisonous tree

descriptive statistics. Measures used to summarize the observations in a sample survey. Because hundreds of individual measurements are impossible to comprehend, statistics are used to reduce and summarize data into more manageable and interpretable forms. The simplest descriptive statistic is a frequency distribution. Where scientists have interval or ratio-level measurement, they probably will use statistics to describe what the typical observation in the sample looks like (for example, some measure of central tendency), as well as a measure of how much variation exists around this typical observation (a measure of dispersion). For example, a researcher might describe a sample by saying that the average respondent is 32 but that persons in the sample range in age from 18 to 73. In addition to describing individual variables in some summary way, the researcher often will also describe relationships between and among variables with other statistics, such as the correlation coefficient.

desecration. The defacing, damaging, or mistreatment of a public structure, monument, or place of worship or burial.

desegregation. In *Brown v. Board of Education of Topeka*, (1954) Chief Justice Earl Warren of the Supreme Court read the unanimous opinion of the Court, which declared that segregation of children in public schools solely on the basis of race, even though physical facilities and other "tangible" factors are equal, deprives such children of equal educational opportunities. In 1955 the Court decreed that the implementation of its earlier decision was to be assumed by the lower federal courts, which were to supervise and enforce desegregation within a reasonable time. In *Bolling v. Sharpe* (1954), the Court also ruled unanimously that segregation deprives children of due process of law under the Fifth Amendment.

desertion. Also called abandonment, the willful abandonment of one spouse by the other without legal cause or intention of returning. In constructive desertion, the misconduct of one spouse forces the end of cohabitation. In most of the United States, desertion of one to two years' duration is grounds for divorce.

designer drugs. Drugs whose molecules are altered to make them legal and more potent. The most potent and deadly are variations, called analogs, of the anesthetic fentanyl. Drug laws define illegal drugs by their exact molecular structure, so it is possible for a chemist to evade the law by making minor changes in these structures. If an analog is identified, but is not on the controlled substance list, it is not illegal.

detain. To stop someone and prevent his or her freedom of action for a short period of time; to interfere with one's freedom of movement or actions.

detainee. Usually, a person held in local, very short-term confinement while awaiting consideration for pretrial release or first appearance for arraignment.

detainer. In corrections, an official notice from a governmental to a correctional agency, requesting that a person wanted by the government but subject to the prison's jurisdiction not be released or discharged without notification, and without giving the government an opportunity to respond.

detective. Usually a plainclothes officer engaged in investigating civil and criminal matters.

detector. A sensor such as those used to detect intrusion, equipment malfunction or failure, rate of temperature rise, smoke, or fire.

detention. The legally authorized confinement of a person subject to criminal or juvenile court proceedings until commitment to a correctional facility or release. Detention describes the custodial status (reason for custody) of persons held in confinement after arrest or while awaiting the completion of judicial proceedings. Release from detention can occur either prior to trial or after trial or adjudication, as a result of a dismissal of the case, an acquittal, or a sentencing disposition that does not require confinement.

detention center. The locked ("secure") facility in which juveniles are detained.

detention hearing. A juvenile court hearing on the issue of limiting a parent's or guardian's custody of a minor by determining where the child is to be housed.

detention, preventive. *See* preventive pretrial detention

detention, protective. Based on a policy of social defense or protection, some countries and states have attempted to keep defective, habitual, and unimprovable offenders in custody for an indefinite or life period after they would qualify for release if they were ordinary offenders. Such an extended stay is in part accomplished by delaying parole or by the use of third- and fourth-time offender acts, under which a prisoner may be detained for periods up to life.

deter. To prevent a person from an act by threat, warning, or, as in imprisonment, example.

deterrence. A theory that swift and sure punishment will discourage others from similar illegal acts. Generally, the term refers to setting examples that discourage criminal behavior in the population at large, but deterrence can be directed at a single individual by incarcerating or supervising him or her.

detoxification center. A public or private facility for the short-term medical treatment of either acutely intoxicated persons or drug or alcohol abusers. Such a center often functions as an alternative to jail for persons who have been taken into custody.

deviance. Behavior that is contrary to the standards of conduct or social expectation of a given group or society. Deviance has been described as being pathological or having roots in social disorganization. *See also* anomie; Merton, Robert

devise. To give or bequeath by will.

devisee. Person or organization to whom a devise or bequest is made.

diagnosis or classification center. A functional unit, within a correctional or medical facility, or a separate facility, which contains persons held in custody for the purpose of determining whether criminal proceedings should continue or whether sentencing, treatment, or disposition to a correctional facility or program is appropriate for a committed offender. Persons may be sent to these centers either before or after court disposition of the case. Parolees returned to prison for alleged or confirmed parole violations may also be placed in diagnostic facilities for study and/or reclassification.

diagnostic commitment. The action of a court ordering a person subject to criminal or juvenile proceedings to be temporarily placed in a confinement facility for study and evaluation of his or her personal history and characteristics, usually as a preliminary to a sentencing or other disposition of the case. This kind of commitment, usually a provisional one that is followed by a final defendant disposition, may occur before judgment and thus be unrelated to any determination of guilt. Diagnostic commitments have various purposes. A court may commit a person for study and observation to determine whether he or she is competent to be tried and, if found incompetent or not guilty by reason of insanity, whether the person is a danger to self or others. There is also the diagnostic commitment to advise the court as to what kind of correctional program, if any, is most suitable for a person convicted of a crime or adjudged to be a delinquent or status offender. This kind of determination is often made for presentation to the court in a presentence (adult) or predisposition (juvenile) report.

dialed number recorders. Devices, also called traps and tracers, used by telephone companies in cooperation with law enforcement agencies to determine either (a) what numbers are being called from a particular phone or (b) what phones are being used to call a particular number. When used in situation (a), the dialed number recorder is attached to the suspect's phone line in a legal wiretap for which the law enforcement agency has obtained a warrant. Situation (b) is the result of a consumer's complaint to local law enforcement that he or she is receiving harassing phone calls; the trap is then placed on the victim's phone line to help determine the source of the calls. *See also* harassing calls; pen register

dichotomy. A division into two parts or lines. In charting the organizational structure (chain of command) of a police agency from the chief downward, there is a dichotomy when "line" and "staff" are shown.

dictum. (1) Formal statement made by a judge. (2) A statement or opinion by the judge on some legal point other than the principal issue of the case.

dies non (Lat.). A day on which the courts do not transact any business, such as a Sunday or legal holiday.

diethyltryptamine. A psychedelic drug found in many South American snuffs, such as yopo (prepared from the beans of the tree *Piptadenia peregrina*); the street name is DET.

differential association. One of the most prominent of the current sociological theories of crime causation, first published in 1939 by Edwin H. Sutherland. The concept of crime as "learned behavior" was formulated by Gabriel Tarde, a French jurist, who in 1890 published his ideas in his *Laws of Imitation.* Sutherland began with this concept; his theory consisted of seven basic correlates (later expanded to nine) explaining the process by which a particular person comes to engage in criminal behavior. Differential association asserts that criminal behavior is learned, and not the result of any concrete condition such as poverty or mental deficiency. This principle forms the crux of a general theory of crime designed to encompass white-collar and professional crime as well as crime ordinarily related to social and psychological disorganization.

differential opportunity. A criminological theory explaining delinquent and criminal behavior, which emphasizes the access or lack of access people have to both legal and illegal ways of meeting their individual goals.

differential pressure sensor. A sensor used for perimeter protection that responds to the difference between the hydraulic pressures in two liquid-filled tubes buried just below the surface of the earth around the perimeter of the protected area. The pressure difference can indicate an intruder walking or driving over the buried tubes.

dilatory. Term that in law describes activity for the purpose of causing a delay or to gain time or postpone a decision.

dilatory exceptions. Those exceptions and motions filed for the purpose of retarding progress of the case but which do not tend to defeat the charges.

dimorphism. Possessing both male and female reproductive organs, sexual characteristics, or responses.

diphenylaminechloroarsine. A solid material that is dispersed by heat to produce an aerosol causing skin and eye irritation, chest distress, and nausea. In popular usage, "adamsite." One of the "vomiting gases," it is relatively nontoxic.

diphenylchloroarsine (DA). This mob- and riot-control gas has a very rapid rate of action. Effects are felt within two or three minutes after one minute of exposure. It causes irritation of the eyes and mucous membranes, viscous discharge from the nose similar to that caused by a cold, sneezing and coughing, severe headache, acute pain and tightness in the chest, and nausea and vomiting. In moderate concentrations the effects last about 30 minutes after an individual leaves the contaminated atmosphere. At higher concentrations the effects may last up to several hours.

diphenylcyanoarsine (DC). This mob- and riot-control gas has a very rapid rate of action. It causes the same symptoms as DA but is more toxic.

diplomatic immunity. The law relating to diplomatic immunity is found in the Vienna Convention on Diplomatic Relations, which went into effect as part of U.S. federal law in 1972. Diplomats are exempt from local jurisdiction. They are free from arrest; trial in local courts; and police, fiscal, and ecclesiastical jurisdiction. Diplomats cannot be required to give evidence. They are entitled to freedom of communication. The diplomatic pouch is inviolate. Immunity extends to diplomats' families, documents, homes, and other personal belongings. Diplomatic immunity is based on common practice and is reciprocal. Because a diplomat cannot be tried in local courts, a host country may ask the diplomat's government to recall the offending official and to punish him or her. If diplomats commit serious crimes, they can be expelled from their host countries. They are expected to give due regard to local laws and regulations for the maintenance of public order and safety, and they may not interfere in domestic matters; if they do, they can be recalled.

dipsomania. Alcoholism; a mental disorder manifested by an uncontrollable desire for intoxicating drink; an irresistible impulse to indulge in intoxication, either by alcohol or other drugs.

direct action. Intimidation or violence (as a sit-in, street demonstration, or riot) in order to overawe the authorities, seize power, or obtain some other political objective.

direct contempt of court. Any contempt committed in the presence of the court, or the failure to comply with a summons, subpoena, or order to appear in court. *See also* contempt of court

direct evidence. Testimony or other proof that expressly or straightforwardly proves the existence of fact.

direct examination. Initial examination of witnesses by the side or party who calls them.

directed verdict. An order or verdict pronounced by a judge during the trial of a criminal case in which the evidence presented by the prosecution clearly fails to show the guilt of the accused.

disability. (1) Legal incapacity that may result from infancy, insanity, or some act in contravention of law. (2) Lack of legal qualifications to hold office, such as want of sufficient age or period of residence, the holding of an incompatible office, foreign citizenship, or, for the U.S. presidency, foreign birth.

Disabled Law Officers Association, National (NDLOA). Founded in 1971. Publishes *NDLOA*, periodic newsletter. Address: 75 New Street, Nutley, NJ 07110.

Disaster Squad. The FBI's Disaster Squad identifies, through fingerprints, the victims of disasters. Its services are available, upon the request of local law enforcement and government agencies or transportation companies, following a catastrophe where the identification of victims is a problem. The squad also assists in identifying Americans in disasters abroad, but only at the specific invitation of the country involved. Address: FBI Disaster Squad, Identification Division, FBI, DOJ, 9th Street & Pennsylvania Avenue, NW, Room 11255, Washington, DC 20537.

discharge. To release a person from confinement, supervision, or a legal status imposing an obligation on him or her.

disciplinary punishment. Punishment to ensure compliance with the rules of a correctional facility.

disclaimer. A denial; disavowal.

discretion. An authority conferred by law on an official or an agency to act in certain conditions or situations in accordance with the named official's or agency's considered judgment and conscience.

Who Exercises Discretion?	
These criminal justice officials…	…must often decide whether or not how to—
Police	Enforce specific laws Investigate specific crimes Search people, vicinities, buildings; Arrest if detain people
Prosecutors	File charges or petitions for adjudication; Seek indictments; Drop cases; Reduce charges
Judges or magistrates	Set bail or conditions for release; Accept pleas; Determine delinquency; Dismiss charges; Impose sentence; Revoke probation
Correctional officials	Assign to type of correctional facility; Award privileges; Punish for disciplinary infractions
Paroling authority	Determine date and conditions of parole; Revoke parole

Source: Bureau of Justice Statistics, *Report to the Nation on Crime and Justice,* 2nd ed. (Washington, DC: U.S. Department of Justice, 1988.)

discrimination. Unfavorable treatment of groups of people on arbitrary grounds such as race or religion, a form of control that keeps the groups socially distant from one another. This separation is accomplished through institutionalized practices that attribute inferiority on the basis of notions that frequently have little or nothing to do with the real behavior of those who are discriminated against.

disfranchisement. (1) State action depriving a designated class or an individual of the privilege of voting, by imposition of new requirements such as a literacy test, as a consequence of conviction for felony or bribery, or by the neglect or refusal of election officers to register otherwise qualified voters. (2) Any act of discrimination or intimidation that has the practical effect of preventing exercise of suffrage; usually used colloquially.

disinter. To remove from the grave; exhume.

dismissal. (1) In judicial proceedings, generally, the disposal of an action, suit, motion, or the like without trial of the issues; the termination of the adjudication of a case before the case reaches judgment. (2) The decision by a court to terminate adjudication of all outstanding charges in a criminal case, or against a given defendant in a criminal case, thus terminating court action and, permanently or provisionally, court jurisdiction over the defendant in relation to those charges. This second definition and usage are more common than the first.

dismissal for want of prosecution. The judicial termination of a case against a defendant, occurring after the filing of a charging document but before the beginning of a trial, on grounds that the prosecuting party has withdrawn or is unable to proceed with the suit.

dismissal in the interest of justice. The judicial termination of a case against a defendant on the grounds that the ends of justice would not be served by continuing prosecution.

disorder. Riotous behavior; confusion of actions; disturbance of the peace.

disorderly conduct. A term of loose and indefinite meaning (except as occasionally defined in state statutes), but signifying generally any behavior that is contrary to law and, more particularly, that tends to disturb the public peace or decorum, scandalize the community, or shock the public sense of morality. In Colorado, for example, the existing disorderly conduct statute includes "disturbing the peace," "breach of the peace," "harassment," "criminal nuisance," and "public display of a deadly weapon." In Uniform Crime Reports, disorderly conduct is the category used to record and report arrests for committing a breach of the peace. Examples include affray; unlawful assembly; disturbing the peace; disturbing meetings; disorderly conduct in state institutions, at court, at fairs, on trains or public conveyances, and so forth, or at prize fights; blasphemy, profanity, and obscene language; desecrating the flag; refusing to assist an officer; and all attempts to commit any of the above.

disorderly house. A house in which people live, or to which they resort, for purposes injurious to public morals, health, convenience, or safety.

disorderly person. One guilty of disorderly conduct, such as a beggar, tramp, or person who deserts his or her family.

disposition. The action by a criminal or juvenile justice agency that signifies either that a portion of the justice process is complete and jurisdiction is terminated or transferred to another agency or that a decision has been reached on one aspect of a case and a different aspect, requiring a different kind of decision, is now under consideration.

disposition hearing. A hearing in juvenile courts, conducted after an adjudicatory hearing and the subsequent receipt of the report of any predisposition investigation, to determine the most appropriate form of custody and/or treatment for a juvenile who has been adjudged a delinquent, a status offender, or a dependent. The possible dispositions of juveniles over whom a court has assumed jurisdiction range from placement, on probation or in a foster home, to confinement.

disqualification. Depriving someone from participating in a proceeding, due to a condition or some irregularity. A juror, because of prejudice or bias, may be disqualified from serving on a jury. Judges may disqualify themselves from conducting a trial because of a personal relationship to one or more of the parties or because of bias or prejudice.

dissent. (1) The opinion of a judge or judges, on a multi-judge court, presenting a view in opposition to all or part of the majority holding in the case being decided. (2) The expression of a judge who does not agree with the verdict of the majority of the court.

dissident. (1) Differing; not in accord with existing policy, rules, or laws; opposing; dissenting. (2) One who disagrees with existing laws, rules, or governmental actions.

dissolve. To annul or set aside an order such as an injunction.

distress. The transferring of a person or piece of property from a wrongdoer to an injured party, in compensation for the wrong done.

district attorney. A locally elected state official who represents the state in bringing indictments and prosecuting criminal cases; the prosecuting attorney or state's attorney. *See also* United States Attorneys

district court. In the federal court system, the court of original criminal jurisdiction and a court of record; one such court is located in each federal judicial district and has jurisdiction over matters of that district. Several states have district courts that are courts of original jurisdiction. The district over which they have jurisdiction may be composed of one or more counties. They are similar to county courts in other states.

District of Columbia Preventive Detention Law. A 1970 bill in Washington, DC, which authorized pretrial preventive detention of offenders for 60 days on the basis of a judge's prediction of dangerousness, based on commission of a dangerous or violent crime, if it is probable that the accused person committed the crime.

distringas writ. A writ issued to a sheriff to seize the property of a defendant and/or the defendant, so that the person or evidence will be available when the suit proceeds.

disturbance of public meeting. In common law it is a misdemeanor to disturb a group of people convening for any lawful purpose, particularly for a distinctly moral or benevolent purpose.

disturbing the peace. Unlawful interruption of the peace, quiet, or order of a community, including offenses called disorderly conduct, vagrancy, loitering, unlawful assembly, and riot.

diversion. (1) In the broadest usage, any procedure which substitutes: (a) nonentry for official entry into the justice process; (b) the suspension of criminal or juvenile proceedings for continuation; (c) lesser supervision or referral to a nonjustice agency or no supervision for conventional supervision; or (d) any kind of nonconfinement status for confinement. (2) In criminal justice usage, the official suspension of criminal or juvenile proceedings against an alleged offender at any point after a recorded justice system intake but before the entering of a judgment and a decision either to refer the person to a treatment or care program administered by a non-justice or private agency or not to make a referral.

diversity jurisdiction. That aspect of the jurisdiction of the federal courts that applies to suits between residents of different states.

Division of Investigation Act. Law passed by Congress on June 18, 1934, empowering certain members of the Division of Investigation of the Department of Justice to serve warrants and subpoenas issued under the authority of the United States; to make seizures under warrant; and to make arrests without warrant for felonies committed, if the person making the arrest has reasonable grounds to believe that the person being arrested is guilty of a felony and where the person is likely to escape before a warrant can be obtained.

divorce. The dissolution, or partial suspension by law, of a marital relationship.

divorce, no-fault. A legal option to dissolve a marriage, in which neither party is required to charge the other with a violation of the marital contract. Instead, both parties can declare they wish to divorce because of irreconcilable differences. In 1970 California was the first state to adopt a no-fault divorce law.

DNA fingerprinting. D(eoxyribo) n(ucleic) a(cid) is an essential component of all living matter and the basic chromosomal material transmitting the hereditary pattern. Investigators can identify suspects by comparing their unique individual genetic codes with the code found in samples of hair, blood, skin, and semen left at crime scenes. There are two principal types of DNA tests. Developed in 1985, the "Long Test," termed the Restriction Fragment Length Polymorphism (RFLP) test, consists of seven steps: (1) DNA is extracted from body tissue or fluids, such as blood, collected from suspects and evidence. RFLP requires 50 nanograms of DNA. (2) The DNA is chemically cut into fragments using restriction enzymes. (3) The resulting fragments are placed in a gel and separated into bands by running an electric current through them, a process called electrophoresis. (4) The pattern, still invisible at this point, is transferred to a nylon membrane. (5) Radioactive DNA probes are applied to the membrane, which bind to matching DNA sequences. Excess, unattached DNA probes are washed away. (6) X-ray film is placed beside the membrane. The film is then developed, revealing a pattern of bands where the radioactive probe has bonded to the DNA fragments. This profile is the genetic fingerprint. (7) The final DNA fingerprint is a pattern of light and dark bands that looks like a supermarket bar code and is compared to DNA from other samples, such as blood found at a crime scene. The second test, the four-step "Quick Test," is called Polymerase Chain Reaction (PCR) typing that can be used on much smaller samples of DNA and is less definitive than the RFLP test. (1) DNA is extracted from tissue or fluids and purified. (2) The intact DNA is combined with short fragments of known DNA, called primers, and other chemicals that cause the DNA to be replicated. The primers cause only certain segments of DNA to replicate. With 30 cycles of replication, the amount of DNA increases 1 million times. (3) Small quantities of the replicated DNA are applied to 8–10 spots on a reagent strip, each spot containing a different segment of known DNA. If the replicated DNA contains a segment matching the known segment, a blue color appears on the spot. (4) The pattern of spots from a sample obtained at a crime scene is compared to that from a suspect. The PCR typing takes a week or less, while the RFLP method takes four to six weeks. Chances of identical results from two different people are between 1 in 500 and 1 in 2,000 with the PCR test; with RFLP typing they are 1 in a million. There is precedent for the admission of RFLP testing as evidence in California and in the U.S. Court of Appeals for the 9th Circuit. The first conviction using DNA mitochondria was on September 3, 1996, when a jury in Chattanooga, TN, found defendant Paul Ware guilty of the felony murder of a four-year-old. Most DNA is found in a cell's nucleus, but mitochondrial DNA is found in the fluid outside the nucleus. It carries its own genetic code and is passed from mother to child. Prosecutors say it allows more precise matching than fingerprinting of traditional DNA.

docket. A formal record of court proceedings.

document. An official paper, deed, manuscript, or any other written or inscribed instrument that has informational or evidentiary value.

documentary evidence. Evidence supplied by papers, books, or other written material.

document, class A. An identification document regarded as generally reliable. Examples include passports and armed forces identification cards.

document, class B. An identification document regarded as often reliable. Examples include photo-bearing drivers' licenses and photo-bearing employee cards issued by national firms.

document, class C. An identification document regarded as doubtfully reliable. This type of document will usually not contain a photo, serial number, or other means of verification.

document, class D. An identification document regarded as unreliable. This type of document can be obtained without proving identity, as in the case of a Social Security card.

document examiner. One who is an expert in the field of handwriting, handprinting, typewriting, inks, printing, and so forth.

Document Examiners, National Association of (NADE). Founded in 1980. Publishes *Journal of NADE* (5/yearly). Address: 20 Nassau Street, Princeton, NJ 08542.

Document Examiners, National Bureau of. Founded in 1984. Publishes *The Exemplar* biannually. Address: 250 W. 57th Street, Suite 2032, New York, NY 10107.

Document Examiners, World Association of. Founded in 1973. Publishes a quarterly journal. Address: 111 N. Canal Street, Chicago, IL 60606.

Doe, John. A fictitious name used to identify a party in a legal action whose true name is unknown or who wishes to remain anonymous. Additional unknown or anonymous parties are sometimes known as Richard Roe and Peter Poe.

Dog Association, North American Police Work. Founded in 1977. Address: 1755 E. Gorman Road, Adrian, MI 49221.

domestic battering. Includes physical abuse between individuals who have an intimate relationship. Although wives are the most frequent victims, the term includes husbands and unmarried individuals.

domestic relations court. A lower judicial tribunal, usually part of a system of municipal courts, the jurisdiction of which extends typically to matters concerned with family support and the care of children. The first domestic relations court was established in Buffalo, NY, in 1909 by Simon Augustine Nash, Judge of Police Court, who privately heard domestic relations cases in his chambers instead of in open court. Chapter 570, Laws of New York State, approved on May 29, 1909, established the City Court of Buffalo; the domestic relations division was opened January 1, 1910.

domestic terrorism. On September 11, 2001, terrorists hijacked four commercial aircraft, flying one into each of the World Trade Center towers in New York City, another into the Pentagon, and a fourth crashing in a field in PA. The death toll at the World Trade Center was approximately 3,000.

domestic violence. Causing physical harm or threatening such harm to a member of one's family or household, including spouses, ex-spouses, parents, children, persons otherwise related by blood, persons living in the household, or persons formerly living there. Persons who have been convicted in any court of a qualifying misdemeanor crime of domestic violence (MCDV) generally are prohibited under federal law from possessing any firearm or ammunition in or affecting commerce (or shipping or transporting any firearm or ammunition in interstate or foreign commerce, or receiving any such firearm or ammunition). This prohibition also applies to federal, state, and local governmental employees in both their official and private capacities. Violation of this prohibition is a federal offense punishable by up to ten years imprisonment. Many states also have laws prohibiting the possession of a firearm by anyone, including law enforcement officers, convicted of a domestic violence offense.

domicile. The permanent place of residence of persons, or the place to which they intend to return even though they may actually reside elsewhere. The legal domicile of a person is important since it, rather than the actual residence, often controls the jurisdiction of the taxing authorities and determines where a person may exercise the privilege of voting and other legal rights.

double jeopardy. Putting a person on trial for an offense for which he or she has previously been indicted and a jury empaneled and sworn to try him or her, provided that the jury did not disagree or was discharged because of the illness of a juror or other sufficient reason. It is prohibited by the Fifth Amendment, which provides in part, "Nor shall any person be subject for the same offense to be twice put in jeopardy of life or limb." The purpose of the prohibition is to prevent repeated harassment of an accused person and reduce the danger of convicting an innocent one. Double jeopardy does not apply when a convicted person appeals to a higher court or when state and federal governments prosecute separately for different offenses arising from the same act. Under state statutes, pleas of not guilty on double-jeopardy grounds can be of two types: either *autrefois* acquit (formerly acquitted) or *autrefois* convict (formerly convicted) of the identical charge involving the same set of facts on a previous occasion before a court of competent jurisdiction.

doubt, reasonable. The state of mind of jurors in which, after the comparison and consideration of all the evidence, they cannot say that they feel an abiding conviction, a moral certainty, of the truth of a criminal charge against a defendant.

Draft Riots. For five days in July 1863, gangs laid siege to New York City. Their goal was to disrupt the process of the newly established draft. Rioters attacked the police and prominent politicians, looted stores, burned buildings, and destroyed railroad cars and telegraph lines. More than 100 people died.

dram law. A liquor law providing that person(s) serving someone who is intoxicated or contributing to the intoxication of another may be liable for subsequent injury or damage caused by the intoxicated person. Such state laws open public bars and, in some cases, private individuals, to liability suits. As of 1988, 38 states had enacted dram laws.

Dreyfus, Alfred. A young Jewish captain in the French army who was framed on a charge of passing secrets to the Germans. He was convicted in a closed-door court martial and sent to Devil's Island with a sentence of life in prison. The so-called Dreyfus Affair occurred during a period of intense nationalism and anti-Semitism in France. When the Army command realized that its case was weak, it manufactured evidence, reasoning that the honor of the army was more important than one man's life and career. **October 10, 1894:** The French minister of war accuses Capt. Dreyfus of being the author of a document sent to the Germans. **October 15:** Dreyfus is arrested, and the army decides that his handwriting is similar to that in the document. **December 12:** He is sentenced to life in prison. **January 5, 1895:** He is stripped of his military rank in the courtyard of the Ecole Militaire. **March 1895–June 1899:** Dreyfus is imprisoned on Devil's Island. **January 13, 1898:** Émile Zola publishes "J'Accuse," telling Dreyfus's story, in the newspaper *L'Aurore*. **June 3, 1899:** Dreyfus's military court sentence is annulled. **September 9, 1899:** The War Council again convicts him, sentencing him to 10 years in prison. **July 12, 1906:** The Supreme Court of Appeals annuls this sentence. **July 13:** He is reintegrated into the army with the rank of commander. Dreyfus returned to active duty, fought beside his son in World War I, and was later awarded the French Legion of Honor medal.

driver. A person who drives or is in physical control of a vehicle. Term does not include the tillerman or other person who, in an auxiliary capacity, assists the driver in the steering or operation of any articulated firefighting apparatus.

driver and pedestrian education. The Department of Transportation provides information and financial assistance to states and local communities for several programs on driver education and pedestrian safety. Research is also conducted on unsafe driving, vehicle occupant restraints, alcohol, pedestrians, and young drivers. The DOT offers driving publications and films. Address: Driver and Pedestrian Education Division, Traffic Safety Programs, National Highway Traffic Safety Administration, DOT, 400 7th Street, SW, Room 5130, Washington, DC 20590.

driving records. The National Driver Register is a compilation of the driver's license suspension and revocations records of participating states, which is available to other states for the purpose of researching new license requests. The kinds of data included are: name, date of birth, Social Security number, driver's license number, height, weight, eye color, date and reason license was revoked, and date of reinstatement. Not all states participate. Address: National Driver Register, Traffic Safety Programs, National Highway Traffic Safety Administration, DOT, 400 7th Street, SW, Room 5206, Washington, DC 20590.

driving under the influence (DUI). Unlawful operation of any motor vehicle while under the influence of alcohol or a controlled substance(s) or drug. In 2002, an estimated 17,419 people died as the result of alcohol-related crashes on the nation's highways. Approximately 41% of all traffic fatalities involve alcohol.

Driving under the Influence Cost Recovery Program. Effort mandated in many states, in which any person under the influence of alcohol or a controlled substance whose negligent operation of a motor vehicle causes any incident leading to an emergency response is responsible for the costs associated with the response. For example, California began billing under a program of this type on January 1, 1989, and from January 1991 through August 1995 had billed approximately $9.3 million in expenses triggered by nearly 39,000 incidents.

Dr. Snow. First indicted in 1984, this drug dealer's real name is Larry Lavin, then a 26-year-old dentist. The case involved a 60-kilogram-per-year cocaine distribution network headquartered in Philadelphia and headed by Lavin. By the time he was indicted under the "drug kingpin" statute, he had personally reaped an estimated $6 million from his drug operations. Lavin was sentenced to 22 years after pleading guilty to 5 counts of drug conspiracy, and also received a 20-year sentence for tax evasion.

drug. This term is derived from the fourteenth-century French word *drogue*, meaning a dry substance. Most pharmaceuticals during that period were prepared from dried herbs. *See also* addiction, amphetamine, anabolic steroids, cocaine, cocaine, crack, gateway drugs, heroin, inhalants, marijuana, methadone, methaqualone, methylphenidate, morphine, nicotine, opium, peyote, phenecyclidine, and Valium and Librium.

drug abuse. The National Clearinghouse for Drug Abuse Information collects and disseminates information on drug abuse and produces information on drugs, drug abuse, and prevention. Address: 1555 Wilson Boulevard, Suite 600, Rosslyn, VA. *See also* drug misuse

Drug Abuse Epidemiology Data Center. Founded in 1973 by the National Institute on Drug Abuse, U.S. Department of Health, Education, and Welfare. Objectives are the preservation of original data of major surveys and records, documentation of these individual files to facilitate further analyses, development and maintenance of a library of drug research reports, and development and implementation of a computer file for retrieval of drug literature based on a refined taxonomy. Publishes *The Drug Abuse Epidemiology Data Center Information Package* (free of charge); *Drug Abuse: A Bibliography of Literature on the Epidemiological and Social Science Aspects of Drug Use and Abuse* (bimonthly); and *DAEDAC Database*, (quarterly newsletter, without charge). Address: Institute of Behavioral Research, Texas Christian University, Fort Worth, TX 76129.

Drugs Are Scheduled Under Federal Law According to Their Effects, Medical Use, and Potential for Abuse				
DEA schedule	Abuse potential	Examples of drugs covered	Some of the effects	Medical use
I	Highest	heroin, LSD, hashish, marijuana, methaqua- lone, designer drugs	Unpredictable effects, severe psychological or physical depen- dence, or death	No accepted use; some are legal for limited research use only
II	High	morphine, PCP, codeine, cocaine, methadone, Demerol®, benzedrine, dexedrine	May lead to severe psychological or phys- ical dependence	Accepted use with restrictions
III	Medium	codeine with aspirin or Tylenol®, some amphetamines, anabolic steroids	May lead to moderate or low physical dependence or high psychological depen- dence	Accepted use
IV	Low	Darvon®, Talwin®, phenobarbital, Equanil®, Miltown®, Libriun®, diazepan	May lead to limited physical or psycholog- ical dependence	Accepted use
V	Lowest	Over the counter or prescription compounds with codeine, Lomotil®, Robitussin A-C®	May lead to limited physical or psycholog- ical dependence	Accepted use

Source: Adapted from DEA, *Drugs of Abuse: 1989.*

Drug Abuse Information, National Clearinghouse for. Operated by the National Institutes of Health, the focal agency for federal information on drugs and their abuse. Provides information through publications and a computerized information service. Address: 5454 Wisconsin Avenue, Chevy Chase, MD 20015.

drug abuse violations. Offenses relating to growing, manufacturing, making, possessing, using, selling, or distributing narcotic and dangerous nonnarcotic drugs. *See also* drug law violations; designer drugs

Drug Abuse Warning Network (DAWN). Begun in 1972 and funded by the National Institute on Drug Abuse, this network identifies and evaluates the scope and magnitude of drug abuse in the United States. More than 900 hospital emergency rooms and medical examiner facilities supply data to the program. DAWN identifies drugs currently being abused, determines existing patterns and profiles of abuse/abuser in Standard Metropolitan Statistical Areas (SMSAs), monitors systemwide abuse trends, detects new abuse entities and polydrug combinations, provides data for the assessment of health hazards and abuse potential of drug substances, and provides data needed for rational control and scheduling of drugs of abuse. Address: Information Systems Section, Office of Compliance and Regulatory Affairs, Drug Enforcement Bureau, DOJ, 1405 I Street, NW, Room 519, Washington, DC.

drug addiction. Defined by the World Health Organization as "a state of periodic or chronic intoxication produced by the repeated consumption of a drug (natural or synthetic), which produces the following characteristics: (1) an overpowering desire or compulsion to continue taking the drug and to obtain it by any means; (2) a tendency to increase the dosage, showing body tolerance; (3) a psychic and generally a physical dependence on the effects of the drug; and (4) the creation of an individual and social problem"

drug and alcohol abuse in the military. The Office of Drug Abuse has identification, treatment, and educational programs on drug and alcohol abuse. It provides quarterly reports that include data on the number of people identified, rejected, discharged, tried, and court-martialed by the military. Address: Office for Drug and Alcohol Abuse Prevention, Health Affairs, Department of Defense, The Pentagon, Room 3D171, Washington, DC 20301.

Drug and Crime Data Center Clearinghouse. This agency distributes all U.S. Department of Justice, Office of Justice Programs, publications, and fact sheets. The Bureau of Justice Statistics provides crime and criminal justice data and publications. The clearinghouse responds to requests by offering database searches, information packages of statistics, and referrals. Telephone: (800) 666-3332 and (800) 732-3277.

Drug Court Resource Center. Funded by the Bureau of Justice Assistance, this office offers technical support for drug court officials and information about drug courts to the public. Address: The American University, Brandywine Building, Suite 660, 440 Massachusetts Ave., NW, Washington, DC 20016-8159.

drug czar. A popular designation for the director of the White House Office on National

Drug Policy, which was created by then vice president George Bush in 1988 to coordinate the 50 U.S. agencies charged with suppressing illegal drugs and their use. The first such director was William Bennett, who served from 1989 to 1990. Next was Robert Martinez, also appointed by Bush, who served from 1990 to 1991; John Walters was acting director from 1991 to 1993; next was Lee Brown, appointed by President William Clinton, who served from March 8, 1993, to November 1994; the fourth director was Barry McCaffrey, a retired four-star general of Gulf War fame, who was appointed by President Clinton and took office in March 1995. John Walters, acting director from 1991 to 1993, was appointed director by President George W. Bush on December 7, 2001. Walters is credited with the launching of an award-winning campaign linking drug trafficking and terrorism.

Drug Dealer Liability Act. A California statute providing a civil damages to people injured as a result of the use of a controlled substance. Such victims can include the parents of a drug user, employers, insurers, governmental agencies, and others who pay for drug treatment programs, as well as infants injured as a result of exposure to controlled substances in utero. Some other states have similar laws.

drug detection. Law enforcement has relied upon several methods in detecting or searching for illegal drugs. They include informants; drug-sniffing dogs; visual and enhanced visual observation (binoculars); and low-flying aircraft and helicopters. However, in June 2001, the Supreme Court (*Kyllo vs. U.S. 99-8508*) ruled that the use of thermal imaging to detect heat from a home violated the 4th Amendment. A thermal imager operates like a video camera, except that it shows white heat spots. This decision dealt only with a private residence, not a car or a work site.

drug education materials. Drug education films are available free of charge to civic, educational, private, and religious groups. For current listings, contact: Preventive Programs, Office of Public Affairs, Drug Enforcement

Administration, DOJ, 1405 I Street, NW, Room 1405, Washington, DC 20537.

Drug Enforcement Administration (DEA). Founded in 1973 by the U.S. Department of Justice, DEA, with approximately 4,100 employees, enforces laws and regulations that apply to legally produced and controlled substances (narcotics, amphetamines, and barbiturates) handled by registered importers, manufacturers, distributors, pharmacists, and doctors. Two DEA operations are Operation SNOWCAP, a joint Peruvian-DEA effort established in 1987 to attack cocaine-producing labs and clandestine airstrips, and located at Santa Lucia, Peru, in the Upper Huallaga Valley, the center of world coca production; and Operation POLAR CAP, code name for a lengthy investigation directed toward the Medellin cartel's key money-laundering network. DEA also aids communities in creating drug abuse prevention organizations and programs, and advises industry on voluntary compliance with regulatory laws. DEA also conducts various internationally oriented seminars for drug law education. The DEA Library provides information on drug abuse, enforcement efforts, diversion efforts, technology, and prevention. Publishes *Drug Enforcement Magazine* (quarterly). Address: Office of Compliance and Regulatory Affairs, DEA, DOJ, 1405 I Street, NW, Washington, DC 20537.

drug enforcement research. The DEA conducts research related to its law enforcement, intelligence, and regulatory functions, including research on drug analysis for prosecution of illicit drug violators and covert surveillance systems. It also provides support to other enforcement agencies in the form of systems studies for voice-privacy requirements and regional communication networks. Contact: Office of Science and Technology, DEA, DOJ, 1405 I Street, NW, Room 418, Washington, DC 20537.

drug enforcement training. Provided by the DEA, the program provides basic and advanced training in drug law enforcement skills for DEA and other federal, state, local,

and foreign officials. The National Training Institute also provides both basic and advanced training in drug law enforcement and related skills to forensic chemists, intelligence analysts, and the foreign drug law enforcement community. Contact: Enforcement Training Division, Office of Training, DEA, DOJ, 1405 I Street, NW, Room 418, Washington, DC 20537.

Drug-Free School Zones, National Coalition for. Address: c/o Chiefs of Police National Drug Task Force, 1514 P Street, NW, Rear, Washington, DC 20005.

drug information, coordination of. In 1989 the CIA established the Counternarcotics Center, responsible for coordinating drug-related intelligence. It employs more than 100 analysts from the CIA, Pentagon, National Security Agency, National Reconnaissance Office, DIA, FBI, DEA, State Department, Customs Service, Coast Guard, and U.S. Marshal's Office.

Drug Information Resources (State Drug Resources: A National Directory). Published in March 1990, this is a comprehensive guide to state agencies listing: Federal Information Centers and Clearinghouses; FBI Drug Demand Reduction Coordinators; U.S. DEA Drug Demand Reduction Coordinators; National Association of State Alcohol and Drug Abuse Directors (NASADAD); National Prevention Network; Treatment Alternatives to Street Crime (TASC) Programs; Drug Abuse Resistance Education (DARE) Regional Training Centers; Regional Centers for Drug-Free Schools; Statistical Analysis Centers; Uniform Crime Reports contacts; and Regional Alcohol and Drug Awareness Resources (RADAR) Network. Since 1987 the Data Center and Clearinghouse has provided data about illegal drug trafficking, drug law violators, drug-using offenders in the criminal justice system, and the impact of drugs on criminal justice administration. Compiled by the Drugs and Crime Data Center and Clearinghouse, 1600 Research Boulevard, Rockville, MD 20850; (800) 6663332.

drug law violations. The unlawful sale, purchase, distribution, manufacture, cultivation, transport, possession, or use of a controlled or prohibited drug or the attempt to commit these acts. The number of incarcerated drug offenders rose by 510 percent from 1983 to 1993. The number of drug arrests tripled from 471,000 in 1980 to 1,247,000 in 1989. Of all adults in 1994 who were on probation or parole, 55 percent, or 1.6 million, were in need of alcohol or drug treatment. Of all the money spent in the United States each year to reduce substance abuse, 78 percent goes to enforce laws, provide punishment, or control drug trade. Only 22 percent is spent on prevention and treatment. *See also* drug monitoring, voice identification

drug misuse. The use of any drug (legal or illegal) for a medical or recreational purpose when alternatives are available, practical, or warranted; drug use endangering either the user or others with whom he or she may interact.

drug monitoring. A new device has been developed to monitor individuals' drug use. It is a sweat patch that collects nonvolatile components of perspiration, including controlled substances. Resembling a 2"x3" bandage, the patch consists of a transparent cover, an absorption pad, and a release liner. A unique number is printed on the underside of the transparent cover to identify the patch. This cover allows small molecules such as water vapor, oxygen, and carbon dioxide to pass through it, while larger molecules, including controlled substances, are caught on the skin side of the patch in the absorbent pad. The patch can be worn on the outside of the upper arm or on the midriff, and after use is sent to a laboratory, where any drugs present are washed into an extraction solvent. The resulting liquid is tested by assays similar to those used for testing urine samples, with immunoassay technology used for screening. Positive results are confirmed with gas chromatography/mass spectometry. *See also* voice identification

drug references and resource. *See* American Association of Probation and Parole; American Bar Association; Bureau of Justice Assistance; Campaign for an Effective Crime Policy; Center for Substance Abuse Treatment; Chiefs of Police National Drug Task Force; Community Anti-drug Coalitions of America; Community Policing Consortium; Criminal Justice Research Institute; Drug Information Resources, Drug and Crime Data Center Clearinghouse; Drug Court Resource Center; Drug Court Resource Center; Drug Strategies; Federal Drugs, Alcohol and Crime Clearinghouse Network; Join Together Online; Justice Management Institute; Minnesota Citizens Council on Crime and Justice; National Alliance for Model State Drug Laws; National Association of Drug Court Professionals; National Association of State Alcohol and Drug Abuse Directors; National Center for Community Policing, National Center for State Courts; National Clearinghouse for Alcohol and Drug Information; National Conference of State Legislatures; National Crime Prevention Council; National Criminal Justice Reference Service; National Drug Prosecution Center; National Judicial College; National League of Cities; Office of National Drug Control Policy; Sentencing Project; Therapeutic Communities of America; United States Conference of Mayors; Western States Information Network; Youth Crime Watch of America.

drug registration. Every person who manufacturers, distributes, or dispenses any drug covered under the Controlled Substance Act or who proposes to do so must register annually with the registration branch of the DEA. A schedule of controlled substances is available. The DEA has more than 540,000 registrants, whom it monitors and periodically investigates to ensure that they are accountable for the controlled substances handled. Contact: Registration Section, Office of Compliance and Regulatory Affairs, DEA, DOJ, 666 11th Street, NW, Room 920, Washington, DC 20001.

drug reporting systems. Three computerized systems are maintained by the DEA: Drug Abuse Warning Network (see entry); Automated Reporting and Consolidated Order System—a comprehensive drug-tracking system that enables DEA to monitor the flow of selected drugs from points of import or manufacture to points of sale, export, or distribution; and Project Label—a system that represents a listing of all marketed drug products containing controlled substances. Contact: Office of Compliance and Regulatory Affairs, DEA, DOJ, 1405 I Street, NW, Room 519, Washington, DC 20537.

Drug Seizure System, Federal (FDSS). This network reflects the combined drug seizure efforts of the DEA, FBI, and U.S. Customs Service within the jurisdiction of the United States, as well as maritime seizures by the U.S. Coast Guard. FDSS eliminates duplicate reporting of a seizure involving more than one federal agency.

drug situation indicators. A retail and wholesale heroin price/purity index is available based on data from the analysis of drug-evidence samples submitted to the DEA. Reports are available on drug-related emergency room admissions and deaths in selected Standard Metropolitan Statistical Areas. Heroin-related death and injury data are published on a quarterly basis for 21 of these areas. All legal drug handlers are registered with DEA and are required to report thefts or losses of controlled substances. Stolen supplies of controlled drugs comprise a substantial portion of the supply of certain substances in the illicit drug distribution network. DEA uses these data to evaluate trends in the overall heroin situation. Contact: Office of Intelligence, DEA, DOJ, 1405 I Street, NW, Room 1013, Washington, DC 20537.

Drug Strategies. A national organization whose mission is to find effective approaches to the nation's drug problems. Address: 1150 Connecticut Avenue, NW, Suite 800, Washington DC 20036.

drugs, synthetic. *See* designer drugs

drug testing, technologies for. The technologies of testing for use of illicit drugs most often used are immunoassay and chromatography. In both tests, the hair is first treated to extract and concentrate the drug-related materials in a solution, which is then chemically analyzed in much the same way as a urine sample would be. Immunoassay testing uses antibodies to detect the presence or absence of drugs in a urine sample or a solution made from hair. An antibody is a protein that reacts only in the presence of a specific substance (the antigen) or group of chemically similar substances. In testing for drugs, a label or "tag," which can be identified and measured after the reaction of the antigen with the antibody, is mixed with the substance being used in the test (the tagged antigen). Commonly used tags include radioactive materials (as in radioimmunoassay tests—RIA and RIAH), enzymes (as in an enzyme-multiplied immunoassay test), or fluorescent materials that glow (as in fluorescent polarization immunoassay tests—FPIA). The tagged antigen, the dissolved hair shaft that may contain drugs (untagged antigens), and the antibodies are mixed. Mixing causes the tagged and untagged antigens to compete to react and bond with the antibodies. The amount of unbonded tag that remains is then compared with a known quantity of the drugs being tested for. If the amount in the sample specimen is higher than or equal to the known quantity, the test is considered positive; if lower, it is considered negative.

Gas chromatography/mass spectometry (GC/MS) is a process in which a nonreactive gas (one that will not react chemically with the substance being tested for) sends the test solution to a special tube that is part of the chromatography instrument. Here the solution is separated into its component chemicals to form a fragmentation spectrum. The components exit the tube and enter a detector (the mass spectrometer) that identifies the drugs present and measures the amount. Each drug has a specific mass spectrum "signature" that eases identification.

drug types. Subclassifications of drugs vary. The Uniform Crime Reports collects data on arrests for drug abuse violations using four drug-type categories: (a) opium or cocaine and their derivatives (morphine, heroin, codeine); (b) marijuana; (c) synthetic narcotics—manufactured narcotics which can cause true drug addiction (Demerol, methadones); and (4) dangerous nonnarcotic drugs (barbiturates, Benzedrine). The Uniform Offense Classifications list eight drug types: (a) hallucinogens (excluding marijuana); (b) heroin; (c) opium; (d) cocaine; (e) synthetic narcotics; (f) marijuana; (g) amphetamines; and (h) barbiturates. *See also* designer drugs

Drug Use Forecasting (DUF) Program. This federal program was established to assist law enforcement agencies in developing programs to combat drug abuse and to expand drug treatment by identifying drug use levels among arrestees, determining what drugs are used in specific jurisdictions, and tracking changes in drug use patterns. Begun in New York City in 1987, the program by 1990 involved 25 of the largest cities in the United States. Data are collected from booked male arrestees in 24 sites across the United States. In 21 sites, data from female arrestees are also collected, and in 12 sites from male juveniles. For about 14 consecutive evenings each quarter, trained local staff obtain anonymous voluntary interviews and urine samples from a new sample of booked arrestees. Response rates are consistently high, with more than 90 percent agreeing to be interviewed and about 80 percent providing urine samples. All specimens are sent to a central laboratory, where they are analyzed for 10 drugs: cocaine, opiates, marijuana, PCP, methadone, benzodiazepines, methaqualone, propoxyphene, barbiturates, and amphetamines. Results are published in quarterly reports, which are summarized in an annual report, available from the National Criminal Justice Reference Service, Box 6000, Rockville, MD 20850; telephone (800) 851-3420.

drunkard. One who is habitually drunk; a "common drunkard" is sometimes legally defined as a person who has been convicted of drunkenness a certain number of times over a specific period of time.

drunkenness. Voluntary drunkenness in a public place is a misdemeanor in most jurisdictions. Although the mere drinking of alcohol is not illegal, appearing in a public place under the influence of alcohol to such an extent that persons endanger themselves, others, or property is classified as an offense in most jurisdictions. In several states, public drunkenness has been decriminalized. Voluntary drunkenness is not grounds for exemption from criminal responsibility except: (a) where the act is committed while laboring under insanity or delirium tremens resulting from intoxication; (b) where a specific intent is essential to constitute a crime, and intoxication may negate such intent; and (c) where provocation for the act is shown, the fact of intoxication may be material.

dual citizenship. Citizenship both of the United States and of a state. The Fourteenth Amendment to the Constitution says, "All persons born or naturalized in the United States, and subject to the jurisdiction thereof, are citizens of the United States and of the State wherein they reside."

duces tecum (Lat., lit. "bring with you"). A writ that requires a party who is summoned to appear in court to bring with him or her some document or piece of evidence to be used or inspected.

ducking stool. A stool or chair in which "common scolds" were tied and then plunged into water. It is mentioned in the Domesday Book and was extensively used throughout England from the fifteenth to the beginning of the eighteenth century. The last recorded instance of its use was in England in 1809.

due process model. A philosophy of criminal justice based on the assumption that an individual is presumed innocent until proven guilty and that individuals ought to be protected from arbitrary power of the state. *See also* crime control model

due process of law. A clause in the Fifth and the Fourteenth Amendments ensuring that laws are reasonable and that they are applied in a fair and equal manner. Essentially, due process guarantees that persons have a right to be fairly heard before they can be deprived of life, liberty, or property. Due process of law restricts the lawmaking powers of the government by banning laws and executive orders that are arbitrary or unreasonable. Due process of law was codified in 1215 in Article 29 of the Magna Carta and appears in an Edward III statute of 1354. Because of the protection afforded in the Bill of Rights against strictures of the federal government, the due process clause of the Fifth Amendment, which applies only to the federal government, is not as important in actual practice as the Fourteenth Amendment's clause, which applies to the states. In fact, this clause has been basic in enforcing the freedoms cherished by Americans; it has been the source of more constitutional law than any other language in the Constitution. The Fourteenth Amendment was passed in 1868 in hopes of applying the Bill of Rights to the states, because, until then, it restricted only the federal government. The first major decision on due process did not come until 1925, when the Supreme Court ruled that the free speech provision of the First Amendment should be brought within the scope of the Fourteenth Amendment and so bind the states. By 1937 all the rights of the First Amendment were covered by the due process clause. In that year Supreme Court justice Benjamin Cardozo held that all Bill of Rights provisions essential to liberty and justice be included under the protections of due process. The provisions of the Bill of Rights that have been included within the due process clause are protection against unreasonable searches and seizures (Fourth Amendment); protection against self-incrimination (Fifth Amendment); the right to have counsel, confront hostile witnesses, and receive a jury trial in criminal cases (Sixth Amendment); and the prohibition of cruel and unusual punishment (Eighth Amendment).

dueling. The fighting of two persons at an appointed time and place, based on a preceding quarrel. It is a misdemeanor in common law to challenge another to fight a duel, be the bearer of such a challenge, or provoke another to send a challenge. To constitute the crime, no actual fighting is necessary. If the duel takes place and one of the parties is killed, the other is guilty of murder, and all who are present abetting the crime are guilty as principals in the second degree. It is immaterial that the duel is to take place in another state.

dumdum; dumdum bullet. A bullet that flattens excessively on contact—a kind of expanding, man-stopping bullet. The name derives from Dum Dum, India, where such bullets were first manufactured. The use of this type of bullet is forbidden under international law.

Duquenois reaction. A chemical test for identifying marijuana.

duress. Unlawful constraint or influence used to force an individual to commit some act that he or she otherwise would not commit; compulsion; coercion.

duress alarm device. A device that produces either a silent or a local alarm under a condition of personal stress such as holdup, fire, illness, or other panic or emergency. The device is normally manually operated and may be either fixed or portable.

Durham rule. A legal precedent of 1954 that altered the concept of *mens rea* by providing for a much broader test of mental illness as a legal defense, stipulating that "an accused is not criminally responsible if his unlawful act was the product of mental disease or defect."

DWI. Driving while intoxicated. A first offense is sometimes referred to as "DWI I" and a second offense as "DWI II."

dyathanasia. The passive form of "mercy killing." It generally involves the discontinuing of extraordinary means of sustaining life, so that the patient expires. *See also* euthanasia; mercy killing

Dyer Act. The federal law dealing with the interstate transportation of stolen motor vehicles; more commonly referred to as the ITSMV.

dyes. Methylene-blue, a chemical dye which is difficult to wash away, is placed in intimate contact with an article or substance likely to be removed or stolen. When disturbed, the article stains the suspect's hand(s) a bluish color. Other materials, such as nitrate of silver, when subjected to light will darken an invisible stain and make it visible. Naphthionate of sodium powder, which is fluorescent, will luminesce under an ultraviolet light. *See also* carbofuchsin

dying declaration. A statement made just before death, or one made by a person who believes that he or she is about to die. The declaration must be a statement of fact as to how the person was injured, and it must appear that the deceased expected to die and was without hope of recovery. Such a statement is admissible evidence only in homicide cases.

E

Eastman Gang. An Irish-organized gang that dominated the Bowery and East River areas of New York City around the turn of the century. It lost power after its leader, Edward Monk Eastman, went to jail on a robbery and assault charge.

eavesdropping. Interception of oral communications in a surreptitious effort to hear/record conversation, without knowledge of at least one of the persons speaking. When hidden electronic equipment is used the process is called "bugging," the equipment is a "bug," and the premises are "bugged."

ecology. Study of the distribution of people and their activities in time and space; used in the study of criminal and other kinds of deviant behavior in relationship to environmental circumstances in which the behavior occurs.

ecotage. A contraction of ecology and sabotage, this term refers to civil disobedience employing violent and nonviolent disruptive actions by radical environmentalists, either to impede depletion/commercial use of natural resources or to destroy existing facilities. Logging efforts have been affected by disabling equipment (sand in gas tanks), inserting plastic or steel spikes in trees, and/or direct physical confrontation. "Earth First!" a Tucson, AZ-based ecotage organization founded in 1980, was infiltrated and investigated by the FBI's domestic counter-terrorism squad in the period from 1987 to 1990.

eco-terrorism. A movement in the United States and Canada that purports to defend the environment and oppose urbanization by setting fires in or attempting to destroy such widely diversified targets as development projects, sport utility vehicles, ski lifts, genetic engineering laboratories, and logging operations. One prominent group is the Earth Liberation Front (ELF), which is suspected of being involved in the arson fire that destroyed an apartment construction project in San Diego in August 2003. The fire caused $20 million in damages and was so intense that it blew out glass panes and melted window shades in residences blocks away. Less than a month later, dozens of sport utility vehicles were vandalized or burned in several simultaneous attacks at auto dealerships in the San Gabriel Valley, east of Los Angeles.

Ecstasy (MDMA). A synthetic methamphetamine compound with both psychedelic and stimulant effects. MDMA Ecstasy was used clinically until 1988, when it was reclassified as a controlled substance. Under the street name Ecstasy, it is most often found in tablet or capsule form.

Edmunds Act. Passed by Congress in 1882, this law provided for the regulation and restriction of Mormon polygamy in Utah. Under the law, Mormons were, to a great degree, excluded from holding local office, and many were indicted and punished for polygamous practices. *See also* polygamy

effigy. The image or representation of a person.

e.g. *Exempli gratia* (Lat., lit.). For the sake of the example.

Egan's Rats. An old-line criminal gang in St. Louis organized by Jellyroll Egan. It eventually became an Irish-organized crime gang that was the forerunner to St. Louis's modern-day Cosa Nostra.

egress. The means of exit from a building or other enclosure.

election law (federal), corrupt practices. The first such law was passed on January 26, 1907, prohibiting corporations from contributing campaign funds in national elections of president, vice president, senators, and representatives. An act passed on March 4, 1909, and effective on January 1, 1910, further prohibited national banks and corporations from contributing campaign funds in connection with any election to any political office.

election law, first. Passed on May 22, 1649, by the General Court in Warwick, RI, it provided that "no one should bring in any votes that he did not receive from the voters' own hands, and that all votes should be filed by the Recorder in the presence of the Assembly." A committee of four freemen was authorized to determine violations of the law and "to examine parties and to present to this court what they find in the case."

electrified fences. Security devices used at prisons that carry several thousand volts and more than the 70 milliamperes necessary to cause death. Such fences are usually placed second in a group of three, and are in use, for example, at 27 California prisons.

electrocution. A method of capital punishment alternative to beheading, hanging, and others, and based on the theory that it is less painful, more certain, and less vulnerable to accident than older methods. It is administered by strapping the convict to a heavy chair wired to conduct an electric current of high voltage to electrodes, one applied to the head and another to the lower leg of the prisoner.

electronic monitoring (EM). EM equipment receives information about monitored offenders and transmits it over telephone lines to a monitoring agency computer. There are two basic types: continuously signaling devices that constantly monitor the offender's presence at a particular location, and programmed contact devices that contact the offender periodically to verify presence. The continuously signaling device has three major parts: a transmitter (attached to the offender), a receiver-dialer, and a central computer. Programmed contact devices use a computer programmed to telephone the offender during the monitored hours, either randomly or at specified times. The first EM program was begun in Palm Beach, FL, in December 1984. All states now use EM programs to supervise offenders. In 2002, 20 companies were manufacturers of EM equipment. For a listing, see *Journal of Offender Monitoring*, published by the Civic Research Institute, P.O. Box 585, Kingston, NJ 08528. *See also* house arrest; net-widening

element of the offense. Any conduct, circumstance, condition, or state of mind which, in combination with other conduct, circumstances, conditions, or states of mind, constitutes an unlawful act. *See also corpus delicti*

eligible for parole. The status of a person who has been committed to the jurisdiction of a federal or state prison system and is usually confined in an institution, and who, by a combination of such factors as sentence effective date, statutory provisions concerning length of sentence to be served in confinement, time credit deductions, and individual sentence, can legally be considered for release from prison to parole.

Elmira Reformatory. The first reformatory built in the United States, it used classification of prisoners, education, vocational training, and indeterminate sentencing.

emancipation. Being freed or set at liberty by (one's) parents, guardian, or master.

embargo. (1) An edict of a government prohibiting the departure or entry of ships; (2) any prohibition imposed by law on commerce.

embezzlement. The misappropriation, misapplication, or illegal disposal of legally entrusted property by the person(s) to whom it was entrusted, with intent to defraud the legal owner or intended beneficiary. In some state codes embezzlement is treated as a form of larceny, that is, theft by taking; in others, as fraud, that is, theft by deception. In Uniform Crime Reports it is described as offenses of "misappropriation or misapplication of money or property entrusted to one's care, custody, or control."

embracery. Any attempt to influence a jury corruptly by promises, persuasions, entreaties, entertainments, and so forth.

embryo. A human fetus in its first three months after conception.

Emergency Programs Center. This office coordinates Department of Justice activities in three main areas: civil disorder, domestic terrorism, and nuclear incidents (criminal aspects only, such as extortion or theft). It also responds to special crises and special security events such as the Olympics. Address: Emergency Programs Center, DOJ, 10th Street & Constitution Avenue, NW, Room 6101, Washington, DC 20530.

emergency strikes. Work stoppages that are especially harmful to the public interest. Most strikes impose an inconvenience on consumers, and they often lead to serious economic damage. But economic harm alone does not create an emergency. Only if a strike seriously jeopardizes the public's safety and well-being does it become an "emergency strike." Such strikes may occur in the public sector, for example, by refusals to work by firemen, policemen, sanitation workers, or nurses, and in the prival sector by food- or fuel-delivery personnel. But strikes by public school teachers or auto and steel workers generally would not constitute emergencies. *See also* strike; job action

eminent domain. The right of a government to take private property for public use. The private owner must be given reasonable compensation for the property, and the government's action must be in accord with the due process of law as outlined in the Fifth and Fourteenth Amendments.

empathy. Broadly defined, the ability to appreciate another's feelings by putting oneself in the other's position and experiencing those feelings. Empathy can be felt by people who have experienced similar situations, who are intimate with the other, or who have special training in interpersonal skills. In empathy training, for example, police officers have posed or role-played as pickets, skid-row inhabitants, prisoners, live-in guests of minority families, and participant-observers in probation or social work.

empirical. Based on experience and observation; based on established facts.

employee assistance programs (EAPs). Originally provided by employers primarily to help workers with alcohol and later drug abuse problems, EAPs now often provide counseling for financial, marital, childrearing, or any other personal or psychological problems that management or human resources feels may be interfering with an individual's productivity. Some EAPs help with career development, weight control, smoking cessation, and a variety of other topics.

empowerment. In business management, giving employees the authority to make decisions within their realm of work operations or scope of employment.

en banc. A French phrase meaning full bench, the term refers to sessions in which the full membership of a court participates. In the U.S., federal districts are single-judge courts; cases in Courts of Appeal are normally heard by a three-judge panel, but important cases may be heard *en banc*; and all cases heard by the Supreme Court are decided *en banc*. The Constitution refers to "one Supreme Court," and the Court has interpreted this to mean that the entire membership should participate as a full bench in each case.

enforcement. An action or process to compel observance of law or the requirements of public policy.

Enforcement Acts. Three laws passed in 1870 and 1871 to enforce the Fourteenth and Fifteenth amendments. The first (May 31, 1870) forbade the use of force, threats of violence, bribery, registration trickery, or economic coercion as tools to prevent eligible voters from exercising their franchise, and set heavy penalties for violations. The law also provided for strict federal supervision of congressional elections, a clause tightened by the second Enforcement Act (February 28, 1871). Congress passed the third act on April 20, 1871, to suppress the Ku Klux Klan and similar Southern organizations. It provided severe penalties for those guilty of terrorist activities and authorized the president to suspend the privilege of the writ of *habeas corpus* and to call out the army and militia to put down such violence.

English common law. The basis of the English common law is immemorial usage and custom, not legislative enactment. For this reason it is often called the "unwritten law." The generic term common law has been well-defined as "those maxims, principles, and forms of judicial proceedings, which have no written law to prescribe or warrant them, but which, founded on the laws of nature and the dictates of reason, have, by usage and custom, become interwoven with the written laws; and, by such incorporation, form a part of the municipal code of each state or nation."

Enoch Arden law. A statute granting permission to remarry without fear of legal penalty to a person whose spouse has been absent, usually for seven successive years (in New York, five), and is presumed dead.

entail. A principle of law originating in medieval England which provided that, upon the death of the owner of an estate, the entire estate was bequeathed to his heir and subsequently to an established line of legatees. The system was imported into the British colonies, where it was met with great resistance because of its undemocratic features. Virginia took the lead in abolishing entail in 1776 and was followed by other states. By the Jeffersonian period, entail had disappeared from the United States.

enterprise. Any individual, partnership, corporation, association, or other legal entity; any union or group of individuals associated in fact although not a legal entity.

entrapment. Inducing an individual to commit a crime he or she did not contemplate, for the sole purpose of instituting a criminal prosecution against the offender. This is a defense to criminal responsibility that arises from improper acts committed against an accused by another, usually an undercover agent. Inducement is the key word; when police encouragement plays upon the weaknesses of innocent persons and beguiles them into committing crimes they normally would not attempt, it can be deemed improper as entrapment and the evidence barred under the exclusionary rule.

entry. Entering a building by going inside; achieved when any part of the body or any instrument or weapon held by hand enters a building.

environmental crimes. Formed in 1983, the environmental crimes section of the Department of Justice's Environment and Natural Resources Division has 30 attorneys. By 1993 the section had convicted more than 500 corporate officers or government employees and won some $245 million in claims. Under 1990 amendments to the Clean Air Act, the government can bring criminal as well as civil suits against violators. The largest civil penalty ($15 million) under the act was assessed against Texas Eastern Natural Gas Pipeline in 1987. The second-largest was an $11.1 million penalty in 1993 against Louisiana-Pacific Corporation for Clean Air Act violations at 14 of its plants.

On March 24, 1989, the tanker *Exxon Valdez* ran aground and spilled more than 10 million gallons of oil into Alaska's Prince William Sound. Two years later, Exxon Corporation settled government claims arising from the nation's worst oil spill by agreeing to pay a record $100 million fine for four environmental crimes and to spend an additional $900 million to complete a cleanup of Alaska's coast. Exxon had already spent $2.5 billion on cleanup efforts. The fine was 20 times larger than the prior record, $5 million paid by Allied Chemical in 1976 for dumping chemicals into Virginia's James River. On May 1, 1991, Pfizer, Inc., paid a $3.1 million fine for dumping pollutants into the Delaware River between 1981 and 1987. This civil settlement covered violations at a Pfizer iron ore plant in Easton, PA, about 50 miles north of Philadelphia. Pfizer admitted no liability in agreeing to the settlement, a record civil penalty under the federal Water Pollution Control Act.

Environmental Protection Agency (EPA). An independent agency in the executive branch, established in 1970 to permit coordinated federal protection of the environment by the systematic control of pollution. Former president George Bush elevated it to cabinet rank in 1990. EPA is responsible for the oversight and enforcement of such legislation as the Clean Air and Water Pollution Control Acts, and for monitoring air and/or water pollution by solid waste, pesticides, radiation, and toxic substances.

ephedrine. Close cousin of the stimulant methamphetamine, this drug is the main ingredient in over-the-counter cold and allergy remedies. "Ripped Fuel" is the trade name of a drug made from the Chinese herb ma huang, which contains 2.5 times more ephedrine than Sudafed and has been used for centuries to treat allergic reactions, including asthma.

episodic criminal. A person who commits a crime under extreme emotional stress, as the single exception to an otherwise lawful life; for example, an individual who kills in the heat of passion.

Equal Employment Opportunity Commission, U.S. (EEOC). The lead federal government civil rights agency, created in 1964 by Congress under Title VII of the Civil Rights Act of 1964. EEOC has primary responsibility for Title VII enforcement. *See also* sexual harassment

equal protection. Guaranteed by Section I of the Fourteenth Amendment, equal protection means that no citizen of any state may be discriminated against by any act or condition. Areas in which equal protection has often been abused include jury selection, voting, use of public facilities, transportation, housing, education, and women's rights. Attempts to eliminate discrimination on the grounds of race, religion, political beliefs, and sex have taken the form of civil rights legislation in Congress and favorable Supreme Court decisions. The equal protection provision, adopted in 1868, was at first interpreted as forbidding a state government to discriminate against any person within its jurisdiction. In 1954 the Supreme Court expanded this interpretation by making it the states' responsibility to remove discriminatory conditions wherever they exist. The Court strengthened its position in 1964 by declaring that, if a state did not do everything it could to eliminate discrimination, action would be enforced by Court decree.

equipment for law enforcement, testing. *See* law enforcement equipment

equitable action. One founded on an equity or in a court of equity; an action arising, not immediately from the contract in suit, but from an equity in favor of a third person, not a party to it, but for whose benefit certain stipulations or promises were made.

equitable right. A right enforceable in a court of equity.

equity jurisdiction. The jurisdiction belonging to a court of equity; all cases, controversies, and occasions which form proper subjects for the exercise of the powers of a chancery court.

equity of redemption. (1) The interest that a mortgagor retains in the property mortgaged. (2) The right of the mortgagor of an estate to redeem the same, after it has been forfeited at law by a breach of the condition of the mortgage, by paying the amount of debt, interests, and costs.

equivocate. (1) To conceal the truth. (2) To use ambiguous words.

ergonomics. The study of human capability and psychology in relation to the employee's working environment and equipment. Also known as human engineering, human factors engineering, or engineering psychology. Ergonomics is based on the premise that tools individuals use and the environment they work in should be matched with their capabilities and limitations, rather than the reverse where people are forced to adapt to the physical environment.

error in fact. In a judicial proceeding, an error not known to the court that may, depending on its seriousness, make a judgment void or voidable.

error in law. An error by the court in applying a law to a particular case on trial, such as allowing evidence that has been established as incompetent, or charging a jury erroneously with respect to the law of the case.

escape. The unlawful departure from official custody of a lawfully confined person. Escapes are either voluntary or negligent. Voluntary escape occurs when the keeper voluntarily concedes to the prisoner any liberty not authorized by law; negligent escape occurs when the prisoner contrives to leave a place of confinement, either by forcing his or her way out or by any other means, without the knowledge or consent of the keeper. Prison breach is the breaking and leaving of confinement. Rescue is the forcible taking of a prisoner from lawful custody by anyone who knows that the person is in custody. The longest recorded escape by a prisoner who was eventually recaptured was that of Leonard T. Fristoe, 77, who escaped from Nevada State Prison on December 15, 1923, and was turned in by his son on November 15, 1969, at Compton, CA. He had 46 years of freedom under the name of Claude R. Willis. He had killed two sheriff's deputies in 1920.

Escobedo, Danny. The Supreme Court's 1964 *Escobedo v. Illinois* decision overturned Escobedo's murder conviction on the grounds that his constitutional rights had been violated when police refused him access to an attorney before he confessed to the slaying of his brother-in-law. The construction of the legal bridge that led to the 1966 *Miranda v. Arizona* decision had its beginning in *Gideon v. Wainwright* (1963), and was completed in *Escobedo*. Within two years of the Supreme Court's decision, Escobedo himself was making regular appearances before Chicago magistrates due to arrests on various charges of disorderly conduct, burglary, weapons violations, and drug sales. On the drug and burglary charges, he was convicted and received concurrent sentences of 22 and 20 years. Subsequent appeals failed to bring about his release.

espionage. The act of covertly obtaining a military secret for a foreign government in time of war or peace. Most countries have organizations engaged in espionage activities even in peacetime. Organizations such as the CIA or the (former Soviet) KGB have been viewed as instruments for subversion, manipulation, violence, and secret intervention in the affairs of other countries.

Espionage Act. A 1917 bill limiting civil liberties, passed as U.S. entry into World War I brought a wave of popular war hysteria and fear. The Espionage Act allowed up to 20 years' imprisonment for disloyalty or opposition to the draft. The Sedition Act of 1918 extended the charges to published writings. These federal laws were copied by the states, with some excesses. Almost 2,000 cases were tried under the acts, but many pardons were granted after war fears had subsided.

espionage, industrial. Agents or paid representatives of one company or industry who obtain secret information about another. This may be accomplished by placing an agent in another company as an undercover employee.

Estes scandal. The rigging of cotton-acreage allotments and contracts for storing government agricultural surpluses by Billie Sol Estes, a Texas manipulator. His indictment in 1962 was followed by the resignation of two federal officials, Republican charges of corruption, and his own conviction for swindling. The conviction was later set aside by the Supreme Court in 1965 because at the preliminary hearing, and to a lesser degree at the trial, the bright lights, numerous strands of television cable, and activities of representatives of news media, which were excessive in relation to the public's interest in the news, had prevented a sober search for the truth and so had denied Estes a fair trial.

estoppel. An impediment or bar that precludes a person from alleging or denying a fact in consequence of his or her own previous act.

ethics. Standards of moral and official conduct; a system of morals. *See also* canons of police ethics; code of ethics

Ethics in Government Act. Established in 1978, this law required financial disclosure by top government officials and applied similar disclosure rules to high-ranking executive and judicial officials as had previously been applied to members of Congress in codes of ethics adopted in 1977.

euthanasia. "The act or practice of painlessly putting to death persons suffering from incurable and distressing disease as an act of mercy." The theory or practice of permitting physicians or other socially authorized persons to give a lethal dose of medicine to persons painfully and incurably ill or hopelessly defective from birth. At present this theory is opposed to the law and the medical code of ethics; but a sample poll has shown that some 46 percent of the people giving opinions favored euthanasia under government supervision. On April 10, 2001, after 30 years of lobbying, the first country to legalize euthanasia was the Netherlands. *See also* dyathanasia; Kevorkian, Dr. Jack; medicide; mercy killing

evidence. All means of giving information to courts trying cases involving factual disputes, including testimony, documents, and physical objects. In the common law system, the law of evidence principally determines when to admit or exclude evidence items, not how much weight to give them. Juries or judges trying facts determine the weight, using their own experience and common sense as guides. Parties' attorneys obtain, select, and present evidence (the adversary system). In constitutional aspects of criminal cases, courts have in recent years greatly restricted evidence admissibility and created a criminal law revolution, which is now beginning to recede. In other respects, the trend is toward broader admissibility, with greater reliance on trial judges' discretion.

Evidence Terms. Direct evidence establishes a fact without the need for inferences or presumptions. *Circumstantial* evidence proves facts that may support an inference or presumption of the disputed fact. *Prima facie* evidence suffices to prove a fact until there is rebuttal evidence. *Relevancy.* Only relevant evidence, which logically tends to prove or disprove a disputed fact, may be admitted. Many exclusionary rules may bar even relevant evidence, however. *Competency.* At one time, parties could not testify in their own lawsuits, nor could witnesses with direct interests in the case; neither convicted felons nor spouses could testify for or against each other in civil or criminal cases. Statutes have since abolished all but one of these restrictions—the one barring survivors, and persons interested in the outcome, from testifying to personal transactions or communications with someone deceased when suing his or her estate. Some variant states either accept survivors' testimony (but require corroboration to support judgments) or accept both survivors' testimony and decedents' written or oral statements on the subject. *Hearsay.* Witnesses ordinarily give oral testimony telling what they have themselves seen, heard, or done. Witnesses' evidence of third parties' statements about things seen, heard, or done are hearsay if used to prove those facts. Documents containing such statements are also hearsay. Such evidence is ordinarily excluded, because the declarants were usually not under oath and not cross-examinable. If all hearsay were barred absolutely, however, needed and trustworthy evidence of persons unavailable as witnesses would often be completely lost; hence, numerous hearsay exceptions have developed. *Opinions.* Witnesses ordinarily testify to facts; opinions or conclusions are excluded. The fact-triers should form opinions and conclusions, but if special training or experience is needed for a reliable opinion (for example on scientific or technical subjects), experts' opinions are admissible if they can assist fact-triers. *Character.* Those accused in criminal cases may prove their good character to imply unlikelihood of their having committed the crime charged. If they do so, prosecutions may afterward show their bad character. In civil and criminal cases, witnesses' credibility may be attacked by proving their bad character for truthfulness or honesty or their prior criminal conviction; only subsequently may their good character be shown. The general rule in criminal cases is that proof of other crimes by the accused should not be received, but many exceptions allow admission when relevant to show more than simply the defendant's criminality. *Privilege.* Though excluding relevant evidence thereby, the law protects against compelled disclosure of confidential communications between spouses, attorney and client, and frequently between physician and patient or clergy and penitent. Similar privileges exist for state secrets, government informants, and, infrequently, accountants and journalists. *Writings.* Documents are inadmissible without proof or concession of genuineness (authentication). All exclusionary evidence rules and some special doctrines apply to documents. The best-evidence rule demands that original documents prove their own contents; secondary evidence (copies or testimony) is inadmissible unless the original's unavailability is properly explained. *Scientific Evidence.* Expanding scientific knowledge and techniques keep enlarging this field. It now includes fingerprints, testing of questioned documents, ballistics, blood grouping, drunkenness tests, carbon dating, radar, lie detection, radiation recordings, medicine, engineering, physics, chemistry, and so on. *Judicial Notice.* Courts consider evidence unnecessary to establish certain obvious facts, like weights-and-measures tables or historical dates. State courts also judicially notice the federal and their own constitutions, statutes, and laws but not those of sister states or foreign countries (except as widely adopted statutes permit). Federal courts judicially notice federal and state provisions. *Burden of Proof.* In trials, parties having the burden of proof lose their cases unless, on their whole claim or defense, they persuade the fact-triers that the facts they allege are true. Parties having the burden of producing evidence must produce some, or additional, evidence supporting their allegations on controverted facts or else have those allegations determined adversely. The burden of proof is fixed at the trial's start and continues unchanged, but the burden of evidence may shift between parties on different matters during trial. *See also* International Association for Property and Evidence, Inc.

evidence aliunde. *See* extraneous evidence

evidence, associative. The establishment of a link between the accused and the crime scene by information obtained from physical evidence found at the crime scene and physical evidence found on the accused or in places traceable to him or her.

evidence, corroborating. Evidence that strengthens or supports other evidence.

evidence, derivative. *See* derivative evidence

evidence given in former proceeding. This is admissible, for the purpose of proving statements made in a later stage of the same proceeding, under the following circumstances: when the witness (a) is dead; (b) is insane; (c) is out of the jurisdiction; (d) cannot be found within the jurisdiction; and (e) could have been, or was, cross-examined earlier by the person against whom the evidence is to be given.

evidence, material. Material evidence must relate to the facts at issue and must also be important enough to warrant its use. Materiality of evidence describes its importance.

Evidence Photographers International Council. Founded in 1967. Publishes *Journal of Evidence Photography* semiannually. Address: 600 Main Street, Honesdale, PA 18431.

evidence, prejudicial. Evidence that is so shocking to the senses of jurors that it may unduly sway their attitude toward one of the parties in a criminal trial; inflammatory evidence.

evidence rule, best. *See* best evidence rule

evidence wrongfully obtained. The fact that articles or admissions were wrongfully obtained from the defendant does not render them inadmissible as evidence.

evidentiary items. Items connected with a crime, not including contraband, profits from, or weapons or other instruments used in, the crime. *See also* mere evidence

examination. The preliminary hearing before the magistrate of the evidence against a person accused of a crime.

examination; cross-examination. Witnesses in open court must first be directly examined by the party that called them; they may then be cross-examined and then reexamined. Both examination and cross-examination must relate to facts at issue or relevant to the case, and in most states the cross-examination must be confined to the facts to which the witness testified on his or her direct examination. The reexamination must be directed to the explanation of matters referred to in cross-examination, and, if new matter is, by permission of court, introduced in reexamination, the opposing party may further cross-examine on the new matter.

examining trial. *See* preliminary hearing

exception. Formal notification to the court during a trial that one party objects to or has reservations about the court's ruling on a request or objection made by the other party to the suit.

exclusionary rule. Legal prohibitions against government prosecution using evidence illegally obtained, such as by illegal search and seizure. Prior the the 1961 *Mapp v. Ohio* decision, several states, by law, had exclusionary rules that precluded the use of such evidence. After *Mapp*, all states were prohibited from its use.

exculpate. To exonerate; to clear of blame or guilt; to prove innocent.

ex delicto (Lat., lit.). From the crime.

execution. (1) A judicial writ directing an officer to carry out the judgment of a court of law. (2) Enforcement of a judgment, especially of the death penalty, following conviction of a capital crime and sentence by a court of law. (3) Rendering valid a legal document by signing and delivering it. *See also* punishment, capital

execution and return of warrant. A search warrant is executed by limiting the search and the authority of the officer in such search named to conduct it, as to the place to be searched and the time and manner of the execution of the warrant; hence, a warrant cannot be extended beyond the privileges granted in its issuance.

execution, methods. *Electrocution*: The prisoner is strapped into a wooden chair and electrodes are attached to the individual's calf and head. A sponge rests on the prisoner's shaved head, beneath a leather and metal headset strapped and bolted into place. Soaked in liquid, the sponge conveys the 2,000 volts and 14 amps of current into the prisoner's skull. Electric current passes through the electrodes in a cycle designed to interrupt the heart's normal electrical pattern and cause it to stop beating, Blood circulation stops, consciousness is lost brain damage is massive, and death results in about four minutes. States in use: AL, CT, FL GA, ID, KY, LA, NB, OH, PA, SC, TN, VA. Some states offer alternatives. *Gas*: The prisoner is strapped into one of two seats in the 7 ½-foot-wide chamber (e.g., San Quentin Prison, CA). Beneath each chair is an empty ceramic reservoir. Suspended above the reservoirs are

What Methods of Execution are Used by the Various States?			
Alabama[b]	Idaho[a,e]	Nebraska[b]	Pennsylvania[a]
Arizona[a,c]	Illinois[a]	Nevada[a]	South Carolina[a]
Arkansas[a,b]	Indiana[a]	New Hampshire[a]	South Dakota[a]
California[a]	Kentucky[a,b]	New Jersey[a]	Tennessee[a,b]
Colorado[a]	Louisiana[a]	New Mexico[a]	Texas[a]
Connecticut[a]	Maryland[a,c]	North Carolina[a,c]	Utah[a,e]
Delaware[a,d]	Mississippi[a]	Ohio[a,b]	Virginia[a,b]
Florida[b]	Missouri[a]	Oklahoma[a]	Washington[a,d]
Georgia[b]	Montana[a,d]	Oregon[a]	Wyoming[a]

Note: Federal executions are to be carried out according to the method of the State in which performed.

a. Lethal Injection
b. Electrocution
c. Lethal gas
d. Hanging
e. Firing Squad

sodium cyanide granules wrapped in foot-square pieces of cheesecloth. At the warden's signal, a valve is turned, releasing distilled water and sulfuric acid into the reservoirs. At a second signal, a switch is thrown and the cyanide granules are lowered into the acid. The prisoner inhales the rising lethal gas. Damaging all tissue it contacts, the gas reaches the lungs. In the lungs, blood is passing through capillaries surrounding the alveoli—tiny, grape-like structures where gas exchange takes place. Normally, the red blood cells drop off carbon dioxide here and pick up oxygen. But cyanide gas binds more readily to blood cells than does oxygen. So the cells travel away to the body's tissues carrying cyanide, rather than their essential cargo of oxygen. As brain tissues begin to die from lack of oxygen and the cyanide's toxicity, the prisoner loses consciousness. Several minutes later, the heartbeat stops. Almost immediately breathing fails and the prisoner dies. The reservoirs are then drained. Caustic soda and water are flushed through the pipes and reservoirs. An exhaust fan sucks the gas up a copper pipe that rises 20 feet above the prison roof. In about 30 minutes, the chamber is opened and the body is removed. States using gas: AZ, CA, MD, MS, NC. *Hanging*: The prisoner stands atop a trap door and a rope is placed around his or her neck. A formula based on the prisoner's weight and height determines the distance of the drop and the rope's thickness. The trap door opens and the prisoner falls. The rope tightens on the person's throat, often breaking the neck and causing paralysis. Simultaneously, the rope's pressure prevents breathing, causing oxygen deprivation and death in about four minutes. States in use: MO, NH, WA. *Lethal Injection*: The prisoner is strapped to a gurney (table) and a combination of drugs is dripped from a bottle into veins in both arms. One drug, potassium, interferes with the heart's normal electrical pattern and makes it stop beating. Another drug paralyzes the body's muscles and makes breathing stop. The resultant oxygen loss causes brain damage and death results in about four minutes. States in use: AZ, CA (which in 1992 began offering prisoners a choice between gas and injection), CO, DE, ID, IL, MO, NV, NJ, NM, NC, OK, OR, SD, TX, UT, WA, WY *Shooting*: Gary Gilmore's 1977 execution in Utah is the only example of death by firing squad in recent history. Of the 37 federal prisoners executed since 1927, 12 were executed by hanging, 15 by electrocution, and 9 by lethal gas. Timothy McVeigh (convicted of the April 1995 bombings of the Federal Building in Oklahoma City), was executed by lethal injection in 2001. The last federal prisoner to be executed was Louis Jones, by lethal injection in 2003.

execution of a warrant. (a) A warrant can only be executed by the officer to whom it is directed, either by name or by description of his or her office; (b) it cannot confer authority to execute it on one officer, where a statute provides for its execution by another; (c) unless a statute so allows, it cannot be executed outside the jurisdiction of the issuing magistrate or court; (d) where the warrant is necessary, it must be in the possession of the officer at the time of search or arrest; and (e) it must be returned after the search or arrest.

executive branch. The part of the government that applies the law. In a separation of powers system, there is an attempt to distinguish the functions of rule initiation, rule application, and rule interpretation, and to assign the primary responsibility for each function to the legislative, executive, and judicial branches respectively, although there is much sharing of functions among branches. Law enforcement is under the executive branch of government.

executive clemency. Authority and power given to certain executive authorities of the government, such as a governor, to set aside a court judgment of sentence. This power is granted by law, usually under provisions of the Constitution.

executive order. A presidential directive that becomes law. Executive orders issued by the president or by administrative agencies must all be published in the *Federal Register*.

executive privilege. An accepted practice that prevents congressional committees from interrogating executive officials without the express consent of the president. A reference case is *United States v. Nixon*.

executor (m.), executrix (f.). An individual appointed in a will to carry out its provisions.

executory process. Proceedings in which, by previous agreement of the parties involved, mortgaged property may be seized and sold without going through the procedure of citing the mortgage debtor into court and obtaining a judgment against him or her. It is an expeditious way of foreclosure and sale of property on which a mortgage or privilege exists.

exemplar. A known specimen of evidence to be used by experts for comparison with other (questioned) evidence.

Exemplary Rehabilitation Certificates. Awarded by the Secretary of Labor to servicemen separated from the armed forces under conditions other than honorable, if it is established that they have rehabilitated themselves. This certificate provides tangible evidence of rehabilitation since discharge, to present to a prospective employer. The certificate does not in any way change the nature of original discharge or alter ex-servicemen's eligibility for veterans benefits. For further information about this procedure, contact: Assistant to the Director for Field Operations, Veterans Employment Service, Employment and Training Administration, Department of Labor, Room 8400, 100 Constitution Avenue, NW, Washington, DC 20212.

ex facie (Lat., lit. "from the face"). Apparently; evidently. A term applied to what appears on the face of a writing.

exhibit. An item of evidence; an item obtained in an investigation, particularly one that is to be used as evidence; a physical object offered in evidence during a trial.

exhibitionist. A person who has a compulsion to show his or her genitals or other body parts in inappropriate circumstances, usually to members of the opposite sex.

exhumation. Disinterment; removing from the earth something that has been buried, especially a human corpse.

exitus. Death.

ex officio (Lat.). By virtue of the office.

exonerate. To prove not guilty; to acquit; to clear of blame or fault.

exonerate bail. To release a surety on a bail bond.

ex parte. A hearing or examination in the presence of only one of the parties to a case, such as a writ of *habeas corpus*.

expatriation. The act of voluntarily leaving, or abandoning allegiance to, one's country.

expert testimony. When there is a question on an aspect of science or other specialized fields, the opinions on that point of persons particularly skilled in that field may be given in court. Expert testimony can be offered on any subject that requires a course of special study or experience in order to form an opinion. The opinions of experts on matters of common knowledge are not admissible, for the jury is as able to judge such facts as experts would be. Where witnesses have expertise in a trade or science beyond that of the average person, they may give their opinions, so that the jury may have this knowledge in arriving at a verdict.

expiation. A theory of the purpose of punishment for crime based originally upon the belief that crime aroused the anger of the gods against the whole community, and that the only way to mollify that anger was to destroy the offender. More recently, the term has been widened in its meaning to include punishing the offender. Used in this way, expiation is virtually synonymous with retribution.

expiration of sentence. The termination of the period of time during which an offender has been required to be under the jurisdiction of a state prison or parole agency as the penalty for an offense.

exploitation. Unequal social relations resulting in the acquisition of a valued commodity by a dominant individual or group. For example, labor, sexual favors, or natural resources have been exploited by historically powerful elites. In the past, radicals have attributed exploitive tendencies to religious institutions, the patriarchal family, economic systems, and racist institutions. The term is often used by those individuals who no longer accept the legitimacy of their inferior status in society.

explosive bullet. A bullet that contains an explosive that is detonated on contact with its target or via a time fuse. Such bullets were banned for small arms by international agreement in 1868.

explosive D. So named from the initial of Col. B.W. Dunn, its inventor, this explosive is also called dunnite. It consists mainly of ammonium picrate and is used in some armor-piercing projectiles because of its comparative insensitivity to shock and friction.

explosive-ordnance disposal unit. Personnel with special training and equipment who render explosive ordnance (such as bombs, mines, projectiles, and booby traps) safe, make intelligence reports on such ordnance, and supervise its safe removal.

explosives classifications. Established by the U.S. Dept. of Transportation: (1) Class A explosives are materials that possess a detonating hazard (such as dynamite, nitroglycerin, picric acid, lead azide, fulminate of mercury, black powder, blasting caps, and detonating primers); (2) Class B explosives are materials that possess a flammable hazard (such as propellant explosives); and (3) Class C explosives are materials that contain restricted quantities of Class A and/or B explosives.

ex post facto **law**. A law retroactively making illegal a certain behavior, increasing punishment for it, or removing lawful protection from it. A basic principle recognized by civilized countries is that of *nulla poena sine lege* (Lat., no punishment without law). Article I of the Constitution forbids Congress and the states to pass any ex post facto law. The Supreme Court used this prohibition to strike down the test-oath laws after the Civil War; civil cases are not, however, affected by this protection.

expropriation. Action by the state, under its sovereign power, to take over property for the use of the people (public use). *See also* eminent domain

expunge. To physically destroy information in files, computers, or other depositories. In juvenile courts, a case can be expunged or erased from the record by a plaintiff or attorney, based on a court order, often because the offender has met certain conditions imposed as a result of the offense. In Massachusetts, for example, an individual who is found to possess marijuana in a first offense may, if found guilty, have the finding continued for six months. If he or she commits no further offenses during that period, the case is brought forward and the record expunged.

ex rel (Lat., lit. "by or on the information of"). In titles of cases, it designates the individual for whom the government or public official is acting.

extenuating circumstances. Particular characteristics of an offender, situation, or offense that partially or entirely excuse the offender or serve to reduce the gravity of the act.

exterior ballistics. The branch of ballistics that deals with the motion of a projectile while in flight.

extortion. Unlawfully obtaining or attempting to obtain something of value from another by compelling the other person to deliver it by the threat of eventual physical injury or other harm to that person, his or her property, or a third person. Extortion differs from robbery in that in robbery, there is an immediate confrontation between offender and victim, and the threatened injury is physical and imminent. Extortion is usually categorized as a type of theft offense in penal codes. Blackmail is the popular name for the kind of extortion where the threat is not physical but relates to exposing some secret true or alleged fact that would do harm to a person's circumstances or damage his or her reputation.

extortion by means of telephone. An act passed by Congress on May 18, 1934, applied the powers of the federal government, under the commerce clause of the Constitution, to extortion by means of telephone, telegraph, radio, oral message, or otherwise.

extradition. The surrender, by one state to another, of an individual accused or convicted of an offense in the second state. (1) Interstate extradition. The Constitution, several acts of Congress, and the statutes of several states provide that a person charged with a crime in one state who flees from that state into another may be returned to the former. In order to be extradited the person: (a) must be judicially charged with a crime in the demanding state; (b) must not be charged with a crime against the state to which he or she has fled; and (c) must have been in the demanding state in order to have "fled from justice." (2) International extradition. By treaties between the United States and most foreign countries, provision is made for the extradition of fugitives from justice in specified cases. The states cannot act in this matter.

extrajudicial. Out of the ordinary course of law. For example, an extrajudicial statement is one made outside of court.

extralegal. Outside or beyond the scope of law.

extraneous. Not germane or relevant to the matter at hand.

extraneous evidence. In reference to any document, a type of evidence that is not derived from anything in the document itself.

extraterritorial operation, of laws. In general, the laws of a country are not effective beyond its territorial limits, on the theory that crime is essentially local and is determined by the law that defines or prohibits it. However, mere physical presence, citizenship, or residence within a state is not always essential to rendering someone subject to its laws and its prosecution. Among the exceptions to the general rule are cases in which a person, being at the time in one state or country, commits a crime that takes effect in another.

extremist group. A group or organization, the avowed purpose of which is to bring about some change in government functions and in society by radical, disorderly, and/or violent methods. Guiding some extremists is *The Turner Diaries*, a fictional plan to finance a racial revolution through robberies, counterfeiting, and other crimes. The Justice Department prosecuted 36 persons for racial violence in 1984, the highest total since 1979. Twenty-nine states have passed laws specifically focused on racial vandalism and intimidation.

extrinsic evidence. External evidence; facts other than those contained in the body of an agreement, document, or other object.

F

facsimile. An exact copy.

fact. A thing done; an actual occurrence.

fact finder (trier of fact). The individual or group with the obligation and authority to determine the facts (as distinct from the law) in a case. In a jury trial, the jury is the fact finder and is charged with accepting the law as given to it by the judge.

fact-finding. A form of third-party intervention in collective bargaining impasses. In public interest disputes, fact-finding by a government-designated board may cut through claims and allegations to the facts. The results of fact-finding may provide an incentive for the parties to settle. *See also* collective bargaining

fair comment. A term used in libel cases, pertaining to statements made by a writer in an honest belief of their truth, although they in fact are not true.

Fair Housing and Equal Credit Opportunity. Title VIII of the Civil Rights Act of 1968 is designed to ensure freedom from discrimination in the sale, rental, and financing of housing. A private suit alleging discrimination may be filed in the appropriate federal or state court. The Attorney General is authorized to bring civil actions in federal courts when there is reasonable cause to believe that any person or group of persons is engaged in a pattern or practice of discrimination or any group has been denied equal rights in a case of general public importance. The Equal Credit Opportunity Act is designed to prohibit discrimination

in all aspects of credit transactions. Persons who believe they are victims of such discrimination may file complaints with one of the appropriate federal regulatory agencies or may bring the information to the attention of the Attorney General. In addition, an aggrieved person may institute suit in federal court. For further information, contact: Chief, General Litigation Section, Civil Rights Division, DOJ, Washington, DC 20530.

fair trade laws. State laws passed under the authorization of the Miller-Tydings Act for the purpose of allowing manufacturers of branded products to establish minimum resale prices.

fait accompli. (Fr.). An action that is regarded as completed and therefore not subject to further negotiation.

false arrest. Unlawful physical restraint of an individual's liberty; such restrictions may occur in prisons, jails, or other maximum security facilities.

False Claims Act. This federal law traces its roots to the Civil War, but it was little used until 1986, when it was strengthened to attract more whistle-blowers, by enabling them to share up to 30 percent of any damage claim paid to the government. By 1993 an estimated $400 million had been recovered by the government on whistle-blower suits since the law was modified.

false impersonation. Also called personation. To impersonate another falsely and to demand or obtain something of value for oneself or someone else is a federal and state violation.

false imprisonment. (1) Detention under false or assumed authority or because of a miscarriage of judicial procedure. (2) Any unlawful restraint of a person's liberty. Isadore Zimmerman (1917–1983) of New York spent 24 years in prison before his conviction for murdering a police officer was overturned because of new evidence. On his release at age 66, he was awarded $1 million, which is equivalent to $42,000 for each year he spent in prison. But, after legal fees and expenses, he ended up with only 60 percent of the money. He decided not to appeal the award, and died a little more than a year later.

false pretenses. False representations and/or statements made with fraudulent design to obtain money, goods, wares, or merchandise with intent to defraud. The distinction between larceny and false pretenses is that in larceny, the owner of something has no intention to part with it, while in false pretenses, the owner does intend to part with the property, but it is obtained from him or her by fraud.

Families with Service Needs. A designation proposed by the Task Force on Juvenile Justice and Delinquency Prevention, in which both status offenders and their families would come under the authority and jurisdiction of the juvenile court.

fascism. An autocratic form of centralized government that represses opposition and rigidly controls finance, commerce, and industry. It can become a dictatorship.

FBI Academy. Founded in 1935, the academy offers programs that include new agents' training; in-service programs for field agents; training for mid-level and senior police administrators; National Executive Institute for top police executives; Senior Executive Program for top FBI executives; and Executive Development Institute for FBI mid-level managers. Custom-designed courses are also available. In conjunction with the Kansas City Police Department, the academy operates the Law Enforcement Satellite Training Network, which annually broadcasts six live teleconferences to an estimated audience of 20,000 officers. The Hostage Rescue Team is also based at the academy. It is a constant-readiness team that can be deployed within four hours to any location in the U.S. or its territories. Address: FBI Academy, Quantico, VA 22135.

FBI field training. Courses available from FBI instructors range from basic recruit training to specialized instruction in such areas as fingerprinting, legal topics, police-community relations, hostage negotiation, white-collar crime, organized crime, computer fraud, management techniques, and so

forth. FBI training assistance is available in complete programs of instruction or as supplemental courses to already-existing, local police training sessions. For further information, contact: Director, FBI, DOJ, Washington, DC 20535.

FBI Laboratory. Facilities are available to duly constituted municipal, county, state, and federal law enforcment agencies in the U.S. and its territorial possessions. Submitted evidence is examined, and the laboratory also furnishes the experts necessary to testify in connection with the results of these examinations. These examinations are made only if the evidence is connected with an official investigation of a criminal matter (for federal agencies, both criminal and civil matters) and if the laboratory report will be used only for official purposes related to the investigation or a subsequent prosecution. The FBI will not accept cases from other crime laboratories that have the capability of conducting the requested examinations. This laboratory is divided into three major sections: Document Section—conducts scientific examinations of all documents submitted as physical evidence as well as shoeprint, tire-tread, and other sophisticated image examinations; Scientific Analysis Section—conducts highly specialized examinations involving chemistry and related matters and has primary responsibility for physical- and biological-science research and forensic-science training; and Special Projects Section—provides visual aids such as demonstrative evidence, 2-dimensional graphics, and 3-dimensional models used in the prosecution of FBI cases. Address: FBI, Laboratory Division, Room 3090, DOJ, Washington, DC 20535.

FBI museum. Features weapons displays, exhibits, and extensive photographic gallery of criminal notables; located within FBI headquarters, Washington, DC, at 9th Street and Pennsylvania Ave.

feasance. A doing; the doing of an act; a performance. *See also* malfeasance; misfeasance; nonfeasance

Administrative review procedures

U.S cases
Includes—
- contracts
- torts
- civil rights
- benefit appeals
- Social Security cases

Handled by—
- Federal agencies with
  —administrative hearing authority
  —direct litigating authority
- U.S. Department of Justice (5 civil litigating divisions; 94 U.S. Attorneys Offices)

Private cases
Diversity of Jurisdiction Cases
Includes—
- torts
- contracts
Federal law cases
Includes—
- maritime
- patents

Handled by—
- private attorneys

Federal agencies	case settled ↑ → Agency reconsideration → case settled ↑ Administrative hearing → case settled ↑ Agency appeal
Department of Justice	
Private attorneys	Case screening → Case filing and pleadings • complaint • answer • counterclaim → Pretrial activities • discovery • motions • pretrial conference

case settled   case settled   case settled

Litigation procedures

Administrative review procedures
- Federal agency administrative procedures are determined by the Administrative Procedure Act or other statues.
- Hearing officials may be administrative law judges (ALJ's) or other statutorily designated officials.
- DOJ litigation divisions and U.S. Attorneys may become involved where case is appealed to District or Appeals Court.
- Appeals of administrative law judges' decisions to the District Court may be "on the record" or de novo, depending upon the relevant statutes.

Litigation procedures
- U.S. actions may be prosecuted o fended by five DOJ litigating divis (civil, tax, antitrust, civil right, lan U.S. Attorneys, any Federal agenc jointly by a Federal agency and a litigating division.

federal administrative review procedures. *See* chart on pages 143–144.

Federal Alcohol Control Board. An agency created by Congress in 1933 for the purpose of regulating the branding and grading of alcoholic beverages and for dealing generally with the new problems of interstate liquor traffic raised by the Twenty-first Amendment. It was authorized to establish proper business standards for the liquor industry and to foster fair trade methods in the interests of producers and consumers. The agency was later reorganized into the Federal Alcohol Administration.

Federal Aviation Act. A law enacted by Congress in 1968. Paragraph 902 of the act makes it a crime for persons with a concealed weapon to board an aircraft operated by an air carrier. Many law enforcement officers, (such as municipal, state, and federal) are exempted.

Federal Aviation Administration. Formerly the Federal Aviation Agency, it is an arm of the U.S. Department of Transportation. Its functions are to issue and enforce safety regulations of air personnel as well as to manufacture and operate aircraft and air-navigation facilities.

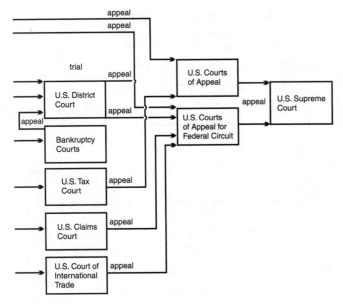

Adjudicative resources
- 1,121 Administrative law judges
- 391,000 cases

Trial Courts
- U.S. District Courts
  94 courts
  575 judges
  467 magistrates
  (including 177 part-time)
  254,828 civil cases
  91,830 U.S. cases
  162,998 private cases
- Bankruptcy Courts
  242 judges
  477,856 cases
- U.S.Tax Court
  28 judges
  15 special trial judges
  48,398 cases
- U.S. Claims Court
  16 judges
  813 cases
- U.S. Court of International Trade
  9 judges
  1,828 cases

Appeals Court
- U.S. Court of Appeals
  12 courts
  156 judges
  24,291 cases
- U.S. Court of Appeals for Federal Circuit
  12 judges 1,163 civil cases
- U.S. Supreme Court
  9 justices
  4,413 cases

Data sources
- Data on the U.S. District Courts, Bankruptcy Courts, and U.S. Courts of Appeal were obtained from the Administrative Office of the U.S. Courts and are for the year ending June 30, 1986.
- Data on the U.S. Tax Court, U.S. Claims Court, and the U.S. Court of International Trade were obtained from the statistical offices of those courts and are for the year ending September 30, 1986.
- Data on the U.S. Supreme Court were obtained from that court and are for the term ending in 1986. The figure is for cases filed and does not include carry-over cases.

- Data on the number of administrative law judges were obtained in August 1986 from the U.S. Office of Personnel Management. Data on the number of administrative law hearings were obtained from the Administrative Conference of the United States. The Administrative Conference conducted a survey of such hearings, and findings are reported in Lubbers, J., "Federal Agency Adjudications," *Federal Bar News and Journal*, vol. 31 (November 1984). The survey findings are the most current available data on administrative law caseloads and apply only to hearings conducted pursuant to the Administrative Procedure Act.

Federal Bureau of Investigation. Established in 1908, the FBI is the investigative arm of the Department of Justice. It investigates all violations of federal law except those specifically assigned to some other agency by legislative action (counterfeiting and internal revenue, postal, and customs violations). This agency is primarily concerned with enforcement of the laws that involve interstate crimes, such as transportation of stolen vehicles across state lines (the Dyer Act) or flight from one state to another to avoid prosecution for a felony (the Fugitive Felon Act); crimes involving federal institutions, such as robbery of a federally insured bank (the National Bank Robbery Act); or crimes on federal property (such as a military reservation). The powers of the FBI are ever-expanding as Congress enacts additional federal criminal laws, such as the National Stolen Property Act (dealing with interstate shipment of stolen goods), the Federal Kidnapping Act, the Hobbs Act (extortion), the White Slavery Act (prostitution), and federal interstate gambling and civil rights laws. The types of crimes under FBI jurisdiction grew from 229 in 1982 to 281 in 1992, including carjackings, drugs, hate crimes, and health care fraud. The number of agents grew from 7,857 in 1980 to 10,366 in 1993, and the FBI's budget grew from $622 million in 1980 to $2 billion in 1993. The FBI's Identification Division houses the largest fingerprint repository in the world.

Federal Bureau of Prisons, history of During the first century of American independence, there were virtually no federal prison facilities. Most federal offenders were incarcerated in state prisons and county jails. After the Civil War, the federal inmate population began to rise. Congress enacted legislation in 1891 to construct three federal penitentiaries. In the 1920s, a women's reformatory, a youth facility, and a detention center were added to the federal system. By the late 1920s, new federal laws such as the Volstead Act (Prohibition) had caused severe overcrowding in the few existing facilities. A special committee of the House of Representatives on federal penal and reformatory institutions met in January 1929, responding to overcrowding, political concerns, and lax management. On May 14, 1930, President Herbert Hoover signed legislation establishing the Federal Bureau of Prisons within the Department of Justice to manage and regulate all federal prisons, authorized the building of new prisons, created a new Board of Parole, and provided prisoner medical treatment by the U.S. Public Health Service. The first director of the Bureau of Prisons was Sanford Bates. The bureau built or acquired several new facilities, ranging from minimum security prison camps, to the maximum security penitentiary at Alcatraz, to a large hospital for federal prisoners in Springfield, MO. In 1934 the Federal Prisons Industries, Inc. (UNICOR) was established. The bureau works closely with the National Institute of Corrections, founded in 1974 to provide advisory and technical support to state and local agencies. In 1992 the bureau supported a prison population of 63,483, served by 23,000 staff members at 68 institutions, with 27 more facilities under construction. *See also* Bates, Sanford

Federal Communications Commission. An independent federal agency that regulates interstate communications and their facilities, including telephone, telegraph, cable, radio, and television.

Federal Deposit Insurance Corporation. A federally created corporation established under the Banking Act of 1933 to provide insurance for deposits in member banks. Banks insured by FDIC are under federal jurisdiction where crimes are involved related to banking. Thus such crimes as bank robbery, embezzlement, and theft are federal criminal violations.

Federal Drugs, Alcohol and Crime Clearinghouse Network. A single point of contact for all related information. Telephone: (800) 788-2800.

Federal Emergency Management Agency. FEMA founded the Arson Resource Center in 1983 to "inform the public about arson" and offer reference service to the general public on arson and related areas of interest. FEMA also founded the National Emergency Training Center Learning Resource Center in 1976. The center's goal is to support the staff and student activities of the National Emergency Training Center. Major subject areas are fire-related fields, management, and education. Address: 16825 South Seton Avenue, Emmitsburg, MD 21727. FEMA's headquarters is at 500 C Street, SW, Washington, DC 20472.

Federal Firearms Act. A law of Congress, enacted June 30, 1938, which forbids any unlicensed person to ship firearms or ammunition in interstate commerce and subjects such shipments to numerous restrictions.

Federal Judicial Center. Investigative organization empowered by Congress to improve the administration of the court system and to develop judicial training programs. The center, located in Washington, DC, was created in 1967 after much public debate about crowded and poorly managed court calendars.

Federal Kidnapping Law. *See* kidnapping; Lindbergh Law

Federal Law Enforcement Training Center. This interagency facility was established in 1970 under the Department of the Treasury. The main center is a 1,500-acre site near Brunswick, GA. Other facilities are located in Artesia, NM, and Charleston, SC. Organization provides basic police and criminal-investigator training for officers and agents of the participating federal organizations, as well as advanced and specialized training that is common to two or more organizations. Its programs include: criminal investigation programs and police programs, criminology skills, investigative techniques, legal courses, communications skills, ethics, and firearms training. Participating agencies include: the Forest Service, National General Service Administration, U.S. Department of Housing and Urban Development, National Park Service, and U.S. Customs Service. Address: Federal Law Enforcement Training Center, Department of the Treasury, Glynco Facility, Brunswick, GA 31524.

federal litigation procedures. *See* chart on pages 143–144.

Federal Motor Vehicle Safety Standards. Mandatory vehicle performance, design features, and objectives established by the National Highway Traffic Safety Administration of the Department of Transportation to enhance vehicle and occupant safety.

Federal Prison Industries, Inc. UNICOR is the trade name under which Federal Prison Industries does most of its business. Its mission is to employ and train federal inmates through a diversified program providing products and services exclusively to other federal agencies. It is a public corporation with six directors, operating under the Department of Justice. Address: Federal Prison Industries, DOJ, 320 1st Street, NW, Room 654, Washington, DC 20534.

Federal Programs Litigation. This office handles litigation against federal agencies, cabinet officers, and other officials. It handles enforcement and litigation aimed at remedying statutory or regulatory violations, the defense of employment policies and personnel actions, and litigation relating to the disposition and availability of government records. Address: Federal Programs Branch, Civil Division, DOJ, 10th Street & Constitution Avenue, NW, Washington, DC 20530.

federal question. Any case with a major issue involving the Constitution or statutes. The jurisdiction of the federal courts is partly controlled by the existence of a federal question.

Federal Register. A U.S. government publication that prints presidential proclamations, reorganization plans, and executive orders. Notices of proposed rules and regulations and administrative orders of public agencies are also published in the *Register*: The Federal Register Act of 1935 requires the publication of presidential proclamations, and the Administrative Procedure Act of 1946 requires compliance by public agencies. Because of the continuing increase in subject matter, the *Federal Register* is an extremely important and widely read publication. Before its existence, citizens and business interests had no way of knowing what new rules applied to them. The publication gives all interested parties the opportunity to be heard prior to the enforcement of any rules and regulations. It is published five times a week, and the documents are codified in the Code of Federal Regulations. Available through the U.S. Government Printing Offices.

Federal Reserve banknotes. The serial numbers on all U.S. currency, also called Federal Reserve banknotes, are preceded by a letter designating which one of the 12 Federal Reserve districts issued the bill.

District	Letter	City
1	A	Boston
2	B	New York
3	C	Philadelphia
4	D	Cleveland
5	E	Richmond
6	F	Atlanta
7	G	Chicago
8	H	St. Louis
9	I	Minneapolis
10	J	Kansas City
11	K	Dallas
12	L	San Francisco

federal security level designations. Level 1—minimum security; Levels 2, 3, 4—medium security; Levels 5, 6—maximum security.

Federal Tort Claims Act. Title IV of the Legislative Reorganization Act of 1946. Under its provisions the federal district courts were authorized to render judgments on claims against the United States because of property damages, personal injury, or death caused by the negligence of a government employee. The heads of federal agencies were required to submit annual reports to Congress of all claims made under the law. The U.S. government was made liable with respect to claims (including costs) tried in the district courts. Employees of the government, however, were exempted from any action by claimants in the event of district court action. The decisions of the district courts were made reviewable on appeal in the courts of appeals or in the U.S. Court of Claims. The attorney general was authorized to arbitrate, compromise, or settle any claim after its institution, with the consent of the court.

Federal Trade Commission. A powerful, five-member, independent, bipartisan commission established in 1915, the FTC exercises extensive quasi-judicial and quasi-legislative functions in enforcing most of the nation's laws related to industrial practices, pricing, food and drug purity, labeling and packaging, and fair credit. The FTC's main objective is to maintain the free enterprise system by preventing unfettered monopoly or corruption by unfair and deceptive trade practices. Much of its work is in guiding industry to voluntary compliance, but the FTC can institute legal cease-and-desist proceedings and impose penalties subject to court appeal. The members, including the chairman, are appointed by the president with senatorial consent.

feigned accomplice. An individual who pretends to act with others in the planning or commission of a crime for the purpose of discovering their plans or compiling evidence against them.

felon. A term derived from the legal classification of crimes as felonies and misdemeanors. The former category includes those crimes regarded as the more heinous, which usually involve as punishment either confinement in a state or federal prison or death. A felon is therefore one who commits a felony or who habitually commits felonies.

felonious. (1) Malignant, malicious. (2) Done with intent to commit a crime.

felony. A criminal offense punishable by death or incarceration in a prison facility.

felony murder rule. The rule stating that an accidental killing that occurs during the commission of a felony may be a murder.

Female Offenders, Bureau of Prisons. This office monitors programs for female inmates. One major area is a psychiatric unit for women, which has been established at the Federal Correctional Institution at Lexington, KY. Address: Correctional Programs Division, Bureau of Prisons, DOJ, 320 1st Street, NW, Room 534, Washington, DC 20534.

femicide. The killing of a woman.

fence. (1) A receiver and seller of stolen property who either pursues this line of work exclusively, or, more often, in connection with a legitimate business. (2) The establishment in which such a person does business.

fencing. The act of receiving stolen goods; the receipt, handling, and sale of stolen goods as a business and occupation.

fetal alcohol syndrome (FAS). A complex of congenital anomalies seen in newborns of women who ingested high doses of alcohol or certain other mood-altering substances, which can easily cross the placenta, during pregnancy. Defects in infants can include premature birth, underweight at birth, retarded growth, brain or other nervous system malformations, including mental retardation, poor coordination, hyperactivity, and facial or skull abnormalities.

feticide. Destroying a fetus; criminal abortion.

fetishism. An unusual form of sexual behavior in which gratification is obtained through the medium of an inanimate object. Common fetish objects are women's lingerie and footwear and garments made entirely of rubber, leather, or fur.

fetus. An unborn animal or human in the womb. In humans, the developing child is referred to as a fetus from the end of the third month until birth.

fiction. Legally, the assumption of a thing as being factual, regardless of its truthfulness.

fiduciary. Referring to one authorized to act for another. Fiduciary trust is the power given to the police by the public to act in its interests.

field interview. Generally, any contact between a private citizen and a law enforcement officer acting in his or her official capacity, whether or not relating to suspicion or criminal activity.

55-mph speed limit. Once a federal law governing drivers nationwide, this statute was repealed in December 1995, returning to the states the right to set their own speed limits.

filing. (1) In recommended general court terminology, the initiation of a case in court by formal submission of a document alleging the facts of a matter and requesting relief. (2) In recommended criminal justice statistical terminology, the initiation of a criminal case in a court by formal submission of a charging document, alleging that one or more named persons have committed one or more specified criminal offenses.

final. A term used in classifying fingerprints. In the classification formula, it appears at the extreme right on the classification line and above the line. It is determined by ridge counts in the little finger. The right hand is used if it has a loop; if not, the left is used if it has a loop. If neither has a loop but each has a whorl, a ridge count between delta and core is made in the right hand.

finding. A conclusion of fact certified after inquiry by a judicial or other body.

fine. The penalty imposed upon a convicted person by a court, requiring that he or she pay a specified sum of money to the court.

fingerprint classification. A system of classifying fingerprints according to the patterns of the friction ridges on the fingertips. This is done by the use of a definite formula. *See also* fingerprint patterns

fingerprint conviction, first. Obtained by the New York Police Department, which arrested Caesar Cella, alias Charles Crispi, for burglary on March 8, 1911. Latent fingerprints found at the scene of the crime were introduced as evidence. He was convicted and sentenced to the NY County Penitentiary by Judge Otto Alfred Rosalsky in General Sessions Court, New York City, on May 19, 1911.

fingerprint identification. The FBI operates a law enforcement assistance service that provides criminal identification by means of fingerprints, determination of the number of previously reported arrests and convictions, fingerprint identification of victims of major disasters (*see* Disaster Squad), and processing of submitted evidence for latent fingerprint impression. Information must be used for official purposes only and is not furnished for public dissemination. The CAL-ID

Automated Fingerprint System, implemented in 1985, uses imaging and database technology. CAL-ID is the largest automated fingerprint system in the world, with storage of over 7 million fingerprint images representing over 1 million individuals. Between 1986 and 1991, the Law Enforcement Data Center's use of the remote access network resulted in the matches of over 64,000 fingerprints lifted from crime scenes. Searches for matches of latent fingerprints can be completed in an average of 25 minutes that, before automation, might have taken more than 40 years. For further information, contact: Assistant Director, Identification Division, FBI, DOJ, Washington, DC 20537.

fingerprint, latent. A chance fingerprint left accidentally or otherwise on a surface.

fingerprint patterns. The configuration of the friction ridges on the fingers is called a pattern. There are basically three patterns: arches, loops, and whorls. An arch is where the ridges come in from one side, do not recurve, and go out the other side. The ridges make an upward thrust at or near the center of the pattern, also called the core. There are two kinds: the plain arch, where the upthrust is smooth and gradual, and the tented arch, where the upward thrust is sharp. A loop has ridge lines that enter from either side, recurve, touch or pass an imaginary line between the delta, or pattern of radiation outward from the center, and the core, and pass out on the side from which the ridge or ridges entered. A plain whorl has one or more ridges that make a complete circuit. It has two deltas, between which, when an imaginary line is drawn, at least one recurving ridge is cut or touched.

These basic patterns are subdivided as follows: Arch: plain arch; tented arch. Loop: radial loop; lateral loop; ulnar loop; central pocket loop; twin loop. Whorl: plain whorl. In addition to the three basic types of fingerprints, there is a catchall or nondescript pattern called accidentals.

fingerprints. Also referred to as dactyloscopy, the prints or impressions produced by the friction ridges of the inner surface of the fingertips. The impressions may be left accidentally or otherwise on objects touched by the fingers or may be taken by two methods: (a) rolled—the fingertips are rolled on a freshly inked surface and then rolled on a white paper; (b) plain—the fingertip is pressed on an inked surface without rolling and the print is made on a light-colored surface. John Vucetichi, born in 1858, is considered the "father of fingerprinting." His system generally followed the Galton-Henry system. The first state prison to take fingerprints of its prisoners was Sing Sing Prison in Ossining, NY, which commenced taking impressions on March 3, 1903. *See also* Galton, Francis; Henry system

fingerprint system, first police department to adopt. The St. Louis (MO) Metropolitan Police Department, on October 28, 1904, adopted the Henry method to fingerprint persons arrested on serious charges. John M. Shea was the first to qualify as a fingerprint expert connected with any police service. He joined the department on May 1, 1899, and was appointed Superintendent of the Bertillon System on September 14, 1903. He remained in office until his death on July 17, 1926. *See also* Bertillon method; Henry system

fire. A state, process, or instances of combustion in which fuel or other material is ignited and combined with oxygen, giving off light, heat, and flame.

firearm. (1) In a general sense, a gun. (2) Specifically, a small arm, such as a pistol or rifle, designed to be carried by an individual. Although it cannot be accepted as proven, the best opinion is that the earliest guns were constructed in North Africa, possibly by Arabs, around 1250. The earliest representation of an English gun is contained in an illustrated manuscript dated 1326 at Oxford University, England.

Firearm Act, Federal. This 1934 legislation regulated possession of submachine guns, silencers, and several other weapons. In 1938 the National Firearms Act was passed, requiring the licensing of firearms manufacturers and dealers. As a result, all new weapons sold legally in the United States since 1938 have been registered and can be traced. The most important federal action was the passage of the Gun Control Act of 1968, as it prohibited interstate retailing of all firearms. Its purpose was to prevent individuals who cannot legally own a gun from ordering guns by mail under false names.

Fireman's Rule. Used as a basis for court decisions as early as 1892, this criterion reflects an effort by courts to reconcile the unique activities of policemen and firemen with the general rule of allowing injured employees to maintain traditional tort actions against third parties for virtually all negligently inflicted injuries. The traditional Fireman's Rule denies a fireman's or policeman's cause of action against any individual whose only negligence was to cause a situation for which the officer was summoned and subsequently injured. Historically underlying the rule are the notions: (a) that firemen and policemen are mere "licensees" in the eyes of the law, and little or no duty is owed them by owners or occupiers of land; (b) that the occupation of policeman and fireman is inherently dangerous, and thus those accepting the position assume the risk of being injured by negligent conduct; (c) that policemen and firemen are compensated for the risks they face; and (d) that public policy demands application of the rule. Despite complaints that it is an anachronism, the rule continues to be followed by most state courts. Once restricted to acts of negligence, it has been expanded in recent years to include willfull, wanton, reckless, and, in some circumstances, intentional conduct, as later interpretations of the risk principles were adopted. The rule remains an important barrier to recovery for injuries policemen receive in the line of duty.

fires, classification. Fires can be grouped into four basic types: Class A: Fires involving ordinary combustible materials (wood, cloth, paper, rubber, and many plastics) requiring the heat-absorbing (cooling) effects of water, water solutions, or the coating effects of certain dry chemicals that retard combustion. Class B: Fires involving flammable or combustible liquids, flammable gases, greases, and similar materials where extinguishment is most readily secured by excluding air (oxygen), inhibiting the release of combustible vapors, or interrupting the combustion chain reaction. Class C: Fires involving energized electrical equipment where safety to the operator requires the use of electrically nonconductive extinguishing agents. Class D: Fires involving certain combustible metals (magnesium, titanium, zirconium, potassium) requiring a heat-absorbing extinguishing medium not reactive with the burning metals. *See* burns.

fires, historic.

The Great Chicago Fire. During October 8–10, 1871, wiped out 3 square miles of the city, killing 120 people, destroying 12,000 buildings, and causing approximately $200 million in damages.

Iroquois Theater, Chicago. On December 30, 1903, the theater caught fire after an overheated spotlight ignited stage riggings; 602 people died.

Triangle Shirtwaist Co., New York. On March 25, 1911, this sweatshop in lower Manhattan, in which 500 immigrants worked on the eighth and ninth floors of a 10-story building, became an inferno when a rag bin caught fire. Exits were blocked and fire hoses were rotted, resulting in 146 deaths.

Coconut Grove, Boston. On November 28, 1942, a small fire in the basement raced through the nightclub, resulting in 491 dead. Approximately 200 died from smoke, fire, and trampling.

MGM Grand Hotel Fire, Las Vegas. On November 21, 1980, a fire caused by a short circuit started in the wall and ceiling of a delicatessen and spread through the lobby. Toxic fumes and dense smoke poured through the air-conditioning ducts and elevator shafts, killing 85 people.

First Interstate Building, Los Angeles. On May 4, 1988, a fire in the 62-story building gutted four floors, killing one person and injuring 40 more. This fire caused over $450 million in damages, and the cause was never determined.

One Meridian Plaza, Philadelphia. On February 23, 1991, three firefighters died battling the flames on the 22nd floor. It raged out of control for 19 hours, causing $100 million in damage.

firing pin impressions. Marks made on the base of a cartridge case or shotgun shell by the firing pin. Such impressions are used by crime laboratories in determining whether a certain cartridge or shell was fired in a specific weapon.

fiscal year. A 12-month financial reporting period for a company or agency that often does not coincide with the calendar year. Government agencies, for example, often have fiscal years running from July 1 to June 30, while retail firms' fiscal years are usually February 1 through January 31.

Fitness for Life. Founded in 1984, the organization develops programs to encourage prison inmates to become responsible for their own physical and mental fitness. Provides self-development training programs and trains qualified inmates to teach other inmates. Address: 751 Kenmoor Ave., SE, #751C, Grand Rapids, MI 49546-2370.

flag, U.S. The word flag comes from the Anglo-Saxon *fleogan*, meaning "to fly in the wind." Flag scholars are vexillologists. The following abbreviated rules are excerpted from the Flag Code of the United States: It is the universal custom to display the flag only from sunrise to sunset on buildings and on a stationary flagpole in the open. However, when a patriotic effect is desired, the flag may be displayed 24 hours a day if properly illuminated during the hours of darkness. When flags of states, cities, or localities, or pennants of societies are flown on the same halyard with the U.S. flag, the latter should always be at the peak. When the flags are flown from adjacent staffs, the U.S. flag should be hoisted first and lowered last. No such flag or pennant may be placed above or to the right of the U.S. flag. When flags of two or more nations are displayed, they are to be flown from separate staffs of the same height. The flags should be of approximately equal size. International usage forbids the display of the flag of one nation above that of another nation in time of peace. The flag should be raised quickly, but lowered ceremoniously. Never allow the flag to touch the ground when it is being raised or lowered for the day.

Local American Legion Centers provide for the destruction of soiled or damaged flags. For a free catalog about flags, call the All Nations Flag Co.; (800) 533-FLAG.

flare, fuzee. A flare having a spike at the bottom and a cap at the top; positioned on or next to roadways and ignited to warn motorists of hazards.

flight. The act of an accused in escaping or fleeing from justice, especially if he or she has been notified as to an officer's intention of arresting him or her. Flight is presumptive evidence of guilt if supported by evidence of the motivation that prompted it.

Florida State University School of Criminology. Established in 1955, it conducts academic research and teaching in criminology and criminal justice. Address: FSU, Tallahassee, FL 32306.

Floyd, Charles Arthur ("Pretty Boy"). Born in Atkins, OK, in 1901. Alias: Jack Hamilton. Between 1925 and his death by FBI agents on October 22, 1934, he was credited with 8 robberies and 13 murders in the midwestern states. Six of the murders occurred in the Kansas City Massacre, in which "Pretty Boy" was claimed to have been a machine gunner.

Food and Drug Administration. A law enforcement agency established in 1907 in the Public Health Service of the former Department of Health, Education, and Welfare. The major responsibilities of FDA are directed toward protecting public health by ensuring that foods are safe and pure, drugs are safe and effective, cosmetics are harmless, and products are honestly and informatively labeled and packaged. These responsibilities are carried out by six bureaus of the FDA: the Bureau of Foods, the Bureau of Drugs, the Bureau of Veterinary Medicine, the Bureau of Radiological Health, the Bureau of Biologics, and the Bureau of Medical Devices.

food stamps. The U.S. Department of Agriculture is charged with the investigation of counterfeiting or misuse of food stamps. Address: Information Office, USDA, Washington, DC 20250.

footcandle. A unit of measure for the intensity of illumination thrown onto a surface one foot away from the light source.

foot rail. A holdup alarm device, often used at cashiers' windows, in which the operator places a foot under the rail and lifts it to give an alarm signal.

force, reasonable. The amount or degree of force that can be reasonably used by persons in protecting themselves or others; the force that can be used by law enforcement officials in the conduct of their duties as authorized by law. The general rule is that an officer can use force no greater than that which is necessary. To effect an arrest, an officer may use reasonable force to overcome resistance.

forcible entry. To enter onto the lands or other property of another by the use of force or fear and without the free consent of the owner or possessor of such property.

forcible rape. Sexual intercourse or attempted sexual intercourse with a female against her will by force or threat of force.

foreclosure. Act of barring a mortgagor's fight to redeem mortgaged property; act of foreclosing a mortgage. *See also* homestead

Foreign Claims Settlement Commission. This DOJ office determines claims of U.S. nationals against foreign governments for losses and injuries sustained by them. Address: Foreign Claims Settlement Commis-

sion of the United States, DOJ, 600 E St., NW, Suite 6002, Washington, DC 20579.

Foreign Litigation, Office of. This DOJ office represents the United States before foreign tribunals in civil cases brought by and against the United States. It represents the government in domestic cases involving questions of international and foreign law. Address: Office of Foreign Litigation, Commercial Litigation Branch, Civil Division, DOJ, 550 11th Street, NW, Room 1234, Washington, DC 20530.

Forensic Center, National. Founded in 1978. Publishes *The Expert and the Law* (6/yearly). Address: 17 Temple Terrace, Lawrenceville, NJ 08648.

forensic medicine. Also called forensic science; an area related to legal medicine (forensic means related to courts of law) that applies anatomy, pathology, toxicology, chemistry, botany, and other fields of science in expert testimony in court cases or hearings. Perhaps the most celebrated case of forensic medicine is the Warren Commission investigation of the assassination of President John Kennedy.

forensic odontology. Investigative branch of dentistry often used to identify cadavers and bite marks, as no two bite marks are identical.

forensic pathologist. A medical doctor, specializing in pathology, who conducts examinations to determine the cause of death in suspected homicide cases and who is in a position to testify to those findings in a court of law. He or she also makes pathology examinations of persons who have been injured or who are suffering from disease, and these findings are also usable in legal proceedings.

forensic psychology and psychiatry. The major concern of forensic psychology is to determine whether legal evidence is reliable. This process involves such factors as perception and memory. Another concern involves decisions, sometimes called the domain of forensic psychiatry, such as whether a person should be judged sane and capable of standing trial or be committed to an institution as mentally disturbed.

forensic science. Science as applied and used in judicial matters. For the highlights of forensic research, the use of crime laboratories and physical evidence in court, and information on how to obtain research documents, newsletters, journals, and names of forensic agencies and organizations, write for the booklet *Forensics—When Science Bears Witness*, available without charge from the National Institute of Justice/NCJRS Distribution Services, Box 6000, Rockville, MD 20850. Specify title and this number: NCJ 93348.

Forensic Sciences Foundation. Founded in 1969. Publishes *Forensic Serology News* (quarterly) and *News and Views in Forensic Toxicology* (quarterly). Address: P.O. Box 669, Colorado Springs, CO 80901.

Forensic Toxicologists, Society of. Founded in 1970. Publishes *Tox Talk* (quarterly newsletter). Address: P.O. Box 5543, Mesa, AZ 85211.

Forest Service. Established in 1905, the service is a division of the Department of Agriculture responsible for managing the more than 150 national forests and 19 national grasslands, protecting them from disease, insect pests, and wildfire. Forest rangers have been given limited peace officer authority to enforce standards of compliance within these protected areas. Address: 3244 South Building, Washington, DC 20250.

forfeiture. The loss of ownership as a civil or criminal penalty for the illegal use of the property in question, or as a sanction for the commission of a crime. *See also* Racketeer Influenced and Corrupt Organizations (RICO); Resolution Trust Corp.

forfeiture, civil. A proceeding against property used in criminal activity, which was first authorized by the First Congress in allowing the forfeiture of vessels that smuggled contraband into the United States. Property subject to civil forfeiture often includes vehicles used to transport contraband, equipment used to manufacture illegal drugs, cash used in il-

legal transactions, and property purchased with criminal proceeds. The government is required to notify registered owners and post notice of the proceedings so that any party who has an interest in the property may contest the forfeiture. If no one claims the property, it is forfeited administratively. If a claim is made, the case must be heard in a civil court, where no finding of criminal guilt is required. *See also* Resolution Trust Corp.

forfeiture, criminal. Criminal forfeiture was first authorized in 1970 as part of the criminal action taken against defendants accused of racketeering, drug trafficking, or money laundering. The forfeiture is a sanction imposed upon conviction that requires the defendant to forfeit various property rights and interests related to the violation. *See also* Resolution Trust Corp.; Racketeer Influenced and Corrupt Organizations.

forgery. The creation or alteration of a written or printed document that, if validly executed, would constitute a record of a legally binding transaction, with the intent to defraud by affirming it to be the act of an unknowing second person; also, the creation of an art object with intent to misrepresent the identity of the creator. The greatest recorded forgery was the German Third Reich government's operation, code named "Bernhard" engineered by S.S. Sturmbannfuhrer Alfred Naujocks in 1940–1941. It involved about $300 million in Bank of England notes.

forgery and counterfeiting. In Uniform Crime Reports terminology, the name used to record and report arrests for offenses of making, manufacturing, altering, possessing, selling, or distributing, or attempting to make, manufacture, alter, sell, distribute, or receive "anything false in the semblance of that which is true."

Fortune Society. Founded in 1967, the society's objectives are to "create a public awareness of the prison system; problems confronting inmates during their incarceration and upon return to society; to work with released prisoners in making their adjustment to society and to develop community involvements by creating alternatives for released convicts." The society sends teams of speakers to schools, churches, and civic groups and provides witnesses and testimony before city, state, and federal legislators. Publishes *Fortune News* (newsletter). Address: The Fortune Society 53 West 23rd Street, 8th Floor, New York, NY 10010.

Fosdick, Raymond Blaine. Lawyer, public servant, and author (1833–1972), Fosdick was born in Buffalo, NY, earning his B.A. in 1905 and his M.A. in 1906. He received his law degree from New York Law School in 1908 and worked for New York City mayor George B. McClellan. Through the Rockefeller Bureau of Social Hygiene, John D. Rockefeller Jr. gave Fosdick a study grant, as a result of which he wrote *European Police Systems*, published in 1915. The following year he rode with "Black Jack" Pershing against Pancho Villa in Mexico. In 1917 he observed military training methods in England, Canada, and France, publishing his findings in *Keeping Our Fighters Fit*. After World War I Fosdick was U.S. representative to the League of Nations. In *American Police Systems*, published in 1920, he declared them inferior to their European counterparts. This book was followed in 1922 by *Criminal Justice in Cleveland*, which termed that city's police department lethargic, inadequate, ragged, and lacking intelligence. In 1933, he published *Toward Liquor Control*, coauthored with Arthur Scott. In all, Fosdick wrote 14 books, received the Distinguished Service Medal and two doctorates, was given the rank of commander of the French Foreign Legion, and earned many other honors.

foster family. A temporary substitute family for a child whose parents cannot provide him or her with an adequate home situation because of such factors as economic hardship, death of a parent, illness, family breakdown, or psychological problems. The child's expenses are generally paid by a private or public agency that has legal custody.

foster grandparents program. A group of low-income people over 60 who work with children who have physical, mental, social, or emotional needs. The volunteers serve in correctional facilities and with dependent and neglected children. In return for the service, foster grandparents receive a tax-free modest stipend, a transportation allowance, hot meals while in service, and an annual physical examination. For general information, contact: Older American Volunteer Program, ACTION, Room 1006, 806 Connecticut Avenue, NW, Washington, DC 20525.

frangible bullet. A brittle plastic or other nonmetallic bullet used for firing practice which, upon striking a target, breaks into powder or small fragments without penetrating. Frangible bullets are usually designed to leave a mark at the point of impact.

frangible grenade. An improvised incendiary hand grenade consisting of a glass container filled with a flammable liquid, with an igniter attached. It breaks and ignites upon striking a resistant target. Sometimes called a "Molotov cocktail."

Frankfurter, Felix. Frankfurter (1882–1965) was an associate justice of the Supreme Court, presidential adviser, and a leading liberal known as a champion of judicial restraint. An emigrant from Austria, he graduated from Harvard Law School with highest honors. In 1914 he joined the school's faculty and remained a classroom teacher for a quarter-century. After World War I, Frankfurter became a legal adviser at the Paris Peace Conference. He also helped to found the American Civil Liberties Union and *The New Republic*; he tried to obtain a new trial for Sacco and Vanzetti. In 1939 Frankfurter, an intimate adviser of President Roosevelt, was made an associate justice of the Supreme Court. Many of his opinions reflect his belief that government by judges is a poor substitute for government by the people.

frankpledge. In old English law, a system whereby the members of a tithing (group who supported their organization or church with 10 percent of their earnings) had corporate responsibility for the behavior of all members over 14 years old.

Fraternal Order of Police. Founded in 1915, this is the oldest and largest of the major police organizations. The group opposes unionization because they view police work as a profession like those of medicine and the law and because they choose a subtle, soft-sell stance at the national level rather than more aggressive tactics to gain their goals.

fratricide. The act of killing or murdering one's brother or sister.

fraud. In Uniform Crime Reports terminology, the name used to record and report arrests for offenses of conversion or obtaining of money or other things of value by false pretenses, except forgery, counterfeiting, and embezzlement.

fraud and white-collar crime. The Fraud Section of DOJ directs and coordinates the federal effort against white-collar crime. The section focuses on frauds involving government programs and procurement, transnational and multidistrict trade, the security and commodity exchanges, banking practices, and consumer victimization. Address: Fraud Section, Criminal Division, DOJ, 315 9th Street, NW, Room 832, Washington, DC 20539.

fraud examiner, certified (CFE). A specialist in the detection and/or deterrence of a wide variety of fraudulent conduct, from identifying employees or executives who misappropriate company assets to assisting investors who are defrauded in the course of commercial transactions. Responsibilities include resolving aggregations of fraud by obtaining evidence, taking statements and writing reports, and testifying to findings in court. Many members are law enforcement personnel, while others are certified public accountants. Referrals and information are available free of charge from the National Association of Fraud Examiners; telephone (800) 245-3321.

fraud, charity. The following organizations can assist law enforcement personnel or con-

sumers by providing information on the operations of charitable organizations and whether they appear to be legitimate, based on complaints and/or filed financial statements: local Better Business Bureaus (check phone directories); Council of Better Business Bureaus, Charities Division, 4200 Wilson Blvd., Suite 800, Arlington, VA 22203; National Charities Information Bureau, 19 Union Square West, New York, NY 10003-3395. Enclose a business size, self-addressed, stamped envelope when requesting information.

fraud, health care. It is estimated that health care quackery amounts to more than $40 billion each year, with approximately 60 percent of individual fraud victims being elderly. Before buying products represented as preventives, treatments, or cures, but not prescribed by your doctor, check with **Cancer:** (800) 422-6237, a toll-free line at the National Cancer Institute; **Arthritis:** (800) 283-7800, the Arthritis Foundation's Information Line; **Products for other illnesses:** Send questions about the products, plus a business-size, self-addressed envelope and $1 to: Consumer Health Research Institute, 300 East Pink Hill Road, Independence, MO 64057. **If you have been harmed by a nonprescription product:** Contact the National Council Against Health Fraud, Victim Redress Taskforce, P.O. Box 1747, Allentown, PA 18105 or your local FBI office.

fraud, investment. The North American Securities Administrators Association (NASAA) estimates that investment fraud in the United States, by telephone alone, reaches $10 billion a year. Telephone numbers for securities agencies in each state can be obtained by calling NASAA at (202) 737-0901. NASAA publishes a free bulletin, *How Older Americans Can Avoid Investment Fraud and Abuse.* Write NASAA, One Massachusetts Ave., NW, Suite 310, Washington, DC 20001. The National Consumers League operates a Fraud Information Center that serves as a clearinghouse for information on consumer fraud; telephone (800) 876-7060. The National Futures Association (NFA) is a self-regulatory organization for all registered individuals or brokerage firms selling commodity futures, such as sugar, gold, petroleum, soybeans, or foreign currencies. To report fraud, write NFA, 200 W. Madison St., Suite 1600, Chicago, IL 60606; telephone (800) 621-3570.

fraud offenses. The type of crime comprising offenses sharing the elements of practice of deceit or intentional misrepresentation of fact, with the intent of unlawfully depriving a person of his or her property or legal rights. On June 3, 1985, financier Jake Butcher was sentenced to 20 years in prison for his theft of $20 million from depositors. Butcher was chairman of a $1.5 billion-financial empire in Tennessee and Kentucky that began to crumble with the 1983 failure of his United American Bank of Knoxville, then the third largest commercial bank failure since the Depression. The Department of Justice indicated this was the most severe sentence given to date for a person convicted of a white-collar crime.

The nation's second-largest law firm—Jones, Day, Reavis & Pogue—agreed (without admitting guilt) on April 19, 1993, to pay a record $51 million to savings and loan regulators for its role in the 1989 collapse of Lincoln Savings & Loan. In a lawsuit, the Resolution Trust Corporation had accused Jones, Day of helping Charles H. Keating, Jr., to keep control of the Irvine, CA-based financial institution even though the firm knew that Keating was looting it. The failure of Lincoln Savings cost taxpayers $2.6 billion. Keating received a 10-year prison term for his December 1991 state securities fraud conviction. Ernst & Young, the nation's largest accounting firm, paid $463 million to regulators who had alleged the firm failed to warn about disastrous problems at major thrifts nationwide. *See also* Resolution Trust Corp.

fraud, postal. The U.S. Postal Service investigates and pursues complaints regarding bogus mail-order investments and other businesses that use, advertise, or sell through the mail. This includes telephone solicitors and newspaper ads, because money sent in response to such ads is usually mailed. Contact your local postmaster or postal inspector.

fraud, telemarketing. The Alliance Against Fraud in Telemarketing (AAFT) was formed by state, federal, trade union, industrial, law enforcement, and consumer groups and will forward complaints to the appropriate agency to investigate and prosecute fraudulent practices. Address: AAFT, 815 15th St., NW, Suite 516, Washington, DC 20005.

fraud, toll. The offense category considered the most costly for telephone companies and their customers, estimated at $4 billion annually by the U.S. Secret Service. Two types of toll fraud predominate: (a) theft of telephone credit card numbers; and (b) theft of business toll codes. Stealing credit card numbers is a multimillion-dollar business involving, among other techniques, binoculars used near busy coin phones to record people's dialing sequences as they charge calls to their cards. In stealing corporate billing codes, thieves tap into a firm's telecommunications switching equipment, use an automatic dialer to try all four-digit codes until it finds the right ones, then sell the codes. Although telephone companies use automated call-tracking equipment to alert staff when a particular credit card or corporate toll code is being used in a heavy and unusual manner, thieves can make thousands of dollars worth of toll calls in the few hours before phone company staff is alerted. Many offenders are prosecuted each year, but most toll fraud must be written off as an expense to phone companies and their customers.

freedom of assembly. One of the fundamental rights guaranteed the individual under the First Amendment. Like other rights in the Constitution, the right of assembly is not absolute or unlimited. In interpreting the extent of these freedoms, the courts have ruled that, although a meeting cannot be prohibited for advocating unpopular views, the right to assemble is subject to reasonable police regulation to ensure general safety and the maintenance of peace and order.

Freedom of Information Act. A 1967 bill designed to give the public greater access to government records. The act, signed by President Lyndon Johnson, superseded the Disclosure of Information Act (1966). The new act permits exemptions only in nine specific areas. Among these are national defense, confidential financial information, and law enforcement files and certain personnel files, in addition to information whose disclosure has been prohibited by statute. The U.S. Department of Justice's Office of Information Law and Policy carries out the DOJ's responsibilities under the act to encourage agency compliance. It also advises other departments and agencies on questions of policy, interpretation, and application of the act. Contact: FOIA/PA Mail Referral Unit, Department of Justice, Room 114, LOC, Washington, DC 20530-0001.

freedom of religion. One of the basic liberties guaranteed by the First Amendment, which states that "Congress shall make no law respecting an establishment of religion, or prohibiting the free exercise thereof."

freedom of speech and press. Basic liberties guaranteed by the First Amendment, which prohibits Congress from abridging them; these are also included among the fundamental rights protected from infringement by the states by the Fourteenth Amendment. In 1978 the confidentiality of news files was lost when it was ruled that a news office could be searched by the police with a search warrant.

free exercise clause. This part of the establishment clause is another name for the First Amendment provision for freedom of religion. It prevents compulsion by law of the acceptance of any creed or the practice of any form of worship. Conversely, it safeguards the free exercise of any chosen form of religion. However, the free exercise clause does not embrace actions that are in violation of social duties or subversive in nature. This interpretation enabled the Supreme Court to uphold Congress's ban on polygamy and, on the other hand, to strike down Wisconsin's law compelling Amish parents to send their children to secondary school.

free venture program. Started by the federal government to encourage the develop-

ment of job opportunities for state prison inmates, the program uses business principles and practices in an attempt to make prison industries profitable and provide transferable work skills.

freeway. A highway to which owners of abutting land have no or only very limited rights of easement or access from their land.

freeway patrol. The law enforcement function concerned with the management and surveillance of traffic on a freeway. This function may include rendering assistance, accident investigation, traffic direction, and traffic law enforcement. It may be accomplished with automobile, motorcycle, or aircraft patrol. Sometimes referred to as the highway patrol or state police.

French Connection. A drug-smuggling operation, the investigation of which began one evening early in 1962. While drinking in a New York nightclub, detectives Eddie Egan and Sonny Grosso, both of the narcotics division, observed a man flashing large sums of money. They followed him and found that he was the proprietor of a small newsstand. What evolved from Egan and Grosso's simple observations was a joint federal–New York Police Department investigation that uncovered a major heroin-importing circuit operating out of Marseilles, France. Raw opium was being transported from Turkey and the Far East to Marseilles, where it was being refined into water-soluble heroin. From there it was being exported to the United States. The Connection was broken, arrests were made, and almost 97 pounds of heroin—valued at $32 million—were confiscated. Sometime between 1962 and 1972, 81 pounds of these narcotics disappeared from the property clerk's office. To this day, the loss remains a mystery.

frequency distribution. A statistical method for organizing and presenting data. The initial procedure consists simply of counting the number of times each item under study occurs. A standard step is to tabulate the number of individuals receiving each possible score, from low to high. Observing the distribution of scores is a step in analyzing test results. For example, when scores on an achievement test given to all students in a school system cluster toward the lower end of the range, several different factors might be accountable: design errors in the test or its scoring, students' lack of motivation, or ineffective teaching. Normal frequency is an ideal situation in which half the scores fall above the midpoint and half below. When this occurs, the mean, the median, and the mode of the results are all the same.

friction, coefficient of. The amount of friction on a roadway surface, determined in calculating the speed of a vehicle as shown by skid marks. Speed and weight of the vehicle are factors, as well as the surface that the vehicle was traveling upon. The coefficient of friction is also referred to as the drag factor.

friction ridges. The ridges of the skin on the palms and palmar side of the fingers. Similar ridges are found on the sole of the foot and lower side of the toes. The prime function of the ridges is to afford friction with surfaces and objects touched by these parts of the body. These ridges are the means by which fingerprints are formed.

Friends Outside. Founded in 1955, this organization's purposes are to: aid prisoners and their families in dealing with traumas and limitations imposed by separation; assist officials in improving conditions of confinement and promote alternatives to confinement; aid ex-offenders in transition; develop public awareness of problems caused by incarceration; and seek volunteers. Publishes a monthly newsletter. Address: 546 E. Market Street, Salinas, CA 93905.

fringe benefits. Sometimes referred to as collateral entitlements, employee benefits are a labor cost to employers incurred in providing compensation above and beyond wages and salaries. Benefits usually include time off with pay (holidays, vacations, sick leave); retirement pensions (deferred payments); life, medical, and hospitalization in-surance; and special incentive pay increases for educational achievement, outstanding performance, or profit sharing. Along with wages and salaries, fringe benefits are usually the topic of collective bargaining.

frisk. A precautionary search of the outer clothing and property (purse or briefcase) in the immediate possession of a suspect. A frisk is usually less intrusive than the full search permitted in a lawful arrest or detention.

fruit of the poisonous tree. A term used by the courts to denote evidence tainted as the result of its being derived from evidence obtained illegally or in such fashion that it was inadmissible. If certain evidence was obtained as the result of an illegal search and, based upon information secured by that search, other evidence was located elsewhere, the latter evidence is also inadmissible even though properly obtained.

fruits of a crime. Any material objects obtained through criminal acts.

fugitive. (1) One who flees (or cannot be located by law enforcement officers) to avoid arrest, incarceration, or questioning concerning an alleged violation of the law. (2) One wanted for a crime who goes outside the state or the territorial jurisdiction of a court.

Fugitive Felon Acts. Acts of Congress, in 1932 and 1934, that make it a federal offense to travel in interstate or foreign commerce in order to avoid: (a) prosecution; (b) confinement after conviction; or (c) giving testimony, where under the laws of the state, the offense charged is a felony (or in NJ, a high misdemeanor).

fugitive from justice. (1) A person who has fled from a state, in which he is accused of having committed a crime, in order to avoid arrest and punishment. (2) A person who has fled from a state in order to avoid giving testimony in a criminal prosecution. *See also* extradition

Fugitive Interception Network Design. A plan established by the Philadelphia Police

Department to prevent the escape of felons from the scenes of major crimes.

fugitive slave laws. Statutes passed by Congress from 1798 to 1850, these laws covered the return of slaves who escaped from one state and were found in another state or territory.

fugitive warrant. An arrest warrant issued for a person wanted for a violation of the criminal law in another state or jurisdiction; a warrant for a fugitive from justice.

full-time temporary release. The authorized temporary absence of a prisoner from a confinement facility, for a period of 24 hours or more, for purposes relating to such matters as the prisoner's employment, education, or personal or family welfare. *See also* furlough

functional authority. The authority to complete a task by virtue of expertise or ability, rather than of power vested by rank.

functional specialization. All functions of a criminal justice agency may be classified as line, auxiliary, or administrative. Operations that a police department is primarily created to perform are called line, primary, or operational duties. Functional specialization further connotes authority and duties based on knowledge and experience rather than rank.

fundamental fairness. The basic principle that crime prevention and control methods must be democratic and fair.

fundamental law. (1) A constitution; statutes or laws that are intrinsically superior to the ordinary law of a state or that the courts regard as law of superior obligation; (2) Natural law, which is sometimes deemed to be morally, if not juridically, superior to positive law.

furlough. Overnight, or longer, leave granted to the inmate of a correctional facility.

G

GAAP. An acronym from the phrase "generally accepted accounting principles," the guidelines used by comptrollers and auditors to ensure that financial records are kept properly and in a manner that can be understood by any accountant.

gag law. Any law abridging freedom of speech, the press, or the right of petition.

Gallup poll. A well-known series of public opinion surveys, Gallup polls since 1950 have been based on a national sample of interviewees. The United States, through categories based on size of communities, population densities, and geographical locations, is divided into approximate blocks of population, with equal probability of selection. A random starting place is selected, and interviewers follow a predetermined pattern until their interview quota is filled. Within each household, the interviewer asks to speak to the youngest man, 18 or older. If no men are home, then the interviewer asks for the oldest woman over 18 years of age. Interviews are conducted at different times of the day and week in order to get a better sample. This procedure is designed to "produce an approximation of the adult civilian population living in the United States, except for those persons in institutions, such as hospitals and prisons." *See also* Harris poll

Galton, Francis. An English scientist and criminologist (1812–1911), Galton was a pioneer in the field of fingerprint science. Although he didn't develop a workable classification system, his work greatly aided Sir Edward Henry in his developments in this area of criminology. *See also* Henry system

galvanometer. An instrument for measuring small amounts of electricity. Used in some types of lie detectors.

Gamblers Anonymous. Self-help group founded in September 1957, reportedly the fourth such group patterned after Alcoholics Anonymous and based on a 12-step recovery model. Now includes some 800 local chapters. Address: P.O. Box 17173, Los Angeles, CA 90017. Families and friends of compulsive gamblers can join Gain-Anon Family Groups. Address: P.O. Box 157, Whitestone, NY 11357.

gambling. Staking or wagering of money or anything of value on a game of chance or an uncertain event. Gambling is the category used to record and report arrests for offenses relating to promoting, permitting, or engaging in gambling. The UCR requires a breakdown by type of gambling as follows: (a) bookmaking (horse and sports betting); (b) numbers and lottery; and (c) all others. The state of Nevada, which legalized gambling in 1931, cites gambling as a major source of income. In 1963 New Hampshire became the first state to adopt a legal lottery. In 1977 North Dakota legalized bingo and a lottery and in 1981 legalized blackjack gambling in bars, restaurants, and motels. In 1978 legal gambling casinos opened in Atlantic City, NJ. Federal law in 1988 allowed Native Americans extensive rights to run their own gaming on Indian reservations. On April 1, 1991, the Diamond Lady, the nation's first legal riverboat casino, was launched at Davenport, Iowa. In 1974, Americans spent $17 billion on gambling activities; by 1992, the figure had risen to $330 billion, growing to $630 billion in 1998, spent in legal activities. The FBI estimates that $40 billion or more is wagered illegally each year. State-sanctioned casino gambling accounts for more than 40 percent of all gaming revenues, followed by gaming on Indian reservations, state-run lotteries, and horse racing. Utah and Hawaii have no legal gambling. In 1996, 37 states had lotteries and 23 allowed some form of casino gambling. In 1996 Congress passed and President Clinton signed a law creating the National Gambling Impact and Policy Commission, which will have nine members— three appointed by the president and three each by the House and Senate.

gaming. An agreement between two or more persons to play together at a game of chance for a stake or wager that is to become the property of the winner and to which all contribute. The words *gaming* and *gambling* in statutes are similar in meaning. To constitute gambling, winner must either pay a consideration for the chance to win or, without paying anything in advance, stand a chance to lose or win. Gaming is properly the act or engagement of the players; if bystanders or other third persons put up a stake or wager among themselves, which will go to one or the other according to the result of the game, this is more correctly termed betting.

gamma hydroxy butyrate (GHB). A drug often referred to as the "date rape drug" because it is used to render women helpless against sexual aggression. GHB is an odorless and tasteless depressant that can cause euphoria, but in large doses leads to breathing problems, seizures, coma, and death. There is no antidote for overdoses. GHB can be either a liquid or a powder.

Gang Crime Research Center, National. Address: P.O. Box 990, Peoptone, IL 60468-0990. *See also* Appendix D

Gantt chart. Developed during World War I by Henry L. Gantt, it is a planning and control instrument that graphically presents work planned and work accomplished in relation to each other and in relation to time.

Gardner, Erle Stanley. A California lawyer (1889–1970), Gardner received his notoriety through his famous Perry Mason novels. The character of Mason later inspired several movies, radio and television series, and over 100 books, which made Gardner an extremely wealthy man. He also started "The Court of Last Resort," an organization which aided persons believed to have been wrongfully convicted.

garnish. To use a legal civil action brought by a creditor, whereby the debtor's money is impounded or attached while in the hands of a third party. The garnishee is warned not to deliver the money or property to the defendant debtor until the lawsuit is concluded.

garnishment. A form of attachment that has as its object the appropriation of money or credits in the hands of a third person.

garrote. To strangle and execute a person by any of several means; the implement or apparatus used to accomplish the strangulation.

gatekeeping. Counting heads; keeping records, as of prisoners; controlling access to or exit from any system, organization, or facility.

gateway drugs. A term for the substances usually tried initially by inexperienced drug users, including inhalants, nicotine, alcohol, and marijuana, so-called because it is theorized that users move on to stronger and more controlled substances after they have passed through the "gateway."

Gatling, Richard Jordan. American inventor (1818–1903) of the Gatling multiple-firing gun, precursor of the machine gun. His name gave rise to the slang word *gat*.

gauge. The unit of bore measurement for shotguns. Originally it referred to the number of solid lead balls of bore diameter that could be cast from one pound of lead; the larger the bore, the lower the number.

gay. A commonly accepted term to describe homosexual males. The Golden State Peace Officer's Association is a California-based association for gay and lesbian peace officers, as is the Gay Officers Action League of New York City. *See also* ACT-UP; Stonewall Riot; White Night

GED (general equivalency diploma). A certificate of secondary educational, or high school, completion that is awarded when an individual has passed standard examinations. Usually used in place of traditional diplomas for individuals who did not finish high school but gained the needed knowledge in other ways.

gendarme. A member of an armed police organization, such as in France; a police officer in France.

Gendarmerie Nationale. A military force in France under the control of the minister of the armed forces, utilized primarily for policing rural areas.

general adaptation syndrome (GAS). A response to stress involving the mobilization of all an individual's biological and psychological resources. Austrian-Canadian physician Hans Selye, born in 1907, first described the GAS, which consists of three stages: (1)

alarm: the person responds to stress as if it were an emergency, releasing adrenalin, increasing blood pressure and heart rate, and becoming more alert; as stress continues, the person develops (2) *resistance* to it, often pretending to relax while actually remaining tense; if under stress for an extended period of time, the person may enter (3) a state of *exhaustion*, in which the physical and mental resources are depleted. This may lead ultimately to a mental breakdown or even, in extreme cases, to death. *See also* stress

general appearance file. A file maintained by law enforcement agencies for photographs and descriptions of persons known to engage habitually in certain types of crime.

general intent. Conscious wrongdoing whose motive is inferred, unless expressly denied, as a method of legal proof.

general law. A statute expressed in general terms and affecting all places, persons, or things within the territory over which a legislature has power to act, but which may include reasonable classifications or categories, provided that all places, persons, or things within each category are treated alike—as distinguished from local legislation and special legislation.

general verdict. A verdict of either guilty or not guilty.

Genovese, Kitty. On March 14, 1964, at 3:20 A.M., 28-year-old Kitty Genovese returned home from work and parked her car 150 feet from her apartment at 82-70 Austin St. (Kew Gardens) in Queens County, NY, a borough of New York City. A man came out of the shadows, stabbed her, and began to sexually assault her. She screamed and lights came on in the apartment houses along Austin St. For the next 25 minutes, the attacker stalked, assaulted, and stabbed Ms. Genovese until she eventually died just before 3:50 A.M. Although 37 witnesses heard her screams for help and watched the assault, the first call to the police did not occur until some minutes after her death. This incident is often used to typify *anomie* as a component of contemporary urban crime. *See also* anomie

geographic base files. Geographically coded database covering, for example, calls for service, field-interrogation/interview cards, offense/ incident records, moving violation citations, and arrest records. The data lend themselves to computer-assisted dispatch, crime-trend analysis, planning, research, and resource allocation. Some agencies have geographic (geo-coded) reporting districts configured to census tracts. *See also* census tract; demography; metropolitan statistical areas

Germanic law. The law of the Teutonic, or Germanic, tribes refers to a family of customary laws in which there were wide variations. Nordic customary laws and the laws of the German barbarians who conquered the Roman Empire in the West are generally included in this category. Although the Germanic tribes are associated with primitive elements of law and the code of bravery, their oral-law tradition contained many elements that would be regarded as democratic. A public assembly or representative body called the Ting acted as the protector of rights of the people. The word *law* is a Norse word, and the concept that no man is above the law is associated with the law speakers of the Germanic tribes. The concept of damages to prevent violent retribution was also an early kind of tort sometimes recommended by the law speakers. The seafaring expeditions of the Vikings in the ninth and tenth centuries did much to promote Germanic customs, and Canute's settlement in England was known for the fairness and impartial application of its laws. Romano-Germanic law stands today as one the three main families of laws.

Gideon, Clarence Earl. Charged with breaking and entering of the Bay Harbor Pool Room in Panama City, FL, with the intent of committing a misdemeanor—a case of petty larceny which, under Florida law, is considered a felony. On August 4, 1961, he was tried, served as his own defense, was found guilty, and sentenced to serve five years in state prison. On January 8, 1962, the U.S. Supreme Court received a large envelope from Gideon containing his petition *in forma pauperis*—in the form of a poor man. Certiorari was granted and the Court assigned Washington, DC, attorney Abe Fortas to argue Gideon's claim. Fortas contended that counsel in a criminal trial is a fundamental right of due process enforced on the states by the Fourteenth Amendment. The Court's decision was unanimous, and in overturning Gideon's conviction, Justice Black wrote: "Any person hailed into court, who is too poor to hire a lawyer, cannot be assured a fair trial unless counsel is provided for him. This seems to be an obvious truth." This ruling on March 18, 1963, after Gideon had served almost two years in prison, entitled him to a new trial. He was retried, represented by counsel, and acquitted. Gideon died in 1972. Abe Fortas, who later served as a Supreme Court justice, died in 1982.

gift *causa mortis*. A gift of personal property made by a party in the expectation that his or her death is imminent.

gift *inter vivos*. A gift from one living person to another.

good faith. With good intention; true and trustworthy, especially in the performance of an obligation or a vow. An honest intention of carrying out a duty without taking any undue advantage.

good samaritan. A person other than a peace officer who is not directly involved in an incident/situation but steps in to prevent injury, aid a victim, or apprehend an offender; usually a bystander or passerby. *See also* victim compensation

goods and chattels. Personal property of every kind, as distinguished from real property.

good-time. The amount of time deducted from time to be served in prison on a given sentence(s) and/or under correction agency jurisdiction, awarded at some point after a prisoner's admission to prison and contingent upon good behavior and/or awarded automatically by application of a statute or regulation. Application of an automatic good-time rule usually reduces the offender's maximum potential term in confinement and/or under correctional jurisdiction, though in many states it reduces the minimum term, and thus the parole eligibility date is affected. Some states have no "good-time" provisions. Good-time can be lost by misbehavior, unless awarded under a statute or regulation providing otherwise. Fixed good-time is called vested good-time. Summary descriptions of each state's good-time rules can be found in *Parole Systems in the U.S.*

Goring, Charles Buckman. A British research scientist and prison physician (1870–1919), Goring published a statistical study of 3,000 male convicts entitled *The English Convict*, in which he claimed criminal tendencies are related to mental deficiencies and psychological factors rather than to physical characteristics as theorized by Cesare Lombroso.

government agency. A subdivision of the executive, legislative, judicial, or other branch of a government, including a department, independent establishment, commission, administration, authority, board, and bureau; or a corporation or other legal entity established by, and subject to control by, a government or governments for execution of a governmental or intergovernmental program.

graffiti. *See* vandalism

graft. Money or valuable privileges gained at the expense of the public or the public interest, usually by officeholders, employees, or persons who possess political influence, and obtained through actions ranging from theft to morally reprehensible acts for which there is no legal penalty.

graft, honest. A term coined by the famous Tammany Hall chieftain George Washington Plunkitt to identify the profit secured by politicians in making use of their foreknowledge of public building projects and improvements. Dishonest graft is payment for nonexistent jobs and services to persons who return a portion of the payment to the politicians who made it. *See also* Tweed, William Marcy

Graham, Jack Gilbert. Constructed a bomb, which he placed in his mother's luggage, set to detonate 10 minutes after her plane departed from Denver's Stapleton Airport bound for Seattle. On the early evening of November 1, 1955, United Airlines flight 629 was blown apart over a beet farm near Longmount, CO, killing all 44 passengers and crew members aboard.

grain. The unit of measurement used to express the weight of a powder charge or a bullet; 437.5 grains equal 1 oz. avoirdupois, and 7,000 grains equal 1 lb.

grandfather clause. Found initially in the Motor Carrier Act of 1935 and often included in legislation that provides for regulatory control of an industry. Such a clause attempts to preserve the rights of firms in operation before enactment of a law by exempting these firms from certain provisions of that law. Grandfather provisions have also been included in protecting existing employees from change(s) made affecting all new hires.

grand jury. The grand jury system apparently originated in England in 1166, when King Henry II required knights and other freemen drawn from rural neighborhoods to file with the court accusations of murder, robbery, larceny, and harboring of known criminals. In time, as the common law developed, the English grand jury came to consist of not fewer than 12 nor more than 23 jurors. Not only did they tender criminal accusations, but they considered them from outsiders as well. The jurors heard witnesses and, if convinced that there were grounds for trial, returned an indictment. Historically, the purposes of the grand jury were to serve as an investigatory body and to act as a buffer between the state and its citizens in order to prevent the Crown from unfairly invoking the criminal process against its enemies. The grand jury was incorporated into the Fifth Amendment of the U.S. Constitution, which provides that "no person shall be held to answer for a capital or otherwise infamous crime, unless on a presentment or indictment of a grand jury." The grand jury has remained unchanged; it is defined as a body of persons who have been selected according to law and sworn to hear the evidence against accused persons and determine whether there is sufficient evidence to bring those persons to trial, to investigate criminal activity generally, and to investigate the conduct of public agencies and officials. It is called a grand jury because it comprises a greater number of jurors than the ordinary trial, or petit, jury. The composition of not less than 12 nor more than 23 members is still the rule in many of the states, though in some the number is otherwise fixed by statute. Thus in OR and UT, the grand jury is composed of 7 persons; in SD, not less than 6 nor more than 8; in TX, 12; in ID, 16 to 23; in CA, 19; and in NM, 21.

grand jury, charging. A grand jury that must decide whether or not to ratify the prosecutor's request for a formal charge against a defendant.

grand jury, investigatory. The grand jury for a court with the authority to conduct investigations into possible crimes.

grand larceny. Larceny of property where the value of the property stolen exceeds the amount fixed by statute in the different states. Often includes larceny from the person and larceny of specific kinds of property. *See also* larceny

grant of probation. A court action requiring that a person fulfill certain conditions of behavior for a specified period of time; often includes assignment to a probation agency for supervision in lieu of either prosecution, judgment, or, after conviction, usually a sentence to confinement.

graphology. Handwriting analysis. Psychologists are interested in this subject because of the hypothesis that handwriting is a projection of personality. Forensic graphology, the study of handwriting to determine who wrote what, is another specialty.

gratuity. A gift or present.

Greek law. Greek contributions to Western thought about law come from the ideas of great philosophers such as Socrates, Plato, and Aristotle. From these men emerged notions of justice that profoundly influenced legal reasoning. The Greeks distinguished, for example, between natural law and positive law. The Socratic method, the use of questions to establish a proposition, is still used in the case method of training lawyers in the United States. The need for equity, a principle to temper the harshness of the law and ensure justice, was recognized by Aristotle; and the principle of equity, continuing in the English courts of chancery, provided one of the founding principles of modern juvenile justice. Another idea to emerge from Greek philosophical thought was Aristotle's Stoic concept of the reasonably prudent man. *See also* Roman legal system

Green Haven Prison. New York's Green Haven Correctional Facility (called Green Haven Prison until 1970) was built as a military prison during World War II and acquired by NY in 1949. It was designed to be an escape-proof institution. Its outer wall of reinforced concrete is 30 feet high, almost 3 feet thick, and is said to go 30 feet below ground. Its 12 towers, reaching to 40 feet above the ground, are evenly positioned along the mile-long wall around the perimeter of the prison. No one has ever managed to escape over the wall at Green Haven.

Green River laws. Laws that prohibit door-to-door selling.

Green River Task Force. Group of law enforcement personnel assembled to investigate what was considered the nation's largest unsolved serial murder cases. The remains of 41 of 49 women reported missing from January 1982 through March 1984 have been found in and around Seattle, WA. At one time the task force involved 56 agents of local, state, and federal law enforcement. Gary Ridgway confessed to killing 48 women over a two-decade period. He pled guilty on November 5, 2003 and was convicted, receiving consecutive life sentences for each murder.

grid search. A technique for searching crime scenes, usually outdoors, in which an area previously searched by the strip method is again searched after being divided into lanes or zones running at right angles to the plots used in the strip search.

grievance. A grievance is any complaint concerning the interpretation or application of a memorandum of understanding or rules or regulations governing personnel practices or working conditions that departmental management has the ability to remedy.

groove diameter. The diameter of a bore of a gun as measured from the bottom of one groove to the bottom of the opposite groove.

grooves. The spiral depressions in the rifling of a gun. They impart a spinning motion to a projectile, which stabilizes it in flight.

gross negligence. Apparent failure to exercise the care demanded by circumstances.

guaranty. A promise or undertaking by one person to answer for the payment of some debt or performance of some contract in case of default by another person.

guardian. One who has legal responsibility for the care and management of the person, estate, or both, of an infant or other incompetent person.

guardian *ad litem.* A guardian appointed for the purpose of a lawsuit.

Guardian Angels. New York City's Guardian Angels were founded by Brooklyn-born Curtis Sliwa, the son of a second-generation Polish-American merchant. To protect the riders on the No. 4 subway, which was known as the muggers' express, he organized a group of his friends called the The Magnificent Thirteen, and, on February 13, 1979, they went on their first subway patrol. They quickly expanded into the Guardian Angels, a group of unarmed but streetwise youths, self-appointed peacekeepers who patrol the city's buses, subways, and streets. Dressed in white T-shirts and red berets, the 700-plus force has had a reassuring effect on many New Yorkers. By 1982, the Guardian Angels had expanded their operations to more than 40 communities across the country, yet only the cities of New York, Boston, Los Angeles,

Miami, and Baltimore have given them official recognition. Numerous cities in Europe, Asia, and South America had requested Sliwa's help in starting similar groups. In May, 1985, he took his group to the U.S.-Mexican border at Tijuana to assist in the protection of illegal aliens. Published the book *Street Smarts: The Guardian Angels Guide to Safe Living.* Address: 982 E. 89th Street, Brooklyn, NY 11236.

guillotine. A machine, invented during the French Revolution, with two upright posts surmounted by a crossbeam grooved so that a weighted and oblique-shaped knife blade falls swiftly and with force when the cord by which it is suspended is released.

guilt by association. The idea, which has sometimes been embodied in statutes, that a person's guilt is prima facie determined by membership in an organization stigmatized as criminal or subversive, regardless of the person's knowledge of the aims and activities of the organization or of his or her own active involvement.

gun. In general, a piece of ordnance consisting essentially of a tube or barrel and used for throwing projectiles by force, usually that of an explosive but sometimes that of compressed gas, a spring, and so forth. The general term embraces such weapons as howitzers, mortars, cannons, firearms, rifles, shotguns, carbines, pistols, and revolvers. *See also* firearm

gun control laws. Federal, state, and local laws that regulate the importation, manufacturing, distribution, sale, purchase, or possession of firearms. The Alcohol, Tobacco, and Firearms Division of the U.S. Treasury Department has jurisdiction over the federal laws. Efforts to pass gun control measures are often referred to as Brady legislation, after former president Ronald Reagan's press secretary, James Brady, who was shot and crippled in the March 1981 assassination attempt on Reagan. The United States has about 20,000 gun control laws, the vast majority of which are state or local ordinances. In June 1993 CT joined CA and NJ as the only three states to ban the sale of semiautomatic assault weapons. The new law bans the sale of 53 weapons based on military designs, including the AK-47, MAC-lO, TEC-9, Colt AR-iS, and the Colt Sporter. *See also* Firearm Act, Federal

H

habeas corpus (Lat., lit. "you should have the body"). The British Parliament formalized the concept with the Habeas Corpus Act of 1679, and Americans wrote it into the U.S. Constitution. Article III, Section 9, reads, "The privilege of the writ of habeas corpus shall not be suspended, unless when in a case of rebellion or invasion the public safety may require it." The writ is a legal device to challenge the detention of a person taken into custody. An individual in custody may demand an evidentiary hearing before a judge to examine the legality of the detention. The writ is purely procedural: it guarantees only a right to a hearing. It has no bearing on the substance of the issue or charge.

habitual criminal laws. Many American states and other countries have passed laws that provide increased penalties for offenders with previous criminal records. The provision for the increased penalty is either permissive or mandatory. The habitual criminal law is invoked after conviction of a second, third, or fourth felony. The advocates of such laws believe the increased severity of penalty will eliminate or considerably reduce serious crime. *See also* Baumes's laws

habitual offender. A person sentenced under the provisions of a statute declaring that persons convicted of a given offense, and shown to have previously been convicted of another specified offense(s), shall receive a more severe penalty than that for the current offense alone. In certain states, under habitual offender acts or so-called Baumes's laws, persons convicted of a certain number of felonies, usually four, are sentenced to imprisonment for life.

habitual offender statutes. *See* recidivism statutes

habituation. A psychological dependence upon a substance such as marijuana or tobacco. Withdrawal from these substances is considered essentially psychological in nature.

hacker. A hacker is a skilled computer user. The term originally denoted a skilled programmer, particularly one skilled in machine code and with a good knowledge of the machine and its operating system. The name arose from the fact that a good programmer could always hack an unsatisfactory system around until it worked.

The term later came to denote a user whose main interest is in defeating password systems. The term has thus acquired a pejorative sense, with the meaning of one who deliberately and sometimes criminally interferes with data available through telephone lines.

halfway house. A term originally given to guidance centers for offenders who are halfway out of prisons, on probation or parole. Today, the term may mean a center to help mental patients readjust to living outside a hospital after discharge, or any therapeutic community for people continuing to recover from drug, alcohol, or other problems after discharge from an in-patient facility. The Isaac T. Hooper Home, the first halfway house in the United States, was opened by the Society of Friends (Quakers) in New York City in 1845.

Haloperidol. A nonnarcotic, nonaddicting drug for treating and controlling withdrawal symptoms associated with both heroin and methadone addiction.

Hand, Learned. Considered one of the greatest jurists of his day, Hand (1872–1961) served over 50 years on the bench as a federal judge. His final post (1924 to 1951) was as chief judge of the Federal Court of Appeals for the Second Circuit.

handicapped parking. On April 10, 1991, the U.S. Department of Transportation established the Informed System for Handicapped Parking. All state license plates issued to people with handicaps must include a three-inch-square image of the international symbol of access—a stick-figure profile of a wheelchair user. States are also required to make available placards of uniform size and color, to be hung from a car's rear view mirror, which clearly display the same symbol. Disabled drivers are entitled to more than one copy of the placard so that it can also be displayed in rental cars. For those with temporary disabilities, a placard will be available, with a doctor's authorization, granting disability parking status for up to six months. The temporary placards are red (placards for permanent disability are blue), and list the issuing state and date of expiration. The dates of state implementation of these regulations are decided by individual state legislatures.

hanging. A method of capital punishment devised in ancient times and currently in use in many countries. Originally, death came about by strangling, but now there is either a drop of about seven feet or a sudden jerk upward, which usually breaks the neck and causes supposedly instantaneous death. *See also* Parker, Isaac C.

harassing calls. Telephone calls, also called nuisance calls, placed repetitively to annoy or frighten a family or individual. Using the telephone in this manner is a criminal offense, and victims can prosecute if calls are frequent and harassing enough to warrant action. Working with local law enforcement personnel, with whom the victim must lodge a complaint, telephone companies can tap the victim's line to determine the source of the calls. *See also* dialed number recorders; pen register

harbor master. An administrator/officer charged with enforcing state harbor laws in addition to city ordinances, rules, and regulations.

Harlan, John Marshall. An associate justice of the Supreme Court (1833–1911) noted for his dissents in decisions upholding racial discrimination and segregation. Although he once supported slavery and strict enforcement of fugitive slave laws, his revulsion at

terrorism helped to convert him to a pro–civil rights position. His support for Rutherford B. Hayes led to Harlan's appointment to the Supreme Court in 1877. He was the Court's outstanding liberal justice during his tenure and the only dissenter in the Civil Rights Cases (1883) and in *Plessy v. Ferguson* (1896), which established the separate-but-equal principle. Harlan built his legal philosophy on a reverence for the Constitution. Aside from civil rights questions, he was against weakening antitrust legislation.

Harlan, John Marshall. An associate justice of the Supreme Court (1899–1971) noted as the conservative conscience of an activist Court and for his strict adherence to prior judicial decisions. He was named for his grandfather. Harlan served as an assistant U.S. attorney and was chief counsel to the New York State Crime Commission. In 1954, President Eisenhower named him to the U.S. Court of Appeals (Second Circuit) and less than a year later nominated him for the Supreme Court. In general, he dissented from the liberal philosophy of his colleagues although siding with the majority on civil rights issues. He also believed that the federal judiciary should not become involved in state and local problems. His conservative philosophy was influential at a time when the majority would have been willing to assert judicial power over other branches of government.

Harrison Narcotics Act. A federal act that requires all persons who deal in narcotics to register with the director of Internal Revenue. The purpose of the act is to regulate the traffic in narcotics for medical and scientific purposes only.

Harris poll. These well-known surveys are based on Bureau of Census information about state and metropolitan populations. Interviews are conducted at a minimum of 100 different locations throughout the country, with usually 16 households contacted in each location. Although the sample is relatively small, it is representative of the civilian population of the United States, excluding Alaska and Hawaii and those in prisons, hospitals, and religious and educational institutions. *See also* Gallup poll

hashish. An extract of the hemp plant (*cannabis sativa*) with a higher concentration of THC than marijuana. It may be inhaled, chewed, or smoked in order to produce a type of exhilaration accompanied by the disorganization of the central nervous system.

Hatch Act of 1939. A law of Congress enacted "to prevent pernicious political activities." It forbids anyone to intimidate, threaten, or coerce any person in order to influence his vote for a federal office. It further prohibits promise of employment or other advantage for political support and makes illegal the soliciting of political contributions by relief workers and federal executive or administrative employees. The latter were also prohibited from engaging in political management or in political campaigns. Exempted from its provisions were certain policy-determining officials. The amendment of 1940 attempted to regulate campaign contributions and expenditures. The act and its amendment, however, have proven unsuccessful. Expenditures and contributions by individual committees and persons have raised the amounts far beyond those laid down in the law, which is also known as the Federal Corrupt Practices Act of 1939. Presently, the federal government has not revised either act.

hate crimes. Statistical category of offenses against minorities included in the annual FBI Uniform Crime Reports. Data include offenses related to victims' race, religion, sexual orientation, and ethnicity. In June 1993 the U.S. Supreme Court upheld hate crime laws in 26 states that permit judges to impose longer sentences on those whose crimes grow out of their biases. The Federal Hate Crimes Sentencing Enhancement Act of 1994 expanded the definition to include women and persons with disabilities. In this statute, hate crimes are those in which "the defendant intentionally selects a victim, or in the case of a property crime, the property that is the object of the crime, because of the actual or perceived race, color, religion, na-

tional origin, ethnicity, gender, disability, or sexual orientation of any person." Created in 1990 by the passage of the Hate Crime Statistical Act of 1990. (18 U.S.C. Sections 241, 242, 245, 247, and 42 U.S.C. Section 3631). *See also* xenophobe

hate crime incident. A "hate incident" is not a crime and cannot be prosecuted because it lacks the element of damage to property, the element of harm or immediate threat of harm, and the element of violence or the immediate threat of violence. Examples could include hostile or hateful speech, or other disrespectful or discriminatory behavior, which although motivated by bias, is not illegal. The First Amendment of the Constitution protects free speech.

Hauptmann, Bruno Richard. A German immigrant (1899–1936) who had been convicted of burglary and armed robbery, he entered the United States illegally in 1923. He kidnapped the son of Colonel Charles Lindbergh; he was convicted and, on April 3, 1936, was electrocuted at the state prison in New Jersey.

Hawes-Cooper Act. A law enacted by the Congress and approved by the president on January 19, 1929, it became operative after five years. It provided that all prison-made goods entering into interstate commerce are subject to the laws of any state or territory of the United States to the same extent and in the same manner as prison-made goods manufactured in that state or territory. It was aimed at the contract, piece-price, and public-account systems of prison labor.

Hawthorne effect. A transitory increase in worker productivity resulting from an expression of management's interest in work group activities. The phenomenon was first recognized in morale-enhancing activities of Elton Mayo and a Harvard University research team during industrial experiments at Western Electric's Hawthorne, IL, plant during the 1920s and 1930s. Recent views hold that a negative Hawthorne effect— decreased productivity because of a perception of lack of management interest—occurs more often than a positive one.

Hawthorne studies. A classic series of experiments conducted at the Hawthorne plant of Western Electric in Chicago from 1924 until 1932. The most famous involved the relay assembly test room, the mica-splitting test room, and the bank-wiring observation room. The research was originally conducted to determine the relationship between working conditions and employee productivity and satisfaction. The major finding was that human factors—perceptions of management interest in workers—were more significant than environmental factors as determinants of productivity and satisfaction. Informal work groups and interactions among employees play a key role in the organization, it was found. This discovery led to the development of the human relations approach to the study of organizations.

Haymarket Massacre. A bombing and shooting incident on May 4, 1886. On May 3, striking workers at the McCormick Reaper works in Chicago attacked strikebreakers; police used guns and clubs to disperse the strikers. August Spies, editor of a German-language anarchist newspaper, called a protest meeting for Haymarket Square the following day. As that meeting was breaking up, a police officer leading 180 men ordered the crowd to disperse. A bomb was thrown among the police, and both sides opened fire with pistols. Seven policemen died, 60 or more were wounded, and a number of civilians were killed or wounded. Police arrested a number of prominent Chicago anarchists, including Spies, Albert Parsons (editor of an English-language newspaper), and Samuel Fielden (a teamster and anarchist leader). Of the seven men sentenced to be hanged, four were hanged, one committed suicide, and two had their sentences commuted. In 1892, Illinois governor John Peter Altgeld released the imprisoned survivors, claiming both judge and jury had shown extreme prejudice. The inci-

dent served to couple the labor movement to anarchic violence in the public mind.

hearing. A proceeding in which arguments, witnesses, or evidence are heard by a judicial officer or administrative body.

hearsay. Evidence that a witness has learned through others.

Hearst, Patricia. The granddaughter of publisher William Randolph Hearst, Patricia was born in 1955. In the company of her boyfriend, she was kidnapped on February 5, 1974, in Berkeley, CA, by the Symbionese Liberation Army. This was the first U.S. political kidnapping. She became the object of one of the most intensive manhunts ever conducted by the FBI. On May 16, 1974, SLA members and the kidnapped Hearst used a red 1970 Volkswagen van in a gunfire-filled getaway after a shoplifting incident at an Inglewood, CA, sporting goods store. When the police found the vehicle, they also discovered a gun nearby—registered to Emily Harris—and a parking ticket inside the van that led them to the SLA's hideout. A day later, six members of the terrorist group—including its leader, Donald DeFreeze—died in a two-hour shoot-out with 500 local and federal officers in south central Los Angeles. FBI agents captured Hearst in San Francisco on September 18, 1975, with others. She was indicted for bank robbery and a San Francisco jury convicted her on March 20, 1976. She was subsequently pardoned by President Gerald Ford.

hebephile. Term for a pedophile who is drawn to young people during the period of puberty and adolescence.

heir at law. One entitled by law to inherit by descent the real estate of a decedent.

Hell's Angels Motorcycle Club. *See* motorcyclists, outlaw

hematoporphyrin test. A chemical confirmation test for the presence of blood.

Hennard, George, Jr. On October 17, 1991, 35-year-old George Hennard drove his 1987 Ford Ranger XLT pickup through a Luby's cafeteria window in Killen, TX, and methodically shot and killed 22 people (14 women and 8 men) and wounded 23 others, using a 9mm Glock 17 and a Ruger P89, both semiautomatic pistols, before taking his own life. This tragedy is considered the worst one-man shooting massacre in U.S. history. *See also* Huberty, James

Henry system. A system of fingerprint classification devised by Sir Edward Richard Henry in 1901. He was a former police commissioner of London. The system divides prints into four main types—arches, loops, whorls, and composites.

heroin. One of the opium family isolated in the search for nonhabit-forming anesthetics to take the place of morphine. Heroin is a trademark name which has become identified with a white crystalline form of morphine derivative. It is definitely habit-forming and has become one of the most widely used of all narcotics. It produces a quiet, pleasant, dreamlike slumber. In February 1989 an investigation, code-named Operation White Mare, seized 838 pounds of heroin valued at $1 billion and $3 million cash in New York City. In June 1991 U.S. Customs agents seized 1,080 pounds of China White (pure heroin) in a Hayward, CA, warehouse near San Francisco, with a street value of between $2.7 and $4 billion. By comparison, about 200 pounds of heroin were seized from the French Connection ring, broken in 1971. It is estimated that U.S. addicts consume four to six tons of heroin a year.

Herzberg's motivation-maintenance theory. Frederick Herzberg postulated, based on his 1950s study *The Motivation to Work*, that there exists a set of extrinsic job conditions that, when not present, result in dissatisfaction among employees. However, the presence of these conditions does not necessarily motivate employees. Potential dissatisfiers (maintenance factors) are: job security; salary; working conditions; status; company policies; quality of technical supervision; quality of interpersonal relations among peers, supervisors, and subordinates; fringe benefits. There

also exists a set of intrinsic job conditions, termed motivators or satisfiers, that include achievement, recognition, work itself, responsibility, advancement, personal growth and development. *See also* motivation

high crimes and misdemeanors. Offenses against law sufficiently grave to warrant impeachment by the House of Representatives.

higher law doctrine. (1) The concept of a law of nature intrinsically superior to positive law. (2) A declaration that "there is a higher law than the Constitution," made by Senator William H. Seward of New York, an abolitionist spokesman, on March 11, 1850, during the debates on the Compromise of 1850.

Highfields. *See* New Jersey Experimental Project for the Treatment of Youthful Offenders

high misdemeanor. In some states, crimes are classified as misdemeanors and high misdemeanors, the latter carrying heavier penalties.

High School Senior Survey. Since 1975, the National Institute on Drug Abuse has sponsored this research, which collects data from 15,000 to 17,000 students in some 135 public and private high schools. Primary uses of the data include assessing the prevalence and trends of drug use among seniors; better understanding the lifestyles and value systems associated with drug use; and monitoring how these attitudes shift over time. *See also* Drug Abuse Warning Network

high seas law enforcement. The U.S. Coast Guard enforces, within the territorial waters, contiguous zones, and special interest areas of the high seas, federal laws and international agreements, except those related to pollution, traffic control, and port and vessel safety. This activity also includes the detection of illegal fishing and other illegal activity. Address: Operational Law Enforcement Division, Office of Operations, Coast Guard, DOT, 2100 2nd Street, SW, Room 3108, Washington, DC 20593.

highway. A way publicly maintained and open to the use of the public for purposes of vehicular travel. The term includes street.

highway patrol. A special state force, known by various names, which enforces motor vehicle and other laws in those states that have not established a state constabulary invested with general law-enforcement powers.

highway statistics. Statistics are available on such topics as: the number of motor vehicles by state; the amount of fuel consumed by state; the number of drivers' licenses issued by age, sex, and state; state finances; and vehicle miles traveled. Contact: Highway Statistics Division, Office of Highway Planning, Federal Highway Administration, DOT, 400 7th Street, SW, Room 3300, HHP 40, Washington, DC 20590.

hijack alert system. A system created by trucking concerns, trucking associations, and law enforcement agencies whereby a theft or hijack is immediately reported to designated law enforcement agencies and to a designated trucking association. The latter, per a prearranged schedule, notifies certain strategically located trucking companies who, in turn, notify others until all truckers in a given area are notified. Truck drivers and others search for and report locations of the stolen equipment.

hijacking. Taking control of a vehicle by the use or threatened use of force or by intimidation; taking a vehicle by stealth, without the use or threatened use of force, in order to steal its cargo. Hijacking is a popular name for behavior that can constitute any of several statutory offenses. Where an occupant of the vehicle is forced to accompany a perpetrator, chargeable offense can be kidnapping or false imprisonment. Where a vehicle is taken by force, with intent to permanently deprive the owner of the vehicle or any of its parts or contents, the chargeable offense can be robbery. Where a vehicle is taken by stealth, the chargeable offense is usually larceny, but such an incident is usually recorded in a separate category of motor vehicle theft. *See also* skyjacking

hit and run. Unlawful departure by a driver from the scene of a motor vehicle accident in which he or she was involved and that re-

sulted in injury to a person or damage to the property of another.

Hobbs Act. An act of Congress passed on July 3, 1947, designed to curb labor racketeering, which imposes penalties on persons found guilty of robbery or extortion when these acts have the effect of obstructing, delaying, or otherwise affecting interstate commerce.

Hoffa, James Riddle. Born in 1913, Hoffa succeeded Dave Beck as Teamsters Union president in 1957, when Beck was jailed for stealing union funds. As a result of Senate hearings, the Teamsters were expelled from the AFL-CIO. In 1964 Hoffa was convicted of jury tampering at the conclusion of a trial begun two years earlier. He was imprisoned in 1967 to serve an eight-year sentence. He disappeared in 1977, and although his body was never found, he was presumed murdered. His son, James Hoffa, currently serves as Teamster Union president.

Holmes, Oliver Wendell, Jr. (1841–1935). Associate justice of the Supreme Court from 1902 to 1932. Known as the "great dissenter," he was appointed by President Theodore Roosevelt and eventually ranked with John Marshall as one of the two greatest justices ever to sit on the Court. A veteran of the Civil War, he was graduated from Harvard Law School in 1866, published *The Common Law* in 1881, and was appointed to the school's faculty in 1882. Within months, however, he had accepted a justiceship on the Massachusetts Supreme Judicial Court and served almost 20 years, the last 3 as chief justice. Holmes became the most outspoken advocate of judicial self-restraint. He believed the Constitution allowed wide latitude for social experimentation by the states and by Congress. It was Holmes who began the Supreme Court's initial involvement with freedom of speech and the meaning of the First Amendment. He formulated the famous rule that an utterance could be punished only if there was a "clear and present danger" that it would lead to an evil that Congress or the states could legitimately try to prevent.

holograph. A handwritten will, or any document completely in the handwriting of the person who has signed it.

home rule. The power of a local government, usually a city, to manage its own affairs and to draft or change its charter. Under home rule of municipalities, the state legislatures voluntarily renounce their power and authorize the cities to manage their affairs, subject only to broad state statutes. More than half of U.S. states allow varying degrees of freedom to their cities.

Homeland Security, Department of. Originally created as the White House Office of Homeland Security in the wake of the 9/11 terrorist attacks on the World Trade Center and the Pentagon, the agency was elevated to cabinet-level status by Congress in March 2003. The new Department of Homeland Security (DHS) brings together over 20 agencies, departments or offices in an effort to coordinate antiterrorism activities. The Secret Service, Coast Guard, Border Patrol, and Immigration and Naturalization Service are examples of major agencies transferred to the new department. In addition, the Bureau of Alcohol, Tobacco, and Firearms (BATF) was moved from the Treasury Department to the Department of Justice. The DHS is organized into four major directorates: Border and Transportation Security, Emergency Preparedness and Response, Science and Technology, and Information Analysis and Infrastructure Protection, plus the traditional functions of the U.S. Secret Service, Coast Guard, and Animal and Plant border inspections. When originally created, the DHS had over 177,000 employees, making it the third largest department in the Federal government, with a budget of over $37 billion. The first Secretary of Homeland Security is Tom Ridge, former governor of Pennsylvania.

homestead. A filing process that protects property against most debts. Among the debts that are not affected by a declaration of homestead are taxes, mortgages, mechanics' liens, child support, alimony, and court judgments recorded before the declaration is filed. The homestead procedure varies from state to state, but generally it protects the first $30,000 of equity if the owner is single; $45,000, if married; and $55,000, if age 65 or disabled.

Homestead Massacre. A fight between strikers and company guards on July 6, 1892. Shooting occurred when Carnegie Steel Company's head manager, Henry Clay Frick, ordered 300 Pinkerton guards sent in to protect strikebreakers at the plant in Homestead, PA. When striking workers forcibly resisted the arrival of the Pinkertons, 10 guards and strikers were killed. The state militia was sent in to maintain order and, incidentally, protect strikebreakers. Both the strike and the union were broken, and the steel industry remained unorganized until the 1930s.

homicide. Any willful killing, including murder and nonnegligent manslaughter.

homicide, excusable. A killing under such circumstances of accident or misfortune that the party is relieved from the penalty attached to the commission of a felonious homicide.

homicide, felonious. A killing committed under such circumstances as to make it punishable.

homicide investigation, computerized. HITMAN, an acronym for homicide information tracing management automation network, was developed in 1985 by Lt. Hocking and Officer Willis of the Los Angeles Police Department. The system can scan Los Angeles homicides since 1983 (with plans to include files back to 1978) and can be asked nearly 100 different questions about each death.

homicide, justifiable. A killing committed with full intent but under such circumstances of duty as to render the act proper, such as in cases of self-defense, defense of property, or an officer lawfully enforcing the law.

homophobia. Fear of homosexuals. Homophobes mistakenly believe that exposure to gay people will cause heterosexual people, especially children, to adopt a gay lifestyle. The AIDS epidemic has increased homophobia and violence against homosexuals. *See also* hate crimes

homosexual. Person(s) attracted sexually to members of one's own sex. In 1989 Denmark was the first country to allow gay marriages. France and Norway soon followed. Germany approved gay marriages in August, 2001. *See* ACT-UP; gay; Stonewall Riot; White Night

Hoover Commissions. The Commission on the Reorganization of the Executive Branch, operating from 1947 to 1949 and from 1953 to 1955 were the third and fourth of a series of commissions to study paralysis, waste, and corruption in the bureaucracy. Named chairman twice because of his eminence as a past president and his record of incorruptible public service, Herbert Hoover was particularly concerned with duplication of responsibilities and inefficiency.

Hoover, J(ohn) Edgar. American public official (1895–1972) who served as first director of the FBI, holding that position for 48 years. Hoover was born in Washington, DC. After receiving a law degree, he began work at the Department of Justice. Within two years, he was named special assistant to Attorney General Palmer. He became the director of the FBI in 1924.

Hoover turned the FBI into a symbol of law enforcement, established the world's largest fingerprint file, and created the FBI National Academy. From the late 1940s, he was known for his uncompromising attitude toward suspected communists and subversives; both the FBI and Hoover came under fire for exceeding their authority. He continued in office, however, until his death. His books include *Masters of Deceit* (1958) and *On Communism* (1969).

horses in law enforcement. *See* Mounted Services Organization

hospice. An institution and a philosophy that offer an alternative to traditional hospital care for terminally ill patients. In a hospice, it is understood that no heroic effort will be made to prolong the patient's life, but that treatment to relieve pain will be provided. The hospice movement began in Great Britain, where St. Christopher's Hospice in London is considered a model. *See also* AIDS; euthanasia

hostage. A person held as a pledge that certain terms or agreements will be kept. The taking of hostages is forbidden under the Geneva Convention of 1949.

hostage-taking. *See* terrorism

hot pursuit. A principle of international law justifying pursuit and arrest of vessels that have infringed the laws of a state, provided such pursuit begins within the territorial waters of the offended state and is continued without interruption. The right of pursuit ceases when the vessel reaches the territorial waters of another state.

hours of work. A major concern of labor as far back as 1840, when efforts were made to limit the number of hours that women and children could be allowed to work. In the early 1890s, wage earners averaged from 54 to 60 hours a week, and it took a quarter-century to enact child labor laws. In the early 1930s, state governments began to enact protective labor legislation in regard to working hours, and in 1938 Congress passed the Fair Labor Standards Act that established the 40-hour work week. From this emerged the concept of overtime pay. Many law enforcement agencies have adopted 10-hour, 4-day (10 plan) work schedules. The 12-hour plan (a 3-day work week) is gaining acceptance, while others maintain the 5-day, 8-hour format or some variation. All work hour models may be either fixed or featuring rotating or overlapping shifts.

house arrest. Monitored restriction to one's residence. St. Paul the Apostle was placed under house arrest, as was Galileo in the 1600s, and, in 1917, the last czar of Russia, Nicholas II, and his family. In contemporary America, it was first used in Wisconsin in 1913 but did not receive much national support until the 1950s.

housebreaking. Breaking open and entering a house with felonious intent.

Household Survey. *See* National Survey on Drug Abuse

house of correction. English institution established in the sixteenth century for vagabonds, prostitutes, rogues, and the unemployed. In the United States, it is a place of confinement for short-term offenders whose violations of the law are of a minor nature.

Huberty, James Oliver. An unemployed security guard, who on July 18, 1984, at a McDonald's fast-food establishment located in San Ysidro, CA, shot and killed 21 persons. The oldest victim was 74 years of age; the youngest 8 months. Huberty was killed by a SWAT sharpshooter on the post office roof 113 feet away. *See also* Hennard, George, Jr.

hue. To sound an alarm by shouting. Colonial citizens would chase a criminal with shouts and cries.

human relations. An understanding of why people act in a certain manner, how they get along together in a group setting, and the characteristics of persons and groups. *See also* community relations; Hawthorne studies

hung jury. A jury which, after long deliberation, is so irreconcilably divided in opinion that it is unable to reach any verdict. A hung jury can lead to the termination of a trial before verdict and judgment when the court is satisfied that the jury is unlikely to agree upon a verdict within any reasonable period of time. Termination of a trial because of a hung jury usually results in retrial on the original charges but is occasionally followed by a dismissal of the charges.

hydrodynamics of blood drops and splashes. The patterns, shapes, and sizes of blood drops and splashes produced by factors such as distance of fall and direction and speed of the body from which they emanated.

hydroplaning. A condition in which the tire tread of a moving vehicle loses contact with the road surface, and thus loses traction, due to a film of water on the road surface.

hypothecation. A right that creditors have to the property of their debtors, through which they can have the property sold. In general terms, hypothecation means simply to place something of value in "hock."

hypothesis. A stated belief or theory, often one that can be tested. For example, one might hypothesize that mean family incomes are different in Los Angeles and in Atlanta. Statistical inference can be used to test such a hypothesis to determine whether any observed difference is reasonably attributable to chance. The testing procedure begins with a null hypothesis and an alternative hypothesis. For example, the null hypothesis is that the true mean incomes are equal, and the alternative is that they are not equal. When we reject the null hypothesis, we accept the alternative.

hypothetical question. A form of question, put to expert witnesses after their competency has been established, containing a recital of facts assumed to have been proved, or proof of which is offered in the case, and requiring the opinion of the witness.

hysteria. A psychological state marked by various symptoms ranging from nervous instability to fits of causeless crying and laughing.

I

iatregenic illness. An adverse mental or physical condition caused by the effects of treatment by a physician or surgeon. The term implies that it could have been avoided by judicious care on the part of the physician.

identification. A photograph showing the head and shoulders, both front and side views, of a person.

identification number. The number assigned to a person whose fingerprints are on file in an identification bureau of a police agency. The record of this person, showing all arrests, convictions, and dispositions of cases, is shown under this number.

identification order. The official wanted notice of the FBI, issued for persons wanted for crime violation. Each is numbered (in sequence), dated, and has the following information: the criminal charge, name, and aliases of the subject; subject's fingerprints; description and photograph; criminal record, information of caution concerning the subject; and request that the FBI be notified of any information concerning the subject. These notices are widely distributed to law enforcement agencies, post offices, and government agencies having frequent contact with the public.

identification record. Criminal record. The record of an individual, as maintained in the identification bureau of a law enforcement agency, which generally contains the person's fingerprints. The record also details the arrests, convictions, and dispositions of the individual.

identify. (1) To recognize a person or thing as being the same as a particular person or thing. (2) In the area of physical evidence, to place markings on evidence or place it in marked containers so it can be positively recognized at a later time.

Identi-Kit. Invented by a former Los Angeles law enforcement officer, this identification device consists of 536 photographic transparencies, enabling investigators to assemble a human face from overlaid combinations of facial features (eyes, beards, hairline, lips, moustache, glasses, etc.). The components are on easy-to-assemble 4 x 5-inch film.

identity theft. A term used to describe the acquisition and use of a person's identification and financial information to make fraudulent credit card purchases, open unauthorized bank accounts, lines of credit or credit cards, and/or make unauthorized purchases in the victim's name. Many cases go undiscovered for long periods of time and some states have modified their laws relating to the statute from the time the crime was discovered, rather than from the time it occurred. In 2001 there were approximately 86,000 cases reported to authorities; in the first 9 months of 2002 that number jumped to over 117,000.

I except. Phrase used in court to register an objection to a ruling, so that the record may show that the exceptor is dissatisfied with the ruling and probably intends to appeal.

ignorance or mistake of fact, common law. In common law, ignorance or mistake of fact, as a rule, exempts a person from criminal liability, if the act done would be lawful were the facts as the actor believes, provided that the ignorance or mistake is not voluntary or due to negligence.

ignorance or mistake of fact, statutory offenses. Where an offense is defined by statute, whether or not ignorance or mistake of fact exempts a person doing a prohibited act from liability, as at common law, depends upon the language and construction of the statute. Unless the intention is clearly expressed, it must be determined by a construction of the statute, in view of the nature of the offense and the evils to be remedied, and of other matters making the one construction or the other reasonable, whether it was the intention to make knowledge of the facts an essential element of the offense.

ignorance of the law is no excuse. The principle, probably originating in Roman law, that a wrongdoer is not freed from criminal responsibility because of lack of awareness that the act was in violation of the law.

illegal detention. The unlawful detention of a person when there is not sufficient cause to believe the person has committed a crime for which he or she could be arrested. Under such conditions courts have ruled that a confession, even though given voluntarily, is not admissible in evidence.

Illinois plan. *See* bail

immediate family member. Spouse, parent, brother or sister, child, or person to whom the person stands *in loco parentis*; or any other person living in the household and related by blood or marriage.

Immigration and Naturalization Service. *See* United States Immigration and Naturalization Service

immigration laws. Certain groups of persons, such as beggars, felons, prostitutes, physically or mentally diseased persons, contract laborers, and others, are excluded by the immigration laws from entrance to the United States. Aliens who enter illegally and are apprehended are immediately returned to the country from which they came at the expense of the carrier that brought them. Aliens may be deported within three years of the time of entry if they become public charges from causes arising after their entry and if they desire to return home. They may be deported within five years if they belong to the excluded groups at the time of their entry into the United States. They may be deported at any time upon proof of their advocating the destruction of property or overthrow of the government or if they (a) are convicted of a crime and sentenced to prison for moral turpitude; (b) become public charges because of some cause which antedates their entrance into the United States; or (c) are found to be connected with illegal traffic in women and children. When there is reason to believe that an individual has gained illegal entry into the United States, it is the duty of a local police officer to refer the facts to the U.S. immigration officers. (This position has been seriously questioned by the chiefs of police of San Jose and Santa Ana, CA.) When a case is accepted by the federal authorities, the responsibility of the police department ceases. If there happens to be a coincidence of violation of federal and state law, the merits of the case are considered by both local and federal officials to determine in whose jurisdiction action shall be instituted. The Immigration Reform Control Act of 1986 stated that any illegal immigrants who could prove they worked and lived in the United States prior to January 1, 1982, could apply for amnesty. In 2002 the U.S. government allowed about 1 million immigrants into the country.

immunity. (1) Exemption of a person from a duty, obligation, service, or penalty (as presidential or diplomatic immunity from judicial process) that is imposed by law on all others not similarly situated. (2) Exemption from prosecution, which is sometimes promised by a prosecutor to a person accused of crime who agrees to "turn state's evidence."

Immunity Act. A 1954 measure that forces witnesses appearing in national security cases to testify by granting them immunity from prosecution for self-incriminatory testimony. If granted immunity, witnesses must testify or face jail terms. Introduced at the height of the communist scare, the bill was aimed at witnesses who refused to testify under the provisions of the Fifth Amendment. The law allows either the House or the Senate, by majority vote, to grant immunity in national security cases if an order has first been obtained from a U.S. district court judge. The attorney general must be notified in advance and given the chance to present any objections he or she might have. Congressional committees, by a two-thirds vote, may also grant immunity, as may U.S. district courts to witnesses coming before either them or grand juries.

immunity bath. The exemption from prosecution of an excessive number of accused persons or principal defendants; the term originated in 1906 when 16 defendants, alleged to have been implicated in a beef trust, were exempted from prosecution because they had aided the government in obtaining evidence against other defendants.

impanel. The process of selecting the jury that is to try a case.

impeach. (1) To accuse, to discredit, or to censure. (2) To remove a public official from office, for reasons of misconduct or illegal activity, by prescribed methods. *See also* impeachment

impeaching credit of witness. The credit of a witness may be impeached either by the adverse party or by the evidence of persons from his or her own community who will swear (a) that they know the general reputation of the witness for truth and veracity; (b) that this reputation is bad; and (c) that they would not believe him or her on oath. In some states the inquiry may be about the witness's general moral character. In most states impeaching witnesses may be asked whether they would believe the other witness on oath; but in a few states this question cannot be asked. In all states the inquiry is confined to general reputation, and specific acts by the witness sought to be impeached cannot be shown. The impeaching witness may be cross-examined and may also be impeached in the manner stated above. Impeaching witnesses cannot, in their examination in chief, give reasons for their belief; but they may be asked their reasons on cross-examination. The party introducing such witnesses cannot thus impeach them, unless they have testified adversely to the party calling them and the party had reason to expect favorable testimony, but a party is not precluded by the testimony of a witness introduced by the former from introducing other witnesses who will testify to the contrary.

impeachment. As authorized by Article I of the Constitution, impeachment is action by the House and Senate to remove the president, vice president, or civil officer of the U.S. from office for crimes of "treason, bribery, or other high crimes and misdemeanors." Alexander Hamilton defined impeachment as a "method of national inquest into the conduct of public men." The procedure dates from fourteenth-century England and was adopted by the colonial government. Impeachment proceedings are initiated in the House of Representatives; if impeachment is approved by the House, the Senate tries the case. If the Senate convicts, the penalty is removal from office and disqualification from holding further office. There is no appeal. Impeachment proceedings have been initiated 51 times in the House, but only 13 cases have reached the Senate. Of these 13 cases, 4 ended in impeachment, 7 in acquittal, and 2 in dismissal. Nine of these cases involved federal judges, who hold lifetime appointments to the bench and can be removed only by impeachment. Charges have ranged from loose morals and insanity to tyranny and advocating secession.

The highest-ranking officials to be impeached by the House were Supreme Court justice Samuel Chase—in 1805 for harsh and partisan conduct on the bench—President Andrew Johnson—in 1868 for violation of the Tenure of Office Act, and President Bill Clinton—in 1998 for loose morals and alleged perjury. All three, however, were acquitted by the Senate.

impersonating an officer. Pretending to be a peace officer, an officer of the armed services, or an official of a federal, state, or local law enforcement agency, usually by wearing a uniform, displaying an identification card or badge, or falsely identifying oneself as an officer.

importation model. A penology theory based on the concept that inmate subculture arises jointly from internal prison experiences and from external patterns of behavior that the offenders bring to prison.

imprisonment. A sentence imposed upon the conviction of a crime; the deprivation of liberty in a penal institution.

imprisonment for debt. Detention on civil process for debt, formerly universal but since 1823, when Kentucky abolished it, prohibited or restricted by state constitutional provisions. Where it exists, it is usually applied against absconding debtors or those who have deliberately entered into a contract without the means of fulfilling their obligations.

impulse. Tendency to act without voluntary direction or reflection; a tendency to act that does not appear to be traceable to stimulation.

impunity. Exemption from punishment or penalty.

inadmissible. Not proper to be admitted; not allowed.

inalienable rights. Rights that inhere in a person and are incapable of being transferred. Such rights have been claimed under natural law.

in articulo mortis (Lat., lit.). At the point of death.

in camera (Lat., lit, in a room). A case heard when the doors of the court are closed and only persons concerned in the case are admitted.

incapable. Legally unable to do something. By law certain persons are considered incapable of violating the criminal law. Among these are children under certain ages, mental incompetents, and those who act through mistake of fact or in ignorance.

incapacitate. In general, to deprive an individual of ability, qualification, or strength; in criminal justice the term often means to deprive an offender of freedom and/or legal power, such as through imprisonment.

incarceration. Confinement or imprisonment in a penal institution.

incendiary. Tending to cause fire; in law, a person guilty of the crime of arson, or the burning of a building.

incest. Sexual intercourse, either with or without marriage, between persons too nearly related by blood to be entitled to marry. In Uniform Crime Reports, incest is included either by name in sex offenses or as "marriage within prohibited degrees."

Incest Anonymous. Either of two support groups for victims of incest. Survivors of Incest Anonymous, Address: World Service Office P.O. Box 190 Benson, MD 21028-9998; or Incest Survivors Anonymous, Address: P.O. Box 17245, Long Beach, CA 90807-7245.

inchoate offense. Also called anticipatory offense, a violation consisting of an action or conduct that is a step toward the intended commission of another offense. *See also* attempt to commit a crime; conspiracy

incidence of crime. Criminality measured in a given population over a definite time span, as during a single day, month, or year. *See also* crime clock

incite. To impel another to particular action; to urge onward, to instigate. In criminal law, to persuade or move another to commit a crime.

included offense, lesser. An offense that is made up of elements that are a subset of the elements of another offense having a greater statutory penalty, and the occurrence of which is established by the same evidence or by some portion of the evidence that has been offered to establish the occurrence of the greater offense.

incompetent evidence. Evidence that is not admissible under the established rules of evidence; evidence that the law does not permit to be presented at all, or in relation to a particular matter, due to lack of authenticity or to some defect in the witness, the document, or the nature of the evidence itself.

incompetent to stand trial. The finding by a court that a defendant is mentally incapable of understanding the nature of the charges and proceedings against him or her, of consulting with an attorney, and of aiding in his or her own defense.

incorrigibility. The unmanageable or uncontrollable behavior of a child or minor, which is generally classified as an act constituting juvenile delinquency; such behavior hence demands that the child be made a ward of the juvenile court.

incriminate. To reflect guilt; to impute guilt or violation of the law; to imply illegal activity or guilt; tend to show guilt; to charge with a crime or a fault.

incrimination. The disclosure of facts that render one liable to criminal prosecution. An accused person cannot be compelled to be a witness against him- or herself in criminal cases, but the accused may waive the privilege and take the stand voluntarily. Witnesses are immune from being required to incriminate themselves in any proceeding, including a congressional investigation, but they may not withhold facts that merely impair their reputations, not even incriminating facts if they have been promised immunity from prosecution under the law. *See also* Immunity Act; search and seizure, unreasonable

inculpate. To imply guilt or wrongdoing; to accuse of crime; to involve in illegal or wrongful activity.

inculpatory. In the law of evidence, facts or opinions showing involvement in criminal activity; tending to establish, indicating, or reflecting guilt; incriminating.

inculpatory evidence. Evidence without which a particular fact cannot be proved.

incumbrance. A claim, lien, or liability attached to a piece of property.

indecent exposure. Unlawful intentional, knowing, or reckless exposing to view of the genitals or anus, in a place where another person may be present who is likely to be offended or alarmed by such an act. Some states specify that the act must be performed in a "lewd or lascivious manner."

indefinite sentence. A system, not used in the United States, in which a person is sentenced without minimum or maximum limitations, with the length of time in prison determined by his or her behavior and other factors. *See also* indeterminate sentence

in delicto (Lat.). At fault.

indemnification. Compensation for loss or damage sustained because of improper or illegal action by a public authority.

indeterminate sentence. A type of sentence to imprisonment in which the commitment, instead of being for a specified single time, such as three years, is for a range of time, such as two to five years or five years maximum and zero minimum.

Index Crimes. Those crimes used by the FBI to measure the incidence of crime in the United States. The statistics appear in the Uniform Crime Reports.

Index Offenses. The eight types of Part I offenses reported by the FBI in the annual Uniform Crime Reports: willful homicide, arson, forcible rape, robbery, burglary, aggravated assault, larceny over $50, and motor vehicle theft.

indictment. A formal, written accusation submitted to the court by a grand jury, alleging that a specified person(s) has committed a specified offense(s), usually a felony Since to indict means to accuse, indictment is sometimes used to mean any accusation of wrongdoing. *See also* charging document; filing; information; presentment

indigent. Poor; destitute; unable to afford legal counsel.

indirect evidence. Evidence that does not actually prove the facts but from which they may be presumed or inferred. *See also* circumstantial evidence

individualized treatment. A philosophy of corrections stating that each individual is different in the causes of his or her criminality and in the particular manifestation thereof; consequently, corrections should look at the individual's unique cluster of traits and devise a treatment program based on needs and deficiencies.

industrial espionage. *See* espionage, industrial

industrial school. Reform school; institution for delinquent or neglected youth.

Industrial Security Organization. *See* American Society for Industrial Security.

inebriate. (1) To make one drunk; to intoxicate. (2) One who is often drunk.

in extremis (Lat.). At the point of death.

in facto (Lat.). In fact; in deed.

infamous crime. Crime punishable by imprisonment in a state penitentiary.

infamous punishment. Punishment by imprisonment or imprisonment at hard labor, particularly if in a penitentiary or state prison; sometimes, imprisonment at hard labor regardless of the location or type of facility.

infancy. In criminal law, the case where the accused has not arrived at such an age as to be able to distinguish between right and wrong.

infanticide. Murder of an infant immediately after its birth.

infantophilia. Tendency to focus one's sexual interest on very young children.

inference. A method of reaching a conclusion based on applying known facts to estimate an unknowable fact, such as estimating total population based on experimental or sample numbers. To estimate total nonreported incidents of burglary of nonwhite families in Denver, for example, researchers could select a sample of a few such families and infer the mean for the total population from the sample mean. Polling every family in Denver to arrive at a true number would be impractical, even if it were possible.

inferential statistics. The techniques used to state the probability that any obtained sample statistic varies from some hypothesized population parameter by some specified amount, and to make estimates about the numerical value of a population parameter, given an obtained sample statistic but with a specifiable degree of confidence. The former branch of inferential statistics is called hypothesis testing and the latter, estimation.

inferiority complex. A term coined by Austrian psychiatrist Alfred Adler (1870–1937) to describe an individual's (generally unconscious) sense that he or she is not equal in competence to other people and is inadequate to meet the demands of the environment. Psychologically, an individual might attempt to compensate for feelings of inferiority by concealing them through feats of courage and achievement. In extreme cases, efforts to compensate may result in aggressive or antisocial behavior.

infibulation. Torture of the genitals.

in flagrante delicto (Lat.). During the commission of a crime; colloquially, caught in the act.

influence. An exercise of power in which one person convinces another to behave in accordance with the first one's preferences.

informant. (1) A person, who, wittingly or unwittingly, provides information to an agent, a clandestine service, or the police. (2) In crime reporting, a person who has provided specific information and is cited as a source.

in forma pauperis. "(Lat., lit. "In the form of a pauper") or as a poor person. Under U.S. law, an indigent or person with insufficient means can bring legal action without paying required fees for counsel, writs, transcripts, subpoenas, and the like.

information. (1) A formal, written accusation submitted to the court by a prosecutor, alleging that a specified person(s) has committed a specified offense(s). (2) Intelligence, or unevaluated material of every description, including that derived from observations, reports, rumors, imagery, and other sources which, when processed, may produce intelligence.

information highway. A term coined by Vice President Al Gore, the information highway, the Internet, an electronic communications network that easily connects all users to one another and provides every type of electronic service possible, including shopping, banking, education, medical diagnosis, video conferencing, and game playing.

infraction. (1) A violation of state statute or local ordinance punishable by a fine or other penalty but not by incarceration, unless it is a specified, unusually limited term. (2) In corrections, a statutory offense or a violation of prison or jail administrative regulations committed by an offender while incarcerated or in a temporary-release program such as work release.

infrared light. A light having a wavelength greater than the visible red. It is in the region of 8,000 to 9,000 angstroms, and is used to read writings that have been erased or obliterated and those that are not visible to the naked eye because of a dark background. It is at the opposite end of the spectrum from ultraviolet light.

infrared (IR) motion detector. A sensor that detects changes in the infrared light radiation from parts of a protected area. Presence of an intruder in the area changes the infrared light intensity from that direction.

inhalants. Chemicals whose vapors cause an intoxicating effect when they are inhaled, acting as central nervous system depressants. Such household products as varnish, paint thinner, and model airplane glue are sources; as are fuels such as gasoline, kerosene, and lighter fluid; along with such chemical gases as nitrous oxide, freon, and butane. Boys aged 12 to 15 are the most common users.

initial appearance. The first appearance of an accused person in the first court having jurisdiction over his or her case.

injunction. An order issued by a court of equity commanding a person (a) to do an act or (b) to refrain from doing an act that would injure another by violating his or her personal or property rights. A mandatory injunction commands the specific performance of an act; a preventive injunction orders a person to desist from an act already commenced or contemplated; a preliminary or interlocutory injunction may be issued when a danger is immediately threatened and there is inadequate opportunity for a court to determine finally the rights of the parties; and a permanent injunction is the final decree of the court. The violation of an injunction is a contempt of court and may be punished by fine or imprisonment.

in loco parentis. (Lat., lit. "In the place of a parent").

inmate. One who is institutionalized in a correctional facility.

inquest. A legal inquiry to establish some question of fact; specifically, an inquiry by a coroner and jury into a person's death where accident, foul play, or violence is suspected as the cause.

inquisitorial system. The system of criminal prosecution prevailing in most of continental Europe, Japan, and other countries, in contrast to the English and American adversary system. In the inquisitorial system, a judicial officer has the responsibility to investigate and examine. Adjudication is not limited to the facts given in proof by the parties. *See also* adversary system

in re (Lat.). In the matter of, concerning; used to label a judicial proceeding in which there are no adversaries.

in re Gault. A Supreme Court case (387 U.S. 1967) concerning the basic right of children to be assured of fair treatment in juvenile courts. A 15-year-old, Gault had been sentenced by a juvenile court to up to six years' imprisonment for making lewd and indecent remarks on the telephone. When committed by an adult, this offense usually carried a maximum sentence of two months. Gault had been taken into custody from his home, no notice or other advice of his arrest was left for his working parents, and the many other elements of due process granted to adults were not observed—a typical incident in juvenile courts at the time. In the opinion of the Court, a juvenile court must adhere to the due process requirements of notice, advice of the right to counsel, advice of the right to remain silent and avoid self-incrimination, offer of the right to confront accusers, and proper procurement of confessions.

in rem (Lat.). Against a thing; a legal proceeding instituted to obtain decrees or judgments against property

Insanity Defense Reform Act of 1984. Federal law under which it is an affirmative defense to a prosecution under any other federal statute that, at the time of the commission the acts constituting the offense, the defendant, as a result of a severe mental disease or defect, was unable to appreciate the nature and quality of the wrongfulness of his or her acts. Mental disease or defect does not otherwise constitute a defense. The defendant has the burden proving the defense of insanity by clear and convincing evidence.

insanity plea. An admission of guilt with the contention that the commission of the crime is not culpable in the eyes of the court because of the insanity of the defendant at the time he or she committed the act. More typically, dual plea of not guilty and not guilty by reason of insanity is entered, which implies, "The burden is on the government to prove I did the act upon which the charge is based, and, even if the government proves that at trial, I still claim that I am not culpable because I was legally insane at the time." One of the most famous insanity pleadings was entered by John W. Hinckley, Jr., when he was tried for the assassination attempt on President Ronald Reagan in 1981. *See also* Insanity Defense Reform Act of 1984

inspectional services. The specialized bureau in a traditionally organized police department responsible for internal affairs, field inspections, supervision of the morals division, an intelligence-gathering activity.

instanter. Immediately; forthwith; without delay. Courts issue subpoenas or other orders specifying that they are returnable instanter meaning the person upon whom papers are served should perform, as ordered, immediately.

Institute for Court Management. Founded in 1971 and cosponsored by the National Center for State Courts, the American Bar Association, the American Judicature Society, and the Institute of Judicial Administration. Lists two major objectives: (a) Education: training and certification of court administrators, continuing education for certified court administrators, and short-term institutes on court management subjects for judges, clerks, court administrator staff, court planners, probationers, and related personnel; (b) Research: extensive and short-term studies of courts and related justice system agencies. Publishes the *Justice System Journal* 3/year. Address: 300 Newport Avenue, Willamsburg, VA 23187-8798.

Institute of Criminal Law and Procedure. Established in 1965 by Georgetown University, the institute provides empirical legal research on criminal law and administration of criminal justice. It maintains databases on plea bargaining, pretrial release, victim assistance, and repeat-offender laws. Address: 605 G Street, NW, Washington, DC 20001.

Institute of Governmental Studies Library. Founded in 1920 by the University of California at Berkeley, the aim of the library is to collect materials concerning all aspects of criminal justice. These materials are then made available to university students, faculty, research staff and other professionals in the field through interlibrary loan. Publishes *Public Affairs Report* monthly. Address: 109 Moses Hall, #2370, University of California, Berkeley, CA 94720.

Institute of Judicial Administration. Founded in 1952 by the New York University School of Law, the institute counts among its major objectives the abilities to promote court modernization; conduct studies of structure, operation, and manpower of courts; provide education programs for appellate and trial judges and court administrators; coordinate efforts of bar associations and judicial councils; and publish results of research in the field of judicial administration. Publishes *IJA Report* (quarterly newsletter). Address: 40 Washington Square South, New York, NY 10012.

institutional capacity. The officially stated number of inmates that a confinement or residential facility is or was originally intended to house.

institutionalized personality. A nonclinical term that refers to an individual who has become so accustomed to existence in an institution that readjustment to life outside the institution is difficult.

insubordination. Defiance; resistance to authority; disobedience; willful failure to obey orders; open refusal to obey orders. Generally a basis of disciplinary action in a law enforcement agency.

insufficient evidence. Evidence that is not enough to constitute proof at the level required at a given point in the proceedings.

Insurance Crime Bureau, National (NICB). In January 1992 the insurance industry established the NICB to combat insurance abuse, especially automobile insurance fraud. The bureau consolidated the previous operations of the National Automobile Theft Bureau and the Insurance Crime Prevention Institute. The NICB estimates insurers are bilked of $17 billion annually by fraudulent claims. Hotline telephone: (800) TEL-NICB (835-1422).

insurgency. A condition, which falls short of civil war, resulting from a revolt or insurrection against a constituted government.

insurrection. A rebellion or uprising of citizens or subjects in resistance to their government. It consists of any group resistance to the lawful authority of the state.

intake. The process by which a juvenile referral is received by personnel of a probation agency, juvenile court, or special intake unit; and a decision is made to close the case at intake, refer the juvenile to another agency, place him or her under some kind of care or supervision, or file a petition in a juvenile court.

Integrated Criminal Apprehension Program. Established in 1976, ICAP is a comprehensive planning, patrol, and investigative program. Initially, ICAP was aimed largely at improving patrol operations but was later expanded to include the investigative process, warrant service, and serious habitual-offender components. ICAP's goals are to increase the clearance rate of violent crime cases as well as the arrest and prosecution of serious offenders by improved allocation and deployment of law enforcement patrols and investigative resources. Address: Bureau of Justice Assistance, Office of Justice Programs, DOJ, 633 Indiana Avenue, NW, Washington, DC 20531.

intelligence. A function of law enforcement agencies concerned with the acquisition of information related to crime.

Intelligence Analysts, International Association of Law Enforcement. Founded in 1981. Publishes *Intelscope* (3 times per year). Address: P.O. Box 6385, Lawrenceville, NJ 08648-0385.

Intelligence Association, National Military. Founded in 1974. Publishes *American Intelligence Journal* (quarterly). Address: 9200 Centerway Rd., Gaithersburg, MD 20879.

intelligence estimate. An appraisal of the elements of information about a specific situation or condition, with a view to determining the courses of action open to the other side or potential adversary and the probable order of their adoption.

Intelligence Officers, Association of Former. Founded in 1975. Publishes *Periscope* (bimonthly newsletter). Address: 6723 Whittier Avenue, Suite 303A, McLean, VA 22101.

intent. (1) The state of mind or attitude with which an act is carried out; the design, resolve, or determination with which a person acts to achieve a certain result. (2) Mere intent to commit a crime is not a criminal violation; an overt act must accompany or follow the intent. Most crimes require intent as an essential element; however, some do not have this requirement, particularly those that are less serious and do not involve moral turpitude. Some crimes, such as theft, require specific intent; others require only general intent; and in still others, constructive intent is sufficient. In cases of culpable negligence and in minor offenses such as traffic violations, no intent is required. *See also* intent, constructive

intent, constructive. Legal term for the situation in which a person intends to commit an illegal act and, in attempting to carry it out, injures someone. For example, if A intends to shoot and kill B but, in shooting at B, hits and kills C, the shooter by law is held to have intended to do what happened. Also called transfer of intent. *See also* intent

intent in cases of negligence. In crimes involving either neglect to observe proper care in performing an act or culpable failure to perform a duty, criminal intent is the state of mind that necessarily accompanies the negligent act or culpable omission. The question of criminal negligence most frequently arises in connection with manslaughter, nuisance, or escape.

intent, specific. There are certain crimes of which a specific intent to accomplish a particular purpose is an essential element and for which there can be no conviction upon proof of mere general malice or criminal intent. In these cases it is necessary for the state to prove the specific intent, either by direct or circumstantial evidence. *See also* intent, constructive; criminal intent

interactionist theory. A key sociological perspective in criminology that focuses on the way in which crime is generated by social control agencies as they attach stigmatizing labels to individual offenders, who often act out or live up to the criminal identity that flows from labels, and who devote themselves to criminal careers. *See also* labeling theory

inter alia (Lat.). Among other things.

interception of prisoners' mail. The constitutional guarantee of the right of privacy does not apply to the interception of a prisoner's mail by the jailer or warden, nor does it prohibit the turning over of such a letter to a prosecuting attorney, for use against the convict, by the warden who had a right to peruse the convict's mail.

interdict. To prevent or forbid.

interdiction. Prevention of movement through rigid enforcement. The U.S. Coast Guard, for example, interdicts drug trade.

interior ballistics. The science of the movement of projectiles within the bore of a gun, along with the combustion of powder, development of pressure, and other factors, to determine the effect of such factors as weight, size, shape, rifling, and others. Also called internal ballistics.

interlocutory. Temporary; not final. An interlocutory decree is a temporary court order pending the final determination of the case or matter.

interlocutory appeal. A request, made at some point before judgment in trial court proceedings, that a court having appellate jurisdiction review a prejudgment decision of the trial court before judgment is reached.

intermediate court. A court, known by various names, falling in a judicial hierarchy between the highest, or supreme, tribunal and the trial court. Its jurisdiction is usually appellate, but some states confer original jurisdiction in special cases such as election contests.

intermittent sentence. A sentence to periods of confinement interrupted by periods of freedom.

intern. (1) To shut up within a prescribed space. (2) A student of a certain profession working within that profession. Several colleges and universities offering criminal justice courses include internship in their respective programs.

Internal Revenue Service. Tax collector for the United States, endowed with discretionary powers in specific tax cases. A division of the Treasury Department, the IRS is decentralized into seven regions (North Atlantic, Mid-Atlantic, Central, Midwest, Southeast, Southwest, and Western) under commissioners and 58 districts under directors. At the district level, the IRS collects and deposits taxes, determines tax liability, certifies refunds, initially processes returns, investigates violations, and provides information to taxpayers. The IRS randomly selects 2,500 employers a year, from among 7.5 million in the nation, for an audit of their workforce records. The national office also supervises the legal alcohol industry and enforces certain explosives and firearms laws. IRS currently has approximately 78,000 employees. For a list of manuals and publications, contact IRS. Address: Department of the Treasury, 1500 Pennsylvania Avenue, NW, Washington, DC 20220.

International Association for Property and Evidence, Inc. Organization that conducts seminars and training. Located at 903 N. San Fernando Blvd., Suite 4, Burbank, CA 91504.

International Association of Asian Crime Investigators (IAACI). Founded in 1987 by two Virginia police officers, James Badey of Arlington and Phil Hannum of Falls Church, the organization adopted by-laws and held elections in San Francisco in 1988. The Secretariat is located in the Office of International Criminal Justice at the University of Illinois at Chicago. Publishes *IAACI News* bimonthly.

International Association of Chiefs of Police. Established in 1893, the association's objectives are to "advance the science and art of police service; to develop and disseminate improved administrative, technical, and operational practices and promote their use in police work; to foster police cooperation and the exchange of information and experience among police administrators throughout the world; to bring about recruitment and training of qualified persons; and to encourage adherence of all officers to high professional standards of performance and conduct." IACP has approximately 14,000 members representing 80 countries. Publishes *The Police Chief.* Address: 515 No. Washington St., Alexandria, VA 22314.

International Brotherhood of Police Officers (IBPO). Organization founded in 1964 by officers in Rhode Island, combined with the National Association of Government Employees in 1969, and with the Service Employees International Union, an AFL-CIO affiliate, in 1982. It is the largest police union in the U.S. National headquarters is at 159 Burgin Parkway, Quincy, MA 02169, with fully staffed offices in other states.

International Brotherhood of Teamsters. The largest labor union in the United States, the Teamsters represent small- to medium-sized police and sheriffs' departments in AK, CA, FL, IA, MA, MI, MN, NY, OK, SD, VA, and WI. Alleged ties between the Teamsters and organized crime, as well as internal corruption, led the AFL-CIO to expel the organization from its ranks in 1958.

International City/County Management Association (ICMA). Founded in 1914, ICMA limits its information services to municipal management officials or police executives. Technical assistance inquiries are limited to ICMA members. ICMA is a professional association of city/county managers. The criminal justice project of ICMA is aimed at increasing the expertise of municipal administrators when dealing with the law enforcement function. In 1938 the ICMA published *Municipal Police Administration*, the first in a series of volumes on police management. The book embodied the principles of administration critical to the reform movement of the era. It was later dubbed the Green Monster by officers using it to prepare for promotion examinations. Along with O. W. Wilson's *Police Administration*, published in 1950, the book is considered the classic police sourcebook. ICMA publishes *Target* (monthly newsletter, free upon request). Address: 777 North Capitol St. NE, Suite 500, Washington, DC 20002.

international code. A code adopted by many countries to facilitate sight communication between persons of different nations. The code uses some 26 flags, each standing for a letter of the Latin alphabet. They may be used in different combinations, each signifying a certain message, or used as letters to spell out a word or sentence. If flags are not used, the international Morse code is employed.

International Court of Justice. Successor to the League of Nations Permanent Court of Justice, established by the United Nations at the 1945 San Francisco Conference. Known now as the World Court. The court's statute is a part of the UN charter, and all UN members are members of ICJ. Each member undertakes to abide by ICJ decisions in cases to which it is a party. The UN Security Council has the right to enforce decisions of the court. The court, seated at The Hague, has 15 judges, who are elected by absolute majorities in the General Assembly and the Security Council. The judges serve for nine-year periods. Nine judges form a quorum. Rulings are by majority vote and are final, without appeal. Only states can be parties in cases before the court, but a state can take up a case in which a national is involved. The court's jurisdiction includes all legal disputes that members refer to it and all matters provided for in the charter, treaties, and conventions.

The court also gives advisory opinions to the General Assembly and the Security Council on request.

International Criminal Police Organization. *See* Interpol

international extradition. By treaties between the United States and most foreign countries and by acts of Congress in accordance with the treaties, provision is made for the extradition of fugitives from justice in special cases. This is a matter in which the states cannot act. A person extradited for one crime cannot be tried for another. By weight of authority, a person can be tried and punished for a crime committed in this country, though he or she has been forcibly abducted from a foreign country.

International Guide to Missing Treasures (IGMT). A central index used by participating art dealers to record art thefts and disseminate reports and special bulletins to subscribers, legitimate art dealers, key persons in the art community, and law enforcement agencies.

international law. An inchoate body of rules, classified as laws of peace, war, or neutrality, that deal principally with relationships between governments of one state and subjects of another. Although various usages existed in the relations between peoples of earlier civilizations, modern international law is a product of the European nation-state system. In the past century, new rules have been decreed by states meeting in conferences and in organizations like the League of Nations and the United Nations and their auxiliary agencies, thereby adding written international law to customary law. Controversies over the existence of international law are due partly to the common misconception that international law defines interstate relations as they ought to be, and partly to the absence of a common superior to make it uniform and enforce it. The test of a rule of international law is its universal acceptance by the community of states and their obedience to its mandates.

International Law Enforcement Instructors Agency. Established in 1976, ILEIA's goal is the "development of uniform professional standards in the training of criminal justice personnel." ILEIA offers educational journeys to training agencies worldwide. Publishes *Torch and Tome* (monthly newsletter). Address: 51 Seven Star Lane, Concord, MA 01742.

International Narcotic Enforcement Officers Association. Established in 1960, the association "promotes and fosters mutual interest in the problems of narcotic control; provides a medium for the exchange of ideas; conducts seminars, conferences, and study groups; and issues publications." Publishes *The NarcOfficer*. Address: Suite 1200, 112 State St., Albany, NY 12207.

International Personnel Management Association. Established in 1973, through the consolidation of the Public Personnel Association, founded in Chicago in 1906, and the Society for Personnel Administration, founded in Washington, DC in 1937, the association aims to provide member agencies with "an advisory service on public personnel administration and to coordinate an exchange of tests, job analyses, surveys, and other personnel materials." Its interest in the criminal justice function is limited to police personnel problems and issues. Publishes *IPMA News* (monthly) and *Public Personnel Management* (quarterly journal) to all members or by subscription. Address: 1617 Duke St., Alexandria, VA, 22314.

international police forces. Contingents of military forces of member states placed under United Nations control, as authorized by the UN Charter, for the purpose of preserving peace and preventing or resisting aggressive actions.

International Union of Police Associations (IUPA). This organization traces its roots to the International Conference of Police Associations, which disbanded on December 4, 1978, over the issue of affiliating with organized labor. The IUPA represents the segment of the earlier group that remained with the AFL-CIO.

Interpol (International Criminal Police Organization). This organization was established in 1914 to facilitate cooperation in fighting international crime, and transferred its headquarters to Paris in 1938, where it became the International Criminal Police Organization. Interpol is a worldwide consortium of 176 countries, but its secretariat is staffed by French police officers. In each member country a point of contact and coordination is established for the Interpol function. It coordinates and facilitates requests between foreign police organizations' law enforcement agencies for information regarding persons, vehicles, and goods that bear on criminal matters within their respective jurisdictions. Interpol exists as a catalyst to provide efficient police communications between the United States and other member countries and the General Secretariat Headquarters in Lyon, France. Investigations can cover criminal-history checks, license plate and drivers' license checks, International Wanted Circulars, weapons traces, and locating suspects. It keeps in daily contact with affiliates through its own radio network and provides assistance to national police within the terms of local laws. Interpol attempts to ensure and promote the widest possible mutual assistance among all police authorities within the limits of the laws existing in the different countries and in the spirit of the Universal Declaration of Human Rights, and to establish and develop all institutions likely to contribute effectively to the prevention and suppression of crime. It is a clearinghouse for international exchange of information, doing no investigation itself. The United States joined the group in 1958. For information, contact: National Central Bureau, Interpol, Department of Justice, 10th Street and Constitution Avenue, NW, Room 6649, Washington, DC 20530. Publishes *International Crime Police Review*, (monthly journal) and *International Crime Statistics* (every two years). Address: General Secretariat, 200, quai charles de Gaulle, 69006 Lyon, France.

interrogation. To probe, with questions, persons believed involved in crime; to question in detail with the purpose of obtaining information relative to the involvement in crime of the person being questioned. *See also* Miranda rights

interrogatory. A question; sets of questions in writing intended to be proposed to a witness.

intersection. An area defined by lateral curb lines or lateral boundary lines of the roadways of two highways that join one another at approximately right angles.

interstate compact. An agreement between states, that, in criminal justice, involves transferring prisoners, parolees, or probationers from one jurisdiction to another, often in order to relieve overcrowding. The state with original jurisdiction retains legal authority to confine or release.

Interstate Commerce Commission. Former U.S. government agency, dismantled in 1995, whose responsibility was to regulate common carriers engaged in transportation.

interstate compact. An agreement between two or more states to transfer prisoners, parolees, or probationers from the physical or supervisory custody of one state to that of another, where the correctional agency that first acquired jurisdiction over a person usually retains the legal authority to confine or release him or her.

Interstate Compact for the Supervision of Parolees and Probationers. This agreement, first instituted in 1937 and entered into by all the states by 1951, allows for the supervision of a parolee or probationer in a state other than the state of conviction, provided that the parolee is a resident of that state, that his or her family lives there, or that the receiving state agrees to accept supervision. Extradition procedural requirements are waived under the compact.

interstate extradition. Provision is made by the Constitution, the acts of Congress in pursuance thereof, and auxiliary statutes in the different states for the extradition of a person, charged in one state with a crime or misdemeanor, who flees from justice and is found

INTERPOL-AFFILIATED COUNTRIES

Albania	Denmark	Laos	Qatar
Algeria	Djibouti	Latvia	Romania
Andorra	Dominica	Lebanon	Russia
Angola	Dominican Republic	Lesotho	Rwanda
Antigua & Babuda	Ecuador	Liberia	St. Kitts & Nevis
Argentina	Egypt	Libya	St. Lucia
Armenia	El Salvador	Liechtenstein	St. Vincent & the Grenadines
Aruba	Equatorial Guinea	Lithuania	Saudi Arabia
Australia	Estonia	Luxembourg	Senegal
Austria	Ethiopia	Macedonia	Seychelles
Azerbaijan	Fiji	Malawi	Sierra Leone
Bahamas	Finland	Malaysia	Singapore
Bahrain	France	Maldives	Slovakia
Bangladesh	Gabon	Mali	Slovenia
Barbados	Gambia	Malta	Somalia
Belarus	Germany	Marshall Islands	South Africa
Belgium	Georgia	Mauritania	Spain
Belize	Ghana	Mauritius	Sudan
Benin	Greece	Mexico	Suriname
Bolivia	Grenada	Moldova	Sri Lanka
Bosnia-Herzegovina	Guatemala	Monaco	Swaziland
Botswana	Guinea	Mongolia	Sweden
Brazil	Guinea-Bissau	Morocco	Switzerland
Brunei	Guyana	Mozambique	Syria
Bulgaria	Haiti	Myanmar	Thailand
Burkina Faso	Honduras	Namibia	Togo
Burundi	Hungary	Nauru	Tonga
Cambodia	Iceland	Nepal	Trinidad & Tobago
Cameroon	India	Netherlands	Tunisia
Canada	Indonesia	Netherlands Antilles	Turkey
Cape Verde	Iran	New Zealand	Uganda
Central African Republic	Iraq	Nicaragua	Ukraine
Chad	Ireland	Niger	United Arab Emerates
Chile	Israel	Nigeria	United Kingdom
China	Italy	Norway	United States
Colombia	Jamaica	Oman	Uruguay
Congo	Japan	Pakistan	Uzbekistan
Congo Republican	Jordan	Panama	Venezuela
Democracy of ex-Zaire	Kazakhstan	Papua New Guinea	Vietnam
Costa Rica	Kenya	Paraguay	Yemen
Croatia	Kiribati	Peru	Zaire
Cuba	Korea (Republic)	Philippines	Zambia
Cyprus	Kuwait	Poland	Zimbabwe
Czech (Republic)	Kyrgyzstan	Portugal	

in another state. Interstate extradition is also called rendition. To be extradited, a person must (a) be judicially charged with a crime in the demanding state, as by indictment or complaint, or (b) have been in the demanding state, in order to be seen as having fled from justice. It is enough that the person was in the demanding state, committed a crime there, and then left that state for any reason. A person may be extradited for any crime against the laws of the demanding state. By the weight of authority, a person may be tried for a crime other than that for which he or she was extradited, and forcible abduction from another state does not prevent this trial.

intestate. Referring to anyone who died without making a will.

in toto (Lat., lit.). In the whole; entirely.

intoxication. A broad and comprehensive term with many definitions: drunkenness; inebriety; inebriation; poisoning; the act of inebriating; the state of being inebriated; the act of intoxicating or making drunk; the state of being intoxicated or drunk; or the state produced by using too much of an alcoholic beverage or using opium, hashish, or the like. The recommended usage is: the offense of being in a public place while intoxicated through consumption of alcohol or intake of a controlled substance or drug.

Intoximeter. Trade name of a device to test the breath to determine the amount of alcohol in the blood.

intrinsic evidence. Evidence that is derived from a document and needs no explanation.

investigate. The term comes from the Latin word *vestigium*, meaning a footprint.

investigation, presentence. An official investigation, ordered by a judge or court subsequent to conviction or a plea of guilty, for the use of the judge or court in arriving at the sentence to be given to the offender.

Investigations, Defense Central Index of. A locator file maintained by the Defense Department. It identifies the location of files concerning past and present military members, DOD civilian employees, and contractors. *See also* Defense Supply Agency File

investigative power of Congress. The power to make inquiries and hold hearings is an essential aspect of the legislative power conferred on Congress by the Constitution. Investigations are conducted by committee rather than by Congress collectively. The congressional power to investigate is rein-

forced by the subpoena power—the power to compel the attendance of witnesses and the delivery of documents—and by the power to cite a reluctant or uncooperative witness for contempt. Some subjects of investigation have attracted considerable attention: the use of security classifications to prevent publication of information, Watergate, Koreagate, ABSCAM, and inquiries into the alleged ties between the Teamsters and organized crime (President's Commission on Organized Crime, April 1985).

Investigators, Association of Federal. Founded in 1957. Publishes *The Investigators Journal* (annual). Address: 1612 K Street, NW, Suite 506, Washington, DC 20006.

Investigators, Society of Professional. Founded in 1955. Publishes an annual bulletin. Address: P.O. Box 3032, Church Street Station, New York, NY 10008.

investigatory stage. That part of a police investigation during which suspicion has not yet been focused on a particular person or persons.

involuntary manslaughter. Unguardedly or undesignedly killing another while committing either an unlawful act, not felonious or tending to great bodily harm, or a lawful act without proper caution or requisite skill.

involuntary servitude. Slavery, peonage, or forced labor to fulfill a contract or debt. The Thirteenth Amendment prohibits involuntary servitude, except as a criminal punishment.

iodine. A chemical element of which the fumes are used to develop fingerprints on paper.

Irish system. A system of punishment, developed by Sir William Crofton, that provided for progressive stages in a prison term and for release under supervision before final termination of sentence.

irresistible impulse. As used in criminal law, the state of a person, due to his or her mental condition, who is driven by an urge to do certain acts that neither willpower nor reasoning is sufficient to prevent.

irritant gas. A nonlethal gas that causes irritation of the skin and a flow of tears. Any one of the family of tear gases used for training and riot control. *See also* tear gas

ISBN. The International Standard Book Number is an ordering and identifying code for book products. The first number designates the language the book is published in, for example, the zero is for English. The second set identifies the publisher, and the last set identifies the particular item. The very last number is a "check number," which mathematically makes certain that the previous numbers have been entered correctly.

issuance of arrest warrants. Authorization to issue an arrest warrant before indictment depends on filing a proper complaint before at appropriate magistrate, showing that a crime has been committed and that there is probably cause to suspect the accused. After indictment the usual practice is to issue a bench warrant. At arrest under an insufficient warrant is in effect at arrest without any warrant at all, and, if a warrant is necessary, such an arrest is illegal.

issuance of search warrants. In general, issuance is regulated by constitutional and statutory provisions to the effect that search warrants must (a) be issued by one authorized to do so, upon application made by a proper party in proper form; (b) show probable cause supported by oath of affirmation; and (c) sufficiently describe the place to be searched and the thing to be seized.

issue. (1) Children, progeny. (2) A single, certain, and material point, deduced from the pleadings of the parties, that is affirmed by one side and denied on the other; a fact put in controversy by the pleadings; in criminal law. a fact that must be proved to convict the accused or that is in controversy.

issue of fact. A question of fact to be determined by the jury.

issue of law. A point to be decided only by the court.

J

jail. A confinement facility administered by an agency of local government, typically a law enforcement agency, intended for adults but sometimes also containing juveniles and persons detained pending adjudication and/or persons committed after adjudication, usually those committed on sentences of a year or less.

jail commitment. A sentence of commitment to the jurisdiction of a confinement facility for adults that is administered by an agency of local government and of which the custodial authority is usually limited to persons sentenced to a year or less of confinement.

Jail Overcrowding/Alternatives to Pretrial Detention Program. Under this program the states of Washington and Arizona (Pima County) have established policies and procedures to meet correctional standards. Federal publications include *Jail Overcrowding: Identifying Causes and Planning for Solutions—A Handbook for Administrators* and *Jail Overcrowding: Guide to Data Collection and Analysis.* Address: U.S. Department of Justice, Bureau of Justice Assistance, Office of Justice Programs, 810 7th St., NW, Washington, DC 20531.

Jail Reform, National Coalition for. Founded in 1978, the organization works to reform the nation's jails but is not involved with prisons. Opposes unnecessary incarceration of the mentally ill and retarded, public inebriates, juveniles, and many pretrial detainees. Address: S. I. Newhouse Center for Law and Justice, 15 Washington St., 12th Floor, Rutgers University, Newark, NJ 07102.

jail time. Credit allowed in a prison sentence for time a defendant spent in jail awaiting trial or mandate on appeal.

James, Jesse Woodson. Born in Clay County, MO, in 1847, James was the famous leader of a western outlaw gang that included his brother Frank, Cole Younger, and others, and that specialized in bank and train robberies. He was killed by gang member Robert Ford for a $5,000 reward in 1882.

Jay, John. Born in New York City in 1745, Jay was the first chief justice of the United States, serving from 1790 to 1795. He was also the New York State delegate to the Continental Congress, 1774–1779; president of the congress, 1778–1779; one of the negotiators and signers of the treaty of peace with Britain, 1783; U.S. secretary of foreign affairs, 1784–1789; author of five essays in *The Federalist*, which urged ratification of the U.S. Constitution, 1787–1789; negotiator of Jay's Treaty, which settled outstanding disputes with Britain, 1794; and governor of New York, 1795–1801. He died in 1829.

Jellinek's Curve. A graphic that represents the progress of the disease of alcoholism, including 43 different steps. Two basic phases, that of Purely Symptomatic and Addictive, are divided into subphases that include prealcoholic, alcohol addiction, chronic, and crucial.

jeopardy. The danger of conviction and punishment that defendants in criminal actions incur when lawfully charged with crimes before a tribunal properly organized and competent to try them. When jeopardy begins may differ slightly among the states; often it is when the petit jury has been impaneled and sworn or, if trial is before a judge without a jury, when the first witness is sworn.

Jesse James Act. Because of Cole Younger, Butch Cassidy and the Sundance Kid, and the Jesse James gangs, who preyed on mail trains during the 1860s, the federal government passed the Jesse James Act, which mandates a 25-year prison sentence for conviction of armed robbery of a postal facility. This is one of the earlier mandatory sentences still in effect and one of the harshest federal statutes for robbery. *See also* James, Jesse

Jim Crow laws. Beginning in the 1880s, a number of ordinances were passed in southern states and municipalities that legalized segregation of blacks and whites. The name Jim Crow is believed to have derived from a character in a minstrel song.

job action. An organized action taken by members of a police association (or other labor union) to exert pressure on city government. Job actions are generally a means of demonstration to coerce public officials to meet union demands after good faith collective bargaining or negotiations have broken down. The issues could include compensation, benefits, or conditions of employment. Job actions can take the form of strikes, "blue flu" (sick-outs), slowdowns, speedups, or a variety of other means.

Johari window. A theoretical model for explaining the concept of an individual's interpersonal disclosure and feedback. The model consists of four quadrants: (1) public self (known by individual and others), (2) blind self (known by others but unknown by the individual); (3) private self (known only by the individual); and (4) unknown area (information that neither the individual nor others are aware of).

John Birch Society. A semisecret, authoritarian, right-wing, extremist organization founded by Robert Welch, a Massachusetts manufacturer, in Indianapolis in 1958. It opposes communism (its announced purpose), impugns the motives of moderate and liberal leaders, and opposes all forms of internationalism; named for a Georgia fundamentalist missionary preacher who was killed by the Chinese Communists following World War II, thus becoming the first U.S. casualty of the cold war. The society is highly supportive of traditional police practices and lobbied against civilian control and civilian review boards. Welch turned over the chairmanship in 1975 to Lawrence P. McDonald (Congressman, D-GA). The aircraft carrying McDonald was shot down by a Soviet fighter plane over the Sea of Japan on August 31, 1983.

John Doe. A fictitious name often used when the true name of a defendant is unknown or to indicate a person for the purpose of argument.

John Howard Association. Founded in 1901 and named after John Howard (1726–1790), an English prison reformer. The organization is devoted to prison reform and the prevention and control of crime and delinquency; provides professional consultation and survey services in crime and delinquency. Publishes a bimonthly newsletter. Address: 300 West Adams Street Suite 617, Chicago, IL 60606.

John Jay College of Criminal Justice Library. Founded in 1962 by the City University of New York, the library serves the "informational needs of criminal justice students, researchers, and professionals from within and outside of its own academic setting." Address: 899 10th Ave., New York, NY 10019.

joinder. (1) In the broadest usage, the combining of multiple defendants and/or charges for purposes of any legal step or proceeding. (2) In criminal proceedings, the naming of two or more defendants and/or the listing of two or more charges in a single charging document.

Join Together Online. This electronic resource was created for communities fighting drug abuse. For a small fee, users can access the latest information about substance abuse and find links to the major online criminal justice resources. Address: One Appleton Street, 4th Floor, Boston, MA 02116-5223. E-mail: info@jointogether. org. Web site: http://www.jointogether.org.

judge. An officer who presides over and administers the law in a court of justice.

Judge Advocate General. The chief legal officer of a branch of the military services who has, among other duties, supervision of military justice and of the proceedings of courts martial and military commissions.

judge-made law. (1) The common law as developed in form and content by judges or judicial decisions. (2) Judicial decisions based on tortured constructions of the Constitution, selecting unusual historical and legal precedents, or using unusual definitions of terms in "discovering" the law applying to a given case—used derogatorily.

judgment. (1) In the broadest usage, any decision or determination of a court. (2) The statement of the decision of a court, that the defendant is acquitted or convicted of the offense(s) charged.

judge pro tem (pro tempore). A judge who sits in lieu of a regularly appointed or elected judge and who is appointed with full authority to hear all cases scheduled for, and exercise all functions of, the regular judge.

judicial notice. An act whereby a court, in conducting a trial or framing its decision, will, of its own motion and without the production of evidence, recognize the existence and truth of certain facts having a bearing on the controversy that are matters of general or common knowledge. Among such matters are the laws of the states, historical facts, the Constitution, and principal geographical features.

judicial officer. Any person authorized by statute, constitutional provision, or court rule to exercise those powers reserved to the judicial branch of the government.

judicial powers. The powers of the courts to interpret laws and constitutions, define the powers of the branches of government, distinguish between the powers of the national government and those of the states, maintain private rights against illegal public encroachment, and void legislative acts. These powers arise either out of constitutional grant or judicial interpretation of the rendering of decisions.

judicial process. The procedures taken by a court in deciding cases or resolving legal controversies.

judicial reprieve. Early form of judicial action that predated the modern-day suspended sentence. In order to give a defendant an opportunity to apply for a pardon from the crown, a judge could grant this temporary suspension of judgment or imposition of sentence.

judicial review. The judiciary's review of the actions and determinations of executive officials of a government. Judicial review is akin to appellate court review of the decisions of lower courts. The principle is an old one in common law. By 1776 the right of judicial review of administrative action had become well enough ingrained to be included in Article III of the Constitution. Although the right to judicial review is guaranteed, its scope is not infinite. In the interest of minimizing litigation and encouraging full utilization of the administrative process, a court will not review administrative actions until all available administrative remedies, such as appeals up the chain of command within an executive department, have been exhausted.

judicial system. Taken together, the federal, state, and municipal courts form a complex judicial system in the United States. The regular federal court structure is three-tiered: the Supreme Court, 11 courts of appeals, and 91 district courts. U.S district courts are the trial courts or courts of original jurisdiction. They can hear cases involving the Constitution, acts of Congress, or treaties with foreign countries; civil suits between citizens of different states, where the amount in controversy exceeds $10,000; cases involving admiralty or maritime jurisdiction; cases where the United States is a party; cases instituted by a state against residents of other states; cases between a state or its citizens and foreign countries or individuals; and cases between two or more states. Decisions of a district court may be appealed to the Supreme Court: (a) if a federal law is held unconstitutional; (b) if a decision in a criminal case goes against the United States; or (c) in certain cases having to do with particular congressional acts or independent agencies. Generally speaking, however, most appeals from district courts are lodged with the courts of appeals. Courts of appeals have appellate jurisdiction over cases from the district courts, the regulatory commissions, and the Tax Court of the United States. The U.S. Supreme Court is the court of last resort for the nation. It hears appeals from the courts of appeals, the district courts, and the highest state courts in cases where a federal question is raised. The Supreme Court can also hear appeals from the special federal courts but rarely does so. It has original jurisdiction when a state is a party and in cases involving ambassadors and ministers. The federal judicial system also contains a number of special courts: the Customs Court, the Court of Customs and Patent Appeals, the Court of Claims, the Court of Military Appeals, and the Tax Court. State judicial systems vary enormously, organizing their courts on three or four levels. At the bottom are magistrate courts and those courts have specifically limited jurisdiction. Magistrate courts are also known as police courts, justice of peace courts, county courts, and municipal courts. Examples of courts of limited jurisdiction include family courts, probate courts, small claims courts, juvenile courts, and domestic relations courts. These courts hear criminal and civil cases, where the crime involved is normally a misdemeanor or the civil claim is quite small. The second-level courts are usually labeled circuit, superior, or district courts. In most states these courts possess both criminal and civil jurisdiction, although 16 states have separate courts for special kinds of jurisdictions. Most states have only three levels of courts, but 14 states have an intermediate level of appellate courts above the circuit, superior, or district courts but below the states' highest tribunal. All states have a court of last resort, usually termed the state supreme court. This tribunal makes final determinations of questions of law on appeal from the lower courts. If a federal question is involved, decision of a state supreme court may be appealed to the U.S. Supreme Court.

Judiciary Acts. The Judiciary Act of 1789 that established the framework of the American judicial system and helped extend the powers of the federal government. The act provided for a Supreme Court, composed of a chief justice and five associate justices; 13 district courts; three circuit courts, each made up of two supreme court justices and a district judge; and an attorney general. The act represented a compromise between two forces:

one wanted a powerful judiciary to administer a uniform United States code of justice, and the other wanted existing state courts to enforce federal laws. Section 25 of the law strengthened federal powers by permitting the Supreme Court to judicially review the states' highest courts when they upheld state laws that conflicted with federal statutes— the Constitution did not explicitly grant the Court these powers.

The Judiciary Act of 1801 was passed by the Federalists after they had lost control of the presidency and Congress in the election of 1800, but before the new government had taken office. The act clearly helped to maintain a Federalist judiciary, but it also introduced reforms that had become necessary in the 1790s. By this act the Supreme Court membership was to be reduced to five, a new set of circuit courts was to be created (with judgeships to be filled), and the number of district court judges was to be increased. This act led to last minute "midnight appointments" by President Adams and caused considerable bitterness among the Democratic-Republicans. In 1802 the new Democratic-Republican administration repealed the act of 1801. The Judicial Act of 1802 restored the Supreme Court membership to six and established a lower number of circuit courts.

Jukes family. The case name given to a New York State family with a notable record for retardation, delinquency, and crime. A study published by R. L. Dugdale and A. H. Estabrook in 1875 reported that more than 2,100 men and women of "Jukes blood" had been traced. Of these, 171 were classed as criminals, 458 were behind their age groups in school, and hundreds of others were labeled paupers, intemperates, and harlots. Like the record of the Kallikak family, the story of the Jukes was taken as proof that heredity is a dominant factor in development. This conclusion has been challenged, however, on several grounds. The investigator based many of his classifications on opinion rather than objective evidence, and he did not allow for the influence of environment on the family members.

jurat. A certificate evidencing the fact or statement that an affidavit was properly made before a duly authorized officer.

juridical. In accordance with law and with due process in the administration of justice; pertaining to the office and functions of a judge.

juridical days. Days in which courts are in session.

jurisdiction. The territory, subject matter, or persons over which lawful authority may be exercised by a court or other justice agency, as determined by statute or constitution. There are four elements of jurisdiction. *Subject-matter jurisdiction* is the authority to consider a particular class of cases. Federal courts, for example, do not have the power to decide cases between citizens of the same state unless a federal question is involved. *Jurisdiction in rem* is jurisdiction over things, typically land. The third element of jurisdiction is the *power to grant the relief* requested. The most difficult element is *jurisdiction of the person*. In common law, jurisdiction over a person is synonymous with power over him or her: it is necessary and sufficient to "serve" the person within the territory over which the court has authority. Civil law, on the other hand, considers a person subject to the court's authority only if the relationship that is the subject of the dispute is within the territory of the court.

jurisdiction in general. Unless extended by statute, a state has jurisdiction only over those crimes committed within its territorial limits and those committed by its own citizens abroad. A crime must be prosecuted in the county in which it was committed, and it is generally held to have been committed in the county in which it was completed or achieved its goal. Thus, where a blow is struck in one county and a death ensues in another, the offense is generally held to have been committed in the latter; and when a person in one county commits a crime in another by means of an innocent agent, such as the post office, the latter county has jurisdiction. Several

The Selection Process for a 12-Person Jury

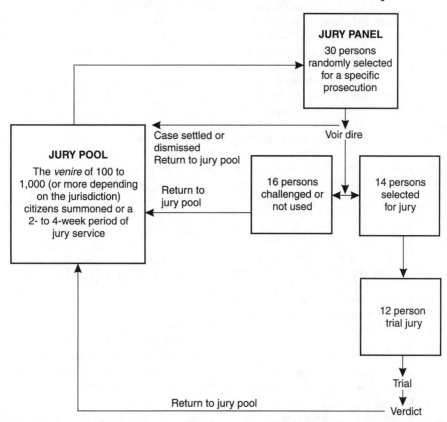

JURY PANEL
30 persons randomly selected for a specific prosecution

JURY POOL
The *venire* of 100 to 1,000 (or more depending on the jurisdiction) citizens summoned or a 2- to 4-week period of jury service

Case settled or dismissed
Return to jury pool

Voir dire

Return to jury pool

16 persons challenged or not used

14 persons selected for jury

12 person trial jury

Trial

Verdict

Return to jury pool

states have special statutes governing the subject of prosecuting homicides in the county where the body is found, giving jurisdiction to either county where the crime is committed partly in one county and partly in another, or to either state under similar circumstances.

jurisprudence. In the strict sense of the term, an act or a technique that comprises the systematized prediction of what the courts will do, with the practical aim of facilitating the work of counselors, judges, and other practitioners. Since there are as many different judicial techniques as there are systems of law and corresponding types of societies, jurisprudence has sometimes been character-

ized as social engineering according to particular social structures and needs. So arose a misleading enlargement of the term jurisprudence, which came to mean a discrete science as well as an art.

jurist. Expert, scholar, or writer in law.

jury. The American jury system is traceable to ninth-century France and was imported to England by William the Conqueror. In its earliest form, a jury was a group of the defendant's neighbors, who were expected to answer questions based on their own knowledge. Such jurors functioned as both witnesses and triers of fact. In colonial America, the jury was the champion of the popular cause. After the Revolution, the right to a trial by jury was guaranteed by the Constitution and by the separate state constitutions. An accused is entitled to a trial by jury whenever the case is originally brought into federal court and involves an offense for which the punishment may exceed six months' imprisonment and in which the defendant is prosecuted as an adult. The size of the federal jury is not constitutionally stipulated. A state jury of 6 persons sitting for a serious offense case has been approved by the Supreme Court in language that clearly indicates constitutional approval of a federal jury of less than 12. Only about 15 percent of all criminal prosecutions result in jury trials. Among those, however, are usually cases in which defendants may receive the most severe punishments. The jury for civil cases has been abolished in Great Britain, and there are pressures to abolish it in the United States. Jury use is time-consuming, and some members of the bench and bar do not believe that a group of laymen is capable of deciding the technical, complex issues raised in civil suits. However, empirical data based on several studies provide an essentially positive image of the jury's competence.

jury, grand. *See* grand jury

jury, hung. A trial jury that, after exhaustive deliberations, cannot agree on a unanimous verdict, necessitating a mistrial and a subsequent retrial. In cases and jurisdictions where unanimity is not required, a hung jury results when the necessary votes for acquittal or conviction cannot be obtained.

jury panel. The group of persons either summoned to appear in court as potential jurors for a particular trial or selected from the group of potential jurors to sit in the jury box, from which a second group, those acceptable to the prosecution and the defense, is finally chosen as the jury. *See also voir dire*

jury poll. A poll, conducted by a judicial officer or by the clerk of the court, after a jury has stated its verdict but before that verdict has been entered in the record of the court, asking each juror individually whether the stated verdict is his or her own verdict.

jury school, first. Opened on January 16, 1937, by federal judge William Clark, U.S. District Court, District of New Jersey, in the post office building at Newark, NJ, to acquaint citizens with courtroom procedures and duties of jurors in considering evidence. The first class was attended by 150 men and women.

jury sentencing. Upon a jury verdict of guilty, the recommendation or determination of a sentence by the jury.

jury wheel. A device for selecting by lot the names of jurors who are to be summoned to attend a particular court.

jus gentium (Lat.). A body of law developed by Roman jurists for the trial of cases between Roman citizens and foreigners or provincials subsequently held by medieval jurists to embody principles of right reason applicable all human relationships and invoked by Dutch jurist Hugo Grotius (1583–1645) and others as authority for rules of international law.

just deserts. A philosophical approach to the administration of justice, which assumes the individuals freely choose to violate criminal laws and therefore the state has a right and duty to punish them according to the nature of their acts.

justice. (1) The title of a judge. (2) The purpose of a legal system. The principles of law applied to the facts of a case should produce justice. There are many conceptions of justice, however, because definitions differ according to types and aims of legal systems. For instance, justice might be equality for all citizens in one system but maintenance of a class system in another. Usually the ethics and morality of a particular society determine the values that make up its idea of justice. Aristotle suggested that justice is equality for equals. He wrote: "Injustice arises when equals are treated unequally and also when unequals are treated equally." Chaim Perelmen, in his *Idea of Justice* (1963), further defines justice as not being arbitrary, as justifying itself, and as flowing from a normative system. Although Aristotelian concepts of justice are based on reason, Platonic concepts usually see justice as a function of a superhuman being, the actual realization of justice being beyond human experience.

Justice Fellowship. Founded in 1983 by Christians supporting criminal justice system reform based on biblical teachings of reconciliation, restitution, and restoration. The organization seeks to develop a system in which criminals are held responsible for their crimes, victims are compensated, and communities are protected from crime. Publishes *The Justice Report* monthly. Address: 1856 Old Reston Ave., Reston, VA 20190.

Justice Management Institute, The. Nonprofit organization that provides special expertise in court management issues. Address: 1900 Grant St., Denver, CO 80203.

justice model. A conservative approach, adopted in the United States in 1974, to the purposes of incarceration. The model's goals are: to legally and humanely control the offender, to provide adequate care and custody, to offer voluntary treatment, and to protect society. This approach views confinement as punishment and does not place great emphasis on rehabilitation. *See also* medical model

justice of the peace. In 1326 Edward II created the office of justice of the peace, designed to assist the "shire-reeve" in his law enforcement function. Noblemen appointed by the Crown, the justices of the peace first policed the counties but soon gained judicial powers and, within a few years, supplanted the constable as the most powerful local law enforcement agent. Today the position is a subordinate magistrate, usually without formal legal training, empowered to try petty civil and criminal cases and, in some states, to conduct preliminary hearings for persons accused of a crime and to fix bail for appearance in court. Justices of the peace are usually elected within a minor civil division, although their jurisdiction normally extends throughout a county. Except in a few states, their compensation is derived from fees, with the result that, in many cases, judgment is for the plaintiff.

Justice Research and Statistics Association. Founded in 1974 and funded by the Bureau of Justice Statistics of the U.S. Department of Justice, the association works to aid in the development, collection, analysis, and use of criminal justice statistics to meet state, interstate, and national needs in the areas of criminal justice administration, management, and planning. CJSA maintains an automated database of State Statistical Analysis Center projects and a library of state statistical reports. Publishes a quarterly newsletter. Address: Suite 122, 444 North Capitol Street, NW, Washington, DC 20001.

justice, sporting theory of. The term applied to the contentious method of judicial procedure in criminal trials. In this method, characteristic of criminal procedure derived from Anglo-Saxon precedents, the prosecution presents all the damaging evidence and the defense all the favorable, while the function of the judge is to act as umpire to see that the game is played fairly, according to the rules of procedure laid down in the law and in court decisions.

Justice, U.S. Department of. A federal department responsible for enforcing federal laws and representing and advising the federal government in legal matters. The Justice Department was established in 1870 with the Attorney General as its head. The department also supervises federal penal institutions, investigates violations of federal laws, and supervises U.S. attorneys and marshals. The department is organized into offices, divisions, bureaus, and boards. The offices of the attorney general, the deputy attorney general, and the associate attorney general oversee the entire department. The Attorney General is the chief law officer of the federal government; the deputy and associate attorneys general act as chief liaisons with other departments, recommend nominations for judicial appointments, and advise on pending legislation. Other offices include that of the solicitor general, the legal counsel, and the pardon at-

AGE AT WHICH CRIMINAL COURTS GAIN JURISDICTION OF YOUNG OFFENDERS RANGES FROM 16 TO 19	
Age of offender when under criminal court jurisdiction	States
16 years	Connecticut, New York, North Carolina
17	Georgia, Ilinois, Louisiana, Massachusetts, Missouri, South Carloina, Texas
18	Alabama, Alaska, Arizona, Arkansas, California, Colorado, Delaware, District of Columbia, Florida, Hawaii, Idaho, Indiana, Iowa, Kansas, Kentucky, Maine, Maryland, Michigan, Minnesota, Mississippi, Montana, Nebraska, Nevada, New Hampshire, New Jersey, New Mexico, North Dakota, Ohio, Oklahoma, Oregon, Pennsylvania, Rhode Island, South Dakota, Tennessee, Utah, Vermont, Virginia, Wisconsin, Federal districts
19	Wyoming

Source: Linda A. Szymanski, *Upper Age of Juvenile Court Jurisdiction Statues Analysis* (Pittsburgh: National Center for Jevenile Justice, 1987).

torney. Prominent divisions in the department include the Antitrust Division, which enforces federal antitrust laws and represents the United States in judicial proceedings involving such agencies as ICC, AEC, and FTC; the Criminal Division, which enforces all federal criminal laws not assigned to other divisions; and the Civil Division, which has a wide range of responsibilities including the Customs Courts. Other divisions are the Community Relations Service, the Civil Rights Division, the Land and Natural Resources Division, and the Tax Division. Most famous of the bureaus is the Federal Bureau of Investigation (FBI). Two other particularly active bureaus are the Drug Enforcement Administration, and the Immigration and Naturalization Service.

justifiable homicide. *See* homicide, justifiable

justification. Any just course or excuse for the commission of an act that would otherwise be a crime.

juvenile. A person subject to juvenile court proceedings because the event or condition for which he or she is in court occurred before the person attained an age specified by statute. The age limit defining the legal categories juvenile and adult varies among states and also, with respect to specified crimes, within states. The generally applicable age limit within a given state is most often the 18th birthday. In statutes establishing criminal-trial-court jurisdiction over persons below the standard age for specified crimes (usually violent crimes such a murder or armed robbery), the age limit may be lowered to 16 or even less.

Juvenile and Family Court Judges, Inc., National Council of. Founded in 1937, with the goal of improving the juvenile justice system through publications, training, and research. Publishes *Juvenile and Family Court Journal; Juvenile and Family Law Digest; Juvenile and Family Court Newsletter* Address: P.O. Box 8970, Reno, NV 89507.

Juvenile Correctional Agencies, National Association of (NAJCA). Founded in 1953; absorbed in 1983 the Association of State Juvenile Justice Administrators. Publishes quarterly newsletter. Address: 55 Albin Road, Bow, NH 03301.

juvenile court. (1) The name for the class courts that have, as all or part of their authority, original jurisdiction over matters concerning persons statutorily defined as juveniles. (2) A specialized court, having jurisdiction in cases of delinquent, neglected, or dependent children, which seeks to determine the underlying causes of misconduct and provides reformation through education, healthful activities, or institutional supervision. Juvenile defendants are entitled to be assisted by counsel and to have all the procedural safeguards that are accorded

The Criminal and the Juvenile Courts: Some Historically Important Contrasts	
Adult Criminal Court	Juvenile Court
Court of law	Social institution, agency, clinic
Constitutional rights	*Parens patriae* approach-supra constitutional rights
Purpose to punish, deter	Purpose to salvage, rehabilitate
Begins with arrest	Begins with apprehension, summons; process of intake
Indictment or presentment	Petition files on behalf of child
Detained in jails or released on bail	Detained in detention centers or released to family or others
Public trial	Private hearing
Strict rules of evidence	Informal procedures
Right to trial by jury	No right to trial by jury
Right to counsel	No right to (or need for) counsel
Prosecuted by state	Allegations frought by state
Plea bargaining	No plea bargaining; state would act in child's best interests
Impartial judge	Judge acting as a wise parent
Pleads guildty, innocent, or *nolo contendre*	Admits or denies petition
Found guilty or innocent	Adjudicated
Sentenced	Disposition of the case
Probation	Probation
Incarcerated in jail or prison	Placed in reformatory, training school, or foster home, etc.
Released on parole	Released to aftercare

to adult defendants at all stages of police and judicial proceedings against them. The first juvenile court was the Juvenile Court of Cook County, known as the Chicago Juvenile Court, authorized on April 21, 1899, and opened on July 1, 1899. *See also* Mack, Julian W.

juvenile court judgment. A decision, terminating an adjudicatory hearing, that the juvenile is a delinquent, status offender, or dependent, or that the allegations in the petition are not sustained.

Juvenile Detention Association, National. Founded in 1968. Seeks to advance the science, processes, and art of juvenile detention services through the overall improvement of the juvenile justice profession. Offices based at Eastern Kentucky University and Michigan State University.

juvenile disposition. The decision of a juvenile court, concluding a disposition hearing, that an adjudicated juvenile be committed to a juvenile correctional facility; placed in a juvenile residence, shelter, or care and treatment program; required to meet certain standards of conduct; or released.

juvenile facility. A building, section of a building, or area that is used for the custody and/or care and treatment of juveniles who have been either administratively determined to be in need of care or formally alleged or adjudged to be delinquents, status offenders, or dependents. These facilities are either short-term, long-term, open, or institutional. The individual juvenile facility types are: (a) training school, "a long-term specialized facility that provides strict confinement for its residents"; (b) ranch, forestry camp, and farm, "a long-term residential facility for persons whose behavior does not necessitate the strict confinement of a training school, often allowing them greater contact with the community"; (c) halfway house and group home, "a long-term facility in which residents are allowed extensive contact with the community, such as attending school or holding a job"; (d) detention center, "a short-term facility that provides temporary care in a physically restricting environment for juveniles in custody pending court disposition and, often, for juveniles who are adjudicated delinquent or are awaiting transfer to another jurisdiction"; (e) shelter, "a short-term facility that provides temporary care similar to that of a detention center, but in a physically unrestricting environment"; and (f) reception or diagnostic center, "a short-term facility that screens persons committed by the courts and assigns them to appropriate correctional facilities."

Juvenile Firesetters Program. A workshop to train fire education specialists, fire investigators, counselors, and law enforcement and juvenile authorities. The program is scheduled through state fire training offices. Address: Office of Planning and Education, Fire Administration, Federal Emergency Management Agency, 16825 South Seton Ave., Emmitsburg, MD 21727.

juvenile information source. The National Directory of Children and Youth Services is compiled by the National Directory fo Children, Youth and Family Services, located at 14 Inverness Drive East, Suite D144, Englewood,CO 80112. It contains lists of organizations and agencies that may be able to provide information on matters concerning juvenile justice.

juvenile justice agency. A government agency, or subunit thereof, of which the functions are the investigation, supervision, adjudication, care, or confinement of juvenile offenders and nonoffenders subject to the jurisdiction of a juvenile court; also, in some usages, a private agency providing care and treatment.

Juvenile Justice and Delinquency Prevention Act of 1974. Federal legislation, amended in 1977 and 1980, that provides funds to states and communities for prevention and treatment programs, emphasizes programs designed to deinstitutionalize status offenders, and provides funding for research on delinquency. This act was further revised with the Juvenile Justice, Runaway Youth, and Missing Children's Act Amendments of 1984. The act also established the Office of Juvenile Justice and Delinquency Prevention and the Missing Children's Assistance Act.

Juvenile Justice, National Center for. Founded in 1973 as the research division of the National Council of Juvenile and Family Court Judges. Maintains library of databases, volumes on juvenile justice. Address: 710 Fifth Ave., Suite 3000, Pittsburgh, PA 15219.

juvenile locators. The National Runaway Switchboard, operated by the Youth Development of Health and Human Services, informs youths what services are available to them and permits them to telephone their parents long distance without charge. Its number is (800) 621-4000. The National Runaway Hotline permits youths to send messages to their parents without revealing their location. Its number is (800) 231-6946; in Texas, (800) 392-3352; and in Alaska or Hawaii, (800) 231-6762.

juvenile offender. A person under 16, 18, or (in some states) 20 years of age who has been found guilty of committing offenses against the law.

juvenile petition. A document, filed in juvenile court, alleging that a juvenile is a delinquent, status offender, or a dependent, and asking that the court assume jurisdiction over the juvenile or that an alleged delinquent be transferred to criminal court for prosecution as an adult.

K

Kansas City Experiment. A study conducted by the Police Foundation in 1972 and 1973 where three different levels of preventive patrol were closely monitored and compared: "normal," "proactive," and "reactive." Normal patrol involved a single car cruising the streets when not responding to calls; the proactive-patrol strategy involved increasing the levels of preventive patrol and police visibility by doubling or tripling the number of cruising cars; reactive patrol was characterized by the virtual elimination of cruising cars, with police entering the designated areas only in response to specific requests. At the conclusion of the study, no significant differences were found in any of the areas—regardless of the level of patrol. In effect this Kansas City experiment suggested that police patrol was not deterring crime.

Keating, Charles. *See* fraud offenses

Kefauver Investigation. An inquiry into organized crime in interstate commerce by the Senate Crime Committee. The five-man committee was established on May 10, 1950, under the chairmanship of Senator Estes Kefauver, to investigate illegal operations, the influence of crime on political leaders, the use of criminal funds for business investments, and the bribery of police by criminal elements. By February 1951, the committee had interviewed 500 witnesses in New York and other large cities. These witnesses included public officers, political leaders, racketeers, and gamblers. In its first report, the committee declared that gambling involved over $20 billion annually. It recommended the establishment of a national crime commission, a federal ban on interstate transmission of bets and gambling information, a strengthening of federal law enforcement, and an improvement in federal tax laws to reach concealed profits from illegal deals. The committee highlighted the work of national crime syndicates, whose control over state and local politics rendered them immune from prosecution. In its final report on August 31, 1951, the committee declared that conditions in smaller cities were similar to those in large cities and recommended attacking crime at the local level.

Kent State University. On May 4, 1970, in response to a weekend of demonstrations that included arson and vandalism, Ohio National Guard troops opened fire on Kent State students who were protesting the U.S. invasion of Cambodia. Four students were killed and nine wounded. Ten days later, on May 14, 1970, a college student and a high school student were killed and seven people wounded at Jackson State University in Jackson, Mississippi. Students had gathered in front of a dormitory to protest the Vietnam War and the student deaths at Kent State. State highway patrol officers and Jackson police ordered the students to disperse and the shooting began.

Kerner Commission. *See* Civil Disorders, National Advisory Commission on

Kevorkian, Dr. Jack. A controversial physician who, with his Mercitron machines, assisted willing patients to end their lives. In February 1993, the state of Michigan enacted legislation making assisted suicide a felony punishable by up to four years in prison and a $2,000 fine. Kevorkian is now in prison. *See also* euthanasia; medicide

key. A term used in fingerprint classification. It is obtained by counting the ridges in the first loop appearing in the set of fingerprints. The loop may be either ulnar or radial and in any finger except the little finger. The thumb may be used. *See also* fingerprint patterns

kidnapping. A federal crime defined by a law enacted in June 1936, referred to as the Lindbergh Law, as it was passed following the Lindbergh kidnapping case. The law makes it a crime to carry away persons against their will, transport them interstate, and hold them for ransom, reward, or otherwise. The law was later amended to create a presumption of interstate transportation after a victim has been kidnapped for 24 hours without release: "Transportation or confinement of a person without authority of law and without his or her consent, or without the consent of his or her guardian, if a minor." *Famous kidnappings:* Robert Franks, 13, in Chicago on May 22, 1924, by two youths, Richard Loeb and Nathan Leopold, who killed the boy. Their demand for $10,000 was ignored. Loeb died in prison and Leopold was paroled in 1958. Charles A. Lindbergh, Jr., 20 months old, in Hopewell, NJ, on March 1, 1932; found dead May 12. The ransom of $50,000 was paid to a man identified as Bruno Richard Hauptmann, 35, a paroled German convict who entered the United States illegally. He was convicted after a spectacular trial at Flemington and electrocuted in Trenton, NJ, April 3, 1936. Frank Sinatra, Jr., 19, from a hotel room in Lake Tahoe, CA, on December 8, 1963. Released on December 11 after his father paid a $240,000 ransom. Three men were sentenced to prison; most of the ransom was recovered. Barbara Jane Mackle, 20, abducted on December 17, 1968, from Atlanta, GA. Found unharmed 3 days later, buried in a coffin-like wooden box 18 inches underground, after her father had paid a $500,000 ransom. Gary Steven Krist was sentenced to life and Ruth Eisemann-Schier to 7 years; most of the ransom was recovered. Victor E. Samuelson, Exxon executive, on December 6, 1973, was kidnapped in Compana, Argentina, by Marxist guerrillas. Freed on April 29, 1974, after the record payment of $14.2 million in ransom. J. Paul Getty III, 17, grandson of the U.S. oil mogul, was released on December 15, 1973, in southern Italy after a $2.8 million ransom was paid. Patricia (Patty) Hearst, 19, was taken from her Berkeley, CA, apartment on February 4, 1974. The Symbionese Liberation Army demanded that her father, publisher Randolph A. Hearst, give millions to the poor. Hearst offered $2 million in food and the Hearst Corporation offered $4 million more. In 1978, William and Emily Harris were sentenced to 10 years to life for the Hearst kidnapping. Samuel Bronfman, 21, the heir to the Seagram liquor fortune, was allegedly abducted on August 9, 1975, in Purchase, NY; the $2.3 million ransom was paid. The FBI and New York City Police found Bronfman on August 17 in Brooklyn, NY, recovered the ransom, and arrested Mel Patrick Lynch and Dominic Byrne. Both were found not guilty of kidnapping, but were convicted of extortion after they claimed Bronfman masterminded the ransom plot. James L. Dozier, U.S. Army general, was kidnapped from his apartment in Verona, Italy, on Dec. 17, 1981, by members of the Red Brigades terrorist organization. He was rescued on January 28, 1982, by Italian police.

killers, serial. *See* serial murders

kilogram. Equals 2.2046 lb.; 1 gram = 1/28 oz.

King, Martin Luther, Jr. Civil rights leader (1929–1968) who won respect around the world for his nonviolent demonstrations and was awarded the Nobel Peace Prize in 1964. Born in Atlanta, GA, he drew national attention by leading a movement against segregation in buses. The 382-day Montgomery boycott in 1955/1956 was successful. Following this event, the Southern Christian Leadership Conference (SCLC) was formed to carry on the peaceful drive for the civil rights of black people. King became president of SCLC and continued leading sit-ins and other forms of protest against discrimination. He was arrested many times for violating state segregation laws. In August 1963, King was a leader of the March on Washington by as many as 250,000 supporters of equal rights. To this gathering he addressed his eloquent "I Have a Dream" speech. The efforts of King and his followers were a major force behind the passage by Congress of the Civil Rights Act of 1964, which has been called a Magna Carta for blacks. In 1968 he went to Memphis, TN, and was assassinated there on April 4 by James Earl Ray. On October 22, 1984, Congress (Senate vote 78-22) designated the third Monday in January, beginning in 1986, as a national holiday in memory of Dr. King. *See also* Ray, James Earl

King, Rodney. The victim in a 1992 case in which an 81-second videotape by amateur photographer George Halliday showed Los Angeles police officers beating King, a motorist. Four officers were indicted, tried in Simi Valley, and acquitted. In the aftermath, the Los Angeles riot left 53 dead and upwards of $1 billion in property damage. Civil rights violations by the officers were filed in federal court, and on April 17, 1993, the verdict was reached and delivered. Officers Koon and Powell were found guilty, and Officers Wind and Briseno were found not guilty. *See also* civil disturbances; Christopher Commission Report; McDuffie, Arthur; Overtown; urban riots

kiting, check. A system of building up deposit balances in a number of banks by drawing on a series of banks where small accounts have been opened. The kiter endeavors to gradually increased the amounts of the deposits. It is a scheme or procedure to defraud and is illegal in many states

kleptomania. Compulsive stealing, usually without any economic motive. Kleptomaniacs, unlike ordinary thieves or shoplifters, do no steal because they intend to use or sell the stolen items. Nor do they plan their crimes carefully to avoid being caught. Rather, they steal on impulse, and as a result they are easily and frequently caught. The great majority of kleptomaniacs are women. The articles they steal frequently have at least symbolic sexual significance, and they tend to steal the same article repeatedly. Boys and men also steal fetishistic items. According to some theories, kleptomania is traceable to emotional deprivation in infancy. The act of stealing is an expression of revenge directed against symbols of the parent.

Knapp Commission. *See* Serpico, Frank

known specimens. Items of physical evidence that are obtained from known sources. Handwriting specimens taken from, or known to be the writings of, a person are such. A pistol taken from a person is a known specimen, contrasted with questioned specimens. A crime laboratory, especially the FBI Laboratory, divides all specimens into known and questioned.

Koga method. A form of self-defense named for Robert K. Koga, a retired Los Angeles Police Department officer who began teaching his techniques in the 1960s. Koga draws heavily on the martial art aikido, and stresses minimal force during confrontations to reduce the likelihood of injury to officers and suspects. It also offers nontraditional ways, such as distraction, to achieve compliance.

Ku Klux Klan. (1) An organization founded in Tennessee in 1866 to reassert white supremacy in the South. Disguised in white masks and robes, members of the Klan rode at night, terrorizing, whipping, and committing other acts of violence (including murder) against blacks who persisted in voting and acting contrary to a white-oriented society. After Congress in 1871 passed the Ku Klux Klan Act and the Force Act, the Klan adopted less violent means to accomplish its purpose. (2) A national organization founded in 1915 and directed against Catholics, Jews, and foreigners, as well as blacks, this Klan was influential in several states for a brief period after World War I. It still exists under several different names. There are several white supremacist organizations, including the White Socialist Party and the Aryan Brotherhood.

L

labeling model in crime. A theoretical approach to deviant behavior, basically stating that applying formal definitions to an individual results in a negative self-concept that may subsequently provide motivation for further acts of deviance. *See also* labeling theory

labeling theory. Frank Tannenbaum in 1938 defined the beginning of a criminal career as the result of a "dramatization of evil,"—the point at which a child is singled out from the group and treated as a delinquent. By 1963 Howard Becker had further developed and renamed Tannenbaum's theory. Now called labeling, Becker's theory held that this interactionist concept could explain deviance in terms of societal reaction to acts of the individual. Labeling theory has come into prominence over the past decade as a major approach to explaining the nature of deviance. The labeling theory stresses that social rules are not clear-cut and that they result in ambiguous evaluations of behavior. Deviance is also emphasized as a process in which deviant rules and self-conceptions are shaped. *See also* self-fulfilling prophecy

labor relations. The relations of employer and employee affecting the conditions of labor. As defined in federal and state labor relations acts, and interpreted by the courts, labor relations include matters dealing with wages, hours, tenure, security, hiring, discharge, union organization and activities, representation, and promotion.

labor union. A combination or association of workers in some trade or industry, or in several allied trades, that exists for the purpose of securing by concerted action the most favorable wages, hours, and conditions of labor, and otherwise improving workers' economic and social status.

laches. An unreasonable delay in pursuing a legal remedy, concurrent with resulting prejudice to the opposing party, whereby the individual who sought the legal remedy forfeits his or her right to do so.

lachrymator. A substance that causes severe weeping or tear production of the eyes. Such chemicals are used in tear gas.

La Guardia Report. Short title for a 1938 study of marijuana ordered by New York mayor Fiorello La Guardia, conducted by the New York Academy of Medicine, with the assistance of the New York Police Department. Headed by George B. Wallace, the committee was composed of 31 eminent physicians, psychiatrists, clinical psychologists, pharmacologists, chemists, and sociologists. The study was in two parts: a clinical study of the effects of marijuana and a sociological study of marijuana users in New York City. The report refuted the stepping-stone hypothesis, and generally stressed that the sociological, psychological, and medical ills commonly attributed to marijuana are exaggerated.

Lanham Act. *See* counterfeiting, trademark

larceny. Unlawful taking or attempted taking of property other than a motor vehicle from the possession of another, by stealth, without force and without deceit, with intent to permanently deprive the owner of the property. Larceny is a UCR reporting category under larceny-theft.

The distinction between larceny as a felony or misdemeanor, or grand larceny versus petty larceny, is of a statutory nature. Grand larceny can range from as little as $20 in IA, OK, and SC, to as much as $2,000 in PA (a value below these amounts constitutes a misdemeanor). The only exception is NC, where the law does not specify a dividing point.

laser. A term based on Light Amplification by Stimulated Emission Radiation, it is an electrical/optical device for producing a coherent parallel beam of light—that is, one in which the light waves are all in phase. Such a beam can be made much more precisely narrow and parallel than can one of ordinary light.

laundering money. Offenses defined as "all activities designed to conceal the existence, nature, and final disposition of funds gained through illicit activities." Money laundering per se did not become a federal crime until passage of the Money Laundering Control Act (MLCA) of 1986 (Pub. L. 99-570, 100 Stat. 3207-18). Until then, the main tools for combating money laundering were provided by the Bank Secrecy Act of 1970. The MLCA of 1986 created two new offenses related to money laundering and currency transaction reporting violations: (1) engaging in financial transactions and international transportations or transfers of funds or property derived from "specified unlawful activity," and (2) engaging in monetary transactions in excess of $10,000 with property derived from proceeds of specified unlawful activity. In addition, the Anti–Drug Abuse Act of 1986 prohibited the structuring of currency transactions to deliberately evade reporting requirements. Also, these offenses and certain violations of the currency reporting requirements are included acts under the Racketeer Influenced and Corrupt Organizations (RICO) statute. It is estimated that between $10 and $100 billion in drug money is laundered in the United States alone. A 1990 report estimated that U.S. and European drug dealers earn about $14 million every hour. *See also* Bank Secrecy Act; Dr. Snow; Mafia; Operation El Dorado; Operation Polar Cap; organized crime; Pizza Connection; Racketeer Influenced and Corrupt Organization.

law. (1) A general rule for the conduct of members of the community, either emanating from the governing authority by positive command or approved by it, and habitually enforced by some public authority by the imposition of sanctions or penalties for its violation. (2) The whole body of such rules, including constitutions, the common law, equity, statutes, judicial decisions, administrative orders, and ordinances, together with the principles of justice and right commonly applied in their enforcement.

law, administrative. Statutes, regulations, and orders that govern public agencies. Essentially these are rules governing the administrative operations of the government—public law as opposed to private law. Administrative law includes social insurance, legislative committee powers, and public authorities such as the Interstate Commerce Commission and the Federal Power Commission. There is no separate legal system of administrative law in the United States, as there is in European law systems, and matters of administrative law are considered by the Supreme Court. The existence of administrative law with legal standing gives the public some control over the administrative activities of the government. Illegitimate interference and abuse by public authorities can be checked, definite standards for public conduct established, and supervision of public authorities provided. Many believe that the increased administrative activities of the U.S. government and the resulting legal problems demand an established system of administrative law with qualified judges and courts. Administrative law has been referred to as the fourth branch of government.

law and order. A catch-phrase for the suppression of crime and violence, used particularly against civil rights activists and antiwar demonstrators during the 1960s and early 1970s. The term conveyed subtle racism where it was used by politicians to appeal to antiblack voters in the South. Later the term was used by the federal government to justify the repression of antiwar demonstrators. Law and order was a particularly useful term for government officials because, with the high crime rate, race-connected riots, bombings, and street violence, few could argue against attempts to maintain law and order in the United States. Historically, the phrase was also heavily used as a convention slogan for the Harding-Coolidge ticket in 1920. Most contemporary politicians emphasize a strong law and order platform.

law and social control. Law imposes formal control on society by setting forth specific rules of conduct, planned sanctions to support these rules, and designated officials to make, interpret, and enforce the rules. The objective is conformity and stability in society. The emphasis on formalism in law makes the regulation of social relations seem more important than the social relations themselves. Nevertheless, formal social controls are considered necessary in modern society because of its complexity and anonymity.

law, blue. *See* blue laws

law book, first published. William Penn's *The Excellent Privilege of Liberty and Property Being the Birth-Right of the Freeborn Subjects of England*, an 83-page book, was printed by William Bradford and published in Philadelphia in 1687. It contained: "(a) the Magna Carta, with a learned comment upon it; (b) the confirmation of the Charters of the Liberties of England and of the Forrest, made in the 35th year of the reign of Edward I; (c) a statute made in the 34th year of the reign of Edward I, commonly called De Tallageo non concedendo, wherein all fundamental laws, liberties, and customs are confirmed, with a comment upon them; (d) an abstract of the patent granted by the king to William Penn and his heirs and assigns for the province of Pennsylvania; and (e) lastly, the charter of liberties granted by the said William Penn to the freemen and inhabitants of the province of Pennsylvania and territories there unto annexed in America."

law, canon. A code governing the organization and operation of a church. The regulations of canon law apply the moral precepts of church doctrine to the daily lives of members.

law, common. Body of rules based on judicial decisions rather than legislation; it is the basis of the Anglo-American legal tradition. The common law judge relies on judicial decisions of the past in rendering rulings. Under the common law approach, the law can change gradually at the hands the judges to meet the changes in society. In the United States, the common law system is evident in the supremacy of the judiciary in determining the constitutionality of legislation. In contrast, the system of civil law prominent on the continent of Europe is based on Roman law and later codes of legislation.

Law, Elizabethan Poor. A law enacted by the English Parliament in 1603, summarizing and consolidating a variety of laws concerning poor relief passed during the preceding century. The law required the local community to assume responsibility for the care of its own poor, established the principle of destitution as a test of eligibility for assistance, and decreed that relief could be granted only in return for work in places provided for housing the poor. The principles of public assistance established by the Elizabethan Poor Law governed the administration of relief in England and the United States for over 300 years.

law enforcement. The generic name for the activities of the agencies responsible for maintaining public order and enforcing the law, particularly the activities of prevention, detection, and investigation of crime and the apprehension of criminals.

law enforcement agency. A federal, state, or local criminal justice agency or identifiable subunit whose principal functions are the prevention, detection, and investigation of crime and the apprehension of alleged offenders.

law enforcement assistance. Funds, equipment, training, intelligence information, and personnel.

Law Enforcement Assistance Administration (LEAA). An agency created by Title I of the Omnibus Crime Control and Safe Streets Act of 1968. In 1965, the Office of Law Enforcement Assistance (OLEA) had been set up within the U.S. Department of Justice to make funds available to states, localities, and private organizations to improve methods of law enforcement, court administration, and prison operations. It was the federal agency charged with channeling federal funds to states to assist local communities in combating crime and improving justice services. In 1969 LEAA assumed these functions and created state planning agencies, block and discretionary grants, and the National Institute of Law Enforcement and Criminal Justice. LEAA also supplied money for the training and education of criminal justice personnel through the Law Enforcement Education Program (LEEP). LEEP, throughout the 1970s, provided more than $40 million per year in loans for educational assistance to some 100,000 persons employed in, or preparing for, careers in criminal justice. Loans were forgiven at 25 percent each year the person was employed in the system. According to the Twentieth Century Fund Task Force, in spite of the billions of dollars spent, LEAA was deemed a failure and ceased operations in 1982. *See also* Comprehensive Crime Control Act of 1984

law enforcement community, federal. The term means the heads of the Federal Bureau of Investigation; Drug Enforcement Administration; Criminal Division of the Department of Justice; Internal Revenue Service; Customs Service; Immigration and Naturalization Service; United States Marshals Service; National Park Service; United States Postal Service; Secret Service; Coast Guard; Bureau of Alcohol, Tobacco, and Firearms;

and other federal agencies with specific statutory authority to investigate violations of federal criminal laws.

law enforcement emergency. A federal term meaning "an uncommon situation which is, or threatens to become, serious or of epidemic proportions, and in which state and local resources are inadequate to protect the lives and property of citizens or enforce the criminal law." The term does not include the perceived need for planning or other activities related to crowd control for general public safety projects or a situation requiring the enforcement of laws associated with scheduled public events, including political conventions and sports events.

law enforcement equipment. The National Bureau of Standards Library has a special division that investigates such products as surveillance cameras, vapor generators, radar, breathohol detection, and clothing worn by law enforcement officers. Address: Law Enforcement Standards Laboratory, National Bureau of Standards, DOC, Physics Building, Room B157, Washington, DC 20234.

law enforcement films. *See* Criminal Justice Audiovisual Materials Directory

Law Enforcement Intelligence Units. An association of law enforcement intelligence officers and units, participated in by officers from some 150 communities who cooperatively exchange information concerning criminal activities and criminals.

law enforcement officer. (1) In some usages, any government employee who is an officer sworn to carry out law enforcement duties, whether or not employed by an agency or identifiable subunit that primarily performs law enforcement functions. (2) An employee of a law enforcement agency who is an officer sworn to carry out law enforcement duties. Federal law enforcement officer: examples of this class are agents of the Federal Bureau of Investigation; the Bureau of Alcohol, Tobacco, and Firearms; and the investigative staff of federal organized crime units and tax law enforcement units. State law enforcement officer: examples of this class are state police officers, state highway patrol officers and state park police. This class should include those campus police officers who are employees of state universities and state colleges. Local law enforcement officer: examples of this class are sheriffs, deputy sheriffs, chiefs of police, city police officers, and sworn personnel of law enforcement subunits of port and transit authorities. This class should include campus police officers who are employees of local city and community college districts. Private campus police are generally excluded.

Law Enforcement Officers Killed and Assaulted (LEOKA). The FBI annually compiles data concerning the felonious and accidental line-of-duty deaths and assaults of law enforcement officers and presents these statistics in *Law Enforcement Officers Killed and Assaulted* (LEOKA). Tabular presentations include weapons used, use of body armor, and circumstances surrounding murders and assaults of officers.

Law Enforcement Officers Memorial, National. The memorial was dedicated by Presideni George Bush in Washington, DC, on October 15, 1991, after seven years of planning. It was built with $10.5 million in private contributions. Inscribed on its two curved marble walls—304 feet long and 3½ feet high—are the 12,561 names of U.S. law enforcement officers who have died in the line of duty since 1794. Statues of lions guard each end, and the site is brimming with trees, grass, and flowers.

Law Enforcement Research Publications. This office of the National Institute of Justice (DOJ) is responsible for the publication and distribution of institute research and evaluation findings and programs. It also oversees the operations of the National Criminal Justice Reference Services. Address: Reference and Dissemination Division, Office of Development Testing and Dissemination, National Institute of Justice, DOJ, 633 Indiana Avenue, NW, Room 810, Washington, DC 20531.

Law Enforcement Training Network (LETN). Established in 1989, LETN is a 24-hour exclusive satellite television network for law enforcement. Programs feature training, daily news, documentaries, and police events. Address: 4101 International Parkway, Carrollton, TX 75007; telephone (800) 535-LETN.

law, natural. An abstract concept of law based on the relation among God, man, and nature. An ideal higher than positive or man-made law, it forms the basis of justice in the ethical sense. It embodies such ideas as the existence of a universal order governing all people and the inalienable rights of the individual. John Locke used natural law principles in setting forth the basic rights of the individual in his social contract theories, and natural law ideas were influential in the framing of the Constitution of the United States.

law of effect. A fundamental concept in learning theory holding that, all other things being equal, a person will more readily learn those habits leading to satisfaction and will not learn (or will learn with greater difficulty) those habits leading to dissatisfaction.

law of nations. Called international law and sometimes public law, it includes those rules that define and regulate the conduct of nations in their intercourse with each other. It consists of: (a) a code of what may be called natural law, dictated by the sentiment that nations should cooperate with each other; (b) a system of unwritten law, depending upon principles of comity or international courtesy; and (c) a code of positive law, derived from ancient codes, treaties, judicial decisions, state papers, and the opinions of great writers upon the subject whose experience as statesmen gives their words authority.

law of the sea. The UN Conference on the Law of the Sea deals with international issues such as navigation, overflight, conservation and management of fisheries' resources, protection of the marine environment, exploitation of oil and gas in the continental shelf, marine scientific research, and a system of compulsory dispute settlement. For further information, contact: Office of the Law of the Sea Negotiations, Office of the Deputy Secretary, Department of State, 2201 C Street, NW, Room 4321, Washington, DC 20520.

law of the situation. A management concept suggesting that one person should not give orders to another person, but both should agree to take their action cues from the situation at hand.

law, poor. An antiquated name still frequently applied to the body of laws governing the administration of public assistance. The name dates from sixteenth-century England and is best known in relation to the Elizabethan Poor Law of 1603. The name was borrowed by the colonies and continued in use to designate various state laws dealing with relief of poor and dependent persons. Public welfare and public assistance are terms that are gradually replacing the term poor law. In a wider sense, poor law is synonymous with a degrading and shortsighted system of poor relief based on severe laws of settlement, pauper oaths, standards of relief below that of the poorest-paid common laborer, and relief in kind.

law reform. Adjustment of legislation to changing social conditions. Reform is called for when a law is not incorporated into the culture of the society and is thus not enforceable. Law reform can take place in the courts, through lawyers, or in legislatures. The courts can initiate basic change by reinterpreting the Constitution or by making decisions that lay the groundwork for legislation. For example, various Supreme Court decisions on civil equality culminated in the Civil Rights Act of 1965. Citizens can also institute law reform through the courts by bringing representative suits—actions against local authorities on behalf of a group—to produce a declaratory judgment. Lawyers play a significant role in law reform through the law revision committees set up by bar associations. Legislative law reform, which generally is slower than court reform, takes place on the state and federal levels.

laws. The individual items within the broad field of law, natural or manmade. Scientific laws are particular statements of generalized truths, especially those having to do with causative sequence. Juristic laws are the items on the statute books of states; in ordinary usage, the current statutes of any particular state. These fall into three main categories: (a) general laws, which apply to all citizens or persons or to all persons within legally recognized groups or classes; (b) special laws, enacted for particular purposes; and (c) private laws, passed for the benefit of particular individuals. Scientific laws are divisible into (a) quantitative laws, which are principles or generalizations explaining the aspects of quantity; and (b) qualitative laws, which are principles or generalizations explaining the aspects of quality.

laws, compilation of colonial, first. *"The Book of the General Lauues and Libertyes*, concerning the inhabitants of Massachusetts, collected out of the records of the General Court for the several years wherein they were made and established and now revised by the same Court and disposed into an Alphabetical order and published by the same Authorities in the General Court held at Boston the fourteenth of the first month Anno 1647." The work was published in Cambridge, MA, in 1648 and sold by Hezekiah Usher in Boston.

laws, compilation of U.S., first. Codifying the laws in force was *The Public Statutes at Large of the United States of America*, from the organization of the government in 1789 to March 3, 1845, arranged in chronological order with references to the matter of each act and to subsequent acts on the same subject and with notes on the decisions of the courts of the United States construing those acts and upon the subjects of the laws, with an index to the contents of each volume.

laws, sumptuary. Laws designed to regulate people's expenditures for food, clothing, and other consumable goods, especially luxuries; to restrict or forbid the use of certain goods. The method usually used today to exercise this type of control is taxation.

leading question. A question asked of a witness during a trial or court proceeding that suggests, and thus may elicit, an answer that might otherwise not be offered by the witness. Leading questions, while not ordinarily allowed, are, under certain conditions, permissible.

learning theory. An explanation of crime and delinquency postulating that criminal behavior, like legal and normative behavior, is learned. Such learning may be acquired from those already engaged in illegal activity, as in differential association theory; learning may be reinforced through rewards and punishments. *See also* differential association

learning, three schools of. (1) Classical conditioning; (2) operant conditioning; and (3) cognitive learning theory. (1) and (2) focus on the stimulus-response connection as the basic unit of analysis in the learning process; (3) suggests that conditioning and learning are one and the same.

leftists, political. Those people in the political spectrum who seek radical, innovative changes in society. Today, socialism is the dominant leftist position. The term derives from the seating arrangements in European legislatures, where radical members sat on the presiding officer's left.

legal aid. Any number of programs designed to provide legal and quasi-legal assistance to persons who cannot afford to hire their own attorneys. The term is frequently used to include only legal assistance of a civil—as opposed to a criminal—nature, particularly since 1963, when *Gideon v. Wainwright* required a publicly appointed defense counsel in criminal cases (*See also* Gideon, Clarence). A large number of organizations, both privately and publicly sponsored, have been established to render this type of legal service. One of the oldest is the Legal Aid Society. In addition, the federal government sponsors the Legal Services Corporation, with headquarters in Washington, DC. One of the most promising developments is union-sponsored legal insurance, which keeps a law firm on retainer, for a fixed annual fee, to handle union members' problems without additional charge.

legal assistants. *See* paralegals

legal counsel for police. Attorneys who work for, and are employed by, law enforcement agencies as legal counselors, advisers, or house counsel.

Legal Counsel for the Elderly. Founded in 1975. Provides direct, free legal services to Washington, DC, residents aged 60 and older. Provides back-up assistance and training to extend legal services and nursing home advocacy to the elderly. Address: 601 E St., NW, Washington, DC 20049.

legal ethics. Customs among those in the legal profession involving their responsibilities toward each other, the courts, and their clients. *See also* code of ethics

legal evidence. A broad, general term meaning all admissible evidence, including both oral and documentary, but with a further implication that it must be of such a character as to reasonably and substantially prove the point, not merely to raise a suspicion or conjecture.

legal fiction. A condition assumed to be true in law, regardless of its actual truth or falsity—sometimes used by judges so that a new subject, for which no rules of law have been formulated, may be embraced within existing rules.

Legal Investigators, National Association of. Founded in 1967. Publishes *Legal Investigator* (quarterly). Address: H. Ellis Armistead & assoc., LLC, 1127 Auraria Parkway #201B, Denver, CO 80204.

legal opinions. The legal opinions of the Department of Justice are published by the Office of Legal Counsel and are made available through the Superintendent of Documents, Government Printing Office, Washington, DC 20402. For further information, contact: Office of Legal Counsel, DOJ, United States Department of Justice, Washington, DC 20530.

legal personality. The legal status accorded a corporation or other artificial person that entitles it to hold and administer property, to sue in the courts, and to enjoy many of the rights and assume many of the liabilities of an actual person.

Legal Points. A monthly publication by the ICAP Police Legal Center, Research Division, Washington, DC 20036. Contains information on legal points of value to the criminal justice community.

legal provocation. Provocation that can be used as a legal defense for an act.

legal realism. A pragmatic approach concerned with the actual working of the rules of law. It centers on identifying the discrepancy between the form of law and the reality of law (or the letter and the spirit) that occurs when laws do not keep up with the changes in society. The basis of legal realism is the scientific method; psychology, sociology, criminology, economics, and statistics are among the disciplines that are incorporated into this method to study the social factors that create the law and its social results.

Legal Services for Children (LSC). Comprehensive, cost-free law firm devoted exclusively to protecting the legal rights of teens, children, and infants who are residents of San Francisco, CA, and other Bay Area counties. Supported by social workers, social work student interns, law students, and support staff. LSC is the first organization of its kind in the nation. Address: 1254 Market Street, 3rd Floor, San Francisco, CA 94102.

Legal Services for the Elderly (LSE). Founded in 1969 and called Legal Services for the Elderly Poor until 1980. Funded through the Legal Services Corporation in New York City, attorney fees, and grants. Publishes *Progress Report* (2/year). Address: 130 W. 42nd St., 17th floor, New York, NY 10036.

legislation. Laws of general application, enacted by a law-making body.

legislative power. The power to make law, generally the power to make policy. In the Constitution, this power is delegated to Congress in Article I. Under the separation-of-powers principle, legislative powers are theoretically exercised only by the legislature. In fact, the president exercises considerable legislative powers, and the Supreme Court's power of judicial review may be considered a legislative power as well.

legitimacy. The belief of a citizenry that a government has the right to rule and that a citizen ought to obey the rules and laws of that government. An illegitimate government must rule either by coercion or by providing material rewards. A legitimate government, on the other hand, should be able to withstand crises, such as economic depressions, when people may feel their needs are not being met and that laws are restrictive. A government can increase its legitimacy by appealing to such symbols as the flag or a constitution. In the United States, elections are probably the most important device for legitimating a government.

Leopold and Loeb. Two men convicted of killing 14-year-old Robert Franks in 1924. Nathan F. Leopold, Jr., was a graduate of the University of Chicago and the son of a multimillionaire shipping magnate; Richard A. Loeb was a University of Michigan graduate and the son of Sears, Roebuck vice president Albert A. Loeb. Leopold and Loeb had structured what they felt would be a "perfect crime"—the kidnapping, ransoming, and killing of a young victim.

lesser included offense. A separate offense, all of the elements of which are alleged, among other elements, in an offense charged in an indictment.

lethal chamber. A room or place, within or adjacent to a prison or jail, where prisoners convicted of capital crimes are put to death.

LETN. *See* Law Enforcement Training Network

LETS. The national Law Enforcement Teletype System, a noncommercial, cooperative interstate system of information exchange between law enforcement agencies, started in the mid-1960s. The system uses common carrier land line circuits.

leuco-malachite test. A preliminary test for the presence of blood. A positive result is not conclusive, but a negative result indicates blood is not the substance being tested.

lewd and lascivious conduct. A statutory term describing criminal sexual behavior codified as depraved and perverse.

lex talionis (Lat., lit.). Law of the claw. (1) Law of retaliation, such as "an eye for an eye and a tooth for a tooth." (2) In modern times, also the acts of one nation in retaliation for the acts of another, which may include amicable retaliatory acts.

Lexow Commission. A committee appointed by the New York State legislature in 1894 to investigate complaints of corruption in the New York City Police Department. The Committee's findings were an important stimulus toward the first major efforts to reform urban police in the United States.

libel and slander. Printed and spoken defamation of character, respectively, of a person or an institution. The laws of libel and slander concern the abuse of free expression guaranteed in the First Amendment. Usually civil offenses, libel and slander may be criminal. In a slander action, it is usually necessary to prove specific damages caused by the spoken words to recover, but in a case of libel, the damage is assumed to have occurred by publication. A slander conviction carries a small fine and a reprimand by the judge, but the more serious libel conviction carries greater penalties. Members of Congress, judges, executive officials of the federal government, and state officials are immune from defamation action in the performance of their duties.

liberals, political. Liberalism is an ideology or philosophy that advocates social reforms designed to increase equality among citizens and greater democratic participation in governance. Liberals generally support the use of governmental power to aid disadvantaged people and groups; take the position that much criminal activity has roots in the social fabric; emphasize alternative sentencing, environmental issues, education, due process, and individual rights; and oppose the death penalty. Liberals are often regarded as proactive, academic, and open-minded.

license. Permission by public authority to perform a certain act, such as driving a car, or to engage in a business or profession; often granted only after the passing of a qualifying examination, the payment of a fee, or both, and revocable if either the terms of the license or the laws or regulations concerning the conduct of the business or profession are violated. Licensing is an administrative device for expediting maintenance of legally stipulated professional or vocational standards or for correction of violations, without the necessity of bringing prosecutions in the courts. The licensee may, however, appeal to the courts to overturn a ruling of the enforcement officers.

lie detector. Often called the polygraph, a device designed for the measurement of many biological responses that are under autonomic control. These biological responses include the EEG (brain waves), heart rate, blood pressure, blood flow, respiration, and skin resistance (galvanic skin response). The courts generally have not allowed lie detector findings to be presented as evidence during a trial, and findings can never be used without the consent of the person tested. Lie detectors are also used by government security agencies and by private personnel departments for such purposes as screening job applicants and investigating leaks of information and thefts of money or goods. Some states allow the use of the device to screen prospective police applicants but prohibit the use of polygraph tests on unwilling police officers undergoing internal affairs investigation(s) that could lead to some form of punishment.

life cycle theory. A concept of leadership holding that the appropriate management style for a particular situation should be primarily dependent upon the maturity level of those being supervised. Maturity is defined as a function of employees' general level of education, experience, motivation, desire to work, and willingness to accept responsibility. Leadership is seen as a combination of two types of behavior: directive and supportive.

Likert Scale. An instrument/technique for measuring feedback concerning employee perceptions of the work organization, especially in the area of job satisfaction (morale). The Likert Scale presents a respondent with a statement calling for a reaction/opinion in one of five or more possible responses. The statement, for example, might be "My supervisor is a good trainer." The responses to choose from might be (1) strongly agree, (2) agree, (3) somewhat agree, (4) not sure, (5) somewhat disagree, (6) disagree, (7) strongly disagree.

limit line. A solid white line not less than 12 nor more than 24 inches wide, extending across a roadway to indicate the point at which traffic is required to stop in compliance with laws.

limitations of actions. The period of time after a crime is committed during which an indictment must be presented.

Lindbergh Law. An act of Congress on May 18, 1934, named for American aviator Charles A. Lindbergh (1902–1974), whose baby son was kidnapped. The law forbids, under penalties of death or imprisonment, the transportation in interstate or foreign commerce of any person who has been kidnapped and held for ransom. Failure to release a person within seven days after he or she has been kidnapped creates the presumption of interstate or foreign transport. *See also* kidnapping

line. In public administration, that portion of the civil service, from highest officials to office employees and field force, that has the responsibility for carrying out the basic functions for which an administrative department is established—distinguished from staff (planning) and housekeeping (auxiliary) functions.

linear design. In penology, a type of jail architecture in which inmate cells are situated along corridors, which requires staff to walk the corridors in order to monitor conditions. This outdated form is also called traditional jail design.

line supervision. Sergeants, in most traditional police departments, are considered first-line supervisors. As such, they serve as links between line and staff employees.

line-up, police. A procedure of placing crime suspects with others, not believed implicated in the crime, in a line or other position so that witnesses can view them for the purpose of making possible identifications. Since 1967, in the case of *U.S. v. Wade*, the Supreme Court has required that an attorney for the accused be present during the line-up.

link network diagrams. Models that provide intelligence analysts with a visual representation of associations between persons and/or organizations. The technique may also be adapted to show associations between telephone numbers, car license plate numbers, and so forth. *See also* Program Evaluation and Review Technique

liquor laws. The Uniform Crime Reports category used to report offenses relating to the manufacture, sale, distribution, transportation, possession, and use of alcoholic beverages, except public drunkenness and driving under the influence.

litigation. A judicial controversy; a contest in a court of justice for the purpose of enforcing a right; any controversy that must be decided upon evidence.

Little Rock riots. Disorders attending efforts to desegregate the Little Rock, AR, schools under a court order that, in September, 1957, led President Dwight Eisenhower to send troops to the city to compel a reluctant Governor Orval Faubus and citizenry to permit black children to attend public schools previously reserved for whites.

livestock, theft. An offense defined as follows: "Whoever obtains or uses the property of another which has a value of $10,000 or more, in connection with the marketing of livestock in interstate or foreign commerce with intent to deprive the other of a right to the property or a benefit of the property or to appropriate the property to his own use or the use of another, shall be fined not more than $10,000 or imprisoned not more than five years or both."

lividity, postmortem. A condition caused by the draining of the blood in a dead body. The blood flows by gravity to the lower parts of the body and causes a peculiar discoloration—usually bluish-red. The condition appears about three hours after death. Due to pressure on the parts of the body touching the surface on which it rests, those parts do not assume the discoloration. If the body is moved after lividity has developed, the change of position will be indicated by lividity.

Livingston, Edward. America's greatest penologist (1764–1836), considered to have been the first legal genius of modern times. Livingston wrote a system of criminal jurisprudence for the state of Louisiana and subsequently served as Secretary of State and minister to France under President Andrew Jackson.

loan shark. One who loans money at a very high—usually an unlawful—interest rate. *See also* usury

local union. An organization of workers that exists independently of any employer, based on other mutual interests. Through authorized agents, a local negotiates with employers the terms of the employees' work agreement, handles grievances, and helps to influence wages.

Locke, John. An English philosopher (1632–1704), Locke supposed that people came to an agreement, or a social contract, with one another to surrender their individual rights of judging and punishing, not to a king, but to the community as a whole. He also advocated that, should the sovereign government violate any of the laws, the community has the right to withdraw from that authority.

logistics. The area of activity in a police operation pertaining to both supplies, equipment, and facilities and to the maintenance and support of personnel.

Lombroso, Cesare. Italian criminologist (1835–1909) and professor of psychiatry, and later of criminal anthropology, at the University of Turin. Lombroso is considered the father of modern criminology and the original spokesman for the positivist viewpoint. In his book *The Criminal Man*, Lombroso maintained that the criminal type can be identified by a number of different physical characteristics. He believed that the victim should be compensated by the criminal and that society should be protected from degenerate and atavistic criminal types. He also advocated the use of indeterminate sentences, but favored the death penalty as a last resort. Contemporary sociologists have criticized his restricted notion of crime and criminal behavior, claiming that, because he focused primarily on the perpetrators of violent crimes against the person, he failed to develop a meaningful theory that would also explain why intelligent people of "normal" appearance and affluent status happen to engage—sometimes routinely—in property crimes, which often require complex legal, business, or organizational skills.

LSD. *See* lysergic acid diethylamide

lynch. To practice the custom of enforcing certain mores by death or of punishing violations of certain fundamental regional mores without due process of law. The avenging group is composed of at least two persons. Following these customs is commonly referred to as operating under lynch law.

lynching. In American history, two types of lynching were common. In frontier areas, with few courts and jails, vigilantes frequently took the law into their own hands and punished (often by death) those accused of crimes. In the South, especially after the Civil War, mobs lynched blacks in the name of white supremacy. Although the practice dates from the eighteenth century, no statistics were kept before 1882. Since then about 5,000 people, 80 percent of them black, have

been lynched. Ninety percent of these lynchings were in the South, with the remainder in bordering states, and most took place in poor rural areas. Frequently victims suffered torture and mutilation before being hanged, shot, or burned. Members of lynch mobs were almost never punished. The alleged crimes committed by lynching victims were homicide (38%), rape (23%), theft (7%), felonious assault (6%), and "insults to whites" (2%). About one-quarter were for miscellaneous offenses, such as a black person's bringing suit or testifying against a white in court, using "offensive" language, boasting, or refusing to pay a debt. Since 1940 lynching has virtually disappeared.

lysergic acid diethylamide (LSD). Derived from lysergic acid, which comes from ergot, a fungus growth on rye. One ounce of LSD is enough to provide 300,000 average doses, each of which is a tiny speck whose effect lasts from 8 to 12 hours. LSD is considered a semisynthetic psychedelic drug.

M

MacDonald, Jeffery Robert. Former Green Beret captain convicted in 1979 of the highly controversial 1970 slaying of his wife and two daughters in their home near the Fort Bragg, NC, army base. He is serving a life sentence in the federal penitentiary at Bastrop, TX. In June 1985, the National Association of Criminal Defense Lawyers filed a brief in Richmond, VA, contending he was wrongfully convicted. Dennis Eisman, a Philadelphia lawyer who served as co-counsel during the army hearings that initially cleared MacDonald, assisted in the preparation of the friend-of-the court brief.

Mace. Trade name for an aerosol irritant projector used to stun an attacker or subdue protesters. *See also* pepper spray

Mack, Julian W. A federal judge for 30 years, Mack (1866–1943) ranks as one of the foremost innovators of juvenile justice. Born in San Francisco, he received his law degree at

Harvard and went into practice in Chicago in 1890. He was elected to a judgeship for the Circuit Court of Cook County, IL, in 1903; between 1904 and 1907, he presided over Chicago's Juvenile Court, the first in the world. This court had been established by the Illinois legislature in 1899. Under Mack, the court dealt with neglected and abused children, runaways, school dropouts, and juveniles who had committed crimes. Mack supported the founding of the National Probation Officers Association. In 1907 he was promoted to the Illinois Appeals Court, and in 1911 he was appointed by President William H. Taft to a seat on the U.S. Court of Appeals for the Seventh Circuit, from which he retired in 1941.

MADD (Mothers Against Drunk Driving). A nationally known organization to combat drunk driving; founded in May, 1980, by Candy Lightner following the death of her teenage daughter Cari. The motorist who killed Cari, Clarence Busch, pleaded innocent to his sixth drunk-driving charge in Sacramento Municipal Court in May, 1985, after spending 16 months in state prison. MADD is a citizens awareness group of approximately 600,000 members, which supports legislation for harsher sanctions against drunk drivers. MADD has grown to a $40 million-a-year corporation with 397 local chapters run by a 16-member board. Located at 669 Airport Way, Hurst, Texas 76053. Similar programs include: SADD (Students Against Drunk Drivers), which was founded in 1983 in Marlboro, MA, by Robert Anastas, a teacher from Wayland High School in Wayland, MA, after two of his students were killed in a car crash (for the free SADD kit, send a long, stamped, self-addressed envelope to SADD, P.O. Box 800, Marlboro, MA 01752); RID (Remove Intoxicated Drivers); VODD (Virginians Opposing Drunk Drivers); DDADD (Drunk Drivers Against Drunk Driving).

Mafia. The largest syndicate of organized crime is the Mafia (*Morte Alla Francia Italia Anela*—Death to France Is Italy's Cry—an acronym devised when the secret society was first organized in the 1860s to combat French

MADD

Mothers Against Drunk Driving

Let's change the meaning of "tie one on . . ." Tie this red ribbon to the left door handle, outside rear view mirror, or antenna of your car as a sign that you join Mothers Against Drunk Driving in our wish for a happy and safe holiday season.

CHOOSE TO MAKE A DIFFERENCE

forces). The organization is also refered to as La Cosa Nostra (our thing). It is a group of organized and generally violent criminals, supposed to have originated in Sicily as an unofficial police system on large estates to protect the owners during the period of disorganization following the Napoleonic invasion, and to have become a distinctly criminal organization when it turned against the owners and became an independent secret group. Its behavior includes tests for admission and an oath not to refer any controversy to legal authorities. The group is said to have started in the United States in New Orleans in 1869 and has now infiltrated the executive, judiciary, and legislative branches of the U.S. government. The single largest Mafia killing was Sept. 11–13, 1931, when Salvatore Maranzano II and 40 allies were liquidated. The greatest breaches of members' vow of silence were by Joseph Valachi in 1963 and by Tommaso Buschetta in 1984.

On February 26, 1985, nine racketeering indictments were returned on 15 counts on the so-called Boss of Bosses, Paul "Big Paul" Castellano of the Gambino family; Anthony "Fat Tony" Salerno of the Genovese family; Anthony "Tony Ducks" Corallo of the Lucchese family; Philip "Rusty" Rastelli of the Bonanno family; Gennaro "Gerry Lang" Langella of the Colombo family; plus four of their top lieutenants. Police said that the charges—extortion, a pattern of racketeering, and conspiracies to commit more than six murders, including the 1979 slaying of Mafia underboss Carmine Galante at a restaurant table—were designed to keep the crime lords in court, if not in prison, for many years to come. Officials did not expect their arrests of the bosses to end Mafia-type crime. Drugs, loan sharking, extortion, gambling, and prostitution are too lucrative to die, and all told there are 3,000 to 5,000 individuals in 25 "families" federated under "The Commission" and an estimated 17,000 confederates.

The federal government, in an attempt to combat organized crime, has placed nearly every major financial institution under scrutiny. During 1984, the Pan American International Bank in Las Vegas pleaded guilty to conspiracy not to file required currency reports on transactions totaling more than $100,000. Six men were indicted in December 1984 for allegedly buying and using the Sunshine State Bank of Miami to launder the profits from a marijuana-smuggling ring. The Global Union Bank of New York City was fined $63,750 and the Rockland Trust

Company of Rockland, MA, was fined $50,000—both for not reporting large cash deposits. The Bank of Boston admitted not reporting $1.2 billion in international cash transactions, most with Swiss banks, over a four-year period ending September 1984. It was fined the maximum, $500,000. The government, from 1976 to 1985, fined 24 banks nearly 1.8 million for failing to report large cash transactions.

magistrate. (1) A public official. (2) A local official exercising jurisdiction of a summary judicial nature over offenses against municipal ordinances or minor criminal cases.

magistrature assise (Fr.). The title of the judge in a French court.

magistrature debout (Fr.). The title of the prosecutor in a French court.

Magna Carta (Lat., lit, great charter). An important thirteenth-century English document that granted rights and privileges to some citizens. It influenced the first 10 amendments to the U.S. Constitution, the Bill of Rights. The Magna Carta originally granted freedoms to barons and the church. It did, however, extend several rights to the common man. Pressured by his rebellious barons, King John issued the charter at Runnymede on June 15, 1215. It has, by liberal interpretations through the centuries, come to be thought of as the basis for constitutional government and as an impartial judicial system in English-speaking countries.

magnetic ink character recognition. A computer technology developed by the American Bankers' Association (ABA) as a machine language that facilitates the processing of checks, drafts, and similar documents required to be processed through the Federal Reserve System. Special numeric MICR groupings, called "fields," are printed in magnetic ink on the check or other instruments. The numbers identify the Federal Reserve routing code, ABA transit number, account number, and the amount.

mail fraud. According to the U.S. Code, a person is not allowed to place in a post office or other authorized depository any scheme or artifice to defraud or obtain money or property by means of false pretenses. There are many types of mail-fraud schemes, including chain letters, pyramid schemes, investment swindles, land sale frauds, work-at-home schemes, medical quackery, fake contests, and charity rackets. Consumers who suspect they have been victims should contact the nearest postmaster or postal inspector or write to: Consumer Advocate, Customer Services Department, Postal Service, 475 L'Enfant Plaza West, SW, Room 5801, Washington, DC 20260.

maim. To willfully inflict upon another an injury that disfigures by mutilation, destroys any limb or organ, or seriously diminishes physical vigor.

maintenance. Offense in which a person unlawfully interferes with a lawsuit in which he or she has no interest, by helping the prosecution or defense, with money, for example.

majority. (1) The greater number; more than half. (2) The condition of being of full or adult age.

maladministration. Corruption in public affairs.

mala in se (Lat., lit. bad in itself). Crimes have been divided, according to their nature, into crimes *mala in se* and crimes *mala prohibita*. The former comprise those acts that are immoral or wrong in themselves, such as murder, rape, arson, burglary, larceny, breach of the peace, forgery, and the like. *See also mala prohibita*

mala fides (Lat.). Bad faith, as opposed to bona fides, or good faith.

mala prohibita (Lat.). Term for crimes that are made illegal by legislation, as opposed to acts that are crimes because they are considered evil in and of themselves, or *mala in se*.

Malcolm X. A leader of the black-consciousness movement. He was born Malcolm Little in Omaha, NE, in 1925, and later lived in MI, MA, and NY. While serving a prison term in 1946, he joined the Black Muslims and took the name Malcolm X. After he was paroled, he had great success in expanding the number of temples and lecturing to many audiences. Conflicts developed, however, between Malcolm X and Elijah Muhammand, leader of the Black Muslims. In 1964 Malcolm X broke away to form his own black nationalist movement, the Organization of Afro-American Unity. In the same year he made a pilgrimage to Mecca. He was assassinated by black gunmen as he was about to make a speech to followers in the Audubon Ballroom in New York City on February 21, 1965.

malfeasance. Commitment of an act forbidden by the moral code or by contract; committing an act that one has no right to do and against which a court action may be instituted. Malfeasance has come to be commonly used in referring to the misconduct of public officials. *See also* misfeasance

malice. Intent to commit a wrong or hurtful act with no reason or legal justification.

malice aforethought. Prior determination, and often planning, to commit a criminal act.

malice, express. Actual, overt, or specific malice.

malice, general. Wickedness; tendency toward wrongdoing.

malice, implied. Malice suggested by the actions of the subject.

malice, legal. Intention or purposefulness to commit a crime, in law.

malicious act. An unlawful act done through malice.

malicious arrest. An arrest made without probable cause.

malicious mischief. A crime consisting of willful damage to, or destruction of, personal property of another and motivated by ill will or resentment toward its owner or possessor.

malicious prosecution. A judicial proceeding instigated by the prosecutor without probable cause to sustain it.

malign. Slander.

malpractice. The mistreatment of disease or injury through ignorance, carelessness, or criminal intent. *See also* fraud offenses

maltreatment. Improper or unskilled treatment or abuse, given willfully or arising from ignorance, neglect, or willfulness.

manacles. Restraining devices such as handcuffs or leg irons.

management functions. The following tasks are usually seen as functions of management: planning, organizing, staffing, directing, coordinating, reporting, and budgeting. A common acronym for these functions is POSDCORB.

managerial style grid. An organizational development or personnel measurement tool that evaluates a manager in terms of how he or she balances the needs of production with employee needs. The grid has 81 blocks: 9 blocks on the horizontal axis represent concern for production, and 9 blocks on the vertical axis represent concern for people. According to the grid, a manager who favors productivity over people is said to "9–1" his or her decisions.

mandate. An order or command; a directive of a superior court, or its judge, to a lower one.

mandate law. A law that imposes a duty upon some public official, agency, or local government body and requires that it be executed without exercise of discretion and in accordance with the express terms of the law.

mandatory sentences. A statutory requirement that a certain penalty shall be set and carried out in all cases upon conviction for a specified offense or series of offenses. Since the mid-1970s, nearly all states have passed some form of mandatory sentencing legislation. In New York, the prison population explosion is laid in part to the 1978 law requiring judges to imprison all those who commit violent felonies. *See also* crime of violence, mandatory penalty

mandatory supervised release. A conditional release from prison required by statute when an inmate has been confined for a period equal to his or her full sentence minus statutory good time, if any.

Manhattan Bail Project. A 1961 experimental release-on-recognizance (ROR) project funded by the Vera Foundation. Its results show that from October 16, 1961, through April 8, 1964, out of 13,000 total defendants, 10,000 were interviewed for the program, 4,000 were recommended, 2,195 were paroled, and 3,000 were not eligible, based on their offenses. Only 15 defendants failed to show up in court, a default rate of less than $7/10$ of 1 percent. This project became the model for nationwide programs, such as the Philadelphia Common Pleas and Municipal Court ROR Program and the San Francisco ROR Program, whose results from August 1, 1964, to July 31, 1968, revealed that 6,377 persons were released on their promise to appear. Ninety percent returned for trial and only one percent evaded justice altogether. *See also* citation to appear

Mann Act. A law passed in 1910 through the efforts of James Robert Mann. Also known as the White Slave Traffic Act, it was passed after various lurid revelations of the growth of prostitution in the United States and in response to fears about the importing of European women for U.S. brothels. Nations had begun to cooperate against prostitution after an international congress on the problem was held in London in 1899. The act, upheld by the Supreme Court in 1913, forbade the transportation of women across state lines for immoral purposes and was so worded because of the federal government's authority over interstate commerce under the commerce clause of the Constitution. The prohibition of prostitution within the states is an exercise of the states' police powers, reserved to them in the Tenth Amendment of the Constitution. At the state level, every government except NV and AZ has outlawed houses of prostitution.

manslaughter. Homicide resulting from culpable recklessness or negligence.

Manson, Charles. On August 8, 1969, five people entered the Beverly Hills home of

Polish film director Roman Polanski and shot or stabbed to death five guests, including Polanski's actress wife, Sharon Tate. The next night, the same killers entered the home of grocery-chain owner Leo LaBianca and murdered him and his wife. Manson did not participate in the killings, but he was charged with ordering his followers, the "Manson family" to commit them. In 1971 Manson and four others were found guilty of the murders and sentenced to death. The sentences were later reduced to life imprisonment.

Mapp, Dollree. The defendant in the landmark 1961 Supreme Court decision *Mapp v. Ohio*, which extended the exclusionary rule to the states. Mapp's conviction for illegal possession of obscene materials was overturned on the grounds of illegal search and seizure. On November 2, 1970, she was arrested by the New York Police Department on suspicion of dealing in stolen property. The detectives, without a search warrant, found 50,000 envelopes of heroin and stolen property valued at over $100,000 in her home. On April 23, 1971, she was convicted of the felonious possession of dangerous drugs and sentenced to a term of 20 years to life. On December 31, 1980, New York Governor Hugh Carey commuted her sentence, making her eligible for parole the next day.

marijuana; marihuana. Drug from the leaves and flowering top of the hemp plant *Cannabis sativa*. When these parts of the female plant are smoked or ingested, they produce an intoxicating effect in some persons. Many states have reduced the criminal penalties for individual use and possession. The Drug Enforcement Administration announced on February 5, 1982, that 3,192 tons of Colombian marijuana had been seized along with 95 vessels and 495 persons arrested in the 14-month long Operation Tiburon.

Eleven states have reduced possession to a minor offense: AK, CA, CO, ME, MN, MS, NE, NY, NC, OH, and OR. Only in Alaska is cultivation for personal use legal. Campaign Against Marijuana Planting is an enforcement program centered around the Emerald Triangle, an area encompassing Humboldt, Mendocino, and Trinity counties in northern California, where marijuana is grown commercially.

The first legal marijuana cigarette in New York's history was smoked by Bonnie Adlman, a patient at North Shore Hospital in Manhasset. Marijuana use was allowed under a 1981 law to combat the nausea that follows chemotherapy treatment given to cancer patients.

Marine Resources. This Department of Justice office handles litigation relating to mineral and biological resources of the adjacent seas and seabed. It is responsible for cases involving the determination of the coastline and other maritime boundaries of the U.S. and those dealing with the rights of the U.S. in submerged lands, particularly as those rights involve increasingly valuable oil and gas resources. The office also has the responsibility for litigation concerning the conservation and management of the living resources of the adjacent seas and the more than 70 species of fish in the 200-mile fishing zone. Address: Marine Resources Section, Environment and Natural Resources Division, DOJ, 950 Pennsylvania Avenue, NW, Washington, DC 20530-0001.

marriage, consanguineous. Unions between people who are considered too closely related by birth, such as first cousins. By 1993, 30 states prohibited such marriages, with 9 states imposing heavy penalties for violation of the statutes.

marshal. (1) An appointed officer in each judicial district of the United States who executes the processes of the court and has law enforcement authority similar to that of a sheriff. (2) An officer sometimes attached to a magistrate's court.

Marshall, John. Fourth chief justice of the Supreme Court (1755–1835), called the Great Chief Justice by Justice Benjamin Cardozo, a title that is hardly ever questioned. Appointed in the last days of President John Adams's administration in 1801, Marshall battled with a series of presidents, nearly all of whom were vigorously opposed to his Federalist interpretation of the Constitution. Although there are some disagreements, it is generally acknowledged that Marshall strengthened both the Supreme Court and the Constitution. During his 34 years as chief justice, he maintained dominance over those justices appointed by presidents opposed to his policies. Marshall helped structure a distribution of the powers of government that has lasted to the present. He died in office, still battling his adversaries in the other branches of government.

marshal, U.S. An official of the federal judicial system whose functions are the following: make arrests of persons charged with federal criminal violations, transport federal prisoners and ensure their incarceration pending trial, maintain order in the federal courts, carry out orders of the federal courts, and serve processes in the federal judicial district in which appointed. Duties correspond to those of a sheriff of a county in many respects.

martial law. Refers to control of civilian populations by a military commander. Commanders are permitted to exercise this control because there is no power sufficient to stop them or to control the situation during war, insurrection, or violence. Martial law replaces all civilian laws, authorities, and courts. It is an exercise of military power that is totally arbitrary and unfettered: the commander is legislator, judge, and executioner.

Maslow's hierarchy of needs. American sociologist Abraham Maslow separated human needs into higher and lower levels. Physiological (hunger, thirst, shelter, sex, and other bodily needs) and safety (security and protection from physical and emotional harm) were described as lower-order needs, and belongingness (affection, belonging, acceptance, and friendship), esteem (self-respect, autonomy, achievement, status recognition), and self-actualization (the drive to fulfill one's potential and self-fulfillment) as higher-order needs. As each need is satisfied, the next level becomes dominant. *See also* Herzberg's motivation-maintenance theory; motivation

mass murder. *See* murder, mass

massacre. The wanton killing of a large number, especially of unresisting human beings or animals. *See* Columbine; Rosewood Massacre

masters/special masters. Court-appointed overseers to ensure that the provisions of decree orders are followed. Masters are usually found in prisons.

material evidence. *See* evidence, material

material fact. A fact necessary to the support of a case or defense.

material witness. One who possesses information of value in the trial of a criminal case. Appropriate magistrates may force such witnesses to post bond to ensure their appearance in court. In lieu of bond being posted, witnesses may be detained. The defense also has rights to ensure the testimony of material witnesses if circumstances suggest they may be unavailable at the time of the hearing or trial.

mathematical theory. Attempts to translate verbal statements of social relationships into mathematical terms in order to introduce greater precision and scientific rigor into sociology and/or criminology.

matic. An alarm system that employs a holdup alarm device, such as a money clip in a cash drawer, in which the signal transmission is initiated solely by the action of the intruder.

matricide. The killing or murder of a mother.

Mattachine Society. Organization founded in the late 1940s by Henry Hay to defend the rights of homosexuals.

maximum sentence. (1) In legal usage, the maximum penalty provided by law for a given offense, usually stated as a maximum term of imprisonment or a maximum fine. (2) In correctional usage, any of several periods (expressed in days, months, or years) that may vary according to whether they were calculated at the point of sentencing or at a later point in the correctional process and according to whether the period referred to is the term of confinement or the total time under correctional jurisdiction.

mayhem. Intentional infliction of injury on another that causes the removal of, disfigures, renders useless, or impairs the function of any limb or organ of the body. In Uniform Crime Reports mayhem is classified as aggravated assault.

McAdoo, William. Lawyer and public official (1853–1930) born in Ireland. Practiced law in New Jersey; member, U.S. House of Representatives (1883–91); appointed by President Grover Cleveland as assistant secretary of the navy; practiced law in New York City; police commissioner (1905–06); chief magistrate (1910–30); largely responsible for a complete reorganization and reform in the municipal court system.

McCarthyism. A tendency to brand all except extreme right-wing ideas as communistic, of indiscriminately leveling false charges of treason, of making new charges instead of furnishing facts, and of attacking the motives of those who question the authenticity of statements. The term arose from the specious charges of Senator Joseph R. McCarthy of Wisconsin, who undermined public confidence in many public officials and private persons until finally censured by the Senate on December 2, 1954.

McDonald's massacre. *See* Huberty, James

McDuffle, Arthur. At 1:59 A.M. on December 17, 1979, in Miami, FL, a lone black male was said to have crashed his motorcycle while evading police at speeds up to 100 miles per hour. He died four days later of head injuries. The victim had been Arthur McDuffle, a 33-year-old insurance salesman and ex-marine. A reconstruction of the case suggested that McDuffle may indeed have tried to elude the police. When he finally slowed down, however, the police pulled him from his vehicle; one officer held him while the others "taught him a lesson." Indicted for manslaughter in the case were four white Miami patrolmen. On May 17, 1980, the officers were acquitted by an all-white

jury, causing the worst outbreak of racial violence the country had seen since 1967. After three days, 15 persons were dead, and the city and its suburbs had suffered a financial toll of some $200 million. *See also* civil disturbances

McGregor, Douglas. *See* Theory X and Theory Y

McGruff. In October 1979 the National Crime Prevention Council began a national media campaign to educate the public about its responsibility for preventing crime. McGruff, a cartoon dog, was adopted as the campaign symbol for crime prevention, urging the public to "take a bite out of crime." McGruff signs were placed in the windows of homes offering sanctuary to children in jeopardy.

McLeod case. An international incident resulting from an arrest of Alexander McLeod, a Canadian deputy sheriff, in New York in 1840 on charges of murder and arson at the time of the destruction of the ship *Caroline*. State authorities refused to release him on demand of the British government, supported by U.S. authorities. He was tried and acquitted. To address such contingencies, Congress empowered federal courts to issue writs of *habeas corpus* for aliens held by state courts.

McNaghten (M'Naghten) rule. A legal decision of 1843 that established the first clear precedent for acquittal based on the defense of insanity. Daniel M'Naghten killed the secretary to England's Sir Robert Peel, but claimed at his trial that at the time he committed the act, he had not been of sound state of mind. From this came the M'Naghten rule, the right-from-wrong test of criminal responsibility: "If the accused was possessed of sufficient understanding when he committed the criminal act to know what he was doing and to know that it was wrong, he is responsible therefore, but if he did not know the nature and quality of the act or did know what he was doing but did not know that it was wrong, he is not responsible." In 1954 the U.S. Court of Appeals for the District of Columbia broadened the M'Naghten test in favor of the Durham rule. *See also* Durham rule

measurement. A set of rules by which numbers are assigned to the different outcomes a group of variables can exhibit. A particular measurement scale is a statement of the rules of correspondence between outcome of the phenomenon under study and the actual numbers of the measuring instrument.

Four basic types of measurement scales are commonly used in criminological research: nominal, ordinal, interval, and ratio. The first two are often classified as discrete measures and the second two as continuous measures. Nominal scales exist when one can say only whether or not the outcomes of a group of variables can be placed in the same measurement class. An ordinal scale exists when, in addition to being able to establish equality among observations, one can say whether or not a particular outcome is greater than, less than, or equal to another outcome. Interval scales, in addition to being able to order variable outcomes from low to high, can indicate by exactly how many units an outcome is greater or lesser than others, although the zero point for such comparisons is an arbitrary one. Ratio scales not only have equal intervals between values, as do interval scales, but they also have true rather than arbitrary zero points. *See also* Likert scale; statistics

mechanic's lien. A legal recourse for a contractor to obtain money owed by attaching the debtor's property or equipment.

mediation. Nonbinding third-party intervention in the collective bargaining process, particularly during a strike considered a public emergency. Unlike an arbitrator, who renders a decision after hearing the positions of labor and management, a mediator endeavors mainly to keep the bargaining from breaking down and to seek paths to an agreement. By clarifying the issues, defining and containing areas of disagreement, offering suggestions, and serving as an intermediary, a mediator can contribute substantially to a settlement.

medical examiner. A qualified physician appointed to examine or perform autopsies on the bodies of persons who are supposed to have met violent deaths and to investigate the causes and circumstances of death. In some states this position has supplanted that of the coroner.

medical jurisprudence. The science consisting of the application of medical and surgical knowledge and skill to the principles and administration of the law. It comprises all medical subjects that have a legal aspect.

medical model. A perspective of certain offenders as sick and in need of treatment; based on the analogy of criminal behavior and disease. The medical model supports rehabilitation as the goal of penalties, and believes criminal behavior can be cured. Beginning in the 1930s, this model was increasingly overshadowed by the justice model, which was adopted in 1974. *See also* justice model

medicide. A legal term used to denote the medical termination of life. The Supreme Court ruled in 1990 that Nancy Cruzan's parents could be permitted to remove the feeding tube keeping their comatose daughter alive, without risking homicide charges. *See also* euthanasia; Kevorkian, Dr. Jack; mercy killing

Megan's Law. A control strategy named after 7-year-old Megan Kanka of Hamilton Township, NJ, who was murdered in 1994. A convicted sex offender who lived across the street from the Kanka family was accused of the crime. In response to her parents' outrage that no one had warned them about their neighbor's past, New Jersey passed a law mandating notification to a community when a convicted sex offender moves in, with different levels of notification required for different levels of offense. On July 1, 1996, a NJ federal district judge upheld the central aspects of Megan's Law. A 1994 federal law included provisions allowing for, but not requiring, similar notifications when a known sex offender is released from prison. Forty-seven states have laws requiring registration of convicted child molesters; 30 have programs to warn communities when offenders move in, and 15 states require community notification. In 1997, California had about 63,000 registered sex offenders; 1 of every 190 adult males in the state is a convicted and registered sex offender.

memorandum of understanding. An official document created in collective bargaining, usually agreed upon by parties involved, clearly delineating the role, tasks, and responsibilities of management and of labor. MOUs are the guiding force in personnel matters and are often bargained or mediated.

Menendez, Lyle and Erik. Brothers who acknowledged having murdered their wealthy parents at the family home in California. Their first trials, in 1994 before two different juries, both resulted in deadlocks. Their second trial, before the same jury in 1995, led to a unanimous verdict of guilt. When juries are hung, as they initially were in this case, the defendants can be tried a second time for the same crime.

mens rea (Lat.). One of the two elements of every crime, which are the criminal act or omission and the mental element or criminal intent, the mens rea. The latter is the state of mind that accompanies the particular act defined as criminal. Hence, the mens rea of each crime will be different. For instance, in the crime of receiving stolen goods, it means knowledge that the goods were stolen; in the case of murder, malice aforethought; in the case of theft, an intention to steal.

mental deficiency. Feeblemindedness; amentia; mental subnormality; mental defectiveness. A state of mental retardation or incomplete development, existing from birth or early infancy, by reason of which one is unable to meet the social expectations of society. Those with mild mental deficiencies can be self-supporting, given guidance, care, and direction. The mentally deficient as a whole are conventionally differentiated into three grades: (a) the mildly retarded, who have an intelligence quotient (IQ) of from 50 to 69 or a mental age (MA) of from 84 to 143 months and who are capable of guided self-support; this category is frequently difficult to distinguish from the population at large; (b) the moderately retarded, who have an IQ

of 25 to 49 or an MA ranging from 36 to 83 months and who are capable of protecting themselves from elemental dangers but not of playing a conventionally mature role in society; and (c) the severely retarded, who have an IQ of less than 25 or an MA of not more than 35 months and whose disabilities demand continual care and attention.

mental element in crime. Criminal intent. Every common law crime consists of two elements, the criminal act, or omission, and the mental element, commonly called criminal intent.

mercy killing. An ethically controversial action involving the removal of a terminally ill patient from life-support systems. The motive in such a case is not generally considered a sufficient defense in a homicide charge. *See also* dyathanasia; euthanasia; Kevorkian, Dr. Jack

mere evidence. Evidence that will aid in the proof of the commission of a crime but that does not fall into the evidentiary categories of contraband or profits of the crime.

merger of offenses. A legal procedure occurring when the same criminal act constitutes both felony and misdemeanor or where one crime culminates in another.

merit system. The method of appointing members of the civil service by open competitive examination. Although temporarily instituted by President Ulysses Grant in 1876, the permanent merit system was not established until the passage of the Pendleton Act in 1883. In 1789, at the beginning of the nation's history, the entire civil service was politically appointed. After passage of the Pendleton Act, 13 percent of civil service workers were appointed on a merit basis; by 1932 the figure had risen to 80 percent. President Harry Truman declared that 93 percent of the federal service at the time of his term in office was on a merit basis. Individual merit systems have been put into effect by some independent bodies, including the Federal Bureau of Investigation and the Tennessee Valley Authority. A merit examination may be written, or, as in recent developments, it may take the form of a performance, oral, or interview examination. The merit system has spread widely to state and municipal governments, and has been adopted in part by private industry.

Merton, Robert K. American sociologist (1910–) who applied the concept and theory of anomie to crime and deviance. He used the term *anomie* to describe the condition of normlessness that occurs when the means of achieving success available to people are not enough for them to achieve what society has deemed success. Individuals who perceive that they cannot succeed conventionally will resort to illegitimate or illegal ways of doing so, Merton believed, and he termed such behavior innovation. *See also* anomie

mesne process. As distinguished from final process, this term is used for any writ issued between the beginning of a case and its conclusion. Mesne, in this context, may be defined as intermediate; intervening; the middle between two extremes.

Mesopotamian laws and codes. The earliest signs of well-developed written law codes emerged from early cultures in Mesopotamia, the land bordered by the Tigris and Euphrates rivers. Although early Sumerian codes no doubt existed as far back as B.C. 3000, the Babylonian Code of Hammurabi—discovered by the French in 1902—is the most famous of the Mesopotamian codes to survive in its entirety. Certain of its legal phrases indicate that the Code of Hammurabi (circa B.C. 1760) was based on prior codes.

methadone (Dolophine). A synthetically produced opiate narcotic.

methadone maintenance. A means of treating addiction to heroin, begun experimentally in 1964 at Rockefeller University Hospital in New York. The addict is given methadone, a synthetic opiate, in an amount (usually 100 milligrams per day) sufficient to satisfy his or her craving for heroin. Once stabilized under hospital observation, the addict can be treated on an outpatient basis, re-turning to the clinic or hospital each day for methadone.

methamphetamine. *See* amphetamine

methaqualone. A synthetic, white, crystal powder processed into tablets or capsules, this addictive central nervous system depressant has been associated with the trade product Quaalude, which is no longer manufactured. Abusers of this drug get high by fighting sleep to experience impaired coordination, lowered inhibitions, and greater sociability. Methaqualone is classified as a sedative-hypnotic and is sometimes prescribed by physicians to relieve anxiety or as a sleep aid.

methodology. The logic of scientific procedure; a system of principles, rules, and techniques of regulating a scientific discipline or inquiry. In criminology, methodology is the logical and theoretical basis for the acceptance of research results by the academic community.

methylphenidate (Ritalin). A central nervous system stimulant chemically and pharmacologically related to amphetamines. Often prescribed for victims of narcolepsy, or the tendency to fall suddenly and deeply asleep at inappropriate times.

Metropolitan Statistical Areas (MSAs). A Census Bureau method of measuring population, formerly called standard metropolitan statistical areas (SMSAs). On June 30, 1988, there were 266 MSAs; 21 consolidated metropolitan statistical areas (CMSAs) comprising 73 primary metropolitan statistical areas (PMSAs). MSAs provide the population aggregates of metropolitan centers to show density, growth and decline, population shifts, and other demographic data, including such variables as age, economics (poverty levels), mobility, occupations, sex, ethnic distributions, transportation, and household data.

The chief reason the Constitution provided for a census of the population every 10 years was to give a basis for apportionment of representatives among the states. This apportionment largely determines the number of electoral votes allotted to each state. The number of representatives of each state in Congress is determined by the state's population, but each state is entitled to one representative regardless of population. A congressional apportionment has been made after each decennial census except that of 1920. *See also* census tract

Mexican American Legal Defense and Education Fund (MALDEF). Founded in 1968 by Pedro "Pete" Tijerina of San Antonio, Texas. MALDEF was created by a $2.2 million Ford Foundation grant. It is based in Los Angeles with offices in San Antonio, Atlanta, Chicago, Houston, Sacramento and Washington. Its services include advocacy, community education and outreach, leadership development, and higher education scholarships.

Miami riots. *See* civil disturbances; McDuffle, Arthur

microchemistry. The field of chemistry involving testing and analysis of minute quantities of substances.

microscope, comparison. A microscope that has two objectives or lens systems converging into a single field of vision. Two separate objects can be seen simultaneously and thus compared. Used in crime laboratories to determine if the markings on two bullets match, which would prove they were fired with the same weapon.

microscopy. Investigation with the use of a microscope.

Midwest Research Institute (MRI). Founded in 1944, MRI has performed contract research for criminal justice agencies since 1968. Its Justice Group was formed to provide assistance in the areas of management and operations. Address: 425 Volker Blvd., Kansas City, MO 64110.

milieu management. A technique of treating deviant behavior that involves the group therapy approach. Therapeutic communities are developed in which inmates and free employees with law-abiding ideals live together and share management responsibilities. Inmates and employees jointly develop the therapeutic program to be used by the community.

military law. Any system of rules and regulations governing military forces. Both the president—by virtue of authority as commander in chief—and Congress may make military law. It also includes certain customary usages that might be called military common law. Military justice is administered by court-martial with no concern for the judicial power or civil law of the U.S. Courts-martial are convened for the duration of a particular case. The regulations governing military justice in the U.S. are set forth in the Uniform Code of Military Justice (1951).

military police. The police force of an army, charged with maintaining law, order, and security. The U.S. Air Force's law enforcement, correctional, and security functions are conducted by the Security Police; the U.S. Navy's counterpart is the Shore Patrol, with the Military Police being the enforcement arm of the U.S. Army.

military prisons. Institutions designed to hold members of the armed forces who have been convicted of violations of the Uniform Code of Military Justice. The term also includes stockades, guardhouses, penitentiaries, and rehabilitation centers.

militia. (1) All able-bodied male citizens and resident male aliens between the ages of 18 and 45, whether members of the organized militia (National Guard) or not. The states retain power to appoint officers, train their militias according to the discipline prescribed by Congress, and call them out for defense and the preservation of order in emergencies. The federal government may provide for their organization, arming, and discipline and may call them into the national service in time of war or other emergencies. (2) Colloquially, the National Guard.

Milton S. Eisenhower Federation. Founded in 1981 with the goal to increase economic and psychological self-sufficiency and reduce crime in inner-city neighborhoods. Address:

1660 L St., Suite 200 NW, Washington, DC 20036.

Minnesota Citizens Council on Crime and Justice. A research, advocacy, and public education organization that has played a key role in helping Minnesota become a national model in the field of criminal justice. Address: 822 South Third St., Suite 100, Minneapolis, MN 55415.

Minnesota Multiphasic Personality Inventory-2 (MMPI-2). A psychological test designed to measure all the more important aspects of personality. It consists of 567 statements covering a wide range of subject matter—from the physical condition to the morale and the social attitudes of the individual being tested. The subject must respond with "true," "false," or "cannot say" to each statement. As the inventory was originally developed in a clinical (treatment) setting, 8 of the 14 scaled responses are based on then-current diagnostic nomenclature: hypochondriasis (Hs), depression (D), hysteria (Hy), psychopathic deviate (Pd), paranoia (Pa), psychasthenia (Pt), schizophrenia (Sc), and hypomania (Ma). The ninth scale is the interest or masculinity-femininity (M-F) scale. The remaining, nonclinical, scales on MMPI-2 are the social introversion-extroversion scale (Si) and the 4 validity scales: the lie (L) score (response inconsistencies indicating subjects' attempts to score well), the question (?) scale (validating "cannot say" responses), the (F) score (another response validity check), and the (K) score (a correction factor for the entire test). The 1989 revision of MMPI includes new clinical scales and new items on topics such as drug abuse, Type A behavior, and eating disorders. Several criminal justice agencies use this instrument in employment prescreening.

minor. A person who has not reached the age, usually between 18 and 21 years, at which the law recognizes adulthood, or a general contractual capacity.

minute order. The official record of orders and findings made by a court.

minutes. Memoranda of what takes place in court, made by authority of the court.

Miranda, Ernesto. The accused in the 1966 prisoners' rights *Miranda v. Arizona* case. An eighth-grade dropout with an extensive criminal record, Miranda was retried on kidnapping and rape charges in February 1967, because while the Supreme Court overturned his original conviction, it had not quashed the indictment. During his second trial, Miranda's common-law wife, Twila Hoffman, testified that he had admitted kidnapping and raping the victim. Miranda was convicted and sentenced to a 20-to-30-year-term in state prison and was paroled in 1972. Two years later he was arrested on a gun charge and for possession of drugs, but the cases were dismissed due to Fourth Amendment violations. In 1975 Miranda was returned for a brief period to Arizona State Prison for parole violation but released later that year. In early 1976, at age 34, Ernesto Miranda was slain in a Phoenix skid-row bar during a quarrel over a card game.

Miranda rights. Set of rights that a person accused or suspected of having committed a specific offense has during interrogation and of which he or she must be informed prior to questioning, as stated by the Supreme Court in deciding *Miranda v. Arizona* in 1966 and related cases. The process of informing persons of their Miranda rights is often called admonition or admonishment of rights, and the information is called the Miranda warning. Many jurisdictions now require a statement, signed by the person to be interrogated, that he or she has heard and understood these rights. An individual's decision to waive these rights and to give information, or the signed statement recording such a decision, is often called admonition and waiver.

misanthropic. Describing behavior or attitudes that are mistrustful or hostile to all others.

miscegenation laws. Statutes formerly on the books in several states, designed to prevent interracial marriages. In 1967 the Supreme Court struck down such laws.

Many police officers carry cards like these, bcause failure to inform suspects of their Miranda rights fully and correctly can result in reversals of convictions. However, when public safety is endangered, the Miranda rights procedure can be suspended.

miscellaneous docket. The docket of the Supreme Court on which are listed all cases filed *in forma pauperis*.

misconduct in office. Negligent, improper, dishonorable, or unlawful behavior on the part of an individual holding a position of public trust, which may result in removal from office.

misdemeanor. An offense punishable by incarceration, usually in a local confinement facility, for a period of which the upper limit, typically a year or less, is prescribed by statute in a given jurisdiction. Also known as *delicta*.

misfeasance. Performance of a lawful act in an improper or illegal manner—distinguished from malfeasance, which is the performance of a wrong act, and nonfeasance, the omission or neglect of duty.

misnomer. A misleading description or mis-identification of someone or something. Courts usually have the right to amend indict-therein. If assent or participation is present,

ments by inserting an individual's correct name.

misogynist. Any person who hates females.

misprision. (1) The concealment of a crime, such as a felony, or treason. (2) In criminal law, a term used to signify any significant misdemeanor that doesn't have a specific legal name.

misprision, negative. The concealment of something which ought to be revealed.

misprision, positive. The commission of something that ought not to be done.

misprision of felony. The offense of concealing a felony committed by another, but without such previous interaction with or subsequent assistance to the felon as would make the concealing party an accessory before or after the fact.

misprision of treason. The knowledge and concealment of an act of treason or treasonable plot, without any assent or participation the party becomes a principal.

misrepresentation. Stating something as a fact while knowing it is untrue; making any deceiving or misleading statement.

missing children. In federal law, any individual less than 18 years of age whose whereabouts are unknown to legal custodians, if (a) the circumstances indicate that the individual may have been removed by another from the control of the legal custodian without consent or (b) the circumstances strongly indicate that the individual is being abused or sexually exploited.

Missing Children Acts. A 1982 federal law requires the U.S. Department of Justice to maintain a central file of missing children that is available to federal, state, and local law enforcement agencies. This act, and the Juvenile Justice and Delinquency Prevention Act of 1974, were amended under the Comprehensive Crime Control Act, leading to the Juvenile Justice, Runaway Youth, and Missing Children's Act Amendments of 1984. The act also established the Office of Juvenile Justice and Delinquency Prevention.

missing children programs. Dairies and supermarkets have placed pictures of missing children on milk cartons and grocery bags. In addition, public utility companies and banks are including pictures of missing children in their monthly statements. The National Center for Missing and Exploited Children can be reached by calling (800) 843-5678. *See also* juvenile locators

missing persons. Policies governing the acceptance of reports of and search for missing persons vary. Generally, immediate attention is given if the missing person is below the age of 11 or elderly, mentally disturbed, or handicapped; or if he or she might be suicidal or the victim of an accident or crime.

Reports of these types of missing persons are usually accepted by telephone, with a formal report generated later. In other cases, generally a 24-hour period of absence must occur prior to investigation or completion of a formal report. The FBI will not look for a missing person but will notify an inquirer of any information received. For further information, contact ID Division, FBI, DOJ, 9th St. and Pennsylvania Ave., NW, Room 11255, Washington, DC 20535.

Missing Person Locator. A service available to the public in 90 countries, provided by the Salvation Army, which offers the following suggestions to inquirers: (1) limit searches to close relatives, rather than old classmates, sweethearts, friends, neighbors, debtors, or runaway adult offspring; (2) you must be able to provide essential information about the missing person; (3) a $10 nonrefundable donation is requested; (4) you may secure information and/or a missing person inquiry form by contacting the nearest Salvation Army office or territorial headquarters. The Salvation Army reserves the right to accept or reject any request for services, based on reasonableness, feasibility, or amount of notice.

mission statement. An increasingly popular means of establishing with and for all employees of a company, agency, or department agreement on the basic and broad purposes of the organization as a whole. Goals and values may also be included in the policy statement or appended as substatements.

Missouri Plan. A plan used in the state of Missouri for the selection of judges. A commission, composed of a judicial officer serving ex officio, lawyers selected by lawyers, and laymen selected by the governor, nominates three candidates for the position. The governor appoints one. At the end of the year, this judge goes before the people at a general election. If receiving a majority vote, the judge serves the remainder of the term, at which time he or she may become a candidate for reelection by certifying the wish to have his or her name placed on the ballot. The judge is not allowed to contribute financially to, nor to participate in, any political campaign.

mistake of fact. Any erroneous conviction of fact or circumstance resulting in some act that would not otherwise have been undertaken. Mistake of fact becomes a defense when an individual commits a prohibited act in good faith and with a reasonable, though false, belief that certain facts are correct. The mistake must be honest and not the result of negligence or poor deliberation.

mistake of law. Any want of knowledge or acquaintance with the laws of the land insofar as they apply to the act, relation, duty, or matter under consideration. Ignorance of the law is no excuse; simple ignorance of forbidden behavior is not usually an acceptable defense. In contrast, however, the Supreme Court ruled in *Lambert v. California* (1957) that ignorance of the law may be a defense, if the law has not been made reasonably well known.

mistrial. A trial that has been terminated and declared invalid by the court because of some circumstance that creates a substantial and uncorrectable prejudice to the conduct of a fair trial or that makes it impossible to continue the trial in accordance with prescribed procedures.

mitigation. Alleviation; abatement; making less rigorous.

mittimus. A court order directing a peace officer to take a person to jail.

mob. A large crowd, particularly one that is violent and disorderly.

mobile command post. A vehicle, containing communications and other operations control equipment, that permits control of an operation to be moved from its normal fixed location to a temporary location.

mobile crime laboratory. A vehicle, usually a van, equipped with investigative instruments, equipment, and supplies. It can be moved to the site of an investigation for immediate analysis of materials and clues found at the scene of an incident.

mode. In statistical research, the most easily obtained measure of central tendency; the score that occurs most frequently in any study.

Model Penal Code. A generalized, modern codification of the principles considered

basic to criminal law, published by the American Law Institute in 1962.

Model Sentencing Act. A document, drawn up by the Advisory Council of Judges of the National Council on Crime and Delinquency (NCCD), outlining a proposed model for sentencing.

modification of probation. A court-ordered change in the terms and conditions of a probation order, making them more, or less, restrictive.

modus operandi. A characteristic pattern of behavior repeated in a series of offenses that coincides with the pattern evidenced by a particular person or group of persons. It is based upon the theory that each professional criminal has a method of committing a crime peculiar to him- or herself. Devised by Major Atcherley of Yorkshire, England, it is used to supplement the fingerprint method. The Atcherley system is a modus operandi file recording offender/suspect peculiarities. Categories may include property, time, location, victim(s), method, and habits.

molding. *See* moulage

Molly Maguires. Terrorist organization of Irish anthracite-coal miners that flourished in east-central Pennsylvania between 1843 and 1876. The Mollies allegedly operated by terrorism—assaulting, even murdering, persons they found offensive. Many of the crimes attributed to the Mollies involved coal-mine supervisory personnel. The group was eventually infiltrated by a Pinkerton detective, who discovered information that led to the arrest of men alleged to be Mollies. Beginning in 1876, 19 of these men were hanged and others imprisoned.

Molotov cocktail. A fire bomb or hand grenade, usually made with a breakable bottle containing a flammable liquid and with a rag wick protruding from the mouth of the bottle. It is used by lighting the wick and throwing the container against an object, causing the bottle to break and thus igniting the fuel.

moot court. A mock court used by criminal justice students to argue hypothetical cases.

moot question. A case that, because circumstances or conditions changed after the litigation was begun, is no longer liable for trial or subject to court jurisdiction.

moral. According to the standards of a society, ethical, good, honest, upright, and virtuous.

moral development. The study of moral development has concentrated on how individuals come to adopt the standards of right and wrong that are laid down by their cultures and how they resist the temptation to transgress the rules of acceptable conduct. The moral developmental theory stems largely from the work of Swiss child psychologist Jean Piaget (1896–1980).

moral evidence. *See* circumstantial evidence

moral turpitude. The quality of a crime that characterizes it as *malum in se*, that is, as inherently vicious and depraved or as offensive to public morals. Foreign citizens convicted of a crime involving moral turpitude are debarred from entry under U.S. immigration laws.

Moran, Thomas Bartholomew. When Moran died in 1971 at the Miami Rescue Mission, he was a vagrant and a derelict, and his pockets were empty. Moran had been a celebrated criminal whom many considered the dean of American pickpockets. His career began in 1906 when, at 14, he would pass through the crowded streets and stores of downtown Kansas City, opening women's purses and removing small change. Moran ultimately achieved the rank of "class cannon," a designation that typified him as a thief with skill and daring. The world-class pickpocket had even been aboard the *Titanic* when it left on its ill-fated maiden voyage, and he was one of the 705 survivors.

mores. Morals; manners.

morgue. A public depository or building for temporarily holding bodies for identification. The morgue was originally a building in Paris, France, where police inspected new prisoners to memorize their features. This is presumably why many newspapers use the term to indicate their archives of clips and photographs.

morphine. A habit-forming narcotic drug; the major sedative and pain-relieving drug found in opium, being approximately 10 percent of the crude opium exudate.

mortis causa (Lat.). In contemplation of death; by reason of death.

Mosaic code. The law of the Old Testament, particularly as expressed in the Ten Commandments, proscribing such actions as murder, adultery, stealing, and bearing false witness.

motion. An oral or written request made to a court at any time before, during, or after court proceedings, asking the court to make a specified finding, decision, or order.

motivation. The term for desired or actual movement toward an identified goal. Four major theories of human goals, drives, or needs are: (1) Abraham Maslow's hierarchy of needs, described in his *Toward a Psychology of Being*; (2) Clayton Alderfer's theory, central to his work with people in organizations, of three core need groups: existence, relatedness, and growth; (3) achievement, power, and affiliation; (4) Frederick Herzberg's motivation-maintenance theory. *See also* Herzberg's motivation-maintenance theory; Maslow's hierarchy of needs

motive. An impulse or emotion toward action. As distinguished from intent, motive is not an essential element of crime. An evil motive will not make an act a crime, nor will a good motive prevent an act from being a crime. Motive may, however, tend to show that an act was willful and done with criminal intent, or tend to incriminate or prove the guilt of the perpetrator.

motorcyclists, outlaw. A south-central Los Angeles motorcycle club called the Booze Fighters was formed in 1946 at a beer cafe on Firestone Blvd., near Watts. On July 4, 1947, the cyclists invaded Hollister, in central California, and, according to *Life* magazine, took over the town. This incident was recreated in the movie *The Wild One*, starring Marlon Brando. The five main motorcycle groups currently are Hell's Angels, Outlaws, Pagans, Bandidos, and Sons of Silence. The Outlaws, also known as the American Outlaw Association, was founded in Chicago in 1959. The Pagans were established in 1959 in Prince Georges County, MD. The Bandidos, or Bandido Nation, came into being in 1966 in Houston. The Sons of Silence was formed in Commerce City, CO, in 1968. The biker philosophy and basic motto is FTW—Fuck the World. The five main gangs only allow white male membership, although all-black outlaw motorcycle gangs do exist. The annual Sturgis, MT, motorcycle rally began in 1938 with a total of nine riders. The rally was canceled for two years during World War II. The 1990 rally, the 50th, drew about 300,000 riders. In 1991 the rally attracted an estimated attendance of 103 motorcycle gangs and clubs, many of them law-abiding. Gang involvement includes narcotics manufacturing and distribution, prostitution, weapons-related violations, extortion, murder, arson-for-hire, pornography, protection rackets, loan sharking, interstate transportation of stolen property and stolen motor vehicles, insurance fraud, and obstruction of justice.

motor vehicle. A vehicle that is self-propelled. The term does not include a self-propelled wheelchair, tricycle, or motorized quadricycle when operated by a person who, because of physical disability, is otherwise unable to move about as a pedestrian.

motor vehicle research. National research is conducted on vehicles under 10,000 lbs., including cars, pickup trucks, and vans. Studies are made on automotive systems, occupant packaging (seating/restraints for driver and passengers), accident avoidance (tires, braking, towing), structures (fuel tanks, crash performance), technology assessment (advanced technology, diesels, emissions, new materials), economic assessment (cost of new technology, production engineering), experimental vehicles, downsizing, and fuel economy. For further

information, contact: Office of Passenger Vehicle Research, Research and Development, National Highway Traffic Safety Administration, DOT, 400 7th St., SW, Room 6226, Washington, DC 20590.

motor vehicle safety standards. The Office of Crashworthiness provides information and sets standards for air bags, seat belts, child restraint safety seats, motorcycle helmets, fuel system integrity, odometers, windshield defrosters, rearview mirrors, tire selection and rims, door locks, school bus rollover protection, seating systems, new pneumatic tires, and more. A publication covering this topic, *Federal Motor Vehicle Safety Standards and Regulations*, is available from: Superintendent of Documents, U.S. Government Printing Office, North Capitol and H Streets, NW, Washington, DC 20401.

motor vehicle theft. Unlawful taking, or attempted taking, of a self-propelled road vehicle owned by another, with the intent to deprive him or her of it permanently or temporarily.

Motor Vehicle Theft Act. An act of Congress on October 29, 1919, that made it a federal offense to transport across state boundary lines a motor vehicle known to have been stolen.

Motor Vehicle Theft Law Enforcement Act of 1984. This law requires car manufacturers, beginning with 1987 models, to mark 14 major components in "high-theft-risk" cars with a 17-character identification number. Major components include the engine, transmission, front fenders, hood, doors, and front and rear bumpers. In addition, replacement parts must bear the manufacturer's registered trademark, or some other unique marking if there is no trademark, and the letter R. The act is designed to combat the sale of parts of stolen vehicles by making components traceable.

moulage. A synonym for molding and casting in criminal investigation work, but the term in criminal justice usually means certain materials used in molding and casting, sold under trade names. Moulage is cast materials manufactured commercially and consisting of types (a) for making a negative mold and (b) for making the positive cast. This process will record fine detail.

Mounted Services Organization, National. Association for law enforcement personnel assigned to patrol on horseback. Address: Box 358, 643 Main St., Sparkhill, NY 10976.

MOVE. Radical group. *See* SWAT

move. (1) To make a motion, or formally ask for something. (2) To apply to a court for an order or a rule.

movement. In corrections, an admission to or a release from a status—prisoner, parolee, or probationer. A transfer between facilities does not, unless specifically noted, count as a movement for reporting purposes.

muckrakers. The name given to a group of early-twentieth-century writers, including Lincoln Steffens and Upton Sinclair, who exposed public corruption and attacked slums, juvenile delinquency, prostitution, and the social evils that produced them.

mug shot. A photograph showing the head and shoulders, both side and front views, of a criminal.

mulet. (1) To punish by fine. (2) To deprive.

multicide. The killing of many individuals. *See also* murder, mass; murder spree; serial murders

municipal charter. A legislative enactment conferring governmental powers of the state upon its local agencies, generally cities.

municipal corporation. A public corporation established as a subdivision of a state for local governmental purposes.

municipal court. A minor court authorized by municipal charter or state law to enforce local ordinances and exercise the criminal and civil jurisdiction of the peace.

municipal home rule. A plan whereby a greater measure of political autonomy is allowed a city within the terms of a charter granted by the state legislature. In 1952 more than 16 states had embodied home-rule provisions in their constitutions. The home-rule charter is forbidden to contain provisions contrary to the Constitution, statutes, or treaties of the United States or to the constitution or laws of the state. The general clauses of a home-rule charter provide for the incorporation of the city, describe its framework of government, and determine its officers, elections, tenure, and similar details. They also prescribe the city's power over contracts, finances, and other purely municipal functions that remain within its jurisdiction. *See also* home rule

municipality. A local area of government in the United States. At various times it has taken the forms of parish, borough, town, township, village, county, and city governments. In the U.S. constitutional system, a municipality is a nonsovereign entity, its powers depending wholly upon state grant. Municipalities may be incorporated or unincorporated. In the former, a state charter provides a degree of autonomy with respect to purely local functions. In the latter, control is generally exercised by the state legislature, operating through a local government. The governments of municipalities vary but consist generally of a legislature in the form of a council, board of trustees or supervisors, or board of selectmen. If there is an executive, it is usually a mayor, although this office is customarily absent from a county. Other municipal offices include those in the court, police, sheriff's, clerk's, and legal sectors.

municipal law. The law of a state or nation, based on the power of the state; also sometimes called arbitrary law, or the power to command what is right and prohibit what is wrong. It is made by people, founded on convenience, and is dependent upon the authority of the legislative body enacting it. The term also designates the law applicable to municipalities. Municipal law is classified as: (a) criminal law and (b) civil law. Criminal law deals with those offenses against the individual or the community that the state recognizes as wrongs to society.

municipal officer. An officer belonging to a municipality—a city, town, or borough—rather than a county.

municipal ordinance. A law created by a municipal corporation to define the proper conduct of its affairs or its inhabitants.

municipal reform. The attempts to increase popular controls over municipal government for the purpose of weakening or eliminating political machines. Some of the developments in this direction include the use of municipal home rule for larger cities, proportional representation, the short ballot, the county executive plan, and the county-manager and city-manager systems.

murder and nonnegligent manslaughter. Intentionally causing the death of another without legal justification or excuse, and/or causing the death of another while committing, or attempting to commit, another crime. Murder appears as a proscription in both the Old and New Testaments, and its designation as a capital offense appears in an early chapter of Genesis. On June 14, 1985, a landmark decision was handed down by the Illinois Supreme Court, in which three corporate officers were found guilty of murder for the cyanide-poisoning death of a worker in a silver recovery plant they managed and operated in suburban Chicago. They were the first company officers to be charged with, and convicted of, murder for management actions and inactions that contributed to the death of a worker. On March 18, 1997, in Ventura, CA, 92-year-old Alfred Pohlmeier was the oldest defendant ever to be convicted in a second-degree murder case. At his sanity hearing, he was found to be legally insane and was ordered to undergo treatment.

murder, mass. The killing of four or more victims at one location, within one event. Famous examples include: Richard Speck's murder of eight nursing students in Chicago on July 14, 1966 (Speck died, one day short of his 50th birthday, of a heart attack at Silver Cross Hospital near the Stateville, IL, Correctional Center, where he had been held for nearly 24 years); Charles Whitman's sniper killings of 16 people by firing from a tower at the University of Texas on August 1, 1966; James Oliver Huberty's killing of 21 people in San Diego; and George Hennard, Jr., who killed 23 people in Killeen, TX. In 1990, 87 people died in an arson fire at the Happy Land social club in the Bronx, NY. On April 28, 1996, Martin Bryant opened fire with an American-made assault weapon in Port Arthur, Tasmania, the site of a nineteenth-century prison, killing 35. This incident spawned a limited U.S. government buy-back of assault weapons, with more than 510,000 turned in. *See also* cults; Hennard, George; Huberty, James; murder spree; National Center for the Analysis of Violent Crime

murder spree. Defined as killings at two or more locations with little or no intervening time and as the result of a single event. For example, in February 1985 Daniel Remeta and two others robbed and killed the manager of a restaurant in Grainfield, KS. An hour later, Remeta shot a sheriff's deputy who was trying to flag down his car. The killer then fled to a nearby grain elevator, shot the manager, and killed two hostages before he was captured. *See also* Starkweather, Charles

museums, police. The New York City Police Museum features narcotics and police exhibits open to the public weekdays without charge; the reference library is available to law enforcement officers and college students; located at 100 Old Slip, New York, NY. The Royal Canadian Mounted Police Museum is open, without charge, daily from June 1 through November 15; located in Regina, Saskatchewan. *See also* Federal Bureau of Investigation

mutiny. An uprising by sailors or soldiers against their commanders. Because of its need for discipline and obedience to authority, the military's most serious offense is mutiny. It has been defined in American military law to mean action by two or more who, with intent to usurp or override lawful military authority, in concert disobey orders,

MODERN MASS MURDERS			
Year	State	Murderer	Death Toll
1949	New Jersey	Howard Unruh	Shot 13 neighbors
1950	Texas	William cook	Shot 5 family members
1955	Colorado	John Graham	Bomb on a plane, 44 died
1959	Kansas	Richard Hickock	Stabbedshot 4 members of Culter family
1959	Kansas	Perry Smith	Stabbed/shot 4 members of Culter family
1966	Illinois	Richard Speck	Stabbed/strangled 8 student nurses
1966	Texas	Charles Whitman	Shot 16, mostly students
1966	Arizona	Robert Smith	Shot 5 women in a beauty salon
1969	California	Charles Watson	Stabbed 9 persons for Charles Manson
1969	California	Patricia Krenwinkel	Stabbed 9 persons for Charles Manson
1969	California	Linda Kasabian	Stabbed 9 persons for Charles Manson
1969	California	Susan Adkins	Stabbed 9 persons for Charles Manson
1971	New Jersey	John List	Shot 5 family members
1973	Georgia	Carl Isaacs	Shot 5 members of a family
1973	Georgia	billy Isaacs	Shot 5 members of a family
1974	Louisiana	Mark Essex	Shot 9, mostly police officers
1974	Long Island	Ronald DeFeo	Shot 6 family members
1975	Florida	Bill Ziegler	Shot 4 adults in a store
1975	Ohio	James Ruppert	Shot 11 family memebers
1976	California	Edward Allaway	Shot 7 coworkers
1977	New York	Frederick Cowan	Shot 6 coworkers
1978	Guyana	Jim Jones	Poisoned/shot 912 cult members
1982	Pennsylvania	George Banks	Shot 13 family and acquaintances
1983	Loisiana	Michael Perry	Shot 5 family members
1983	Washington	Willie Mak	Shot 13 people in the head
1983	Washington	Benjamin Ng	Shot 13 people in the head
1984	California	James Huberty	Shot 21 at McDonald's
1985	Pennsylvania	Sylvia Seigrist	Shot several at a mall, 2 died
1986	Oklahoma	Patrick Sherrill	Shot 14 coworkers
1986	Arkansas	Ronald Simmons	Shot 16 family members
1987	Florida	Willaim Cruse	Shot 6 persons at a mall
1988	California	Richard Farley	Shot 7 in a computer company
1988	Illinois	Lauri Dann	Shot, poisoned many, 1 death
1988	California	James Purdy	Shot 5 children in a playground
1988	N. Carolina	Michael Hayes	Shot 4 neighbors
1989	Kentucky	Joseph Wesbecker	Shot 8 coworkers
1990	Michigan	Lawrence DeLisle	Drowned his 4 children
1990	Florida	James Pough	Shot 13 in an auto loan company
1990	New York	Julio Gonzalez	87 people died in a nightclub fire
1991	Michigan	Ilene Russell	4 adults and 1 dhild in a fire
1991	Kentucky	Michael Brunner	Shot girlfriend, her 2 children
1991	New Jersey	Joseph Harris	Shot 4 people at post office
1991	New York	Andrew Broods	Shot father and 3 men
1991	Hawaii	Orlando Ganal	Shot 4 people including inlaws
1991	Texas	George Hennard	Shot 22 people in a restaurant
1991	Iowa	Gang Lu	Shot 5 college students and officials
1991	New Hampshire	James Colbert	Strangled wife, suffocated 3 daughters

(continued)

Year	State	Murderer	Death Toll
1991	Kentucky	Robert Daigneau	Shot wife and three strangers
1995	California	Willie Woods	City electrician fatally shoots four supervisors. Sentenced to life in prison.
1995	Texas	James Simpson	Kills five people at a refinery inspection station then kills self
1996	Australia	Martin Bryant	Shot 35 visitors to historic prison site
1996	Mississippi	Kenneth Tornes	A firefighter kills four superiors. Dies on death row
1997	South Carolina	Arthur H. Wise	Fired assembly line worker opens fire in plant filling four
1997	California	Arturo R. Torres	Fired employee kills four former co-workers at a maintenace yard, and is shot to death by police
1998	Conneticut	Matthew Beck	Former CT Lottery Corp. accountant fatally shoots four executives, then himself
1999	Georgia	Mark Barton	Former day trader kills nine people at two Atlanta brokerage offices and commits suicide
1999	Alabama	Alan E. Miller	Truck driver fatally shoots two co-workers at a Pelham office then kills a former co-worker
1999	Hawaii	Bryan Uyesugi	Copier repairman fatally shoots sven people at the Xerox Corp. Sentenced to life in prison.
1999	Florida	Silvio Izquierdo-Leyva	Housekeeper allegedly fatally shoots five co-workers at the Radisson Bay Harbor hotel. He pleads not guilty
2000	Texas	Robert Harris	Fired employee fatally shoots five people at a Dallas-area car wash. He is sentenced to death.
2000	Massachusettes	Michael "Mucko" McDermott	Killed seven people at Edgewater Technology (Internet firm) in Wakefield, Mass. Company was set to dock his salary over unpaid taxes. He was convicted April 24, 2002 and sentenced to life without parole.
2001	Japan	Mamoru Takuma	Stabbed eight first- and second-graders to death with a kitchen knife and injured 15 other people.
2001	Switzerland	Friedrich Leibacher	Wearing a ploice vest, shot and killed 14 people and committed suicide.

Source: *Federal Probation*, Vol. 56, No. 1 March 1992, pp. 53-61, and media reports.

shirk their duty, or create any violence or disturbance. The maximum penalty for mutiny is death.

mutual agreement program. A program, providing a form of contract between a prisoner and state prison and parole officials, wherein the prisoner undertakes specified self-improvement programs in order to receive a definite parole date, and the agency promises to provide the necessary educational and social services.

mutual aid. In law enforcement, a contractual agreement among .various contiguous agencies to provide back-up assistance to one another in emergency situations. Agencies could include the highway patrol, state police, county sheriff's department, and other local agencies. Beyond such contractual agreements, situations may demand the next higher level of imposing control, use of the state's National Guard troops, or, as a last resort, federal intervention. *See also* National Guard

mutual transfer. When two or more objects come in contact with one another, trace evidence from each may be left on the other. This is called mutual transfer. This is often the case when one vehicle is struck by another; each usually leaves some evidence on the other, such as an exchange of paint traces.

mysoped. An aggressive and sadistic child molester.

N

nalline test. A test used to determine whether or not a person is using narcotics.

Napoleonic Code. The code of laws adopted in France by the regime of Napoleon Bonaparte in 1810 and revised in 1819. The code became the basis for the criminal code in most continental European and Latin American countries.

narcotic. Offenses of Uniform Crime Reports relating to narcotic drugs, such as their unlawful possession, sale, use, growing, and manufacturing.

narcotic drugs. The term *narcotic drug* means any of the following, whether produced directly or indirectly by extraction from substances of vegetable origin, independently by chemical synthesis, or by a combination of the two: (a) opium, opiates, and their derivatives, including their isomers, esters, ethers, and salts, but not including the isoquinoline alkaloids of opium; (b) poppy straw and concentrate of poppy straw; (c) coca leaves, except those and their extracts from which cocaine, ecgonine, and derivatives of ecgonine or their salts have been removed; (d) cocaine, its salts, isomers, and salts of isomers; (e) ecgonine, its derivatives, their salts, isomers, and salts of isomers; and (f) any compound, mixture, or preparation that contains any quantity of any of the substances referred to above. The scope of illicit drugs and drug profits was illustrated when, in January 1985, a federal grand jury indicted 26 persons in a $100 million, nationwide, drug-trafficking ring.

narcotic prohibition act, first federal. The first federal narcotic regulation was enacted by Congress as part of the McKinley Tariff Act on October 1, 1890. This act provided for an internal revenue tax of $10 a pound on all smoking opium manufactured in the United States for smoking purposes and limited the manufacture, keeping of books, rendering of returns, and so forth. Section 1 of the federal act of February 9, 1909, read: "After the first day of April 1909, it shall be unlawful to import into the United States, opium in any form or any preparation or derivative thereof… other than smoking opium for medicinal purposes."

narcotic regulation, first state. Adopted on March 10, 1933, by Nevada.

narcotics and dangerous drugs training. This program is designed to acquaint appropriate professional and law enforcement personnel with: (a) techniques in the conduct of drug investigations; (b) aspects of physical security in legitimate drug distribution; (c) techniques in analysis of drugs for evidentiary purposes; and (d) pharmacologic and sociopsychologic aspects of drug abuse, drug education, and investigative techniques. DEA Training Academy, Quantico, VA.

Narcotics Anonymous. Founded in July 1953, this is the third largest self-help group, after Alcoholics Anonymous and Al-Anon. NA has approximately 18,000 local chapters across the nation and 2,000 more abroad. Address: P.O. Box 9999, Van Nuys, CA 91409.

narcotic tariff, first. The first federal law governing the importing of narcotics into the United States was the Tariff Act of August 30, 1842, which placed a levy of 75 cents a pound on opium. Prior to this act, opium was exempted from duty by the acts of July 14, 1832, and March 2, 1833.

National Advisory Commission on Criminal Justice Standards and Goals. Appointed in 1971 by the administrator of the Law Enforcement Assistance Administration to formulate, for the first time, national criminal justice standards and goals for crime reduction and prevention at the state and local levels. In 1973 the Commission recommended guidelines covering all areas of police practices.

National Advisory Committee for Juvenile Justice and Delinquency Prevention and Treatment. A committee appointed within the U.S. Department of Justice that developed new standards for the administration of juvenile justice.

national agency check. A Department of Defense (DOD) personnel security investigation consisting of a records review of certain national agencies, including a technical FBI fingerprint search.

national agency check and inquiry. A Department of Defense (DOD) personnel security investigation conducted by the Office of Personnel Management, combining a national agency check (as above) and written background inquiries to law enforcement agencies, former employers and supervisors, references, and schools.

National Alliance for Model State Drug Laws. Organization created by Congress to develop a uniform code for state drug laws. This resource center is dedicated to helping governors, state legislators, and others to create comprehensive, effective state substance abuse laws based on the findings of a presidential commission on the subject. Focus are economic weapons against drug traffickers, community empowerment and coordinated state drug-planning mechanisms, treatment, drug-free schools, and drug-free families. Address: 700 North Fairfax Street, Suite 550, Alexandria, VA 22314.

National Association of Drug Court Professionals. Formed under the auspices of Community Antidrug Coalitions of America, this organization comprises judges, prosecutors, defense attorneys, drug treatment providers, educators, and others with the goal of pressing drug courts to place offenders in treatment and rehabilitation programs rather than incarcerate them. Address: 901 North Pitt St., Suite 370, Alexandria, VA 22314.

National Association of Legal Assistants, Inc. (NALA). NALA, incorporated in April 1975, is the leading professional association for legal assistants, or paralegals, providing continuing education, professional development, and certification programs in the field. Begun by NALA in 1976, the Certified Legal Assistant (CLA) examination and program

has become the national professional credential for legal assistants, ensuring uniformity of professional standards and permitting legal assistants to move among states without losing certification. In 1987 the CLA program was recognized by the American Bar Association's Standing Committee on Legal Assistants, and subsequently recognized by 47 legal assistant organizations and many other bar associations. The program is taught three times a year by a board of CLAs, attorneys, and paralegal educators. The two-day examination covers verbal and written communication skills, judgment and analytical abilities, ethics, human relations, legal terminology, and legal research, as well as substantive knowledge of law and procedures, including one section on the American legal system and four subtests chosen from among eight areas of specialization. In 1982 the certifying board began offering specialty certifications in civil litigation and in probate and estate planning. Other areas of concentration are corporate and business law, real estate, bankruptcy, and criminal law and procedure. Address: NALA, 1516 S. Boston Ave., Suite 200, Tulsa, OK 74119; telephone (918) 587-6828.

National Association of Police Organizations (NAPO). Formed after the International Conference of Police Associations, which was affiliated with organized labor, was disbanded, NAPO has no such affiliations. Lobbying group for rank-and-file police officers, composed of independent police associations, including those from Dallas, TX; Detroit, MI; San Jose, Los Angeles County, and San Diego, CA; Suffolk County, NY; and several statewide organizations such as the Peace Officers Association of Michigan and the New Jersey State PBA, all of whom pool fees to retain lobbyists in Washington. Address: 750 First St., NE, Suite 920, Washington, DC 20002.

National Association of State Alcohol and Drug Abuse Directors. Organization for heads of state agencies. Address: 808 17th St., NW, Suite 410, Washington, DC 20006.

National Audiovisual Center. Part of National Technical Information Service, an agency of the U.S. Department of Commerce, the center is the central distribution source of audiovisual programs produced by the U.S. government on fire, law enforcement, and emergency medical services. Address: Springfield, VA 22161.

National Center for Community Policing. Hosts training sessions and conferences, and provides on-site technical assistance to police agencies, community groups, and civic officials. Address: School of Criminal Justice, Michigan State University; 324 Nisbet Bldg.,1407 S. Harrison Rd., East Lansing, MI 48823, telephone: (800) 892-9051.

National Center for State Courts. Provides technical assistance and funding for a wide variety of court programs and services. Address: 300 Newport Ave., Williamsburg, VA 23185.

National Center for the Analysis of Violent Crime (NCAVC). The FBI's NCAVC provides special resources to local law enforcement agencies. Its behavioral science unit provides training and research in criminal profiling, a process to identify major offender personality and behavioral characteristics based on analyses of the crime or crimes committed. The NCAVC operates the Violent Criminal Apprehension Program (VCAP), a national clearinghouse for information about unsolved violent crimes, particularly murder. Local law enforcement agencies report unsolved violent crime data to the FBI, which analyzes the data, seeking to identify similarities with other unsolved crimes. If similarities exist, the participating agencies are notified to coordinate their investigations.

National Clearinghouse for Alcohol and Drug Information. The information service of the Center for Substance Abuse Prevention, this organization offers bibliographies, free computer searches, treatment referrals, and other resources on alcohol, drugs, prevention, and education. Telephone: (800) 729-6686. Address: P.O. Box 2345, Rockville, MD 20847-2345.

National College of District Attorneys. Established in 1970 by the University of Houston, the college is cosponsored by the American Bar Association, the National District Attorneys Association, the American College of Trial Lawyers, and the International Academy of Trial Lawyers. NCDA provides continuing legal education for prosecuting attorneys in all areas of criminal law. Address: University of South Carolina, Carolina Plaza, 937 Assembly Street, Columbia, South Carolina 29208.

National Commission on Law Observance and Enforcement. A commission created by President Herbert Hoover in 1929, and composed of 10 attorneys and a woman college president. Its purpose was to study crime as a national problem. It was called the Wickersham Commission after its chairman, George W. Wickersham, former U.S. attorney general. It completed its last report, of a total of 12, in 1931.

National Commission on the Causes and Prevention of Violence. Created by President Lyndon B. Johnson on June 10, 1968, to investigate and make recommendations pertaining to causes and prevention of violence, with the cooperation of other executive departments and agencies; to report its findings and recommendations not later than June 10, 1969. Its term was extended by President Richard M. Nixon on May 23, 1969, to completion of its report or to December 10, 1969, whichever was earlier.

National Computerized Criminal History System. Inaugurated by and through the National Crime Information Center, U.S. Department of Justice, in 1971. By that November, approximately 15 states were participating. The goal is to have all 50 states participate. To do so, each state must have the following: (a) a computer capable of interfacing with the NCIC computer for the interstate exchange of criminal history information under the management control of a criminal justice agency authorized to function as a control-terminal agency; (b) a communication network serving all criminal justice agencies throughout the state; (c) a central state agency capable of processing all fingerprint cards generated in that state and updating the NCIC files; and (d) a computerized state criminal history capability certified by the NCIC as meeting national standards.

National Conference of State Legislatures. Serving legislatures and staffs nationwide, this agency offers status reports on state legislation and analyses of public safety and drug-related issues. Address: 1560 Broadway, Suite 700, Denver, CO 80202.

National Crime Commission (President's Commission on Law Enforcement and Administration of Justice). Established by President Lyndon B. Johnson on July 23, 1965, to study the whole field of criminal justice, making comments on its findings and recommendations. The study was divided into five task forces: Assessment of the Crime Problem, Police and Public Safety, Administration of Justice, Corrections, and Science and Technology. Its first report, "The Challenge of Crime in a Free Society" was released on February 18, 1967.

National Crime Coordinating Council. *See* Kefauver Investigation

National Crime Information Center. Begun on January 27, 1967, by the FBI as a service to all criminal justice agencies. NCIC terminals are located in the major cities of the United States and Canada. Its goal is to maintain a computerized filing system of documented criminal justice information. Eight files pertain to Wanted Persons, Stolen Property (serialized), and Computerized Criminal Histories (individuals arrested and fingerprinted for serious or significant offenses). The 9th, or Missing Persons, file is not criminal data but is used to assist in the location of missing juveniles. The Criminalistics Laboratory Information System (CLIS) prototype is a 10th file. Address: 1000 Custer Hollow Road, Clarksburg, West Virginia 26306.

National Crime Prevention Council. address: 1700 K Street, NW, Second Floor, Washington, DC 20006-3817. *See* Crime Prevention Council, National

National Crime Victimization Survey (NCVS). A statistical program instituted in 1972, which serves as a second source, along with the Crime Index, which is based on the FBI's Uniform Crime Reports (UCR) of incidents reported to the police, to gauge the national incidence of crime. NCVA data are collected by the Bureau of Census and provide information on the extent to which persons 12 years of age and older and households have been the victims of selected crimes.

Percent of Crime Reported to the Police, 2000–2001

	2000	2001	Percent Change
Violent Crime	47.9	49.4	3.1
Rape/secual assault	48.1	38.6	-19.8*
Robbery	56.3	60.5	7.5
Aggravated assault	56.7	59.2	4.4
Simple assault	43.6	44.9	2.3
Personal Theft	35.0	35.2	0.6
Property Crime	35.7	37.0	3.6
Burglary	50.7	53.7	6.9
Motor Vehicle Theft	80.4	81.6	1.5
Theft	29.5	30.1	2.0

*based on a limited sample.

National Criminal Justice Reference Service. *See* National Institute of Justice

National District Attorneys Association. Founded in 1950, the NDAA strives to further the professionalism of prosecutors, sponsors annual conferences, and has advisory committees on juvenile justice, civil law, child support, organized crime, and metropolitan prosecution. Address: 99 Canal Center Plaza, Suite 510, Alexandria, VA 22314.

National Drug Enforcement Board. The National Narcotics Act of 1984 established the NDEB. Its chairman is the attorney general, with the remaining members composed of the secretaries of state, treasury, defense, transportation, and health and human services; the directors of the Office of Management and Budget and of the Central Intelligence Agency; and other officials as appointed by the president. The board was established to facilitate coordination of U.S. operations and policy on drug law enforcement.

National Drug Prosecution Center. This group is part of the American Prosecutors Research Institute, a nonprofit, public education and technical assistance affiliate of the National District Attorneys Association. The center's mission is to train prosecutors to investigate and prosecute drug cases more effectively, to identify and evaluate drug control and demand-reduction strategies, to provide technical assistance regarding task forces or anti-drug abuse programs, and to develop model legislation on drugs. *See also* National District Attorneys Association.

National Federation of Paralegal Associations (NFPA). Organized by eight associations in 1974, NFPA by 1992 represented more than 50 member associations with total membership exceeding 17,500. Its mission statement describes NFPA as a nonprofit, professional organization of state and local paralegal associations throughout the United States that supports increased quality, efficiency, and accessibility in the delivery of legal services, with the paralegal profession as an integral partner in that delivery. Publishes *National Paralegal Reporter* quarterly. Address: 2517 Eastlake Avenue East, Suite 200, Seattle, Washington 98102.

National Fire Academy. The academy trains over 6,000 students each year. Courses include executive development, fire data collection and analysis, fire-fighting technologies, arson investigation and detection, and disaster planning for hazardous materials. Many of the courses are made available to paid and volunteer firemen. Contact: NFA,

Fire Administration, Federal Emergency Management Agency, U.S. Fire Administration, 16825 S. Seton ave., Emmitsburg,MD 21727; telepone: (206) 652-4120.

National Firearms Act. An act passed by Congress on June 26, 1934, which restrained the importation and interstate transportation of sawed-off shotguns, machine guns, and silencers for any type of weapon and placed a tax on dealers of firearms.

National Fire Prevention and Control Administration Fire Reference Service. Created in 1974 by the U.S. Department of Commerce to "provide the fire prevention and control community with an extensive repository of fire-related information that can assist them in the performance of their duties." Publishes *Fireword* (monthly newsletter), *Fire Technology Abstracts* (available from U.S. Government Printing Office), and *Fire in the U.S.* (annual). Address: P.O. Box 19518, Washington, DC 20036.

National Fire Protection Association. Publishes and periodically updates a manual, *Life Safety Code* that specifies minimum standards for fire safety necessary for the public interest. Two chapters of the manual are devoted to correctional facilities.

National Fraudulent Check File. Maintained by the FBI Laboratory, this file serves as a "clearinghouse" for information on worthless checks. Checks sent in by law enforcement agencies are searched against reproductions of checks on file to determine if the writing, printing, check protector, and so forth are identified with that or other checks in the file. If an identification is made, a copy of the check is recorded for future reference.

National Guard. The volunteer militia of the states, which in 1916 was organized as an auxiliary of the regular army, armed and trained by the federal government, and made subject to federal service in wartime or other emergencies on call of the president. At other times, the respective state contingents may be called out by the governor when, in his or her judgment, the regular police forces are unable to maintain order.

national incident-based reporting system (NIBRS). In 1988 the FBI announced it had a new reporting plan in collecting crime data. In this system, a crime is viewed along with all of its components, including type of victim, type of weapon used, location of the crime, alcohol and/or drug influence, type of criminal activity, relationship of victim to offender, residence of victims and arrestees, and a description of property and its value. This system includes 22 crimes, rather than the 8 that constitute the FBI's UCR Part I crimes. *See also* Index Crimes

National Institute of Corrections. Gives technical assistance and provides training to state and local correctional programs. Grants finance projects in the institute's priority areas. The NIC Information Center functions as the base for information collection and dissemination on correctional programs, policies, practices, and standards. Publishes *Annual Program Plan*. For technical assistance specifically related to jails, contact: NIC Jail Center, 1960 Industrial Cir., Suite A, Longmont, CO 80501. For general technical assistance, contact: NIC, Bureau of Prisons, DOJ, 320 1st Street NW, Washington, DC 20534.

National Institute of Justice. The National Institute of Justice/NCJRS—the National Criminal Justice Reference Service—is the centralized national clearinghouse serving the criminal justice community since 1972. NCJRS also operates the Juvenile Justice Clearinghouse (telephone: 800.638.8736) for the National Institute for Juvenile Justice and Delinquency Prevention; the Dispute Resolution Information Center for the Federal Justice Research Program; and the Justice Statistics Clearinghouse (telephone: 800.732.3277) for the Bureau of Justice Statistics. NCJRS maintains a steadily growing computerized database of more than 75,000 criminal justice documents, operates a public reading room, and offers complete information and referral services. Among the products and services provided by NCJRS are custom searches, topical searches and bibli-

ographies, research service, audiovisual and document loans, conference support, selective dissemination of information, and distribution of documents in print or microfiche. A Visiting Fellowship Program is open to senior-level criminal justice professionals and researchers. Registered users of NCJRS receive *NIJ Reports* bimonthly. Address: 810 Seventh St., NW, Washington, DC 20531

National Institute of Mental Health. One of the major operating divisions of the Alcohol, Drug Abuse, and Mental Health Administration in the U.S. Department of Health and Human Services. The institute has conducted or supported research on alcoholism, narcotics addiction, suicide, delinquency and crime, and problems of city living. NIMH began operations in 1949, under plans authorized by the National Mental Health Act of 1946.

National Judicial College. Offers courses for judges, including several that focus on substance abuse. Address: Judicial College Building/MS 358, University of Nevada, Reno, NV 89557.

National Laboratory Response Network. *See* bio-terrorism

National Labor Relations Board. Independent, regulatory agency empowered under the Wagner Act (1935), the Taft-Hartley Act (1947), and the Landrum-Griffin Act (1959). The NLRB consists of 5 members appointed by the president for 5 years and a general counsel appointed for 4 years. The board performs quasi-judicial and quasi-legislative functions aimed at preventing and remedying unfair labor practices by employers or union organizations and at protecting fair union representation. The board maintains 31 regional and subregional offices. It is the agency most responsible for ending violent labor-management confrontations.

National League of Cities. A membership organization of local elected officials, the NLC has created an awards program to study and honor innovative local public safety initiatives with the National Institute of Justice. Address 1301 Pennsylvania Ave., NW, Suite 550, Washington, DC 20004.

National Legal Aid and Defenders Association. Founded in 1911, NLADA has as major function the "maintenance and improvement of high quality legal representation to indigent defendants at all stages in criminal and quasi-criminal proceedings." Publishes *Cornerstone* (monthly) and *Briefcase* (quarterly).Address: 1140 Connectiut Ave. NW, Suite 900, Washington, DC 20036.

National Narcotics Act of 1984. The purpose of this act is to ensure that (a) a national and international effort against illegal drugs are maintained; (b) the activities of the federal agencies involved are fully coordinated; and (c) a single, competent, and responsible high-level board of the U.S. government is charged with this coordination. *See also* National Drug Enforcement Board

National Narcotics Border Interdiction System. Established in 1983 and headed by then Vice President George Bush, former head of th CIA, the NNBIS is a federal effort to combat drug smuggling. The program coordinates the activities of the CIA, military intelligence agencies, and domestic crime officials.

National Narcotics Intelligence Consumers Committee. A federal interagency consortium to coordinate drug intelligence collection and produce estimates. The consortium issues periodic reports on the status of illicit drugs worldwide, including production and availability estimates for marijuana, cocaine, opiates, and synthetic drugs. Reports also cover drug-trafficking routes and methods and money trails. *See also* National Survey on Drug Abuse

National Organization for Women. A civil rights pressure group formed in 1966 to campaign for legislative and economic reforms that will ensure equality for women; admits men as well as women. NOW has strived for a "fully equal partnership of the sexes" by promoting such measures as the Equal Rights Amendment (ERA), equal employment op-

portunities, an end to laws restricting abortion, free day-care centers, and an end to discriminatory educational quotas. NOW also seeks to revise state protective laws for women; to change Social Security, divorce, and alimony laws; and to change the mass media's portrayal of women.

National Referral Center. Founded in 1962 by the Library of Congress, the center refers individuals making requests to the agency or organization that can provide the answer. Publishes the *Directory of Information Resources in the United States, U.S. GPO* and *NRC Switchboard* (periodically, both available free). Address: Library of Congress, Science and Technology Division, Washington, DC 20540.

National Retired Teachers Association/ American Association of Retired Persons. Established in 1947; maintains a criminal justice services information center that "develops and implements programs designed to educate and demonstrate protection of person and property and crime resistance." The center also conducts seminars for law enforcement personnel on problems of the elderly. Address: 601 E St., NW, Washington, DC 20049.

National Runaway Switchboard. *See* juvenile locators

National Security Agency (NSA)/Central Security Service (CSS). Federal security agencies that are components of the Department of Defense (DOD). The NSA was established by a presidential directive as a separately organized agency within the DOD in 1952; the CSS was created in 1972 in accordance with a presidential memorandum. The NSA director is also chief of the CSS. The NSA/CSS is responsible for coordination, direction, and performance of technical functions in support of government activities to protect U.S. communications and to produce foreign intelligence data. For example, in the course of its work NSA can intercept and decipher electronic communications.

National Stolen Property Act. A federal law of May 22, 1934, to extend the provisions of the National Motor Vehicles Theft Act to other stolen property, such as securities, which includes any note, stock certificate, bond, debenture, check, draft, warrant, travelers check, letter of credit, warehouse receipt, negotiable bill of lading, or evidence of indebtedness. The law also covers money—U.S. or foreign legal tender or counterfeit. Any person violating this act may be punished in any district into or through which such property has been transported or removed.

National Survey on Drug Abuse. Sometimes referred to as the Household Survey, this research is funded by the National Institute on Drug Abuse and has been conducted every 2–3 years since 1972, with the 10th version done in 1990. Data provided include drug use incidence, prevalence, and trends for people aged 12 and over in selected households. Results cover a random sample of some 8,000 households, each of whom returns a self-administered questionnaire. These data are combined with those of the High School Senior Survey. *See also* High School Senior Survey; Drug Abuse Warning Network

Nation of Islam. The name given to the original Black Muslim movement in the United States by its founder, Elijah Muhammad. His son later changed the name to American Muslim Mission. The earlier name has been adopted by a splinter group under Louis Farrakhan.

naturalization. The conferring upon an alien of the rights and privileges of U.S. citizenship. This is achieved through federal laws administered by the Bureau of Immigration and Naturalization and the federal courts.

natural law. A set of principles and rules discovered by human reason that, it is supposed, would govern people in a state of nature (before formal law existed), or provide rational principles for the government of people in society. It has also been considered a valuable supplement to formal law in setting moral standards by which the conduct of governments may be judged. Natural law theories originated with Stoic philoso-

phers and statesmen. In the eighteenth century, natural law was variously derived from reason, the Bible, and the fundamental principles of the common law. *See also* common law; positive law

natural rights. Those rights believed to be intrinsic to the individual before the creation of the state. They were developed in the political philosophies of John Milton, John Locke, and Jean Jacques Rousseau and modified in America by Thomas Jefferson, Samuel Adams, and Thomas Paine. In the early Revolutionary period, these rights were conceived of as part of the heritage of British constitutionalism, although Paine considered natural rights as independent of constitutions. As developed in the United States, natural rights included popular sovereignty, the right of revolution against tyranny, democracy, liberty, the pursuit of happiness, and property rights. Varying emphases on the importance of natural rights have played significant roles in U.S. history. Alexander Hamilton, for example, emphasized property rights. Jefferson and Paine emphasized personal civil rights. Later, South Carolina statesman John C. Calhoun (1782–1850) repudiated the entire doctrine of natural rights as unsound.

natus (Lat.). Born.

Naval Investigative Service. A law enforcement organization staffed mostly by civilians and responsible for providing investigative support in matters involving serious crimes committed by or against Navy personnel. The descendant of a small undercover unit formed in New York City in 1916, today's NIS was established in 1966 with the personnel resources of the old district intelligence offices of the Office of Naval Intelligence. NIS has 154 locations worldwide and 10 regional offices, 6 in the U.S. and 4 overseas.

Nazi war criminals. The Office of Special Investigations detects, identifies, and takes appropriate administrative action leading to denaturalization and/or deportation of Nazi war criminals. It provides historic research, investigations, and proceedings before both administrative bodies and U.S. courts. For further information, contact: OSI, Criminal Division, DOJ, 950 Pennsylvania Ave., Washington, DC 20530-0001.

N.B. (Lat., lit.). Abbreviation for *nota bene*, take note, or note well.

ne exeat (Lat., lit.). (In order) that he or she does not depart.

negligent. Culpably careless; doing something, or omitting to do something, which a person of ordinary prudence would not have done, or omitted to do. Negligent conduct may be defined as acting without the due care required by the circumstances. *See also* vicarious liability

negligent manslaughter (manslaughter by negligence). Causing the death of another by recklessness or gross negligence.

negotiable. Capable of being transferred to another by assignment or endorsement.

negotiable instrument. A written promise or request for the payment of a certain sum, such as a check or promissory note.

neighborhood (team) policing. Assigning a team of officers to police a specific geographic area on a 24-hour basis.

neighborhood watch. Procedure started in the United States in the early 1970s to foster community-based crime prevention. The London Metropolitan Police defines neighborhood watch as involving three elements: (1) public surveillance (the community serves as the eyes and ears of the police); (2) property marking (the police provide marking kits to facilitate return of stolen property); and (3) home security (free police inspections). *See also* radio watch

nemo (Lat.). No one.

neoclassicism. A trend in the history of criminology that flourished in Europe during the early nineteenth century. It modified the views of the classical school of criminology by introducing the concepts of diminished criminal responsibility and less severe punishment due to the age or mental condition of the offender.

nepotism. Favoritism granted to relatives without due regard for merit; family favoritism. Used to describe the employment of any immediate family member by his or her relative; especially, to hire close relatives regardless of their qualifications.

net-widening. A correctional concept suggesting that community control alternatives to incarceration, such as electronic monitoring and house arrest, are options that merely expand the number of people under sentence, or prisoner population, without a corresponding expansion of facilities.

Neutrality Laws. Acts of Congress that forbid the fitting out and equipping of armed vessels or the enlisting of troops for the aid of either of two belligerent powers who are at war with each other, but with whom the United States is at peace.

neutron activation analysis. A test using radioactive materials to detect the presence and quantities of chemical elements in a substance even when quantities are minute (trace elements). It is useful in crime laboratories for analyzing substances such as poisons, traces of contaminants, and residues on the hands of homicide suspects to determine if a handgun has been recently fired.

new court commitment. The readmission to prison of a person entering on one or more new sentences rather than on any prior sentence still in effect.

New Jersey Experimental Project for the Treatment of Youthful Offenders. This project and facility, commonly known as Highfields, was established in 1950. Its philosophy is that rehabilitation of offenders is facilitated by close interpersonal contact among the boys in small groups, and between the boys and the staff. The program operates on a four-month incarceration program, and evaluations have been positive.

newly discovered evidence. Evidence of a new and material fact, or new evidence in relation to a fact at issue, discovered by a party to a cause after the rendition of a verdict or judgment therein.

new trial. Any trial in which issues of fact and law are examined that have already been the subject of an earlier trial.

next friend. Anyone who enters a legal case or conducts a suit on behalf of an infant.

next of kin. Nearest in relationship according to the degrees of consanguinity.

nicotine. The poison contained in tobacco leaves. When tobacco products are smoked, dipped, or chewed, nicotine chemically attaches to receptors in the user's brain, which can cause either relaxation or arousal. Continued use leads to addiction, and smoking is the leading preventable cause of death in the United States. Some 50 million Americans smoke tobacco, while another 12 million chew or dip it.

Nicotine Anonymous. Self-help group for smokers. Address: 419 Main Street, PMB# 370, Huntington Beach,CA 92648.

Niederhoffer, Arthur. A leading author (1917–1981) on police work, Niederhoffer graduated from Brooklyn College in 1937, earned his law degree from Brooklyn Law School, and was admitted to the bar in New York in 1940, joining the New York City Police Department that year. He was promoted to sergeant in 1951 and to lieutenant in 1956, earning that year an M.S. in sociology. His first book, written with another author, was *The Gang: A Study of Adolescent Behavior*, published in 1958. He earned a Ph.D. from New York University in 1963, two years after retiring from the NYPD. Niederhoffer then became an instructor at the New York City Police Academy. Based on his doctoral dissertation, *The Mobile Force: A Study of Police Cynicism*, he devised a "cynicism scale," which has been widely replicated. Other books include *Behind the Shield: The Police in Urban Society* (1967), with Abraham Blumberg; *The Ambivalent Force: Perspectives on the Police* (1970), with Smith; *New Directions in Police-Community Relations*,

(1974); and with his wife, Elaine, *The Police Family: From Station House to Ranch House* (1974). He became a professor of sociology at John Jay College of Criminal Justice and in 1980 was elected a fellow of the American Society of Criminology.

night court. A criminal court which, in certain cities, sits during the early evening hours for the immediate disposition of petty offenses and the granting or withholding of bail in more serious cases. The first night court was opened in New York City on September 1, 1907.

nightstick. *See* baton

nihil (Lat.). Nothing; shortened to nil.

nihilism. (1) A political or social position involving total rejection of belief in laws. (2) Use of force and violence against authority or those representing such authority.

nine-one-one (911). The uniform national emergency telephone number established by AT&T and the (former) Bell System—by default, since all other 3-digit codes below that number had been assigned or were in use. The first digit, 9, distinguishes emergency calls in the nationwide switched telecommunications network from long-distance calls or attempts to reach an operator; when the 9 is followed by 1 + 1, the network has been programmed to route calls to appropriate fire, police, and ambulance personnel. While more and more communities have 911 service, current estimates are that it is available to fewer than 60 percent of all Americans. A variety of local difficulties, such as disagreements among public safety departments, out-of-date switching equipment, or budget constraints, can prevent the service from being installed.

Nineteen Eighty-three. Jargon for a section of federal civil rights law, which reads: "Every person who, under color of any state or territory, subjects, or causes to be subjected, any citizen of the U.S. or other person within the jurisdiction thereof to the deprivation of any rights, privileges, or immunities secured by the Constitution and laws, shall be liable to the party injured in an action at law, suit in equity, or other proper proceedings for redress." The name comes from the U.S. Code, in which this provision is Section 1983 of Title 42.

***nisi prius* court**. A court in which trials of issues of fact are held before a jury and a single presiding judge.

"no knock" law. A law that empowers an officer to enter a home or other place, with a suitable court order, without knocking or announcing his or her identity, when to give warning would imperil the officer's safety or allow evidence to be easily and quickly destroyed.

nolle prosequi (Lat.). A prosecutor's decision not to initiate or continue prosecution.

nolo contendere (Lat., lit., I will not contest it). A plea in a criminal action having the same legal results as a plea of guilty. This plea is usually used in a criminal proceeding from which possible civil proceedings and liabilities might result.

nominal damages. A trifling sum, awarded to a plaintiff who has sued for damages, that shows a breach of duty on the part of the defendant but no serious loss resulting therefrom.

non compos mentis (Lat.). Meaning not of sound mind.

nonfeasance. Omission to do something; not doing what ought to be done. *See also* malfeasance; misfeasance

nonjuror. A person who declines to take an oath required in a proceeding.

nonlethal force. Also referred to as less than lethal force, this includes devices or agents used to induce compliance without substantial risk of permanent injury or death. Three general categories are: (I) electrical: TASER, stun gun; (2) chemical: tear gas, Mace; and (3) impact: water cannon, baton, rubber bullets, and shot-filled bean bags. *See also* Koga method

nonlethal weapons. Weapons that will not cause death. These are contrasted with less-than-lethal weapons, which, although designed only to incapacitate, may cause death under unusual circumstances or if inappropriately used. *See also* nonlethal force; TASER

non prosequitor (Lat., shortened to *non pros*). He or she does not prosecute.

nonsecretor. A person whose saliva and other bodily fluids do not contain blood group antigens. Hence, it is not possible to type the person's saliva and other bodily fluids, an important technique in criminal justice.

non sequitur (Lat., lit.). It does not follow.

nonsuit. A judgment given against a plaintiff for failure to establish a case.

nonviolence. A policy adopted by an adversarial group that refrains from the use of overt force, either as a matter of principle or expediency.

norm. A statistical term for the common or average score or performance in a given group; the result that occurs most often.

normal curves. Bell-shaped symmetrical distributions of statistics. The precise shape of any such curve will depend on the mean and standard deviation used in the study. The standard normal curve has a mean of 0 and a standard deviation of 1; that is, a standard normal curve is one in which all the observations have been converted to standard scores. The symmetrical shape of the normal curve gives it certain useful properties for statistical research. For example, it is known that in a normal curve, 68 percent of all observations fall within one standard deviation, plus or minus, of the mean, 95 percent fall within two standard deviations, and 99 percent fall within three standard deviations. Thus, any observation varying from the mean by three standard deviations is atypical in a normal distribution. *See also* frequency distribution

normative power. The ability of any leader to obtain compliance from followers by using symbolic rewards.

Northwestern University Traffic Institute. Begun in 1932 as a two-week training program for traffic officers, this organization eventually spawned the National Highway Traffic Safety Administration in 1966, which became a U.S. Department of Transportation Agency. The Traffic Institute itself was founded in 1936; early texts were *Evidence Handbook* and *The Traffic Accident Investigation Manual*, which was the first of its kind. First revised in 1981, it then adopted an "accident reconstruction" approach. The Traffic Institute now has 12 divisions: Police Administration Training Program; School of Police Staff and Command, Police Training, Field Services, Transportation Engineering, Accident Investigation, Motor Vehicle Administration, Research and Development, Legal, Traffic Safety School, Public Information and Publications, and Research Center for Aviation Safety and Security. Along with the FBI Academy and the Southern Police Institute, it is one of the major law enforcement training centers in the United States.

notary public. A public officer authorized to authenticate and certify documents such as deeds, contracts, and affidavits with his or her signature and seal.

not-guilty plea. *See* plea

notice. An advice, or written warning, in more or less formal shape, intended to apprise persons of some proceeding in which their interests are involved or to inform them of some fact that it is their right to know and the duty of the notifying party to communicate.

nuisance. Generally defined as any activity that interferes with the quality of life in a community, such as an establishment or practice that offends public morals or decency or menaces public health, safety, or order. Indications that a nuisance exists include any documented activity commonly associated with narcotics or vice violations. *See also* abatement

null. Of no legal or binding force.

nulla poena sine crimine (Lat.). No punishment without a crime.

null hypothesis. A statement that there is no relationship between two things being studied, or that results were negative. Researchers expect to be able to reject null hypotheses if they prove their scientific hypotheses; that is, proof of one hypothesis nullifies its opposite.

numbers, obliterated. Serial or identification numbers on objects that have been removed or made unreadable by being hammered or punched. Thieves use this technique on such things as guns, motor vehicles, and other items of value that have identification numbers, thus making it difficult or impossible to identify the objects. Crime laboratories can restore such numbers in many instances by use of acid etching, the application of heat, or other methods.

Nuremberg trials. A series of trials conducted by an international military tribunal at Nuremberg, Germany, after World War II. The defendants were Nazi party and military officials and other persons intimately associated with the Hitler regime, who were accused of violations of the laws of war, crimes against humanity, and other international crimes, based on their involvement with the Holocaust. Trials of the most serious offenders began November 21, 1945, and ended on September 30, 1946. Twenty-two defendants were found guilty, of whom 11 were sentenced to be hanged.

O

oath. A solemn appeal to God or the Supreme Being as to the truth of a statement. A false oath is punishable as perjury.

obit (Lat., lit.). He died.

obiter (Lat.). Something incidental in an opinion rather than the principal question.

obiter dictum (Lat.). A belief or opinion included by a judge in his or her decision in a case.

objectivity. A claim intended to ensure the legitimacy of a statement describing empirical reality; the quality of belonging to the sensible world and of being observable or verifiable, especially scientific methods.

obligatory. Binding in law or conscience; requiring performance or forbearance of some act.

obscenity. First defined in law in *Miller v. California*, 1973, which carefully limited the scope of state statutes designed to regulate obscene material. Basic guidelines established were (a) whether the average person, applying contemporary community standards, would find that a work, taken as a whole, appeals to the prurient interest; (b) whether the work depicts or describes, in a patently offensive way, sexual conduct specifically defined by the applicable state law; and (c) whether the work, taken as a whole, lacks serious literary, artistic, political, or scientific value.

OBSCIS. An acronym for Offender-Based State Corrections Information System, OBSCIS is a multistate program for the development of prisoner information systems for state correctional agencies. Data elements and basic OBSCIS code structure are presented in the OBSCIS Data Dictionary.

observation. The procedure by which a researcher gathers data. Whereas measurement is the assignment of numbers to the various outcomes that variables can exhibit, observation is the method of undertaking to measure a phenomenon. It may be direct, where a researcher actually observes behavior or individuals, or indirect, through the use of questionnaires, interviews, projective techniques, or physiological reactions. *See also* participant observation

Obsessive-Compulsives Anonymous. Support and self-help group for people afflicted with this illness. Address: P.O. Box 215, New Hyde Park, NY 11040.

obstruction of justice. All unlawful acts committed with intent to prevent or hinder the administration of justice, including law enforcement, judicial, and corrections functions.

OBTS. An abbreviation for Offender-Based Transaction Statistics, OBTS are derived from information concerning law enforcement, court, and corrections proceedings, recorded in such a way that the method of identifying the person subject to the proceedings is uniform throughout data collection and analysis. This system serves to link the output of one agency to the input of another agency, and the flow of offenders through the system can be observed over long periods of time. Some states have developed OBTS programs, and a national statistical program using OBTS data is being developed by the Bureau of Justice Statistics.

occasional property crime. Those types and instances of burglary, larceny, forgery, and other thefts undertaken infrequently, irregularly, and often quite crudely. Offenders who engage in this level of property crime do not pursue it as a career. Edwin M. Lemet's study of "naive check forgers," undertaken many decades ago, clearly illustrates the factors associated with occasional property crime as a behavior system.

occult. *See* Crowley, Aleister; satanic cult

Occupational Safety and Health Administration (OSHA). A federal agency established by act of Congress in 1970. OSHA is responsible for developing standards of workplace safety, issuing regulations to protect workers, and enforcing these laws, regulations, and standards. OSHA is empowered to inspect workplaces and to issue citations and fines for noncompliance.

o'clock. The position of points on a target or at a scene when compared to the face of a clock. As the target is viewed from the front, it is compared with a clock face held in front of the viewer. Three o'clock position is the right side of a horizontal line drawn through the center of the target; six o'clock is the bottom of the target and in line with a vertical line drawn through the center of the target.

odometer tampering. Federal law prohibits tampering with a vehicle's odometer (often misidentified as a speedometer, it measures the distance traveled by a vehicle). No one, including the vehicle owner, is permitted to turn back or disconnect the odometer, unless performing repairs. When a broken odometer cannot be adjusted to reflect the true mileage, the odometer must be set at zero and a sticker indicating the true mileage before service and the date of service attached to the left door frame. Federal law also requires disclosure of the vehicle mileage upon transfer of ownership. Purchasers who suspect tampering should contact: Administrator, National Highway Traffic Safety Administration, Department of Transportation, Washington, DC; Consumer Affairs Section, Antitrust Division, DOJ, Washington, DC; or local or state law enforcement authorities.

offender. An adult who has been convicted of a crime.

offender groups, in federal prisons. Comprised of (1) Drug offenders: all individuals sentenced for violation of the federal narcotics laws according to the Federal Bureau of Prisons. This includes offenses pertaining to the use, manufacture, sale, and distribution of drugs or controlled substances. (2) Violent offenders: all individuals sentenced for the commission of violent crimes, which include assault, homicide, kidnapping, rape, robbery, injuries resulting from explosives, and threats against the president. (3) Property offenders: all individuals sentenced for the violation of property crimes, which include burglary, violation of customs laws, destruction of property, embezzlement, forgery, larceny theft, lottery, mailing or otherwise transporting obscene material, robbery theft, and violations of the Interstate Commerce Act. (4) Other offenders: all individuals sentenced for offenses other than drug, violent, and property offenses.

offenders, sex. Sex offenders may be divided into two classes: persons committing illegal acts such as rape, sodomy, and indecent exposure that indicate physical or mental abnormality; and those committing similar acts that in themselves do not indicate abnormalities but that may have been declared unlawful, such as solicitation, maintaining disorderly houses (commercial vice), and seduction.

offense. (1) A felony, misdemeanor, or a less serious violation of the law of a state. (2) A breach of international law that Congress is authorized to punish.

offenses against the family and children. Offenses relating to desertion, abandonment, nonsupport, neglect or abuse of spouse or child, nonpayment of alimony, or other similar acts. *See also* child support

Office of National Drug Control Policy. Agency that coordinates federal, state, and local efforts to control illegal drug use and devises national strategies to carry out anti-drug programs. Prepares the annual National Drug Control Strategy and accompanying budget. Address: P.O. Box 6000, Rockville, MD 20849-6000. Web site: http://www.whitehousedrugpolicy.gov/

oligarchy. Rule by a select few, especially by those at the top of an organizational hierarchy.

ombudsman. In criminal justice, an individual who operates within the prison institution but is ideally independent of both the administration and the inmates. This individual acts as an intermediary between the prison inmates and the staff in airing grievances, investigating them, and so forth. The function is a tension-relieving device that allows inmates to feel they have an outlet for their complaints.

Omnibus Crime Control and Safe Streets Act of 1968. A series of acts passed by Congress to deal with the rise of crime in the United States. The acts established the Law Enforcement Assistance Administration (LEAA) to carry out a broad program of aid to the states and localities for crime control—with particular attention to street crime, riots, and organized crime. Other provisions of the acts and their subsequent amendments include a ban in federal court against evidence gained from wiretaps or listening devices; the regulation of firearm sales, transport, and possession; grants for the construction and renovation of correctional facilities, courtrooms, treatment centers, and so forth; and the establishment of the Bureau of Justice Statistics. This act was amended by the Comprehensive Crime Control Act of 1984.

Onion Field, The. A nonfiction book authored by Joseph Wambaugh, depicting the murder of a Los Angeles policeman, Ian Campbell. Officers Campbell and Karl Hettinger, while on routine patrol, were kidnapped at gunpoint from Hollywood, CA, on the night of March 9, 1963, and driven 95 miles to an onion field 30 miles south of Bakersfield, CA, by Gregory Powell and Jimmy Lee Smith. Powell shot Campbell in the mouth and then four more times, as the officers stood with their hands over their heads. Hettinger fled when a cloud obscured the moon. Powell and Smith twice were sentenced to death, but their sentences were reduced to life in prison with the possibility of parole in 1972 when the California state Supreme Court declared the death penalty law unconstitutional. Smith was paroled in 1982 but later returned to prison on a heroin charge. The state parole board in 1977 found Powell suitable for release and affirmed the finding in 1978 and 1979. But intense public and political pressure caused the board to withdraw Powell's parole date shortly before his scheduled release in June 1982. After the episode and trials, Hettinger committed a series of shoplifting offenses and was forced to resign from the LAPD. A psychiatrist reported this was due to an unconscious need to be punished. Hettinger was unemployed for a time, worked as a gardener in LA, and took a job as a greenhouse manager in Bakersfield some nine years after the killing. In 1977 he became an aide to Kern County (Bakersfield) Supervisor Harvey.

open court. (1) A court whose sessions may be attended by spectators. (2) A court that is in session for the transaction of judicial business.

opening statement. First statement made by prosecutors to the jury, in which they outline the case, pointing out the general proof that will be offered. The purpose is to give the jury a brief summary of the case, enabling it to understand the evidence.

Operation El Dorado. A task force headquartered in New York and launched in 1992 by the U.S. Treasury Department to interdict illegal, drug-generated, bulk cash transfers. During its first six months, the task force seized more than $52 million in cash, arrested 128 suspected money launderers, and dismantled financial networks responsible for processing hundreds of millions of dollars.

Operation Greylord. An unprecedented, four-year-long FBI undercover investigation of the Cook County, IL, court system (the nation's largest unified court system). As of June 7, 1985, the inquiry had resulted in the indictments of 28 persons, including 6 judges and 13 lawyers; 17 of the 28 have either pleaded guilty or been found guilty, while 3, including a judge, have been acquitted.

In the trial of former Circuit Judge Murphy it was disclosed that he fixed more than 100 drunk-driving cases for $100 each. He was convicted of 24 counts and sentenced to 10 years in prison. A former narcotics court judge boasted in conversations recorded by the FBI that he could "make $1,000 a week fixing cases." This is believed to be the first time the FBI bugged the private chambers of a judge. Circuit Judge Devine received one-third of lawyers' legal fees in a kickback scheme. He was convicted of 47 charges related to bribery and extortion and is serving 15 years in prison.

Operation Guatemalan Auto Theft Enforcement (GATE). This multiagency task force involves the states of Texas, New Mexico, Arizona, and California. A November 1995 operation resulted in the recovery of 31 vehicles and the arrest of seven suspects. *See also* Cargo CATS

Operation Identification. A program of engraving or otherwise marking property with a unique identification number that is intended to deter potential burglars and increase the probability of recovering stolen property. The National Sheriffs' Operation Identification Registry provides the computer storage service for individuals to register their property. This file is accessible to law enforcement agencies on a round-the-clock basis.

Operation Intercept. A program instituted on the U.S.-Mexican border on September 21, 1969, to cut off the flow of narcotics, marijuana, and dangerous drugs into the United States. The program was jointly undertaken by the U.S. Treasury and Justice departments, with the Bureau of Customs, Immigration and Naturalization Service, Bureau of Narcotics and Dangerous Drugs, Coast Guard, Navy, Federal Aviation Administration, and General Services Administration participating.

Operation Polar Cap. In March 1989 federal agents seized three boxes of documents from the New York City branch of Continental Illinois Bank. The seizure was the culmination of a two-year investigation that broke up a Colombian Medellin Cartel money-laundering organization operating in Europe, South America, and the United States. Colombian cocaine manufactured by the Medellin Cartel was sold on the streets of New York. The cash from sales was packed in boxes, labeled as jewelry, and delivered by armored car to La Guardia Airport for shipment to Los Angeles. It was then delivered to nearby banks and deposited as if it were the proceeds of jewelry sales; later it was transferred by wire back to NY banks, which unsuspectingly wired it to accounts in other NY banks. Ultimately, the money was wire-transferred to banks in Colombia. During the first phase of the investigation, 127 persons were arrested. A federal grand jury in Atlanta returned indictments against two South American banks, charging their involvement in laundering more than $300 million in drug proceeds from the United States. On November 25, 1991, 50 people in five states were charged with operating a coast-to-coast ring. More than $10 million in cash and bank accounts was seized.

Operation Rescue. A militant antiabortion group founded by Randall Terry that uses civil disobedience in its attempts to close abortion clinics. Major confrontations with the police have occurred in Wichita, Los Angeles, Pittsburgh, Milwaukee, south Miami, Philadelphia, Phoenix, and throughout New Jersey. The National Abortion Federation collects data regarding violence against abortion clinics.

operations. In criminal justice, the activity resulting from planning and controlling the current ongoing activities of a police force. This term may also refer to the office or communications center from which current operations are controlled.

opiate. Any natural or synthetic drug that exerts actions on the body similar to those induced by morphine, the major pain-relieving agent obtained from the opium poppy.

opiate narcotic. A drug that has both sedative and analgesic actions.

opinion. The official announcement of a decision of a court, together with the reason for that decision. An oral opinion is usually very brief. A full (or written) opinion is usually lengthy, presenting in detail the reasoning leading to the decision. A memorandum opinion (or memorandum decision) is also in writing but is a very brief statement of the reasons for a decision, without detailed explanation. A *per curiam* opinion is one issued by the court as a whole, without indication of individual authorship, while a signed opinion is one bearing the name of the individual judge who authored it, whether or not issued on behalf of the whole court. A majority opinion is that of the majority of the judges hearing the case; a dissenting (or minority) opinion is that of one or more judges who disagree with the decision of the majority; a concurring opinion states the reasoning of one or more judges who agree with the majority decision, but on different grounds.

opinion evidence. The fact that a person is of an opinion that a fact in issue, or relevant to the issue, does or does not exist is admissible only in exceptional cases. Generally, witnesses must testify to facts rather than stating their opinions or conclusions.

opium. The dried-out juice obtained from parts of the poppy *Papaver somniferum*, whose petals may be white, red, mauve, or purple. Nineteenth-century scientists isolated and intensified the poppy's strengths. Opium gum and poppy-straw concentrate hold the natural alkaloid morphine, still regarded as unsurpassed in treating severe pain. Heroin, chemically treated morphine, is now a worldwide problem as a street drug. Heroin is usually a powder, white or beige or chocolate brown, nearly always produced by criminals, primarily from poppies illicitly grown in remote corners of Asia or Mexico. Illegal fields of poppies alternate with wheat in Pakistan's Northwest Frontier Province. In 1979, when opium was declared illegal, 32,376 hectares (80,000 acres) were planted. In 1984, fewer than 2,500 hectares were said to remain. Federal authorities estimate they seize less than 10% of the heroin entering the U.S.—believed to be more than four metric tons each year. The El Paso Intelligence Center in Texas was created in 1974 to deter the renewed influx of heroin from Mexico, following the severing of the trade that led from Turkey through Marseilles, France, to the U.S.—the so-called French Connection. The center now collects and dispenses worldwide narcotics information and is staffed by U.S. agencies: Immigration, FBI, Coast Guard, FAA, Internal Revenue, DEA, Marshals Service, and Customs.

O.R. Own recognizance. *See also* Manhattan Bail Project

oral evidence. Evidence given by the spoken word, as contrasted with documentary or real evidence. Sometimes referred to as parol evidence.

order. A communication, written, oral, or by signal, that conveys instructions from a superior to a subordinate. In a broad sense, the terms order and command are synonymous. However, an order implies discretion as to the details of execution, whereas a command does not.

order *nisi*. A conditional order.

order of recognizance or bail. In New York, an order setting bail or releasing a person on his own recognizance.

order to show cause. A court order calling on the opposing side to give a reason why a request of the petitioner should not be granted.

ordinance. A law of an authorized subdivision of a state, such as a city or a county.

ordinary care. The degree of care exercised by ordinarily prudent persons.

ordnance. Weapons, ammunition, explosives, vehicles, and confrontation material collectively, together with the necessary maintenance and equipment.

Oregon boot. A device placed on the ankle and foot of a person to impede his or her walking or running. It has been used on convicts working outside of prison, such as on road gangs, and also in transferring prisoners. It consists generally of heavy metal contrivances, something like shoes or boots, that are joined by a chain of such length that a person can take only short steps.

organic law. The fundamental law or constitution.

organized crime. A complex pattern of activity that includes the commission of statutorily defined offenses, in particular the provision of illegal goods and services, but also carefully planned and coordinated instances of offenses by fraud, theft, and extortion groups, which are uniquely characterized by the planned use of both legitimate and criminal professional expertise and the use, for criminal purposes or organizational features, of legitimate business, including availability of large capital resources, disciplined management, division of labor, and focus upon maximum profit; also, the persons engaged in such a pattern of activity. Organized crime is not a statutory offense (a defined offense to which a penalty is attached). The Federal Omnibus Crime Control Act of 1970 defines organized crime for administrative purposes as: "the unlawful activities of the members of a highly organized, disciplined association engaged in supplying illegal goods and services, including but not limited to gambling, prostitution, loan-sharking, narcotics, labor racketeering, and other unlawful activities of members of such organizations." On July 28, 1984, then-president Reagan named a 20-member commission, headed by Judge Irving R. Kaufman, to analyze organized crime and recommend remedies. The President's Commission on Organized Crime (PCOC) defines the criminal group involved in organized crime as "a continuing, structured collectivity of persons who utilize criminality, violence, and a willingness to corrupt in order to gain and maintain power and profit." Characteristics are organizational continuity; hierarchical structure; restricted membership; criminality, violence, and power; legitimate business involvement; and use of specialists. A survey for the PCOC estimates that 1986 net income from organized crime activity ranged between $26.8 billion and $67.7 billion. The Treasury Department estimates that $110 billion in narcotics profits are laundered in the United States annually. Between 1982 and 1989, 60 banks were convicted of laundering money and 25 were fined $10,000 or less. In 1989, the Bank of Commerce and Credit International (BCCI) paid a $15 million settlement after pleading guilty to conspiring to launder drug proceeds. Based in Luxembourg, BCCI had offices in 73 countries and over $20 billion in assets. *See also* laundering money; Mafia

Organized Crime and Racketeering (OCR) Section. In 1951, the Kefauver Committee concluded that "there is a sinister criminal organization known as the Mafia operating throughout the country." The OCR office of the Department of Justice was established in 1954 to lead coordinated investigations of organized crime. By 1957 there were only 10 attorneys in OCR. In 1961 Attorney General Robert Kennedy took an active interest in the investigation and prosecution of organized crime figures. That year, only 49 such people were convicted, but by the time Kennedy left the DOJ in 1965, convictions had increased to

468. The Intelligence and Special Services Unit provides a comprehensive, central intelligence file devoted exclusively to organized crime. The OCR section develops and coordinates nationwide enforcement programs to suppress the illicit activities of organized criminal groups, including narcotics trafficking; loan-sharking; vice; and the illegal infiltrating of legitimate businesses, labor unions, and the political process. For further information, contact: Organized Crime and Racketeering Section, Criminal Division, DOJ, Criminal Division, 950 Pennsylvania Ave., Washington, DC 20530-0001.

Organized Crime Control Act of 1970. Signed into law by President Nixon on October 15, 1970, the law broadens the fight against organized crime and charges the FBI with investigating bombings of, and bombing attempts on, any property of the federal government or that of any institution or organization receiving federal financial assistance.

Organized Crime, National Council on. Created by President Richard M. Nixon on June 4, 1970, for the purpose of controlling organized crime by coordinating efforts of the various federal agencies. Attorney General John N. Mitchell was named chairman. The council was composed of the postmaster general, the secretaries of labor and the treasury, and the heads of all federal investigative agencies.

organized deception of the public. Certain crimes against trust and ethics involving conspiracy by persons in high office to deceive the public concerning particular events. *See also* Teapot Dome Scandal; Tweed, William Marcy; Watergate affair

organoleptic. Testing or identification by means of the senses—commonly smell or taste.

original jurisdiction. The authority of a court to hear and determine a lawsuit when it is initiated.

orphanage. A facility, generally county or state funded, for children who become wards of the state due to abandonment or any form of abuse or neglect. The first orphanage in North America was founded by Ursuline nuns in 1792 after Indians massacred adult settlers in Natchez, Mississippi.

orphans' court. A court, so-called in NJ, PA, DE, and MD, that has jurisdiction over probate, administration of estates, and guardianship of minors. Called also surrogate's court. *See also* surrogate

Osborn, Albert Sherman. An American handwriting analyst (1858–1946) whose testimony was of substantial importance in the conviction of Bruno Hauptmann in the Lindbergh kidnapping case. *See also* kidnapping

ostracism. A form of punishment administered within a social or community group, in contrast with banishment. Neighborly help is forbidden, and even aid by the members of one's family is denied. Often it is accompanied by sneers and contemptuous attitudes or by complete indifference. Today the attitude of the public toward the ex-convict or the parolee is one of ostracism.

O.T.B. (OTB). Abbreviation for off-track betting. Legalized in New York City, where it started operations in April 1971. Now operated under government direction in many cities.

other crimes. When a person is being tried for one crime, the state cannot prove the commission by the accused of another crime in no way connected with the crime charged. But if the other crime was committed as part of the same transaction and tends to explain or qualify the fact in issue, it may be shown. The rule may also be stated thus: when it is legally permitted to prove a fact, such evidence cannot be excluded merely because it tends to prove a crime other than that for which the accused is on trial. Whenever the existence of any particular intention, knowledge, good or bad faith, malice, or other state of mind is in issue and the commission of another crime tends to prove its existence, the other crime may be shown.

overcriminalization. Enactment of legislation making marginal acts criminal and re-sulting in more criminal laws than can be enforced or are necessary for the protection of society and the safety of life and property.

Overeaters Anonymous. Support and self-help group for people struggling with weight problems. Address: P.O.Box 44020, Rio Rancho, NM 87174-4020.

overt act. In criminal law, an act done to further a plan, conspiracy, or intent. In a criminal conspiracy case, mere planning is insufficient to constitute the crime; an overt act to further the plan must be done. The same applies in a criminal attempt case.

Overtown. A civil disturbance in 1989 that began when Miami police officer William Lozano shot the driver of a speeding motorcycle, which then crashed into a car, killing both drivers. Within an hour of this incident, residents of the city's Overtown neighborhood began pelting police officers and emergency workers with rocks and bottles. Three days of rioting followed. Lozano, claiming self-defense, was tried on two counts of manslaughter, convicted in December 1989, and sentenced to seven years in prison. An appeals court ordered a new trial in Orlando in 1991, ruling that the Miami jury was pressured into its decision by the possibility of more violence. A not-guilty verdict was reached on May 28, 1993, in the appeal. *See also* McDuffie, Arthur

oyez. Means hear ye; a phrase often used to begin sessions in court.

P

paedophilia. *See* pedophilia

pandering. The activity of procuring another person for the purpose of prostitution. The Los Angeles Police Department during May 1985 began arresting producers of hardcore sex films under the state's pandering law, which carries a mandatory three-year prison term.

panel. Schedule or roll containing the names of jurors summoned for service.

panhandle. To approach people and beg, especially in a public place.

Panoptican plan. Model for prison architecture developed by Jeremy Bentham in 1791. The model was circular, with all cells on the outside. It was thought that a guard stationed at the center of the circle could observe all the prisoners on the many-tiered circular structure. Although the idea proved much less efficient than expected and was not widely adopted, an example of this structure is still in use in Joliet, IL.

paradigm. A collection of the major assumptions, concepts, and propositions in an area of business or research that suggests how organizational structure or operations should be approached. A paradigm resembles a model in that it serves to orient research and theorizing.

paraffin test. A technique of coating the hands of a person with melted paraffin. After the paraffin cools and hardens, the "glove" is removed by cutting with scissors and the inside surface is treated with a diphenylamine solution. If nitrates or nitrites are present a distinctive color is produced, thus indicating the presence of gun-powder residue. This test is not considered reliable due to the prevalence of nitrates and nitrites.

paralegals. Employees, also known as legal assistants, of law firms, who assist attorneys in the delivery of legal services. Through formal education, training, and experience, legal assistants gain knowledge of the legal system and substantive and procedural law. Paralegals may conduct interviews, investigations, and legal research, and perform limited functions in court, such as filing motions. They may not represent or give legal advice to clients. *See also* National Association of Legal Assistants; National Federation of Paralegal Associations

parameter. (1) A measurable quantity whose magnitude can vary, depending on the areas or objects being compared, such as a predetermined length for a piece of string or for the cylinder capacity of a motor vehicle; similar to a benchmark. (2) A quantity in a mathematical calculation that may be assigned any arbitrary value.

pardon. There are two kinds of pardons of offenses: the absolute pardon, which fully restores to the individual all rights and privileges of a citizen, and the conditional pardon, which requires a condition to be met before the pardon is officially granted. Article II, Section 2, of the Constitution gives the president full pardon power in all cases involving federal infractions. In the Department of Justice there is an Office of the Pardon Attorney with responsibility for handling all administrative procedures concerning pardons. In most states the governor has full pardoning power, although in some states he or she must share this power with the state senate or some other body. In 1979, Governor Ray Blanton of Tennessee was removed from office after pardoning 52 prisoners; he was subsequently convicted in 1981 of 11 counts of extortion, fraud, and conspiracy. *See also* clemency

Pardon Attorney. This federal office receives all petitions for executive clemency; initiates the necessary investigations; and prepares recommendations of the attorney general to the president involving all forms of executive clemency, including pardon, commutation, reduction of sentence, remission of fine, and reprieve. For further information, contact: Office of the Pardon Attorney, DOJ, 500 First Street, NW, Suite 400, Washington, DC 20530.

parens patrine (Lat., lit.). Father of his country; a doctrine under which a government supervises children and other persons who have been termed legally incapable. It often takes the form of supervision analogous to that of a parent.

parenteral. Introduced into the human body by some means other than through the intestines as a result of ingestion, such as by piercing the skin or mucous membrane with a needle, bite, cut, or abrasion.

parity pay. Generally, the same pay for the same job classification. Police associations and unions in collective bargaining survey surrounding and similar jurisdictions to ensure their members are compensated as well or better than their counterparts in other locations.

Parker, Isaac C. On May 2, 1875, federal judge Parker arrived in Fort Smith to reestablish the federal court in the Western District of Arkansas. Eight days after his arrival, he opened his first term of court. Eighteen persons were brought before him charged with murder, 15 were convicted, and 8 were sentenced to die. One was later shot during an escape attempt and another had his sentence commuted to life imprisonment. The mass hanging of the remaining 6 brought international attention to the court and its judge, who became known as "the hanging judge." In 21 years, Parker sentenced 168 persons to death, of whom 88 where actually hanged. He died in 1896 at the age of 58.

Parker, William H. (1902–1966). Born in Lead, SD, this law officer began his career with the Los Angeles Police Department in 1927, earned a law degree and became a member of the California bar in 1930, and was promoted to sergeant in 1931. Rising to the rank of inspector in 1940, he served in the army during World War II and participated in the reorganization of police forces in several German cities while overseas. After the war he returned to the LAPD, becoming deputy chief of internal affairs in 1949. He was named chief in 1950 and a year later, amid charges of vice-squad corruption, he disciplined more than 40 officers, freeing the department from political interference. He was admitted to the federal bar in 1956. The LAPD headquarters building was named the Parker Center in his memory.

Park Police. The U.S. Park Police are part of the Department of the Interior, and most are assigned within the Washington, DC, metropolitan area. They have the same police powers as local police and act as hosts to park visitors. For further information, contact: National Capital Region, Park Service, Department of the Interior, 1100 Ohio Dr., SW, Room 117, Washington, DC 20242.

Park Rangers. The rangers of the National Park Service carry out conservation efforts to protect plant and animal life from fire, disease, and visitor abuse. They plan and conduct programs of public safety, including law enforcement and rescue work. For further information, contact: Ranger Activities and Protection Division, National Park Service, 1849 C Street NW, Washington, DC 20240.

parole. A method of completing a prison sentence in the community rather than in confinement. The paroled offender can legally be recalled to prison to serve the remainder of his or her sentence if he or she does not comply with the conditions of parole. Parole has its roots in the English tradition. In 1617, the privy counsel of the English Parliament standardized the previously subjective practice of some English judges to spare the lives of condemned felons by exiling them to the newly created colonies of Australia and America. Alexander Maconochie and his disciple, Sir Walter Crofton, were early reformers. In the United States the first real parole system was begun in Philadelphia in 1822. The force behind American parole methods was Zebulon Brockway.

parole agency. A correctional agency that may or may not include a paroling authority, and whose principal functions are pre-release investigations, parole-plan preparation for prospective parolees, and the supervision of adults having parole or other conditional-release status.

parole board. An administrative board that by law has charge of granting paroles and of supervising parolees. Such boards usually follow laws governing who may be granted parole and the length of time parolees remain under its control. The concept was originally devised by Alexander Maconochie, called ticket-of-leave, and applied to prisoners transported to Norfolk Island as a method of improving discipline.

parole clinic. A facility that provides intensive aid to parolees who require continued mental health services and therapy after re-

STATE OF CONNECTICUT BOARD OF PAROLE

PAROLE AGREEMENT

You have been granted a parole by the Board of Parole. It will be effective on the date indicated or as soon thereafter as your parole program is approved by the Division of Parole.

Parole gives you the opportunity to serve the remainder of your sentence outside of the instiution. The Board of Parole may grant you a certifictate of early discharge from your sentence at the recommendation of your parole officer after you have shown satisfactory progress while you are on parole. Until that time, or until the maximum expiration date of your sentence, you will remain in the legal custody of the Board of Parole and under the supervision of the Division of Parole of the department of Correction.

A parole officer will be assigned to work with you and help you adjust to life in the community. The parole officer will attempt to help you and will be available for counseling should any problems arise. You are urged to talk over any difficulties with the parole officer. The parole officer will also submit reports on your progress to the Commissioner of Correction, and, if requested, to the Board of Parole.

It is also the parole officer's duty to make sure that you abide by the conditions of parole found on the other side of this page. Those conditions have been carefully designed as guidelines for acceptable behaviour while you are on parole. If you should violate any of those conditions of parole, the officer has the authority from the Chairman of the board of Parole and the Commissioner of correction to return you to custody so that your parole status may be reviewed by the Board of Parole. By signing your name to the other side of this page you indicate your consent to abide by the standard and individual conditions of your parole listed there, as well as your awareness that failure to abide by those conditions will constitute a violation of parole and may result in your return to custody. It is the hope of the Board of Parole in granting you this parole that you will accept it and its conditions as a opportunity to prove to yourself and to others that you are capable of living as a responsible, law-abiding citizen of society and of your community.

Parolee_____ No._____ Release on or after _____

CONDITIONS OF PAROLE

1). Upon my release I will report to my parole officer as directed and follow the parole officer's instructions.
2). I will report to my parole officer in person and in writing whenever and wherever the parole officer directs.
3). I agree that the parole officer has the right to visit my residence or place of employment at any reasonable time.
4). I will maintain such gainful employment or other activity as approved by my parole officer.
5). I will notify my parole officer within 48 hours of any changes in my place of residence, in my place of employment, or of any change in my marital status.
6). I will notify my parole officer within 48 hours if at any time I am arrested for any offense.
7). I will not at any time have firearms, ammunition, or any other weapon in my possession or under my control.
8). I will not leave the State of Connecticut without prior permission of my parole officer.
9). I will obey all laws, and to the best of my ability fulfill all my legal obligations.
10). I will not at any time use, or have in my possession or control, any illegal drug or narcotic.
11). Your release on parole is based upon the conclusion of the Parole Panel that there is a reasonable probability that you will live and remain at liberty without violating the law and that your release is not incompatible with the welfare of society. In the event that you engage in conduct in the future which renders this conclusion no longer valid, then your parole will be revoked or modified accordingly.
12). I also agree to abide by the following INDIVIDUAL CONDITONS:

Signed _____

Witness _____ Date_____

(Chairman   *Secretary)*

For the Board of Parole _____

lease. This facility is usually maintained by a governmental agency, such as a mental health or social service.

Parole Commission. *See* United States Parole Commission

parole contract. A statement of the conditions that a parolee is to observe while on parole. Violation of these conditions is grounds for the revocation of the parole and for the return of the parolee to the institution.

parolee. A person who has been conditionally released by a paroling authority from a prison prior to the expiration of his or her sentence, placed under the supervision of a parole agency, and required to observe conditions of parole.

parole officer. An employee of a parole agency whose primary duties are the supervision of parolees and pre-parole investigation or planning.

parole revocation. The administrative action of a paroling authority removing a person from parole status in response to a violation of lawfully required conditions of parole, including the prohibition against commission of a new offense, and usually resulting in a return to prison.

parole supervision. Guidance, treatment, or regulation of a convicted adult who is obliged to fulfill conditions of parole or other conditional release, authorized and required by statute, performed by a parole agency, and occurring after a period of prison confinement.

parole supervisory caseload. The total number of clients registered with a parole agency or officer on a given date or during a specified period.

parole suspended. The withdrawal by a paroling authority or parole agent of a person's effective parole status, usually accompanied by a return to confinement, pending a determination of whether parole should be revoked or pending resolution of some problem that may require a temporary return to confinement.

parole evidence. Oral or verbal evidence; that which is given by word of mouth; the ordinary kind of evidence given by witnesses in court.

parole violation. An act, or a failure to act, by a parolee that does not conform to the conditions of parole.

paroling authority. A board or commission that has the authority to release on parole adults committed to prison, to revoke parole or other conditional release, and to discharge from parole or other conditional release status.

parricide. The murder of one's father, mother, or legal guardian.

participant observation. A technique with which a researcher attempts to develop a theory through direct exploration or confirm a hypothesis through participation in and observation of the group under study, in the group's natural environment. Often only a few members of the group serve as informants, while all others are simply observed.

parsimony (law of). The law of parsimony, also called the law of economy or Ockham's razor, proposes that a problem should be stated in its basic and simplest terms. Credit for outlining the law is usually given to William of Ockham (1284–1347?).

parties to offense. All persons culpably concerned in the commission of a crime, whether they directly commit the act constituting the offense or facilitate, solicit, encourage, aid, or abet its commission; also, in some penal codes, persons who assist one who has committed a crime to avoid arrest, trial, conviction, or punishment.

Part I offenses. In Uniform Crime Reports, the group of offenses, also called major offenses, for which UCR publishes counts of reported instances and which consist of those that meet the following five-part criterion: (a) are most likely to be reported to police, (b) can easily be established by police as to whether they occurred, (c) occur in all geographical areas, (d) occur with sufficient frequency to provide an adequate basis for comparison, and (e) are serious crimes by nature and/or volume. Part I offenses are: 1. criminal homicide (murder and nonnegligent or voluntary manslaughter); 2. forcible rape (actual or attempted); 3. robbery (firearm, knife or cutting instrument, other dangerous weapon, or strongarm); 4. aggravated assault (firearm, knife or cutting instrument, other dangerous weapon, hands, fist, feet, etc.—aggravated injury); 5. burglary (forcible entry, unlawful entry—no force, attempted forcible entry); 6. larceny theft; 7. motor vehicle theft; and 8. arson (added to the Part I offenses in 1979 by congressional action).

Part II offenses. In Uniform Crime Reports, crimes that are less serious than Part I offenses, with numbers continuing after the 8 Part I categories: 9. simple (in contrast with aggravated) assault; 10. forgery and counterfeiting; 11. fraud; 12. embezzlement; 13. stolen property (buying, receiving, possessing); 14. vandalism; 15. weapons (carrying, possessing, etc.); 16. prostitution and commercialized vice; 17. sex offenses (except forcible rape, prostitution, and commercialized vice); 18. drug abuse violations; 19. gambling; 20. offenses against the family and children; 21. driving under the influence; 22. liquor law violations; 23. drunkenness; 24. disorderly conduct; 25. vagrancy; 26. all other offenses (except traffic law violations); 27. suspicion (no specific offense; suspect released); 28. curfew and loitering violations (juveniles); and 29. runaways (juveniles). Uniform Crime Reports publishes both reported-crime and arrest data for Part I offenses, but only arrest data for Part II offenses.

party. (1) A person or group of persons constituting one side of an issue, undertaking, or dispute. (2) A person or persons constituting one or more sides of a contractual agreement.

party-dominated process. The aspect of the adversary system that gives to the judge the passive role of umpire and allows the adversaries (prosecution and defense) to be the major forces in the trial. In a party-dominated process, the judge cannot initiate or continue proceedings. The parties control the factual,

and, to a large extent, the legal boundaries of a case.

passive alcohol sensor. Passive alcohol sensing as a concept dates from the early 1970s, becoming technically feasible only recently through microchip technology. The Honda Motor Company developed a passive alcohol sensor based on a semiconductor sensor; but it had limitations for police applications, as the unit was not specific to alcohol, was sensitive to other contaminants such as cigarette smoke, and would not hold a constant calibration. The ALCO-Sensor III breath analyzer, made in St. Louis, MO, by Intoximenters Inc., has been purchased by the California Highway Patrol and Ventura, CA, Police Department. The hand-held tester allows on-the-spot alcohol detection to determine probable cause for further mandatory testing (blood, breath, or urine) under the implied consent law. Firms are also marketing portable self-administered breath analyzers. One, called Ensure, delivers readings of blood-alcohol content accurate within plus or minus 10 percent (not admissible as evidence in court).

The Insurance Institute for Highway Safety (IIHS), in collaboration with Lion Laboratories, Ltd., U.K., and Prototypes, Inc., MD, developed a unit based on an electrochemical fuel cell sensor with a pump that draws air from in front of a person being tested over the sensor. The alcohol content of the air is analyzed and the result shown on a three-digit light-emitting diode display. Laboratory tests indicate that the system is relatively unaffected by cigarette smoke or other anticipated contaminants. The unit is built into a standard police flashlight so that it can be operated at night. The device was demonstrated and evaluated with the assistance of the Charlottesville Police Department.

passive intrusion sensor. A passive sensor in an intrusion-alarm system that detects an intruder within the range of the sensor. Examples are a sound-sensing detection system, a vibration detection system, an infrared motion detector, and an E-field sensor.

passive ultrasonic alarm system. An alarm system that detects the sounds in the ultrasonic frequency range caused by an attempted forcible entry into a protected structure. The system consists of microphones, a control unit containing an amplifier, filters, an accumulator, and a power supply. The unit's sensitivity is adjustable.

pastoral counseling. A special field that combines insights and procedures from religion, psychiatry, and the social sciences. Major seminaries offer courses in principles of psychology and methods of counseling. Clergy trained by such courses work with students, patients in hospitals, inmates of prisons, and members of the armed forces. The nation's first "clergy malpractice" lawsuit was dismissed in mid-trial, on May 16, 1985, by a Glendale, CA, superior court judge who ruled that any judicial effort to set standards for pastoral counseling would violate the First Amendment's separation of church and state.

patent. A form of property right giving an inventor of a new product, design, or process (or the owner of the patent, if sold) the sole legal right to use, not use, or dispose of the invention. Patents in the United States are issued for a period of 17 years by the U.S. Patent Office, with renewal possible after significant modification of the original design. One very large settlement in a patent-infringement suit was $55.8 million in *Pfizer Inc. v. International Rectifier Corp. and Rochelle Laboratories* over the antibiotic dioxycycline on July 5, 1983.

patent and copyright policy. Advice is supplied to the Department of Justice and other agencies on government patent policy by the Intellectual Property Section, which also determines improper uses of copyrights and patents as marketing devices. Address: Intellectual Property Section, Antitrust Division, DOJ, 10th & Constitution Ave., NW, Criminal Division,(Computer Crime & Intellectual Property section), John C. Keeney Building, Suite 600, Washington, DC 20530.

path analysis. A technique for estimating the effects that a set of independent variables has on a dependent variable from a set of observed correlations, given a set of hypothesized causal, asymmetric relations among the variables. Path diagrams indicate causality among variables with arrows. With causal ordering among the variables assumed, intercorrelations among them can be analyzed to obtain estimates of the path coefficients, one for each arrow. The path coefficients indicate the effect that each independent variable has on the dependent variable. The major limitation of this technique is the quality of the researcher's assumption regarding the causal ordering among the variables.

pathogenic. Causing disease.

pathologist. A person who is educated, trained, and certified/licensed in pathology, the area of medicine dealing with the nature and causes of illness or injury.

pathology. (1) The science dealing with causes, development, and effects of disease. (2) The disease or abnormal condition itself.

patricide. The murder or murderer of one's father.

patrol beat. An area to which a patrol is assigned and to which it has primary responsibility for responding to calls for police assistance.

patrol car. An automobile, usually modified with special equipment, used by law enforcement agencies in performing the patrol function. The first patrol car was a Model "T" Ford used in Detroit in 1909.

patrol district. A geographical area that consists of more than one patrol beat and that may have its own police station and vehicle maintenance facilities.

patrolman. (1) The law enforcement officer who walks a beat or patrols areas by motor vehicle. (2) An official rank of a police officer, generally the beginning rank.

patronage, political. The promise or provision of public sector jobs by politicians, usually to individuals who have made significant campaign contributions or otherwise aided the politician to be elected.

patron saints. Since the early days of Christianity, certain saints and angels have been regarded as patrons of specific occupations, groups, localities, and nations. Patron saints and their constituents include: falsely accused, St. Raymund Nonnatus; firemen, St. Florian; jurists, St. Catherine of Alexandria and St. John Capistrano; lawyers, St. Ivo and St. Thomas More; mentally ill, St. Dympna; motorcyclists, Our Lady of Grace; motorists, St. Christopher and St. Frances of Rome; policemen, St. Michael; prisoners, St. Dismas, St. Barbara, and St. Joseph Cafasso; and social workers, St. Louise de Marillac.

pauper. One without means; one supported at the public expense.

PCBs (polychlorinated hiphenyls). PCBs are a group of chemicals that were widely used before 1970 in the electrical industry as a coolant. They caused environmental problems as they do not break down and can spread through the water, soil, and air. They have been linked to cancer and reproductive disorders and can cause liver function abnormalities. Government action has resulted in the control of the use, disposal, and production of PCBs in nearly all areas of the world, including the United States.

PCP. *See* phencyclidine

peace bond. A bond or bail fixed by a magistrate to ensure that the person bonded will keep the peace and not molest or injure someone against whom he or she has made threats or tried to harm. In 1970 a Hawaiian court declared the peace bond unconstitutional.

peaceful picketing. A right protected by Congress on June 24, 1936, with an act making it a felony to transport in interstate or foreign commerce persons to be employed to obstruct or interfere with the right of peaceful picketing during labor controversies. Amended in 1939. The provisions of the act do not apply to common carriers.

peace officers. This term is variously defined by state statutes, but generally includes sheriffs and their deputies, constables, marshals, members of municipal police forces, and other officers whose duty is to enforce and preserve the public peace.

Peace Officers' Memorial Day. A national observance day; May 15th of each year (during Police Week, established in 1962).

peculation. The wrongful conversion of property in one's custody or control to one's own use; embezzlement.

pecuniary value. Monetary value, such as that of a negotiable instrument, a commercial interest, or anything else whose primary significance is economic advantage.

pederasty. Anal sexual intercourse, usually defined in law as occurring between a man and a boy; sodomy.

pedestrian. Any person who is on foot or who is using a means of conveyance propelled by human power other than a bicycle. The term includes anyone who is operating a self-propelled wheelchair, tricycle, or motorized quadricycle because the individual is otherwise unable to move around because of disability.

pedomania. Additional term for pedophilia.

pedophile. One who indulges in pedophilia.

pedophilia. The use of a minor for sexual gratification by an adult. Sexual conduct between adult females and nonadult males is known to occur, but persons convicted of the crime of pedophilia are, almost without exception, males. They constitute a third of all institutionalized sex criminals, one of the largest classifications. Approximately two-thirds of the victims of pedophilic acts are prepubescent and adolescent girls, in about equal numbers. The act itself is seldom more than fondling. Sexual intercourse is rarely attempted, and actual penetration occurs only in about 2 percent of known cases. Genital acts, such as anal coitus and fellatio, occur more often when the pedophile's object is male. Pedophiles who have contact with boys under 12 tend to have a basic heterosexual orientation, while those whose objects are older boys are more likely to be homosexuals. Contrary to general belief, a large majority of pedophilic acts, especially involving females, are performed by relatives, neighbors, and acquaintances of the victim. A man who is sexually interested in young children is usually a shy, nonaggressive individual, while pedophiles who choose teenage girls have more assertive personalities.

peeling. A system used by safe burglars, whereby the outer surface of the safe door is peeled off, thus making access to the locking device available.

Peel, Sir Robert. (1788–1850). Born in Bury, Lancashire, England, and educated at Oxford. In 1812, Peel accepted the post of chief secretary for Ireland and, during his term of office, made his reputation as an able and incorruptible administrator. He sought passage of the Peace Preservation Act of 1814, which made possible the formation of a body of national police, later to become known as the Royal Irish Constabulary, popularly called The Peelers. In 1822, he accepted a seat in the cabinet of Parliament. As the British Home Secretary in 1829, Peel introduced into Parliament an act for improving the police in and near London. He believed that a community needed a protective body of well-selected and trained men in order to prevent crime and institute social control. He reformed criminal laws by limiting their scope and reducing unfair penalties. Peel removed the death penalty from more than 100 offenses. Most important, he established 12 fundamental principles of quality policing that are still applicable today.

Peeping Tom. A popular name for a person who trespasses for the purpose of observing persons inside a dwelling.

peer. (1) An equal. A trial jury must be composed of persons who are peers (members of the general class) of the accused. (2) A member of the British House of Lords.

penal. Of or pertaining to punishment or penalties.

penal administration. The maintenance and management of institutions and programs (as probation and parole) for the punishment and correction of criminals. Personnel include prison and parole board staffs; wardens; guards; medical, pedagogical, and psychiatric staffs; and probation and parole officers.

penal codes. Many states have adopted penal or criminal codes, the purpose of which is to define what acts shall be punished as crimes. In some, the code is intended to cover the whole law, and no act is a crime unless it is expressly declared so. In others, the code does not entirely abrogate the common law, insofar as it makes acts crimes, but merely sets it aside for expressly prohibited acts, leaving common law in force for other acts.

penal laws. The set of statutes imposing penalties of confinement for the commission of prohibited acts, the terms of that confinement, and the operations of the places of confinement. In the United States, the dominant penal law is the prison system.

penal servitude. Punishment that consists of confinement and hard labor.

penalty. A punishment by fine, imprisonment, or both, inflicted for violation of a law.

penalty, death. *See* execution; punishment, capital

pendens (Lat.). Pending; hanging.

Pendleton Act. *See* merit system

penetration. The insertion of the penis into a woman's body; in criminal law, the action is important in rape cases.

penitentiary. An institution for the imprisonment of convicted offenders.

penitentiary science. Jean Jacques Vilain, who founded the Maison de Force built in Ghent in 1773, is called the father of penitentiary science.

Pennsylvania (separate) system. Based on Quaker beliefs, a penal system espousing the individual isolation of prisoners to avoid their harmful influences on others. This approach to corrections was symbolized by the Eastern State Penitentiary, erected in 1829 at Cherry Hill in Philadelphia. Resembling a medieval fortress and containing an individual, walled-in exercise yard at the rear of each cell, the prison was designed for "separate and solitary confinement at labor, with instruction in labor, morals, and religion." To further ensure isolation and anonymity, prisoners were enshrouded in hoods.

penology. The study of various programs, social structures, and administrative organizations for the treatment of criminal offenders, along with the evaluation of the effectiveness of such programs.

pen register. In telephone company jargon, a dialed number recorder. The name pen register is derived from an older, manual system of recording numbers dialed from a particular phone. *See also* dialed number recorders

Pentagon Papers. On June 13, 1971, a series of articles was launched by the *New York Times* and the *Washington Post*, based on documents called the Pentagon Papers, which detailed how the United States had made key decisions regarding its involvement in the Vietnam War. The administration of President Richard Nixon obtained an injunction on June 15 against further articles in the series, but the Supreme Court disallowed the injunction on June 30. The Pentagon Papers' espionage trial of Dr. Daniel Ellsberg was dismissed by a federal judge on May 11, 1973, after disclosure that White House agents had committed burglary in seeking evidence.

penumbral right. A constitutional right that is not specifically articulated or guaranteed but is implied from other guarantees.

peonage. A condition of enforced servitude in which individuals are deprived of liberty and compelled to labor to repay some debt or other obligation, real or imagined, against their will.

pepper spray. A nonlethal product containing capsicum oleoresin, the essence of hot chili peppers, as its active ingredient. Originally developed by the U.S. Forestry Service to incapacitate bears, pepper spray acts as an inflammatory agent rather than an irritant. Popular brand names are CAP-STUN and Mace.

per annum (Lat.). By the year.

per capita (Lat., lit.). By heads; per person; by or for each person.

per curiam (Lat., lit.). By the court; an opinion of the full court, rather than one of an individual judge.

per diem (Lat.). By the day.

peremptory challenge. In the selection of jurors, challenges made by either side to certain jurors without assigning any reason, and which the court must allow.

perfidious. False; untrustworthy; disloyal.

perfidy. Treachery or faithlessness.

perimeter security. Perimeter security systems are based on all or any of these components: (1) a fence or wall, (2) towers, (3) electronic detection, and (4) patrols. In 1985, 717 inmates escaped from high- or medium-security prisons; 1,945 escaped from low- or minimum-security facilities. In that year, maximum security prisons used the following combinations of perimeter security: fence or wall, 92.7 percent; towers, 80.2 percent; detection, 38.4 percent; and patrols, 87.0 percent. The Green Haven Correctional Facility in New York (opened in 1949) has, as perimeter security, a 35-foot-high reinforced stone and concrete wall and 12 towers. Its wall has never been breached. Due to high costs, new prison construction relies on security systems other than masonry walls.

perjury. The intentional making of a false statement as part of testimony by a sworn witness in a judicial proceeding on a matter material to the inquiry.

permanent circuit. An alarm circuit that is capable of transmitting an alarm signal whether the alarm control is in access mode or secure mode; used, for example, on foiled fixed windows, tamper switches, and supervisory lines. *See also* permanent protection; supervisory alarm system

permanent protection. A system of alarm devices such as foil, burglar alarm pads, or lacing connected in a permanent circuit to provide protection whether the control unit is in the access mode or secure mode.

permit. An official paper identifying a person as one who is entitled to exercise some privilege under the law; also a license.

perpetrator. The chief actor in the commission of a crime, that is, the person who directly commits the criminal act. In law enforcement usage, culprit is a synonym. Where a crime involves two or more chief actors, they may be called co-perpetrators, cohorts, or accomplices.

perquisites. Anything of value—such as a car and driver, generous expense account, or free parking—that is derived from a position of employment or office in addition to the regular salary; often shortened to perks.

per se (Lat.). By itself alone, or in and of itself.

person. A human being, or a group of human beings considered a legal unit, having the lawful capacity to defend rights, incur obligations, prosecute claims, or be prosecuted or adjudicated. Examples of a legal unit constituting a legal person are a state, a territory, a government, a country, a partnership, a public or private corporation, or an unincorporated association.

personal property. Goods, money, and all movable property, as distinguished from real property—land and/or buildings.

personate. In law, a synonym for impersonate: with fraudulent intent, to assume the character and/or identity of another, without the latter's consent, and to gain some advantage or obtain something of value as a result. To pretend to be or assume the identity of another.

personnel security. A program or procedure whereby an organization seeks to protect its technology, materials, or equipment from loss or embezzlement by its own employees and nonemployees who have contact with personnel of the organization. Employees who are considered "not good risks" are precluded from access to certain types of information and materials.

PERT. *See* Program Evaluation and Review Technique

Peter Principle. A business theory formulated by Laurence Peter and suggesting that corporate employees tend to be promoted to their level of incompetence. The concept is that employees who perform their jobs well are rewarded with promotions, so that they ultimately reach positions just beyond their capabilities and skills. Since they no longer perform well in those jobs, promotions cease. The end result is that those who do their jobs poorly continue to do them, while those who do their jobs well are soon promoted out of them.

petit jury. A body at common law of 12 disinterested and impartial persons, chosen from the community in which the trial is held, who render a verdict on questions of fact submitted in the trial of a case. Later modified in many states by reduction in number of jurors, especially in civil cases, and by provisions for less-than-unanimous verdicts, except in the trial of persons accused of capital crimes. Called *petit* (Fr., small) because fewer in number than a grand jury; called also trial jury.

petition. (1) A written request made to a court asking for the exercise of its judicial powers, or asking for permission to perform some act for which the authorization of a court is required. (2) The First Amendment grants the privilege to petition the government for redress of grievances. The petition is the principal means by which an American citizen can inform an elected official of his or her opinions. Petition, in the form of letters to members of Congress, provides representatives with the opinions of their constituents.

petition not sustained. The finding by a juvenile court in an adjudicatory hearing that there is not sufficient evidence to sustain an allegation that a juvenile is a delinquent, status offender, or dependent.

petit larceny. Also called petty larceny; any larceny that is less than grand larceny. *See also* larceny

petty jury. Petit jury.

peyote. A spineless cactus with a small crown or button that is dried and then swallowed. Just as other churches use bread and wine as a sacrament, members of the Native American Church of North America, a 10,000-year-old faith with 250,000 members, use peyote in their religious sacraments, where it is seldom abused. The U.S. Supreme Court in April 1990 ruled that state drug laws may prohibit such religious use by Native Americans. But on July 1, 1991, Idaho enacted a bill allowing Native Americans to transport peyote, and 23 other states and the federal government now have similar laws allowing the religious use of peyote on reservations. The active ingredient in peyote is mescaline. When eaten, mescaline affects the brain within 30 to 90 minutes, and effects may persist for 12 hours. The average dose may produce clear and vivid hallucinations, including brightly colored lights, animals, and geometric designs. There is no delirium or amnesia, although there may be nausea. Three compounds are derived from mescaline— DOM (often referred to as STP), TMA, and MMDA. These induce similar effects at higher doses, but may be toxic.

pharmacognogy. The identification of plant materials used in pharmacy by means of their microscopic appearance.

pharmacology. The branch of science that deals with the study of drugs and their effects on living systems.

phencyclidine (PCP). A psychedelic surgical anesthetic also called angel dust. It is manufactured as a tablet, capsule, liquid, flake, spray, or crystal-like white powder. PCP can be ingested, smoked, sniffed, or injected. It is often sprinkled on crack, marijuana, tobacco, or parsley and smoked. The greatest danger of this drug is what it causes users to do to themselves and others: It can trigger psychotic attacks, rendering victims temporarily violent. Half of all PCP deaths are from drowning, as the substance raises the body temperature and lends a hot, dry feeling to the skin, prompting

users to swim. PCP chemicals associated with illegal laboratories include: cyclohexanone, sodium metabisulfite, potassium cyanide, piperidine, anhydrous ether, bromobenzene, magnesium turnings, iodine crystals, petroleum ether, hydrochloric acid, and sodium carbonate.

phenobarbital. A barbiturate, in white powder form, which has hypnotic and sedative properties.

phenol. A poison or antiseptic-carbolic acid.

phenolphthalein test. A preliminary test to determine if a stain is blood. If a positive reaction is obtained, further confirmation tests are conducted.

phobia. A persistent, irrational fear of a specific object, activity, or situation that leads to a compelling desire to avoid it.

Phobia subject	Phobia term
Animals	Zoophobia
Beards	Pogonophobia
Books	Bibliophobia
Churches	Ecclesiaphobia
Dreams	Oneirophobia
Flowers	Anthophobia
Food	Sitophobia
Graves	Taphphobia
Infection	Nosemaphobia
Lakes	Limnophobia
Leaves	Phyllophobia
Lightning	Astraphobia
Men	Androphobia
Money	Crometophobia
Music	Musicophobia
Sex	Genophobia
Shadows	Sciopphobia
Spiders	Arachnophobia
Sun	Heliophobia
Touch	Haptophobia
Trees	Dendrophobia
Walking	Basiphobia
Water	Hydrophobia
Women	Gynophobia
Work	Ergophobia
Writing	Graphophobia

phonetic alphabet (standard).

Letter	Phonetic equivalent
A	Alpha
B	Bravo
C	Charlie
D	Delta
E	Echo
F	Fox Trot
G	Golf
H	Hotel
I	India
J	Juliet
K	Kilo
L	Lima
M	Mike
N	November
O	Oscar
P	Papa
Q	Quebec
R	Romeo
S	Sierra
T	Tango
U	Uniform
V	Victor
W	Whiskey
X	X-ray
Y	Yankee
Z	Zulu

phonoscopy. The study of voice prints, voiceprint analysis, and identification.

photoelectric alarm system. An alarm system that employs a light beam and photoelectric sensor to provide a line of protection. Any interruption of the beam by an intruder is detected by the sensor. Mirrors may be used to change the direction of the beam. The maximum beam length is limited by many factors, some of which are the light source intensity, number of mirror reflections, detector sensitivity, beam divergence, fog, and haze.

photoengraving. A method of producing etched printing plates by photographic means.

photogrammetry. The process of obtaining measurements from photographs. It requires the use of two cameras to produce photographs from slightly different but known points of reference. Precise measurements are determined from an analysis of the photographs.

photomacrograph. A photograph of an object large enough to be seen by the naked eye but in which the lens of a microscope enlarges the size and detail of the object. This process is used in the examination of the cut surfaces of metal wire, in tool mark examinations, or firearm examinations.

photomicrograph. A photograph taken through a microscope of an object so small as to be invisible to the naked eye.

photostat. The trademarked name of a camera that makes copies of documents, letters, or drawings, on sensitized paper; also the copies made by means of this camera.

physical security. The portion of security concerned with physical measures designed to safeguard personnel; to prevent unauthorized access to equipment, facilities, material, and documents; and to safeguard equipment, facilities, material, and documents against espionage, sabotage, damage, and theft.

pickpocket. Generally, a highly skilled and professional thief who specializes in stealing valuables from the garments of victims. *See also* Moran, Thomas

PIE (Prison Industry Enhancement). A private-sector certification program that permits some states to sell prison-made goods in the open market.

Pill Addicts Anonymous. Support and self-help group for substance abusers. Address: P.O. Box 278, Reading, PA 19603.

Pinkerton, Allan. (1819–1884). Son of a Glasgow police sergeant, Pinkerton emigrated to the United States in 1842 and is considered the first professional detective in the United States. During a series of railway and express robberies in 1850, he opened his own firm (with E.G. Rucker as a partner), the Pinkerton National Detective Agency. He also organized the secret service division of the U.S. Army in 1861 and was made its first chief. Later, while employed by the Wilmington and Baltimore Railroad, he saved Abraham Lincoln's life by uncovering an assassination plot directed against the president.

PINS/CHINS/JINS/MINS. Acronyms used to name a class of juveniles often consisting of status offenders but variously defined in different jurisdictions. The INS portion of the acronym means in need of supervision, and P = Person, CH = Child, J = Juvenile, and M = Minor.

piquers. Criminals who use sharp instruments to stab their victims.

piracy. An act of violence committed at sea by individuals or groups from armed vessels, who are not acting under the authority of a state.

pirate. One who commits robbery on the high seas.

pistol. (1) In popular usage, any firearm, usually short-barreled, designed to be held and fired in one hand. Pistols came into use early in the sixteenth century, when the wheel lock first made them practical; (2) more precisely, such a firearm in which the chamber is an integral part of the barrel, especially a self-loading pistol, as distinguished from a revolver.

Pizza Connection. This case, investigated by the FBI in the early 1980s, involved the smuggling and distribution of heroin from Southeast Asia's Golden Triangle by various elements of the Sicilian Mafia. The proceeds from East Coast heroin sales were collected from pizza parlors in Queens, NY. The money was then deposited in commodities accounts held by New York City brokerage firms and frequently transported to banks in gym bags and suitcases. In addition, some of the cash, usually in small-denomination bills, was taken to Bermuda on private jets. Money was then wire-transferred from New York and Bermuda to Switzerland and from there to Italy, where it was used to buy more heroin. It was believed that at least $25.4 million was laundered in this case between 1980 and 1982. In 1984, 38 individuals were indicted. *See also* laundering money; Mafia

placement. The commitment or assignment of a person to a facility, or to any supervisory care or treatment program, as the result of either official or unofficial actions.

plagiarism. Theft of another's written work and/or ideas—whether intentional or accidental—and subsequent presentation of those words or ideas as the thief's own. Common ground rules: (1) You cannot use another writer's exact words without using quotation marks and offering a complete citation, indicating the source of the words so that a reader could find it in its original context. (2) It is unacceptable to edit or paraphrase another's words and present the revised version as your own work. (3) It is unacceptable to present another's ideas as your own, even if you use completely different words to express those ideas.

plain arch. A fingerprint pattern in which the ridges come in from one side and go out the other without recurving or turning back, and in which there is a smooth upward thrust of the lines at or near the center of the pattern. *See also* fingerprint patterns

plaintiff. A person who initiates a court action.

plain view rule. A procedure that permits police who are conducting a search to seize contraband if it is in plain view of the officers. Evidence seized in such a way may be admitted in a trial even if the search as a whole is found to be illegal.

plain whorl. A fingerprint pattern.

planning. The process of articulating expectations or goals using current and past data, and structuring or operating in order to achieve those goals. The most common types of planning are *Reactive planning*: a response to an immediate event, which may serve as a guide to future action in similar situations; *Contingency planning*: a method of responding to anticipated accidents, disasters, or other extraordinary events; *Operational efficiency planning*: a review of existing procedures in order to improve them; *Short-range planning*: solutions for immediate problems; *Long-range* or *Strategic planning*: the setting of goals for at least five years and creating methods to achieve them. *See also* Program Evaluation and Review Technique

plant security. The protection of a business or industrial plant from fire, burglary, sabotage, theft, or liability.

plaster of paris. A powdery substance used in police work for making casts of impressions in the earth and other soft surfaces. Such impressions are usually caused by shoe or tire imprints. Plaster of paris is composed of gypsum and can be obtained in pharmacies.

plasticized white phosphorus (PWP). A common ingredient in incendiary devices, PWP is produced by melting white phosphorus (WP) and stirring it into cold water. This produces small granules that are then mixed with a viscous solution of synthetic rubber. All the granules become coated with a film of rubber and thus are separated from one another. This rubbery mass is dispersed by an exploding munition, but does not break up to the extent that WP does.

platoon system. The division of policemen or firemen into shifts, or platoons, each of which is on duty during certain hours of a 24-hour day.

plea. A defendant's formal answer in court to the charge contained in a complaint, information, or indictment, that he or she is guilty or not guilty of the offense charged, or does not contest the charge. Among the possible pleas are *Initial* or *first plea*: the first plea to a given charge entered into the court record by or for the defendant; *Final plea*: the last plea to a given charge entered into the court record by or for the defendant; *Not-guilty plea*: a defendant's formal answer in court to the charge(s) contained in a complaint, information, or indictment, claiming that he or she did not commit the offense(s); *Not guilty by reason of insanity*: a defendant's formal answer in court to the charge(s) contained in a complaint, information, or indictment, claiming that he or she is not legally accountable for the offenses listed in the charging document due to insanity at the time they were committed; *Guilty plea*: a defendent's formal answer in court to the charge(s) contained in a complaint, information, or indictment, admitting that he or she did in fact commit the offense(s) listed; *Nolo contendere*: a defendant's formal answer in court to the charge(s) contained in a complaint, information, or indictment, stating that he or she will not contest the charge(s), but neither admits guilt nor claims innocence.

plea bargaining. The practice involving negotiation between prosecutor and defendant and/or his or her attorney, which often results in the defendant's entering of a guilty plea in exchange for the state's reduction of charges, or in the prosecutor's promise to recommend a more lenient sentence than the offender would ordinarily receive. Plea bargaining was allowed by the Supreme Court in *Brady v. United States.*, 197 U.S. 742 and by the California Supreme Court in *People v. West* (1970). Alaska abolished plea bargaining in 1975.

pleadings. Pleadings in criminal cases are comparatively simple, and, contrary to popular opinion, reversals of criminal cases on appeal are very infrequent. The pleadings used by the state in felony and some misdemeanor cases are the indictment and the information; in other misdemeanor cases, affidavits and complaints; by the defendant, usually an oral plea of guilty or not guilty. Other pleas, such as "former jeopardy' "autrefois acquit," "insanity," or "alibi" are available or required in particular states. Pleas in abatement, demurrers, motions to quash the indictment, and in arrest of judgment are also available under some circumstances.

pleasure-pain principle. The utilitarian concept that people endeavor to maximize pleasure (profit) and minimize pain (loss); making the anticipated penalty greater than the expected gain is believed to deter people from committing crimes.

pledge, legal. The process in which a debtor puts up or turns over to the creditor certain property to be held until the debt is satisfied, with property title remaining with the debtor. The creditor must have a lien on the property.

plenary. Full; entire; complete.

poach. To trespass, or to take game or fish illegally.

podular units. Separate jail or prison areas within the facility and containing cells and at least one common recreational area. Pods can house varying numbers of prisoners and are observed by a centrally located custodian.

poena (Lat.). Punishment; penalty.

pogrom. A massacre or wholesale slaughter spontaneously generated or incited and organized by a government or ruling class against a group of unarmed persons because of popular hatred or some sort of prejudice. It refers especially to the large-scale killing of Jews in czarist Russia, which from time to time was carried out by the governing class.

points of identification. In fingerprints, identical or matching ridge formations on more than one set of or copies of prints, used, for example, when comparing a latent print with known prints of a person. Eight to 12 matching points of identification are enough to establish that two or more prints were made by the same person; some courts require a minimum of 12 points.

poison. A substance that on being applied to the human body, internally or externally, is capable of causing illness or death by destroying or damaging vital functions.

police. As a means of social control, agents of the law charged with the responsibility of maintaining law and order among citizens. The policing function began to emerge in connection with military operations, and particularly for military occupation of conquered territories. Civil policing made its appearance in the form of the first guard system established by Pisistratus, ruler of Athens from 605 to 527 B.C. The Vigiles of Rome, in existence from 63 B.C. to A.D. 14, was the title

of the first police-fire integrated service under Caesar. With the decline of central authority, organized police forces disappeared in Europe until the late Middle Ages. Until well into the seventeenth century, civil authorities relied for the most part on the military to curb civil disorders. By the nineteenth century, most European nations were well on the road to developing modern professional police forces. These were usually centralized and under the control of an interior minister. England, an exception to this pattern, developed decentralized British police forces under the jurisdiction of local authorities. The reforms of Sir Robert Peel instituted in 1829 are seen as the beginning of England's modern police system. The United States, which traces its law enforcement system to colonial times, also has a decentralized police system featuring independent local, county, state, and federal agencies, each with a high degree of autonomy. Police in western Europe, as well as in many parts of Asia, Africa, and Latin America, are usually under complete central control. There are also several kinds of private, industrial, and railroad police. *See also* Peel, Sir Robert

police advisory boards. A citizens' group overseeing general policies of the police; sometimes organized on a neighborhood basis. *See also* civilian review boards

Police Athletic League. A program of police officers working with young people of the community. One of the first such programs was established by New York City's police department.

police bureau of criminal alien investigation, first. Started by the New York City Police Department on December 23, 1930. Its purpose was to bring to the attention of the U.S. immigration authorities any undesirable aliens subject to deportation under immigration laws, either because of their criminal records or their illegal entry into the United States.

police bureau of identification, first. Established by Captain Michael Patrick Evans on

January 1, 1884, for the Chicago Police Department. At its inception, only photographs were used. On June 1, 1887, the Bertillon system of identification was adopted; on November 1, 1904, the Sir E. R. Henry system of fingerprinting was added. Evans was in charge of the Bureau of Identification from its inception until his death on October 6, 1931. *See also* Bertillon method; Henry system

police civilian review boards. *See* civilian review boards; police advisory boards

police commission. Generally a body of appointed community members, approved by council, functioning to establish police policy and to review operational practices.

police corruption. Behavior by a police official that is unethical, dishonest, or criminal. Corruption is generally manifested in nine specific areas: (a) meals and services, (b) kickbacks, (c) opportunistic theft, (d) planned theft (e) shakedowns, (f) protection, (g) case fixing (h) private security, and (i) patronage. *See also* Serpico, Frank

police court. A municipal tribunal that tries those accused of violating local ordinances, acts as a tribunal for the preliminary examination and commitment of those accused of graver offenses, and is essentially equivalent to the criminal court of a justice of the peace in rural communities.

police decoys. In decoy operations, nonuniformed officers pose as potential high-risk victims—drunks, tourists, young women, the elderly, and the disabled—in high crime areas in order to attract and apprehend street criminals. *Blending* involves the use of police officers, posing as ordinary citizens, who are strategically placed in high-risk locations to observe and intervene should a crime occur. Among the more effective decoy and blending operations was New York City's Taxi-Truck Surveillance Unit, launched in 1970 to combat the growing number of nighttime assaults on truck and cab drivers. From 1970 to 1975, this approach reduced those assaults and robberies by almost 50 percent. *See also* SWAT

police department. A municipal—city, town, or village—law enforcement agency.

Police Executive Research Forum (PERF). A national organization of police chiefs from larger jurisdictions, the forum seeks to improve the professional quality of police services through discussion and debate among members, as well as research and development. Since larger jurisdictions encounter special problems in law enforcement, PERF provides a unique insight into cities with populations between 100,000 and 500,000. Address: 1120 Connecticut Ave., NW, Suite 930, Washington, DC 20036.

police jury. The administrative board of a parish in Louisiana, equivalent to a county's police commission elsewhere.

police power. The authority to legislate for the protection of the health, morals, safety, and welfare of the people. In the United States, police power is a reserved power of the states, provided for in state constitutions. The federal government can legislate for the welfare of its citizens only through specific congressional powers, such as taxation and the regulation of interstate commerce. Police power is the most important power exercised by individual state governments. Although resting in the executive branch of government, police power has been largely dependent on the judgment of the judiciary. During the twentieth century, the increasing power of both legal corporations and criminal enterprises whose business crosses state boundaries has created a greater need for federal authority. The Eighteenth, or Prohibition, Amendment (1920) was the most extensive attempt to grant police power to the federal government. In recent years further attempts have been made to exercise police powers on both national and state levels.

police review boards. A citizens' group composed of representatives of particular ethnic, racial, or other groups whose task is to investigate allegations of police misconduct.

police state. A state (as a totalitarian state or one operating under a dictatorship) that

Police organization

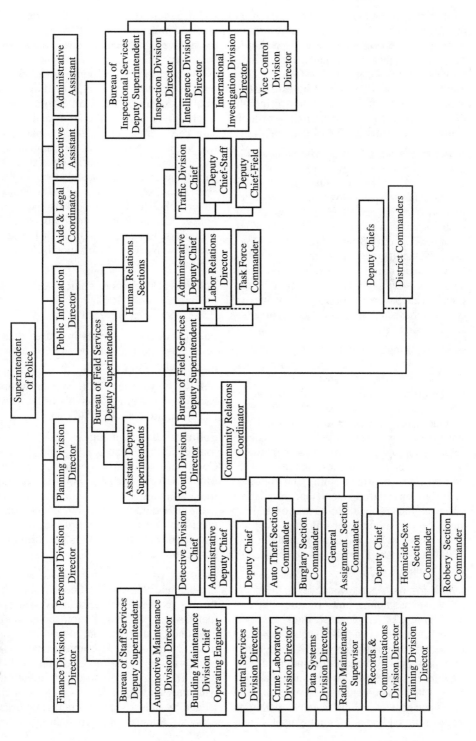

confers special powers over the rights of individuals upon its ordinary or secret police or military, vesting them with discretion to arrest, detain, incarcerate, and sentence individuals without formal trial or forms of law, and that refuses to be bound by established canons of due process or by the principle that the rights of individuals shall be adjudicated in established courts of justice.

police traffic squad, first. The famous old Broadway Squad of New York City was organized in 1860. This was the first unit of the police department to have special functions in traffic regulation. The members of the squad were stationed on the sidewalks along Broadway, from Bowling Green to 59th Street, at the intersections of the cross streets. It was their purpose to escort pedestrians across the streets and to stop traffic while so doing. The pavement of Broadway was of cobblestones, and most of the traffic consisted of slow-moving, horse-drawn vehicles.

police training school, first. Begun on July 29, 1935, by the Federal Bureau of Investigation, U.S. Department of Justice. The courses, similar to those given in the training bureau for newly appointed special agents of the FBI, provide a program of training for local and state law enforcement officials and include subjects under the following headings: scientific and technical; statistics, records, and report writing; firearms training and first aid; investigations, enforcement, and regulatory procedure; and police administration and organization. The course of training lasts for a period of 12 weeks and is given without cost to those enrolled. The first class consisted of 23 students.

police unions. At the local level these are collective bargaining units representing certain classes of employees. Rank and file (labor) employees in a police agency generally include officer through sergeant. Higher levels are represented by management-oriented associations. In some states, police unions have the right to "meet and confer, in good faith, with city management on all matters relating to wages and conditions of employment' a radical departure from the traditional practice of chiefs of police serving as sole bargaining representatives. At the county level, municipal associations may affiliate and network for common purposes. Umbrella labor organizations exist at the state level, providing services smaller departments cannot afford, such as legal representation, false arrest and other insurance coverage, medical/dental plans, arbitration, and lobbying. At the national level, such as the National Association of Police Organizations, they monitor and lobby for favorable federal legislation. *See also* Fraternal Order of Police; International Brotherhood of Police Officers; International Brotherhood of Teamsters; International Union of Police Associations; National Association of Police Organizations

Police Week. Second or third week of May, proclaimed since 1962; includes Peace Officers' Memorial Day, May 15th.

political question. Issues in a case that the court believes should be decided by a nonjudicial unit of government.

poll the jury. A procedure in court whereby each juror is asked to state his or her verdict and is required to make it known.

Pollutant Standard Index. The U.S. Environmental Protection Agency and the South Coast Air Quality Managment District of El Monte, CA, devised the Pollutant Standard Index to monitor concentration of pollutants in the air and inform the public concerning related health effects. The scale measures the amount of pollution in parts per million and has been in use since 1978.

pollution control. At the federal level, the responsibility of a DOJ office that supervises the prosecution and defense of civil and criminal cases involving pollution abatement and environmental protection. Much of the caseload includes civil and criminal-enforcement actions under the various environmental statutes. The rest is composed of litigation in which regulations or permits have been challenged by industry or environmental organizations. Address: Environmental Defense

Section, Land and Natural Resources Division, DOJ, 950 Pennsylvania Avenue, NW, NW, Washington, DC 20530-0001.

Pollutant Standard Index. The U.S. Environmental Protection Agency and the South Coast Air Quality management District of El Monte, CA, devised the Pollutant Standard Index to monitor concentration of pollutants in the air and inform the public concerning related health effects. The scale measures the amount of pollution in parts per million, and has been in use since 1978.

PSI Index	Health Effects	Cautionary Status
50	Moderate	
100	Unhealthful	
101	Very unhealthful	Alert: elderly or ill should stay indoors and reduce physical activity.
300	Hazardous	Warning: general population should stay indoors and reduce physical activity.
400	Extremely hazardous	Emergency: all people remain indoors, windows shut, no physical exertion.
500	Toxic	Significant harm. Same as above.

polyandry. The practice of a woman's having more than one husband.

polygamy. The practice of having more than one spouse. On July 1, 1862, polygamy, which was practiced by the Mormons in Utah, was made a federal crime by an act of Congress. The attempted federal enforcement caused decades of strife. Finally, on October 6, 1890, the Mormon Church renounced the practice, and on September 7, 1894, President Grover Cleveland proclaimed pardon and restoration of civil rights for persons disfranchised by antipolygamy laws. *See also* Edmunds Act

polygraph. Most modern polygraphs, or lie detectors, have three capacities for recording anatomical responses: the pneumograph—for recording respiration; the galvanograph—for recording skin electrical-resistance changes; and the cardiograph—for recording changes in blood pressure and pulse rate. The first police department to use the polygraph was that of Berkeley, CA, in 1934. Deceptograph is the commercial name of a polygraph instrument manufactured by the Stoelting Company. The results of polygraph tests have not been universally accepted as evidence. New Mexico is the only state in which polygraph evidence is routinely admitted in criminal trials. The recent trend in federal courts has been to leave the question up to judges in individual cases, a trend that has accelerated in the years since the Supreme Court in its 1993 *Daubert v. Merrell Dow Pharmaceuticals* decision gave federal trial judges more leeway to evaluate scientific evidence. *See also* FBI Laboratory

Polygraph Association, American. Founded in 1966. Address: P.O. Box 8037, Chattanooga, TN 37414; telephone (800) APA-8037.

Ponzi, Charles. During the 1920s Ponzi, a $15-a-week stock clerk in Boston, told acquaintances he had found a way to make money by buying postal coupons in Spain for 1 cent and redeeming them in the United States for 5 cents. He promised investors a 50 percent return on their money in 45 days and 100 percent in 90 days. In fact, he simply paid off early investors with money obtained from later victims. Within a year, Ponzi had taken $15 million from gullible people and moved into a palatial home. Since then, any operation that pays off old investors from new investors' money is known as a "Ponzi scheme."

poor laws. See Law, Elizabethan Poor; law, poor

popular justice. Attempts by local communities to devise informal and nonbureaucratic alternatives to the official justice system. These alternatives may include unofficial neighborhood or community courts and community patrols.

population. *See* sampling

pornography. Often equated in general usage with the ambiguous term obscenity, pornography has not been defined precisely enough to withstand legal challenges and court tests. Most attempts to define it refer to the portrayal of particular sexual acts or to excessive violence in sex. The ambiguity was perhaps best illustrated by Supreme Court justice Potter Stewart's statement that he cannot define hardcore pornography, but he knows it when he sees it. A landmark case was *Roth v. Alberts* in 1957, in which it was ruled that, in general, laws forbidding obscenity are constitutional. A three-part test evolved to define what is obscene: 1) the dominant theme of the material must appeal to a prurient interest in sex; 2) the material must be patently offensive in that it affronts contemporary community standards; 3) the material must be utterly without redeeming social value. In 1972 the second and third criteria were changed by the Supreme Court in a decision holding that community standards were to be defined locally rather than nationally, and that material need not be "utterly without redeeming social value" to be pornographic, but need only be lacking, when "taken as a whole in serious literary, artistic, political or scientific value." *See also* pandering

pornography received through the mail. Receipt of unsolicited sexually oriented ads can be halted by filling out Form 2201 at your local post office. A mailer who sends sexually oriented ads to any person whose name has been on this postal list for 30 days is subject to legal action by the U.S. government. Notice for Prohibitory Order Against Sender of Pandering Advertisement in the Mails can also be filled out to stop any further mailings considered "erotically arousing or sexually provocative." Contact the nearest post office or: Office of Consumer Affairs, Customer Service Department, Postal Service, 475 L'Enfant Plaza West, SW, Room 5910, Washington, DC 20260.

poroscopy. The study of the arrangement and individual characteristics of sweat pores as seen in fingerprint impressions as a means of fingerprint identification. These sweatpore characteristics are especially important when there is only a fragment of the fingerprint impression available.

portrait parle (Fr., lit.). A speaking likeness; a means of recording the descriptions of persons, used in France.

port warden. Individual or group responsible for protecting a port against all hazards and keeping it safe and secure. For example, the Port Warden Section of the Los Angeles, CA, Harbor Department consists of 47 sworn peace officers and 10 civilian personnel. This section has safety and security responsibility for land and water patrol of approximately 11 square miles (28 miles of waterfront).

POSDCORB. Acronym for the primary management functions of planning, organizing, staffing, directing, coordinating, reporting, and budgeting.

positive evidence. Evidence that directly proves the fact or point at issue.

positive law. Law consisting of definite rules of human conduct with appropriate sanctions for their enforcement, both prescribed by a human superior or sovereign; defined by English jurist John Austin (1790–1859) and others of the positive school of jurisprudence, which owed much of its inspiration to the French social theorist, Auguste Comte.

posse. A company; a force; a body with legal authority.

posse comitatus. (1) The power of the county. (2) The whole body (under common law, all male persons over 15 years of age) that the sheriff may summon to assist him in law enforcement; also, any group that is actually summoned.

Posse Comitatus Act of 1878. Prohibits the use of military personnel for the purpose of assisting civil authorities in the execution of civil law enforcement. However, this federal law does not prohibit the use of a state's National Guard or Air National Guard troops if their use is authorized by the governor.

possession. Having certain articles prohibited by law constitutes the criminal offense of possession, such as possession of narcotics by persons not legally entitled to have them.

possession, writ of. A term generally used to designate any writ by which the sheriff is commanded to place a person in possession of real or personal property.

post. (1) A position. (2) A place of assignment for an officer. (3) To record or make a record of. (4) Afterward in time; following. (5) Postmortem. (6) Abbreviation for commission of Peace Officers Standards and Training, such as the one established in California in 1959.

postal robbery. *See* Jesse James Act

postconviction remedy. The procedure or set of procedures by which a person who has been convicted of a crime can challenge in court the lawfulness of the conviction judgment or penalty or of a correctional agency action, and thus obtain relief in situations where this cannot be done by a direct appeal.

posterity. Descendants.

post facto (Lat.). After the fact.

posthumous. Occurring to an individual after his or her death. A posthumous child is one born after the death of the father.

postmortem. (1) Subsequent to death. (2) An autopsy.

postmortem lividity. *See* lividity, postmortem

post obit (Lat.). After death.

post-traumatic stress disorder (PTSD). A mental disorder manifested by persistent and intense distress, increased arousal, and a blunted enthusiasm for life. PTSD can be triggered by a crisis or trauma that is beyond the usual or typical range of human experience, such as war or other kinds of violence.

potency. A measure of drug activity expressed in terms of the amount required to produce an effect of given intensity. Potency varies inversely with the amount of the drug required to produce its effect—thus the more potent the drug, the lower the amount required to produce the effect.

powder, black. A propellant for firearms ammunition, composed of charcoal, sulfur, and nitrate of potassium. It was used in firearms of the past but has been largely replaced by smokeless powder.

powder pattern. The pattern of powder deposited on an object when fired onto by a firearm. At contact range there is little or no powder deposited and what is there is in a small circle. As the distance between the gun muzzle and the object increases, the size of the powder pattern increases until a distance is reached where the discharge of powder particles does not reach the object. *See also* powder pattern test

powder pattern test. A crime laboratory test of garments to determine the pattern of powder residue and thus determine the distance between the muzzle of the weapon and the person shot. It is a useful test in homicide cases, especially where suicide is suggested or alleged.

powders. The powders used in weapon loading are three types: black, semi-smokeless, and smokeless. Smokeless powders are divided into two types; the first is known as bulk, meaning that its charge corresponds in bulk, or nearly so, to the charge of black powder; the second is the dense type, which means that it is denser and of much less bulk.

powder, smokeless. A modern gunpowder consisting primarily of nitrocellulose or a combination of nitroglycerin and nitrocellulose.

power. The ability to do or act; political or national strength; great or marked ability to do or act; legal ability, capacity, or authority.

power of attorney. An instrument authorizing a person to act as the agent or attorney of the person granting it.

power of Congress. Unlike a state legislature, the U.S. Congress has no inherent powers; instead it derives them, including the power to define and punish crimes, from the

Constitution. Under the Constitution, Congress may define and punish crimes in the District of Columbia, U.S. territories, and elsewhere within the jurisdiction of the federal government.

power of municipalities. By the weight of authority, municipal corporations may, by ordinance, prohibit and punish acts that are not prohibited and punishable as misdemeanors under the general statutes of a state or that may involve a common law offense. In some jurisdictions, however, this power cannot be exercised in the absence of express legislative authority.

prearraignment lockup. A confinement facility for arrested adults awaiting arraignment or consideration for pretrial release, in which the duration of stay is usually limited by statute to two days or until the next session of the appropriate court.

precedent. Decision by a court that may serve as an example or authority for similar cases in the future.

precept. (1) A process or warrant. (2) A writ directed to the sheriff or other officer directing him or her to do something.

precinct. (1) A minor division for police administration in a city or ward. (2) A county or municipal subdivision for casting votes in elections.

precipe (Lat.). A document containing the particulars of a writ.

precipitant reaction test. A crime laboratory test to determine if blood is of human origin.

predatory crime. Illegal activity, usually but not exclusively robbery or burglary, in which the offender preys upon, exploits, attacks, or in another way takes advantage of the victim. Juveniles and the elderly are often targets.

predisposition investigation. An investigation undertaken by a probation agency or other designated authority at the request of a juvenile court into the past behavior, family background, and personality of a juvenile

who has been adjudicated a delinquent, a status offender, or a dependent, in order to assist the court in determining the most appropriate disposition.

preempt. To move into a field or area and take possession or jurisdiction with priority ahead of others.

preliminary hearing. The proceeding before a judicial officer in which three matters must be decided: whether a crime was committed, whether the crime occurred within the territorial jurisdiction of the court, and whether there are reasonable grounds to believe that the defendant committed the crime. *See also* jurisdiction

preliminary jurisdiction. A criminal court has preliminary jurisdiction of an offense and may conduct criminal proceedings with respect to the offense when the proceedings lead or may lead to prosecution and final disposition of the case in a court having trial jurisdiction.

premeditation. A design to commit a crime or commit some other act before it is done; deliberation.

preponderance of evidence. Evidence that is the most impressive or convincing of any offered; the burden of proof required in a civil proceeding, which is less stringent than the requirement of "beyond a reasonable doubt;' which is the requirement for criminal proceedings. For example, former pro football player O.J. Simpson was acquitted of murdering his ex-wife and her friend in his criminal trial, when a jury could not find him guilty beyond a reasonable doubt. A civil jury, however, found him liable for the two murders when using the lesser burden of proof. Preponderance of evidence is also the standard required at probation or parole violation proceedings.

prescription. (1) Acquiring some advantage or title to property by possession for specified periods of time. (2) In law, something proscribed by negative prescription, such as the time limitations within which prosecutions must be commenced after the commission of a crime, and after which such prosecutions are said to be prescribed, or invalidated. *See also* statute of limitations

presentence investigation. An investigation undertaken by a probation agency or other designated authority at the request of a court into the past behavior, family circumstances, and personality of an adult who has been convicted of a crime, in order to assist the court in determining the most appropriate sentence. Presentencing information may reach the court in various ways. For example, a confidential report may be prepared in addition to the usually public presentence report, or the defendant may submit information.

presentence report. A report prepared from the presentence investigation to aid the sentencing authority in passing sentence.

presentment. Historically, written notice of an offense taken by a grand jury from its own knowledge or observation; in current usage, any of several presentations of alleged facts and charges to a court or a grand jury by a prosecutor.

President's Crime Commission. Officially known as the President's Commission on Law Enforcement and Administration of Justice, the commission was established on July 25, 1965, by President Lyndon Johnson, who had "declared war on crime." The commission, consisting of 19 commissioners, 63 staff members, 175 consultants, and hundreds of advisers, studied most aspects of the crime problem and the machinery of criminal justice. The commission released a series of task force reports on the police, courts, corrections, juvenile delinquency, organized crime, science and technology, drunkenness, narcotics and drugs, and the assessment of crime, all of which were summarized in its general report, *The Challenge of Crime in a Free Society*. The commission introduced the *Crime Commission Model*, which applied the systems approach to the process of criminal justice. It provided a conceptual framework and focused on the flow of cases between agencies. The main stortcoming is that it portrays a single justice system, handling all cases the same. *See* wedding cake model.

press, freedom of the. Guaranteed in the First Amendment of the Constitution. Until 1925, this guarantee was generally considered to apply against infringement by Congress. As a result of the Supreme Court's decision in 1925 in the case of *Gitlow v. New York*, the free press clause of the First Amendment has since been applied to the states as well. The principle of the freedom of the press was originally set down in North America in 1734 in the famous trial of Peter Zenger.

pressure. The force exerted in the cartridge chamber and bore of a barrel by powder gases is known as the pressure and measured in pounds per square inch. The amount of pressure permissible in pistol and revolver charges is governed by safety factors— 15,000 lbs. per square inch represents about the maximum pressure that may safely be used in the best grades of revolvers and 30,000 lbs. in high-velocity automatics like the Mauser. The method of ascertaining pressures is rather complicated and requires special equipment. The method generally used by ammunition companies is known as the Radial System.

pressure alarm system. An alarm system that protects a vault or other enclosed space by maintaining and monitoring a predetermined air pressure differential between the inside and outside of the space. Equalization of pressure resulting from opening the vault or cutting through will be sensed and will initiate an alarm signal.

presumed dead. *See* artificial presumption

presumption. Inference drawn from some fact or group of facts.

presumption, legal. The law providing that the judiciary shall assume certain facts exist from a set of circumstances. These assumptions or inferred facts persist until disproven. *See also* presumption, rebuttable

presumption of innocence. The defendant is presumed to be innocent and the burden is on the state to prove his guilt beyond a reasonable doubt. *See also* burden of proof

presumption, rebuttable. A legal presumption that relieves the person in whose favor it exists from the necessity of offering proof; however, it can be disproven or rebutted. Such is the presumption of innocence of an accused.

presumptive evidence. (1) The presumption of incapacity in a minor to act, which is conclusive and irrebuttable. (2) Evidence that may be disproved or rebutted by other evidence. Presumptions of fact can be determined by the judge from the existing evidence.

pretermit. To pass by, disregard, or take no action concerning. In relation to a grand jury, it means the jury passes a matter before it without finding a true bill or no true bill. This is brought about by lack of agreement among the grand jurors or by the intentional act of the grand jury. The next grand jury may consider the case.

STEPS IN THE CRIMINAL JUSTICE PROCESS BEFORE TRIAL

1). Report of a crime
2). Investigation prior to arrrest
3). Arrest
4). Booking
5). Postarrest investigation
6). Prosecutor's decision to charge suspect with a crime
7). Initial appearance
8). Preliminary hearing
9). Grand jury review
10). Arraignment
11). Pertrial motions
12). Pretrial conferences

---

pretrial conference. A meeting of the opposing parties in a case with the judicial officer prior to trial for the purposes of stipulating those things that are agreed upon and thus narrowing the trial to the things that are in dispute, disclosing the required information about witnesses and evidence, making motions, and generally organizing the presentation of motions, witnesses, and evidence.

The matters dealt with in a pretrial conference may instead be taken up in a procedure called an omnibus hearing. In criminal proceedings, this type of pretrial activity takes place before the trial judge following an arraignment in which the defendant has pled not guilty. It may include consideration of reduction of the charges.

pretrial detention. Any period of confinement occurring between arrest or other holding to answer a charge, and the conclusion of prosecution.

pretrial discovery. Disclosure by the prosecution or the defense prior to trial of evidence or other information that is intended to be used in the trial.

pretrial publicity. Media information about a crime, a defendant, or a forthcoming trial that is sometimes claimed by the defense to be inordinate, prejudicial, and precluding a fair trial. It is often used by the defense in its request that the place of trial be moved (motion for a change of venue).

pretrial release. The release of an accused person from custody for all or part of the time before or during prosecution, upon his or her promise to appear in court when required.

pretrial screens. Steps in the criminal justice process to apply quality control to police arrests and prosecutors' charges to reduce the number of unwarranted trials.

prevalence of crime. Criminality measured in a given population during a specified period of time. For example, the prevalence of juvenile delinquency in a city or state in 1999 is the number of juveniles in that area in 1999 who have ever been judged delinquent, relative to the total number of juveniles in the city or state at that time.

preventive pretrial detention. A procedure that allows an individual to be held in police custody without benefit of bail. The practice of granting bail originated in thirteenth-century English common law and is guaranteed by the Eighth Amendment. Historically, the only condition for denying bail in other than capital cases has been that the accused might flee in order to avoid trial. Preventive detention allows the courts to detain individuals without possibility of bail on another condition: that an acused might, if set free, commit serious crimes while awaiting trial.

prima facie (Lat.). At first glance; without investigation or evaluation. That which, if not rebutted, is sufficient to establish a fact or case.

prima facie case. One in which the evidence in favor of a proposition is sufficient to support a finding in its favor, if all the evidence to the contrary is disregarded.

prima facie evidence. Evidence that is sufficient to support a fact or group of facts.

primary classification. A term used in classifying fingerprints. A numerical value is given to each of the 10 fingers, and that value is entered in the classification formula after the major division, such as 1/1.

primary evidence. Primary evidence is that kind of evidence which, under every possible circumstance, affords the greatest certainty of the fact in question. Thus, a written instrument is itself the best possible evidence of its existence and contents. It means original or firsthand evidence, the best evidence that the nature of the case admits of; the evidence that is required in the first instance, and which must fail before secondary evidence can be admitted.

primogeniture. A social system centering on the firstborn child among all children born of the same parents. In law, primogeniture is the rule of inheritance and succession by the firstborn, particularly the firstborn son.

principal. A person held accountable for a crime. The person who actually commits the crime is a principal. In some states, persons who aid or assist the principal in committing a crime are also considered principals, even though they did not actively participate in the crime itself.

principal and accessories. Parties concerned in the commission of felonies are principals or accessories according to whether they are present or absent when the act is committed. Principals are either (a) principals in the first degree or (b) principals in the second degree. Accessories are either (a) before the fact or (b) after the fact.

principal in the first degree. A principal in the first degree is the person who actually perpetrates a deed, either by his or her own hand or through an innocent agent.

principal in the second degree. One who is actually or constructively present, aiding and abetting another in the commission of a deed: (a) he or she must be present, actually or constructively; (b) he or she must aid or abet the commission of the act; (c) there must be community of unlawful purpose at the time the act was committed; and (d) such purpose must be real on the part of the principal in the first degree.

principal registration. A system of classifying and identifying fingerprints based on all 10 fingers of the hands. It is necessary to have the same kind of fingerprints in order to search for and locate a duplicate set of fingerprints on file in this type of registration. Provisions for amputees are made in the classifying system. *See also* single-fingerprint registration

principal's liability for acts of agent. As a rule, no person is criminally liable for the act of another unless he or she has previously authorized or assented to it; consequently a principal is not liable for acts of his or her agents or servants that were not authorized or assented to, although they are done in the course of employment.

prison. A state or federal confinement facility having custodial authority over adults sentenced to confinement. Prisons are a relatively recent development. Until the reforms growing out of the eighteenth-century Enlightenment, those convicted of crime were more often fined, banished, publicly whipped, or executed than imprisoned. And although colonial jails were established in the seventeenth century, they hardly resembled the institutions that the term *prison* implies today. Such places were solely for detention and made no pretense of rehabilitation. Prisons as they are now known in America and Europe had their beginning in the eastern United States in the early nineteenth century. They were intended to stress reform instead of punishments and to correct the poor conditions and inmate idleness that characterized the jails. It was no accident that the first prison in Pennsylvania was called a penitentiary, for the prisoner was kept in complete isolation so that, alone with his Bible and work, he could do penance. Auburn Prison in New York opened in 1819. Here prisoners lived in separate cells but worked in groups. First introduced at Lewisburg, PA, in 1932, the Lewisburg plan, also termed the telephone-pole design, resembles a telephone pole with its crossarms; cellblocks and workshops are at right angles to a central corridor. This design provides flexibility in layout and coordination of elements for control and supervision of the inmates. The long connecting corridor (the pole) extends from the administrative building past dining rooms and shops, and is bisected by cellblocks.

European prisons developed largely after the Pennsylvania model, but, for economic reasons, most American prisons in the nineteenth century were patterned on the Auburn model. They evoked criticism by reformers in the 1870s, the "golden age of penal reform." In this decade, the National Prison Association was founded, one of its principles being that "reformation not vindictive suffering" should be the purpose of prisons. These theoretical advances were not followed in practice, although one lasting reform was parole. (Maine abolished parole in 1976.) Reform received renewed impetus in the 1930s, when the federal prison system demonstrated that effective programs of rehabilitation could be established if qualified personnel were recruited. The era after World War II brought more reforms. Changes in California were so notable that American prisons once again served as models for those of Europe.

The United States has 53 prison systems, made up of those of the Federal Bureau of Prisons, the 50 states, the District of Columbia, and Puerto Rico. Jackson prison, near Jackson, MI, is considered the world's largest walled prison, enclosing more than 57 acres. *See also* prison reform

prison-ashram project. Founded in 1973, this organization sponsors workshops in prisons and universities, and a pen pal project to match people on the basis of spiritual interests. (An ashram is an institution similar to a monastery, except that most residents stay for only a brief period of time.) *Publishes Prison-Ashram Project of the Human Kindness Foundation* (quarterly newsletter). Address: P.O. Box 61619, Durham, NC 27715.

prison commitment. A sentence of confinement to the jurisdiction of a state or federal confinement system for adults, of which the custodial authority extends to persons sentenced to more than a year of confinement, for a term expressed in years or for life, or to await execution of a death sentence.

prison community. Social structure, relationships, and processes in a prison: the quality of staff-staff, inmate-inmate, and inmate-staff relationships; class stratification, informal group life, leadership, folkways in prisoner society, and the role of gossip and public opinion as means of social control; the processes whereby the guards become institutionalized and the inmates "prisonized."

prison, discipline in. All those measures used by the prison administration—the grade system, degradation and advancement in grade, privileges and denial thereof, isolation in cell or in solitary cells, "good time," and so forth—designed to promote good behavior in the institution.

prisoner. A person in physical custody in a confinement facility, or in the personal physical custody of a criminal justice official while being transported to or between confinement facilities.

Prisoner's Rights Union. Founded in 1971. Formerly Prisoner's Union. Convicts, exconvicts, and other advocates interested in improving the conditions of those incarcerated in California prisons. Publishes *California Prisoner* (bimonthly). Address: P.O. Box 1019, Sacramento, CA 95812.

prison escape, largest. In February 1979 U.S. Army Colonel Arthur "Bull" Simons (ret.) led a band of 14 to break into Gasre prison, Teheran, Iran, to rescue two Americans. Some 11,000 other prisoners took advantage of this event and the national chaos, in what became history's largest jail break.

prison farms. Farms for convicts, of four general varieties: (a) those owned by counties or municipalities where misdemeanants are committed who would otherwise serve short terms in a county or city jail; (b) those run as auxiliaries to state prisons, partially as a means of segregating a special group of offenders, as for example, first offenders or habitual offenders, and partially to provide meat and vegetables for the prison kitchens; (c) those privately owned in the South, to which the states leased convicts at considerable profit and which assumed the responsibility for guarding and disciplining the men and providing their food and shelter in return for their labor, most of such farms having been abolished because of abuses; (d) those owned and operated by a number of southern states, including AR, LA, TX, and MS, as a basic part of their prison system, to which prisoners are sent from a receiving center that allocates them to different farms, according to their types.

prison, federal. From 1950 to 1980, the federal prison population increased less than 40 percent. From October 1980 to May 1989, the population almost doubled, growing from 24,162 to 48,017 inmates in 67 facilities. In September 1992 the inmate population was 70,998, or 144 percent of capacity. By mid-1998, however, federal prisons were at 119 percent of capacity. The average bureau-wide yearly cost per inmate in 1988 was about $15,270; in 1992 it was $20,072, including central and regional office overhead. In 1992 approximately 60 percent of inmates had been sentenced for drug-related offenses, and that percentage held through 1997. The next most common offense was robbery, at 11 per-

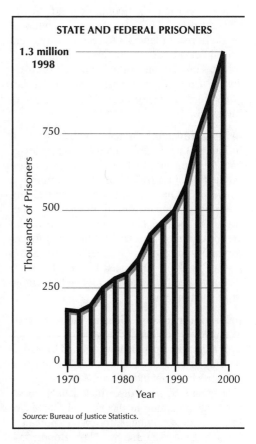

STATE AND FEDERAL PRISONERS

Source: Bureau of Justice Statistics.

cent; 88 percent had violated U.S. Codes. 57 percent are held at minimum or low security levels; 10 percent are high-security inmates. In 1993 there were 27 additional federal prison facilities under construction. Other confinement of federal prisoners includes military prisons and facilities such as halfway houses under contract to the federal prison system.

Prison Fellowship International. Founded in 1976 and devoted to Christian ministry, both in prisons and in communities, for the welfare of inmates, ex-prisoners, and their families. Publishes *World Report* (bimonthly). Address: P.O. Box 17434, Washington, DC 20041.

Prison Fellowship Ministries. Founded in 1976. Affiliated with the American Correctional Association; Economic and Social Council of the United Nations; Evangelical Council for Financial Accountability; and Prison Fellowship International. Sponsors in-prison seminars and Bible studies. Publishes *Jubilee* (monthly newsletter) and *Justice Report* (quarterly). Address: P.O. Box 1550, Merrifield, VA 22116-1550.

prison, industrial. A term, more common in Europe than in the United States, to designate a prison in which the inmates carry on production of useful articles, with a minimum emphasis upon vocational or other training intended to prepare the discharged prisoner for life in society. The inmates are those who are looked upon as relatively hopeless for reformatory methods. Originally it meant a prison for those sentenced to hard labor, as distinguished from those sentenced to simple imprisonment.

prison information. General information is available on prisons, including statistics, such as percentage of population confined to institutions by offense, and history of federal prisons. Free brochures include *Federal Prison System Education for Tomorrow*, which details the educational programs in the Federal Bureau of Prisons. Contact: Public Information, Bureau of Prisons, DOJ, 320 1st St., NW, Room 554, Washington, DC 20534, or visit the DOJ's web site: http://www.usdoj.gov/.

prisonization. The more indirect, negative effects of imprisonment—adopting, in greater or lesser degree, the values, orientation, and lifestyle of the prison subculture. *See also* prison psychosis

prison labor. As a tool within the correctional institution, labor by inmates has roots in both the retributive and rehabilitative philosophies. Some avow that prison labor should be as hard and unpleasant as possible, while others maintain that it should be useful and should train the inmate in marketable skills. Nearly all agree that it should be financially beneficial to the state. Methods of utilizing prison labor have ranged from a system of leasing prisoners and their labor to private

users to a state-use system, in which the state retains control of the prisoners and their labor and alone uses their products.

Prison Ministry, International. Founded in 1969. Conducts prison crusades and produces a weekly television program. Address: Box 63, Dallas, TX 75221.

prison/parole population movement. Entries and exits of persons committed to prison, into or from prison facility systems into conditional release or supervisory programs.

prison psychosis. Characteristic attitudes on the part of some inmates due to the rigid system of discipline in many prisons. Prisoners can become either apathetic and dull or rebellious and violent. Extreme personality deviations of these sorts have been observed in prisons throughout the world. The longer the period of confinement, the more marked are the reactions. There is little opportunity for initiative; the prison atmosphere is repressive and the daily program, monotonous. Inmates are robbed of will. They compensate by day-dreaming and fantasizing or by marked aggressive behavior that sometimes takes the form of destroying everything in the cell. This kind of stupor or aggression has been labeled prison psychosis, a term not used to criticize its victims.

prison reform. Prison conditions in colonial America retained medieval characteristics. Punishments included whipping, the stocks, pillories, and ducking. Prisoners were confined to unsanitary quarters and not segregated by gender or age. The first prison reform society to bring about changes in prison administration was the Philadelphia Society for Alleviating the Miseries of Public Prisons, formed May 8, 1787, in the German School House on Cherry Street, Philadelphia, PA, by Quakers. The first president was William White. In 1791, the first penitentiary was established in Philadelphia. Overcrowded conditions, nevertheless, prevented any serious reform. It was not until the humanitarian revolt of the Jacksonian period that fundamental prison reform was undertaken. In 1824, the Auburn System of silent confinement was established. Correction houses and reform schools were founded to meet the special needs of juvenile offenders. By the opening of the Civil War, Auburn-type prisons had been established in all states except NJ and PA. The American Prison Association was founded in 1870 to carry out the ideas of such reformers as Enoch C. Wines and Zebulon R. Brockway. These leaders had been strongly influenced by the Irish penal system, which maintained rehabilitation rather than punishment as the aim of imprisonment. In 1877 the New York State Reformatory at Elmira was opened under Brockway's administration to further this experiment. Youthful offenders were separated from hardened criminals and encouraged to reduce their terms through good conduct. Parole and probation were introduced to provide continuing supervision after release. The Elmira plan was quickly adopted in many northern and western states. In the twentieth century, psychology, psychiatry, sociology, and medicine have contributed to reform concepts in penology. These have emphasized occupational therapy, psychiatric care, social work, classification of inmates, the suspended sentence, and compensated labor. Postrelease supervision has stressed adjustment to society through employment services, hospitalization, and family care.

prison riots. In a four-day revolt in 1971 by 1,200 inmates of the Attica Correctional Facility in New York, prisoners held 38 guards hostage. During an assault by more than 1,000 NY state troopers and police to retake the prison, 9 hostages and 28 inmates were killed.

The New Mexico State Penitentiary Riot of February 2 and 3, 1980, is noted as one of the worst prison riots in U.S. history. The 36-hour rebellion claimed 33 lives and caused more than $50 million in damage. The penitentiary was restored to order by New Mexico National Guard troops, state police, Santa Fe County Sheriff personnel, and city police.

From April 11 to 21, 1993, 409 maximum-security prisoners at the Southern Ohio Correctional Facility held 5 guards hostage. They surrendered after killing 1 guard and 9 inmates.

Prisons, Federal Bureau of, directors. First: Sanford Bates, 1930–1937; Second: James V. Bennett, 1937–1964; Third: Myrl E. Alexander, 1964–1970; Fourth: Norman A. Carlson, 1970–1987; Fifth: J. Michael Quinlan, 1987–1992; Sixth: Kathleen Hawk Sawyer, 1992–present.

Prisons, Federal Bureau of, Library. A free publication, *Correctional Bookshelf*, is a bibliography of some of the books and periodicals in the library, covering such areas as administration and organization, programs for offenders, community corrections, jails, the prison social system, institutions for female offenders, and law and history. Reference and research services are also available. Contact: Federal Bureau of Prisons Archives, 320 First St., NW, Building 500, 7th Floor, Washington, DC 20534.

prisons, receiving. Induction centers to which prisoners are sent for assignment to the particular prison or prison facilities that best suit them. Some prison systems have reception prisons; others have facilities at larger prisons. A reception center is designed to enable classification committees to assign each admitted offender to the proper custody, work, and education. During the period of reception, often called the period of quarantine, the offender is given any preventive and corrective medical attention necessary, interviewed for social and criminal background, examined psychologically, and processed for identification.

privacy, records. The Privacy Act of 1974 required the *Federal Register* to describe every system of records kept on individuals. More than 9,000 have been identified; 20 percent are automated. There are five volumes devoted to explanations of these systems, including how a person can obtain copies of records.

privacy, right of. The right to be left alone; not to be interfered with as to conversations, activities within one's own home, or the possession and use of property. The largest sum awarded for invasion of privacy was $40 million to author-actress Jackie Collins by a federal jury of six women on June 16, 1983, in New York City for use of nude photos published in 1980 by the magazine *Alelina* and incorrectly identified as being of Collins.

private law. The law that regulates the relations of individuals to one another.

private rehabilitation agency. An independent organization providing care and treatment services, that may include housing, to convicted persons, juvenile offenders, or persons subject to judicial proceedings.

private right. A right enjoyed by the individual under law. Many such rights are enumerated in bills of rights of the federal and state constitutions.

private sector. In general, citizens' residential and business activities that are not part of the government, or public sector. The first response to crime may come from any part of the private sector: individuals, families, neighborhood associations, business, industry, agriculture, educational institutions, the news media, or any other private service to the public. Public sector involvement includes crime prevention and participation in the justice process once a crime has been committed and reported. Private crime prevention is more than providing private security, or burglar alarms, or participating in a neighborhood watch. It includes a moral commitment to stop criminal behavior by refusing to engage in it or condone it when it is committed by others. Citizens take part directly in the criminal justice process by reporting crime to the police, or by being reliable participants (such as witnesses or jurors) in criminal proceedings. As voters and taxpayers, citizens also participate in criminal justice through policymaking that affects how the process operates, the resources available to the process, and the process's goals and objectives. At every stage, from the original formulation of objectives, to political decisions about where to locate jails and prisons, the private sector has a role to play. Without such involvement, many feel that the criminal justice

process cannot effectively serve the citizens it is designed to protect.

private security agency. An independent or proprietary commercial organization whose activities include employee screening investigations, maintaining the security of persons or property, and/or performing the functions of detection and investigation of crime and criminals and apprehension of offenders.

Private security is defined as: a private patrol operator or operator of such a service within a premise's boundaries; a person other than an armored contract carrier, who, for any consideration whatsoever agrees to furnish, or furnishes a watchman, guard, patrolman, or other person to protect persons or property or to prevent the theft, unlawful taking, loss, embezzlement, misappropriation, or concealment of any goods, wares, merchandise, money, bonds, stocks, notes, documents, papers, or property of any kind or perform the service of such watchman, guard, or other person, for any said purposes.

During 1985, it was estimated that in the United States there were 6,500 security firms competing in a $500 million–private patrol market. Homeowners were expected to spend an additional $125 million on residential alarm systems. In California there were 1,787 firms, including 794 companies in Los Angeles and Orange counties. In the city of Los Angeles there were 39 private security firms.

privilege. A right or protection granted to persons in special statuses and not extended to others. Privileges may be held by the defendant, defense counsel, judge, spouse of the accused, and others.

privilege, absolute. A legal prohibition against prosecution for criminal libel, regardless of malice, generally limited to official participants in the governmental process. This prohibition is based on the belief that the public benefits by having officials who are free to exercise their function with independence and without fear of litigation. *See also* libel and slander

privileged communications. No husband is compelled to disclose any communication made to him by his wife during the marriage, and no wife is compelled to disclose any communication made to her by her husband during the marriage. No one can be compelled to give evidence relating to any affairs of state, as to official communications between public officers upon public affairs, except with the permission of the officer at the head of the department concerned. In cases in which the government is immediately concerned, no witness can be compelled to answer any question, the answer to which would tend to discover the names of persons by or to whom information was given as to the commission of offenses. No *legal adviser* is permitted, whether during or after the termination of employment as such, unless with the client's express consent, to disclose any communication, oral or documentary, made to such legal adviser. The term legal adviser includes lawyers, their clerks, and interpreters between them and their clients.

proactive. A broad criminal justice concept embracing the activities of planning, community involvement, and crime prevention with a view toward the future; as opposed to reactive.

probable cause. A set of facts and circumstances that would induce a reasonably intelligent and prudent person to believe that a particular person had committed a specific crime; reasonable grounds to make or believe an accusation.

probable cause, writ of. A writ that in criminal prosecution operates as an order to stay execution pending an appeal.

probable evidence. Presumptive evidence.

probate. Proving and establishing a will.

probate court or surrogate's court. A state court having jurisdiction over probate (proving) of wills and administration of the estates of those who die intestate (without leaving a will), and supervision of financial matters relating to estates. In some states probate courts have jurisdiction over the estates of minors and are thus called orphans' courts.

probation. The conditional freedom granted by a judicial officer to an alleged or adjudged adult or juvenile offender, as long as the person meets certain conditions of behavior. This form of judicial disposition was in use in all states by 1957.

probation agency. A correctional agency of which the principal functions are juvenile intake; the supervision of adults and juveniles placed on probation status; the investigation of adults or juveniles; and the preparation of presentence or predisposition reports to assist the court in determining the proper sentence or juvenile court disposition.

Probation and Parole Association, American (APPA). Membership consists of practitioners in probation, parole, and community-based corrections from the United States and Canada. Publishes *Perspectives.* Address: APPA, P.O. Box 11910, Lexington, KY 40578.

probationer. A person who is placed on probation and required by a court or probation agency to meet certain conditions of behavior, and who may or may not be placed under the supervision of a probation agency.

probation officer. An employee of a probation agency whose primary duties include one or more of the agency's functions.

probation revocation. A court order in response to a violation of conditions of probation, taking away a person's probationary status and usually withdrawing the conditional freedom associated with the status.

probation supervisory caseload. The total number of clients registered with a probation agency on a given date or over a given period of time who have received grants of probation and are under active or inactive supervision.

probation supervisory population movement. Entries to and exits from the population for whom a probation agency has supervisory responsibility.

probation termination. The ending of the probation status of a given person by routine expiration of the probationary period, by special early termination by court, or by revocation.

Order for Probation Conditions

In the District court of _____ County
STATE OF _____

CASE NUMBER _____
DEFENDANT _____
OFFENSE _____
DATE _____

RULES AND CONDITIONS OF PROBATION:

1). I will until my final relaese, make a report in writing and in person as directed by the Supervising Authority.

2). I will not use or be in possession of intoxicants or illicit drugs of any kind, or visit places where illicit drugs are unlawfully sold, dispensed or used. I undersand that I am not allowed to enter or loiter around beer taverns or clubs.

3). I will not leave the State of _____ without written permission of the Supervising Authority. I will not leave _____ County without permission of the Supervising Authority.

4). I will not communicate with persons on Parole or inmates of penal institutions, nor will I associate with persons having a criminal record or involved in criminal activity. I understand that it is my responsibility to know whether an associate has a criminal record.

5). I will allow the Supervising Authority to visit me at my home, place of employment or elsewhere. I will notify the Supervising Authority prior to changing residence or employment.

6). I will carry out all instructions the Supervising Authority may give me, including but not limited to, urinalysis, curfew, and treatment.

7). I understand it will be a violation of my Probation to own, carry or possess firearms or ammunition of any type or to be in a vehicle where firearms are located.

8). I will work reularly at a lawful occupation and support my legal dependents without public assistance as long as I am physically able to do so.

9). I will refrain from violating City, State or Federal laws and I will report within 48 hours if I am arrested or questioned by any law enforcement agency.

10). I hereby agree to pay the sum of $10.00 per month for the term of my probation to the Department of Corrections to defray the costs of my supervision.

11). SPECIAL CONDITIONS

( ) TREATMENT/URINALYSIS   ( ) MAIL-IN PENDING INTERSTATE
( ) DRUG/ALCOHOL COUNSELING   ( ) STAY AWAY_____
( ) RESTITUTION-EXHIBIT A ATTACHED   ( ) WAIVE RULE(S)_____
( ) PSYCHIATRIC COUNSELING   ( ) MEDIATED AGREEMENT
( ) COMMUNITY SERVICE _____ HOURS   ( ) OTHER

I understand and agree that the continuance of my probation depends entirely on my conduct. I understand that shoud I violate the terms and conditions of my probation, the court may revoke my sentence and I may be required to serve imprisonment of the sentence imposed by the Court.

I hereby certify that I have carefully read or have been read and explained the above Ruels and Conditions and fully understand what my obligations are while under supervision of the Department of Corrections. I further acknowledge receipt of a copy of these Rules and conditions which I agree to study from time to time so that I will be fully informed at all times regarding my obligations while under supervision.

_____
ATTORNEY FOR DEFENDANT

_____
DEFENDANT-PROBATIONER
Department of Corrections, Probation and Parole

Source: Reid, 1996. *Criminal Justice*, 5th ed., Dubuque, IA Brown & Benchmark.

probation violation. An act or failure to act by a probationer that does not conform to the conditions of his or her probation.

probation workload. The total set of activities required in order to carry out the probation agency functions of intake-screening of juvenile cases, referral of cases to other service agencies, investigation of juveniles and adults for the purpose of preparing predisposition or presentence reports, supervision or treatment of juveniles and adults granted probation, assistance in the enforcement of court orders concerning family problems such as abandonment and nonsupport cases, and such other functions as may be assigned by statute or court order.

probative value. Having value as proof; value of absolute proof.

problem-oriented policing. A strategy to develop long-range plans to reduce recurrent crime and disorder problems and to assist in mobilizing public and private resources to that end. Requires the ability to analyze social problems, coordinate design solutions, appraise alternatives, advocate the adoption of programs, and monitor the results of cooperative efforts.

procedural law. A branch of law that prescribes in detail the methods or procedures to be used in determining and enforcing the rights and duties of persons toward each other under substantive law. *See also* substantive law

procedural rights. Guarantees granted to every citizen by the Bill of Rights. Procedural rights are concerned with the methods by which citizens are protected against arbitrary actions by public officials. No one may be deprived of his or her life, liberty, property, or other rights except according to carefully stated procedures. No person may be tried or condemned without due process of law, and convictions may be rendered void if procedural errors occur. *See also* due process of law

procedure. Court procedure is a development from custom, while customs have their origin in the habits, mode of life, and special circumstances of the people among whom they prevail. The chief merit of any system of procedure lies in (a) the generality of its application; (b) the uniformity of its rules; and (c) the certainty of its course. Courts must adhere to established modes of procedure.

proceeding. Action in conducting judicial business in a court or before a judicial officer.

process. In law, generally defined as a means of compelling a defendant in an action to appear in court; a means whereby a court compels compliance with its demands, and, when actions were commenced by original writ instead of, as at present, by writ of summons, a means of compelling the defendant to appear by what was termed *original process*, so called to distinguish it from *mesne* or intermediate *process*, which was a writ or process issued during the progress of the suit. The word process now commonly refers to all writs. The writ of summons is now used for commencing personal actions. Writs used to carry the judgments of the courts into effect and called *writs of execution* are also called *final process*, because they are usually issued at the end of a suit.

process in practice. A writ, summons, or order issued in a judicial proceeding to acquire jurisdiction of a person or his or her property, expedite the cause, or enforce the judgment.

procurement policy. An expressed or written statement that defines the terms, conditions, and other relevant criteria under which the user, such as a law enforcement agency, procures goods or services. In corporations, also called purchasing policy.

productivity. A term used to describe the relationship between work accomplished and the resources used to accomplish it. The work to be done is often called input, while the results of efforts are called output. Productivity is measurable by a variety of means, and high productivity is often associated with job satisfaction or good morale. Frequent employee absence, overtime, turnover, disciplinary actions, and equipment abuse can all reduce productivity and/or indicate poor morale.

profession. Term often used to distinguish such careers as law, medicine, and theology from all other careers, which may be called trades, skills, labor, or by a variety of other names. In broader usage, the designation of any line of work as a profession depends on such criteria as: high admission standards, a specialized body of knowledge, advanced education, social acceptance, licensing, autonomy of performance, portability of skills, scholarly research and publication, lengthy training or apprenticeship, and trade groups or professional associations.

professional. In criminal justice usage: the humane constitutional application of legitimate authority in the best interests of the community; acknowledgment and adherence to the concepts and application of fiduciary trust and altruism; performance on the highest ethical plane.

professional crime. Regular participation in criminal activity that involves complex skills and relies on a specialized system of status and organization. The *modus operandi* of professional crime usually emphasizes manipulating victims with cleverness rather than using force.

professionalization. Upgrading the standards of any occupation. In law enforcement, for example, professionalization includes rigorous admission standards, higher education, public acceptance, specialized training, ethical behavior, and a commitment to excellent community service and quality of life.

profiles, criminal. *See* National Center for the Analysis of Violent Crime

profiteer. One who demands and secures exorbitant profits in the sale of goods or services.

pro forma (Lat.). For form's sake or as a matter of form.

Program Evaluation and Review Technique (PERT). A popular management technique of diagramming the logical, sequential steps in a program, operation, or function. This method, usually referred to as creating PERT charts, was applied to police investigations

by Gilbert Burgoyne (LAPD ret.) in his application of VIA (Visual Investigative Analysis). *See also* link network diagrams

prohibition. Generally denotes the ban of alcoholic beverages containing 0.5 percent or more of alcohol. In a broader sense, the term applies to the prohibition by law of the manufacture and use of certain foods, clothes, and other articles considered injurious to the population.

An example of a complete prohibition of the manufacture, transportation, and sale of liquor containing more than 0.5 percent alcohol was the Eighteenth Amendment ("The Great Social Experiment"), which was in effect from January 16, 1919, to December 5, 1933, when it was repealed by the Twenty-First Amendment. While it was in effect, Prohibition gave rise to organized crime and government corruption at all levels.

prohibition, writ of. In practice, the name of a writ issued by a superior court, directed to the judge and parties to a suit in an inferior court, commanding them to cease prosecution of the suit, because the original cause of the suit or collateral issue does not belong to that jurisdiction.

promulgate. To announce formally and officially or make known something such as a law.

proof. The method of establishing the truth of an allegation; establishment of a fact; evidence when used to establish a fact.

property. Property falls into two general categories: (a) real property, including things growing on, affixed to, and found in land; and (b) tangible and intangible personal property, including rights, privileges, interests, claims, and securities.

The origin of the word property shows something about Western society's attitude toward possession. The Latin *proprius* means "one's own," and the French *propre* means "close" or "near."

property clerk. Law enforcement employee responsible for all property, lost or unclaimed, coming into police custody, and all evidence of crimes that is delivered to the police for safekeeping. Property unclaimed after a minimum of 90 days, or unclaimed evidence from crimes, upon disposition of the case and with the approval of the district attorney, is sold at public auction. Proceeds are generally turned over to the department pension or relief fund.

Property Crime Program (Sting). The Sting program was begun in 1974 to penetrate criminal fencing operations through undercover techniques. A 1980 evaluation disclosed that it was highly effective against career burglars, larceny, and motor vehicle theft. The study concluded that arrests, convictions, and dollar value of recoveries amounted to a substantial return on the initial investment. For example, an investment of $32 million in 68 Sting projects resulted in more than 11,900 arrests, an average conviction rate of 93 percent, the arrests of more than 8,900 career criminals, a savings of $109 million in court costs through guilty pleas, and the recovery of $398 million in stolen property, most of which was returned to its rightful owners. For further information, contact: Bureau of Justice Assistance, Office of Justice Programs, DOJ, 633 Indiana Avenue NW, Washington, DC 20531.

property rights. As developed in English common law and in the political philosophy of Thomas Hobbes and John Locke, this term refers to the right of ownership of private property against public restraint. Property rights, in the evolution of Anglo-American law, are now subject to public control when necessary to protect the public welfare. This has become particularly important in public utilities such as transportation, power, communication, and waterworks. Public restraints are based on reconciling police power with due process doctrines. *See also* Locke, John

proponent. One who makes a proposal; one who puts forward a document as a will for probate.

proprietary alarm system. An alarm system that is similar to a central station alarm system except that the equipment is located in a constantly manned guard room maintained by owners for their own internal security operations. The guards monitor the system and respond to all alarm signals, alert law enforcement agencies, or do both.

prosecute. To bring a matter or person into a court of law with a view to obtaining justice.

prosecution. (1) The conduct of a criminal proceeding before a judicial tribunal including all steps from the indictment or information to the final decision. (2) The party, usually the state, that conducts a criminal proceeding against an accused person.

prosecution agency. A federal, state, or local criminal justice agency or subunit whose principal function is the prosecution of alleged offenders.

prosecutor. An attorney who is the elected or appointed chief of a prosecution agency and whose official duty is to conduct criminal proceedings on behalf of the people against persons accused of committing criminal offenses. Also called district attorney, DA, state's attorney, county attorney, U.S. Attorney; any attorney deputized to assist the chief prosecutor.

prosecutorial screening decision. The decision of a prosecutor to submit a charging document to a court, seek a grand jury indictment, or decline to prosecute.

prosecutor's information. A written statement by a district attorney, filed with a local criminal court, accusing one or more defendants with the commission of one or more nonfelonious offenses. This accusation serves as a basis for prosecution.

prostitution. Offering or agreeing to engage in, or engaging in, a sex act with another in return for a fee. The California Penal Code defines it as anyone "who solicits or who engages in any act of prostitution (including) lewd acts between persons for money or other consideration." Prostitution is not illegal unless prohibited by state statute. The states of AZ and NV are the only two that have left the choice to each county rather than prohibiting prostitution. The status of being a prostitute does not per se cause a person to forfeit any constitutional or legal rights. For example, a prostitute who has been raped can bring charges against the attacker. Prostitutes have created several special interest groups, such as COYOTE, Cast Off Your Old Tired Ethics (San Francisco), and DOLPHIN, Dump Obsolete Laws—Prove Hypocrisy Isn't Necessary (Honolulu). One of the most famous madams was Polly Adler, who lived from 1900 to 1962 and in 1953 published her autobiography, *A House Is Not a Home*.

protest. Unconventional and often collective public action taken to show disapproval of, and the need for change in, some policy or condition. Protest may be aimed at the government, but it usually goes beyond voting to a variety of legal or illegal, peaceful or violent, forms of dissent.

provincial courts, criminal division. Criminal courts of limited jurisdiction located in urban areas in Canada.

provisional exit. An authorized temporary exit from prison for appearance in court, work furlough, hospital treatment, appeal proceedings, or other purposes that require absence with the expectation of return.

provocation. Incitement to commit an act.

provost marshal. A military officer whose duties correspond to those of a chief of police.

proxy. A person appointed to represent another; the document used by a shareholder or other individual authorizing someone to act on his or her behalf, such as in voting shares.

prurient. Having lustful interests or desires. This term is used in the legal definition of obscene or pornographic material.

psilocybin. Obtained from the so-called magic mushroom of Mexico, *Psilocybe Mexicana*, psilocybin is not as potent as LSD, but it can produce hallucinations and distortions of time and space at higher doses (5 to 15 mg). The drug was popular among Indians in Central America for religious use. Psilocybin sold on the streets is likely to be supermarket mushrooms sprayed with LSD or PCP.

psychedelic drug. Any drug with the ability to alter sensory perception.

psychiatric social worker. A professional who works with psychiatrists or psychologists to help patients with mental disorders. Typical duties include interviewing patients and members of their families (interview reports are part of the background material used by doctors in diagnosis and planning treatment), counseling patients' families, and helping in rehabilitation programs. Required training for a psychiatric social worker consists of four years of college (B.S. degree) plus two years in an accredited school of social work (M.S.W.) and a period of supervised experience.

psychiatry. The specialized branch of medical practice that deals with the diagnosis, treatment, and prevention of mental and emotional disorders. A psychiatrist is a physician who is qualified through training and clinical experience in the specialty of psychiatry.

psychoactive drug. Any chemical substance that alters mood or behavior as a result of alterations in the functioning of the brain. Classes of such drugs include: *Antidepressants*, introduced in the early 1960s, are used to treat long-term clinical depression. Some common ones are tricyclic antidepressants (TCAs). They generally increase brain levels of norepinephrine or serotonin or both. First-generation TCAs Elavil (amitriptyline) and Tofranil (imipramine) are used to treat depression and sleep disorders. Antidepressants that act to inhibit the enzyme monoamine oxidase are called MAO inhibitors. They increase the neurotransmitters that lead to emotional stability. MAO inhibitors can interact with hot dogs, cheese, alcoholic beverages, and other foods to produce dangerously adverse side effects. The newest antidepressants are serotonin reuptake blockers or serotonin uptake inhibitors. The best-known of these drugs is Prozac (fluoxetine). Lithium carbonate is still another type of antidepressant, often used to stabilize moods in bipolar disorder. *Antipsychotics* block the dopamine receptors in the brain. Also called major tranquilizers, they include

Thorazine (chlorpromazine), Trilafon (perphenazine), and Haldol (halperidol). *Antianxiety drugs*, also called minor tranquilizers, act by depressing the limbic system and the gababenzodiazepine complex of the brain. Common examples are Librium (chlordiazepoxide), Valium (diazepam), and Xanax (alprazolam). This class of drugs is often misused, accounting for the majority of addicts among prescription-drug users. Stimulants, which were formerly prescribed as antidepressants and appetite suppressants, are now used primarily to treat both hyperactivity and narcolepsy. They can also supplement other treatments for depression. Common stimulants include Dexedrine, Ritalin, Cylert, and Pondimin.

psychological fact. In evidence, a fact perceived mentally rather than through documents or other physical evidence.

public defender. An attorney appointed by a court to represent individuals in criminal proceedings who do not have the resources to hire their own defense counsel. The appointment of public defenders is now required in most criminal cases as a result of the Supreme Court's *Gideon v. Wainwright* decision and later cases. Public defenders are not provided to defendants in civil suits.

public defender's organization. A federal, state, or local criminal justice agency or subunit whose principal function is to represent in court persons accused or convicted of a crime or crimes, and who are unable to hire private counsel. Since its beginnings in Los Angeles County in 1914, it has become the most typical method of representing indigent defendants in U.S. court systems. *See also* assigned counsel system

public interest disputes. Strikes that may jeopardize the national health and safety, or the public interest, such as policemen's and firemen's strikes, sometimes called emergency strikes. In order to protect the public in these situations, the emergency strike provisions of federal and state laws may be invoked. The Taft-Hartley Act provides for government intervention in these disputes.

public interest law. A term describing legal and quasi-legal (such as administrative) activities, rather than a branch of law. Such activities are undertaken to protect a sizable group of people or a community at large rather than a single individual; in this sense public interest law includes class action suits structured to spread legal costs among all affected people who are parties to the suit. Another definition of public interest law is the practice of law to accomplish social change. Major areas of such law have been environmental and consumer protection, but the term includes such traditional fields as legal aid. Consumer advocate Ralph Nader has been a leading figure in this type of legislation. *See also* class action

public law. (1) A general classification of law—the principal branches are constitutional, administrative, criminal, and international—that is concerned with the organization of the state; the relations between the state and the people who compose it; the responsibilities of public officers to the state, to each other, and to private persons; and the relations of states to one another. (2) A statute that applies to all people and in all locations in a state.

public nuisance. An activity or set of conditions that negatively affects the rights, health, safety, or peace of others.

public opinion survey. A type of quantitative research, usually conducted by telephone with random samples of the population, to assess attitudes. Knowledge of the opinions of Americans on criminal justice issues is useful, for example, in revealing the public's mood and priorities, and such information may also assist in forecasting public pressure for legislative changes. *See also* Gallup poll; Harris poll

public order offenses. Violations of the peace or order of the community or threats to the public health through unacceptable public conduct, interference with governmental authority, or violation of civil rights or liberties. These violations include weapons offenses, bribery, escape, and tax evasion.

public relations. A specialty within the field of communications and/or marketing whose goal is to improve the public image of or promote public acceptance or support of an organization or service or product. Primary public relations tactics include developing good relationships with media reporters and editors, targeting particular audiences within the public at large, staging news events, and generating publicity. Crisis public relations can be focused on helping an organization weather a problem situation such as bankruptcy or product tampering. Public relations conducted by large organizations is normally part of a larger communications program that includes marketing, advertising, lobbying, and customer, investor, and employee relations.

public safety department. An agency organized at the state or local level of government and incorporating, at a minimum, various law enforcement and emergency service functions. An example of this type of agency is the Sunnyvale, CA, Public Safety Department; police and fire personnel are cross-trained and serve in the same department.

public sector unions. Labor unions that represent employees in public service occupations, whose employers are generally local or state government. In 1962 President John F. Kennedy issued an executive order granting federal civil service employees the right to organize. Since the mid-1970s, public sector unions have grown faster than those in the private sector. Public employees' unions differ from those in the private sector only in their types of employer and the tactics they use; many private sector unions have members in public employment. Unions of educators, police, and firefighters are now common. Public sector workers and their unions lack the protections granted by the National Labor Relations Act, and they cannot use the services of the National Labor Relations Board. Public employees are instead covered by various state labor laws, and at the federal level by the Civil Service Reform Act of 1978 and other legislation. Over 50 percent of federal employees are covered by collective bargaining agreements, and almost 40 percent at the state and local levels are so covered. *See also* collective bargaining

pulling method. A safe-cracking technique involving a screw-type device with a long handle used by burglars to pull the combination wheel and its attached spindle from the safe. *See also* punching tool

Pullman strike. One of the most significant strikes in labor history, it began in May 1894 when the Pullman Palace Car Co. cut wages without reducing workers' rents in the company town of Pullman, IL. When the company refused to discuss grievances or arbitrate, Eugene Debs's American Railway Union joined the strike, and rail transportation in 27 states was paralyzed. The government used the Sherman Antitrust Act to obtain a blanket injunction against the union. Violence followed, and President Grover Cleveland sent federal troops to crush the strike. Debs emerged from jail a dedicated foe of American capitalism.

punching tool. A tool used by safe burglars to batter away the safe lock and spindle so that the locking bars can be released and the safe opened. *See also* pulling method

punishment. In criminal law, any pain, penalty, suffering, or confinement inflicted upon a person by the authority of the law and the judgment and sentence of a court, for some crime or offense committed by him, or for his omission of a duty enjoined by law.

punishment, capital. Death penalty for crime; executions by the state for purposes of social control or defense. A wide variety of crimes have come under the purview of the death penalty from ancient times to the present, and methods of execution have included hanging, crucifixion, quartering, beheading, gas, electric chair, lethal injection, and the firing squad. In England during the eighteenth century it was estimated that 240 crimes were punishable by death.

Capital punishment was an early part of American colonial life. William Penn's Great Law of 1682, although essentially humani-

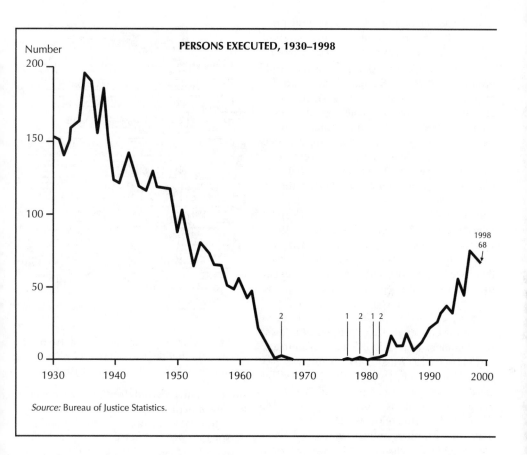

PERSONS EXECUTED, 1930–1998

Number

Source: Bureau of Justice Statistics.

tarian, retained the death penalty for first de-gree murder. In the early 1840s reform movements such as the Anti-Gallows Societies and the National Society for the Abolition of Capital Punishment were formed. The first execution by electrocution occurred on August 6, 1890, at Auburn Prison, NY, when William Kemmler was put to death for murder. Caryl Chessman spent 12 years on death row in California before his execution in 1960.

In 1972, the Supreme Court argued and decided three cases involving the use of capital punishment in a prejudicial manner. Each of the three petitioners was black and had been sentenced to death, with juries having determined the sentence in each case. Lucius Jackson had been convicted of murder, and

William Furman and Elmer Branch had been convicted of rape. All three eventually appealed their convictions to the Supreme Court. Prior to the ruling in *Furman v. Georgia*, a total of 3,859 persons had been executed since 1930, when national statistics were first used. Of that total, 53.5 percent were black, lending credence to the charge that capital punishment had been used discriminately; only 32 were women. The largest single year for capital punishment in modern history was 1935, when 199 offenders were executed. The South used capital punishment more often than all the other regions of the nation combined—between 1930 and 1965, of 3,856 executed, 2,305 were in the South, 608 in the Northwest, 507 in the West, and 403 in the North Central states. The remaining 33 were federal prisoners. The last execution before the 1972 ruling took place in June 1967 in Colorado.

Furman v. Georgia did not end the death penalty. In 1976 the Supreme Court in a 7-2 majority ruling (*Gregg V. Georgia*) upheld the constitutionality of new state capital punishment laws, which had been rewritten to avoid racial discrimination and to require separate consideration of the guilty-or-innocent decision and the penalty decision in potential capital cases. Convicted murderer Gary Gilmore was executed by a Utah firing squad on January 16, 1977, in the first exercise of capital punishment in the United States since 1967. Gilmore had opposed all attempts to delay his execution. At the time of Gilmore's death there were approximately 450 persons under the death sentence, one in federal prison and the others in prisons in 23 states. Of that number, 233 had been sentenced to death in 1976, most under revised death penalty laws. In 2002 there were 3,557 death row inmates, and between 1977 and 2001, there were 743 executions. During those years, 270 died by causes other than execution, and 2,161 received other dispensation. On February 14, 1989, 70 drug smugglers were hanged in Tehran and 25 other Iranian cities; 67 were hanged in public at dawn and 3 women were executed inside Iranian prisons. *See also* execution, methods

punishment, corporal. (1) Bodily pain or suffering inflicted as punishment for crime, such as flogging. (2) The larger category of punishment that includes deportation or imprisonment, as distinguished from capital punishment or punishment by monetary penalty.

punishment, cruel and unusual. The Eighth Amendment to the Constitution says: "Excessive bail shall not be required nor excessive fines imposed, nor cruel and unusual punishment inflicted." Such punishment has been defined by the courts as those things that are cruel and inhuman, especially if such forms of punishment have not been specifically provided for by law; however, this definition is no guarantee that a particular punishment

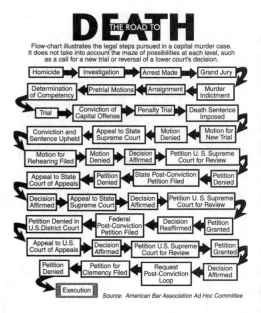

D**EATH**
THE ROAD TO

Flow-chart illustrates the legal steps pursued in a capital murder case. It does not take into account the maze of possibilities at each level, such as a call for a new trial or reversal of a lower court's decision.

Source: American Bar Association Ad Hoc Committee

will not be determined cruel and unusual. The Court held that the use of convict guards in a penitentiary fell within this classification.

punishment, individualization of. Corrective treatment of offenders based on an analysis of the interrelated factors in the background and personality that led to the particular conflict with the law of each offender. Such treatment can be termed making the punishment fit the criminal rather than making the punishment fit the crime.

punishment, infamous. Punishment for what is held by society at a given time to be an infamous crime. The Supreme Court has decided that death, or imprisonment in a state prison for a term of years at hard labor, especially for treason or felony, are infamous punishments, and that disqualification for public office as a punishment for crime is infamous.

punishment, mitigation of. The reduction in severity of the sentence normally imposed for an offense because of some special aspect of, or surrounding circumstances in, the case.

punitive damages. The awarding of damages in a tort action to punish the one at fault, usually but not always as a monetary award. Not all states allow such damages.

Pure Food and Drug Act. Federal law of 1906 supported by President Theodore Roosevelt in response to mounting criticism of the food preparation industries. It was passed in conjunction with the Meat Inspection Act. The food and drug act barred the sale or manufacture of adulterated or falsely labeled drugs and food involved in interstate commerce, while the meat act required federal inspection of meat plants engaged in interstate commerce.

The campaign for the Pure Food and Drug Act had attacked the use of dyes and artificial preservatives in foods sold to the public. As early as 1898, public health officials banded together in the National Association of State Dairy and Food Departments to agitate for federal food controls, and in the Spanish-American War a huge public scandal over the "embalmed" beef supplied for U.S. troops aroused public outrage. However, the most effective propaganda came in 1906 with Upton Sinclair's shocking novel about the Chicago stockyards, *The Jungle*.

Later amendments strengthened these reforms, and in 1938 the Wheeler-Lea Act required clearer labeling of food, drugs, and cosmetics and provided for prosecution of false advertisers.

pyromania. Usually referred to as pathological firesetting, pyromania is a compulsion to start fires. This disorder has been called an obsessive-compulsive reaction or a symptom of an antisocial personality. It has been called the "fire-water complex" and can involve sexual pleasure. Some aggressive sex offenders, for example, engage in voyeurism, sadism, and pyromania. Whatever the cause, persons with this disorder have been responsible for millions of dollars of fire damage and innumerable deaths.

The unconscious motivation for pyromania may be defiance of a particular authority figure or of society in general, a more general expression of aggression, or of sexual drives that do not find another outlet.

Q

quasi-judicial powers. Law-making powers granted by Congress to administrative and regulatory agencies. Although the doctrine of separation of powers calls for judicial powers to be exercised only by courts and judges, Congress can empower a commission or agency to hold hearings and make decisions that have the force of law.

quasi-military organization. Generally referring to law enforcement agencies modeled after the military: with strong emphasis on hierarchy, uniformity, chain-of-command, division of labor, accountability, and control. The structure is attributed to Sir Robert Peel, who in his Peelian Reform stated that police should be organized "along military lines."

Queer Nation. The organization formed during May 1990 in New York City after M-80 bombs were exploded in trash cans adjacent to a gay nightclub. Protesters formed a loose-knit organization dubbed Queer Nation that describes itself as "militant and uncompromising in the fight against homophobia in all its manifestations." *See also* ACT-UP

Questioned Document Examiners, American Society of. Founded in 1942. Address: P.O. Box 382684, Germantown, TN 38183.

questioned specimens. Physical evidence specimens, the origin or ownership of which is unknown; as contrasted with known specimens. For example, a bullet found in the body of a deceased is a questioned specimen, whereas one fired from a gun by an officer or a laboratory technician is a known specimen. The FBI Laboratory and some others number specimens and assign to each either a Q number, for questioned, or a K number, for known.

questionnaire. The most commonly used research tool to elicit information, in writing or by telephone, from respondents in surveys. Normally survey questions are carefully worded and ordered to avoid biasing respondents. Answers may be based on agree-disagree scales, rank-ordering of items, choosing preworded statements that most closely match the respondent's opinions, or open-ended questions requiring brief or one-word responses. All research questionnaires should be pretested for reliability, veracity, and content. *See also* Likert Scale; reliability

questions, lawful in cross-examination. When witnesses are cross-examined, they may be asked any questions that tend to (a) test their accuracy, veracity, or credibility or (b) damage their credibility. Witnesses have been compelled to answer such questions; the court has a right to exercise a discretion in such cases and to refuse to compel such questions to be answered when the truth of the matter suggested would not, in the opinion of the court, affect the credibility of witnesses as to the matter to which they are required to testify.

quid pro quo (Lat., lit.). This for that; a phrase meaning a direct exchange of services or things of similar value.

quorum. A number or percentage of the officers or members of any body that has been determined as legally competent to transact business or make decisions on behalf of the entire organization.

quo warranto (Lat.). A proceeding requiring a person to show by what right he or she exercised any office or liberty.

R

race relations. A special DOJ office has been created to help people settle race-related differences voluntarily rather than in the courts or on the streets. Agency professionals enter troubled communities, with no investigative power or authority to dispense funds, and try to mediate or arrange voluntary settlements of disputes. For instance, they have conciliated problems in education, law enforcement, and sentencing disparities. Several free publications are available. For the list, contact: Community Relations Service, DOJ, 600 E. Street, NW, Suite 6000, Washington, DC 20530.

Racketeer Influenced and Corrupt Organizations (RICO). The federal RICO statute was enacted in 1970 and amended in 1986. Unlike other laws that address individual criminal acts such as murder or robbery, the RICO statutes were specifically designed to target the overall and continuing operations of organized crime. Specifically, the act prohibits the use of racketeering activities or profits to acquire, conduct, or maintain the business of an existing organization or enterprise. Racketeering activities are defined as any act or threat involving murder, kidnapping, gambling, arson, robbery, bribery, extortion, dealing in narcotics or dangerous drugs, fraud, and other crimes. The act provides for forfeiture of illegally obtained gains and interests in enterprises. Twenty-three states had enacted RICO statutes by 1986. Most are very similar to the federal statute. RICO charges were filed against a brokerage firm for the first time in a suit brought against Princeton/Newport Partners by NY U.S. attorney Rudolph W. Guiliani in August 1988.

racketeering. The type of crime involving obtaining money illegally, especially through extortion, but also by bootlegging, fraud, or other criminal activities. In the twentieth century, racketeering became more common in large cities in prostitution, gambling, liquor, and narcotics. Sharp practices such as swindling schemes, the coercive collection of tolls from reputable businessmen, hijacking, protection rackets, slot-machine control, and bookmaking were developed in the easy money efforts of gangsters. The high point was reached during the Prohibition era, when national gangster syndicates ruled over large empires of crime, extending their control into government, labor unions, and industry. Important rackets arose in poultry, laundries, milk, and other industries. Accompaniments to racketeering were bribes, bombings, assassinations, and corruption. Alphonse Capone was the recognized king of the underworld. Other prominent racketeers were "Legs" Diamond, "Dutch" Schultz, "Waxey" Gordon, Frank Yale, "Lucky" Luciano, "Nocky"

Johnson, and Frank Costello. From time to time public drives against racketeering have been undertaken, generally with little success. Among these campaigns have been those of special prosecutor Thomas E. Dewey in New York County, William O'Dwyer in Kings County, and the federal Kefauver Committee. *See also* Kefauver Investigation

radar. (1) Any of certain methods or systems of using beamed and reflected radio-frequency energy (radio waves) to detect and locate objects or to measure distance or altitude. (2) The electronic equipment, sets, or devices used in any such system. The term derives from the words *radio detection* and *ranging*. The National Bureau of Standards has conducted tests in order to measure the reliability and performance of police radar systems. For further information on these tests, including details on devices that affect the reliability of radar systems, contact: National Bureau of Standards, Public Information Division, Department of Commerce, Washington DC 20234.

radial design. An architectural plan for penal institutions in which prisons are constructed in the form of wheels, with "spokes" or branches radiating from the center.

radical. One who advocates immediate and fundamental changes in governments and laws, especially laws relating to economic and social welfare.

radical criminology. A contemporary school of criminology that focuses on the political nature of crime and criminal law and that emphasizes the repressive function of the criminal justice system.

radicalism. A term derived from the Latin word *radix*, or root, radicalism literally means an attitude that goes to the heart or root of a problem or situation. Political radicalism represents an extreme difference from the point of view of those in power; that is, it questions the fundamentals of an economic or governmental system and implies advocacy of profound change in the institutions in question.

radio call letters. Generally those stations east of the Mississippi River begins with the letter "W" and the stations west of the Missssippi having the first letter as K."

radio frequency motion detector. A sensor that detects the motion of an intruder through the use of a radiated, radio frequency, electromagnetic field. The device operates by sensing a disturbance in the generated RF field caused by intruder motion, typically a modulation of the field referred to as a Doppler effect, which is used to initiate an alarm signal. Most radio frequency motion detectors are certified by the FCC for operation as field disturbance sensors at one of the following frequencies: 0.9 15 GHz (L-Band), 2.45 GHz (S-Band), 5.8 GHz (XBand), and 22.125 GHz (K-Band). Units operating in the microwave frequency range are usually called microwave motion detectors.

radio watch. Volunteer, mobile, citizen band (CB) radio operators and drivers who augment police surveillance and detection capacities. Screened CB volunteer operators are generally under the direct supervision of an official watch commander or supervisor and take no action other than notifying that official of suspicious activity or the location of a suspect.

railroad police. Largest private police group in the United States, numbering about 8,000, including personnel in Canada, whose function is to protect the passengers, property, cargo, and reputation of the railroads.

railroad safety. The Office of Safety Programs inspects tracks, equipment, signals, and general railroad operations. It investigates accidents and complaints. Publishes *Safety Report*, which includes a list of completed or pending judicial actions for the enforcement of any safety rules, regulations, orders, or standards issued. Address: Office of Safety Programs, Safety, Federal Railway Administration, Department of Transportation, 400 7th St., SW, Room 7330, Washington, DC 20590. Information on railroad accidents can be obtained through accident data maintained in a database and through free publications. Contact the Reports and Analysis Division, Safety RR-32, same address.

Railroad Strike. During the two-week Railroad Strike of 1877, service on two-thirds of the nation's rail lines in 11 states was disrupted, some 100 people died, and millions of dollars worth of property was destroyed.

Randolph, Edmund. Born in Williamsburg, VA, in 1793, Randolph served as the first U.S. attorney general under President George Washington from 1789 to 1794; he was secretary of state from 1794 to 1795, resigning after being falsely charged with accepting a bribe from France. Aaron Burr was his counsel and won an acquittal in Randolph's treason trial in 1807. He lived until 1813.

randomization. A technique for controlling all other variables that might confuse the relationship between the independent variable(s) and the dependent variable in an experimental situation. Randomization is accomplished by assigning the people or phenomena to be observed randomly to experimental and control groups; that is, each individual has an equal probability of being assigned to either type of group. This procedure guarantees with measurable probability that the characteristics associated with the individuals being observed, such as age, gender, or race, that might confuse or interfere with the relationship between the variables being tested, will be uniformly distributed among experimental and control groups.

ransom. The demanding of money for the redemption of captured persons or property.

rape. Unlawful sexual intercourse, by force or without legal or factual consent. Date rape is forcible rape in which the victim has consented to the company of the offender but has not agreed to have sexual intercourse. *See also* Rape, National Center for the Prevention and Control of

Rape, National Center for the Prevention and Control of. Founded in 1976 by the U.S. Department of Health and Human Services, National Institute of Mental Health, the center supports research on the causes of rape and sexual assault, mental health consequences, treatment of victims (adults and children), and offenders. The center also evaluates programs that are intended to prevent and reduce sexual assaults. Address: 5600 Fishers Lane, Rockville, MD 20857.

rap sheet. Popularized in many early crime movies and novels, rap is an acronym for record of arrest and prosecution.

rate, crime. A measure of reported crime in given geographical areas or population groups, expressed in numbers proportionate to a population unit. Such rates may be crude (per 100,000 population), refined (per 100,000 persons capable of committing a crime), or specific (such as per 100,000 native-born males, 21–30 years of age). No generally accepted terminology to distinguish different types of rates exists. The unit of crime or criminality employed in computing these rates varies.

rationalization. The process of explaining behavior or attitudes prompted by unrecognized motives by excuses or reasons that place the person in a more favorable light. In using this mechanism, an individual defends himself against truths that are uncomfortable or painful.

ratio scales. Measurement systems for intervals that have true, rather than arbitrary, zero points, allowing each outcome to be stated as *n* times greater or lesser than other outcomes. Fahrenheit and Centigrade scales both have arbitrary zero points, as do many other common systems.

Ray, James Earl. Convicted of assassinating the Rev. Martin Luther King Jr. in Memphis, TN, on April 4, 1968, Ray had been the subject of one of the most intensive manhunts in history when he was captured in London. Returned to Memphis, he initially pleaded guilty and then recanted his confession, claiming that he was victimized in a conspiracy. Sentenced to prison, he was not given his first parole hearing until May 25, 1994, at which he continued to deny his guilt. The parole board rejected his request, and Ray died in prison in Nashville, TN, of liver disease at the age of 70, on April 23, 1998. By that time, he had convinced a group of Dr. King's heirs that the case should be reopened.

reaction time (RT). The interval between the beginning of a stimulus and the initiating of a response. For example, the length of time it takes to put your foot on the brake is one measure of your RT to a red light. The RT experiment was invented by the physiologist Hermann von Helmholtz more than 100 years ago.

real evidence. Evidence produced by actual inspection of material objects or physical characteristics.

reasonable man. Judicial review is sometimes guided by the precept that a "reasonable man" considering the evidence would make the same determination as the court. Reasonable-man standards are applied in administrative law matters and in determining patterned evasion of vice codes, racial equality laws, and other cases in which public sentiment may disagree with legal rules.

rebellion. The open, organized, and often armed resistance to government or authority. Like insurrection or revolt, rebellion does not imply the radical political and social changes of a revolution.

rebutting evidence. When the defense has produced new evidence that the prosecution has not dealt with, the court, at its discretion, may allow the prosecution to give evidence in reply to rebut or contradict it. When such rebutting evidence is given, the defense is entitled to comment on it. For example, evidence may be called to rebut or contradict an alibi.

recall. A procedure for dismissing elected officials before their term of office has officially terminated. *See also* impeachment

receiver. One who is legally appointed with custody of property belonging to others, pending judicial action; also sometimes an illegal activity, such as receiver of stolen goods, or fence.

reception. In criminal justice, the indoctrination and classification process used in the prison system for newly received inmates.

recidivism. The repetition of criminal behavior.

recidivism statutes. Laws that provide for increased penalties for persons who commit additional specific crimes after conviction for previous criminal acts. Included are career criminal and habitual criminal statutes. In a 5–4 decision in *Solem v. Helm*, the Supreme Court on June 28, 1983, invalidated a life-term sentence that had been imposed in South Dakota on a man who had passed a bad check for $100. The man had been sentenced under a habitual criminal law because he previously had been convicted of six crimes, including burglary, grand larceny, and drunk driving.

recidivist. A person who has been convicted of one or more crimes and who is alleged or found to have subsequently committed another crime or series of crimes.

recognizance. Pledge by an individual found guilty of an offense to refrain from certain acts or to appear at a set time, usually in court.

record. (1) The records of a court: the formal history of the proceedings before it, entered by the clerk, which are the only evidence of what has been done by the court. They cannot be amended or contradicted. (2) A collection of information about an individual, including arrests and dispositions. (3) Any collection of data that all pertains to a particular person, place, or thing.

record expungement. The process whereby a youth who has a delinquent record can request that the record be destroyed or sealed.

recuse. (1) To challenge or object to a judge or other person officially involved in the trial of a case on the grounds that he or she is prejudiced, or has an interest in the case. (2) The nonparticipation of a judge or other official or person officially involved in the trial of a case because of personal interest, prejudice, or close relationship to an involved party.

redirect examination. The questioning of a witness, by the party who called him or her, after the witness has been cross-examined. In a criminal trial, the party offering a witness questions him or her first on direct examination. The opposing party questions on crossexamination, and the first party then questions on redirect examination.

Red Light Abatement Law. A California law enacted in 1913 and amended, stating that "any building or place used for the purpose of illegal gambling, lewdness, or prostitution is a nuisance that shall be enjoined, abated and prevented whether it is a public or private nuisance." Such abatement is a civil process, although contained in the penal code. This law has been a device to combat prostitution operating under the guise of massage parlors. If the police can show cause, the place of business can be closed for up to two years.

redress of grievances. The correction of abuses in the government of a state. The right of the individual to petition for redress of grievances, one of the oldest of British constitutional rights, is guaranteed in the First Amendment of the U.S. Constitution. Historically, such petitions were considered by the British parliament before it voted appropriations for governmental services.

reeve. Historically, the top law enforcement officer of a district or shire in England. It was from "shire reeve" that the title sheriff evolved.

reformatory. A correctional institution for youthful offenders; the term is based on the concept that juvenile criminal behavior can be reformed.

refreshing memory. A witness, while on the stand and testifying, may look at memoranda or other documents on any subject for the purpose of aiding his or her memory and recalling facts.

refugee. Traditionally a person fleeing his or her country to avoid persecution or hardship. Individual governments establish their own policies on the admission of refugees, despite the obligations imposed by United Nations conventions. Increasingly, states have begun to distinguish between political refugees, who are admitted, and those fleeing economic hardship, who are often refused entry.

regulation. (1) A rule or instruction to be followed by members of an organization. (2) Approved, accepted, or specified by the employing agency.

rehabilitate. To restore a person or thing to its original state or capacity, such as a slum area to a desirable neighborhood.

rehabilitation. A widely accepted but seldom achieved goal of penal systems, generally relying on three basic elements: (a) individualization—emphasis on the offender, not the violation; (b) indeterminacy—the release of the individual when cured rather than after a sentence has been served; (c) discretion—flexibility in managing the treatment of offenders.

Rehabilitation Act of 1973. Legislation covering recipients of federal contracts or financial assistance programs that prohibits discrimination on the basis of disability and requires affirmative action to include and accommodate disabled participants.

Rehabilitation of Errants, Citizens United for (CURE). Founded in 1972 for prisoners and former prisoners, their families, and others concerned with prison reform. Aims to reduce crime through reform of the criminal justice system. Publishes a quarterly newsletter. Address: CURE National, P.O. Box 2310, National Capitol Station, Washington, DC 20013.

release on own recognizance. The pretrial release of an arrested person on his or her pledge to reappear for trial at a later date, granted to those who are presumed likely to reappear.

release to parole. A release from prison by discretionary action of a paroling authority, conditional upon the parolee's fulfillment of specified conditions of behavior.

reliability. In statistical research, the consistency with which items are ordered on a measuring instrument to ensure that experiments can be replicated. That is, an instrument is reliable if, when no true change in a variable has occurred, items measured by the instrument will have the same relative placement in all experiments. *See also* replication

remand. *See* bind over

remedial. Curative, ameliorative; describes a level of social casework, group work, or custodial care that is above the merely palliative, in that the situation of the client becomes better than it was when the treatment was initiated and may even be brought into the range of average or normalcy.

remission. In criminal justice, a release; pardon of an offense.

removal proceedings. A procedure used by the federal judicial system to transfer an accused from one judicial district to another, prior to his or her conviction for an offense. After a hearing on the matter, a federal judge signs a removal order, which authorizes a U.S. marshal to transfer the accused to another district.

reparation. The provision that a convicted offender make restitution to the victim in accordance with the damage the latter suffered. Thus, one of the conditions of probation in some jurisdictions is that the offender make weekly or periodic payments to the victim for the injury done.

reparole. A release to parole occurring after a return to prison from an earlier release to parole, on the same sentence to confinement.

repeal. The abrogation of a law by the enacting body, either by express declaration or implication by the passage of a later act whose provisions contradict those of the earlier law.

replevin. An action in court brought by an individual to recover possessions unlawfully taken or detained.

replication. The repetition or duplication of procedures followed in a particular study, in order to determine whether or not the findings obtained correspond to those of earlier studies. *See also* reliability

report. (1) The accurate recording of facts, usually transcribed in written form. (2) Data processing output that has high information content; more broadly, any planned and organized output from a system.

reprieve. The temporary postponement of the execution of a sentence, usually in order for an appeal to be brought.

requisition. In law, the demand made by one governor of another for a fugitive from justice.

research. An objective, painstaking, and careful investigation of a matter; a studious examination of a problem with a view toward finding facts.

research, applied. Scientific inquiry directed toward practical use or application.

research design. The strategy used by researchers to collect and analyze the data necessary to test hypotheses. Designing a study or experiment entails choosing the fundamental unit of analysis, basic research method, time-ordering of variables, data collection procedures, and techniques for data analysis. The research methods most often used by criminologists are sample surveys, experiments, and field research.

research, pure. Inquiry directed toward the solution of a scientific problem of theory. The results may have no current practical application.

res gestae (Lat.). Events that speak for themselves; the words spoken by participants during an occurrence, rather than later in retelling; spontaneous words spoken during or immediately after an act, so that the speaker has no opportunity to rationalize or explain what was said. Any part of the *res gestae* is admissible as an exception to the hearsay rule.

resident. A person required by official action or his or her own acceptance of placement to reside in a public or private facility established for purposes of confinement, supervision, or care.

residential commitment. A sentence of commitment to a correctional facility for adults, in which the offender is required to reside at night but from which he or she is regularly permitted to depart during the day, unaccompanied by any official.

residential facility. A correctional facility from which residents are regularly permitted to depart, unaccompanied by any official, for the purposes of using community resources, such as schools or treatment programs, and seeking or holding employment.

resisting an officer. Resisting or obstructing a law enforcement officer in the performance of an official duty.

Resolution Trust Corp. (RTC). A federal agency formed in 1989 to oversee failed savings and loan banks and to administer seized or forfeited property. RTC is a private corporation whose board includes the secretary of the treasury, the chairman of the Federal Reserve Board, and other government officials.

respondent. The person who formally answers the allegations stated in a petition that has been filed in a court; in criminal proceedings, the one who contends against an appeal. In research, anyone who answers a questionnaire or other survey instrument.

response time. The interval period between the receipt of information and the arrival of authorities.

restitution. A court requirement that an alleged or convicted offender pay money or provide services to the victim of the crime or provide services to the community.

restorative justice. A framework for justice reform that seeks to engage victims, offenders and their families, other citizens, and community groups both as clients of criminal justice services and as resources in an effective response to crime. Three basic questions

are asked: (1) What is the nature of the harm resulting from the crime? (2) What needs to be done to "make it right" or repair the harm? and (3) Who is responsible for this repair?

restraining order. An order, issued by a court of competent jurisdiction, forbidding a named person, or a class of persons, from doing specified acts.

retaliation. The term applied to private vengeance for wrongs. The avenger attempts to make the offender suffer as much as the victim had suffered. The term carries the idea that punishment for an injury should be like the injury. *See also* revenge

retentionist. One who favors the retention or reinstitution of the death penalty, in contrast to the abolitionist, who favors its abolition.

retreatism. A mode of adaptation in Robert Merton's anomie theory in which the individual rejects both the goal of economic success and the legitimate means of attaining it. *See also* anomie

retreat to the wall. A phrase used in criminal justice to mean that an individual must avail him- or herself of any reasonable avenue of escape to eliminate the necessity of killing an assailant.

retribution. A concept that implies the payment of a debt to society and thus the expiation of one's offense. It was codified in the biblical injunction, "an eye for an eye, a tooth for a tooth."

return. A return in writing must be made by the person to whom a writ is directed. In most states it is required by statute to be verified, though in many states this is not necessary if the person is in the custody of a peace officer.

reus. The individual formally accused of a crime.

revenge. The infliction of suffering upon an offender by a private individual who has been injured. It is a broader term than retaliation in that revenge has no limits as to kind or degree of suffering returned upon the offender. *See also* retaliation

reversal. The action of an appellate court in rendering judgment in a case under review that has the effect of invalidating a judgment of a lower court or tribunal or of requiring a new trial. Such action is usually based on an error by the lower tribunal in interpreting the law applicable to the case.

review. (1) A reexamination of some matter (as the findings of a board or the valuation of property by an assessor) by a higher officer or tribunal. (2) Reconsideration of applicable law in a judicial decision by a higher court.

review, writ of. A general designation of any form of process issuing from an appellate court and intended to bring up for review the record or decision of the lower court. In code practice, a substitute for, or equivalent of, the writ of *certiorari*.

revocation. In application to either probation or parole, the withdrawal of the privileges of either status because the behavior of the individual was in violation of the conditions agreed upon. In both instances, a body of case law has developed that defines the constitutional rights the probationer or parolee retains in revocation proceedings.

revolution. A far-ranging, pervasive, radical change in part, or in many parts, of society; the violent or nonviolent replacement of one power elite by another in the climactic phase of such a change.

rewards. Under the 1984 Currency and Foreign Transactions Reporting Act Amendments, "The Secretary of Treasury may pay a reward to an individual who provides original information which leads to a recovery of a criminal fine, civil penalty, or forfeiture, which exceeds $50,000, for a violation. The Secretary may not award more than 25 percent of the net amount of the fine, penalty, or forfeiture collected or $150,000, whichever is less. An officer or employee of the United States, a state, or local government who provides information in the performance of official duties is not eligible for a reward."

ridge. A mark or line constituting part of a fingerprint.

ridge count. The number of ridges intervening between the delta and the core of a fingerprint. Ridges counted must cross or touch an imaginary line from the delta to the core. *See also* fingerprint patterns

right of allocution. The right of the defendant to speak in his own defense before judgment is pronounced. *See also* allocution

right, political. Those individuals in the spectrum of political views who oppose drastic or radical change in society. Right-wing groups supporting the maintenance of the status quo are often termed conservatives, while those who advocate a return to an earlier set of conditions are termed reactionaries. *See also* conservative; leftists, political; liberals, political

Rights, Bill of. The first 10 amendments to the Constitution, prohibiting the federal government or, in certain amendments, the states from interfering with political liberties and guaranteeing to persons charged with crime the protections of fair procedure. The Civil War amendments (Thirteenth, Fourteenth, and Fifteenth) are also commonly classed as part of the Bill of Rights. Most state constitutions also include the equivalent of the federal guarantees, and, when codified together, these are referred to as bills of rights. The phrase was used earlier in England in the course of the struggle between king and commoners and covers similar guarantees won by the people.

rights of accused. *See* accused persons, rights of

rights of defendant. Those powers and privileges that are constitutionally guaranteed to every defendant.

right to bear arms. The right of citizens under the Second Amendment to the Constitution to possess arms in order to provide a militia. The courts have held that this right is not infringed by the Federal Firearms Act, or by statutes in most of the states that make unauthorized possession of lethal weapons a criminal offense.

right to counsel. A fundamental right of an accused person to be represented by an attorney at any stage of a criminal proceeding, including the rights (a) to have an attorney assigned as counsel by the court if the accused is financially unable to pay counsel fees, (b) to consult privately with counsel, and (c) of counsel to have sufficient time to prepare the case.

right-to-know laws. State laws that entitle genuine representatives of radio, television, newspapers, and magazines and certain other citizens access to official meetings, records, and other information. Although the First Amendment states that "Congress cannot make laws which threaten freedom of speech or freedom of the press," there is no enforceable constitutional right to know, nor is there any hard and fast regulation of what each branch of government and its agencies must disclose. *See also* Freedom of Information Act

right to release on bail. In common law it was within the discretion of the magistrate, judge, or court having jurisdiction and power to allow or deny bail in all cases. It could be allowed whenever it was deemed sufficient to ensure the appearance of the accused, but not otherwise, and was therefore always allowed in cases of misdemeanor, less frequently in cases of felony, and almost never in cases of felony punishable by death. It is now generally declared by the state constitutions, or provided by statute, that the accused shall have an absolute right to give bail in all cases except where the punishment may be death and in those cases, too, except where the proof of guilt is evident or the presumption great.

Rikers Island Penitentiary. Located in New York City, it is the largest penal colony in the nation. It consists of six facilities, each holding a separate population of offenders. Built in 1933 to house sentenced offenders, some of its cell blocks are the length of a football field.

riot. The coming together of a group of persons who engage in violent and tumultuous conduct, thereby causing or creating either a serious, imminent risk of injury to persons or property or public alarm. *See also* Draft Riots

Riot Act. A statute that originated in England for the purpose of dispersing unlawfully assembled persons. The statute states that if 12 persons or more are unlawfully assembled and disturbing the peace, they are guilty of a felony if they do not disperse within one hour when ordered to do so by a duly authorized officer.

riot-control agent. A chemical that produces temporary irritating or disabling effects when in contact with the eyes or when inhaled.

riot grenade. A grenade of plastic or other nonfragmenting material containing a charge of tear gas and a detonating fuse with short delay. The grenade functions and the gas is released by a bursting action.

riot gun. Any shotgun with a short barrel, especially one used in guard duty or to scatter rioters. A riot gun usually has a 20-inch cylindrical barrel.

riots, urban. The anticonscription (draft) riot of New York City from July 13 to 16, 1863, resulted in an estimated 1,200 deaths. The first ghetto riots in modern history occurred in the early 1960s in New York City's Brownsville, Bedford-Stuyvesant, and Harlem areas and were followed by the Watts riot in Los Angeles, CA, in August 1965. The Watts riot began with an alleged incident of police brutality and ended with 34 fatalities, 1,032 injuries, $40 million in property destroyed, 600 buildings damaged or demolished, and 4,000 arrests. By 1967 there had been 164 disorders (and 83 deaths); outbreaks of violence in Newark, NJ, and Detroit, MI, were especially serious. On April 29, 1992, following the reading of the Rodney King verdict, the nation's worst riot of the twentieth century broke out in an area of Los Angeles known as Mid-city. The three-day disorder spread from Hollywood to Long Beach, taking at least 53 lives, injuring 2,300 people, and damaging more than 1,100 stores, which were looted and/or burned. *See also* civil disturbances

ripping method. A method of opening safes by burglars. A can opener-type tool is used to remove the metal from the top, bottom, back, or side of a safe. *See also* pulling method

risk management. A business function that in large organizations is limited to the management of corporate property, liability, and casualty insurance and processing of claims. In smaller firms, risk management also includes loss prevention and loss control-programs to contain employee or customer theft of merchandise and other company property.

robbery. The unlawful taking or attempted taking of property that is in the immediate possession of another, by force or threat of force.

The largest amount lost in a robbery was on November 25, 1983, when $35 million worth of gold in the form of 6,800 bars in 76 boxes were removed by six masked men from a vault of Brinks Mat Ltd. at Heathrow Airport, England.

The greatest recorded train robbery occurred between 3:03 A.M. and 3:27 A.M. on August 8, 1963, when a General Post Office mail train from Glasgow, Scotland, was ambushed at Sears Crossing and robbed at Bridego Bridge near Mentmore, Buckinghamshire, England. The gang escaped with about 120 mailbags containing $6,053,103 worth of bank notes being taken to London for pulping. Only $961,654 was recovered.

On April 29, 1985, $7.94 million in untraceable bills was taken from a Wells Fargo vault in New York City. The largest armored-car robbery in the United States occurred in Jacksonville, FL, on April 4, 1997, when a Loomis armored-car driver fled with up to $20 million in used banknotes.

The largest armed robbery was committed by five individuals in Los Angeles, CA, in September 1997. They escaped with $18.9 million in cash, in a takeover at Dunbar's armored truck depot. On June 18, 2001, Allen Pace III, a fired Dunbar Armored Co., security worker and mastermind of the heist, was sentenced to 24 years and 2 months in federal prison.

role playing. This procedure, which has a multitude of uses in clinical psychology, is widely used in sensitivity and therapeutic groups. The individual is required to adopt the role of another person and experience the world in a way that is not usual for him or her. This experience is designed to produce new insights into an individual's perception of his or her own behavior and that of others.

Role playing has been effectively used, for example, in programs to establish better police-community relations. In such cases police play the roles of protesters, while protestors play those of police officers. This use of role playing is thought to increase empathy by providing individuals with some ability to relate to others' experiences. *See also* empathy

Roman legal system. A system that favored the interests of citizens with higher social status, similar to the Babylonian system. The law of the Twelve Tables (circa 450 B.C.) represented Rome's first attempts to codify the law and to satisfy the grievances of the lower classes; the tables set forth the citizen's basic rights. Roman procedure was highly formalized, with precise steps for filing courses of action and the drafting of pleas and remedies. After the fall of Rome, the Byzantine Empire, with its new capital at Constantinople, continued to develop sophisticated legal systems by codifying the Roman law. The Justinian Code (circa A.D. 530) consisted of four sections: the Code, the Digests, the Institutes, and the Novels. Adapting or absorbing previous laws, the Justinian Code represented a high point in reflective jurisprudence, revealing analytical thinking and authoritative commentary. The code later influenced the study of law in the first law school in Bologna, Italy, and at Oxford and Cambridge universities in England.

Roman lawyers and magistrates also developed a system of equity, known as *jus gentium*, the law of nations. This system was to be used in cases involving foreigners. Although not equivalent to what we now refer to as international law, the system represents early attempts to solve conflict-of-laws questions. *See also* canon law; common law; Germanic law; Greek law; Mesopotamian laws and codes.

Rosewood Massacre. On January 1, 1923, a white mill worker's wife stated that her husband was assaulted by a black male. A posse was formed and marched to a small Florida town of Rosewood, the black section of town. When no suspect was found, the posse turned into a vigilante mob, pulling blacks from their homes and burning structures. The siege continued for six days with the mob growing to approximately 300 people. The official death toll was six blacks and two whites although it was alleged that many blacks were buried in mass graves.

Royal Canadian Mounted Police. The federal police force of Canada.

rule of four. Prior to granting of *certiorari*, a potential case must pass the rule of four; that is, a case is accepted for Supreme Court review only if four or more members of the bench feel that it merits full consideration by the court. *See also certiorari*

rules. Social standards that are agreed upon by the members of a social organization and that concern acceptable and unacceptable actions but contain no moral implications.

runaway. A juvenile who has been judged by a judicial officer of a juvenile court to have committed the status offense of leaving the custody and home of his or her parents, guardians, or custodians without permission and failing to return within a reasonable length of time.

Rush, Benjamin. American psychiatrist, surgeon, and politician born in Philadelphia in 1746. After studying medicine at the University of Edinburgh, he became professor of chemistry at Dickinson College from 1769 to 1789. He was a signer of the Declaration of Independence. Regarded as the father of American psychiatry, Rush devoted much of his life to the reform of treatment for the mentally ill, particularly at Pennsylvania Hospital. Following his military career, he was the organizer and leader of the Philadelphia Society for Alleviating the Miseries of the Public Prisons, which was founded in 1787. In *An Enquiry Into the Effects of Public Punishment Upon Criminals*, 1787, he maintained that excessive cruelty served only to harden criminals. Opposed to capital punishment, he wrote *On Punishing Murder By Death* in 1792, condemning the practice as an offspring of monarchical divine right, a principle contrary to a republican form of government. Rush and his organization were influential in gaining penal reforms, including the establishment of the Walnut Street Jail, the first penitentiary. He is probably best known for advocating the penitentiary as a replacement for capital and corporal punishment. He lived until 1813.

S

sabotage. Willful acts designed to obstruct and interfere with the normal course of industrial operations by destroying their productive mechanisms. The purpose of sabotage in wartime is to interfere with the physical production of war goods. In labor, it is an intentional form of slowing or discontinuing production by using illegal and often violent means, sometimes including machine wrecking. The first recorded act of sabotage is said to have been the slipping of a workman's shoe into a loom to slow down production in the early days of the Industrial Revolution. In international law, sabotage may be punished by jail terms or death if the perpetrators are not lawful combatants.

Sacco-Vanzetti case. Celebrated trial and execution that has been considered a microcosm of the social, political, and economic issues of the 1920s. On April 15, 1920, two men were murdered in South Braintree, MA, in the course of a payroll robbery. On May 5, Nicola Sacco, a fish peddler, and Bartolomeo Vanzetti, a factory worker, were arrested for the crime. Both were Italian immigrants who were well known for their anarchist views. They were tried on July 14, 1921. From that time until their execution on August 23, 1927, the question of the justice of the trial, conviction, and execution of Sacco and Vanzetti agitated the country; the issue was whether or not members of unpopular minority groups are treated fairly by the American criminal justice system. To this day the case can arouse the most heated passions because the issue is still very much alive.

SADD. Students Against Drunk Driving. *See also* MADD

Safe, Class 1. A General Services Administration (GSA)-approved insulated security filing cabinet designed for 30 minutes of protection against surreptitious entry; 10 minutes against forced entry; 1 hour against fire damage to contents; and 20 hours against lock manipulation and radiological attack.

Class 2. A GSA-approved insulated security filing cabinet affording protection for 20 minutes against surreptitious entry; 5 minutes against forced entry; 1 hour against fire damage to contents; and 20 hours against lock manipulation and radiological attack.

Class 3. A GSA-approved noninsulated security filing cabinet affording protection for 20 minutes against surreptitious entry; 20 hours against manipulation of the lock and radiological attack; and no protection against forced entry.

Class 4. A GSA-approved noninsulated security filing cabinet affording protection for 20 minutes against surreptitious entry; 5 minutes against forced entry; and 20 hours against manipulation of the lock and radiological attack.

Class 5. A GSA-approved noninsulated security filing cabinet affording protection for 30 minutes against surreptitious entry; 10 minutes against forced entry; 20 minutes against manipulation of the lock; and 20 hours against radiological attack.

Class 6. A GSA-approved noninsulated security filing cabinet affording protection for 30 minutes against surreptitious attack and 20 hours against manipulation of the lock and radiological attack. It has no forced entry protection.

Safer Society Foundation. National network/clearinghouse on sexual abuse prevention, assessment, and treatment programs. Address: P.O. Box 340, Orwell, VT 05733.

Saint Valentine's Day Massacre. The murder of members of a gang of bootleggers in Chicago in 1929. This act against the "Bugs" Moran gang enabled Al Capone to consolidate his control in the city.

sally port. A double-gated security entrance into a jail or prison facility in which one gate is always closed. This permits identification, searches, and so forth, to be conducted before the remaining gate is opened.

Sam Browne belt. A broad waistband of leather designed to carry police pistol, handcuffs, ammunition, and baton. The belt was designed by General Samuel J. Browne (1824–1901).

same act may be both a crime and a tort. In such a case the offender is subject both to a civil action by the state and to a civil action by the injured party. These two actions are separate and distinct; the object of the former is to punish as an example, of the latter, to compensate the injured party. If the offense committed is a misdemeanor, either action may precede the other or both may be carried on at the same time. In case of a felony, the same rule applies generally in this country; but, in England and a few U.S. states, the civil action may not precede the criminal action. *See also* tort

sample. A part of a thing presented as evidence of the quality of the whole; a specimen.

sampling. The technique by which a researcher chooses some subset of a prespecified population to observe and measure, as a statistically valid representative group of the whole. A population is the aggregate of all individuals having some designated set of characteristics, such as all parents of preschoolers in Chicago or all inmates of Rikers Island Penitentiary.

sanction. A legal penalty assessed for the violation of law. Sanctions can include censure, community service, fines, forfeiture, suspension of privileges, probation, or imprisonment. The term also includes social methods of obtaining compliance, such as peer pressure and public opinion.

sanctioned. (1) Socially permitted or approved. (2) Subject to social, particularly legal or conventional, restraints, prohibitions, or penalties.

sanity hearing. A procedure, ordered by the court or other official, for the purpose of determining whether a person is sane and legally capable of being held responsible for offenses.

sans (Fr.). Without.

satanic cult. A group of individuals usually allied with a charismatic leader who leads them to believe in him or her as a visible deity. The term also describes practitioners of satanic beliefs and black-mass worship. Practitioners believe that Satan was an archangel who protected the throne of God, and that because of his rebellious attitude, he and many other "fallen angels" were cast out of heaven. *See also* Church of Satan; Crowley, Aleister

satisfactory evidence. Evidence that is sufficient to produce a belief that a thing is true; credible evidence; evidence that is, in respect to its amount or weight, adequate or sufficient to justify the court or jury in adopting the conclusion in support of which it is adduced.

saving clause. An exception of a special thing out of general things mentioned in a statute.

scaffold. A platform on which convicted criminals are executed by being hanged. Also termed the gallows.

scale, nominal. A measuring format that indicates whether or not outcomes of a variable can be placed in the same measurement class, but not how they can be ordered from low to high. *See also* scale, ordinal

scale, ordinal. A measuring format that, in addition to establishing equality among observations, also indicates whether an individual outcome is greater than, lesser than, or equal to other outcomes.

scapegoat. A person or community that is made the undeserving object of aggressive energies of others, which are generated by the need to place blame for misfortunes they have experienced. The term derives from the goat allowed to escape after a Jewish chief priest had symbolically laid the sins of the people on it. (Lev. 16)

scared straight. On November 2, 1978, the film "Scared Straight!" was shown for the first time on public television (KTLA, Los Angeles). It showed the inside of the maximum-security state prison in Rahway, NJ, and followed 17 juvenile offenders "as they learn, at first hand, about the realities of prison life." The program won the Academy Award for best documentary in April 1979.

scientific management. The branch of classical management theory associated with U.S. industrial engineer Frederick Winslow Taylor (1856–1915). Taylor studied the physiological principles of work and was primarily concerned with discovering methods to improve efficiency and productivity. Techniques included detailed task performance instructions, extensive supervisory control, and economic incentives. In this model, workers were viewed as analogous to complex machines that must be well-programmed if they are to produce efficiently.

scintilla of evidence. A spark or shred of evidence. Any material evidence that, if true, would tend to establish an issue in the mind of a reasonable jury.

Scopes, John Thomas. John T. Scopes, a 24-year-old teacher in Dayton, TN, was charged with "undermining the peace and dignity of the state" by teaching his students the Darwinian theory of evolution, that man had descended from the apes. His famous trial is known as The Monkey Trial. Scopes was defended by Clarence Darrow but on July 21, 1925, was found guilty and fined $100. The decision was reversed on technical grounds by the Tennessee Supreme Court.

scopolamine. An alkaloid, produced from nightshade plants like belladonna, which creates a hypnotic state. It has been used in lie detection work to create a quasi-sleep in suspects who are then questioned, and will allegedly tell the truth as their inhibitions are removed. The value of this procedure is highly questionable.

Scotland Yard. The popular name for the headquarters (established in 1829) of the London Metropolitan Police (MPO). The office was located in a building at Whitehall Place and took its name from the rear premises, Scotland Yard, through which the public had access to the building. The MPO is now located on Victoria Street.

Scottsboro cases. On March 25, 1931, a group of nine young black men, ranging in age from 13 to 21 years, were riding in an open gondola car aboard a freight train crossing Alabama. Also aboard the train were seven other boys and two young women, all of whom were white. At some point a fight broke out between the two groups and six of the white boys were thrown from the train. A message was relayed, and as the train pulled into the station at Paint Rock, AL, a sheriff's posse was waiting. The two women, Victoria Price and Ruby Bates, claimed they had been raped by a number of the black youths. All nine were taken into custody and placed under military guard in the local jail at Scottsboro.

The Scottsboro boys, as they became known in history, were indicted on March 31, arraigned on the same day, and entered pleas of not guilty. On the morning of the trial, a local attorney offered reluctantly to represent the defendants.

Of the nine youths arrested, one had not been indicted because he was only 13. The remaining eight were joined into three groups for separate trials, each lasting a single day. Medical and other evidence was presented establishing that the two women had not been raped. The jury nevertheless sentenced all eight defendants to death. After conviction and sentence of death, the case remained pending for six years as a result of nationwide protest. The evidence was clear that the defendants were innocent of the charges, and many groups and individuals sought retrials on the basis of new evidence. A second trial was ordered by the U.S. Supreme Court in November 1932 and again in 1934 on the grounds that the defendants had been denied adequate counsel and that black citizens had been excluded from the juries at the three original trials. Continued appeals led to a decision in 1938 by the Court to deny new trials for four of the defendants (three eventually won parole, and one escaped). The other four had been released.

search and seizure. As the interpretation of the Fourth Amendment varies, it is necessary to study the statutes and case law governing each state. In California, for example, searches and seizures are considered reasonable if made under any of the following circumstances: (a) "With a valid search warrant"; or (b) "Incidental to a valid arrest made pursuant to a warrant of arrest or on probable cause (exception: a search warrant is required for materials having possible protection as free speech by the First Amendment)"; or (c) "By an officer lawfully on the premises (e.g., with probable cause to make an arrest; with consent; to render aid, in hot pursuit of escaping felon; pressing emergency; search of parolee's premises; or on public premises), though no arrest is in fact made, and who sees the evidence or contraband in plain sight"; or (d) "With consent voluntarily obtained"; or (e) "By an officer who searches a vehicle with reasonable cause to believe the vehicle contains contraband or evidence of crime even though not incidental to valid arrest (justified because of mobility)." On July 6, 1984, in a 6–3 decision, the Supreme Court ruled that police can conduct a "protective search" of the passenger area of a car without a warrant if they believe that concealed weapons are in the auto. Probable cause to believe a search will reveal contraband does not justify a search of a home or personal effects without a warrant, unless the search is incidental to a valid arrest based on probable cause.

search and seizure, unreasonable. Searches of persons and places and seizure of papers and effects without search warrants properly sworn to, issued by judicial officers, and, particularly, describing the place to be searched and the persons or things seized. Wiretapping and the use of a stomach pump are considered unreasonable searches; but blood tests for alcohol and seizures made immediately after a proper arrest, when objects wanted as evidence are in plain sight or the danger exists that offenders might escape because of the delay necessary to obtain a warrant, are not considered unreasonable. Since 1967 the courts have broadened the range of items that can be seized in a lawful search and used as evidence. The Fourth Amendment prohibits unreasonable searches and seizures, and the provision against self-incrimination in the Fifth Amendment prohibits the use of illegally seized articles as evidence against an accused person.

searching places outside of curtilage. Curtilage means the enclosed ground and buildings surrounding a dwelling. As a rule, no search warrant is needed for a lawful search of an open place not within the curtilage of, or in close proximity to, a dwelling, or unenclosed grounds not essential to the dwelling, where a search in no way invades or disturbs the privacy of a home or legitimate business.

search of curtilage or appurtenant premises. Usually considered to be a part of a dwelling, its curtilage or nearby premises, like the dwelling itself, cannot be searched without a valid search warrant.

search of place of business. While officers are vested with the same rights as the general public in entering a business establishment, a search warrant may be necessary to search an office or store or a room in a plant, and this rule extends to the premises of the business.

search warrant. A document issued by a judicial officer that directs a law enforcement officer to conduct a search at a specific location for specified property or persons relating to a crime(s), to seize the property or persons if found, and to account for the results of the search to the issuing judicial officer. On June 8, 1984, the Supreme Court voted 6–3 to expand police powers to obtain search warrants on the basis of anonymous tips; the court avoided ruling on whether illegally seized evidence could be admissible in court if police acted in good faith. *See also* search and seizure

search warrant, second search (same warrant). A warrant once served cannot, of course, be used for the purpose of additional searches; but, where a search is continuous—not having been abandoned or completed—it will not be held void because the officers go over the premises a second time.

secondary classification. A term used in classifying fingerprints. In the classification formula, it follows the primary classification and is a code of two upper-case letters, such as T/W. It describes the type of pattern in each of the index fingers.

secondary deviance. A term describing the situation that arises when a person publicly labeled as a deviant for some initial behavior (primary deviance) begins to use deviant behavior, or a role based on it, as a means of defense or adjustment to the problems created by society's reactions to the primary behavior.

secondary evidence. Evidence that is inferior to primary evidence, such as a copy of an instrument, or oral evidence of its contents. Either would be secondary to the original document.

secondhand evidence. Hearsay evidence.

secret. (1) Well-kept information or knowledge concerning a particular thing. (2) In government service, material or information that is disclosed without authority and that could result in serious damage to the nation by endangering its international relations; jeopardizing the effectiveness of a program or policy of great importance to the national defense; exposing important military or defense plans, technological developments of importance to the national defense, or information relative to important intelligence operations.

Secret Service. With approximately 3,500 employees under the direction of the secretary of the treasury, the service is responsible for the protection of the president and members of his immediate family, the president-elect, the vice president or other officer next in order of succession to the presidency, the vice president-elect, major candidates for the offices of president and vice president during their campaigns, the minor children of a former president until they reach age 16, and visiting heads of a foreign state or government. The Secret Service is also authorized to detect and arrest persons committing offenses against the laws of the United States relating to coins, obligations, and securities of the United States and foreign governments, and persons who forge government requests for transportation to be furnished by a common carrier. The director of the service is also responsible for the Protective Service and the Treasury Security Force.

The Secret Service is organized into five main divisions: (1) administrative; (2) inspection; (3) the Division of Investigations, which has four units, (a) the investigation unit, which coordinates and directs activities against organized crime; (b) counterfeit unit; (c) forgery unit; and (d) a special unit to supervise the uniformed guards who provide security for the Treasury and Treasury Annex buildings; (4) Office of Protective Services; and (5) Office of Protective Intelligence. Address: DOT, 950 H Street, NW, Suite 8400, Washington, DC 20223.

The first colonial Secret Service agency was organized by Aaron Burr and Major Benjamin Tallmadge in June 1778 for the United Colonies. It was known as the Headquarters Secret Service and developed into the first organized intelligence department of the Army of the United Colonies. On July 4, 1778, General George Washington in a special order made Burr head of the Department for Detecting and Defeating Conspiracies and ordered him "to proceed to Elizabeth Town to procure information of movements of the enemy's shipping about New York." Information about the activities of the British, however, had been secretly gathered previously by patriotic individuals and societies.

The first federal Secret Service agency under the Treasury Department was created by act on June 23, 1860, to suppress counterfeiting in U.S. coins. The act was extended to include counterfeiting of notes, obligations, and securities of the government by act on July 11, 1862, and an appropriation act approved July 2, 1864. Since the assassination of Abraham Lincoln, one of the duties of the Secret Service has been to guard the president and family. The FBI was created in 1908 under the Department of Justice to supplement the work of the Secret Service.

sector search. *See* zone search

Securities and Exchange Commission (SEC). Independent federal agency that supervises all aspects of the securities industry—including brokers, investment companies, the stock exchanges, and the actions of corporate officials. The SEC, which consists of five members appointed by the president for five-year terms, was established by the Securities Exchange Act of 1934. The main purpose of the commission is to preserve the integrity of the securities industry. Generally emphasizing prevention of abuses over punishment, the SEC relies heavily on the industry for self-regulation.

securities violations. In December 1988 the New York brokerage and investment banking firm of Drexel Burnham Lambert pleaded guilty to six felony counts of securities violations and was fined $650 million. Others involved in securities fraud cases and who have admitted to felonies are Ivan F. Boesky, Boyd L. Jefferies, Dennis B. Levine, and Martin Siegel.

security. (1) The restriction of inmate movement within a correctional facility, usually divided into maximum, medium, and minimum levels. (2) Measures taken for protection against espionage, observation, sabotage, annoyance, or surprise. (3) With respect to classified matter, the condition that prevents unauthorized persons from having access to official information that is safeguarded in the interests of national defense. (4) Item(s) deposited as a guarantee for payment of money. (5) Any of a wide variety of documents of monetary value, including but not limited to bills, stock certificates, bonds, certificates of deposit, checks, money orders, letters of credit, or certificates of interest in tangible or intangible property.

Industrial security is a business function with the responsibility of safeguarding the physical plant, properties, and products of the business.

security and privacy. As an exception to the general right of U.S. citizens to security and privacy, the Supreme Court found in its 1976 *Paul v. Davis* decision that arrest records do not qualify for protection under the Constitution, because they do not relate to private conduct. This decision meant that confidentiality standards concerning criminal histories are largely a matter of legislative discretion.

security classifications. The following are used in the Department of Defense Industrial Security Program: *Confidential*: information or material for which unauthorized disclosure could reasonably be expected to cause damage to national security; *Restricted*: information concerning the design, manufacture, or utilization of atomic weapons; the production of special nuclear material; and the use of special nuclear material in the production of energy; *Secret*: information or material whose unauthorized disclosure could [reasonably] be expected to cause serious damage to national security. *Top Secret*: information or material whose unauthorized disclosure could reasonably be expected to cause exceptionally grave damage to national security.

security for costs. The security that a defendant in an action may require of a plaintiff who does not reside within the jurisdiction of the court.

security index files. A card file maintained by the U.S. Civil Service Commission listing persons investigated by the commission and other agencies since 1939. Information from the index is available to investigators with a bona fide employment or investigative interest.

sedition. Issuing any false, scandalous, and malicious statement against the government, the president, or Congress with the intent to defame, disrupt, encourage contempt, or excite hatred of citizens for the United States Laws against sedition, however, may not violate First Amendment guarantees. The United States faced its first conflict over sedition between 1798 and 1801, when there was a conflict between the Federalists and Republicans over defining the role of public criticism in a representative government. Historically, sedition laws were based on the philosophy that the government is superior to the people. With the election of President Thomas Jefferson in 1800, this idea was superseded by the Populist theory that the people are superior to the government and that First Amendment rights are stronger than sedition laws. Since that time Congress has revived the sedition laws only twice—during World War I and World War II.

seditious conspiracy. The agreement of two or more persons to act together in promoting unlawful means of changing the government or of encouraging the violation of law for the purpose of promoting disloyalty or disaffection to the government.

seduction. The offense of inducing someone to consent to sexual intercourse under promise of marriage or other promises or pretences.

segregation. In penology, the part of a prison where inmates are held in solitary confinement as punishment.

seizin. Possession of real estate or personal property.

seizure. The taking into custody, by a law enforcement officer or other person authorized to do so, of objects relating to, or believed to relate to, criminal activity. *See also* forfeiture

selective enforcement. The deploying of police personnel in ways to cope most effectively with existing or anticipated problems. If data show that residential burglaries occur most frequently in certain areas at certain times, officers are assigned to such areas at the critical times under a program of selective enforcement.

self-actualization. A concept attributed to Abraham Maslow, it has been described as the process of becoming all that one is capable of being, of developing into an individual who is motivated primarily by an unselfish need for growth rather than by the appraisals of others; a process of becoming conscious of one's unique self. *See also* Maslow's hierarchy of needs

self-defense. The protection of oneself or one's property from unlawful injury or the immediate risk of unlawful injury; the justification for an act that would otherwise constitute an offense and that the doer reasonably believed was necessary to protect self or property from immediate danger.

self-fulfilling prophecy. An event that was predicted, and then occurred because the prediction became the cause. For example, an individual who is convinced that something bad will happen may unconsciously cause the anticipated mishap. Some criminologists believe a person doesn't become deviant until so labeled by authorities. In this view, someone who has initially been labeled deviant, through arrest and conviction, may find the pattern of behavior difficult to alter.

self-incrimination. In constitutional terms, the process of becoming involved in or charged with a crime by one's own testimony. The Constitution prohibits forced self-incrimination under the Fifth Amendment. This amendment has been widely used by witnesses in congressional investigations of subversive or criminal activities, who refuse to answer questions on the grounds that such answers would be self-incriminating. In 1972 the Court upheld the constitutionality of the Organized Crime Control Law of 1970, which protects witnesses from prosecution only to the extent that what they say will not be used against them; they are still liable to prosecution on other evidence.

self-report studies. A modern survey technique designed to measure the number of criminals by asking respondents if they have committed crimes within a specific period.

Although their truthfulness may be somewhat suspect even with firm pledges of confidentiality, as many as 91 percent of the respondents surveyed by some studies have admitted one or more criminal acts.

Sellin Center for Studies in Criminology and Criminal Law. Founded in 1960 at the Wharton School of the University of Pennsylvania and called the Center for Studies in Criminology and Criminal Law until 1986. The center operates with foundation and federal support and conducts research on crime, delinquency, police, judicial systems, prisons, social control, and social deviance. Address: University of Pennsylvania, 440 Vance Hall, Philadelphia, PA 19104.

semiautomatic. A firearm or gun that uses part of the force of an exploding cartridge to extract the empty case and chamber the next round, but requires a separate pull of the trigger to fire each round; hence, the phrase semiautomatic fire.

Senate crime investigations. The first committee set up specifically to investigate crime was the Kefauver Committee of 1950–1951. The committee was aided by an executive order from President Harry Truman that gave it access to income tax returns, which were the starting point for many investigations. The committee discovered considerable evidence of a nationwide crime syndicate and its operations. Numerous Senate crime committees have been formed since 1950.

sensitivity training (T-groups). Generic term for a variety of (primarily verbal) group-interaction experiences for individuals and organization staffs. The group sessions are intended to help people function more effectively in their jobs through understanding group dynamics, increasing awareness of their own and other people's feelings, becoming more direct in talking about those feelings, and exchanging feedback with others about styles of interaction.

sentence. (1) The penalty imposed by a court on a person convicted of a crime. (2) The court judgment specifying the penalty imposed on a person convicted of a crime. (3) Any disposition of a defendant resulting from a conviction, including the court decision to suspend execution of a sentence.

sentence credit time. Time already spent in confinement in relation to a given offense(s), which is deducted at the point of admission on a sentence to jail or prison from the maximum jail or prison liability of the sentence for the offense(s).

sentence effective date. With respect to a term of confinement, the date from which time served is calculated, not necessarily coincident with the date sentence was pronounced or the date of entry to confinement after sentencing.

sentence, flat. Also called a straight sentence; a fixed sentence with no maximum or minimum range indicated.

sentence, indeterminate. A sentence to incarceration indicating a range of time between minimum date of parole eligibility and a maxi mum discharge date. A completely indeterminate sentence has a minimum of one day and a maximum of natural life.

sentence, maximum. The longest period of time the prisoner can be held in custody. The longest prison sentence was a 10,000-year sentence imposed on Dudley Wayne Kyzer, 40, on December 4, 1981, in Tuscaloosa, AL, for triple murder in 1976 that included his mother-in-law. The longest time served was by Paul Geidel (born April 21, 1894), a 17-year-old porter employed by a New York City hotel. He was convicted of second-degree murder on September 5, 1911, and released from the Fishkill Correctional Facility in Beacon, NY, aged 85, on May 7, 1980, having served 68 years, 8 months, and 2 days—the longest recorded term in U.S. history. He had first refused parole in 1974.

sentence, minimum. The shortest period of time an offender must spend in prison before becoming eligible for parole.

sentence review. The reconsideration of a sentence imposed on a person convicted of a crime, either by the same court that imposed the sentence or a higher court.

sentence, short. A sentence that runs from a few days to a few months, imposed on petty offenders who often cannot afford to pay a fine, if one is offered as an alternative to imprisonment. Short sentences are usually served in municipal or county jails, except in those few places where special institutions for misdemeanants are maintained.

sentence, suspended. Technically a sentence, but based on unconditional, unsupervised release of the convicted defendant.

sentencing councils. A panel of three or more judges sometimes used instead of a trial judge to determine a criminal sentence, in an attempt to make sentencing more uniform. Sentencing councils were first used in 1960 in the Eastern District of Michigan.

sentencing dispositions. Court dispositions of defendants after a judgment of conviction, expressed as penalties, such as imprisonment or payment of fines; or any of a number of alternatives to actually executed penalties, such as suspended sentences, grants of probation, or orders to perform restitution; or various combinations of the above.

sentencing hearing. A hearing during which the court or jury considers relevant information, such as evidence concerning aggravating or mitigating circumstances, for the purpose of determining a sentencing disposition for a person convicted of an offense(s).

sentencing jury. The trial jury attached to a court that imposes sentence.

sentencing postponed. The delay for an unspecified period of time, or to a remote date, of the court's pronouncement of any other sentencing disposition for a person convicted of an offense, in order to place the defendant in some status contingent on good behavior in the expectation that a penalty need never be pronounced or executed.

Sentencing Project, The. Leading national effort to develop alternative sentencing programs to reform criminal justice policy. The organization has provided technical assistance and helped to establish alternative sentencing schemes in more than 20 states. Address: 918 F St., NW, Suite 501, Washington, DC 20004.

sentinel. A person charged with standing guard and giving notice of danger if it is threatened.

sentry. A guard, especially one who stands at a point where only properly authorized and identified persons are permitted to pass.

sepulture. Burial; interment.

sequester. To keep a jury together and in isolation from the public under charge of the bailiff during a trial; sometimes called separation of the jury. Also, to keep witnesses apart from other witnesses and therefore unable to hear their testimony.

sergeant. A police officer whose rank is higher than patrolman and lower than lieutenant. The sergeant is the first supervisory officer in the ascending chain of command. He is the line officer who is in closest contact with the field operations of a department.

serial murders. The phenomenon of serial killings has been recognized since a man dubbed "Jack the Ripper" murdered seven London prostitutes in 1888. The FBI terms serial murders as the killing of several victims in three or more separate events. These may occur over several days, weeks, or years, and reveal similarities of pattern, such as where the murders occurred, the type of victim, or the method of killing. The elapsed time between murders separates serial killers from other multiple killers. John Wayne Gacy, a serial murderer, planned the separate killings of 33 boys and young men in Chicago over a span of two to three years in the late 1970s. Other serial murders have been attributed to Albert De Salvo, the Boston Strangler, although he was never charged with murder; Theodore Robert Bundy; Juan Carona; David Berkowitz, Son of Sam; Wayne Williams of Atlanta; and Randy Kraft. Aileen Wournos, a hitchhiking prostitute who killed six men, was executed in Florida by lethal injection on October 10, 2002. The FBI has compiled profiles of several types of repeat criminals, and analysts study data on more than 200 suspects each year. Professor Ronald Holmes of the University of Louisville is coauthor of a book on this subject titled *Serial Murder* from Sage Publications. *See also* Green River Task Force; mass murder; murder spree; National Center for the Analysis of Violent Crime

serious misdemeanor. A class of misdemeanors having more severe penalties than other misdemeanors, or being procedurally distinct; sometimes a statutory name for a type of misdemeanor having a maximum penalty much greater than the customary maximum one-year incarceration for misdemeanors.

Serpico, Frank. A New York police officer who broke the code of silence regarding corruption in his department and was transferred to the Midtown Manhattan prostitution detail in retaliation. He released his story to the *New York Times*, in response to which the mayor convened the Knapp Commission to investigate the department during the summer of 1970. Serpico was shot in the face by a drug dealer but survived and continued his work with the commission. The group's findings were staggering: 15,000 officers were involved in some sort of corruption. In May 1972, after the commission had disbanded, a new scandal hit the New York Police Department: 20 plainclothesmen, one policewoman, and three sergeants were indicted for accepting $250,000 a year in bribes from gamblers linked to organized crime.

service of process. The act of delivering a written summons or notice of a judicial proceeding to the person who will be affected by it.

session. A meeting; a sitting of a court, legislative body, or other assembly.

severance. In criminal proceedings the separation, for purposes of pleading and/or trial, of multiple defendants named in a single charging document, or of multiple charges against a particular defendant listed in a single charging document.

sexism. The domination and/or exploitation of one sex by the other, or generalized bias against a group of people based solely on their common gender. The term is usually used to mean the subordination of women by men through ideology, stereotyping, family structures, and unfair legislation.

sex offender notification systems. Computerized systems that will automatically contact victims of sexual crimes that the perpetrators have escaped or are about to be released. Once victims have registered their telephone numbers, the systems are programmed to call, be activated by a code number, and play a taped message. In 1996, 135 counties had such systems, including the cities of San Antonio, Fort Worth, Detroit, Miami, Tampa, San Jose, Oakland, and Atlanta.

sex offender registration. *See* Megan's Law

sex offenses. Defined by law as "offenses against chastity, common decency, morals, and the like," except forcible rape, prostitution, and commercialized vice.

sexual deviations. Deviations such as exhibitionism and rape are penalized by law, but many other forms of sexual behavior are arbitrarily called deviant because they depart from what is considered normal by a society. Deviation is a label applied at a given time and does not imply a condemnation of everything so termed. Some authorities have suggested that sexual anomaly would be a preferable term.

sexual harassment. The Supreme Court granted *certiorari* to review *Metitor Saving Bank v. Vinson* in 1985, heard the case the following March, and handed down its first sexual harassment decision on June 19, 1986. *Vinson* did not resolve all legal inconsistencies, but it did establish some important sexual harassment laws and deserves to be termed a landmark decision. Illinois defines sexual harassment as "any unwelcome sexual advances or requests for sexual favors or any conduct of a sexual nature when (1) submission to such conduct is made either explicitly or implicitly a term or condition of a person's emplyment; (2) submission to or rejection of such conduct by an individual is used as the basis for employment decisions affecting such individual; or (3) such conduct has the purpose or effect of substantially interfering with an individual's work performance or creating an intimidating, hostile, or offensive working environment" (Ill. Ann. State, ch. 68, Sec. 2-102(E) [Smith-Hurd]). For another example of a state statute dealing expressly with sexual harassment, see Michigan's Elliott-Larsen Act. Mich. Comp. Laws Ann., Sec. 37.211103 (h) (iii). The National Association for Working Women maintains a hotline:(800) 522-0925.

shakedowns. Forms of extortion in which officials accept money from citizens in lieu of enforcing the law. The term comes from the nineteenth-century British underworld, where shakedown was a common temporary substitute for a bed in many prostitutes' rooms; hence, their rooms also became known as shakedowns.

shall. In law this verb means must: mandatory actions or requirements. If the law states something shall be done, it is a positive and definite requirement. If the word may is used, discretion is allowed.

shanghai. To drug, intoxicate, or knock out someone in order to put him aboard ship as a seaman.

shell game. A swindling game in which the operator manipulates a pea-sized object under three walnut shells. Victims wager they can tell which shell it is under. The object is generally concealed in the crook of the finger of the swindler, so that bettors always lose their money. The term is often used to connote any manipulative scheme that defrauds or misleads people.

sheriff. The elected chief officer of a county law enforcement agency, usually responsible for law enforcement in unincorporated areas and for the operation of the county jail; in some states, collects taxes. Sheriffs are popularly elected in all states except Rhode Island and are often not re-eligible. *See also* reeve

Sheriff's Association, National. Founded in 1940. Publishes *Sheriff* magazine (bimonthly). Address: 1450 Duke St., Alexandria, VA 22314.

sheriff's department. A local law enforcement agency, organized at the county level, and directed by a sheriff, which exercises its law enforcement functions at the county level, usually within unincorporated areas, and operates the county jail in most jurisdictions. Sometimes referred to as the "SO" or Sheriff's Office.

Sherman Antitrust Act. An 1890 federal law providing that "Every contract combination in the form of a trust or otherwise, or conspiracy in restraint of trade or commerce, is hereby declared to be illegal." Combinations of labor are included within the terms of this act, as are similar combinations of capital.

Sherman report. A report by the National Advisory Commission on Higher Education for Police Officers, which criticized programs that concentrate heavily on training and that make a practice of employing law enforcement practitioners as part-time instructors.

shield law. (1) Protects professionals, such as doctors, lawyers, and ministers, from making public those facts that have been related to them in confidence by people who have sought their professional counsel. Journalists now cannot legally protect their news sources from public or court exposure and may contend that a shield law is necessary to ensure the flow of vital information. (2) The Supreme Court during May 1985 held that judges can be sued for violating constitutional rights and, if they lose, be forced to pay attorneys' fees. It affirmed an award against a Virginia magistrate who ordered two men jailed because they were unable to raise money for bail that she had illegally imposed on them for nonjailable misdemeanors. While permitting attorneys' fees against court officers, the justices left mostly intact the doctrine of judicial immunity, which shields judges, magistrates, and even prosecutors from damage suits related to their official acts. *See also* privileged communications

shock incarceration. Military-style boot camps designed for short-time and generally first-time offenders are part of the federal penal system and operated by 29 states, including FL, TX, and SC. The concept was first introduced in GA and OK during the early 1980s and has become a widespread response to overcrowding in existing prisons. NY has the largest boot-camp system.

shock probation. A type of split sentence used in some states, by which imprisoned offenders sentenced to long terms may be released to the community to serve the remainder of the sentence under supervision. It is hoped that the impact of the initial incarceration will have caused offenders to reevaluate their behavior. Failure to complete the probation satisfactorily generally results in reconfinement for the full duration of the sentence. *See also* split sentence

shoplifting. The theft of goods, wares, or merchandise from a store or shop (in retailing, such losses are included in the euphemism "inventory shrinkage"). Shoplifting has been the most common form of occasional property crime in the United States during the twentieth century, accounting for approximately 10 percent of all larceny theft. Shoplifting includes commercial shoplifters and so-called boosters, who steal merchandise to resell it, as well as pilferers, who steal for their own personal use. The pressures of inflation and recession in the late 1970s and early 1980s initiated higher levels of amateur shoplifting. During the 1979 Christmas season alone, it was estimated that shoplifting losses in the United States amounted to some $2 billion.

short ridge. In fingerprint patterns, a short, broken ridge or line. *See also* fingerprint patterns

shotgun. A smoothbore shoulder weapon that fires shot pellets or slugs. The usual classes are riot gun, skeet gun, and sporting gun.

Boot Camp Programs in the United States

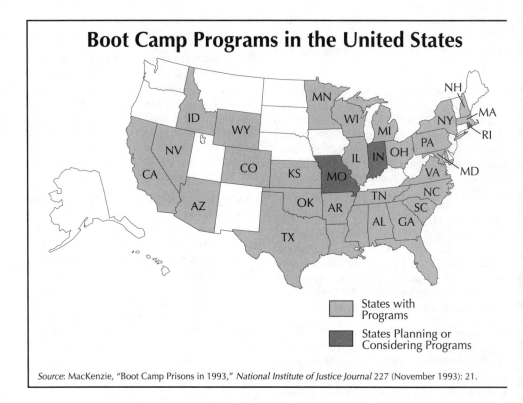

States with Programs

States Planning or Considering Programs

Source: MacKenzie, "Boot Camp Prisons in 1993," *National Institute of Justice Journal* 227 (November 1993): 21.

shot pattern. The dispersion pattern of shot fired from a shotgun; pellets that separate from one another in flight. The shot pattern is determined by shooting at a target or other surface that will register the impact of the shots when they strike.

show cause. An order to appear in court and deliver reasons why certain circumstances continue either to be allowed or prohibited.

shrapnel. (1) Strictly speaking, small lead or steel balls contained in certain shells, which are discharged in every direction upon explosion of the shell. The system was invented by Lieutenant (later Gen.) Henry Shrapnel in 1784. (2) A popular term for munition fragments.

sidewalk. That portion of a highway set apart by curbs, barriers, markings, or other delineations for pedestrian travel.

siege. The act or process of surrounding and attacking a fortified place so as to compel the surrender of its defenders and involving a prolonged effort to overcome resistance. One of the longest law enforcement sieges in American history was the 81-day standoff between the FBI and "freemen" in Jordan, Montana, extending from March 25 to June 13, 1996. Three other notable sieges were the 69-day American Indian Movement action at Wounded Knee in 1973; the 11-day standoff involving white separatist Randy Weaver and his family at Ruby Ridge, Idaho, in 1992; and the 51-day siege of the Branch Davidian compound near Waco, Texas, in 1993.

signal. (1) As applied to electronics, any transmitted electrical impulse. (2) Operationally, a type of message, the text of which consists of one or more letters, words, characters, signal flags, visual displays, or special sounds with prearranged meanings and which is conveyed or transmitted by visual, acoustical, or electrical means.

signal security. A generic term that includes both communications security and electronic security.

signals, 10-dash. A system of signals used in law enforcement that consists of the numeral 10 followed by other numbers. Such codes have prearranged meanings and are used frequently in radio communications.

silencer. A device designed to silence the explosive report caused by the discharge of cartridges by a small-arms weapon. It incorporates integral chambers or baffles that allow the gases to expand gradually.

"Silver platter" doctrine. The name given to the controversial practice of circumventing rules prohibiting the introduction at federal trials of evidence illegally seized by federal officers. Federal officers exploited a loophole in the wording of a 1914 Supreme Court decision, *Weeks v. United States*, which said, "Evidence illegally seized by federal officers is inadmissible." Until curbed by the *Elkins v. United States* decision of 1960, federal police officers simply requested state or local officers to make seizures on their behalf. *See also* Court Cases: *Elkins v. United States; Weeks v. United States*

simple assault. Unlawful threatening, attempted inflicting, or inflicting of less than serious bodily injury, in the absence of a deadly weapon. *See also* aggravated assault

simple contract. A contract not under seal or record.

simulated forgery. Forgery of writing accomplished by someone who practices the genuine writing until the forged writing is similar to the genuine.

simulation. Any model a researcher builds to convey his or her hypothesis of how variables interrelate. The simulation model is then used to make predictions, in contrast with the research technique of empirically examining relationships among variables and estimating relations among them based on data.

sine (Lat.). Without.

sine qua non. An indispensable thing; a necessity.

single action. A method of fire in some revolvers and shoulder arms in which the hammer must be cocked by hand, in contrast to double action, in which a single pull of the trigger both cocks and fires the weapon.

single-fingerprint registration. A system of classifying single fingerprints to permit identification of prints left at the scene of a crime. *See also* primary classification

Sing Sing. The New York State Penitentiary at Ossining, NY, "up where the jailbirds warble twice"; the Ossining Correctional Facility.

Sirhan Sirhan. Convicted of assassinating Senator Robert F. Kennedy on June 5, 1968, in the pantry of the Ambassador Hotel in Los Angeles, CA. His release date was set for 1984, but revoked. On June 26, 1985, Sirhan was denied parole for the seventh time.

sketching. The drawing or charting of objects, places, or scenes to show the details and/or relative positions of objects and other evidence.

skewness. In quantitative research, the amount by which a distribution departs from the symmetry of a bell-shaped curve. If the pattern of results has a longer tail on the right, it is said to be positively skewed; a long tail on the left indicates negative skewing.

skid. A controlled or uncontrolled slide by a vehicle, resulting from the loss of friction between the road surface and the tires.

skid marks. The marking or imprints left on a traveled surface by vehicle tires as a result of sliding or skidding. Calculations can be made of the direction and speed of a vehicle prior to a collision by examining the skid marks.

skyjacking. The hijacking of an airplane first occurred in the United States in 1961. The skyjacker typically: (a) wants to be flown to a destination other than that scheduled; (b) attempts to extort large sums of money from the airline; or (c) holds the passengers hostage for political purposes. Most U.S. skyjackings in the early 1960s involved people who wanted to fly to Cuba. From 1961 to 1968, there was an average of one skyjacking each month.

sky marshals. A group of officers who travel aboard passenger airplanes to protect against hijackers. They worked in a federal program started in 1970 under the direction of Lt. Gen. Benjamin O. Davis, Director of Civil Aviation Security. On December 23, 1970, a group of specially trained officers started replacing 1,200 marshals then in service. This program was deactivated, but due to increased international hijacking, the State Department activated its airline hijacking task force on June 14, 1985, after Muslim militants seized a TWA jetliner with 153 people aboard. Now part of the Federal Aviation Administration, sky marshals are called aviation security inspectors, and their role has been expanded to include such other tasks as airport security.

slander. The oral utterance or publication of a falsehood that is intended to defame a person or injure his or her reputation. *See also* libel and slander

slum. An area of urban blight marked by decaying buildings, abandoned businesses, widespread poverty, and accompanying social disorganization. Crime and violence and family disintegration are characteristic of slums. Renovation and rehabilitation are only partial solutions, for slums are symptoms of broad and deep problems of society.

small arms. All arms, including automatic weapons, up to and including those of .60 caliber and shotguns.

small claims court. A special court that provides expeditious, informal, and inexpensive adjudication of small contractual claims. In most jurisdictions, attorneys are not permitted for cases, and claims are limited to $1,500 ($2,000 in CA). Sometimes referred to as peoples' court.

smoke bombs. Smoke bombs have a threefold purpose: they are used for screening movement, for creating an antipersonnel effect in the open or in dug-in positions, and for making targets. They also have an incendiary effect, in that they will set fire to materials that are easily ignited, such as clothing, dry brush, and canvas. The bodies of the bombs are filled with plasticized white or white phosphorus. The functioning of a fuse and burster shatters the bomb on impact, dispersing the filler over a wide area. Atmospheric oxygen ignites the particles, which produce a dense white smoke.

smoke detector. A device that detects visible or invisible products of combustion. Types of smoke detectors include: ionization, photoelectric beam-type, photoelectric spot-type, and resistance bridge.

smoke grenade. A hand grenade or rifle grenade containing a smoke-producing mixture and used for screening or signaling. It is sometimes charged with colored smoke, such as red, green, yellow, or violet.

smuggle. To import or export without paying duty.

smuggling. Unlawful movement of goods across a national frontier or state boundary or into or out of a correctional facility.

sneeze gas. A gas that causes sneezing; specifically, diphenylchloroarsine.

sniperscope. An electronic device for use on a carbine or rifle that permits a shooter to aim at a target at night without being seen. Infrared rays illuminate the target, which is then viewed through a combination telescopic sight and fluorescent screen (in which all objects appear as various shades of green). The system was developed by the U.S. Army during World War II. It has an angle of view of 14 degrees and a range of 125 yards.

sobriety checkpoints. Temporary police locations in areas or on occasions noted for a high frequency of alcohol- or drug-impaired driving. For example, the California Highway Patrol began such checkpoints in 1984 and by December 31, 1995, had set up 2,036 locations, resulting in 1,150,180 vehicles screened, 28,940 field sobriety tests administered, 9,777 impaired drivers arrested, and 2,944 drivers cited or arrested for other violations. *See also* driving under the influence cost recovery

social case work. A method of providing social services and personal counseling in order to improve the personal and family adjustments of clients. Each individual or family constitutes a case for the social worker.

social indicators. Every three years, the book *Social Indicators* is published, providing statistical information about the population of the United States as a whole, including information on public safety. Contact: Bureau of the Census, DOC, FOB3, Room 3705, Washington, DC 20233.

Social Security numbers. Numbers were first issued in 1936 by the Social Security Administration. The first three digits of numbers issued since 1972 have indicated the state of residence of the person to whom the number was issued. The Social Security Administration's hot-line telephone number is (800) 772-1213.

SOCIAL SECURITY NUMBERS

Initial #	Issuing State	Initial #	Issuing State
001-003	NH	433-439	LA
004-007	ME	440-448	OK
008-009	VT	449-467, 627-645	TX
010-034	MA	468-477, 525	MN
035-039	RI	478-485	IA
040-049	CT	485-500	MO
050-134	NY	501-502	ND
135-158	NJ	503-504	SD
159-211	PA	505-508	NE
212-220	MD	509-515	KS
221-222	DE	516-517	MT
223-231	VA	518-519	ID
232-236	WV	520	WY
237-246	NC	521-524	CO
247-251	SC	526-527, 600-601	AZ
252-260	GA	528-529, 646-647	UT
261-267, 589-595	FL	530	NV
268-302	OH	531-539	WA
303-317	IN	540-544	OR
318-361	IL	545-573, 602-626	CA
362-386	MI	574	AK
387-399	WI	575-576	HI
400-407	KY	577-579	DC
408-415	TN	580	U.S. Virgin Islands
416-424	AL	581-584, 596-599	PR
425-428, 587-588	MS	585, 648-649	NM
429-432	AR	586	Guam, American Samoa, Northern Marianas, Philippines

Society for the Reformation of Juvenile Delinquents. This organization opened the House of Refuge for young offenders in 1824, in New York City. It was the first institution in the United States whose function was to remove children from the primarily adult jails and prisons.

sociological law. A statement of scientifically established causal relations and of causal sequences and continuity; a social theory that has been proven. *See also* law

sociology. A term first used by Auguste Comte (1798–1857), who attempted to outline a new discipline modeled on the natural sciences. The scientific study of the phenomena arising out of the group relations of human beings; the study of humans and their human environment in relation to each other. Different schools of sociology lay varying emphasis on the related factors, some stressing the relationships themselves, such as interaction and association; while others emphasize human beings in their social relationships, focusing on the individual in varying roles and functions. Whether sociology, as developed so far, is entitled to the rank of a science is still a matter of some disagreement, but it is uniformly recognized that the methods of sociology may be strictly scientific, and that the verified generalizations that are the earmark of true science are being progressively built up out of extensive and painstaking observation and analysis of the repetitious uniformities in group behavior.

sociopath. A person with a character disorder; an antisocial personality.

sodium amytal. So-called truth serum.

sodomy. (1) Scientifically, this term applies only to insertion of the penis into the rectum of another person. (2) In the laws of a number of states, however, sodomy includes oral-genital acts and bestiality: unlawful physical contact between the genitals of one person and the mouth or anus of another person or with the mouth, anus, or genitals of an animal. These laws were struck down by the U.S. Supreme Court in *Lawrence v. Texas*

(decided June 2003), in which the Court held that laws proscribing behavior between consenting adults in the privacy of their own home were a denial of due process.

solicit. To ask earnestly; to petition.

solicitation. *See* inchoate offense

solicitor. A practitioner of the law who practices law in a court of chancery.

solicitor general (federal). Conducts and supervises government litigation in the Supreme Court. He or she reviews every case litigated by the federal government in which a lower court has decided against the United States to determine whether to appeal, and also decides whether the United States should file a brief as *amicus curiae* in any appellate court. For more information, contact: Office of the Solicitor General, DOJ, 950 Pennsylvania Ave., NW, Washington, DC 20530-0001.

solicitor general (state). In states having no attorney general, the ranking law officer. Where there is an attorney general, the solicitor general is the next ranking law officer.

Son of Sam. *See* Berkowitz, David

sound-sensing detection system. An alarm system that detects the audible sound caused by an attempted forcible entry into a protected structure. The system consists of microphones and a control unit containing an amplifier, accumulator, and a power supply. The unit's sensitivity is adjustable so that ambient noise or normal sounds will not initiate an alarm.

sovereign immunity. A doctrine under which a government and its subdivisions, in the conduct of governmental functions, is immune from civil liability resulting from wrongful acts of its agents. In 1946 the Federal Tort Claims Act abolished this immunity for the federal government; some states have also abolished the immunity, and courts in other states are striking it down.

SP. State Police; Shore Patrol (U.S. Navy); Security Police.

span of control. Management principle suggesting that supervisors should supervise no more than three to six subordinates to remain effective. As the number of subordinates increases arithmetically, the number of possible interpersonal interactions increases geometrically. More generally, the term is used to describe any manager's level of responsibility in order to rank the job by comparison with others and/or determine the appropriate salary level.

special judge. A judge who is appointed to hear, and exercise all judicial functions for, a specific case. Special judges are appointed in addition to, not in lieu of, regularly appointed or elected judges. They conduct all criminal proceedings pertaining only to a specific case.

special verdict. A verdict by which the jury finds the facts only, leaving the judgment to the court.

specific intent. When a crime consists not merely in doing an act, but in doing it with a specific intent, the existence of that intent is an essential element of the case that must be proven; the existence of criminal intent is not presumed from the commission of the act.

special master. A master in chancery appointed to act as the representative of the court in some assigned action or transaction, such as collecting information, to aid the court in deciding if a constitutional violation has occurred, and to assist in developing or monitoring a remedial decree that involves constitutional violations. Prison inmates have been appointed as special masters to monitor consent decrees and report their findings to the court. *See also* consent decree, decree

specimen. An item of physical evidence, or that which might be evidence, in a criminal case, especially any item submitted to a crime laboratory. The laboratory may list or record the item as a questioned (Q) specimen or a known (K) specimen, according to its nature and whether it came from a known source.

spectrograph. A device used to photograph elements of the light spectrum. It is used in a crime laboratory to make a spectrogram, produced when various inorganic substances are examined to determine their composition, and can detect the presence of minute quantities of materials.

speedy trial. The right of the defendant to have a prompt trial is guaranteed by the Sixth Amendment of the Constitution, which states, "In all criminal prosecution, the accused shall enjoy the right to a speedy and public trial." In 1970, the Supreme Court held that Florida did not give a defendant a speedy trial when he was not tried for six years while serving a term in federal prison, during which time the state maintained a detainer against him and the defendant repeatedly asked for a trial (*Dickey v. Florida*). Most states and the federal government (Speedy Trial Act of 1974, sponsored by Senator Sam J. Ervin of NC) have enacted statutes setting forth the time within which a defendant must be tried following the date of his or her arrest, detention, first appearance, or the filing of charges in court. Currently, if the accused is not brought to trial within 100 days, the case is dismissed. Jurisdictions differ, however, on whether dismissal on these grounds constitutes a bar to subsequent prosecution for the same offense(s).

spindle. A part of the combination-lock mechanism on a safe. The combination dial fits onto the outer end of the spindle, and its function is to turn the lock mechanism when the dial is rotated. On some types of safes, burglars gain entry by punching in or pulling out the spindle. *See also* pulling method; punching method

spiral rifling. The cutting of spiral grooves in the surface of the bore of a gun barrel. Invented about 1520 by G. Koller (or Kollner) of Vienna, this rifling imparts a rotary motion to the longitudinal axis of the bullet as it passes through the barrel, which is maintained during its flight. This rotation equalizes any defects or irregularities in the form of the bullet and in its density, thus tending to keep it in a straight course in its flight.

split sentence. A sentence explicitly requiring the convicted person to serve a period of confinement in a local, state, or federal facility followed by a period of probation. Shock probation is frequently used as another name for the split sentence, although neither term is recommended for reporting purposes.

spoils system. Practice by which political party loyalists are rewarded for their support with government offices. The Jacksonian senator William Marcy of New York proclaimed in 1831, "To the victor belong the spoils."

spontaneous declaration. An utterance made as a result of some sudden and/or shocking event, such as an accident or crime. *See also res gestae*

spoofing. The defeat or compromise of an alarm system by "tricking" or "fooling" its detection devices, such as by short-circuiting part or all of a series circuit, cutting wires in a parallel circuit, reducing the sensitivity of a sensor, or entering false signals into the system. Spoofing contrasts with circumvention.

spot protection. Protection of objects such as safes, art objects, or anything of value that could be damaged or removed from the premises.

spur. A ridge detail in a fingerprint, also called a hook; a hook-like ridge or small branch emanating from a single ridge line. *See also* fingerprint patterns

spy. Generally, anyone employed by a government to obtain secret information about another government; anyone who engages in espionage.

staff. Personnel in the administrative functions of an organization and who are responsible for investigative, advisory, planning, accounting, and other functions.

staff functions. Doing things of an advisory, specialized, or technical nature that are not concerned directly with carrying out the main objectives of the organization or department. Such tasks include fiscal matters, personnel hiring and training, or planning and research.

stalking. A crime involving repeated following, spying on, or otherwise harassing someone such that the victim experiences a "credible threat" of bodily harm. California passed the first anti-stalking law in the United States in 1990. In 2004, 49 states and the District of Columbia had anti-stalking laws.

standard deviation. In a distribution of scores or observations gathered in a survey or experiment, two descriptive measures are particularly significant—indices of central tendency (mean, median, mode) and variability. Basically, the standard deviation reveals the degree to which scores in a distribution are clustered around the mean.

Standard Metropolitan Statistical Areas (SMSAs). *See* Metropolitan Statistical Areas

standard muzzle velocity. The velocity at which a given projectile is designed to leave the muzzle of a gun. The velocity is calculated on the basis of the particular gun, the propelling charge used, and the type of projectile fired from the gun. Firing tables are based on standard muzzle velocity.

standing. The qualifications needed to bring legal action. These qualifications relate to the existence of a controversy in which the plaintiff has suffered or is about to suffer an injury to or infringement upon a legal protected right that a court is competent to redress. Hence, a specific issue is said to have, or lack, legal standing.

standing order. An order that remains in force indefinitely, until it is amended or canceled.

star chamber proceeding. A secret proceeding in which a person is given little or no opportunity to present his or her case or defense, and in which the proceedings are conducted and conclusions reached without observing usual judicial formalities. The term comes from the Star Chamber, an English court established by King Charles I and abolished by Parliament in 1641. The Star Chamber had no jury and was permitted to apply torture.

Starkweather, Charles Raymond. On January 21, 1958, Starkweather set out on a murderous rampage across the American plains states. His mass slaughter lasted eight days and claimed the lives of 10 people. Three of the victims were the parents and baby sister of Charles's 14-year-old girlfriend, Carol Ann Fugate, who accompanied him on his trail of violence. Starkweather was electrocuted in the Nebraska State Penitentiary on June 14, 1959.

state and federal jurisdiction. The constitutional power of Congress to enact legislation, define crimes, and provide for their punishment implies that such legislation supersedes state statutes, and that the states cannot punish violations of federal law as offenses against the state. Where these provisions are not made explicit in federal laws, either expressly or by necessary implication, a state statute is not superseded by a federal law, and the same act may be punished as an offense against the United States and also as an offense against the state.

state constitutions. These differ materially from the U.S. Constitution. The state constitutions comprise, for the most part, restrictions or limitations of powers, whereas the federal document constitutes, for the most part, grants of powers.

state courts. The courts in the various states are created, and their jurisdiction is conferred and defined, by state statutes rather than federal or constitutional law.

state highway patrol. A state law enforcement agency whose principal functions consist of prevention, detection, and investigation of motor vehicle offenses, and apprehension of traffic offenders.

state legislatures. These elected bodies have the inherent power to prohibit and punish any act as a crime, provided they do not violate the restrictions of the state and federal constitutions; and the courts cannot look further into the propriety of a penal statute than to ascertain whether the legislature had the power to enact it.

state police. A state law enforcement agency whose principal functions usually include maintaining statewide police communications,

aiding local police in criminal investigation, police training, and guarding state property, and may include highway patrol.

The earliest state police organization was the Texas Rangers, formed in 1835. In 1865 state constables were appointed in Massachusetts, with Connecticut adopting a similar force in 1903. The Arizona Rangers were established in 1901, followed by the New Mexico Mounted Police and the Pennsylvania State Police in 1905. The years after World War I saw a great expansion of state police forces: NY and MI in 1917; WV, 1919; NJ, 1921; and RI, 1925. Today all states except Hawaii have some form of state police force.

state prisons. State prisons held 732,651 prisoners at year-end 1991, up from 689,596 in 1990, not including those in the custody of state correctional authorities but held in jails or other facilities.

Louisiana: an example of a state prison system. At year-end 1991, the Louisiana prison system was responsible for 20,003 inmates, 8,351 of whom were newly admitted to confinement during that year. Just over 5,000 of the total, or more than 25 percent, were housed in jails because of overcrowding in state facilities. African Americans outnumbered whites by a ratio of nearly three to one. The rate of confinement was 462 for every 100,000 people in the state's total residential population. During 1991, 19 inmates had escaped, including 12 from minimum-security facilities; all 19 had been recaptured. Among Louisiana's inmates on September 30, 1992, were 2,158 men and 72 women serving life sentences: 602 for first-degree murder, 952 for second-degree murder, 33 for kidnapping, 101 for drug charges, 504 for sex offenses, and 38 for other offenses. The average grade of school completed by all inmates was 5th, no prisoner education programs were mandatory, and the state employed 58 full-time teachers in its prison system. The state maintained 57 drug and alcohol treatment programs for prisoners, serving 13,468 inmates.

state's attorney. An officer, usually locally elected within a county, who represents the state in securing indictments and in prosecuting criminal cases; called a prosecuting attorney.

state's evidence. Testimony by a participant in the commission of a crime that incriminates others involved, given under the promise of immunity.

states' rights. As stated in the Tenth Amendment, "powers not delegated to the United States by the Constitution, nor prohibited by it to the States, are reserved to the States respectively, or to the people." In Article I, Section 8, however, the framers recognized the need for flexibility. This so-called elastic clause granted the federal government the power to enact legislation "necessary and proper for carrying into Execution the foregoing Powers." The battle about what is appropriately a concern of the states alone and what is a proper topic of federal legislation is a key and ongoing issue in American history and politics. Most key decisions limiting states' rights have been justified by the "due process" clause of the Fourteenth Amendment.

statistical analysis, multivariate. A set of techniques for analyzing the relationships among three or more variables. Multivariate analysis can have any of three major purposes: (1) to explain the variance in one dependent variable by two or more different independent variables; (2) to explain the variance in a set of dependent variables by some unmeasured construct; or (3) to explain a set of dependent variables by a set of independent variables.

statistical hypothesis. In research, a speculation as to the value of an unknown parameter in a population. The null hypothesis is the opposite of the hypothesis, which is ordinarily the conclusion that there is no relationship among or between the variables being tested. Because absolute proof of a scientific hypothesis is impossible, researchers rely on indirect proof by demonstrating that an observed sample statistic is so different from the results that would be predicted from the null

hypothesis that it must be rejected in favor of the statistical hypothesis. However, there is always the possibility that the null hypothesis is true, and falsely rejecting it is called a Type I error; the opposite, or failing to reject a false null hypothesis, is called a Type II error. *See also* statistics

statistical inference. Generalized statements about the characteristics of a population made on the basis of information obtained from the study of one or more samples of the population. Such inference is necessary whenever a researcher wishes to test a hypothesis but cannot study an entire population. *See also* sampling

statistical model. One or more equations expressing the relationship between two or more variables. These equations must be capable of fitting in with observed data, and the precision of the fit is evaluated. Statistical models are expressions of hypothetical statements derived from theories; as such, they assume that the observable world works in the way predicted by the theory. If the model can be shown to fit observed data well, it lends support to the theory. A poor fit casts doubt on the theory.

statistical significance. A demonstration that the probability that a null hypothesis is true is very small. When a researcher states that a result is statistically significant at the 0.05 level, he or she means that the probability of obtaining a sample statistic as large as or larger than that achieved if the null hypothesis is true is less than 0.05, which is grounds for rejecting the null hypothesis. Statistical significance depends not only on the discrepancy between an observed sample statistic and hypothesized population parameter, but also on the size of the sample taken. Specifically, the larger the sample size, the easier it is to attain statistical significance. Care must be taken not to confuse statistical significance with substantive significance. Some substantively trivial relationships may well be statistically significant if one's sample size is large enough. For example, in a large enough sample of state prison inmates, a statistically significant number might have moles somewhere on their bodies—a substantively trivial relationship. *See also* statistics

statistical theory. Like a hypothesis, a theory states relationships in statistical as well as verbal terms in order to lend precision to research.

statistics. A method of analyzing data gathered from observations of samples in order to (1) describe the amount of variation in each of two or more variables; (2) describe relationships hypothesized to exist between or among the variables; and (3) make inferences from the results to the larger population from which the sample was drawn. A numerical value summarizing a characteristic of a sample (such as the sample mean) is called a sample statistic, whereas the comparable value computed in the population, such as the population mean, is called a population parameter.

status offense. An act that is declared by statute to be an offense, but only when committed or engaged in by a juvenile, and that can be adjudicated only by a juvenile court. Typical status offenses are violation of curfew, running away from home, truancy, possession of an alcoholic beverage, "incorrigibility," "having delinquent tendencies," "leading an immoral life," and being "in need of supervision." Status offense ordinarily refers to juvenile conduct, but the term has also been used to refer to adults who were charged with the status offense of being vagrant or an addict.

status quo (Lat.). The situation in which a case was at any given date; sometimes referred to as *in status quo*. In general, the term connotes any existing condition or set of circumstances.

statute. A law enacted by, or with the authority of, a legislature.

statute law. An act of a legislature; a particular law enacted and established by the will of the legislative department of government; the written will of a legislature, solemnly expressed according to the forms necessary to constitute it a law of a state.

statute of limitations. A term applied to numerous statutes that set a limit on the length of time that may elapse between an event giving rise to a cause of action and the commencement of a suit to enforce that cause. The purpose is to settle people's affairs so that they are not forever subject to doubt. These statutory requirements simply mean that, within the prescribed period of the statute, an indictment, a complaint, or information must be filed. The time requirement does not run when the defendant is out of the state. Crimes specified as felonies have a three-year statute of limitations from time information is filed, not from filing of complaint. A one-year statute of limitations is specified for misdemeanors from the time a complaint is filed. When these time limits have expired, the defendant cannot be tried for the offense. This is jurisdictional, and a conviction after time has run out is void, even if the defendant does not plead this as a defense. The time starts to run from the date a crime was committed. The statute of limitations for the offense of "acceptance of bribe by a public official or employee" is six years. There is no statute of limitations for murder, embezzlement of public money, or falsification of public records. The federal statute of limitations regarding the liability to pay a fine expires (a) 20 years after the entry of the judgment or (b) on the death of the person fined.

statutes, repeal of. Except in jurisdictions where neither English nor American common law is in force, the general rule is that, if a statute is repealed without a saving clause, there can be no prosecution or punishment for a violation of it that occurred before the repeal. The repeal of an existing statute or law under which a proceeding is pending puts an end to the proceeding, unless it is saved by a proper saving clause in the repealing statute. Even when the statute is repealed after the accused has been convicted, judgment may be arrested, and, if an appeal from a conviction is pending when the statute is repealed, the judgment of conviction must be set aside and the indictment quashed. But a repeal after final judgment of an appellate court will neither vacate the judgment nor prevent the carrying out of the sentence.

statutory. Pertaining to a law or statute, that is, to a law enacted by a legislative body.

statutory rape. Consensual sexual intercourse with any female who is under the age of consent specified by statute. In some jurisdictions, the definition includes males as potential victims.

stay. A halting of judicial proceedings by court order.

stay *ad interim*. A temporary stoppage of proceedings, pending the completion of another action or proceeding.

stay of execution. The stopping by a court of the carrying out or implementation of a judgment, that is, of a court order previously issued.

steal. To appropriate or take something of value that is the property of another, without the consent of the owner; to commit theft.

stet (Lat.). Let it stand.

stereotype. An exaggerated or oversimplified set of beliefs about a particular category, especially a national, ethnic, or racial group of people. Stereotypes are a characteristic feature of prejudiced thinking. Biased people have a fixed mental image of the group or class against whom they are prejudiced, and that they apply to all members of the group or class without attempting to test their preconceptions against reality. The term is derived from the molded cast used in the printing process.

stigmata. In criminology, physical defects or characteristics that were once believed to be influential in producing or indicating criminal conduct. *See also* Lombroso, Cesare

stimulant. A drug or other substance that speeds up the physiological processes of the body.

sting operation. The typical sting involves using various undercover methods to control large-scale theft. Police officers pose as pur-chasers (fences) of stolen goods, setting up contact points and storefronts wired for sound and videotape. Perhaps the best known was the Washington, DC, sting operation in 1975, in which local police joined with the FBI and the Treasury Department in posing as members of the "New York Mafia." During a five-month period, they purchased some $2.4 million in stolen property (for $67,000) and arrested a total of 180 "customers." *See also* Property Crime Program (Sting)

stipend. A salary; fixed payment for work done.

stipulation. An agreement between attorneys representing opposing parties to perform or refrain from something in connection with a case in progress in court or pending court action.

Stockholm syndrome. A term for misplaced empathy or compassion experienced by victims of terrorists, who may tend to identify with their captors or abductors, as was the case with a group held captive in a bank vault in Stockholm in August 1973. One of the female hostages later married her captor.

stolen property; buying, receiving, possessing. The terminology used in the annual Uniform Crime Reports to designate and measure the frequency of this type of offense.

stolen property offenses. The unlawful receiving, buying, distributing, selling, transporting, concealing, or possessing of the property of another by a person who knows that the property has been unlawfully obtained from the owner or other lawful possessor.

Stone, Harlan Fiske. American jurist (1872–1945) who was the 11th chief justice of the Supreme Court. He began his law practice in New York City in 1899. In 1924 President Calvin Coolidge appointed Stone attorney general, and in 1925 he became an associate justice of the Supreme Court. In 1941 President Franklin Roosevelt, ignoring partisan politics and Stone's basically Republican philosophy, selected him to succeed Charles Evans Hughes as chief justice. During World War II, he presided over cases of martial law, military courts, and treason. One of his more famous dissents (1935) involved the constitutionality of the first Agricultural Adjustment Act of the New Deal. Stone wrote that "while unconstitutional exercise of power by the government is subject to judicial restraint, the only check upon our exercise of power is our own sense of restraint."

Stonewall riot. On June 28, 1969, New York City police conducted a routine raid at the Stonewall Inn, a gay bar in Greenwich Village. The officers had a search warrant to investigate reports that liquor was sold illegally, but patrons maintained the police harassed them because they were homosexual. A melee ensued, leading to the injury of 13 patrons and 4 policemen. Two more riots erupted that week; one the next day, involving hundreds of protesters. The Stonewall riots are considered the birth of the gay rights movement. The anniversary of the Stonewall riots is celebrated each year by gay rights activists and civil libertarians. *See also* gay; White Night

stop and frisk. The detaining of someone by a law enforcement officer for the purpose of investigation, accompanied by the officer's superficial examination of the person's body surface or clothing to discover weapons, contraband, or other objects relating to criminal activity. It is intended to stop short of any activity that could be considered a violation of a citizen's constitutional rights.

stoppage in transit. The right of a seller who has not yet been paid for his or her goods to stop the merchandise in transit after it has been removed from his or her possession.

strain-sensitive cable. An electrical cable that is designed to produce a signal whenever the cable is strained by a change in applied force. Typical uses including mounting it in a wall to detect any attempted forced entry through the wall, or fastening it to a fence to detect climbing on the fence, or burying it around a perimeter to detect walking or driving across the perimeter.

street. A way publicly maintained and open to the use of the public for purposes of vehicular travel. The term includes highway.

street crime. A class of offenses, sometimes formally defined as those that occur in public locations, are visible and assaultive, and thus constitute a special risk to the public and a special target for law enforcement preventive efforts and prosecutorial attention. Typically included are robbery, purse snatching, and any kind of assault outside a residence. *See also* treatment alternatives to street crime

stress. There are four general types of stress: (1) hyperstress, caused by an overload of change; (2) hypostress, caused by isolation and stimulus deprivation; (3) eustress, created by positive or favorable change; and (4) distress, caused by negative or unfavorable change. Stress occurs whenever individuals must adapt to demands placed on them. When they are placed under a great deal of adverse stress, they may no longer be able to function normally. Most frequently the result of prolonged distress is a breakdown in the hemostatic mechanisms that normally keep the body working as a whole. An individual who is plagued by excessive tension and anxiety may develop headaches, ulcers, high blood pressure, or muscular ailments. These symptoms, generally referred to as psychophysiological disorders, reflect true organic malfunctions that are caused by the body's efforts to cope with unusually high stress levels. Successfully dealing with stress involves such coping mechanisms as exercise, relaxation techniques, recreation, meditation, diet changes, and psychological counseling. Most stressors fall into three main categories: personal, environmental, and organizational/social. *See also* general adaptation syndrome; Type-A personality

strict construction. Doctrine that the Constitution should have only its traditional literal meaning and that constitutional changes should be made through the amendment process.

strike. A collective refusal by employees to work; a work stoppage. A " stoppage" is any interruption of employee activity lasting a full shift or day or longer and involving six or more workers. In 1981, 14,000 Minnesota state employees walked off their jobs. The strike lasted 22 days and resulted in wage increases. Although the first major police strike was in Boston in 1919, the police in Cincinnati, OH, had struck in September 1918. According to the Bureau of Labor Statistics, between 1970 and 1980, 215 police strikes occurred in U.S. cities, and job actions were threatened in many others. The Police Association of New Orleans led a 15-day strike that ended on March 4, 1979. The strike caused the city to reorganize the association, but the furor over cancellation of Mardi Gras turned public opinion against the union and resulted in no contract, 200 disciplinary actions, fines of $600,000, and disbanding of the Teamsters local. The first police strike in California was in 1969 in the city of Vallejo. On January 14, 1971, approximately 2,100 New York City police officers walked off the job. *See also* Boston police strike; job action; Railroad Strike

stripes. Chevrons used on uniforms to indicate an officer's rank.

strip search. (1) A search of a crime scene, usually outdoors, where the terrain to be searched is divided into strips and searched carefully strip by strip; generally followed by a grid search, which consists of dividing the area into strips at right angles to the lines used in the strip search. (2) A search of a person whose wearing apparel is removed so that both the clothing and the individual's body (including cavities) can be thoroughly examined.

struck jury. A trial jury of 12 secured by having opposing counsel each strike out 12 names from a list of 48 veniremen and thereafter eliminate 12 more from the list by exercising the right of challenge.

strychnine. A poison, bitter in taste, composed of white crystals, derived from nux vomica and certain other plants.

Students for a Democratic Society (SDS). Student organization that was influential during the 1960s. It evolved from a small radical study group of socialists who attracted liberal and idealistic students disenchanted with the American establishment. SDS grew into the largest, most powerful national white leftist organization, which had, at its peak, an estimated 70,000 to 100,000 members. SDS became a major national force when it led white students to take action (mostly sit-ins and a few violent incidents) against racism, poverty, and war on major college campuses across the nation in the spring and summer of 1968.

Due in large part to factionalism, SDS had declined in power and influence by summer 1969, at which time a small, tightly organized, revolutionary fighting force of white youth, called Weathermen, emerged. They engaged in bombings, street fighting, and other offensive action. They were the first organization in recent years to stress publicly the importance of armed social protest in the United States. In 1970 the Weathermen moved underground. *See also* Weathermen

stun bomb. A device designed not to inflict permanent injury but to disable, for several seconds, those exposed to its concussive effect.

stun gun. A correctional riot control device that fires a flat shot bag with the ability to knock someone down without penetrating his or her body. The original model, manufactured by Nova Technologies of Austin, TX, was the handheld Nova XR 5000 Stun Gun, producing 45,000 volts of electricity and a bit larger than an electric razor, is said to be capable of immobilizing a person for up to 90 seconds. The Union City Police department was the first in California to employ stun guns.

subject. (1) The person under investigation or about whom information is being sought by a peace officer. (2) In moulage or casting, the object or impression to be reproduced or cast.

sub justice. Under or before a judge or court undetermined.

suborn. To cause, persuade, or bribe a person to give false testimony while under oath in judicial matter.

subornation of perjury. Procuring another to commit legal perjury.

subpoena. A written order, issued by a judicial officer, prosecutor, defense attorney, or gram jury, requiring a specified person to appear in a designated court at a specified time in order to testify in a case under the jurisdiction of that court or to bring material to be used as evidence to that court. Subpoenas may be served in person by a law enforcement office or by another person authorized to do so, but generally not by a person involved in the action. In some jurisdictions some types of subpoenas may be served by mail or by telephone. Failure to obey a subpoena is contempt of court. A subpoena issued for the appearance of a hostile witness or person who has failed to appear in answer to a previous subpoena and authorizing a law enforcement officer to bring that person to the court is often called an instanter. A subpoena to serve as a witness is called a subpoena *testificatum*. A subpoena to bring material is called a subpoena *duces tecum*.

subrogation. The substitution of one person for another insofar as legal claims or rights an concerned.

sub rosa (Lat.). Privately, or in a manner no open to public scrutiny.

substantive evidence. Evidence offered for the purpose of proving a fact at issue, as opposed to evidence given for the purpose of discrediting a witness.

substantive felony. An independent felony; one not dependent on the conviction of another person for another crime.

substantive law. The part of law that creates defines, and regulates rights.

substantive rights. Guarantees granted to all U.S. citizens under the Constitution. These rights, essential to personal liberty, are listed in the First, Thirteenth, and Fourteenth Amendments and include freedom of speech, press, religion, assembly, and petition. They also include freedom from involuntary servitude and equal protection under the law. These rights may be limited, but only in accordance with due process.

substitutionary evidence. Evidence allowed as a substitute for original or primary evidence.

subterfuge. Any plan, strategy, or action used to evade something unpleasant or difficult or to gain an unfair advantage.

suburb. From the Latin *sub urbe*, for below the city, a term meaning any community that is part of a metropolitan area but outside the city limits. Suburb has always implied proximity to the city, leading to the term exurb for dependent communities farther away from the urban center.

subversion. Demolition; overthrow; destruction; a cause of destruction or overthrow, especially of a government.

sue. To bring a lawsuit against another; to commence a legal action.

sufficiency of bail. The amount of bail is required to be enough, but not more than enough, to ensure the appearance of the accused.

sufficient evidence. Adequate   evidence; such evidence in character, weight, or amount as will legally justify the judicial or official action demanded; according to circumstances, it may be *prima facie* or satisfactory evidence, according to the definitions of those terms.

suicide. The human act of intentional, self-inflicted death. Self-killing is one of the 10 leading causes of death in most Western countries. Approximately 28,000 suicides are recorded in the United States each year, but experts estimate the true number is closer to 40,000 annually. More men than women take their own lives by a ratio of three to one, but more women attempt suicide. Suicidologists are criminologists, sociologists, psychologists, and others who specialize in the study of suicide. A major preventive focus was provided in 1966 when the federal government established the Center for Studies of Suicide

Prevention as part of the National Institutes of Mental Health. The first full-scale, professionally staffed suicide prevention center was established in Los Angeles in 1958.

Weapons Used in 1990
(Percentage of total U.S. suicides)

Firearms	61.0
Hanging & Strangulation	14.5
Gas Poisoning	7.5
Other Poisoning	10.0
Other	7.0

Suicide Demographics in 1990

White Mailes	22.0
Black Males	12.0
White Females	5.3
Black Females	2.3

Instance and Age of Suicides in 1996
(per 100,000)

305	5–14	0.8
4,369	15–24	12.1
12,536	25–44	15.00
7,714	45–64	14.4
5,938	65 and over	11.6

suit. Prosecution of some claim or demand in a court of justice.

Sullivan Act. A law of New York State making it a felony to possess firearms without legal authority.

summary. (1) Done without delay or ceremony; done instantly or quickly; without formality. (2) In law, a hasty or arbitrary procedure, such as a trial without a jury.

summary jurisdiction. The jurisdiction of a court to give a judgment or make an order itself, forthwith; for example, to commit to prison for contempt; to punish malpractice in a solicitor; or, in the case of justices of the peace, a jurisdiction to convict offenders themselves instead of committing them for trial by jury.

summary proceeding. A judicial action, usually a judgment or decision, that is taken without benefit of a formal hearing. Summary decisions of the Supreme Court are those made without the Court's having heard oral arguments on the issue.

summons. A written order issued by a judicial officer requiring a person accused of a criminal offense to appear in a designated court at a specified time to answer the charge(s). A document issued by a law enforcement officer requiring court appearance of an accused person, is, in this terminology, classified as a citation.

sunset laws. Legislation enacted and designed to disband agencies that do not serve the public. The nation's first sunset law was enacted in 1976. Sunset legislation typically specifies that a government program will automatically expire, along with its administrative bureaucracy, after a certain number of years, often seven, in the expectation that it will have served its purpose within that time. The burden is then on the government and the program's advocates to justify the agency's existence beyond the expiration.

sunshine legislation. In recent years both state and federal governments have adopted significant legislation requiring that key meetings and hearings take place "in the sunshine"—or publicly—so that democratic participation and influence on government can be more effectively exercised at critical points in the policy-making process. Such laws are a reaction against government secrecy. In the Sunshine Act of 1977, the federal government required that some 50 executive agencies, regulatory commissions, advisory committees, and independent offices hold public meetings or publish minutes of their meetings. The act also banned all unofficial contracts between agencies and persons affected by them. Cabinet departments are exempted, but Congress has since passed rules requiring more sunshine on many of its internal deliberations.

superior court. (1) A court of record or general trial court in some states, superior to a justice of the peace or magistrate's court. (2) In other states, an intermediate court between the general trial court and the highest appellate court.

superior court warrant of arrest. In New York, a subpoena that a police officer delivers to the defendant.

supersede. To set aside; annul.

supersedeas, writ of. An order to stay the proceedings. It is either expressed, by the issuance of a writ of *supersedeas*, or implied, by the issuance of a writ, as of *certiorari*.

supervised probation. Guidance, treatment, or regulation by a probation agency of the behavior of a person who is subject to adjudication or who has been convicted of an offense, resulting from a formal court order or a probation agency decision. Supervision of adults may be in lieu of prosecution or judgment or after a judgment of conviction. Supervised probation may be a substitute for confinement or may occur after a period of confinement in jail or prison. Probation supervision differs according to the degree of intensity of supervision and amount of services provided to subjects. A common, broad distinction is between active supervision (contact between the agency and the client occurs on a regular basis) and inactive supervision (contact occurs only when initiated by the client or other interested party outside the probation agency and is not on a regular basis). Inactive cases are sometimes called "banked" cases.

supervision. Authorized and required guidance, treatment, and/or regulation of the behavior of a person who is subject to adjudication or who has been adjudicated to be an offender, performed by a correctional agency.

supervisory alarm system. An alarm system that monitors conditions or persons or both and signals any deviation from an established norm or schedule. Examples are the monitoring of signals from guard patrol stations for irregularities in the progression along a prescribed patrol route and the monitoring of production or safety conditions, such as sprinkler water pressure, temperature, or liquid level.

supporting evidence. Evidence that will bolster and strengthen such evidence as eyewitness testimony, transfer evidence, and statements of the accused. Supportive evidence includes such things as proof of motivation, similarity of modus operandi to other crimes known to have been committed by the accused, the accused having possession of the stolen property, and so forth.

suppression hearing. A hearing to determine whether or not the court will prohibit specified statements, documents, or objects from being introduced into evidence in a trial.

supra (Lat). Above; previously referred to.

supreme court, state. Usually the highest court in the state judicial system.

Supreme Court, U.S. Heads the judicial branch of the American government and is the nation's highest law court. It also performs a political function as the official interpreter and expounder of the Constitution. Because many of the most important provisions of the Constitution are extremely broad and offer much room for difference of interpretation (such as due process of law or equal protection of the laws), the Court's role in the political development of the American republic has been great, often exceeding that of the president or Congress. The Supreme Court was created by Article III of the Constitution and is headed by the chief justice of the United States. The size of the Court is determined by Congress; since 1869 it has been composed of nine justices appointed by the president with the advice and consent of the Senate. They serve during good behavior and are removable only by death, resignation, or impeachment. The Supreme Court is primarily an appellate court. It reviews decisions of the lower federal courts by writ of *certiorari*, a discretionary writ granted on the affirmative vote of four of the nine justices (Rule of Four). The Court also hears appeals against decisions of state supreme courts that involve interpretation of the Constitution, federal laws, or treaties. In addition, a few types of cases, principally suits

SUPREME COURT IN 2004		
	Birth Year	Appointment Year
Chief Justice William Rehnquist	1924	1972: Nixon
John Paul Stevens	1920	1975: Ford
Sandra Day O'Connor	1930	1981: Reagan
Antonin Scalia	1936	1986: Reagan
Anthony Kennedy	1936	1988: Reagan
David Souter	1939	1990: Bush
Clarence Thomas	1948	1991: Bush
Ruth Bader Ginsburg	1933	1993: Clinton
Stephen G. Breyer	1938	1994: Clinton

between states, can be filed directly in the original jurisdiction of the Supreme Court without having gone through any other court. When President George Washington made his nominations for the Supreme Court in 1790, his six selections were all white, male, and Protestant. The first Roman Catholic justice appointed (in 1836) was Roger Brooke Taney, the son of a Maryland plantation owner. Another 80 years passed before the barrier against Jews was finally breached. In 1916 President Woodrow Wilson filled a vacant seat with Louis Dembitz Brandeis. The barrier against blacks fell in 1967 with President Lyndon B. Johnson's appointment of Thurgood Marshall, a former U.S. Court of Appeals judge. And after almost two centuries, the barrier against women also fell. The "brethren's" first "sister" was Sandra Day O'Connor, an Arizona Court of Appeals judge nominated by President Ronald W. Reagan in 1981 and confirmed by the Senate on September 28, 1981, by a unanimous vote.

surety. One who undertakes to become responsible for the debt of another; one who binds him- or herself for the performance of some act of another.

suretyship. An undertaking to answer for the debt, default, or miscarriage of another.

surprise. A procedural pleading available to parties to a trial when something unexpected, which could not be prevented by due diligence, develops. The side that is disadvantaged by such a development may plead surprise.

surreptitious. Covert, hidden, concealed, or disguised.

surrogate. A judicial officer who has jurisdiction over the probate of wills, the settlement of estates, and so forth.

surveillance. (1) Control of premises for security purposes through alarm systems, closed circuit television, or other monitoring methods. (2) Supervision or inspection of industrial processes by monitoring those conditions that could cause damage if not corrected. (3) Police investigative technique involving visual or electronic observation or listening directed at a person or place (such as stakeout, tailing suspects, or wiretapping). *See also* supervisory alarm system

surveillance cameras. The National Institute of Standards provides advice on how to select surveillance cameras for specific needs, including tips on storing processed film, improving photo quality, and selecting film and lens size. For information, contact: Office of Law Enforcement Standards Institute, National Bureau of Standards, 100 Bureau Drive, M/S 8102, Gaithersburg, MD 20899-8102.

survey. A study that selects a sample from some larger population in order to ascertain the prevalence, incidence, and interrelations of table   **335**

selected variables. The survey is used primarily to determine the distribution of persons on some variable, such as the percentage of them opposed to capital punishment, and to determine other variables accompanying that opinion or position. A researcher begins by deciding what populations to study—from an entire country or state to a particular subgroup such as prisoners, women police officers, or juvenile arrestees. Next, the surveyor designates a sample of persons representing this population, who will be studied. Depending on the research design, this may be a simple random sample, a stratified sample, a cluster sample, or a quota sample. Additionally, depending on research aims, a cross-sectional or panel study may be used. *See also* sampling

suspect. An adult or juvenile considered by a criminal justice agency to be one who may have committed a specific criminal offense but who has not yet been arrested or charged.

suspended sentence. A court disposition of a convicted person, pronouncing a penalty of a fine or commitment to confinement but unconditionally discharging the defendant or holding execution of the penalty in abeyance upon good behavior.

suspension of judgment. A court action pronouncing a fine or a prison sentence followed by an order that, upon certain conditions, the payment of the fine, the prison term, or either of them need not be met.

suspicion. Category of annual Uniform Crime Reports used to record and report arrests made on grounds of suspicion, in jurisdictions where the law permits, in which the arrestee is later released without being charged. Suspicion is not an offense.

Sutton, Willie. Willie "the actor" Sutton was America's most famous bank robber, who, during his half-century career, plundered almost 100 banks using a variety of ruses, disguises, pioneering safe-cracking techniques, and precision timing. He was arrested, for the fourth time, in New York for possession of a gun in 1952.

SWAT. An acronym for Special Weapons and Tactics. The forerunner was apparently New York City's Tactical Patrol Force (TPF). During the 1960s and 1970s, the TPFs viewed their 1,000-member force as the elite of incorruptible law enforcement. In addition to mob and riot control, the TPFs swept into high crime areas to apprehend muggers and robbers, often using a variety of decoy units that readily blended into the street life. More visible and controversial are the newer, commando-style police units known as SWAT teams, carefully chosen and trained in the use of weapons and strategic invasion tactics and typically used in situations involving hostages, airplane hijackings, and prison riots. The first of these police units was the Philadelphia Police Department's 100-man SWAT squad, organized in 1964 in response to a growing number of bank robberies. That team, on May 19, 1985, in an effort to arrest members of a black radical group called MOVE, dropped a bomb on the group's "fortress," which resulted in the deaths of 11 people and left 270 homeless when 61 rowhouses burned. It was alleged that in the United States this was the first time. that a home was bombed in pursuit of criminals. On May 3, 1988, a grand jury cleared Mayor W. Wilson Goode and all other city officials of criminal liability. But the jury referred to their actions as "morally reprehensible behavior," as well as "incompeten[t]" and "coward[ly]."

swindler. One who defrauds others by cheating and deception or through fraudulent schemes.

syndicate. A name applied to the Mafia and other organizations whose purpose is to accomplish unlawful or questionable objectives. It also applies to legal and legitimate organizations whose activities are joined together for business purposes.

T

table. A dual series of similar items—for example, the names of cities, their current crime rate, and one or more prior rates; a two-dimensional array.

tales. Persons summoned as jurors.

talesman. A bystander who is chosen to serve on a jury when the jury is not filled by those who had been summoned for jury duty. The person chosen need not be present in court.

Taney, Roger Brooke. Born in 1771, Taney was the fourth chief justice of the United States, whose decision in the Dred Scott case in 1857 became a controversial issue. Descended from a prominent Maryland Tidewater family, Taney studied law for three years in Annapolis. In 1836, as reward for his political loyalty, President Andrew Jackson appointed him chief justice, succeeding John Marshall. Taney held this position for nearly three decades. The Dred Scott case, which maintained that blacks did not possess rights of citizenship entitling them to sue in federal courts, caused the prestige of the Court to fall to its lowest point and, with it, the reputation of Taney, a position from which he never recovered. Although unpopular at his death in 1864, today Taney is considered one of the great justices by conservatives and liberals alike.

TASER. An acronym for Tom Swift's Electric Rifle (the "a" was added for phonetic purposes). The Taser, introduced in early 1975, is designed as a nonlethal weapon resembling a handgun. Once the trigger is depressed, two small barbed contacts, trailing fine conducting wires, are shot from one of the cassettes along the line of aim into the target. The dart-like contacts need not actually touch the skin. If the darts are imbedded in clothing, the electrical charge is capable of reaching the body, since the Taser provides a 1½-inch spark from its high-voltage power supply. Taser performance was tested by the U.S. Consumer Product Safety Commission in 1976. More than 100 penal and law enforcement agencies are using the Taser Police Special (PS-81A), including the Los Angeles and Nashville police departments.

Task Force on Juvenile Justice and Delinquency Prevention. A group of persons, representing a wide variety of professional services and disciplines serving youth, appointed in 1975 to develop national standards for juvenile justice and delinquency prevention.

tattooing. In law enforcement, gunpowder patterns; the marks left on the surface of a skin of the person who has been shot at fairly close range. They are caused by the residue of unburned powder in the propellant. From little or no pattern at contact range, the design or pattern increases in size with the increase in the distance of the muzzle of the weapon from the body, up to a distance from which none of the particles reach the body. The markings caused by these particles are black or red.

team policing (tp). A decentralized form of policing, popularized in the 1970s, that uses a self-contained group of officers who are permanently assigned to a neighborhood and are responsible for all its crime problems. These officers follow through to case or incident completion. The process relies on functional authority (individual expertise) rather than traditional rank structure. Tp encourages community participation in solving crime, with less emphasis on response time and greater emphasis on follow-through for each case, and involves many nontraditional police methods. Tp is no longer popular because (a) by increasing community participation and trust in law enforcement, it led to higher levels of crime-reporting, which appeared statistically as increases in crime; and (b) the law enforcement hierarchy perceived the method as reducing the control of middle- and senior-management officers.

Teapot Dome Scandal. An affair that disclosed corruption in high levels of government, shocking the American public. The findings of a Senate committee in October 1923, inquiring into how the rich naval oil reserves at Teapot Dome, WY, and Elk Hills and Buena Vista, CA, were leased to Harry S. Sinclair's Mammoth Oil Co. and Edward L. Doheny's

PanAmerican Petroleum and Transport Co. led to the prosecution for conspiracy and bribery of Senator Albert B. Fall of New York. As secretary of the interior under President Warren Harding, he had authorized the award of the leases to the two oil companies; he was confined in the New Mexico State Penitentiary at Santa Fe, but a $1 million fine was never paid. After his release, he survived in relative poverty until 1944.

tear gas. A substance, usually liquid, that, when atomized and of a certain concentration, causes temporary but intense eye irritation and a blinding flow of tears in anyone exposed to it. Also called a lachrymator.

technical services. The specialized bureau in a traditionally organized police department responsible for communications, records, identification, laboratory activities, and temporary detention.

telegraph channel. A low-capacity communication channel with a maximum data transmission rate of 10 characters per second.

telephone. The first commercial telephone exchange in the United States, possibly in the world, opened in New Haven, CT, in 1876. The first police department to install a telephone exchange to replace the telegraph was that of Cincinnati, OH.

telephone channel. A medium-capacity communication channel with a maximum capacity of 300 characters per second.

teletypewriter. An electric typewriter that can be operated manually or by reading and reperforating paper tape; it is connected to a leased or dial-switched telegraph grade circuit for transmitting text and data messages in readable form.

Ten-Codes. The officially suggested ten-codes by the Associated Public Safety Communications Officers are:

ten-1 Cannot understand your message
ten-2 Your signal is good
ten-3 Stop transmitting
ten-4 Message received ("OK")
ten-5 Relay information to _____

ten-6 Station is busy
ten-7 Out of service
ten-8 In service
ten-9 Repeat last message
ten-10 Negative ("no")
ten-11 _____ in service
ten-12 Stand by
ten-13 Report _____ conditions
ten-14 Information
ten-15 Message delivered
ten-16 Reply to message
ten-17 En route
ten-18 Urgent
ten-19 Contact _____
ten-20 Unit location
ten-21 Call _____ by telephone
ten-22 Cancel last message
ten-23 Arrived at scene
ten-24 Assignment completed
ten-25 Meet _____
ten-26 Estimated time of arrival is _____
ten-27 Request for information on license
ten-28 Request vehicle registration information
ten-29 Check records
ten-30 Use caution
ten-31 Pick up
ten-32 Units requested
ten-33 Emergency! Officer needs help
ten-34 Correct time

tender. To offer money in payment of a debt or in fulfillment of a contract.

territorial court. Any one of a number of different courts established from time to time by Congress for territories subject to U.S. jurisdiction. These courts are legislative because their creation is an exercise of the power of Congress to make rules for U.S. property, under Article IV, Section 3 of the Constitution.

territorial jealousy. A concern with protecting the turf of one's own agency, which sometimes makes cooperation among criminal justice agencies difficult or impossible. Sometimes termed the *not-invented-here* or *NIH syndrome*.

territorial jurisdiction. The right of a state to exercise exclusive control over (a) all lands within its boundaries; (b) its territorial waters; (c) an extensive portion of the air space over its territory; and (d) all persons or things not covered by diplomatic immunity within any of the foregoing areas. Among the territories administered by the United States are: American Samoa; Baker, Howland, and Jarvis Islands; Canton and Enderburg Islands; Guam; Johnston Island; Kingman Reef; Midway Island; Navarra Island; Northern Mariana Islands; Palmyra Island; Puerto Rico; the U.S. Virgin Islands (St. Croix, St. John, and St. Thomas); and Wake Island. For further information, contact: Office of International Affairs, Department of the Interior, 1849 C Street, NW, Washington, DC 20240.

territorial waters. The waters under the jurisdiction of a nation or state, including the offshore waters lying between its shores and the high seas, an area called the territorial belt or marginal sea; inland lakes and rivers entirely within the state; and boundary rivers, straits, lakes, and bays up to the middle point, measured from shore to shore. The jurisdiction of a state extends over territorial waters in matters of fishing rights, navigation, coastal trade, sanitation, and custom duties. Historically, the territorial belt was generally three to six miles, although some nations tried to enforce much wider limits. In December 1988 the United States became the 105th nation to proclaim a 12-mile limit, an action taken by President Ronald Reagan in accordance with the 1982 UN Law of the Sea Convention, created to curb Soviet spy ships. Ships of other nations have the right of innocent passage through the territorial waters of any nation as long as the vessels observe the navigation, customs, and sanitation regulations of the countries having jurisdiction. During war the marginal seas of neutral territories are off-limits to battling warships of the nations at war.

terrorism. (1) The calculated use of violence to obtain political goals through instilling fear, intimidation, or coercion. It usually involves a criminal act, often symbolic in nature and intended to influence an audience beyond the immediate victims. (2) A climate of fear and intimidation, created by means of threats or violent actions, causing sustained fear for personal safety, in order to achieve social or political goals. (3) An organized pattern of violent behavior designed to influence government policy or to intimidate the population for the same purpose. (4) Violent, criminal behavior designed primarily to generate fear in the community, or a substantial segment of it, for political purposes. In 1980, the U.S. Army established an elite antiterrorist group, under a top-secret Joint Special Operations Command, called The Delta Force or Blue Light, and based in Fort Bragg, NC. Pentagon counterterror units are said to number 2,000 elite troops with their own air and naval units. Major acts of terrorism with the United states as a main target include:

April 1983, the bombing of the U.S. embassy in Beirut, killing 63.

October 1983, the bombing of military barracks in Beirut, killing 241.

December 1988, the destruction of Pan Am Flight 103 over Scotland, killing 270.

February 1993, the bombing of the World Trade Center, killing 6.

April 1995, the Oklahoma City bombing, killing 168.

June 1996, the bombing of military barracks in Saudi Arabia, killing 19.

August 1998, attacks on U.S. embassies in East Africa, killing 147.

October 2000, the bombing of a warship in Yemen, killing 17.

September 2001, coordinated attacks by hijacked commercial airliners on the Pentagon and World Trade Centers leaving about 3,000 dead. *See also* bioterrorism

terrorism abroad. Acts of international terrorism rose from 322 incidents in 1994 to 440 in 1995, making that the worst year since 1991. However, the number of deaths involved was only 165 in 1995, down from 314 the prior year. The number of injuries was 6,291 in 1995, including approximately

5,500 people injured in a single incident, a gas attack in the Tokyo subway system that was attributed to the Aum Supreme Truth cult, a group based in Japan with branches in other nations. Attacks on U.S. government and military facilities peaked in 1986 at 200, declining to 39 in 1995. The greatest civilian death toll from a terrorist bomb was 329 killed when an Air India 747 was destroyed by a bomb over the North Atlantic while approaching Shannon, Ireland, on June 23, 1985. In 1997, the U.S. government listed seven countries as perpetrators of state-sponsored terrorism: Iran, Iraq, Libya, North Korea, Sudan, Cuba, and Syria. In 1995, 440 acts of terrorism killed 163 people, while in 1996 there were 256 acts that killed 311 and wounded 2,652, making it one of the highest casualty years on record. On January 31, 1996, 90 people died and 1,400 were injured when an explosive-laden truck driven by Tamil separatists smashed into the Sri Lanka Central Bank. In June 1996, a large fuel truck exploded outside the U.S. military's Khobar Towers housing complex near Dharain, Saudi Arabia, killing 19 and wounding 500. In 1996 President Clinton signed a bill that expanded the authority of U.S. courts to prosecute terrorists for crimes against Americans committed outside U.S. borders. Assistance is available to help design corporate security programs for businesses in foreign countries. Information is available on the security climate within a given country. *Countering Terrorism* is a free pamphlet providing security suggestions for U.S. business representatives abroad; it describes precautionary measures, as well as suggested procedures in case of kidnapping. Additional information is also available from: D/DT, DOS, 2201 C St., NW, Room 2238, Washington, DC 20520. Contact: Overseas Security Advisory Council, Bureau of Diplomatic Security, DOS, Room 3422 (same address).

terrorism, rewards for information on. The U.S. State Department created an interagency task force in 1989 to pay bounties for tips on terrorist attack plans. As of August 1992 the task force, which combines the efforts of the National Security Agency, the FBI, CIA, Interpol, and other agencies, has been contacted by informants in 60 nations and has paid out more than $2 million in bounties.

terrorist groups. John F. Fay, in his book, *Security Dictionary*, lists over 350 international terrorist organizations believed to be responsible either by claim or attribution for terrorist acts. On February 26, 1993, a bomb explosion in New York City's World Trade Center was pronounced a terrorist attack, with a group calling itself the Liberation Army Fifth Battalion claiming responsibility. For more information, see the appendix "Worldwide Historical Evolution of Terrorism Since World War II," *Annual Editions: Violence and Terrorism*, 7th ed., 2004/05, Dubuque, IA: McGraw-Hill/ Dushkin Companies.

terrorist targets worldwide. April 1983, the destruction of an Air India flight over the Irish coast, killing 329.

October 1983, bombing of a bus station in Sri Lanka, killing 150.

December 1988, the destruction of a UTA flight over Chad, killing 170.

February 1993, bombing of the Jewish center in Buenos Aires, killing 96.

April 1995, a bus bomb in Tel Aviv killed 22.

June 1996, 62 tourists were gunned down in Egypt.

August 1998, a bombing in Omagh, Ireland, killed 29.

October 2000, apartments were bombed in Moscow, killing 118.

Terror Warning Color Codes. The White House Office of Homeland Security established five levels of terrorist alerts:

Red: Severe risk of terrorist attacks
• Deploy specifically trained teams.
• Watch and adjust transportation systems.
• Close public and government facilities.

Orange: High risk of terrorist attacks
• Take additional precautions at public events.

- Prepare to work at an alternative site.
- Restrict access to essential personnel only at some facilities.

Yellow: Elevated condition. Significant risk of terrorist attacks.

- Increase surveillance of key locations.
- Coordinate emergency plans with nearby jurisdictions.

Blue: Guarded condition. General risk of terrorist attack.

- Check communications.
- Review and update emergency response procedures.
- Give the public necessary information.

Green: Low risk of terrorist attacks.

- Train emergency personnel.
- Reduce vulnerabilities at key facilities.

testamentary. Having to do with a will or testament; obtained by or through a will.

testimony. Evidence given by a witness, under oath or affirmation. All persons are competent to testify in cases except: if, in the opinion of the judge, they are prevented by extreme youth, disease affecting the mind, or any other cause of the same kind from recollecting the matter on which to testify, from understanding the questions put to them, from giving rational answers to those questions, or from knowing that they ought to speak the truth. Witnesses unable to speak or hear are not incompetent and may give evidence by writing, signs, or any other manner in which they can make it intelligible, but the writing or signs must be made in open court. Evidence so given is deemed to be oral evidence. Generally neither a husband nor wife can be a witness against the spouse, but the laws on this subject vary in different states. In most states, the accused is allowed to testify in his or her own behalf, but cannot be compelled to testify.

Texas Rangers. A semimilitary, mounted police force first organized in 1836 as a local body of settlers with the purpose of defense against Indian attacks. When, in 1845, Texas was admitted to the union, the Rangers became the first official state police agency in America. During the Mexican War, they were reorganized by General Sam Houston, who built up their strength to a force of 1,600 men. They served in the Civil War as an element of the Confederate Army and were reorganized in the 1870s. As a police force at that time, the Rangers protected hundreds of miles of the Texas frontier against Indians, hold-up men, rustlers, and bandits. They operated without uniforms or standard procedures, being authorized as roving commissioners for specific duties. The Rangers were famous for their skill and ability and exercised great moral influence in the state. *See also* state police

Texas Syndicate. A group formed of Texas-born Mexican American inmates at San Quentin Prison in 1975. Membership spread to other California prisons and then to those in Texas.

thanatology. The study of death and dying. *See also* AIDS

theft. Generally, the taking of the property of another with intent to permanently deprive the rightful owner of possession; in the broadest legal usage, the name of the group of offenses featuring larceny, fraud, embezzlement, false pretenses, robbery, and extortion. Theft offenses can include larceny; shoplifting; pickpocketing; embezzlement; fraud; forgery; counterfeiting; confidence games; blackmail; usury; ransom; buying, receiving, or possessing stolen goods; plagiarism; removal of landmarks; and criminal bankruptcy. In March 1960 Miami's Trendline Jewelry, a large wholesaler of precious metals, was the victim of a still-unknown and highly sophisticated group of thieves, who thwarted complex alarm systems that used sonar equipment and electric eyes and carried off thousands of 14-karat gold bracelets and ring mountings, plus over 800 pounds of gold and 3,000 pounds of silver. The $7 million loss was the largest theft of precious metals in the nation's history, exceeding even the Lufthansa robbery in 1978 at New York City's Kennedy Airport, in which thieves stole $5.8 million worth of currency and jewelry; and the famed 1950 Brinks robbery in Boston, which netted thieves some $2.8 million. The Philippine government announced on April 23, 1986, that it had identified $860.8 million that had been salted away by former president Ferdinand Marcos and his wife Imelda. The total allegedly stolen since November 1965 was believed to be between $5 and $10 billion.

Theory X and Theory Y. A nonempirical assumption by management theorist Douglas McGregor (1906–1964) regarding how managers perceive the people they direct. *Theory X*, the conventional concept, says that the average human being has an inherent dislike of work and will avoid it if possible. Because people inherently dislike work, they must be coerced, controlled, and threatened with punishment to elicit adequate effort toward the achievement of company objectives. The average human being prefers to be directed, wishes to avoid responsibility, has relatively little ambition, and wants security above all. In *Theory Y* by contrast, the expenditure of physical and mental effort in work is as natural as play and rest. External control and the threat of punishment are not the only means for eliciting effort toward company objectives. Commitment to objectives is a function of the rewards associated with their achievement. The most significant types of rewards are ego satisfaction and self-actualization. The average human being will learn, under proper conditions, not only to accept but to seek responsibility. The human capacity to exercise a relatively high degree of imagination, ingenuity, and creativity in the solution of company problems is widely, not narrowly, distributed in the population. Under the conditions of modern industrial life, the intellectual potentialities of the average human being are only partially utilized. In an influential 1960 book, McGregor urged American industry to adopt Theory Y as quickly as possible in managing especially manufacturing operations.

Therapeutic Communities of America (TCA). A chain of facilities that treats, among others, so-called "hard-core" substance abusers, clients who lack education, vocational skills, and family support systems, and who have criminal backgrounds and long histories of illicit-drug use. TCA offers residential and out-patient programs, crisis intervention, case management, education, and relapse prevention. Address: 1601 Connecticut Ave., NW, Suite 803, Washington, DC 20009.

therapeutic community. A concept for treatment of people with emotional problems, especially in the rehabilitation of drug addicts. Centers for drug addicts include Synanon, Kinsman Hall, Odyssey House, and Phoenix House. They operate on the principle, similar to that of Alcoholics Anonymous, that recovered addicts can understand, relate to, and communicate effectively with addicts.

thief-takers. Private detectives who were paid by the Crown on a piecework basis. In England during the seventeenth century, highway robbery was prevalent and associated with persons such as Claude Duval, Jack Sheppard, Dick Turpin, and Captain Lightfoot. As a result, in 1693 an act of Parliament established a reward of 40 pounds sterling for the capture of any highwayman or road agent. The reward was payable upon conviction, and to the thief-taker also went the highwayman's horse, arms, money, and property, unless these were proven not to have been stolen. Thief-takers had no official status and were akin to the bounty hunters of the American West. Thief-makers often became thief-takers. They would seduce youngsters into committing crimes, then have another thief-taker arrest the youth in the midst of the offense.

THOR. An acronym for the Target Hardening and Opportunity Reduction project. This was one the the most comprehensive and well-funded of all Law Enforcement Assistance Administration–funded, community crime-prevention programs. Atlanta, GA, was one of eight cities selected for the anti-crime impact program.

threat. The declaration by words or actions of an unlawful intent to do some injury to another, together with an apparent ability to do so.

Three Prisons Act. Passed by Congress in 1891, it authorized the establishment of three federal penitentiaries: first, Leavenworth, opened in 1895 and fully operational in 1906; second, Atlanta, opened in 1902; the territorial jail at McNeil Island, which had begun operations in 1875, was designated the third penitentiary in 1907 and has since been deactivated.

three-strikes laws. A type of mandatory minimum-sentencing structure in which judges have no discretion and must impose lengthy incarceration on defendants who have two serious or violent felonies on record prior to being convicted of a third. In California, for example, a defendant prosecuted under the three-strikes law must be sentenced to a term of 25 years-to-life for a third serious or violent felony conviction. Such laws are designed to incapacitate violent or career criminals, but they are controversial. Critics say they represent excessive and unnecessary punishment in many cases, as well as contributing to prison overcrowding. By 1995 13 states had adopted such laws. Georgia enacted a two-strike law on January 1, 1995, requiring people convicted of a "second strike" for any of seven types of crimes—murder, rape, kidnapping, armed robbery, aggravated child molestation, aggravated sodomy, or aggravated sexual battery—to be sentenced to life in prison without parole.

ticket-of-leave. Method of conditional release from prison, used in the 1840s by Alexander Maconochie of England and Sir Walter Crofton of Ireland. The ticket-of-leave allowed conditional release from prison.

time served. Generally, time spent in confinement in relation to conviction and sentencing for a given offense(s), calculated in accord with the rules and conventions specific to a given jurisdiction; also, total time served under correctional agency jurisdiction. "Dead time" or "nonrun time" is time that does not count as prison time served toward a required term in confinement or as time served on parole toward total time under correctional jurisdiction. Time elapsed after escape and before apprehension is dead time in counting time in confinement. Time spent out of confinement pending an appeal decision may also be declared dead time in counting prison time, depending on the rules of a jurisdiction or decisions made in individual cases. "Street time" is time spent on conditional release. If parole or other conditional release is revoked and the person reconfined, all or part of this time may become dead time in calculations of time served under correctional jurisdiction, according to administrative or court decision.

tokenism. The practice of permitting a very limited number of minority group members into schools, neighborhoods, businesses, and other organizations, often with the purpose of meeting only the minimum requirements of civil rights legislation or public opinion.

tong. *See* war, tong

top secret. In government service, information that is ranked of extreme importance and which if divulged without authority, might cause irreparable harm, which would bring about a break in diplomatic relations with another country, cause an armed attack upon the nation or its allies, or compromise military or defense plans or other developments vital to the national defense.

Top Ten Most Wanted Criminals. An FBI program in which 10 persons charged with major crimes are targeted through publication of their photos and descriptions. They are each the subject of an Identification Order. This program has proven effective, and many wanted persons have been identified by members of the public, which has resulted in their apprehension. John Dillinger was America's first "public enemy #1." In 1985, the Los Angeles Police Department established a similar program and took into custody its #1 suspect within two months. The syndicated TV show "America's Most Wanted," begun in the late 1980s, has still further increased the effectiveness of the program.

tort. The breach of a duty to an individual that results in damage to him or her. Crime, in contrast, may be called the breach of a duty to the public. An act that offends both society and an individual receives the classification of the person who seeks justice. Moreover, damage need not result for the act to constitute a crime, as in an attempted murder. Note that a tort involves only duties owed to an individual as a matter of law, not duties arising from an agreement (contract) with him or her. *See also* same act may be both a crime and a tort

total quality management (TQM). An organizational concept of management that first appeared in W. A. Shehart's "Economic Control of Quality of Manufactured Products" in 1931 and was refined and made widely popular by management consultant W. Edwards Deming in the 1980s. The concept, promulgated in U.S. corporations through training programs, involves: (1) customer focus, (2) focusing on processes as well as results, (3) prevention of defects or mistakes as opposed to post-production inspection, (4) mobilizing the expertise of the workforce, (5) fact-based decision making, and (6) feedback. TQM has been seen as the force behind Japanese domination in many markets—an important reason for its popularity. Several law enforcement departments have implemented TQM concepts to enhance the efficiency, delivery, and quality of service. As a customer-focused process emphasizing employee capabilities, TQM meshes well with community-oriented policing.

toxicology. The study and science of toxic substances and their characteristics, effects, and antidotes.

Toxic Release Inventory (TRI). TRI is a government mandated, publicly available compilation of information and data on the release of over 300 individual toxic chemicals and 20 categories of chemical compounds by manufacturing facilities in the United States. The law requires manufacturers to state the amounts of chemicals they release directly to air, land, or water, or that they transfer to off-site facilities that treat or dispose of wastes. The U.S. Environmental Protection Agency compiles these reports into an annual inventory and makes the information available in a computerized database. *See* Pollutant Standard Index

traced forgery. Forging by tracing genuine writings onto another document. This is usually accomplished by placing the genuine document over a lighted glass or other transparent surface and tracing the original onto a document placed over it. A qualified document examiner can detect this type of forgery because of the waviness of the forged writing.

trace elements. Minute quantities of chemical elements present in or on objects or materials. Crime laboratories have developed techniques for finding and analyzing such small amounts of chemicals, which can be useful in identifying two or more specimens as having come from the same source.

tracking. The following of an individual through the entire criminal justice process.

traffic. Term that includes pedestrians, ridden animals, vehicles, streetcars, or other conveyances, either singly or together, while using any highway for purposes of travel.

traffic law, first. Passed on June 27, 1652, by New Amsterdam (New York City): "The Director General and Council of New Netherland in order to prevent accidents do hereby ordain that no Wagons, Carts or Sleighs shall be run, rode or driven at a gallop within this city of New Amsterdam, that the drivers and conductors of all Wagons, Carts and Sleighs within this city (the Broadway alone excepted) shall walk by the Wagons, Carts or Sleighs and so take and lead the horses, on the penalty of two pounds Flemish for the first time, and for the second time double, and for the third time to be arbitrarily corrected therefore and in addition to be responsible for all damages which may arise therefrom."

traffic management. The function of law enforcement to assist in the orderly flow of vehicles on streets and highways and to enforce the laws regulating vehicle use.

traffic offenses. A category of motor vehicle offenses considered as infractions and minor misdemeanors and excluded from most databases of criminal and correctional proceedings.

traffic regulation, first. The first one-way traffic regulation appears to have been issued in New York City on December 17, 1791, when a regulation incidental to a performance at the John Street Theatre requested that "Ladies and Gentlemen will order their Coachmen to take up and set down with their Horse Heads to the East River, to avoid Confusion."

traffic signals. The use of mechanical devices to control traffic flow predates the invention of the automobile. One was installed outside the British Parliament in 1868 to regulate pedestrian traffic. This signal, and early American variations, had two semaphore arms, like a railroad signal, that acted as physical impediments to oncoming traffic. For night visibility, red and green gas lamps would signify when one could proceed or must stop. It is not clear where the first modern traffic signal to control automobile traffic was installed. Salt Lake City and St. Paul both lay claim to the event, but the green-red signal installed on Euclid Ave. in Cleveland in 1914 is generally credited with being the first of its kind. The mechanisms of signals are uniformly vertical, with the red light always on top to assist color-blind drivers.

traffic signs and markings. Information and expertise is available on the design of traffic control device standards. A free 45-minute slide presentation describes symbol signs and traffic-signal meanings. Contact: Signs and Markings Branch, Traffic Control System, Office of Traffic Operations, Federal Highway Administration, DOT, 400 7th St., SW, Room 3419, Washington, DC 20024.

Trainers, American Society of Law Enforcement (ASLET). Address: 10 Dock Rd., Box 361, Lewes, DE 19958.

training schools. State institutions providing education and vocational training programs to prison inmates and juvenile offenders.

transcript. The official description of a court proceeding recorded by the court reporter.

transfer. In criminal justice, the movement of a person from one correctional facility or caseload to another.

transfer hearing. A preadjudicatory hearing in juvenile court for the purpose of determining whether juvenile court jurisdiction should be retained over a juvenile alleged to have committed a delinquent act or whether it should be waived and the juvenile transferred to criminal court for prosecution as an adult.

transient. One who comes to a place for a temporary period of time and then moves on.

transit police. As most rapid transit systems cross jurisdictional boundaries, it was necesary to create special forces of transportation officers with law enforcement powers. The New York City Transit Police Department, policing over 700 miles of track and 460 stations, is the second largest police force in New York State, and one of the largest in the nation. It began in 1936 when Mayor LaGuardia signed a resolution creating the post of "special patrolman" on the subway system. These patrolmen were granted peace officer status in 1947 and the department made a separate entity in 1955.

transnational crime. Illegal activity involving more than one sovereign nation, or in which national borders are crossed, as in organized crime, money laundering, international terrorism, drug operations, and illegal traffic in armaments.

transponder warrant. A search warrant allowing the covert placement of a transponder (beeper) on property to track its movement.

trap. (1) A device, usually a switch, installed within a protected area, which serves as secondary protection in the event a perimeter-alarm system is successfully penetrated. Examples are a trip-wire switch placed across a likely path for an intruder, a mat switch hidden under a rug, or a magnetic switch mounted on an inner door. (2) A volumetric sensor installed so as to detect an intruder in a corridor or pathway that is likely to be traveled. (3) A tracing device placed on a telephone line to identify the numbers from which calls are placed to that line; often used by law enforcement agencies and telephone companies in harassing call cases.

traverse method. A method of sketching a scene, especially an outdoor scene, where distances, contours, and locations of objects need to be shown. It requires the use of a sketchboard, a compass, and a telescopic surveying instrument.

treason. As cited in the Constitution: "Treason against the United States shall consist only in levying war against them, or in adhering to their enemies, giving them aid and comfort. No person shall be convicted of treason unless on the testimony of two witnesses in the same overt act or on confession in open court." A person convicted of treason is given the death penalty or sentenced to at least five years in prison and fined at least $10,000.

Treatment Accountability for Safer Communities (TASC). A response to the problems of crime related to alcohol or drug abuse, TASC was developed over several years of testing, demonstration, and modification. It identifies substance-abusing offenders, refers them to community treatment resources, and monitors their treatment. TASC was initially conceived in the Special Action Office for Drug Abuse Prevention in the early 1970s; tested in Wilmington, DE, in 1972; and became operational that year in Philadelphia and Cleveland. For further information, contact: Office of Justice Programs, DOJ, 810 7th St., NW, Washington, DC 20531.

trespass. Unlawful entry into someone's property.

trial. The examination in a court of the issues of fact and law in a case for the purpose of reaching a judgment. *Jury trial*: in criminal proceedings, a trial in which a jury is empaneled to determine the issues of fact in a case and to render a verdict of guilty or not guilty.

Nonjury trial: in criminal proceedings, a trial in which there is no jury and in which a judicial officer determines all issues of fact and law in a case. (This type of trial is also called a judge trial, bench trial, or court trial.) *Trial on transcript*: also called trial by the record; a nonjury trial in which the judicial officer makes a decision on the basis of the record of pretrial proceedings in a lower court. *Consolidated trial*: one in which either two or more defendants named in separate charging documents are tried together or a given defendant is tried on charges contained in two or more charging documents.

trial court case. A case that has been filed in a court of general jurisdiction or a court of limited jurisdiction.

trial *de novo*. A new trial before a provincial court—criminal division—granted to a defendant in Canada following a successful appeal from a conviction on a summary offense by a justice of the peace. A trial *de novo* is a new trial, the rehearing of a case that has been appealed from a decision made in a court of limited jurisdiction.

trial judge. A judicial officer who is authorized to conduct jury and nonjury trials and who may or may not be authorized to hear appellate cases; the judicial officer who conducts a particular trial.

trial jury. A statutorily defined number of persons selected according to the law and sworn to determine, in accordance with the law as instructed by the court, certain matters of fact based on evidence presented in a trial, and to render a verdict. The size of a trial jury is set by statute and, depending upon jurisdiction, is 12 or a specific smaller number. Some jurisdictions specify a minimum of 6 jurors and allow for fewer if a juror falls ill.

tribunal. A court or other body in which decisions binding on litigants are made.

trifurcation. In fingerprinting, a single ridge line that divides into three lines. *See also* fingerprint patterns

triple (or treble) damages. A remedy in antitrust law (federal Sherman and Clayton Acts) whereby a competitor, damaged as a result of the proven illegal, anticompetitive behavior of a defendant, may recover from the defendant three times the amount of actual monetary damages sustained. In California Small Claims Court, a judgment for three times the face value of an insufficient funds check can be awarded to the defendant, with a limit of $2,000.

truancy law, first. The first state legislation was "an act to provide for the care and instruction of idle and truant children," enacted by New York on April 12, 1853. A fine of $50 was levied against parents whose children between the ages of 5 and 14 were absent from school.

truant. A juvenile who has been adjudicated by a judicial officer of a juvenile court as having committed the status offense of violating a compulsory school attendance law.

truant officer. An employee of a board of education who enforces compulsory schoolattendance laws; also called attendance officer.

true bill. An endorsement made by a grand jury on a bill of indictment submitted by a prosecuting officer when the grand jury finds that sufficient reason exists to bring an accused person to trial.

trusty. An inmate of a jail or prison who has been entrusted with some custodial responsibilities or who performs other assistance services in the operation of the facility.

Truth-In-Lending Act. A detailed federal law of 1968 to protect consumers by enabling them to compare various credit terms realistically. The main provisions regarding installment buying and open-end credit plans (such as credit cards) call for clear and full disclosure of all credit charges and of conditions under which the creditor acquires security from the borrower. The act prevents the creditor from hiding lending violations and fraud behind a collection agency. The act's straightforward wording prohibits issuing unrequested credit cards and limits a cardholder's liability in the case of unauthorized card use to $50. Credit reports are open to review by their subjects, but issuing agencies cannot be prosecuted for including false information unless malice is proven.

Truth-In-Packaging Law. Federal legislation of 1966, also called the Fair Packaging and Labeling Act, is designed to help consumers compare products and be accurately informed. The law provides that all commodity labels must identify the product, give the name and place of business of the manufacturer, packer, or distributor, and list the net quantity of smaller packages. The law prohibits nonfunctional slack fill and regulates cents-off promotional labeling as well as size and type of labels.

truth-in-sentencing laws. Statutes passed in many states and in the federal code that require offenders to serve all or most of sentence time imposed by the court. Such laws are gaining popularity because, in many states, offenders have been serving 50 percent or less of the time to which they were sentenced, because of generous good-time policies and/or in efforts to avoid overcrowding in prisons. The federal system, for example, now requires that offenders serve 85 percent of the time imposed by judges. Most truth-in-sentencing laws do, however, provide for some time off for good behavior.

Tweed, William Marcy (Boss). A New York political leader (1823–1878) who came to symbolize the corruption of political bosses. He was one of the New York City aldermen known as the Forty Thieves, a congressman, and finally Grand Sachem of Tammany Hall (1863). The Tweed Ring monopolized all parts of the government. Contracts submitted to the city were approved only after payments of 10 to 85 percent went to the ring. In 1867 Tweed, as a state senator, broadened his system to include the legislature. When John Hoffman, Tweed's protégé, was elected governor in 1869, the ring's power encompassed all New York State. Their downfall was initiated by a series of cartoons by Thomas Nast, printed in *Harper's Weekly* from 1869 through 1871. Only when disgruntled ring members made documentary evidence available was a Committee of Seventy, led by Samuel Tilden, able to break the ring. Tweed served a short jail term then fled to Spain to avoid a trial to recover the stolen money. After extradition, he died in jail.

twist. In firearms, the inclination of the spiral grooves (rifling) to the axis of the bore of a weapon. It is expressed as the number of calibers of length in which the rifling makes one complete turn.

two-strikes law. *See* three-strikes laws

Type-A personality. A personality profile that was believed to lead to higher levels of stress and resulting heart disease than the contrasting Type B personality. According to this theory, Type A individuals tend to be competitive, hostile, impatient people who are constantly under stress, while Type B people demonstrate more patience and an ability to react to environmental demands and deal with stress more effectively. Later research has tended to show that only the underlying hostility of Type A personalities, rather than their competitiveness or impatience, is important in increasing the risk of heart disease. *See also* stress

typographic printing. A type of printing used in the making of paper currency, stock certificates, and similar items susceptible to counterfeiting. The typographic process allows for overprinting the permanent (intaglio) features with changeable characteristics such as serial numbers, seals, and authorizing signatures.

typology. A classification scheme containing two or more categories (types), based on characteristics of the things being classified that the classifier considers important. Typologies are useful in organizing data; any set of concepts can be used to classify. People can be grouped, for example, according to age, sex, race, weight, height, hair color, or shoe size.

U

ulnar loop. A fingerprint pattern.

ultrasonic motion detector. A sensor that detects the motion of an intruder through the use of ultrasonic generating and receiving equipment. The device operates by filling a space with a pattern of ultrasonic waves; the modulation of these waves by a moving object is detected and initiates an alarm signal.

ultraviolet light. Light located beyond the violet end of the visible spectrum. Sometimes referred to as black light. Used in law enforcement to detect certain fluorescent substances such as semen, invisible laundry marks, and other invisible writings. It is at the end of the spectrum opposite infrared light. An ultraviolet filter transmits ultraviolet light by the reflected ultraviolet light method.

ultra vires. An action beyond the legal power or authority of a corporation, governmental agency or official.

Unabomber. Self-given title of an individual, now presumed to be Theodore Kaczynski, who perpetrated an 18-year rampage of letter bombs that killed 3 and injured 29 other people. The first bombing occurred on May 26, 1978, when a package found at the University of Illinois in Chicago was returned to the addressee at Northwestern University, where it exploded and injured one victim. Between 1978 and 1985, several more people were injured by bombs planted at or mailed to addresses in Illinois, Utah, Tennessee, California, Washington, Michigan, and aboard an airplane. The first fatality occurred on December 11, 1985, when Hugh Scrutton was killed when he moved a bomb disguised as discarded lumber. On February 20, 1987, the Unabomber was seen in Salt Lake City wearing a hooded sweatshirt and aviator sunglasses while placing a bomb. There were no further attacks for six years. On June 22, 1993, University of California at San Francisco geneticist Charles Epstein was severely injured by a bomb mailed to his home. Two days later, Yale University computer scientist David Gelernter suffered extensive injuries when a bomb exploded in his office. On December 10, 1994, advertising excecutive Thomas Mosser was killed by a bomb sent to his home in New Jersey. On April 24, 1995, timber industry executive Gilbert P. Murray was killed when he opened a package in his Sacramento office. On June 27, 1995, the Unabomber threatened to blow up an airliner out of Los Angeles, which led to lasting changes in airport and postal security. On September 19, 1995, the Unabomber's 35,000-word, so-called manifesto against technology was published. Through information given by his brother, Theodore Kaczynski was taken into custody by federal officers on April 3, 1996. In April 1998, the 55-year-old former math professor, long a recluse, was sentenced to life in prison without parole.

underground. An organized group of people who carry on some regular operation without effective discovery by those in authority; the network to which these people belong.

underground economy. Unreported, untaxed, unregulated, and often illegal economic transactions in goods and services that take place outside the official and legal economy. This includes the practice of tradeouts, where goods or services are traded by businesses without cash transactions or record. The underground economy consists of persons who report less income than earned and those who file no income tax returns. Drug trafficking and organized crime are major segments of this economy.

underground press. Much of the political and cultural dissent in the United States during the 1960s was expressed in some 500 weekly, monthly, and irregularly published non-establishment newspapers. Originating with New York's *The Village Voice* in 1955, the underground press flourished until the 1970s when many of its media disappeared.

underworld. A semipopular designation for the *sub rosa* existence of criminal activity, commercialized vice, gambling houses, places trafficking in contraband narcotics, and other interconnected illicit enterprises, such as boot-legging and numbers rackets. The criminal and pseudocriminal elements constitute an underworld to the extent that association and activity take place outside the bounds of respectable society; hence, they form a sort of pariah caste. *See also* organized crime

unfair and deceptive practices. Those activities of business firms that damage consumers and/or have an adverse effect on competition. Examples are bait and switch advertising, deceptive pricing, and misbranding and mislabeling. Under Section 5 of the original Federal Trade Commission Act, the FTC was authorized to proceed against business practices doing potential or actual damage to competition (a less rigorous test of damage than the restraint of trade provisions found in the Sherman Antitrust Act). With the Wheeler-Lea Act of 1938, the prohibition was extended to include unfair practices outside the normal antitrust category as well as practices unfair to the general consuming public.

unfair labor practices. Antiunion actions by employers. The 1930s marked a great turning point for organized labor, and no law aided its cause more than the Wagner Act (1935), which allowed unions to organize and bargain collectively. It also specified unfair labor practices in which employers were forbidden to engage. No comparable restrictions, however, were imposed on unions.

unfounding. The process in statistics of declaring that certain unsolved crimes were never crimes in the first place. *See also* defounding

Uniform Code of Military Justice. A comprehensive statement of the laws governing all the armed forces, containing 140 articles, signed by President Harry Truman and enacted by Congress. It replaced the Articles of War and the Articles for the Government of the Navy. (Articles 77 through 134 are considered the punitive articles.) The code also provides for a review of decisions of courts martial and for appeals to the United States Court of Military Appeals, which was created by the code.

Uniform Crime Reporting Program (UCR). In 1927, the International Association of Chiefs of Police (IACP) formed a committee to create a uniform system for gathering statistics on crimes known to the police. Led by August Vollmer and Bruce Smith, it was called the Committee on Uniform Crime Records, it developed the UCR, which was adopted by the IACP. In 1930 the FBI was authorized to serve as the national clearinghouse for the UCR. This was the first standardized crime-related record keeping on a national level.

The national UCR program produces a major annual report called *Crime in the United States*. The bulk of the information in these reports relates to reported instances (offenses known to police) of the FBI's Crime Index offenses, reported arrests for all crimes, and law enforcement agency employee data. The detail includes information concerning crimes cleared by arrest, arrests and dispositions of arrested persons, and dispositions of juveniles taken into custody. The reported crime and reported arrest data are categorized by geographical area and related to various factors. UCR also produces three other annual publications, *Law Enforcement Officers Killed, Assaults on Federal Officers, and Bomb Summary*.

The FBI's Uniform Reporting Program offers its annual *Crime in the United States—Uniform Crime Reports*. These can be obtained online at www.fbi.gov/ucr/ucr.htm, or by writing the Uniform Crime Reporting Section, Room 7437, FBI, 935 Pennsylvania Avenue, NW, Washington, DC 20535.

Uniform Juvenile Court Act. A 1968 act of Congress, which recommended standards for the processing of delinquent and status offenders in the juvenile justice system.

uniform state laws. Model statutes drafted by the Conference of Commissioners on Uniform Laws and enacted without amendment by all or several state legislatures, which are designed to substitute a series of uniform enactments for conflicting state laws on subjects like bills of lading, negotiable instruments, motor vehicle registration, and liability for accidents.

Unitarian Universalist Service Committee. This committee established the National Moratorium on Prison Construction in 1975. "NMPC works toward a halt to all prison and jail construction until alternatives to imprisonment are fully evaluated and implemented." Address: 2000 P St., NW, Suite 505, Washington, DC 20036.

United Nations Criminal Justice Information Network. Established in 1989, UNCJIN provides the latest reports of research and activities of worldwide UN institutes, calendars of events and meetings, legislative and court updates, and UN World Crime Survey data. It publishes several directories, a bibliography of other criminal justice statistics, and a computerized selection of U.S. Bureau of Justice Statistics reports, available before they are printed. UNCJIN is funded in part by the U.S. Bureau of Justice Statistics and operates under the auspices of the UN Crime Prevention and Criminal Justice Branch, Vienna International Center, Austria. Address: UNODC Liaison Office, United Nations Headquarters, Room DC1-613, 1 United Nations Plaza, New York, NY 10017.

United Nations Information Centre. Founded in 1946, under the Office of Public Information of the UN, the centre aims "to bring about an informed understanding of the United Nations, including its work in the field of criminal justice." Publishes: *Standard Minimum Rules for the Treatment of Prisoners and Related Recommendations; International Review of Criminal Policy #6;* and *Reports of the First–Sixth UN Congress on the Prevention of Crime and Treatment of Offenders.* Other lists of UN publications in the field of criminal justice are printed in the United Nations Documents Indexes issued monthly. Address: United Nations Secretariat, Room 1060F, New York, NY 10017.

United Nations Standard Minimum Rules for the Treatment of Prisoners. Adopted on August 30, 1955, by the First United Nations Congress on the Prevention of Crime and the Treatment of Offenders, this document provides recommendations for the operation of penal facilities, as well as for the treatment of offenders.

United States Associate Attorney General. This office is under the Department of Justice, employing approximately 11,000 persons, and is located at Suite 570, Flag Building, Department of Justice, Washington, DC 20530-0001.

United States Attorneys. U.S. attorneys are the chief law enforcement representatives of the attorney general, in the federal judicial district. There is one in each federal judicial district, enforcing federal criminal law and handling most of the civil litigation in which the United States is involved. The attorneys are involved with white-collar crime, official corruption, narcotics, organized crime, and criminal and civil litigation. The position is appointive, and usually has one or more assistants carrying the title assistant U.S. attorney.

United States Attorneys, Executive Office for. This office provides general executive assistance and supervision to 93 officers of the U.S. attorneys. Address: Executive Office for U.S. Attorneys, DOJ, 950 Pennsylvania Ave., NW, Room 2616, Washington, DC 20530.

United States Bureau of Alcohol, Tobacco and Firearms. With approximately 4,000 employees, under the Department of the Treasury, the bureau enforces and administers laws regarding firearms and explosives, as well as those laws covering the production, use, and distribution of alcohol and tobacco products. Data are available on the domestic manufacturing and importation of all types of alcohol, tobacco, and firearms. The data are broken down monthly by state and include statistics on establishments qualified to manufacture these items and the number of permits issued. The *Alcohol, Tobacco and Firearms Bulletin* (quarterly), available through the U.S. Government Printing Office, informs all permit holders and licensees on current alcohol, to-

bacco, and firearms and explosive matters. It contains regulatory, procedural, and administrative information as well as items of general interest.

The law enforcement office works with state and local agencies in curtailing the flow of firearms to criminal elements.

For information concerning any activity in the Bureau of ATF, contact: Office of Public and Governmental Affairs, 650 Massachusetts Avenue, NW, Room 8290, Washington, DC 20226.

United States Bureau of Prisons. The bureau "protects society through the care and custody of those persons convicted by the courts to serve a period of time incarcerated in a Federal penal institution." The bureau in October 1998 employed 30,250 people. Address: Department of Justice, 320 First St., NW, Washington, DC 20534.

United States Citizenship and Immigration Services. First established as the Bureau of Immigration under the Treasury Department in 1891, the service expanded to include naturalization functions in 1933, finally moving under the Justice Department in 1940. Currently, with approximately 11,000 employees, the service has a mission to "administer the immigration and naturalization laws relating to the admission, exclusion, deportation, and naturalization of aliens; inspect aliens to determine their admissibility into the United States; adjudicate requests of aliens for benefits under the law; guard against illegal entry into the United States; investigate, apprehend, and remove aliens in this country in violation of the law; and examine alien applicants wishing to become citizens." Address: DOJ, Citizenship and Immigration Services, 425 I Street, NW, Washington, DC 20536.

United States Claims Court. Established in 1982 to replace the Court of Claims that had been founded February 24, 1855, it assumed all jurisdiction previously held by its predecessor. It serves as the court of original and exclusive jurisdiction over claims brought against the federal government, except for tort claims, which are heard by district courts.

Claims Court can render money judgments in cases concerning the application of the Constitution, acts of Congress, regulations of an executive department, or on express and implied contract with the federal government. The court takes testimony and depositions at locations convenient for claimants and witnesses. It comprises 16 judges, all appointed by the president and confirmed by the Senate. One, designated by the president, serves as chief judge. *See also* United States Court of Claims

United States Coast Guard. The Revenue Cutter Service was established in 1789 to deal with the problem of smuggling. Today the Coast Guard is an essentially autonomous unit of the public forces of the United States, subject to the jurisdiction of the Department of Transportation in time of peace and of the Navy in time of war or national emergency. Although it is especially charged with the enforcement of the customs, navigation, and neutrality laws, it serves as a general law enforcement agency on navigable waters and high seas and protects life and property at sea. It develops regulations on commercial vessel safety, recreational boating safety, port safety and security, and marine pollution.

The U.S. Coast Guard, as authorized by a 1972 act of Congress, maintains three regional strike forces to assist in handling oil spills or hazardous substance leaks that are too large for other agencies to handle. The Pacific Strike Team, consisting of eight members, is based at Hamilton Air Force Base near San Francisco, and covers 14 contiguous states, Hawaii, Alaska, and the trust territories of the Pacific islands. The Gulf Coast Strike Team and the Atlantic Coast Strike Team handle the rest of the country. When on land, the force works with the Environmental Protection Agency. For further information, contact: Commandant, U.S. Coast Guard, 2100 Second St., SW, Washington, DC 20593. *See also* high seas law enforcement

United States Code (USC). A consolidation and codification of all the general and permanent federal laws in effect, classified by subject matter under 50 titles, prepared under the direction of the Judiciary Committee of the House of Representatives. A revision has appeared every six years since 1926, and a supplementary volume is issued after each session of Congress. Many of the titles have been enacted as law and, when all have been enacted, the code will constitute the entire body of federal law.

United States Code Annotated (USCA). A commercially published edition of the U.S. Code.

United States Commissioner. A federal magistrate whose functions in the federal field are comparable to those in state matters of the justice of the peace. The officeholder is not a judge and does not hold court but may issue certain warrants, act as a committing official, set bail, and bind over for trial. All functions of the position are prescribed by statute.

United States Conference of Mayors. Organization that facilitates cooperation between cities and the federal government on urban social and health issues such as substance abuse, by providing mayors and municipal agencies with resources, technical assistance, and legislative services. Address: 1620 I St. NW, Washington, DC 20006.

United States Court of Claims. A special court consisting of a chief justice and four associates set up in 1855 with recommendatory powers only, granted jurisdiction in 1866 to decide claims against the government arising under contracts, and empowered in 1946 to decide certain kinds of cases involving torts by government employees. *See also* United States Claims Court

United States Court of Customs and Patent Appeals. A specialized court established in 1909 as the U.S. Court of Customs Appeals, given its present title and duties in 1929, and consisting of five justices, which reviews (a) decisions of the U.S. Customs Court on classifications and duties on imported merchandise; (b) decisions of the Patent Office on applications for, and interference with, patents and trademarks; and (c) legal questions in findings of the U.S. Tariff Commission concerning unfair practices in import trade.

United States Customs and Border Protection. Determines and collects duties and taxes on merchandise imported into the United States, controls exporters and importers and their goods, and works to control smuggling and revenue fraud. Created as a division of the Department of the Treasury in 1927, the Customs Service is authorized to collect customs and revenue by the second, third, and fifth acts of the First Congress (1789). The service helps enforce environmental protection programs involving the discharge of oil or refuse into coastal waters, the safety standards of imported motor vehicles, and the regulation by quarantine of animals and plants entering the country. Currently with approximately 15,250 employees, the service works closely with the Drug Enforcement Administration and the Immigration and Naturalization Service. U.S. Customs maintains a force of special agents at 66 domestic and 8 foreign offices. They investigate violations of customs and related laws and regulations—fraud, currency reporting violations, cargo theft, neutrality violations, narcotics, and bird smuggling. The service's Public Information Department contains publications (*Customs Today* is a free quarterly) on all component activities of the U.S. Customs Service. Address: Department of the Treasury, 1300 Pennsylvania Ave., NW, Washington, DC 20299.

United States Customs Court. A court created in 1890 as the Board of the United States General Appraisers and given its present title in 1926, which consists of nine judges sitting in New York City, and which has sole jurisdiction over the interpretation of tariff laws, the classification of merchandise, and the determination of the dutiable valuation of imported goods. In 1956 it was made a court of record under Article III of the Constitution.

United States District Courts. Trial courts with original jurisdiction over diversity-of-citizenship cases and cases arising under U.S. criminal, bankruptcy, admiralty, patent, copyright, and postal laws. There are 89 district courts in the United States and Puerto Rico, each having from 1 to 24 judges, a total of 303.

Normally, one district judge presides over each trial, but three-judge district courts are necessary for the issuance of injunctions concerning certain subjects. From district courts, the normal course of appeals is to a court of appeals, but some decisions—holding statutes unconstitutional, certain criminal cases, and the injunction orders of three-judge district courts—may be appealed directly to the Supreme Court.

United States Fish and Wildlife Service. A division of the Department of the Interior, dating from the consolidation in 1940 of the Bureau of Biological Survey and the Bureau of Sport Fisheries and Wildlife, that carries on research and wildlife conservation programs and is charged especially with the preservation of the fishing industry; the enforcement of international agreements relating to fur seals and commercial fish; and the conservation, for economic and recreational purposes, of various kinds of wildlife. For further information, contact: Public Affairs Office, Fish and Wildlife Service, DOI, Room 3240, Interior Building, Washington, DC 20240.

United States Internal Revenue Service. *See* Internal Revenue Service

United States Marshals Service. With approximately 7,200 employees, the service serves to protect witnesses to organized crime whose lives and those of their families are jeopardized by their testimony; provide physical security for U.S. courtrooms and personal protection for federal judges, jurors, and attorneys; perform federal law enforcement functions for the attorney general; execute all civil and criminal processes emanating from the federal courts; disburse appropriate funds to satisfy government obligations incurred in the administration of justice at the federal level; maintain custody of federal prisoners from the time of their arrest to their commitment or release; transport federal prisoners under writs and direction from the Bureau of Prisons; and maintain custody and control of evidence, as well as money and property, seized under federal statutes. A free publication, *United States Marshals Service Then ... and Now*, is available. Address: United States Marshals Service Headquarters, Washington, DC 20530-1000.

United States–Mexico border. This border extends 1,952 miles or 3,141 kilometers from Brownsville, TX (opposite Matamoros, Tamaulipas), to San Diego, CA (opposite Tijuana, Baja California Norte).

United States Parole Commission. An independent agency in the Department of Justice with approximately 175 employees. Its primary function is to administer a parole system for federal prisoners and develop federal parole policy. The commission is authorized to: (a) grant or deny parole to any eligible federal prisoner; (b) impose reasonable conditions on the release of any prisoner from custody or discretionary parole or mandatory release by operation of "good-time" laws; (c) revoke parole or mandatory release; and (d) discharge offenders from supervision and terminate their sentences prior to expiration. The commission also determines whether or not persons convicted of certain crimes may serve as officials in the field of organized labor or in labor-oriented management positions and whether they may provide services to, or be employed by, employment-benefit plans. Address: Department of Justice, 5550 Friendship Blvd., Suite 420, Chevy Chase, MD 20815.

United States Reports. The official printed record of cases heard and decided by the Supreme Court, which usually includes a statement of the essential facts of each case; the opinion of the Court, concurring and dissenting opinions, if any; the disposition of each case and occasionally an abstract of counsels' briefs. Originally, a series of reports, with volumes numbered consecutively, was issued during the incumbency of each successive court reporter. These are cited as Dallas (1790–1800), Cranch (1801–1815), Wheaton (1816–1827), Peters (1823–1843),

Howard (1843–1860), Black (1861–1862), and Wallace (1863–1874). By 1874, when the number of volumes so identified totalled 90, the practice began of eliminating the reporter's name and citing them as United States Reports.

United States Secret Service. *See* Secret Service

United States Sentencing Commission. Established by the Comprehensive Crime Control Act of 1984, this independent commission in the judicial branch of the U.S. consists of seven voting members and one nonvoting member. The president, after consultation with representatives of judges, prosecuting attorneys, defense attorneys, law enforcement officials, senior citizens, victims of crime, and others interested in the criminal justice process, appoints the voting members of the commission, including its chairman, by and with the advice and consent of the Senate. At least three of the members are federal judges in regular active service selected after considering a list of six judges recommended to the president by the Judicial Conference of the United States. No more than four commission members may be members of the same political party. The purposes of the commission are to (a) establish sentencing policies and practices for the federal criminal justice system and (b) develop means of measuring the degree to which sentencing, penal, and correctional practices are effective in meeting the purposes of sentencing.

United States Statutes at Large. An official compilation of the acts and resolutions of each session of Congress published by the Office of the Federal Register in the National Archives and Records Service. It consists of two parts: the first comprises public acts and joint resolutions, the second, private acts and joint resolutions, concurrent resolutions, treaties, and presidential proclamations.

United States Supreme Court. *See* Supreme Court, U.S.

United States Trustee Program. Officials charged with administering bankruptcy cases in their respective regions. There is a trustee for each of 10 regions who has the responsibility for appointing private trustees as well as committees of creditors in order to insulate bankruptcy judges from the day-to-day administration of cases. For further information, contact: Executive Office for U.S. Trustees, DOJ, 20 Massachusetts Ave., NW, Washington, DC 20530.

unity of command. A traditional management principle recommending that employees should report directly only to one supervisor.

University of Chicago Center for Studies in Criminal Justice. Established in 1965 with goals to "conduct criminal justice research on the criminal justice system and to give specialized education at the graduate level." Address: Law School, 1111 East 60th St., Chicago, IL 60637.

unlawful entry. A less serious crime than burglary, it involves entering an open or unlocked building without authority or legal right.

unlawful flight to avoid giving testimony. In federal law it is a felony to travel to another state or nation to avoid giving testimony as a material witness in a criminal proceeding in which a felony is charged under the state laws. The law is called the Fugitive Witness Act.

unlawful flight to avoid prosecution. A federal law making it a felony for any person, charged by a state with a felony, to travel to another state for the purpose of avoiding prosecution. Also called the Fugitive Felon Act.

UOC. An abbreviation for the Uniform Offense Classifications, used by the FBI's National Crime Information Center to represent offense types in automated record systems of individual criminal histories.

UPR. An abbreviation for Uniform Parole Reports. UPR is a statistical program sponsored by the Bureau of Justice Statistics and administered by the National Council on Crime and Delinquency. It was established in 1964 by the National Institutes of Health. It has published statistical information on parolees, parole authority decisions, and parole agency workloads.

urban riots. As old as cities themselves. Colonial seaports were frequently plagued by roving mobs. Development of professional city police systems was speeded as a response to urban rioting in the Northeast in the 1840s and 1850s. In 1863 there were massive draft riots in New York City. Until the 1960s, riots by blacks in urban areas had largely been expressions of self-defense and retaliation against white oppression. The ghetto riots of the 1960s were different, in that they apparently erupted spontaneously out of seemingly minor incidents involving blacks and white police. *See also* Civil Disorders, National Advisory Commission on; civil disturbances; King, Rodney; McDuffie, Arthur, Overtown

usury. The charging of interest greater than that permitted by law in return for the loan of money.

V

Vacutainer. Trade name for a blood collection system used for laboratory testing of blood for its alcohol content.

vagrancy. Except where defined by statute, the behavior of a person without permanent social attachments; aimless wandering of an individual without visible means of legitimate self-support. In common law, vagrancy means wandering about from place to place by an idle person who has no visible means of support, subsists on charity, and does not work, though able to do so. But the connotations of vagrancy have been extended by statutory regulations to include other forms of behavior. Vagrancy is the broadest of offense categories, which could include: prostitution, gambling, fortune-telling, drunkenness, begging, and many other forms of behavior deemed socially undesirable, if not dangerous. Though the charge of vagrancy may not be sustained if the alleged offender has regular employment or is wandering in search of it, in times of economic recession, convictions for vagrancy increase sharply. The vagueness of vagrancy laws was demonstrated on May 2, 1984, when the California Supreme Court struck down the vagrancy law in a 7–2 decision, holding that the state cannot give police power to arrest persons who fail to produce proper identification on demand.

vagrant. An unattached, itinerant, and indigent person. Several types are variously described on the basis of behavior or appearance, as in this old text: "The hobo works and wanders; the tramp dreams and wanders; and the bum drinks and wanders." The hobo, an itinerant worker who may occasionally panhandle, is now virtually nonexistent. Homeless indigent types change from one period to another and are different in different localities. Vagrants are perceived to be a problem to the security of a community because they are homeless, voteless, and without local interests, and there is strong presumption that they are or may become offenders.

Valentine's Day. Named after St. Valentine, patron saint of lovers, who was a third-century Roman bishop who defied imperial law by performing marriage rites for military-eligible young men and their brides and advising them to pursue domestic, rather than army, life. Roman law decreed that young men were better soldiers if they remained single. St. Valentine's activities led to his execution by Roman authorities on February 14, 269.

Valium and Librium. Prescription drugs that act as sedatives and minor tranquilizers. They are central nervous system depressants and directly affect the brain, relaxing large skeletal muscles and causing tranquility or sleepiness. Both are commonly prescribed and often abused.

values. A term distinguished from attitudes, needs, or wants, that refers to the degree to which an event is perceived to be positive or negative. As guides to behavior, values link actions to attitudes, needs, or interests. Some investigators link values to what ought to be, in contrast to what is. As a result, much values research has addressed morals and ethics. The three major theories of how people acquire values are psychoanalytic, social learning, and perceptual. Many law enforcement agencies have adopted organizational values statements to clarify their mission, vision, and purposes.

vandalism. Willfully destroying or defacing the property of another. The word is derived from Vandals, the Germanic tribe responsible for destroying Rome in the fifth century. Vandalism in the United States is predominantly, though not exclusively, perpetrated by juveniles and is responsible for losses of millions of dollars each year. The City of New York spent $10 million in 1973 to paint and clean surfaces defaced by graffiti.

variable. A dynamic trait or characteristic that can change in value or magnitude from case to case. The term is contrasted with constant, a static and unchanging characteristic. Variables can be qualitative, such as male or female; quantitative and stated numerically, such as age or height; continuous, involving such uninterrupted progressions as aging or traveling certain distances; or discrete. A discrete variable can be quantitative or qualitative; if it is quantitative, its values increase or decrease by definite steps. A continuous variable must be quantitative, but not all quantitative variables are discrete.

VASCAR. Abbreviation for Visual Average Speed Computer and Recorder. An electronic device, manually activated, that measures quantities of distance and time and computes the resultant speed. Used in CO and several other states by the highway patrol.

vaults. **Class 1:** Vault doors equaling the Underwriters' Laboratories, Inc. (UL) standard for 30-minute resistance to expert burglary attack using common mechanical devices, electric tools and cutting torches, or combinations of these. The door lock meets UL standard 768 or 887.

    Class 2: Vaults meeting UL standards for one-hour resistance to expert burglary attack using common mechanical or electric tools and cutting torches. The door lock meets UL standard 768 or 887.

Class 3: Vaults meeting UL standards for two-hour resistance to expert burglary attack using common mechanical or electric tools and cutting torches. The lock meets UL standard 768 or 887.

Class 5: A Department of Defense (DOD)–approved door built to resist 30 minutes against surreptitious entry; 10 minutes against forced entry; 20 minutes against lock manipulation; and 20 hours against radiology techniques.

Class 6: A DOD-approved vault door designed to protect for 30 minutes against surreptitious entry; 30 minutes against lock manipulation, and 20 hours against radiology techniques.

vehicle. A device by means of which any person or property can be propelled, moved, or drawn on a highway, except a device moved exclusively by human power or used exclusively on stationary rails or tracks.

vehicle identification number (VIN). A permanent and unique number assigned to, and placed on, each vehicle by an automotive manufacturer for identification purposes. It may indicate the vehicle's model, engine displacement, place and year of manufacture, and sequence in the manufacturer's production.

vehicle theft. Unauthorized taking of a motor vehicle belonging to another person. *See also* Cargo CATS; Community Effort to Combat Auto Theft; Operation Guatemalan Auto Theft Enforcement

venireman. A member of a jury; a juror summoned by a writ of *venire facias.*

venue. The locality in which a suit may be tried.

Vera Institute of Justice. Formerly the Vera Foundation, a research organization with objectives "to achieve a more equal and fair criminal justice system." It was founded in October 1961 in New York by Louis Schweitzer. The Manhattan Bail Project, the Bronx Sentencing Project, the Manhattan Bowery Project, the Victim/Witness Assistance Project, and the Court Employment Project are well-known endeavors. Address: 233 Broadway, 12th Floor, New York, NY 10279.

verbal judo. In law enforcement, managing a person's behavior only through verbal commands and responses, rather than physical restraint. It is a noncombative method of easing tension and encouraging compliance. In some law enforcement agencies, verbal judo training is mandatory.

verdict. The decision of the jury in trials of either civil or criminal cases.

verdict, directed. A jury decision rendered by an order of a trial judge; in modern criminal procedure the directed verdict is always to acquit, although it may be limited to specific counts or specific defendants.

vibration detection system. An alarm system that employs one or more contact microphones or vibration sensors fastened to the surfaces of the area or object being protected to detect excessive levels of vibration. The contact microphone system consists of microphones, a control unit containing an amplifier and an accumulator, and a power supply. The unit's sensitivity is adjustable so that ambient noises or normal vibrations will not initiate an alarm signal. In a vibration sensor system, the sensor responds to excessive vibration by opening a switch in a closed-circuit system.

vicarious liability. Liability for the actions of another in the absence of fault, as where the persons neither knew of, encouraged, nor assisted in the act(s) of the other; usually imposed because of a person's general duty of supervision over another. There are several situations in which the theory of vicarious liability has been applied: negligent appointment or hiring, negligent retention (of an employee), negligent assignment, negligent supervision, negligent entrustment, and failure to train. *See also* negligent

vice, commercialized. As customarily used in sociological studies and crime statistics, the business of prostitution. Prostitution shows varying degrees of commercialization, ranging from independent conduct of prostitution by individuals to exploitation of prostitutes in brothels or syndicated houses of prostitution. In some Asian countries the business of prostitution has been accepted as an institution, with practitioners called business girls. In Western countries, it is either tolerated through police policy or has illegal status; in the latter case it is the object of suppressive measures of law enforcement.

vice squad. A special detail of police agents, charged with raiding and closing houses of prostitution and gambling resorts. Vice squads are likely to become unusually active in selective enforcement or law and order campaigns. *See also* Red Light Abatement law

vicinage. The county, district, or subdivision in which a court has the power or authority to hear cases.

victim. A person who has been killed or suffered physical or mental anguish or loss of property as a result of an actual or attempted criminal offense committed by another person.

Victim and Witness Protection Act of 1984. The federal VWP Act and state laws protect crime victims and witnesses against physical and verbal intimidation where such intimidation is designed to discourage reporting of crimes and participation in criminal trials. Laws generally protect all subpoenaed witnesses but may also protect persons the offender believes will be called to testify or who may have knowledge of the crime. Some laws also permit courts to forbid defendants from communicating with or approaching victims and witnesses.

Victim Assistance Program. A synthesis of several years of experience with prosecutor- or police-based victim-witness programs, rape crisis centers, domestic violence programs, and other independent victim assistance projects. The program incorporates recommendations, developed by the 1982 President's Task Force on Victims of Crime, that have an immediate impact on victims. The goals are to improve the treatment of victims of crime by providing assistance and services necessary to speed their recovery from a criminal act and to support and aid them as they move through the criminal justice process. For further information, contact: Office for Victims of Crime Resource Center, National Criminal Justice Reference Service, P.O. Box 6000, Rockville, MD 20849-6000.

victim compensation. State compensation programs are funded with state-administered funds. The 1984 federal Victims of Crime Act provides for federal grants to assist states that have established qualifying victim compensation programs. Forty-four states, the District of Columbia, and the U.S. Virgin Islands provide compensation for medical bills and lost wages for victims. In general, awards may be made to persons injured as a direct result of the crime. If the victim dies, payments to cover burial and related expenses are generally available to dependent survivors. In many cases, good samaritans—persons injured while trying to prevent a crime or apprehend an offender—are also eligible for payment. Most states establish upper limits on payments and do not provide compensation for property losses. In general, payment can be made whether or not the offender has been apprehended or convicted, but most states require that the crime be reported to proper authorities. *See also* Victims of Crime Act

victimization. The harming of any single victim in a criminal incident. The first national victimization survey was conducted in 1965 by the University of Chicago. More detailed surveys were undertaken in medium- and high-crime areas in Washington, DC, Boston, and Chicago by the Bureau of Social Science Research in Washington, and the Survey Research Center of the University of Michigan.

victimless crimes. Illegal acts that harm no one, or where harm occurs, it is negated by the informed and legal consent of the participants in the crime. In this context, harm can take several forms: (1) harm to the person, (2) harm to property, (3) psychological harm, (4) social harm, and (5) harm to an individual's freedom. The category commonly includes gambling, individual drug use, prostitution, and consensual sexual acts.

COMPENSATION PROGRAMS TO HELP VICTIMS OF VIOLENT CRIME

State	Victim compensation board location[a]	Financial award	To qualify, victim must—		
			show financial need	report to police within:	file claim within:
Alabama	Alabama Crime Victim Compensation Commission	$0-10,000	No	3 days	12 mos.
Alaska	Department of Public Safety	$0-40,000	Yes	5	24
Arizona	Arizona Criminal Justice Commission	**	Yes	3	**
California	State Board of Control	$100-46,000	Yes	*	12
Colorado	Judicial district boards	$25-10,000	No	3	6
Connecticut	Criminal Injuries Compensation Board	$100-10,000	No	5	24
Delaware	Violent Crimes Board	$25-20,000	No	*	12
D.C.	Office of Crime Victim Compensation	$100-25,000	Yes	7	6
Florida	Department of Labor and Employment Security, Workmen's Compensation Division	$0-10,000	Yes	3	12
Hawaii	Department of Corrections	$0-10,000	No	*	18
Idaho	Industrial Commission	$0-25,000	No	3	12
Illinois	Court of Claims	$0-25,000	No	3	12
Indiana	Industrial Board	$100-10,000	No	2	24
Iowa	Department of Public Safety	$0-20,000	No	1	6
Kansas	Executive Department	$100-10,000	Yes	3	12
Kentucky	Victim Compensation Board	$0-25,000	Yes	2	12
Louisiana	Commission on Law Enforcement	$100-10,000	No	3	12
Maryland	Criminal Injuries Compensation Board	$0-45,000	Yes	2	6
Massachusetts	District court system	$0-25,000	No	2	12
Michigan	Department of Managment and Budget	$200-15,000	Yes	2	12
Minnesota	Crime Victims Reparation Board	$100-50,000	No	5	12
Missouri	Division of Workmen's Compensation	$200-10,000	No	2	12
Montana	Crime Control Division	$0-25,000	No	3	12
Nebraska	Commission on Law Enforcement and Criminal Justice	$0-10,000	Yes	3	24

victimology. The study of the psychological and dynamic interrelationships between victims and offenders, with a view toward crime prevention. Interest in the study of the victim arose in the 1940s, and the works of such scholars as Mendelsohn (1947) and Von

State	Victim compensation board location[a]	Financial award	To qualify, victim must—		
			show financial need	report to police within:	file claim within:
Nevada	Board of Examiners and Department of Administration	$0-15,000	Yes	5	12
New Jersey	Executive Branch	$0-25,000	No	90	24
New Mexico	Executive Branch	$0-12,500	No	30	12
New York	Executive Department	$0-30,000*	Yes	7	12
North Carolina[b]	Department of Crime Control and Public Safety	$100-20,000	Yes	3	24
North Dakota	Workmen's Compensation Bureau	$0-25,000	No	3	12
Ohio	Court of Claims Commissioners	$0-25,000	No	3	12
Oklahoma	Crime Victims Board	$0-10,000	No	3	12
Oregon	Department of Justice/Workmen's Compensation Board	$250-23,000	No	3	6
Pennsylvania	Crime Victims Board	$0-35,000	No	3	12
Rhode Island	Superior court system	$0-25,000	No	10	24
South Carolina	Crime Victims Advisory Board	$100-3,000	No	2	6
Tennessee	Court of Claims Commission	$0-5,000	No	2	12
Texas	Industrial Accident Board	$0-25,000	No	3	6
Utah	Department of Administrative Services	$0-25,000	**	7	12
Virgin Islands	Department of Social Welfare	Up to 25,000	No	1	24
Virginia	Industrial Commission	$0-15,000	No	5	24
Washington	Department of Labor and Industries	$0-15,000+	No	3	12
West Virginia	Court of Claims Commissioner	$0-35,000	No	3	24
Wisconsin	Department of Justice	$0-40,000	No	5	12

[a]If location of the board is not indicated in the state statute, the board itself is noted.
[b]North Carolina's program is administratively established but not funded.
*Must report but no time limit specified.
**No reference in statute.
+Plus unlimited medical expenses.

Source: Bureau of Justice Statistics, 1987 update of *Victim/Witness Legislation: An Overview* (Washington, DC: U.S. Department of Justice, 1984), with assistance from National Organization for Victim Assistance.

Hentig (1948) underlined the importance of studying criminal-victim relationships in understanding crime.

victim precipitation. A criminal act in which the victim was responsible, at least in part, for initiating, encouraging, or escalating the altercation that resulted in his/her own loss, injury, or death.

Victims of Crime Act. On October 12, 1984, President Ronald W. Reagan signed into law the Victims of Crime Act, which established a Crime Victims Fund in the Treasury Department that can receive up to $100 million annually from four sources: criminal fines collected from convicted federal defendants; new penalty assessments imposed on convicted federal defendants; forfeited appearance bonds, bail bonds, and collateral security posted by federal criminal defendants; and literary profits due certain convicted federal defendants. The act authorized deposits in the fund through September 30, 1988. Address: Office for Victims of Crime, Office of Justice Programs, 810 7th Street, NW, Washington, DC 20531.

victim-witness programs. County- and/or state-funded agencies to provide assistance to victims or witnesses of crime. For example, in 1976 the Evanston, IL, police department received a grant to establish the victim-witness advocacy unit, with goals to provide comprehensive social services to crime victims and witnesses, assist with problems resulting from victimization, support victims and witnesses through the criminal justice system, and to provide assistance to those who come into contact with the police in noncrime-related situations and who could benefit from social service intervention. Program services included crisis intervention, counseling, court advocacy, referrals, emergency funding, and education in crime prevention. Most major urban areas have similar programs within the office of the district attorney.

victim/witness relocation program. *See* Witness Protection Plan

video surveillance. Electronic cameras capable of viewing targeted areas, which fall into two categories, clearly visible systems and those hidden from view. Police-monitored public video surveillance systems are in place in Tacoma, WA; Newark, NJ; Baltimore, MD; and Santiago, Chile. The Baltimore system employs 16 black-and-white fixed-position cameras to monitor a 16-block area in the downtown business sector. The cameras are mounted on light poles at intersections, 15 feet high, and equipped with zoom lenses to deter muggings, drug deals, and car thefts.

HOW DO CRIME RATES COMPARE WITH THE RATES OF OTHER LIFE EVENTS?

Events	Rate per 1,000 adults per year*
Acidental injury, all circumstances	242
Accidental injury at home	79
Personal theft	72
Accidental injury at work	58
Violent victimization	31
Assault (aggravated and simple)	24
Injury in motor vehicle accident	17
Death, all causes	11
Victimization with injury	10
Serious (aggravated) assault	9
Robbery	6
Heart disease death	4
Cancer death	2
Rape (women only)	2
Accidental death, all circumstances	.5
Pneumonia/influenza death	.3
Motor vehicle accident death	.2
Suicide	.2
Injury from fire	.1
Homicide/legal intervention death	.1
Death from fire	.03

These rates approximate your chances of becoming a victim of these events. More precise estimates can be derived by taking account of such factors as your age, sex, race, place of residence, and lifestyle. Findings are based on 1982–84 data, but there is little variation in rates from year to year.

*These rates exclude children from the calculations (those under age 12–17, depending on the series). Fire injury/death data are based on the total population, because no age-specific data are available in this series.

Sources: Current Estimates from the National Health Interview Survey: United States, 1982, National Center for Health Statistics; "Advance Report of Final Mortality Statistics, 1983"; *Monthly Vital Statistics Report,* National Center for Health Statistics; *Estimates of the Population of the United States, by Age, Sex, and Race: 1980 to 1984,* U.S. Bureau of the Census; *The 1984 Fire Almanac,* National Fire Protection Association. *Criminal Victimization 1984,* BJS Bulletin, October 1985.

vigilante. An individual or member of a group who undertakes to enforce the law and/or maintain morals without legal authority. From the 1760s through the beginning of the twentieth century, vigilante activity was an almost constant factor in American life. The better-known vigilante groups, such as the South Carolina Moderators (1767) and the East Texas Regulators (1840–1856), were highly structured and served in all phases of their own criminal justice proceedings. *See also* lynching

Vinson, Frederick Moore. Born in 1890, Vinson was the 12th chief justice of the United States, noted for his support of the broad interpretation of the powers of the federal government. He began his law practice in 1911 in his hometown of Louisa, KY. He became an influential congressman, supporting Franklin Roosevelt's New Deal. In 1938, President Roosevelt appointed Vinson to the U.S. Circuit Court of Appeals for the District of Columbia. In 1943, he moved to the executive branch, serving in several posts, including secretary of the treasury (1945–1946). He was appointed to the Supreme Court by President Harry S. Truman in 1946. Vinson's failure to unite a faction-ridden court led critics to consider him one of the less successful justices. He died in 1953.

violence. That force that is employed against common right, against law, and against public property.

vitiate. To impair the quality of.

voice identification. The ability to distinguish individual voice patterns using telecommunications technology. Banks use this technique to protect currency and securities transfers made by telephone. It is also used in adult and juvenile community supervision programs.

voiceprint. A spectrographic record of the energy output produced by the sound of words or sounds made by a person when speaking. Allegedly, it is distinctive for each person.

voir dire (Fr.). The preliminary examination of a prospective juror in order to determine his or her qualifications to serve as a juror.

Vollmer, August. Born in 1876, Vollmer began his distinguished law enforcement career in 1905 when he was elected town marshal for the city of Berkeley, CA. He assisted in the creation of the State Bureau of Criminal Identification. He promoted a police school in conjunction with the University of California, San Jose, in 1916. He was appointed Professor of Police Administration at the University of Chicago in 1929, accepting a full professorship at the University of California in 1931. Vollmer introduced the bicycle for patrol (soon to be followed by motorcycles), radio-equipped police cars, and the police telephone-callbox system. During his career, he served as a consultant to survey and reorganize police departments in 75 American and foreign cities. He inaugurated the use of automatic tabulating machinery to marshal the facts of crime and established the first scientific crime-detection laboratory. He is considered the "father of modern American police" and the "dean of American police chiefs." He lived until 1955. The August Vollmer University is located in Santa Ana, CA.

Volstead Act. Also known as the National Prohibition Act; passed by Congress in 1919. Its enactment was a result of the authorization conferred upon Congress by the Eighteenth Amendment. The law prohibited the manufacture, transportation, and sale of beverages containing more than 0.5 percent alcohol. It fixed penalties for sales of liquor and provided for injunctions against public places that dispensed liquor in violation of the law. Private stocks bought before the act went into effect could be retained. The act was roundly condemned by a large segment of the American people as an invasion of their constitutional rights. The most unfortunate consequences of its passage were the development of widespread political corruption and the emergence of organized crime. The act was repealed by the passage of the Twenty-first Amendment in 1933.

voluntariness. The state of having autonomy over one's actions; it is allegedly diminished or negated by such conditions as physical or psychological duress, illness, hypnosis, or mental defect.

volunteer. One who serves or acts, usually without compensation, of his or her own free will or accord. The American Association of Retired People (AARP), for example, has pioneered in the field of law enforcement volunteering. AARP provides training, organizational tips, teaching guides, and other help for volunteer associations. One group they are involved in is TRIAD, an alliance of AARP, the National Sheriffs' Association, and the International Association of Chiefs of Police. Address: AARP Criminal Justice Services-VOL, 601 E St., NW, Washington, DC 20049.

vomiting agents. War gases and mob- and riot-control gases, such as DA, DM, and DC. These three vomiting agents are normally solids that, when heated, vaporize and then condense to form toxic aerosols. Under field conditions, vomiting agents cause great discomfort to their victims; when released indoors, they may cause serious illness or death.

vote of no confidence. An extralegal and nonbinding procedure used by police labor associations and unions to voice their dissatisfaction with agency personnel such as the Chief of Police and appointed officials such as city managers regarding leadership or policy. In some instances such votes may influence community and political decisions.

voting laws. The Voting Section of the Civil Rights Division, Department of Justice, enforces voting laws designed to ensure that all qualified citizens have the opportunity to register and vote without discrimination on account of race, color, membership in an ethnic minority group, or age. It also enforces the overseas Citizens Voting Rights Act. Address: DOJ, 950 Pennsylvania Avenue, NW, Washington, DC 20530.

voyeurism. In its broadest sense, gratification from watching sexual objects and acts. At one time voyeurism was defined only as looking at individual people, while observing sexual acts was called *scoptophilia* or *scotophilia*. This distinction is no longer made.

W

wage and hour enforcement. The Wage and Hour Division administers and enforces the law with respect to private employment, state and local government, and federal employees of the Library of Congress, U.S. Postal Service, Postal Rate Commission, and the Tennessee Valley Authority. It has the authority to conduct investigations and gather data on wages, hours, and other employment conditions, as well as supervise the payment of back wages. For further information, contact: Division of Fair Labor Standards Policy and Procedure, Office of Fair Labor Standards, Wage and Hour Division, Employment Standards Administration, Department of Labor, ESA Wage & Hour Division, Room 207, Appraisers Stores Building, 103 South Gay Street, Baltimore, MD 21202-4061.

Waite, Morrison Remick. Sixth chief justice of the United States, who is generally regarded as having had only fair capabilities. Born in Connecticut in 1816, Waite was educated at Yale. He moved to Ohio to practice law and soon became successful as a bank and railroad lawyer. Waite was loyal to President Abraham Lincoln and in 1874 was appointed chief justice by President Ulysses S. Grant. Waite died in office in 1888.

wait, lie in. To conceal oneself, or stay hidden, ready to attack. A Louisiana statute provides that lying in wait with a dangerous weapon with intent to commit a crime constitutes an attempt to commit the offense intended.

walking line. An imaginary line that, in normal and ideal walking, fuses with the direction line and runs along the inner sides of both heelprints. It is one of the elements of an individual's walking profile. *See also* walking picture

walking picture. The study of the characteristics of footprints left by a person walking. Included in this study are the direction line, the walking line, and the foot line.

Walnut Street Jail. Erected in Philadelphia in 1773, it was later called a penitentiary. Unlike previous prisons, it received convicted felons from a statewide area and kept its prisoners at hard labor in solitary confinement. It was expected that prisoners in solitary confinement could meditate on their evil ways and become penitent, leading to the term *penitentiary*. This institution served as a model of humane penal reform that was widely adopted by European penologists. Among the characteristics that were most impressive were the facts that prisoners were paid for their work, men and women prisoners were separated, corporal punishment was forbidden, and religious instruction was required.

wanton. Reckless; malicious; without regard to the rights of others.

war crimes. During World War II, the first statement by the United Nations that war crimes would be punished after the war was made in the Moscow Declaration on October 30, 1943. Subsequently the UN Commission for the Investigation of War Crimes was established to compile lists of suspected war criminals. It classified two groups of crimes: those against the nationals of a state, the trials of whom were to be held by national courts or military tribunals, and those international in scope, to be tried by special international courts under military law. In August 1945 the United States, the United Kingdom, France, and the Soviet Union adopted a statute for trying the principal Nazi civil and military leaders. These nations established the Nuremberg Tribunal, which opened its hearing on November 20, 1945. War crimes had been defined as plotting aggressive war, atrocities against civilians, genocide, slave labor, looting of occupied countries, and the maltreatment and murder of war prisoners. On June 3, 1946,

trial was also opened in Tokyo by an 11-man international tribunal against 28 Japanese indicted as war criminals. During this period, concurrent trials were held in German and Japanese courts, which by 1950 had tried more than 8,000 war criminals and executed 2,000 of them. Altogether about 150,000 war criminals—members of the Gestapo, SS, and their collaborators—were suspected of crimes against humanity. Only about 40,000 were ever formally charged, and only about 10,000 were convicted. There may be as many as 50,000 Nazi criminals still alive around the world—about 10,000 in the United States and over 3,000 in Canada. The best known is Josef Mengele, dubbed by his victims as the Angel of Death. Rewards for his capture total more than $2.3 million, including $1 million each from the Friends of the Wiesenthal Center and the *Washington Times*. According to June 1985 reports, Mengele lived in Brazil for at least 15 years and allegedly drowned on February 7, 1979, at Bertioga, about 47 miles from São Paulo. The body was said to have been buried the next day under the name of Wolfgang Gerhard, an Austrian who served in the German army.

warden. The official in charge of operating a prison; the chief administrator of a prison; the prison superintendent.

Wardens and Superintendents, North American Association of. Founded in 1870. Bestows National Warden of the Year Award; promotes improved prison management and prison conditions. Publishes *The Grapevine* (bimonthly). Address: P.O. Box 11037, Albany, NY 12211.

warrant. In criminal proceedings, any of number of writs, issued by a judicial officer that direct law enforcement officers to perform specified acts and afford them protection from damage in carrying them out. *See also* execution and return of warrant; execution of the warrant; search and seizure

Warren Commission. The commission assigned to report on the assassination of President John F. Kennedy, headed by Chief Justice

Earl Warren. It was established by executive order in November 1963 to study and report on the Kennedy shooting and subsequent shooting of Lee Harvey Oswald, the man arrested in connection with the assassination. The September 1964 commission report, submitted to President Lyndon B. Johnson, rejected the possibility of an assassination conspiracy, finding that Oswald acted alone. The commission further determined that Jack Ruby, the man convicted of killing Oswald, also acted alone. Several other theories had been postulated, several of which still have substantial following.

Warren, Earl. Fourteenth chief justice of the United States from 1953 to 1969. Not since John Marshall has a chief justice been credited with engendering as many social and political changes as Earl Warren, who was appointed by President Dwight D. Eisenhower. Born in Los Angeles in 1891, Warren graduated from the University of California Law School at Berkeley. From 1920 on he spent his entire career in appointive and elective political offices: deputy district attorney, attorney general, and governor of California. He was also the Republican candidate for vice president in 1948. The so-called Warren Revolution began in 1954, when Warren argued that state-imposed segregation of public schools was unconstitutional because it fostered feelings of inferiority (*Brown v. Board of Education of Topeka*). The Warren Court expanded First Amendment freedoms and the requirements for counsel for defendants (*Gideon v. Wainwright*, 1963), ruled on the necessity of informing defendants of particular rights (*Miranda v. Arizona*, 1966), invalidated illegally seized evidence at trial (*Mapp v. Ohio*, 1961), and outlawed prayers in public schools (*Engel v. Vitale*, 1962). Warren died in 1974.

war, tong. Violent conflict between rival Chinese groups or tongs. Such groups or societies in the United States are a transfer from China, where they are based upon kinship, district, or other forms of affiliation. They often serve useful purposes in business or social welfare. But through business rivalry, or efforts to control illicit forms of gain in relation to vice, gambling, or opium traffic, some of the tongs become involved in criminal violence. Membership in the tongs may consist in part of merchants who are forced to join in order to get protection from rival tongs who seek control over their businesses.

watch and ward. During the reign of Edward I (1272–1307), the first police forces—the watch and ward—were created in England. They appeared in the larger walled towns of England, usually under the control of the constable and with responsibility to protect the town against fire, to guard the gates, and to arrest those who committed offenses at night. Thus, they were equivalent to today's night watchmen or private security guards. The first night watch in the United States was established in Boston, MA, in 1636.

watchdog committee. Congressional special committee, or a subcommittee of a standing committee, charged with investigation, in contrast with the standing committee's routine consideration of bills. Watchdog committees are usually authorized by each house independently, although on occasion both houses have acted concurrently to set up a joint watchdog committee. The committees have inquired into lobbying activities, corrupt practices and campaign expenditures, and government stockpiling of strategic materials.

Watergate affair. One of the most sensational political scandals of the twentieth century, involving numerous prominent Republicans. During the 1972 presidential campaign, the Democrats had their party headquarters in the Watergate Complex in Washington, DC. In June 1972 burglars, originally thought to be anti-Castro Cuban refugees who opposed George McGovern, were caught in Democratic headquarters. The Nixon administration and the Republican campaign organization at first denied complicity, but, following President Richard M. Nixon's landslide reelection and the conviction of the burglars, more revealing details began to emerge. In addition to wide-ranging financial irregularities, the affair involved the use of independent government agencies for partisan, political purposes and widened the gulf between the executive branch and Congress, which held its own investigation into Watergate. Maurice Stans, exsecretary of commerce, and John N. Mitchell, ex-attorney general, as well as John Ehrlichman and H. R. Haldeman, the president's top White House advisers, and the president's personal lawyer and his White House counsel were all implicated. The Nixon administration's effort to cover up its involvement provoked the Justice Department and Senate to investigate even further, and, in 1973, impeachment proceedings were begun against Nixon. When the Supreme Court ordered him to hand over tape recordings that implicated him in the coverup, Nixon resigned in 1974. Several of his top officials were convicted for their parts in the Watergate affair and were sentenced to prison. Nixon was eventually granted a general pardon by his successor, Gerald R. Ford.

watermark. A design worked into certain kinds of paper. It can be seen by holding the paper against a bright light and is usually put there by the paper manufacturer, whose logo it may be.

weapon. An instrument used in fighting; an instrument of offensive or defensive combat. The term is chiefly used in law in the statutes prohibiting the carrying of concealed or deadly weapons. *See also* nonlethal weapons

weapon identification. *See* Criminalistics Laboratory Information System

weapons: carrying, possessing, and so forth. The name of the Uniform Crime Reports category used to record and report arrests for offenses relating to the regulation of the manufacture, sale, distribution, possession, use, or transportation of deadly weapons and accessories.

Weathermen. A militant faction of the Students for a Democratic Society (SDS). It splintered from SDS in June 1969 at Ann Arbor, MI. *See also* Students for a Democratic Society

We Care. Founded in 1983, an organization interested in deterring teenagers from a life of crime. Members believe the best deterrent against crime is convicted criminals' telling of their own experiences; their stories emphasize what a prisoner loses as a result of a criminal life. Influenced by a videotape made by John Lewis Evans III, who was executed April 22, 1983, for the slaying of an Alabama pawnbroker. Evans's tape is a plea against crime and drugs, aimed at school children aged 10 to 15. Publishes *We Care* (newsletter every 4–6 weeks). Address: 5825 Highway 21, Atmore, AL 36502.

wedding cake model. This criminal justice model was formulated by Lawrence Friedman and Robert V. Percival. The "cake" model consists of four layers: (1) celebrated cases, (2 & 3) serious felonies, and (4) misdemeanors. The fourth layer far outnumbers the felonies. The celebrity cases receive massive media coverage and give the public a distorted view of the actual criminal justice system. *See* crime commission model

Weed and Seed Operation. On July 20, 1992, the U.S. attorney general created the Executive Office for Weed and Seed as an arm of the Office of the Deputy Attorney General. Operation Weed and Seed is a neighborhood revitalization program that coordinates law enforcement with social services, housing, and community redevelopment programs. The purpose is to "weed out" undesirable elements through aggressive law enforcement and to "seed" neighborhoods through economic revitalization and restoration.

weight of evidence. The preponderance of evidence.

Welch, Joseph Nye. Born in Primghar, Iowa, on October 22, 1890, Welch graduated from Grinnell College and Harvard Law School and was admitted to the Massachusetts bar in 1918. He gained national fame in 1954 as special counsel for the U.S. Army in the congressional McCarthy hearings on the spread of Communism and Communist plots in the United States. then being alleged by Senator Joseph McCarthy. When McCarthy made a particularly nasty accusation, Welch responded with the most memorable statement to come out of the sessions: "Until this moment, Senator, I think I never really gauged your cruelty or recklessness.... Have you no sense of decency?" The hearings were McCarthy's undoing. Welch returned to his law practice in Boston, a national figure. He died in Hyannis, MA, on October 6, 1960.

Wells Fargo and Co. Founded in 1852 by Henry Wells and William G. Fargo as a joint stock association, Wells, Fargo was actually a banking institution, an express and mail-carrying service, and a stage line that operated out of more than 100 offices in the western mining districts. The company carried millions of dollars in gold dust in an area beset with bandits and, since it had advertised that there would never be a loss to any customer, it was forced to structure its own elaborate security system. Treasure boxes and express coaches were protected by armed guards, and outlaws who held up Wells Fargo banks and carriers were relentlessly hunted down by specially trained and equipped couriers and agents.

Werther effect. Additional term for the copycat syndrome in which people are spurred to commit suicide by media reports of others who have done so. Werther was a character in a novel by Goethe who committed suicide, and the story was said to have triggered imitative deaths throughout Europe in the nineteenth century.

Western States Information Network. Established by Congress in 1981 as one of six regional intelligence systems in the United States. WSIN serves the narcotics intelligence needs of law enforcement agencies in Alaska, California, Hawaii, Oregon, and Washington.

WETIP. Acronym for We Turn In Pushers, founded in 1972. Conducts a program for witnesses who wish to remain anonymous. Publishes a periodic bulletin, *Counterattack* (quarterly) and *Eyewitness Newsline* (monthly). Address: P.O. Box 1296, Rancho Cucamonga,

CA 91729: (800) 78-CRIME, (800) 47-ARSON, and (800) US-FRAUD.

Wharton Rule. Legal restriction that two people who agree to commit a crime cannot be prosecuted as conspirators when the crime naturally requires the participation of two people, such as dueling or adultery.

whistleblowers. *See* False Claims Act

white-collar crime. Nonviolent crime for financial gain committed by means of deception by persons whose occupational status is entrepreneurial, professional, or semiprofessional and who use their special occupational skills and opportunities; also, nonviolent crime for financial gain using deception and committed by anyone having special technical and professional knowledge of business and government, irrespective of the person's occupation. The term was first used by criminologist Edwin H. Sutherland to cover business crimes such as embezzlement, price fixing, antitrust violations. Actual instances of white-collar crime are prosecuted as the offenses defined in statutes under such headings as theft, fraud, and embezzlement. On May 2, 1985, the brokerage firm of E. F. Hutton wrote at least $4 billion in overdrafts—cheating 400 banks of tens of millions in interest. The case resulted in a $2 million fine. According to the U.S. Department of Justice, white-collar criminals rake in a minimum of $200 billion annually, far overshadowing the $11 billion cost of violent crimes. Criminal acts played a part in half of the more than 100 bank and savings and loan failures in 1989. Specific white-collar crimes include embezzlement, bribery, fraud (including procurement fraud, stock fraud, fraud in government programs, and investment and other schemes), theft of services, theft of trade secrets, tax evasion, and obstruction of justice. *See also* securities violations

White, Edward Douglass. Eighth chief justice of the United States, appointed by President Grover S. Cleveland. He is noted for opinions reflecting a conservative and nationalistic viewpoint. Born in Louisiana in 1845,

White was admitted to the bar in 1868. In 1874 he was elected to the state senate and served on the Louisiana Supreme Court from 1879 to 1880 before his election to the U.S. Senate in 1890. White served as an associate justice from 1894 to 1910, when he was elevated to chief justice by President William H. Taft. His chief distinction lies in his dissenting opinion in the Income Tax Cases and his concurring and dissenting opinions in the Insular Cases. He died in 1921.

White Night. On May 21, 1979, after former San Francisco county supervisor Dan White was convicted of voluntary manslaughter rather than murder for killing Mayor George Moscone and gay supervisor Harvey Milk, thousands of gay men and women attacked San Francisco City Hall, smashing windows and torching patrol cars. Police, in a retaliatory action, stormed the Castro, the city's gay ghetto. *See also* Queer Nation

white slave traffic. A term meaning selling or procuring others for the purpose of prostitution. The federal law known as the Mann Act punishes, by the fine of $5,000 or imprisonment for five years or both, any person who knowingly transports, or causes to be transported or assists in obtaining transportation for, any woman or girl for the purpose of prostitution or debauchery or for any other immoral purpose or with the intent to do so, in interstate or foreign commerce. The act includes inducing, enticing, or coercing a woman or girl to go from one place to another in interstate or foreign commerce for immoral purposes. The act received the cooperation of many foreign nations at the Paris conference on May 18, 1904. It has been used as an instrument for blackmail by prostitutes working bordering states and has proven difficult to enforce, although it is a very effective weapon for the suppression of the vice it was designed to suppress. The importation of women from foreign countries for the purpose of prostitution or for any other immoral purpose is prohibited by the federal law governing aliens and immigration; the law prohibits such traffic and includes within its scope the keeping, controlling, or harboring of any woman imported for such purposes.

Wickersham Commission. Informal name for the National Commission on Law Observance and Enforcement, which was created by President Herbert Hoover in 1931 as the first national commission to deal with crime and the police. It ultimately produced a series of 13 reports, on the following subjects: Observance and Enforcement of Prohibition, Enforcement of the Prohibition Laws of the U.S., Criminal Statistics, Prosecution, Enforcement of the Deportation Laws of the U.S., The Child Offender in the Federal System of Justice, Progress on the Study of the Federal Courts, Criminal Procedure, Crime and the Foreign Born, Lawlessness in Law Enforcement, Cost of Crime, Causes of Crime, and Police. The report on police noted that the average police chief's term was too short and that his responsibility to political officials made his position insecure. The commission also felt there was a lack of competent, efficient, and honest patrolmen. It said that no intensive effort was being made to educate, train, and discipline prospective officers, or to eliminate those shown to be incompetent. The commission found that with perhaps two exceptions, police forces in cities with populations over 300,000 had neither an adequate communications system nor the equipment necessary to enforce the law effectively. It said that the police task was made much more difficult by the excessively rapid growth of U.S. cities in the prior 50 years, and by the tendency of different ethnic groups to retain their languages and customs in large cities. The report added that there were too many duties cast upon each officer and patrolman. The commission report also excoriated the police for the practice of giving suspects the "third degree," and expressed concern about whether or not criminal investigations were conducted lawfully.

Wilson, Orlando W. A police reformer who has often been credited with the promotion of police professionalism. Wilson learned police reform while a patrolman under August Vollmer at Berkeley, CA, in 1921. He was police chief in Wichita, KS, in 1928 and convinced the Kansas League of Municipalities to create a statewide police training school in 1931, and to appoint him the director. He drafted the Square Deal Code of Wichita, which has since been adopted as a code of ethics by the International Association of Chiefs of Police. By 1939 Wilson had achieved national prominence, but he had also irritated too many Wichita politicians. He resigned as Chief of Police and accepted a professorship in police administration at the University of California, Berkeley, and founded the first professional school of criminology there after World War II ended. As dean, Wilson became an extremely influential reformer. Wilson was appointed Chief of Police for Chicago in 1960 and retired in 1967.

witness. Anyone called to testify by either side in a trial. The witness is sworn in and offer evidence deemed relevant to the case. More broadly, a witness is anyone who has observed an event.

witness, alibi. *See* alibi

witness, character. *See* character

witness, expert. *See* expert testimony

witness list. A list of all individuals intended to be called as witnesses by either side in trial. It is usually demanded of the prosecution by the defense during discovery, so that counsel for the accused can adequately prepare a case and not be taken by surprise. In many jurisdictions, the defense must furnish a list of alibi and expert witnesses it intends to call.

Witness Protection Plan (WPP). This progran was established in 1970 under Title V of the Organized Crime Control Act. It provides for the health, safety, and welfare of witnesses who have offered valuable testimony in investigations or prosecutions of organized crime. Services are provided to witnesses and their families by the U.S. Marshals Service. (Between 1974 and 1978, an estimated 10 percent of all murders linked to organized crime were of prosecution witnesses.) The Witness Security Reform Act was passed in 1984, extending protection under the WPP to witnesses who provided information in other serious crimes not involving organized crime. In 1998, more than 6,700 witnesses were receiving services under the program. The budget for the program in fiscal year 1997 was $61.8 million, comprising $41.6 million for witness expenses and $20.2 million for Marshals Service salaries and expenses. More than 80 percent of current WPP cases involve drug prosecutions, compared to approximately 33 percent of such cases in 1983.

Workaholics Anonymous. Support and self-help group for people who feel they are addicted to their jobs or to spending time in the offices. Address: P.O. Box 289, Menlo Park, CA 94026-0289.

work release (furlough) programs. Change in prisoners' status to minimum custody with permission to work outside prison. Many such prisoners are housed in local communities. The concept was first applied in Wisconsin in 1913 but did not receive much support until the 1950s. Work release, work furlough, house arrest, and electronic monitoring are all economical alternatives to incarceration and prison overcrowding. They also provide a supervised transition period from prison to life on the outside.

World Court. Formally known as the International Court of Justice, the court was formed in 1945 by the United Nations to deal with disputes involving international law. Its 15 judges are elected for nine-year terms from UN countries under rules ensuring a political balance. It sits in the Peace Palace built in The Hague, the Netherlands, in 1903 with money donated by industrialist Andrew Carnegie. Although the court has had no power to enforce its rulings over the past four decades, it has decided barely 50 cases and given a dozen advisory opinions. The United States has been involved directly in only five cases, winning the most important in 1980 when the court condemned Iran's seizure of the U.S. embassy in Teheran and demanded the release of 50 American hostages. Iran ignored the findings. The United States won another victory in the 1960s when the court told the Soviet Union to pay its share of costs for Mideast peacekeeping forces approved by the General Assembly. Moscow refused. The most recent case was Nicaragua's charge that the CIA was trying to "overthrow or destabilize" the Sandinista government by supplying aid, money, and training to contra forces. In April 1985 the United States stated that it would not accept, for the next two years, the court's jurisdiction on matters concerning Central America.

X

xenophobe. A person who fears, mistrusts, and dislikes foreigners or things he or she perceives as strange and foreign. *See also* hate crimes

x-ray. This technique is used in some examinations conducted by a crime laboratory. The process was invented by German professor Wilhelm Roentgen in 1895 by accident. He received the Nobel Prize in 1901 for his work.

XYY chromosomes. Mass murderer Richard Speck tried unsuccessfully to use a form of heredity—a claim that he had an unusual chromosome pattern—as a defense in his case. Speck, convicted of the 1966 murders of eight Chicago student nurses, produced medical testimony indicating that he had an XYY-chromosome pattern. In claiming an extra "Y" chromosome, he charged that this additional "maleness" made him overly aggressive and prone to violence and that, since it was an inherited trait, he could not be blamed for his subsequent actions. Speck lost his case and his appeals.

Y

youth. A person from the age of adolescence to full maturity. As a collective term, youth refers especially to young persons of high school and early college age. Persons aged 15 through 24 are usually considered the youth group by researchers dealing with census data. The National Youth Administration considered persons aged 16 through 25 as eligible for assistance.

youth correction authority. An administrative agency for the treatment of convicted youthful offenders. Designed by a committee of the American Law Institute and described in a model act approved by the institute in 1940, the agency meets many of the demands for reform in penal treatment urged by social scientists and lawyers in recent times. The model act was, with modifications, adopted by California in 1914.

Youth Correction Authority Act. A model act, published by the American Law Institute in 1940, which served as an impetus to several state youth authority laws. Among other proposals, the act gave ultimate sentencing authority to an administrative board, and provided for an indefinite commitment until the maximum age of 25.

Youth Crime Watch of America. Organization that trains students, teachers, school administrators, and other community members to develop youth-led crime prevention groups. Offers a video and accompanying manual, "Guns and Teens." Address: 9200 Dadeland Blvd., Suite 417, Miami, FL 33156.

Z

zero-based budgeting (ZBB). A procedure requiring departments and agencies to justify all annual expenditures by starting each cost category at 0 rather than using the prior year's expenditures as a framework. More traditional budgeting requires justification of changes from the prior year's expenditures. Under ZBB, money allocated each year is based on predetermined department or agency goals as they relate to proposed expenditures.

zone search. A method of searching a crime scene where the area to be searched is divided into sectors and each one is carefully examined. This is also called a sector search.

zoning. The division of municipalities into distinct districts, the use of each of which is regulated by statute. Zoning laws specify what types of buildings may be constructed and to what use existing buildings and land may be devoted—residential, commercial, light industrial, mixed, and other categories. In addition, zoning laws may regulate the height and densities of buildings, as well as their size in relation to amount of property and the placement of buildings on lots. Zoning is the main procedure local government uses to control the socioeconomic character and the development of a community.

The first comprehensive zoning ordinance was adopted in New York City in 1916 and patterned on earlier, smaller-scope ordinances in Boston and Los Angeles. The Supreme Court approved zoning as a proper use of governmental powers when it was challenged in 1926. The enactment of zoning laws falls under the police power of communities to protect the health, safety, and welfare of the citizens.

zoophilia. Unnaturally strong attachment to specific animals for generating sexual pleasure through stroking, petting, or smelling.

zoosadism. The practice of deriving sexual pleasure through killing or torturing animals.

BIBLIOGRAPHY OF SOURCES

Abadinsky, H. (1993). *Drug abuse.* Nelson-Hall.

Annual editions: Criminal justice 85/86; 86/87; 87/88; 88/89; 89/90; 90/91; 91/92; 92/93; 93/94. Guilford, CT: Dushkin Publishing Group.

Annual editions: Violence and terrorism. (3rd ed.). Guilford, CT: Dushkin/McGraw-Hill.

Bopp, W.J., & Schultz, D.O. (1972). *Short history of American law enforcement.* Springfield, IL: Charles C. Thomas.

Burek, D., Koek, K.E., & Novallo, A. (Eds.). (1989). *Encyclopedia of associations.* Detroit, MI: Gale Research.

Champion, D.J., & Rush, G.E. (1997). *Policing in the community.* Englewood Cliffs, NJ: Prentice Hall.

Cole, G.F. (1983). *The American system of criminal justice* (3rd ed.). Pacific Grove, CA: Brooks/Cole.

Cox, S.M., & Wade, J.E. (1985). *The criminal justice network: An introduction.* Dubuque, IA: Wm. C. Brown.

DeAngelis, F.J. (1980). *Criminalistics for the investigator.* Mission Hills, CA: Glencoe.

Department of Defense industrial security program manual. (1984). Washington, DC: Defense Investigative Service.

De Sola, R. (1982). *Crime dictionary* (revised and expanded ed.). New York: Facts on File Publications.

Eldefonso, E., Coffey, A.R., & Grace, R.C. (1982). *Principles of law enforcement* (3rd ed.). New York: John Wiley & Sons.

Encyclopedic dictionary of American government (4th ed.). (1991). Guilford, CT: Dushkin Publishing Group.

Encyclopedic dictionary of American history (4th ed.). (1991). Guilford, CT: Dushkin Publishing Group.

Encyclopedic dictionary of economics (4th ed.). (1991). Guilford, CT: Dushkin Publishing Group.

Encyclopedic dictionary of psychology (4th ed.). (1991). Guilford, CT: Dushkin Publishing Group.

Encyclopedic dictionary of sociology (4th ed.). (1991). Guilford, CT: Dushkin Publishing Group.

Facilities 1992. Washington, DC: U.S. Department of Justice, Federal Bureau of Prisons.

Fairchild, H.P. (1977). *Dictionary of sociology and related sciences.* New York: Philosophical Library.

Family legal guide. (1981). Pleasantville, NY: Reader's Digest Association.

Fay, J.J. (1988). *The police dictionary and encyclopedia.* Springfield, IL: Charles C. Thomas.

_____. (1987). *Security dictionary.* Stoneham, MA: Butterworth Publishers.

Feldman, David. (1991). *Do penguins have knees?* New York: Harper Perennial.

_____. (1989). *When do fish sleep?* New York: Harper Perennial.

_____. (1987). *Why do clocks run clockwise?* New York: Harper & Row.

Folley, V.L. (1976). *American law enforcement* (2nd ed.). Rockleigh, NJ: Holbrook.

Fox, V. (1977). *Introduction to corrections.* Englewood Cliffs, NJ: Prentice Hall.

Fricke, C.W. (1968). *5000 criminal definitions, terms, and phrases.* Los Angeles: Legal Books.

Geller, W.A., Ed. (1991). *Local government police management* (3rd ed.). International City Management Association.

Germann, A.C., Day, F.D., & Gallati, R.J. (1981). *Introduction to law enforcement and criminal justice.* Springfield, IL: Charles C. Thomas.

Goldfarb, R.L., & Singer, L.R. (1973). *After conviction.* New York: Simon & Schuster.

Gregory, R.H., & Van Horn, R.L. (1981). *Automatic data-processing systems* (2nd ed.). Belmont, CA: Wadsworth.

Guinness book of world records. (1988). New York: Sterling.

Hale, C.D. (1977). *Fundamentals of police administration.* Rockleigh, NJ: Holbrook.

Holmes, R.M. (1991). *Sex crimes.* Sage.

Holmes, R.M., & De Burger, J. (1988). *Serial murder.* Newbury Park, CA: Sage Publications.

Inciardi, J.A. (1993). *Criminal justice* (4th ed.). Fort Worth, TX: Harcourt Brace Jovanovich College Publishers.

Join Together. (1996) "Fixing a failing system."

Julien, R.M. (1981). *A primer of drug action* (3rd ed.). New York: W.H. Freeman and Company.

Kadish, S.H. (Ed.). (1983). *Encyclopedia of crime and justice* (Vol. 4). New York: The Free Press.

Kane, J.N. (1975). *Famous first facts of records.* Bronx, NY: H.W. Wilson.

Kratowski, P., & Walker, D. (1984). *Criminal justice in America: Process and issues* (2nd ed.). New York: Random House.

Leet, D.A., Smith, A.M., & Rush, G.E. (1997). *Gangs, graffiti and violence: A realistic guide to the scope and nature of gangs in America.* Copperhouse.

Lesko, M. (1983). *Information USA.* New York: Viking.

Littlejohn, R.F. (1983). *Crisis management: A team approach.* New York: American Management Association.

Mannheim, H. (Ed.). (1972). *Pioneers in criminology.* Montclair, NJ: Patterson Smith.

Martin, J.A. (1980). *Law enforcement vocabulary.* Springfield, IL: Charles C. Thomas.

Martin, M., & Gelber, L. (1981). *Dictionary of American history.* New York: Philosophical Library.

Mathias, W., Rescoria, R.C., & Stephens, E. (1980). *Foundations of criminal justice.* Englewood Cliffs, NJ: Prentice Hall.

Mauer, M. (1995). "Young Black Americans and the criminal justice system: Five years later." The Sentencing Project.

McEwen, J.T. (1989). "Dedicated computer crime units." Washington, DC: National Institute of Justice.

Murton, T., & Hayams, J. (1969). *Accomplices to the crime.* New York: Grove.

National Institute of Justice. (1984). *National criminal justice thesaurus.* Washington, DC: Author.

National Institute of Justice. (1984). *A network of knowledge.* (Directory of Criminal Justice Information Sources). Queenstown, MD: Aspen Systems.

Nice, R. (1965). *Dictionary of criminology.* New York: Philosophical Library.

Palmer, J.W. (1984). *Constitutional rights of prisoners.* Cincinnati, OH: Anderson.

Pellicciotti, J.M. (1988). *Title VII liability for sexual harassment in the workplace.* Alexandria, VA: International Personnel Management Association.

Pursley, R.D. (1987). *Introduction to criminal justice* (4th ed.). New York: Macmillan.

Quick, J. (1973). *Dictionary of weapons and military terms.* New York: McGraw-Hill.

Reid, S.T. (1996). *Criminal justice* (4th ed.). Guilford, CT: Brown & Benchmark

Ross, R.S. (1996). *American national government* (4th ed.). Guilford, CT: Dushkin Publishing Group.

Rubin, S. (1973). *Law of criminal correction* (2nd ed.). St. Paul, MN: West.

Salottolo, L.A. (1976). *Modern police service encyclopedia* (2nd ed.). New York: ARCO.

Sansone, S.J. (1977). *Modern photography for police and firemen.* Cincinnati, OH: Anderson.

Scott, Sir H. (Ed.). (1961). *Crime and criminals.* New York: Hawthorne Books.

Senna, J.J., & Siegel, L.J. (1990). *Introduction to criminal justice* (5th ed.). St. Paul, MN: West Publishing.

Sills, D. (Ed.). (1977). *International encyclopedia of social sciences.* New York: Macmillan.

Smith, E., & Zurcher, A. (1968). *Dictionary of American politics* (2nd ed.). New York: Harper & Row.

Sourcebook of criminal justice statistics 1992. Washington, DC: U.S. Department of Justice, Office of Justice Programs, Bureau of Justice Statistics.

Sutherland, E.H., & Cressey, D.R. (1966). *Principles of criminology* (7th ed.). Philadelphia: J.B. Lippincott.

U.S. Department of Justice. (1976). *Law enforcement and private security sources and areas of conflict.* Washington, DC: Author.

U.S. Department of Justice: Bureau of Justice Statistics. (1990). "Drugs and crime facts." Washington, DC: Author.

U.S. Department of Justice: Bureau of Justice Statistics. (1981). *Dictionary of criminal justice data terminology* (2nd ed.). Sacramento, CA: SEARCH group.

Vold, G.B., & Bernard, T.J. (1986). *Theoretical criminology* (3rd ed.). New York: Oxford University Press.

Walker, S. (1989). *Sense and nonsense about crime: A policy guide* (2nd ed.). Pacific Grove, CA: Brooks/Cole.

Walls, H.J. (1974). *Forensic science: An introduction to scientific crime detection.* New York: Praeger.

Wedge, T.W. (1988). *The Satan hunter.* Canton, OH: Daring Books.

Weston, P.B., & Wells, K.M. (1981). *The administration of justice* (4th ed.). Englewood Cliffs: NJ: Prentice Hall.

Whisenand, P.M. (1981). *The effective police manager.* Englewood Cliffs, NJ: Prentice Hall.

Whisenand, P.M., & Ferguson, R.F. (1973). *The managing of police organizations.* Englewood Cliffs, NJ: Prentice Hall.

Whisenand, P.M., & Rush, G.E. (1988). *Supervising police personnel: Back to the basics.* Englewood Cliffs, NJ: Prentice Hall.

Whisenand, P.M., & Rush, G.E. (1993). *Supervising police personnel: The fifteen responsibilities.* Englewood Cliffs, NJ: Prentice Hall.

Wilson, J.R., & Wilson, J.A. (1992) *Addictionary.* New York: Simon & Schuster.

Woods, G. (1993). *Drug Abuse in society.* ABC-CLIO.

World almanac and book of facts. (1988). New York: Newspaper Enterprise Association.

You and the law: A practical guide to everyday law and how it affects you and your family. (1971). Pleasantville, NY: Reader's Digest Association.

Part II

SUMMARIES OF SUPREME COURT CASES AFFECTING CRIMINAL JUSTICE

Summaries of
United States Supreme Court
Cases Affecting Criminal Justice

Judy Hails Kaci, J.D., LL.M.

Department of Criminal Justice
California State University, Long Beach

PREFACE

The United States Supreme Court has decided hundreds of cases that relate to criminal justice. This summary includes cases decided to the middle of the 1998–99 term. Although it focuses on cases decided in the last 25 years, other landmark cases have been included for the sake of completeness. Due to their historical impact, some cases have been included even though they have been subsequently overruled.

The materials in this summary are organized by topic. Cases within each topic are chronological, with the most recent cases given first. When looking up a case, it will be necessary to glance through the more recent cases to determine if the holding has been modified or overruled. It must be emphasized that these brief summaries are presented as a reference point, not as a substitute for studying the text of the cases. A complete alphabetical index to all cases follows the summaries.

Each Supreme Court case has three citations:

U.S.   United States Reports (official published source of United States Supreme Court decisions)

L.Ed.   United States Supreme Court Reports, Lawyers Edition (published by Lawyers Co-operative Publishing Company)

S.Ct. or
Sup.Ct.   Supreme Court Reporter (published by West Publishing Company)

Current L.Ed. citations contain the reference "2d," which refers to the Second Series (volumes were numbered sequentially until 1957, then the Second Series was initiated starting with volume 1 again). The Supreme Court Reporter has one number for each term of the Supreme Court; the entire term is paginated consecutively, but for ease in binding, two or three volumes appear on the shelf (109 S.Ct. will be bound as 109, 109A and 109B). United States Reports usually are printed later than the other two sources; an example of a citation for a case which has not appeared yet in the official reports is *California v. Greenwood* 486 U.S. ___, 100 L.Ed. 2d 30, 108 S.Ct. 1625 (1988).

A student looking for the text of a Supreme Court decision should check to see which of these reference works his or her local library has. Due to the fact that Supreme Court opinions are printed verbatim in each of them, it is not necessary to look up a case in more than one source. Once this is determined, the number preceding the abbreviated title of the book is the volume number, the number following it is the page number, and the number in parentheses is the year the case was decided. For example, the citation for *Miranda v. Arizona* is 384 U.S. 436, 16 L.Ed. 2d 694, 86 S.Ct. 1602 (1966). *Miranda* can be found starting on page 436 of volume 384 of the United States Reports; page 694 of volume 16 of the United States Supreme Court Reports, Lawyers Edition, Second Series; or page 1602 of volume 86 of the Supreme Court Reporter.

U.S. SUPREME COURT CASES

I FIRST AMENDMENT ISSUES

A. Freedom of Speech

Buckley v. American Constitutional Law Foundation 525 U.S. ___, 142 L.Ed. 2d 599, 119 S.Ct. 636 (1999) the Court, in an opinion by Stevens for 5 justices, held that a Colorado law violated the First Amendment by requiring ballot initiative-petition circulators to be registered voters in the state and wear identification badges bearing their names; initiative proponents were also required to report the names and addresses of all paid circulators and the amount paid to circulators. These controls excessively restricted political speech.

Arkansas Educational Television Commission v. Forbes 523 U.S. 666, 140 L.Ed. 2d 875, 118 S.Ct. 1633 (1998) the Court, 6–3 in an opinion by Kennedy, held that a state-owned public television broadcast of a candidate debate that excluded independent candidates with little popular support did not violate the candidates' First Amendment rights. The decision to exclude the candidates was a reasonable, viewpoint-neutral exercise of journalistic discretion.

Schenck v. Pro-Choice Network of Western New York 519 U.S. 357, 137 L.Ed. 2d 1, 117 S.Ct. 855 (1997) the Court, in an opinion by Rehnquist for 5 justices with the 4 remaining justices joining in parts of the opinion, held that "fixed bubble" or "fixed buffer zone" limitations in an injunction against pickets at an abortion clinic did not violate the First Amendment, but provisions for a "floating bubble" or "floating buffer zone" violated the First Amendment. The "fixed buffer zone" in question was a 15-foot space around doorways, driveways, and parking lots associated with the clinic. The "floating buffer zone" was a 15-foot space around any person or vehicle entering or leaving the building; it in effect prohibited "sidewalk counselors" from approaching people within a normal conversational distance or handing leaflets to them. The Court found the "floating buffer zones" unduly inhibited free speech and leafleting but did not state that such buffer zones were unconstitutional under all circumstances.

O'Hare Truck Service, Inc. v. City of Northlake 518 U.S. 712, 135 L.Ed. 2d 874, 116 S.Ct. 2353 (1996) the Court, 7–2 in an opinion by Kennedy, held that although the government has broad discretion in formulating its contracting policies, it cannot retaliate against a contractor or a regular provider of services for exercising the rights of political association or expression of political allegiance.

Board of County Commissioners, Wabaunsee County v. Umbehr 518 U.S. 668, 135 L.Ed. 2d 843, 116 S.Ct. 2342 (1996) the Court, 7–2 in an opinion by O'Connor, held that the First Amendment protects independent contractors from termination of at-will government contracts in retaliation for their exercise of freedom of speech.

44 Liquormart, Inc. and Peoples Super Liquor Stores, Inc. v. Rhode Island and Rhode Island Liquor Stores Association 517 U.S. 484, 134 L.Ed. 2d 711, 116 S.Ct. 1495 (1996) the Court, in an opinion by Stevens for 6 justices with concurring opinions by the remaining justices, held that Rhode Island's statutory prohibition against advertisements that provide the public with accurate information about retail prices of alcoholic beverages is an unconstitutional violation of the First Amendment that is not shielded from constitutional scrutiny by the Twenty-first Amendment.

Rosenberger v. Rector and Visitors of the University of Virginia 515 U.S. 819, 132 L.Ed. 2d 700, 115 S.Ct. 2510 (1995) the Court, 5–4 in an opinion by Kennedy, held that the University of Virginia violated the petitioner's First Amendment right to free speech when it paid for the cost of printing student publications but denied funding for petitioner's paper because of its religious orientation.

Florida Bar v. Went for It, Inc. 515 U.S. 618, 132 L.Ed. 2d 541, 115 S.Ct. 2371 (1995) the Court, 5–4 in an opinion by O'Connor, held that the Florida Bar's prohibition on personal injury lawyers sending targeted direct-mail solicitations to victims and their relatives for 30 days following an accident or disaster did not violate the First Amendment. The Court noted that this case concerns pure commercial advertising; added to this was the fact that the actions of lawyers have always been subject to extensive regulation by the states.

Hurley v. Irish-American Gay, Lesbian, and Bisexual Group of Boston 515 U.S. 557, 132 L.Ed. 2d 487, 115 S.Ct. 2338 (1995) the Court, in a unanimous opinion by Souter, held Massachusetts violated the First Amendment rights of private citizens who organized a St. Patrick's Day parade when it required that the organization include among the marchers a group imparting a message that the organizers did not wish to convey.

McIntyre v. Ohio Elections Commission 514 U.S. 334, 131 L.Ed. 2d 426, 115 S.Ct. 1511 (1995) the Court, in an opinion by Stevens for 6 justices with 2 justices dissenting, held that an Ohio statute that prohibits the distribution of anonymous campaign literature violates the First Amendment.

Rubin v. Coors Brewing Company 514 U.S. 476, 131 L.Ed. 2d 532, 115 S.Ct. 1585 (1995) the Court, in an opinion by Thomas for 8 justices with 1 justice concurring, held that provisions of the Federal Alcohol Administration Act of 1935 that prohibit beer labels from displaying alcohol content are inconsistent with the protections granted to commercial speech by the First Amendment.

Madsen v. Women's Health Center, Inc. 512 U.S. 753, 129 L.Ed. 2d 593, 114 S.Ct. 2516 (1994) the Court, in an opinion by Rehnquist

for 6 justices, held portions of state court's injunction on demonstrations at abortion clinics were valid. Establishing a 36-foot buffer zone around the clinic entrances and driveway and noise restrictions were constitutional. An "in concert" provision that applied to all persons acting "in concert" with protesters was upheld. The following restrictions were found unconstitutional: 36-foot buffer zone as applied to "private property" on the back and side of the clinic; the restriction on using "images observable" to patients during such hours; the prohibition against uninvited approaches of persons seeking the services of the clinic; and the prohibition against picketing within 300 feet of the residences of clinic staff.

City of LaDue v. Gilleo 512 U.S. 43, 129 L.Ed. 2d 36, 114 S.Ct. 2038 (1994) the Court, in a unanimous opinion by Stevens, held that a content-neutral city ordinance that prohibited nearly all signs in residential areas violated the First Amendment rights of residents. It distinguished this decision from those permitting regulation of signs on commercial and public property, saying the government's need to regulate temperate speech from the home was much less pressing than the government's need to mediate among various competing expressive uses for public streets and facilities.

United States v. Edge Broadcasting Co. 509 U.S. 418, 125 L.Ed. 2d 345, 113 S.Ct. 2696 (1993) the Court, in an opinion by White for 7 justices, held that a statute in a state in which lotteries were illegal, which prohibited the broadcast of information about lotteries in states where they are legal, did not violate the First Amendment protection of commercial speech.

Wisconsin v. Mitchell 508 U.S. 47, 124 L.Ed. 2d 436, 113 S.Ct. 2194 (1993) the Court, in a unanimous decision by Rehnquist, held that a "hate crime" law that permitted enhancement of a sentence if the defendant selected the victim due to race, religion, color, disability, sexual orientation, national origin, or ancestry was not an impermissible infringement of free speech.

The conduct forbidden by the statute, battery, is not protected by the First Amendment.

El Vocero de Puerto Rico v. Puerto Rico 508 U.S. 147, 124 L.Ed. 2d 60, 113 S.Ct. 2004 (1993) the Court, in a unanimous *per curiam* opinion, held that a rule which provided that preliminary hearings be held in private unless the defendant requests otherwise violates the First Amendment.

City of Cincinnati v. Discovery Network, Inc. 507 U.S. 410, 123 L.Ed. 2d 99, 113 S.Ct. 1505 (1993) the Court, 6–3 in an opinion by Stevens, held that a city ordinance prohibiting distribution of commercial publications in freestanding newsracks on public property, enacted in the interest of safety and maintaining the attractive appearance of streets and sidewalks, violated First Amendment protection of commercial speech.

International Society for Krishna Consciousness v. Lee 505 U.S. 672, 120 L.Ed. 2d 541, 112 S.Ct. 2701 (1992) the Court, 5–4 in an opinion by Rehnquist, held that solicitation inside a public airport terminal could be restricted.

Lee v. International Society of Krishna Consciousness 505 U.S. 830, 120 L.Ed. 2d 669, 112 S.Ct. 2709 (1992) the Court, 5–4 in a *per curiam* opinion, held that distribution of literature within a public airport terminal could not be restricted.

R. A. V. v. City of St. Paul, Minnesota 505 U.S. 377, 120 L.Ed. 2d 305, 112 S.Ct. 2538 (1992) the Court, 5–4 in an opinion by Scalia, held a "hate crime" ordinance unconstitutional; statutes attempting to regulate "fighting words" must be content-neutral.

Forsyth County, Georgia v. The Nationalist Movement 505 U.S. 123, 120 L.Ed. 2d 101, 112 S.Ct. 2395 (1992) the Court, 5–4 in an opinion by Blackmun, held that an ordinance regulating parade permit fees based on the anticipated amount of hostility generated by the demonstration was invalid because it unconstitutionally tied the amount of the fee to the content of the speech and lacked adequate procedural safeguards.

Simon & Schuster Inc. v. Members of the New York State Crime Victims Board 502 U.S. 116, 116 L.Ed. 2d 476, 112 S.Ct. 501 (1991) the Court, 6–2 (Thomas not participating) in an opinion by O'Connor, held that a Son of Sam law, which prohibited convicted criminals from profiting from publishing their stories, is not content-neutral and therefore violates the First Amendment.

Barnes v. Glen Theatre, Inc. 501 U.S. 560, 115 L.Ed. 2d 504, 111 S.Ct. 2456 (1991) the Court, in a case without a majority opinion, held that a city ordinance prohibiting nude dancing as entertainment did not violate the First Amendment.

United States v. Eichman 496 U.S. 310, 110 L.Ed. 2d 287, 110 S.Ct. 2404 (1990) the Court, in an opinion by Brennan for 5 justices, held that while the federal government may create national symbols, promote them, and encourage their respectful treatment, the Flag Protection Act was unconstitutional because it criminally proscribed expressive conduct because of its likely impact.

Johnson v. Texas (1989) 491 U.S. 397, 105 L.Ed. 2d 342, 109 S.Ct. 2533 (1989) the Court. 5–4 in an opinion by Brennan, held that a state statute that prohibited burning the United States flag in protest violated the First Amendment by restricting expressive conduct.

City of Dallas v. Stanglin (1989) 490 U.S. 19, 104 L.Ed. 2d 18, 109 S.Ct. 1591 (1989) the Court, 7–2 in an opinion by Rehnquist, held that the First Amendment does not prohibit regulation of purely social conduct. Case involved local ordinance regulating dance halls attended by juveniles.

Frisby v. Schultz (1988) 487 U.S. 474, 101 L.Ed. 2d 420, 108 S.Ct. 2495 (1988) the Court, 5–4 in an opinion by O'Connor, held that the First Amendment was not violated by a local ordinance that prohibited picketing focused on a single residence. Case involved anti-abortion picketing in front of the home of a doctor.

City of Houston v. Hill 482 U.S. 451, 96 L.Ed. 2d 398, 107 S.Ct. 2502 (1987) the Court, in an opinion by Brennan for 5 justices, held that a municipal ordinance that made it unlawful for a person to "willfully or intentionally interrupt a city policeman... by verbal challenge during an investigation" was facially invalid under the First Amendment. The Court noted that the statute did not deal with "core criminal conduct," and that the First Amendment protects a significant amount of verbal criticism and challenge directed at police officers.

Arcara v. Cloud Books, Inc. 478 U.S. 697, 92 L.Ed. 2d 568, 106 S.Ct. 3172 (1986) the Court, in an opinion by Burger for 6 justices, held that the First Amendment does not bar enforcement of the New York Public Health Law authorizing closure of a premises found to be used as a place for prostitution and lewdness because the premises are also used as an adult bookstore.

Los Angeles City Council v. Taxpayers for Vincent (1984) 466 U.S. 789, 80 L.Ed. 2d 772, 104 S.Ct. 2118 (1984) the Court, 6–3 in an opinion by Stevens, held that a local ordinance prohibiting posting of signs on public property during political campaigns did not violate the First Amendment.

Connick v. Myers 461 U.S. 138, 75 L.Ed. 2d 708, 103 S.Ct. 1684 (1983) the Court, 5–4, in an opinion by White, held that the First Amendment did not require a public employer to tolerate action by an employee that the employer reasonably believed would disrupt the office, undermine the authority of the employer, and destroy close working relationships within the office.

Village of Hoffman Estates v. Flipside, Hoffman Estates, Inc. 455 U.S. 489, 71 L.Ed. 2d 362, 102 S.Ct. 2023 (1982) the Court, in an opinion by Marshall for 7 members of the Court, upheld an ordinance requiring businesses to obtain licenses if they sell any items that are "designed or marketed for use with illegal cannabis or drugs."

Village of Schaumberg v. Citizens for Better Environment 444 U.S. 620, 63 L.Ed. 2d 73, 100 S.Ct. 826 (1980) the Court, 8–1 in an opinion by White, held that a local ordinance was unconstitutional under the First Amendment because it barred solicitation of charitable contributions unless at least 75 percent of the money collected went to charitable purposes.

Hynes v. The Mayor and Council of the Borough of Oradell 425 U.S. 610, 48 L.Ed. 2d 243, 96 S.Ct. 1755 (1976) the Court, in an opinion by Burger for 5 members of the Court, held that cities possess the authority to regulate soliciting and canvassing by the use of narrowly drawn ordinances.

Greer v. Spock 424 U.S. 828, 47 L.Ed. 2d 505, 96 S.Ct. 1211 (1976) the Court, 6–2 with Stevens not participating, in an opinion by Stewart, held that civilians do not have a generalized constitutional right to make political speeches or distribute political leaflets at a military post. The regulations involved were found to be constitutional because they did not discriminate against candidates on the basis of political views. The record showed a consistent policy of keeping military activities free of entanglement with partisan political campaigns.

Gooding v. Wilson 405 U.S. 518, 31 L.Ed. 2d 408, 92 S.Ct. 1103 (1972) in a 6–2 opinion by Brennan, the Court held unconstitutional a Georgia statute making it an offense to use "opprobrious words or abusive language tending to cause a breach of the peace." The construction given the Georgia statute by the state courts had not limited it to "fighting words" and so it did not come under the narrow exception to the constitutional right of freedom of expression sanctioned by *Chaplinsky v. New Hampshire.*

Brandenburg v. Ohio 395 U.S. 444, 23 L.Ed. 2d 430, 89 S.Ct. 1827 (1969) Chief Justice Warren in a *per curiam* opinion that overruled

Whitney v. California, 274 U.S. 357 (1927), found the Ohio Criminal Syndicalism Act (Ohio Rev. Code, section 2923.13) unconstitutional and unconstitutionally applied to the appellant, a leader of the Ku Klux Klan group. The First Amendment bars laws prohibiting the "advocacy" of force or lawlessness that is not directed to inciting or producing imminent lawless action and not likely to incite or produce such action. Mere urging the moral propriety or even the moral necessity of a resort to force is distinguished from preparing a particular group for violent action.

Shuttleworth v. City of Birmingham 394 U.S. 147, 22 L.Ed. 2d 162, 89 S.Ct. 935 (1969) the Court, in an opinion by Stewart, found an ordinance to be unconstitutional on its face. The ordinance conferred "virtually unbridled and absolute power to prohibit any 'parade, procession,' or 'demonstration' on the city's streets or public ways."

Gregory v. City of Chicago 394 U.S. 111, 22 L.Ed. 2d 134, 89 S.Ct. 946 (1969) in a short opinion by Warren, the Court reversed, concluding that since there was no evidence that the petitioner's conduct was disorderly, the march was protected by the First Amendment.

Cameron v. Johnson 390 U.S. 611, 20 L.Ed. 2d 182, 88 S.Ct. 1335 (1966) the Court held, 7–2, that while picketing cannot be made a crime, blocking the entrance to a public building can constitute a criminal act.

Cox v. Louisiana 379 U.S. 536, 13 L.Ed. 2d 471, 85 S.Ct. 453 (1965) the Court emphatically rejected the notion that the First and Fourteenth Amendments afford the same kind of freedom to those who would communicate ideas by conduct such as patrolling, marching, and picketing on streets and highways as these amendments afford to those who communicate ideas by pure speech.

Poulos v. New Hampshire 345 U.S. 195, 97 L.Ed. 1105, 73 S.Ct. 760 (1953) the Court held that a state or municipality may require a permit to conduct a meeting in a public park.

Dennis v. United States 341 U.S. 494, 95 L.Ed. 1137, 71 S.Ct. 857 (1951) the Court held that teaching and advocating the overthrow of the government is protected by the First Amendment except when it advocates "a rule of principle to incite persons to such action, all with the intent to cause the overthrow or destruction of the Government of the United States by force and violence as speedily as circumstances will permit."

Kovacs v. Cooper 336 U.S. 77, 93 L.Ed. 513, 69 S.Ct. 448 (1949) the Court held that the state or municipality may prohibit the operation of sound trucks and loudspeakers on public streets.

Chaplinsky v. New Hampshire 315 U.S. 568, 86 L.Ed. 1031, 62 S.Ct. 766 (1942) the Court held unanimously that states may punish "fighting words."

Cox v. New Hampshire 312 U.S. 569, 85 L.Ed. 1049, 61 S.Ct. 762 (1941) the Court held unanimously that states may regulate parades incident to regulating streets for traffic purposes.

Gitlow v. New York 268 U.S. 652, 69 L.Ed. 1138, 45 S.Ct. 625 (1925) the Court upheld the validity of New York's Criminal Anarchy Act of 1902.

Schenck v. United States 249 U.S. 47, 63 L.Ed. 470, 39 S.Ct. 247 (1919) Holmes enunciated his famous clear-and-present danger test. The well-known words about shouting fire in a crowded theater are used to illustrate a situation in which free speech may be limited.

B. Freedom of the Press

Gentile v. State Bar of Nevada 501 U.S. 1030, 115 L.Ed. 2d 888, 111 S.Ct. 2720 (1991) the Court, 5 in an opinion by Rehnquist, held that a Nevada rule that prohibited attorneys from making statements to the press that posed a substantial likelihood of material prejudice to the case did not violate the First Amendment.

Press-Enterprise Company v. Superior Court of California for the County of Riverside 478 U.S. 1, 92 L.Ed. 2d 1, 106 S.Ct. 2735 (1986) the Court, in an opinion by Burger for 7 justices, held that the qualified First Amendment right of access to criminal proceedings applies to preliminary hearings as they are conducted in California. The judge may not close the preliminary hearing based on a cursory assertion that publicity might deprive the defendant of the right to a fair trial. Any limitation on access to the preliminary hearing must be narrowly tailored to serve First Amendment interests.

Press-Enterprise Company v. Superior Court of California, Riverside County 464 U.S. 501, 78 L.Ed. 2d 629, 104 S.Ct. 819 (1984) the Court, in an opinion by Burger signed by 8 justices, held that the guarantees of open public proceedings in criminal trials included the right of the press to cover *voir dire* examination of potential jurors. Closure of *voir dire* proceedings may be allowed rarely and only on a showing of cause that outweighs the value of openness.

Globe Newspaper Company v. Superior Court for the County of Norfolk 457 U.S. 596, 73 L.Ed. 2d 248, 102 S.Ct. 2613 (1982) the Court, in an opinion by Brennan for 5 justices, held that a Massachusetts statute providing for exclusion of the general public from trials for specified sexual offenses involving a victim under the age of 18 was unconstitutional. The Court found that the state court interpretation of the statute to mandate the exclusion of the press and public during the testimony of minor victims of sex offenses could not stand.

Chandler v. Florida 449 U.S. 560, 66 L. Ed. 2d 740, 101 S.Ct. 802 (1981) the Court, in an opinion by Burger for 6 justices, held that states could experiment with the use of electronic media and still photographic coverage of public judicial proceedings without violating the constitutional rights of the defendant.

Richmond Newspapers, Inc. v. Virginia 448 U.S. 555, 65 L.Ed. 2d 973, 100 S.Ct. 2814 (1980) 7 members of the Court, although unable to agree upon an opinion, held that the trial judge's order, at request of defendant

and without objection by the prosecution, that the defendant's murder trial be closed to the public and press violated the First and Fourteenth Amendments.

Gannett Co., Inc. v. DePasquale 443 U.S. 368, 61 L.Ed. 2d 608, 99 S.Ct. 2898 (1979) the Court, in an opinion by Stewart for 5 justices, held that where the trial judge had adequately considered the balance of the right of the defendant to a fair trial against the right of the press and public to attend a suppression hearing, the order closing the suppression hearing to the press and public was constitutional.

Zurcher v. The Stanford Daily 436 U.S. 547, 56 L.Ed. 2d 525, 98 S.Ct. 1970 (1978) the Court, 5–3 with Brennan not participating, in an opinion by White, held First Amendment protections of the press did not require that evidence in the hands of third-party press be obtained by the use of subpoena *duces tecum* rather than a search warrant.

Landmark Communications, Inc. v. Virginia 435 U.S. 829, 56 L.Ed. 2d 1, 98 S.Ct. 1535 (1978) the Court, in an opinion by Burger for 6 members of the Court, held that the First Amendment did not prohibit punishing members of the press for divulging or publishing truthful information regarding an official commission's confidential proceedings.

Nebraska Press Association v. Stuart 427 U.S. 539, 49 L.Ed. 2d 683, 96 S.Ct. 2791 (1976) the Court, in an opinion by Burger for 5 justices, held that a court order prohibiting the publication or broadcasting of accounts of confessions or admissions made by the accused, or facts strongly implicating him, was unconstitutional. The record did not show an adequate consideration of alternatives to prior restraint that might have mitigated the adverse effect of pretrial publicity. Prohibition on reporting and commenting on court proceedings that were held in public is clearly invalid.

Murphy v. Florida 421 U.S. 794, 44 L.Ed. 2d 589, 95 S.Ct. 2031 (1975) the Court, in an opinion by Marshall for 7 justices, held that denial of a motion for change of venue on grounds of pretrial publicity did not violate the defendant's constitutional rights. Defendant had failed to show that the setting of the trial was inherently prejudicial or that the jury selection process permitted an inference of actual prejudice.

Pell v. Procunier 417 U.S. 817, 41 L.Ed. 2d 495, 94 S.Ct. 2800 (1974) the Court, 6–3 in an opinion by Stewart, held that a prison regulation prohibiting face-to-face press interviews did not violate the First Amendment because other avenues were available to the media.

Branzburg v. Hayes 408 U.S. 665, 33 L.Ed. 2d 626, 92 S.Ct. 2646 (1972) the Court, 5–4 in an opinion by White, held that news reporters have no constitutional privilege against appearing before a grand jury and answering questions as to the identity of their sources or information received in confidence.

Sheppard v. Maxwell 384 U.S. 333, 16 L.Ed. 2d 600, 86 S.Ct. 1507 (1966) this decision contains an extensive discussion of the effect of unfair, distorted publicity upon the jurors at the time of trial. The decision notes that neither prosecutors, counsel for defense, the accused, witness, court staff, nor enforcement officers coming under the jurisdiction of the trial court should be permitted to frustrate its function by actions or statements threatening the fair trial of the defendant.

C. Obscenity and Related Issues

Reno v. American Civil Liberties Union 521 U.S. 844, 138 L.Ed. 2d 874, 117 S.Ct. 2329 (1997) the Court, in an opinion by Stevens for 7 justices with the remaining justices filing a concurring and dissenting opinion, held that portions of the Communications Decency Act of 1996 that attempted to protect minors from dissemination of "indecent" and "patently offensive" communications on the Internet violated the First Amendment because the act infringed upon the free speech rights of adults.

Denver Area Educational Telecommunications Consortium v. Federal Communications Commission 518 U.S. 727, 135 L.Ed. 2d 888, 116 S.Ct. 2374 (1996) the Court, in a portion of an opinion by Breyer signed by 7 justices but without a majority opinion, held that portions of the Cable Television Consumer Protection and Competition Act of 1992 relating to blocking "patently offensive" sex-related material on cable television is consistent with the First Amendment. The First Amendment was violated by provisions that require leased channel operators to segregate and to block this type of programming and by portions of the act that are applicable to public, educational, and governmental channels because these portions of the act are not appropriately tailored to achieve the basic, legitimate objective of protecting children from exposure to "patently offensive" material.

Osborne v. Ohio 495 U.S. 103, 109 L.Ed. 2d 98, 110 S.Ct. 1691 (1990) the Court, 6–3 in an opinion by White, held that states had sufficient interest in the prevention of sexual exploitation of children to give them the right to regulate possession and viewing of child pornography. A statute must require *scienter* and not be overbroad; mere nudity cannot be banned.

New York v. P J. Video 475 U.S. 868, 89 L.Ed. 2d 871, 106 S.Ct. 1610 (1986) the Court, in an opinion by Rehnquist for 6 justices, held that a higher standard of probable cause is not required for search warrants for allegedly obscene materials than for items not protected by the First Amendment.

City of Renton v. Playtime Theaters 475 U.S. 41, 89 L.Ed. 2d 29, 106 S.Ct. 925 (1986) the Court, 6–3 in an opinion by Rehnquist, held that the First Amendment was not violated by a zoning ordinance that required adult movie theaters to be at least 1,000 feet from any residence, church, park, or school.

Maryland v. Macon 472 U.S. 463, 86 L.Ed. 2d 370, 105 S.Ct. 2778 (1985) the Court, in an opinion by O'Connor for 7 justices, upheld the actions of undercover officers who entered an adult bookstore during business hours, without a warrant, examined items offered for sale, and purchased two allegedly obscene magazines.

New York v. Ferber 458 U.S. 747, 73 L.Ed. 2d 1113, 102 S.Ct. 3348 (1982) the Court, in an opinion by White for 5 members of the Court, with all other members of the Court concurring in the result, held that child pornography is unprotected by the First Amendment if it involves *scienter* and a visual depiction of sexual conduct by children without serious literary, artistic, political, or scientific value.

Young v. American Mini Theaters, Inc. 427 U.S. 50, 49 L.Ed. 2d 310, 96 S.Ct. 2440 (1976) the Court, 5–4, in an opinion by Stevens, held the city's interest in regulating the use of property for commercial purposes was adequate to support licensing and zoning restrictions that would not permit an adult theater to be located within 1000 feet of any two other "regulated uses" (10 different kinds of establishments in addition to adult theaters were considered to be "regulated uses"). "Adult theater" was defined as one that presents material "characterized by an emphasis" on matter depicting or relating to "specified sexual activities" or "specified anatomical areas" (as defined in the ordinances).

Erznoznik v. City of Jacksonville 422 U.S. 205, 45 L.Ed. 2d 125, 95 S.Ct. 2268 (1975) the Court, 6–3, in an opinion by Powell, held that the city failed to satisfy the rigorous constitutional standards that apply to regulation of expression when it enacted an ordinance prohibiting the showing of films containing nudity by a drive-in movie theater whose screen was visible from a public street.

Miller v. California 413 U.S. 15, 37 L.Ed. 2d 419, 93 S.Ct. 2607 (1973) the Court, in an opinion by Burger for 5 justices, held that the First Amendment does not protect obscene matter. The Court established the following standards for obscenity: the average person, applying contemporary community standards, would find that the work, taken as a whole, appealed to prurient interest; the work depicted or described, in a patently offensive way,

sexual conduct specifically defined by the applicable state law, as written or authoritatively construed; and, the work, taken as a whole, lacked serious literary, artistic, political, or scientific value. The work need not be shown to be "utterly without redeeming social value."

D. Freedom of Religion

City of Boerne v. Flores 521 U.S. 507, 138 L.Ed. 2d 624, 117 S.Ct. 2157 (1997) the Court, 6–3 in an opinion by Kennedy, invalidated the Religious Freedom Restoration Act of 1993. The act prohibited "government" from "substantially burdening" a person's exercise of religion even if the burden results from a rule of general applicability unless the government can demonstrate the burden (1) is in furtherance of a compelling governmental interest; and (2) is the least restrictive means of furthering that compelling governmental interest. The decision was based on an analysis of the Fourteenth Amendment as being self-executing and not giving Congress the right to pass substantive legislation to protect constitutional rights except in remedial situations. The Religious Freedom Restoration Act was seen as disrupting the separation of powers created by the Constitution.

Agostini v. Felton 521 U.S. 203, 138 L.Ed. 2d 391, 117 S.Ct. 1997 (1997) the Court, 5–4 in an opinion by O'Connor, held that the use of public school employees for remedial education in private schools as part of the Elementary and Secondary Education Act of 1965 did not violate the establishment clause of the First Amendment. The Court reversed its holding in *Aguilar v. Felton* (1985) and portions of *School District of Grand Rapids v. Ball* (1985).

Capital Square Review and Advisory Board v. Pinette 515 U.S. 753, 132 L.Ed. 2d 650, 115 S.Ct. 2440 (1995) the Court, in an opinion by Scalia, portions of which were joined by 7 justices, held that the First Amendment was violated by a denial of the Ku Klux Klan request for a permit to display a cross during the Christmas holidays in the square surrounding the statehouse in Columbus, Ohio. The First Amendment establishment clause was not violated by allowing the display of a cross on state property by a private party. The Court noted that the state did not sponsor the cross, the display was on public property that had been opened for public speech, and the petitioners had complied with the application process as required by the law in question.

Church of the Lukumi Babalu Aye, Inc. v. City of Hialeah 508 U.S. 520, 124 L.Ed. 2d 472, 113 S.Ct. (1993) the Court, in an opinion by Kennedy, relevant parts of which represented the views of 7 justices, held that an ordinance that subjects a person to criminal punishment if he/she "unnecessarily or cruelly… kills any animal" violated the Free Exercise Clause. The Court found that the object of the ordinance was suppression of the central element of the Santeria worship service. The ordinance was both overbroad and underinclusive; analogous nonreligious conduct was not covered.

Employment Division, Department of Human Resources of Oregon v. Smith 494 U.S. 872, 108 L.Ed. 2d 876, 110 S.Ct. 1595 (1990) the Court, in an opinion by Scalia for 5 justices, held defendant could be denied unemployment compensation when he was fired based on use of peyote in violation of Oregon's law. The Court rejected defendant's argument that the ingestion of peyote for sacramental purposes at a ceremony of the Native American Church was protected by the Free Exercise Clause.

II FOURTH AMENDMENT ISSUES

A. Aerial Surveillance

Florida v. Riley 488 U.S. 445, 102 L.Ed. 2d 835, 109 S.Ct. 693 (1989) the Court, without a majority opinion, held that surveillance of the interior of a partially covered greenhouse in a residential backyard from the vantage point of a helicopter located 400 feet above the greenhouse did not constitute a search for which a warrant is required under the Fourth Amendment. *In dicta*, four justices indicated the result would have been different if the flying altitude had been in violation of law or regulations.

Dow Chemical Company v. United States 476 U.S. 227, 90 L.Ed. 2d 226, 106 S.Ct. 1819 (1986) the Court, in an opinion by Burger for 5 justices, held that the Environmental Protection Agency's aerial photography of Dow's 2,000-acre plant complex from navigable airspace without a warrant was not a search under the Fourth Amendment. The Court also held that the use of aerial photography is within the EPA's statutory authority.

California v. Ciraolo 476 U.S. 207, 90 L.Ed. 2d 210, 106 S.Ct. 1809 (1986) the Court, in an opinion by Burger for 5 justices, held that the Fourth Amendment was not violated by aerial observation without a warrant from an altitude of 1,000 feet of a fenced-in backyard within the curtilage of a home.

B. Arrest and Booking

Wilson v. Layne ___ U.S. ___, ___ L.Ed. 2d ___, S.Ct. ___ (1999) the Court, in an opinion by Rehnquist that was unanimous in part and divided 8–1 in part, held that federal marshals and sheriff's deputies violated plaintiffs' Fourth Amendment privacy rights in executing an arrest warrant. The officers invited a news reporter and a photographer to accompany them to the suspect's home to record the arrest. The pictures were never published, because the suspect was absent, but the Court ruled that his parents' right to privacy had been violated by the media presence.

Knowles v. Iowa 525 U.S. ___, 142 L.Ed. 2d 492, 119 S.Ct. 484 (1998) the Court, in a unanimous opinion by Rehnquist, held that an Iowa law that allowed officers to conduct a full search, equivalent to that authorized in *United States v. Robinson* (1973), when a motorist is detained for the purpose of issuing a traffic citation, violates the Fourth Amendment. The Court reaffirmed the right to have people exit the vehicle but required a showing of reasonable suspicion of danger to the officer in order to justify any type of search.

Minnesota v. Olson 495 U.S. 91, 109 L.Ed. 2d 85, 110 S.Ct. 1684 (1990) the Court, in an opinion by White for 7 justices, held that police entry, without a warrant or consent, into a home where the suspect was an overnight guest violated the suspect's rights under the Fourth Amendment.

Maryland v. Buie 494 U.S. 325, 108 L.Ed. 2d 276, 110 S.Ct. 1093 (1990) the Court, in an opinion by White for 7 justices, held that incident to an arrest the officers could, as a precautionary matter and without probable cause or reasonable suspicion, look in closets and other spaces immediately adjoining the place of arrest from which an attack could be immediately launched. To go beyond that area, there must be articulable facts which, taken together with the rational inferences from those facts, would warrant a reasonably prudent officer to believe that the area to be swept harbors an individual posing a danger to those on the arrest scene.

Brower v. County of Inyo 489 U.S. 593, 103 L.Ed. 2d 628, 109 S.Ct. 1378 (1989) the Court, in an opinion by Scalia for 5 justices, held that the act of placing a roadblock across all lanes of traffic in order to stop a fleeing suspect was sufficient to establish a seizure under the Fourth Amendment. If such a seizure was unreasonable, it would establish liability under 42 U.S.C. §1983.

Welsh v. Wisconsin 466 U.S. 740, 80 L.Ed. 2d 732, 104 S.Ct. 2091 (1984) the Court, in an opinion by Brennan joined by 5 other justices, held that absent exigent circumstances, a warrantless nighttime entry into the home of an individual to arrest him for a civil, nonjailable traffic offense is prohibited by the Fourth Amendment. The opinion went on to say, "... [A]pplication of the exigent-circumstances exception in the context of a home entry should rarely be sanctioned when there is probable cause to believe that only a minor offense, such as the kind at issue in this case, has been committed.... [A] warrantless home

arrest cannot be upheld simply because evidence of the petitioner's blood-alcohol level might have dissipated while the police obtained a warrant."

Illinois v. Lafayette 462 U.S. 640, 77 L.Ed. 65, 103 S.Ct. 2605 (1983) the Court, in an opinion by Burger for 7 members of the court with Marshall and Brennan concurring, held that routine inventory and search of any container or article in the possession of a person during booking at a police station was not unreasonable.

Washington v. Chrisman 455 U.S. 1, 70 L.Ed. 2d 778, 102 S.Ct. 812 (1982) the Court, 6–3, in an opinion by Burger, held that a police officer has the right to monitor the movements of an arrested person following arrest. In this case the officer accompanied student back into dormitory room so that he could retrieve necessary identification and upon entering the room saw contraband in plain view.

Stegald v. United States 451 U.S. 204, 68 L.Ed. 2d 38, 101 S.Ct. 1642 (1981) the Court, in an opinion by Marshall joined by 5 justices, held that defendant's right of privacy had been invaded when, absent consent or exigent circumstances, officers entered his house to search for another person. During search incriminating evidence leading to defendant's arrest was found. The Court held that an arrest warrant adequately protected rights of person to be arrested but did not justify intrusion into privacy of another.

Payton v. New York 445 U.S. 573, 63 L.Ed. 2d 639, 100 S.Ct. 1371 (1980) the Court, 6–3, in an opinion by Stevens, held that police are prohibited from making warrantless, nonconsensual entry into a suspect's home in order to make a routine felony arrest. Warrant may be dispensed with in exigent circumstances.

Michigan v. DeFillipo 443 U.S. 31, 61 L.Ed. 2d 343, 99 S.Ct. 2627 (1979) the Court, 6–3, in an opinion by Burger, held that warrantless arrest in good-faith reliance on ordinance was valid regardless of fact that ordinance was later held to be unconstitutional.

Pennsylvania v. Mimms 434 U.S. 106, 54 L.Ed. 2d 331, 98 S.Ct. 330 (1977) the Court, 6–3, in a *per curiam* opinion, held that when a police officer lawfully stops a motorist for a traffic violation, the officer may order the motorist out of the car without reason to suspect foul play from the particular driver at the time of the stop. "Pat down" search for weapons requires reasonable suspicion that the person is armed.

United States v. Santana 427 U.S. 38, 49 L.Ed. 2d 300, 96 S.Ct. 2406 (1976) the Court, 7–2, in an opinion by Rehnquist, held that a person in the threshold of his/her house was in a public place and could be arrested without a warrant. Police may pursue suspect into house when suspect attempts to avoid arrest.

United States v. Watson 423 U.S. 411, 46 L.Ed. 2d 598, 96 S.Ct. 820 (1976) the Court, in an opinion by White joined by 4 justices, held that a felony arrest could be made without a warrant in a public place. Facts that there were no exigent circumstances and that officers could have first obtained a warrant were immaterial.

United States v. Edwards 415 U.S. 800, 39 L.Ed. 2d 771, 94 S.Ct. 1234 (1974) the Court, 5–4 in an opinion by White, held that sending clothing worn at the time of booking to a crime laboratory for examination did not violate the suspect's rights. Clothing was not taken away from suspect until morning after booking because there was no jail clothing in an appropriate size on hand.

Gustafson v. Florida 414 U.S. 260, 38 L.Ed. 2d 456, 94 S.Ct. 488 (1973) (companion case to *United States v. Robinson* (1973)) the Court, 6–3 in an opinion by Rehnquist, held that a full search may be made incident to a custodial arrest even though the officer had no fear for his/her own safety and the offense was one for which there was no physical evidence that could be revealed by the search.

United States v. Robinson 414 U.S. 218, 38 L.Ed. 2d 427, 94 S.Ct. 467 (1973) the Court upheld, 6–3, searches incident to full custodial arrests in which arrests had been made on traffic code violations. Court rejected argument that a search incident to an arrest must be based on belief that search will produce weapon, evidence of crime, or contraband.

Whiteley v. Warden 401 U.S. 560, 28 L.Ed. 2d 306, 91 S.Ct. 1031 (1971) the Court, 6–3 in an opinion by Harlan, held that a police radio broadcast based on an affidavit insufficient for issuance of an arrest warrant cannot furnish probable cause to arrest the suspect described in the broadcast.

Vale v. Louisiana 399 U.S. 30, 26 L.Ed. 2d 409, 90 S.Ct. 1969 (1970) the Court, 7–2 in an opinion by Stewart, held that an arrest outside the house, even if made on the front steps as the suspect was about to enter the house, did not justify the search of the house as part of the search incident to the arrest.

Chimel v. California 395 U.S. 752, 23 L.Ed. 2d 685, 89 S.Ct. 2034 (1969) the Court, 6–2 in an opinion by Stewart, held that a search incident to a lawful arrest in a home must be limited to "the area into which an arrestee might reach in order to grab a weapon or other evidentiary items." *Chimel* expressly overrules *Harris* (1947), and *Rabinowitz* (1950).

Davis v. Mississippi 394 U.S. 721, 22 L.Ed. 2d 676, 89 S.Ct. 1394 (1969) a landmark case holding that fingerprints taken as a result of an illegal arrest were inadmissible in evidence.

Warden v. Hayden 387 U.S. 294, 18 L.Ed. 2d 782, 87 S.Ct. 1642 (1967) in an 8–1 decision, the Court decided that items such as clothing may be seized by the police during lawful searches of the suspect's residence or other locations. This case abrogated the "mere evidence" rule.

Schmerber v. California 384 U.S. 757, 16 L.Ed. 2d 908, 86 S.Ct. 1826 (1966) the Court, 5–4 in an opinion by Brennan, held that in a drunk driving case the prosecution can use as evidence the analysis of a blood sample taken without the consent of the accused without violating his Fourth, Fifth, Sixth, and Fourteenth Amendment rights. The Court distinguished between the production of compelled physical evidence and testimonial compulsion, i.e., words produced by someone's lips.

C. Border Searches

United States v. Montoya de Hernandez 473 U.S. 531, 87 L.Ed. 2d 381, 105 S.Ct. 3304 (1985) the Court, in an opinion by Rehnquist for 6 justices, held that detention of a traveler at the international border, beyond the scope of the routine Customs search and inspection, is justified at its inception if Customs agents, considering all the facts surrounding the traveler and his/her trip, reasonably suspect that the traveler is smuggling contraband in his/her alimentary canal. Incommunicado detention for almost 16 hours to allow suspect, who refused to be x-rayed, to have a bowel movement, prior to seeking a search warrant, was justified under the circumstances.

Immigration and Naturalization Service v. Delgado 466 U.S. 210, 80 L.Ed. 2d 247, 104 S.Ct. 1758 (1984) the Court, in an opinion by Rehnquist for 6 justices, held that INS "factory surveys" and questioning of individual employees did not constitute detention or seizure under the Fourth Amendment. "Factory surveys" consisted of entry into factories, pursuant to a warrant, and questioning employees regarding immigration or citizenship status. Exits to the factory were guarded by INS agents while this procedure took place.

United States v. Villamonte-Marquez 462 U.S. 579, 77 L.Ed. 2d 22, 103 S.Ct. 2573 (1983) the Court, 6–3 in an opinion by Rehnquist, held that the Fourth Amendment is not violated when Customs agents board vessels to conduct document checks without suspicion that a statute is being violated.

United States v. Cortez 449 U.S. 411, 66 L.Ed. 2d 621, 101 S.Ct. 690 (1981) the Court, in an opinion by Burger for 7 justices, held that border patrol officers investigating a specific person for smuggling aliens into the United States could stop a vehicle based on reasonable suspicion for the purpose of questioning the occupants about their citizenship, immigration status, and the reasons for their presence in the area.

United States v. Ramsey 431 U.S. 606, 52 L.Ed. 2d 617, 97 S.Ct. 1972 (1977) the Court, in an opinion by Rehnquist for 6 justices, held that Customs officers could open and search mail entering the United States without probable cause or a warrant.

United States v. Martinez-Fuerte 428 U.S. 543, 49 L.Ed. 2d 1116, 96 S.Ct. 3074 (1976) the Court, in an opinion by Powell for 7 justices, held that the Fourth Amendment was not violated by stops of vehicles at permanent border patrol checkpoints for brief questioning of their occupants regarding immigration status, even though there was no reason to believe that the particular vehicle contained illegal aliens. Fixed checkpoints do not need to be authorized in advance by judicial warrant.

United States v. Brignoni-Ponce 422 U.S. 873, 45 L.Ed. 2d 607, 95 S.Ct. 2574 (1975) the Court, in an opinion by Powell, held that at roving border patrol checkpoints a car may be briefly stopped for questioning and investigation if the officer's observations establish reasonable suspicion that a particular vehicle may contain aliens who are illegally in the country. The officer may question the driver and passengers about their citizenship and immigration status and may ask them to explain suspicious circumstances, but any further detention or search must be based on consent or probable cause.

United States v. Ortiz 422 U.S. 891, 45 L.Ed. 2d 623, 95 S.Ct. 2585 (1975) the Court, in an opinion by Powell for 6 justices, held that the search of a car at a fixed checkpoint required consent, probable cause, or a warrant. Searches must not be done on a random basis.

Almeida-Sanchez v. United States 413 U.S. 266, 37 L.Ed. 2d 596, 93 S.Ct. 2535 (1973) the Court, in an opinion by Steward for 5 justices, held that a search of an automobile more than 20 miles from the Mexican border at a roving border patrol checkpoint, without a search warrant, consent, or probable cause to believe there was evidence in the automobile, violated the Fourth Amendment.

D. Car and Other Vehicle Searches

Pennsylvania v. Labron 518 U.S. 938, 135 L.Ed. 2d 1031, 116 S.Ct. 2485 (1996) the Court, 7–2 in a *per curiam* opinion by Rehnquist, held that the Fourth Amendment right to search a car without a warrant was not contingent upon there being exigent circumstances necessitating rapid action.

Whren v. United States 517 U.S. 806, 135 L.Ed. 2d 89, 116 S.Ct. 1769 (1996) the Court, in a unanimous opinion by Scalia, held that the constitutionality of the detention of a motorist at a traffic stop depends on objective reasonableness, not the subjective motivation of the individual officers. Plainclothes officers' use of a traffic violation as grounds to stop a motorist, even though the department policy indicated they should not make such a stop, did not violate the Fourth Amendment because there was probable cause to believe a traffic violation had occurred.

California v. Acevedo 500 U.S. 565, 114 L.Ed. 2d 619, 111 S.Ct. 1982 (1991) the Court, 5–4 in an opinion by Blackmun, overruled *Arkansas v. Sanders* 422 U.S. 753 (1979) and held that police may conduct a warrantless search of a closed container in a vehicle if there is probable cause that evidence is in the container searched.

Florida v. Wells 495 U.S. 1, 109 L.Ed. 2d 1, 110 S.Ct. 1632 (1990) the Court, in an opinion by Rehnquist for 5 justices, held that the search of closed containers during the inventory of an automobile is only valid if the law enforcement agency has a policy regulating the actions of its officers in this type of situation.

Colorado v. Bertine 479 U.S. 367, 93 L.Ed. 2d 739, 107 S.Ct. 738 (1987) the Court, in an opinion by Rehnquist for 7 justices, held that the search of a closed backpack found in an impounded vehicle during a warrantless inventory search of the vehicle did not violate the Fourth Amendment.

New York v. Class 475 U.S. 106, 89 L.Ed. 2d 81, 106 S.Ct. 960 (1986) the Court, in an opinion by O'Connor for 5 justices, held that the Fourth Amendment was not violated by a police officer's finding a gun while reaching into a car to move papers obscuring the vehicle's identification number.

California v. Carney 471 U.S. 386, 85 L.Ed. 2d 406, 105 S.Ct. 2066 (1985) the Court, in an opinion by Burger for 6 justices, held that the warrantless search of a motor home did not violate the Fourth Amendment. Motor homes fall within the vehicle exception to the warrant requirement if they are readily mobile.

Michigan v. Long 463 U.S. 1032, 77 L.Ed. 2d 1201, 103 S.Ct. 3469 (1983) the Court, in an opinion by O'Connor for 5 members of the Court, held that during a stop of a vehicle on reasonable suspicion an officer may make a protective search of the passenger compartment, limited to those areas in which a weapon may be placed or hidden, if the officer reasonably believes that the suspect is dangerous and may gain immediate control of weapons.

United States v. Ross 456 U.S. 798, 72 L.Ed. 2d 572, 102 S.Ct. 2157 (1982) the Court, in an opinion by Stevens for 6 members of the Court, held the scope of a search of a vehicle under the probable cause exception is the same as the search that could be authorized by a magistrate under the circumstances.

New York v. Belton 453 U.S. 454, 69 L.Ed. 2d 768, 101 S.Ct. 2860 (1981) the Court, in an opinion by Stewart for 5 members of the Court, held that incident to a lawful custodial arrest of the occupant of a vehicle, an officer may search the entire passenger compartment including containers such as glove compartment, console, luggage, and clothing. Case overruled by *Robbins v. California* 453 U.S. 420 (1981).

South Dakota v. Opperman 428 U.S. 364, 49 L.Ed. 2d 1000, 96 S.Ct. 3092 (1976) the Court, 5, in an opinion by Burger, held routine inventories of cars taken into police custody do not violate the Fourth Amendment. Inventories must follow standard police procedures, not be pretexts for investigatory police motive, and be reasonable in scope.

Chambers v. Maroney 399 U.S. 42, 26 L.Ed. 2d 419, 90 S.Ct. 1975 (1970) is a U.S. Supreme Court landmark case on searches of automobiles, holding that if the officer has probable cause to believe that a car contains evidence of a crime and the car is mobile, the officer may search the car at the scene or move it to the police station or impound lot and search it there, in both instances without a warrant.

Cooper v. California 386 U.S. 58, 17 L.Ed. 2d 730, 87 S.Ct. 788 (1967) in this 5–4 opinion, the Court held that a search of an automobile is reasonable when by statute it is impounded for the purpose of forfeiture due to transportation of contraband, narcotics, alcohol, and unregistered firearms.

Preston v. United States 376 U.S. 364 11 L.Ed. 2d 777, 84 S.Ct. 881 (1963) a unanimous Court held that to qualify as a search incident to an arrest, an automobile must be searched at the time and place of arrest.

E. Closed Containers

California v. Acevedo 500 U.S. 565, 114 L.Ed. 2d 619, 111 S.Ct. 1982 (1991) the Court, in an opinion by Blackmun for 5 members, overruled *Arkansas v. Sanders* 422 U.S. 753 (1979) and held that police may conduct a warrantless search of a closed container in a vehicle if there is probable cause that evidence is in the container searched.

Florida v. Wells 495 U.S. 1, 109 L.Ed. 2d 1, 110 S.Ct. 1632 (1990) the Court, in an opinion by Rehnquist for 5 justices, held that the search of closed containers during the inventory of an automobile is only valid if the law enforcement agency has a policy regulating the actions of its officers in this type of situation.

Colorado v. Bertine 479 U.S. 367, 93 L.Ed. 2d 739, 107 S.Ct. 738 (1987) the Court, in an opinion by Rehnquist for 7 justices, held that the search of a closed backpack found in an impounded vehicle during a warrantless inventory search of the vehicle did not violate the Fourth Amendment.

Illinois v. Lafayette 462 U.S. 640, 77 L. Ed. 2d 65, 103 S.Ct. 2605 (1983) the Court, in an opinion by Burger for 7 members of the Court, held that during booking all items in the possession of a lawfully arrested person may be inventoried and searched without a warrant.

United States v. Ross 456 U.S. 798, 72 L.Ed. 2d 572, 102 S.Ct. 2157 (1982) the Court, in an opinion by Stevens for 6 members of the Court, held that a probable cause search of a car may include the contents of closed containers including glove compartments and consoles as well as luggage, packages, and clothing found in the vehicle.

New York v. Belton 453 U.S. 454, 69 L.Ed. 2d 768, 101 S.Ct. 2860 (1981) the Court, in an opinion by Stewart for 5 members of the Court, held that incident to a lawful custodial arrest of the occupant of a vehicle, an officer may search the entire passenger compartment including containers such as glove compartment, console, luggage, and clothing. Case overruled by *Robbins v. California* (1981).

United States v. Chadwick 433 U.S. 1, 53 L. Ed. 2d 538, 97 5. Ct. 2476 (1977) the Court, 7–2, in an opinion by Burger, held that a warrant was necessary to search a closed container.

F. Consent Searches

Ohio v. Robinette 519 U.S. 33, 136 L.Ed. 2d 347, 117 S.Ct. 417 (1996) the Court, 8–1 in an opinion by Rehnquist for 7 justices, held that consent obtained from a lawfully detained person before he is advised that he is "free to go" is valid; voluntariness of the consent is a question of fact to be determined from all the circumstances of the case.

Florida v. Bostick 501 U.S. 429, 115 L.Ed. 2d 389, 111 S.Ct. 2382 (1991) the Court, in a 6–3 opinion by O'Connor, held that a police officer may approach a person on a bus without cause and request consent to search luggage. Whether valid consent is given depends on the totality of the circumstances.

Florida v. Jimeno 500 U.S. 248, 114 L.Ed. 2d 297, 111 S.Ct. 1801 (1991) the Court, 7–2 in an opinion by Rehnquist, held that consent to search a vehicle includes consent to search closed containers found in the vehicle unless restrictions were placed on the consent when it was given.

Illinois v. Rodriguez 497 U.S. 177, 111 L.Ed. 2d 148, 110 S.Ct. 2793 (1990) the Court, in an opinion by Scalia for 6 justices, held that a consent search was valid when consent was obtained from a third party whom the police, at the time of the entry, reasonably believed to possess common authority over the premises, but who in fact did not have such authority.

Lo-Ji Sales, Inc. v. New York 442 U.S. 319, 60 L.Ed. 2d 920, 99 S.Ct. 2319 (1979) the Court, in a unanimous opinion by Burger, held that the fact that the defendant exhibited allegedly obscene items to the general public in an area of a store open to the public did not amount to consent for a sweeping search of the store.

United States v. Matlock 415 U.S. 164, 39 L.Ed. 2d 242, 94 S.Ct. 988 (1974) a majority of the Court in an opinion by White upheld the introduction into evidence of materials seized during the warrantless search of a bedroom because the common law wife of the defendant had consented to the search.

Schneckloth v. Bustamonte 412 U.S. 218, 36 L.Ed. 2d 854, 93 S.Ct. 2041 (1973) the Court, 7–2 in an opinion by White, held that advisement of Fourth Amendment rights is unnecessary as a prerequisite to a consent search in a noncustodial situation. The standard for the

evaluation of consent is voluntariness as determined from all the circumstances.

Bumper v. North Carolina 391 U.S. 543, 20 L.Ed. 2d 797, 88 S.Ct. 1788 (1968) the Court, 7–2 in an opinion by Stewart, held that no valid consent was obtained when permission to enter was given immediately after officers informed the occupant that they had a search warrant for the premises.

Stoner v. California 376 U.S. 483, 11 L.Ed. 2d 856, 84 S.Ct. 889 (1964) the Court held (with only Black dissenting, in part, on other grounds) that the search of defendant's hotel room without his consent and with neither search nor arrest warrants, violated his constitutional rights, even though the search was done with the consent of the hotel clerk.

G. Plain View and Open Fields Doctrines

California v. Hodari D. 499 U.S. 621, 113 L.Ed. 2d 690, 111 S.Ct. 1547 (1991) the Court, 7–2 in an opinion by Scalia, held that the seizure of a item discarded by a person who was being pursued by the police did not violate the Fourth Amendment where the police had not touched the person in order to make an arrest at the time the item was discarded.

Horton v. California 496 U.S. 128, 110 L.Ed. 2d 112, 110 S.Ct. 2301 (1990) the Court, in an opinion by Stevens for 7 justices, held that evidence does not need to be inadvertently discovered in order to be covered by the Plain View Doctrine. Case involved application for warrant to search for proceeds of robbery and weapons used by the robbers. Warrant was issued for proceeds but not weapons. When warrant was executed no proceeds were found but weapons discovered in plain view were seized.

California v. Greenwood 486 U.S. 35, 100 L.Ed. 2d 30, 108 S.Ct. 1625 (1988) the Court, in an opinion by White for 6 justices, held that the Fourth Amendment does not prohibit warrantless search and seizure of garbage left for collection outside the curtilage of a home.

Arizona v. Hicks 480 U.S. 321, 94 L.Ed. 2d 347, 107 S.Ct. 1149 (1987) the Court, in an opinion by Scalia for 6 justices, held that although the mere recording of serial numbers does not constitute a "seizure," moving a stereo found in plain view in order to obtain its serial number came within the Fourth Amendment as a "search" independent of actions that justified exigent entry into dwelling.

United States v. Dunn 480 U.S. 294, 94 L.Ed. 2d 326, 107 S.Ct. 1134 (1987) the Court, in an opinion by White for 6 justices, held that peering into the front of a barn without a search warrant did not violate the Fourth Amendment, because the barn was not within the curtilage of a dwelling, and observations made from open fields do not violate any other privacy expectations.

Dow Chemical Company v. United States 476 U.S. 227, 90 L.Ed. 2d 226, 106 S.Ct. 1819 (1986) the Court, in an opinion by Burger for 5 justices, held that the Environmental Protection Agency's aerial photography of Dow's 2,000-acre plant complex from navigable airspace without a warrant was not a search under the Fourth Amendment.

California v. Ciraclo 476 U.S. 207, 90 L.Ed. 2d 210, 106 S.Ct. 1809 (1986) the Court, in an opinion by Burger for 5 justices, held that the Fourth Amendment was not violated by warrantless aerial observation from an altitude of 1,000 feet of a fenced-in backyard within the curtilage of a home.

Oliver v. United States 466 U.S. 170, 80 L.Ed. 2d 214, 104 S.Ct. 1735 (1984) the Court, in an opinion by Powell for 5 members of the Court, held that Fourth Amendment protections do not extend to open fields beyond areas immediately surrounding a home.

Texas v. Brown 460 U.S. 730, 75 L.Ed. 2d 502, 103 S.Ct. 1319 (1983) the Court, although unable to agree upon an opinion, held that seizure of evidence in plain view did not violate the warrant requirement of the Fourth Amendment.

H. Stop-and-Frisk

Maryland v. Wilson 519 U.S. 408, 137 L.Ed. 2d 41, 117 S.Ct. 882 (1997) the Court, 7–2 in an opinion by Rehnquist, held that police officers may routinely order passengers out of vehicles that are legally stopped. No showing of suspicion or probable cause regarding the passengers' activities need be present. The Court did not address the issue of whether a passenger could be detained or searched once out of the vehicle.

Minnesota v. Dickerson 508 U.S. 366, 124 L.Ed. 2d 334, 113 S.Ct. 2130 (1993) the Court, in an opinion by White in which all justices concurred on the rule but not the application to the facts of this case, held that an officer may seize nonthreatening contraband detected during a protective patdown search under *Terry v. Ohio* only if, by the object's contour or mass, its identity is immediately apparent. Six justices agreed that the actions of the officer in "squeezing, sliding and otherwise manipulating the contents of the defendant's pocket" to identify a lump of crack cocaine that weighed one-fifth of a gram went beyond what was permissible.

Alabama v. White 496 U.S. 325, 110 L.Ed. 2d 301, 110 S.Ct. 2412 (1990) the Court, in an opinion by White for 6 justices, held that a modified version of the *Gates* "totality of the circumstances" test could be used to establish reasonable suspicion. Both the content of information possessed by police and its degree of reliability are considered in accessing the "totality of the circumstances."

United States v. Sokolow 490 U.S. 1, 104 L.Ed. 2d 1, 109 S.Ct. 1581 (1989) the Court, in an opinion by Rehnquist for 7 justices, held that an investigative stop could be based on the totality of the circumstances even though each individual item was a legal act.

Pennsylvania v. Bruder 488 U.S. 9, 102 L.Ed. 2d 172, 109 S.Ct. 205 (1988) the Court, in a *per curiam* opinion for 7 justices, held that no Miranda warnings are required during a routine traffic stop because the motorist's freedom of action is not curtailed to a degree associated with formal arrest.

Michigan v. Chesternut 486 U.S. 567, 100 L.Ed. 2d 565, 108 S.Ct. 1975 (1988) the Court, in a unanimous opinion by Blackmun, held that, under the facts of this case, an "investigatory pursuit" of a suspect during which officers drove alongside the suspect but did not stop him did not amount to a seizure within the meaning of the Fourth Amendment because it would not have communicated to a reasonable person that he/she was not at liberty to ignore the police presence and go about his/her business.

Hayes v. Florida 470 U.S. 811, 84 L.Ed. 2d 705, 105 S.Ct. 1643 (1985) the Court, in an opinion by White for 5 justices, held that police acting without probable cause, a warrant, or consent cannot transport a suspect to the police station for fingerprinting. Brief detention in the field based on reasonable suspicion for purpose of fingerprinting may be permissible under Fourth Amendment.

United States v. Sharpe 470 U.S. 675, 84 L.Ed. 2d 605, 105 S.Ct. 1568 (1985) the Court, in an opinion by Burger for 6 justices, held that the Fourth Amendment imposes no rigid time limitations on investigative detentions. Given the circumstances of the case, the investigation was conducted in a diligent and reasonable manner, and a 20-minute stop was not unreasonable.

New Jersey v. T.L.O. 469 U.S. 325, 83 L.Ed. 2d 720, 105 S.Ct. 733 (1985) the Court, in an opinion by White, relevant parts of which were signed by 8 justices, held that the Fourth Amendment applies to searches by public school officials. These searches are judged on reasonableness under all the circumstances and do not require probable cause if school officials believe that a student is currently violating, or has violated, a school regulation or the law.

United States v. Hensley 469 U.S. 221, 83 L.Ed. 2d 604, 105 S.Ct. 675 (1985) the Court, in a unanimous decision by O'Connor, held that police officers may make an investiga-

tive stop in objective reliance on a "wanted flyer" issued by another police department, so long as the flyer was issued on the basis of reasonable suspicion that the wanted person had committed an offense.

Michigan v. Long 463 U.S. 1032, 77 L.Ed. 2d 1201, 103 S.Ct. 3469 (1983) the Court, in an opinion by O'Connor for 5 justices, held that a protective search of the passenger compartment of a vehicle is permissible when the vehicle has been stopped on reasonable suspicion and the officer reasonably believes the occupants are dangerous and may gain immediate access to weapons inside the vehicle. The fact officers intended to release the suspect(s) is immaterial.

United States v. Place 462 U.S. 696, 77 L.Ed. 2d 110, 103 S.Ct. 2637 (1983) the Court, in an opinion by O'Connor for 6 justices, held that the Fourth Amendment was not violated by temporary detention of personal luggage based on reasonable suspicion for the purpose of allowing a dog trained in narcotics detection to sniff it. The Court found that a 90-minute detention in this case was unreasonable and invalidated the search.

Brown v. Texas 443 U.S. 47, 61 L.Ed. 2d 357, 99 S.Ct. 2637 (1979) the Court, in a unanimous opinion by Burger, held a Texas law was invalid insofar as it allowed officers to require a person to identify him/herself when there was no reasonable suspicion that the person was, or had been, engaged in criminal activity.

Dunaway v. New York 442 U.S. 200, 60 L.Ed. 2d 824, 99 S.Ct. 2248 (1979) the Court, in an opinion by Brennan for 6 justices, held that a suspect cannot be detained and transported to a police station for interrogation without probable cause to arrest.

Delaware v. Prouse 440 U.S. 648, 59 L.Ed. 2d 660, 99 S.Ct. 1391 (1979) the Court, 8–1 in an opinion by White, held that police may not stop the driver of a vehicle in order to check his driver's license and car registration absent at least reasonable suspicion that the driver is unlicensed, the vehicle is unregistered, or it is otherwise subject to seizure for violation of the law.

Terry v. Ohio 392 U.S. 1, 20 L.Ed. 2d 889, 88 S.Ct. 1868 (1968) the Court held, 8–1, that a person may be detained without probable cause to make an arrest if there is reasonable suspicion that criminal activity is afoot. Reasonable suspicion must be based on specific, articulable facts from which reasonable inferences may be drawn. When a reasonably prudent officer has a reasonable suspicion that he/she or others in the area are in danger, a "frisk" may be justified when its purpose is to "discover guns, knives, clubs, or other hidden instruments for assault of the police officer." The "frisk" must be limited in scope to a patdown of the outer clothing of the suspect for weapons.

I. Warrants

Griffin v. Wisconsin 483 U.S. 868, 97 L.Ed. 2d 709, 107 S.Ct. 3164 (1987) the Court, in an opinion by Scalia for 5 justices, held that the warrantless search of a probationer's home by probation officers was "reasonable" within the meaning of the Fourth Amendment because it was conducted pursuant to a valid regulation governing probationers. Information provided by a police officer, whether or not on the basis of firsthand knowledge, may be used to justify searching a probationer.

New York v. Burger 482 U.S. 691, 96 L.Ed. 2d 601, 107 S.Ct. 2636 (1987) the Court, in an opinion by Blackmun for 6 justices, held that the warrantless search of an automobile junkyard conducted pursuant to state statutes falls within the exception for warrantless administrative inspections of pervasively regulated industries.

O'Connor v. Ortega 480 U.S. 709, 94 L.Ed. 2d 714, 107 S.Ct. 1492 (1987) the Court, in an opinion by O'Connor for 5 justices, held a public employee has a reasonable expectation of privacy in his/her desk and file cabinets which he/she did not share with any other employees and where personal materials are kept.

New York v. P J Video 475 U.S. 868, 89 L.Ed. 2d 871, 106 S.Ct. 1610 (1986) the Court, in an opinion by Rehnquist for 6 justices, held that the same standard of probable cause should be used for obtaining a search warrant authorizing the seizure of allegedly obscene material as is required for items not protected by the First Amendment.

Winston v. Lee 470 U.S. 753, 84 L.Ed. 2d 662, 105 S.Ct. 1611 (1985) the Court, in an opinion by Brennan for 6 justices, using a balancing test held that surgery was an unreasonable search under the Fourth Amendment. The Court found that the state had failed to show a compelling need for the bullet that would have had to be surgically removed from the defendant. Court order for the surgery might be approved if there was a compelling showing of need for the evidence and the medical risk to the suspect was low.

Thompson v. Louisiana 469 U.S. 17, 83 L.Ed. 2d 246, 105 S.Ct. 409 (1984), the Court, in a unanimous *per curiam* opinion, held that there is no exception to the warrant clause that enables police officers to conduct a two-hour search of the scene of a recent homicide in the defendant's home even though the police were called to investigate by a family member who did not live there.

Illinois v. Andreas 463 U.S. 765, 77 L.Ed. 2d 1003, 103 S.Ct. 3319 (1983) the Court, 6–3 in an opinion by Burger, held that no warrant was required to reopen a package containing drugs that had been discovered at an airport by customs inspectors. The package had been resealed, delivered to the addressee, and kept under surveillance except for about 30–45 minutes between delivery to the defendant and his arrest.

Illinois v. Gates 462 U.S. 213, 76 L.Ed. 2d 527, 103 S.Ct. 2317 (1983) the Court, in an opinion by Rehnquist for 5 justices, held that the reliability of an informant in search warrant cases should be based on the "totality of the circumstances" instead of the rigid "two-pronged test" of *Aguilar* and *Spinelli.* Prior reliability does not have to be established if the information provided is sufficiently detailed and has indicia of credibility.

Michigan v. Summers 452 U.S. 692, 69 L.Ed. 2d 340, 101 S.Ct. 2587 (1981) the Court, 6–3 in an opinion by Stevens, held that a valid warrant for the search of a dwelling implicitly contains the authority to detain the occupants of the premises while the warrant is being lawfully executed.

Ybarra v. Illinois 444 U.S. 85, 62 L.Ed. 2d 238, 100 S.Ct. 338 (1979) the Court, 6–3 in an opinion by Stewart, held that the search of patrons of a bar, during the execution of a search warrant directed at the seizure of narcotics to be found in the bar or on the person of the bartender, violated the Fourth Amendment.

Franks v. Delaware 438 U.S. 154, 57 L.Ed. 2d 667, 98 S.Ct. 2674 (1978) the Court, 7–2, in an opinion by Blackmun, held that a defendant could attack the validity of a search warrant based on the fact that officers had knowingly and intentionally, or with reckless disregard of the truth, used false statements in the affidavit supporting said warrant. If the defendant established that such statements were in the affidavit by a preponderance of the evidence, the remaining untainted information in the affidavit must be reassessed to determine if there is probable cause to support the issuance of the warrant.

Mincey v. Arizona 437 U.S. 385, 57 L.Ed. 2d 290, 98 S.Ct. 2408 (1978) the Court, in an opinion by Stewart for 7 justices, held that there is no "murder scene" exception to the requirement that police obtain a search warrant.

Michigan v. Tyler 436 U.S. 499, 56 L.Ed. 2d 486, 98 S.Ct. 1942 (1978) the Court, although unable to agree upon an opinion, held that no search warrant was required when firefighters entered a building to extinguish a fire, or to conduct an investigation of the cause of the fire immediately after the fire was out and for a reasonable amount of time

thereafter. Re-entry at later times requires a search warrant.

Marshall v. Barlow's Inc. 436 U.S. 307, 56 L.Ed. 2d 305, 98 S.Ct. 1816 (1978) the Court, 5–3 with Brennan not participating, in an opinion by White, held nonconsensual inspections by Occupational Safety and Health Administration inspectors violated the Fourth Amendment unless conducted pursuant to a search warrant or an administrative warrant as described in *Camara.*

Connally v. Georgia 429 U.S. 245, 50 L.Ed. 2d 444, 97 S.Ct. 546 (1977) the Court, in a unanimous *per curiam* opinion, held a state law unconstitutional that permitted the issuance of search warrants by an unsalaried justice of the peace who received a fee when a search warrant was issued, but none if the application for a warrant was denied.

United States v. Miller 425 U.S. 435, 48 L.Ed. 2d 71, 96 S.Ct. 1619 (1976) the Court, 7–2, in an opinion by Powell, held that bank records could be subpoenaed for use in a criminal case and that a search warrant was not required.

Coolidge v. New Hampshire 403 U.S. 443, 29 L.Ed. 2d 564, 91 S.Ct. 2022 (1971) the Court, in an opinion by Stewart, held that search warrants must be issued by a "neutral and detached magistrate." State law authorizing a deputy attorney general or a police captain, who were designated justices of the peace, to issue search warrants was found to be invalid.

Spinelli v. United States 393 U.S. 110, 21 L.Ed. 2d 637, 89 S.Ct. 584 (1969) the Court, 5–3 in an opinion by Harlan, applied the two-pronged *Aguilar* test to cases where the informant had not been previously proven to be reliable. The test established in this case was later replaced by the "totality of the circumstances test" in *Illinois v. Gates* (1983).

Camara v. Municipal Court 387 U.S. 523, 18 L.Ed. 2d 930, 87 S.Ct. 1727; *See v. Seattle* 387 U.S. 541, 18 L.Ed. 2d 943, 87 S.Ct. 1737

(1967) the Court, in an opinion by White for 6 justices, held that health and fire inspectors are not entitled to search a home or business without warrant or consent. A diluted probable cause standard based on reasonable legislative or administrative standards for conducting an inspection of the area must be satisfied. *Frank v. Maryland*, 359 U.S. 360, was expressly overruled.

McCray v. Illinois 386 U.S. 300, 18 L.Ed. 2d 62, 87 S.Ct. 1056 (1967) the Court, 5–4 in an opinion by Stewart, held that a reliable informant's identity generally need not be disclosed pretrial on a motion to suppress.

Aguilar v. Texas 378 U.S. 108, 12 L.Ed. 2d 723, 84 S.Ct. 1509 (1964) the Court held that the magistrate issuing the warrant must be advised: (1) of the underlying circumstances from which the affiant concluded that probable cause existed; and (2) of the underlying circumstances from which the affiant concluded that the informant, whose identity need not be revealed in the affidavit, was "credible" or his/her information "reliable." This established the so-called *Aguilar* two-prong test, which was replaced by the "totality of the circumstances test" in *Illinois v. Gates* (1983).

J. Wiretapping and Electronic Surveillance

United States v. Karo 468 U.S. 705, 82 L.Ed. 2d 530, 104 S.Ct. 3296 (1984) the Court, in an opinion by White for 4 justices with other justices concurring in relevant parts, held that the installation of an electronic beeper in a container, with the consent of the person who owned it at the time the beeper was installed, does not violate the Fourth Amendment rights of the purchaser of the container even though it was purchased without knowledge that it contained a monitoring device. It was also held that monitoring of this beeper after it entered the residence of the suspect, and was out of view from common areas, violated the right of privacy of the suspect.

United States v. Knotts 460 U.S. 276, 75 L.Ed. 2d 55, 103 S.Ct. 1081 (1983) the Court, in an

opinion by Rehnquist for 5 justices, held that the monitoring of a beeper, installed inside a container of chloroform, did not invade the suspect's reasonable expectation of privacy. The Court found no difference between this method of tracking a person's movements and visual surveillance.

Smith v. Maryland 442 U.S. 735, 61 L.Ed. 2d 220, 99 S.Ct. 2577 (1979) the Court, 5–3, in an opinion by Blackmun, held that the installation and use of a pen register, at the offices of the telephone company, did not violate the suspect's reasonable expectation of privacy and did not require the authorization of a warrant. (A pen register is a device that records the telephone numbers called but not the audio portion of the conversation.) NOTE: Congress later passed laws requiring a court order to install a pen register. See 18 U.S.C. §3121 et al.

Dalia v. United States 441 U.S. 238, 60 L.Ed. 2d 177, 99 S.Ct. 1682 (1979) the Court, in an opinion by Powell for 5 justices, held that the right to covertly enter a private premises in order to install an electronic listening device was implicit in an electronic surveillance warrant issued under Title Ill of the Omnibus Crime Control and Safe Streets Act. No specific authorization for such activity need be mentioned in the warrant itself.

United States v. Caceres 440 U.S. 741, 59 L.Ed. 2d 733, 99 S.Ct. 1465 (1979) the Court, 7–2, in an opinion by Stevens, held that tape-recorded nontelephonic conversations between the defendant and an IRS agent were admissible into evidence despite the fact that the conversations were tape-recorded in violation of agency regulations and without the defendant's consent.

Scott v. United States 436 U.S. 128, 56 L.Ed. 2d 168, 98 S.Ct. 1717 (1978) the Court, 7–2, in an opinion by Rehnquist, held that compliance with the minimization requirement for monitoring electronic surveillance, pursuant to a warrant obtained under Title Ill of the Omnibus Crime Control and Safe Streets Act, should be judged by an objective assessment of the actions of the officer(s) involved in light of the relevant circumstances. The subjective bad faith of the officer involved was not controlling.

United States v. New York Telephone Company 434 U.S. 159, 54 L.Ed. 2d 376, 98 S.Ct. 364 (1977) the Court, in an opinion by White for 5 justices, held that a telephone company must comply with a federal court order, issued under the All Writs Act, requiring it to assist law enforcement officers by installing a pen register.

United States v. Donovan 429 U.S. 413, 50 L.Ed. 2d 652, 97 S.Ct. 658 (1977) the Court, in an opinion by Powell for 5 justices, held that the application for a Title III warrant must give the names of all persons whom the government has probable cause to believe will engage in the criminal activity under investigation and whose conversations will be intercepted. Listing of "principal targets" is inadequate.

United States v. Kahn 415 U.S. 143, 94 S.Ct. 977, 39 L.Ed. 2d 225 (1974) the Court, 6–3, in opinion by Stewart, held that Title III requires the naming of a person as the target of a wiretap in the application or interception order only when the law enforcement authorities have probable cause to believe that that individual is "committing the offense" for which the wiretap is sought. Names of person known to be using the line to be tapped, but not known to be involved in the crime investigated, need not be included.

United States v. United States District Court, Eastern Michigan 407 U.S. 297, 32 L.Ed. 2d 752, 92 S.Ct. 2125 (1972) the Court, 6–2, in an opinion by Powell, refused to approve warrantless electronic monitoring of domestic "subversives."

United States v. White 401 U.S. 745, 28 L.Ed. 2d 453, 91 S.Ct. 1122 (1971) Justice White's opinion approves the warrantless use of informants who carry electronic recording devices.

Katz v. United States 389 U.S. 347, 19 L.Ed. 2d 576, 88 S.Ct. 507 (1967) the Court, with Black dissenting, held that the Fourth Amendment "protects people, not places," and as a result, eavesdropping carried on by electronic means (equivalent to wiretapping) constitutes a "search" and "seizure" and is subject to the warrant requirements of the Fourth Amendment-overruling *Olmstead v. United States* (1928).

Berger v. New York 388 U.S. 41, 18 L.Ed. 2d 1040, 87 S.Ct. 1873 (1967) the Court, 5–4, held New York State's permissive wiretap statute violated the Fourth and Fourteenth Amendments. The Court criticized the statute for allowing an electronic surveillance warrant to be issued without sufficient justification, authorizing nearly automatic renewal of the original order upon its expiration, and authorizing wiretaps for up to 90 days.

Osborn v. United States 385 U.S. 323, 17 L.Ed. 2d 394, 87 S.Ct. 429 (1966) the Court, 7–2 in an opinion by Stewart, held that a tape recording of incriminating conversation, obtained by a "friend" of the defendant, was admissible even though no warrant was obtained. Tapes of privileged conversations between defendant and attorney would not be admissible.

Hoffa v. United States 385 U.S. 293, 17 L.Ed. 2d 374, 87 S.Ct. 408 (1966) the Court, in an opinion by Stewart, held that the Fourth Amendment does not protect a wrongdoer's misplaced belief that a person to whom he voluntarily confides his wrongdoing will not reveal it.

Olmstead v. United States 277 U.S. 438, 73 L.Ed. 944, 48 S.Ct. 564 (1928) the Court, 5–4, in an opinion by Taft, held that messages passing over telephone wires were not within the protection of the Fourth Amendments, and for this reason, the Amendment did not apply unless there was a physical trespass on premises owned by, or under the control of, the defendant. Overruled by *Katz v. United States* (1967).

K. Other Fourth Amendment Issues

1. Use of Force

Graham v. Connor 490 U.S. 386, 104 L.Ed. 2d 443, 109 S.Ct. 1865 (1989) the Court, in an opinion by Rehnquist for 6 justices, held that in suits under 42 U.S.C. §1983, allegations of excessive force in a nonprison setting should be analyzed under the Fourth Amendment's "objective reasonableness" standard rather than under a substantive due process standard.

Tennessee v. Garner 471 U.S. 1, 85 L.Ed. 2d 1, 105 S.Ct. 1694 (1985) the Court, in an opinion by White for 6 justices, held that the Fourth Amendment prohibits the use of deadly force by police officers to prevent the escape of a suspected felon unless the force is necessary to prevent the escape and the officer has probable cause to believe that the suspect poses a significant threat of death or serious physical injury to the officer or another person.

2. Drug Testing

Chandler v. Miller 520 U.S. 305, 137 L.Ed. 2d 513, 117 S.Ct. 1295 (1997) the Court, 8–1 in an opinion by Ginsburg, held that Georgia's requirement that candidates for state office pass a drug test does not fit within the closely guarded category of constitutionally permissible searches that may be done without suspicion of wrongdoing.

Vernonia School District 47J v. Acton 515 U.S. 646, 132 L.Ed. 2d 564, 115 S.Ct. 2386 (1995) the Court, 6–3 in an opinion by Scalia, held that random urinalysis drug testing of students who participate in the school district's athletics programs did not violate the Fourth Amendment. The Court noted that prior notice that athletes would be tested decreased the students' expectation of privacy, the relative unobtrusiveness of the search, and the severity of the need the search was designed to meet, and concluded that the district's actions were reasonable.

Skinner v. Railway Labor Executives' Association 489 U.S. 602, 103 L.Ed. 2d 639, 109 S.Ct. 1402 (1989) the Court, in an opinion by Kennedy for 6 justices, held that regulations of the Federal Railroad Administration that mandate blood and urine tests of employees involved in certain train accidents did not violate the Fourth Amendment. The government's interest in testing without a showing of individualized suspicion was compelling because the employees subject to testing discharge duties fraught with such risks of injury to others that even a momentary lapse of attention could have disastrous consequences.

National Treasury Employees Union v. Raab 489 U.S. 656, 103 L.Ed. 2d 685, 109 S.Ct. 1384 (1989) the Court, in an opinion by Kennedy for 5 justices, held that the Fourth Amendment was not violated by a practice of the United States Customs Service that required a urinalysis test of employees who sought transfer or promotion to positions involving drug interdiction or the mandatory carrying of firearms.

3. Trash Searches

California v. Greenwood 486 U.S. 35, 100 L.Ed. 2d 30, 108 S.Ct. 1625 (1988) the Court, in an opinion by White for 6 justices, held that the Fourth Amendment does not prohibit warrantless search and seizure of garbage left for collection outside the curtilage of a home.

4. Sobriety Tests

Pennsylvania v. Muniz 496 U.S. 582, 110 L.Ed. 2d 528, 110 S.Ct. 2638 (1990) the Court, in an opinion by Brennan with 8 justices joining relevant parts, held that Miranda warnings were not required prior to videotaping sobriety test. Slurring of speech and evidence of lack of muscular coordination are not testimonial in nature. Questions that test recall or the ability to solve problems are testimonial and require Miranda warnings; standard booking questions (name, address, birth date, etc.) do not.

Michigan Department of State Police v. Sitz 496 U.S. 444, 110 L.Ed. 2d 412, 110 S.Ct. 2481 (1990) the Court, in an opinion by Rehnquist for 5 justices, held that sobriety checkpoints do not violate the Fourth Amendment. The Court addressed only the initial stop of each motorist passing through a checkpoint and the associated preliminary questioning and observation by checkpoint officers.

5. Knock and Announce

United States v. Ramirez 523 U.S. 65, 140 L.Ed. 2d 191, 118 S.Ct. 992 (1998) the Court, in a unanimous opinion by Rehnquist, reaffirmed that "no-knock" entries are justified when police officers have a "reasonable suspicion" that knocking and announcing their presence before entering would "be dangerous or futile, or… inhibit the effective investigation of the crime." The Court held that the standard is the same whether or not entry would result in the destruction of property.

Richards v. Wisconsin 520 U.S. 385, 137 L.Ed. 2d 615, 117 S.Ct. 1416 (1997) the Court, in a unanimous opinion by Stevens, held that it was an error to make a blanket exclusion from the "knock-notice" requirement for the execution of search warrants in felony drug investigations.

Wilson v. Arkansas 514 U.S. 927, 131 L.Ed. 2d 976, 115 S.Ct. 1914 (1995) the Court, in a unanimous opinion by Thomas, held that the common-law "knock and announce" principle forms a part of the reasonableness inquiry under the Fourth Amendment. The Court stated that there may be countervailing reasons why law enforcement would be excused from "knock and announce" in some cases but left the development of such exceptions to the lower courts.

6. Other Issues

Soldal v. Cook County 506 U.S. 56, 121 L.Ed. 2d 450, 113 S.Ct. 538 (1992) the Court, in a unanimous decision by White, held that law enforcement officers violated the Fourth Amendment by preventing interference by the tenant when the landlord of a private mobile home park towed away a trailer home. The officers involved knew that the eviction was unlawful and refused to assist the victim or take a trespassing complaint.

III IDENTIFICATION PROCEDURES

Manson v. Brathwaite 432 U.S. 98, 53 L.Ed. 2d 140, 97 S.Ct. 2243 (1977) the Court, 7–2, in an opinion by Blackmun, permitted the introduction into evidence of pretrial identification of the defendant, based on the totality of the circumstances, even though the method of making the identification was suggestive and unnecessary. This case involved identification made from a single photograph by an undercover police office who had purchased narcotics from the suspect.

United States v. Ash 413 U.S. 300, 37 L.Ed. 2d 619, 93 S.Ct. 1568 (1973) the Court, 6–3 in an opinion by Blackmun, held that a defendant has no right to the presence of counsel at a pretrial photographic lineup.

Neil v. Biggers 409 U.S. 188, 34 L.Ed. 2d 401, 93 S.Ct. 375 (1972) the Court, in an opinion by Powell for 7 justices, held that a stationhouse identification based on the viewing of a single suspect was admissible into evidence based on the totality of the circumstances. The factors to be considered in evaluating the likelihood of misidentification include: the opportunity of the witness to view the criminal at the time of the crime; the witness's degree of attention to the suspect during the crime; the accuracy of the witness's prior description of the criminal; the level of certainty demonstrated by the witness at the confrontation; and the length of time between the crime and the confrontation.

Kirby v. Illinois 406 U.S. 682, 32 L.Ed. 2d 411, 92 S.Ct. 1877 (1972) in a 4–4 opinion by Stewart (Powell concurring in the result), the Court held that after the formal charge is made (whether by preliminary hearing, indictment, information, or arraignment) a person is entitled to have counsel present at a lineup. The rule of *Wade* and *Gilbert* does not apply to pre-indictment confrontations.

Gilbert v. California 388 U.S. 263, 18 L.Ed. 2d 1178, 87 S.Ct. 1951 (1967) the Court restated the basic principle announced in *Wade* and refined it to clearly indicate that testimony that is the direct result of an illegal lineup is inadmissible.

United States v. Wade 388 U.S. 218, 18 L.Ed. 2d 1149, 87 S.Ct. 1926 (1967) held that the Sixth Amendment right to counsel applies to indicted defendants who are required to participate in lineups. The rule is applicable to the states through the due process clause of the Fourteenth Amendment.

IV FIFTH AMENDMENT ISSUES

A. *Self-Incrimination*

1. Confessions

Stansbury v. California 511 U.S. 318, 128 L.Ed. 2d 293, 114 S.Ct. 1526 (1994) the Court, in a unanimous *per curiam* opinion, held that for the purposes of determining whether Miranda warnings are required, the initial determination of custody depends on the objective circumstances of the interrogation, not on the subjective views harbored by either the interrogating officer or the person being questioned.

Davis v. United States 512 U.S. 452, 129 L.Ed. 2d 362, 114 S.Ct. 2350 (1994) the Court, in an opinion by O'Connor for 5 justices, held that Naval Investigative Service did not violate the suspect's Fifth Amendment rights by asking him to clarify his ambiguous remark, made during an interrogation session preceded by a valid Miranda waiver, about talking to a lawyer.

McNeil v. Wisconsin 501 U.S. 171, 115 L.Ed. 2d 158, 111 S.Ct. 2204 (1991) the Court, in a 6–3 opinion by Scalia, held that a defendant's invocation of his Sixth Amendment right to counsel during a judicial proceeding to set bail and schedule a preliminary examination did not constitute an invocation of the Miranda right to counsel.

Arizona v. Fulminante 499 U.S. 279, 113 L.Ed. 2d 302, 111 S.Ct. 1246 (1991) the Court, 5–4 in an opinion by White, held that a confession obtained by a prison informant, under circumstances where there was a credible threat of physical harm by other inmates unless the informant intervened, was coerced and violated due process; and 5–4 (a different majority) in an opinion by Rehnquist held that convictions from trials in which coerced confessions were introduced are subject to the harmless error rule rather than mandatory reversal.

Minnick v. Mississippi 498 U.S. 146, 112 L.Ed. 2d 489, 111 S.Ct. 486 (1990) the Court, 6–2 in an opinion by Kennedy, held that questioning may not resume without an attorney present if a person has been given Miranda warnings and invoked the right to counsel.

Pennsylvania v. Muniz 496 U.S. 582, 110 L.Ed. 2d 528, 110 S.Ct. 2638 (1990) the Court, in an opinion by Brennan with 8 justices joining relevant parts, held that Miranda warnings were not required prior to videotaping sobriety test. Slurring of speech and evidence of lack of muscular coordination are not testimonial in nature. Questions that test recall or the ability to solve problems are testimonial and require Miranda warnings; standard booking questions (name, address, birth date, etc.) do not.

Illinois v. Perkins 496 U.S. 292, 110 L.Ed. 2d 243, 110 S.Ct. 2394 (1990) the Court, in an opinion by Kennedy for 7 justices, held that Miranda warnings were not required when a suspect is unaware that he/she is speaking to a law enforcement officer and voluntarily gives a statement.

Michigan v. Harvey 494 U.S. 344, 108 L.Ed. 2d 293, 110 S.Ct. 1176 (1990) the Court, in an opinion by Rehnquist for 5 justices, held that while statements made during police-initiated interrogation after a suspect invokes his/her right to counsel cannot be used as substantive evidence, they can be used to impeach.

Duckworth v. Eagan 492 U.S. 195, 106 L.Ed. 2d 166, 109 S.Ct. 2875 (1989) the Court, in an opinion by Rehnquist for 5 justices, held that the statement "We have no way of giving you a lawyer, but one will be appointed for you, if you wish, if and when you go to court" as a portion of the Miranda warnings did not render the confession inadmissible. The warnings must be considered in their totality.

Pennsylvania v. Bruder 488 U.S. 9, 102 L.Ed. 2d 172, 109 S.Ct. 205 (1988) the Court, in a *per curiam* opinion for 7 justices, held that no Miranda warnings are required during a routine traffic stop.

Patterson v. Illinois 487 U.S. 285, 101 L.Ed. 2d 261, 108 S.Ct. 2389 (1988) the Court, in an opinion by White for 5 justices, held that giving Miranda admonitions and obtaining a valid waiver of these rights prior to post-arraignment interrogation is sufficient to apprise the defendant of the nature of his/her Sixth Amendment rights and of the consequences of abandoning those rights.

Arizona v. Roberson 486 U.S. 675, 100 L.Ed. 2d 704, 108 S.Ct. 2093 (1988) the Court, in an opinion by Stevens for 6 justices, held that the rule in *Edwards v. Arizona*, which prohibits officers from questioning a person who has invoked his/her Miranda rights by requesting counsel, applies whether subsequent interrogations concern the same or different offenses. It also applies whether the same or different law enforcement authorities are involved in the subsequent interrogation.

Arizona v. Mauro 481 U.S. 520, 95 L.Ed. 2d 458, 107 S.Ct. 1931 (1987) the Court, in an opinion by Powell for 5 justices, held that statements the defendant made to his wife in the presence of a police officer were admissible even though he had invoked Miranda prior to the officer's agreeing to let him talk to his wife.

Colorado v. Spring 479 U.S. 364, 93 L.Ed. 2d 954, 107 S.Ct. 851 (1987) the Court, in an opinion by Powell for 7 justices, held that the suspect's awareness of all possible subjects of questioning in advance of interrogation is not relevant in determining whether Miranda waiver was valid.

Connecticut v. Barrett 479 U.S. 523, 93 L.Ed. 2d 920, 107 S.Ct. 828 (1987) the Court, in an opinion by Rehnquist for 6 justices, held that the Fifth Amendment does not require suppression of an oral confession where suspect was given Miranda warnings and agreed to make oral, but not written, statements to the police without an attorney present.

Colorado v. Connelly 479 U.S. 157, 93 L.Ed. 2d 473, 107 S.Ct. 515 (1986) the Court, in an opinion by Rehnquist for 5 justices, held that coercive police activity is a necessary predicate to finding a confession was not voluntary. A Miranda waiver need only be proven by preponderance of evidence.

Kuhlman v. Wilson 477 U.S. 436, 91 L.Ed. 2d 364, 106 S.Ct. 2616 (1986) the Court, in an opinion by Powell, pertinent parts of which were signed by 6 justices, held that in order to reverse a conviction in a case where a jailhouse informant testified that he was instructed to listen to defendant's statements but not to ask questions, defendant must demonstrate that the police and their informant took some action beyond mere passive listening to defendant's incriminating remarks.

Crane v. Kentucky 476 U.S. 683, 90 L.Ed. 2d 636, 106 S.Ct. 2142 (1986) the Court, in a unanimous opinion by O'Connor, held that a defendant may introduce evidence about the physical and psychological circumstances under which the confession was obtained in order to show lack of trustworthiness of a confession; this is based on constitutional guarantees of "a meaningful opportunity to present a complete defense," and is independent of a ruling on Miranda issues.

Michigan v. Jackson 475 U.S. 625, 89 L.Ed. 2d 631, 106 S.Ct. 1404 (1986) the Court, in an opinion by Stevens for 5 justices, held that a request for counsel at arraignment is presumed to be a request to be represented by counsel at all future proceedings, including interrogation.

Moran v. Burbine 475 U.S. 412, 89 L.Ed. 2d 410, 106 S.Ct. 1135 (1986) the Court, in an opinion by O'Connor for 6 justices, held that the failure of police to inform suspect of his attorney's telephone call did not affect validity of uncoerced waiver of Miranda rights; Sixth Amendment right to counsel and right to have counsel intercede does not attach until the first court appearance.

Wainwright v. Greenfield 474 U.S. 284, 88 L.Ed. 2d 623, 106 S.Ct. 634 (1985) the Court, in an opinion by Stevens for 7 justices, held that prosecutor's use of post-Miranda silence in closing arguments in not guilty by reason of insanity case (as evidence of defendant's degree of comprehension, which was inconsistent with defense's contention that defendant was paranoid schizophrenic) violated due process because it was fundamentally unfair, having violated the promise that "silence will carry no penalty."

Oregon v. Elstad 470 U.S. 298, 84 L.Ed. 2d 222, 105 S.Ct. 1285 (1985) the Court, in an opinion by O'Connor for 6 justices, held an uncoerced confession admissible where police officers had properly administered Miranda and obtained a waiver even though the officers had previously obtained damaging statements from the defendant in violation of Miranda.

Smith v. Illinois 469 U.S. 91, 83 L.Ed. 2d 488, 105 S.Ct. 490 (1984) the Court, in a *per curiam* opinion for 7 justices, held that when deciding whether a request for counsel during interrogation was ambiguous, an accused's post-request responses to further interrogation may not be used to cast doubt on the clarity of the initial request itself.

Berkemer v. McCarty 468 U.S. 420, 82 L.Ed. 2d 317, 104 S.Ct. 3138 (1984) the Court, in an opinion by Marshall for 8 members of the Court, held that every person is entitled to Miranda warnings prior to custodial interrogation regardless of the severity of the offense for which he/she is arrested or suspected.

New York v. Quarles 467 U.S. 649, 81 L.Ed. 2d 550, 104 S.Ct. 2626 (1984) the Court, in an opinion by Rehnquist for 5 members of the Court, held that an overriding consideration of public safety justified the officer's failure to provide Miranda warnings before asking questions regarding the location of a weapon the defendant had apparently abandoned immediately prior to arrest.

Minnesota v. Murphy 465 U.S. 420, 79 L.Ed. 2d 409, 104 S.Ct. 1136 (1984) the Court, in an opinion by White for 6 members of the Court, held that a probation officer does not have to give a probationer Miranda warnings prior to meetings required as a condition of probation.

Wyrick v. Fields 459 U.S. 42, 74 L.Ed. 2d 214, 103 S.Ct. 394 (1982) the Court, in a *per curiam* opinion expressing the views of 7 members of the Court, held that a suspect who requests a polygraph examination waives the right to have counsel present during the examination and post-polygraph questioning by the polygraph examiner.

Taylor v. Alabama 457 U.S. 687, 73 L.Ed. 2d 314, 102 S.Ct. 2664 (1982) the Court, in an opinion by Marshall for 5 members of the Court, held a confession obtained through custodial interrogation, after an illegal arrest, should be inadmissible unless the confession is sufficiently an act of free will to purge the taint of the illegal arrest.

California v. Prysock 453 U.S. 355, 69 L.Ed. 2d 696, 101 S.Ct. 2806 (1981) the Court, 6–3, in a *per curiam* opinion, held police do not need to give a verbatim rendition of Miranda warnings so long as the suspect is fully advised of his rights and no suggestion of any limitation of those rights is made.

Edwards v. Arizona 451 U.S. 477, 68 L.Ed. 2d 378, 101 S.Ct. 1880 (1981) the Court, in an opinion by White for 6 members of the

Court, held custodial interrogation can only be resumed, after a suspect has requested a lawyer, if the suspect has had an opportunity to consult with a lawyer or if the suspect initiates the conversation. See *Minnick v. Mississippi* 498 U.S. 146 (1990).

Rhode Island v. Innis 446 U.S. 291, 64 L.Ed. 2d 297, 100 S.Ct. 1682 (1980) the Court, in an opinion by Stewart for 5 members of the Court, held Miranda warnings are required whenever a suspect in custody is subjected to either express questioning or its functional equivalent. Interrogation includes both questioning and any words or actions on the part of the police that the officer(s) should know are reasonably likely to elicit an incriminating response.

Fare v. Michael C. 442 U.S. 707, 61 L.Ed. 2d 197, 99 S.Ct. 2560 (1979) the Court, in an opinion by Blackmun for 5 members of the Court, held that a juvenile's request to speak with his probation officer did not per se constitute an invocation of his Fifth Amendment right against self-incrimination.

North Carolina v. Butler 441 U.S. 369, 60 L.Ed. 2d 286, 99 S.Ct. 1755 (1979) the Court, 5–3 with Powell not participating, in an opinion by Stewart, held a waiver of Miranda rights should be determined by looking at the facts to see if the defendant knowingly and voluntarily waived his rights. An explicit waiver is not required.

Brewer v. Williams 430 U.S. 387, 51 L.Ed. 2d 424, 97 S.Ct. 1232 (1977) the Court, in an opinion by Stewart for 5 justices, held that indirect questioning of a suspect, after arraignment and without counsel present, violated his right to counsel.

Oregon v. Mathiason 429 U.S. 492, 50 L.Ed. 2d 714, 97 S.Ct. 711 (1977) the Court, in a *per curiam* opinion for 6 members of the Court, held that Miranda warnings were not required prior to interrogation of a parolee who voluntarily came to the police station and was allowed to leave the station without being arrested.

Michigan v. Mosley 423 U.S. 96, 46 L.Ed. 2d 313, 96 S.Ct. 321 (1975) the Court, in an opinion by Stewart for 5 members of the Court, held statements by a suspect who was in custody, made during an interrogation session two hours after invoking Miranda, may be used in court if the right of the suspect to cut off questioning has been scrupulously honored.

Brown v. Illinois 422 U.S. 590, 45 L.Ed. 2d 416, 95 S.Ct. 2254 (1975) the Court held, through Justice Blackmun, that the mere giving of the warnings required by Miranda does not dissipate the taint of a defendant's illegal arrest and render admissible statements given after the arrest.

Harris v. New York 401 U.S. 222, 28 L.Ed. 2d 1, 91 S.Ct. 643 (1971) the Court, 5–4, in an opinion by Chief Justice Burger, held that a prosecutor may use an illegally obtained confession to prove that a defendant who takes the witness stand is lying.

Orozco v. Texas 394 U.S. 324, 22 L.Ed. 2d 311, 89 S.Ct. 1095 (1969) the Court, 6–2 in an opinion by Black, held that once an accused is in custody, regardless of where he/she is in custody, Miranda warnings must be given, if a statement, or evidence derived therefrom, is to be admissible.

Gardner v. Broderick 392 U.S. 273, 20 L.Ed. 2d 1082, 88 S.Ct. 1913 (1968) the Court held that a policeman who refused to waive his Fifth Amendment privilege against self-incrimination cannot be dismissed from office solely because of his refusal. See *Lachance v. Erikson* 522 U.S. 262 (1998), page xxx.

Miranda v. Arizona 384 U.S. 436, 16 L.Ed. 2d 694, 86 S.Ct. 1602 (1966) the Court, 5–4, held that the privilege against self-incrimination is available outside of criminal court proceedings and applied to police interrogations of persons "in custody." Prior to custodial interrogation the following warnings must be given: (1) you have the right to remain silent; (2) anything you say can be used in a court of law against you; (3) you have the right to have an attorney with you during the interrogation; (4) if you are unable to hire an attorney one will be provided for you without cost during questioning.

Griffin v. California 380 U.S. 609, 14 L.Ed. 2d 106, 85 S.Ct. 1229 (1965) the Court held, 6–2, that the Fifth Amendment forbids a state prosecutor's comments on failure of a defendant to take the stand and explain evidence and bars an instruction from the Court that such silence may be evidence of guilt.

Escobedo v. Illinois 378 U.S. 478, 12 L.Ed. 2d 977, 84 S.Ct. 1758 (1964) the Court, held 5, "that when the process shifts from investigatory to accusatory and its purpose is to elicit a confession—our adversary system begins to operate, and, under the circumstances here, the accused must be permitted to consult with his lawyer."

Malloy v. Hogan 378 U.S. 1, 12 L.Ed. 2d 653, 84 S.Ct. 1489 (1964) the Court, 7–2, made the self-incrimination privilege of the Fifth Amendment applicable to the states through the due process clause of the Fourteenth Amendment. This case overruled *Adamson v. California*, 353 U.S. 46 (1947).

Massiah v. United States 377 U.S. 201, 12 L.Ed. 2d 246, 84 S.Ct. 1199 (1964) the Court held, 6–3, that no indicted defendant can be interrogated under any circumstances in the absence of his/her attorney without having his Sixth Amendment right to counsel impaired. *McLeod v. Ohio*, 381 U.S. 356 (1965) made the *Massiah* doctrine binding on the states under the Fourteenth Amendment.

2. Other Self-Incrimination Issues

United States v. Balsys 524 U.S. ___, 141 L.Ed. 2d 575, 118 S.Ct. 2218 (1998) the Court, 7–2 in an opinion by Souter for 5 justices, held that a person could not claim the Fifth Amendment privilege against self-incrimination based on fear of prosecution by a foreign nation.

United States v. Dunnigan 507 U.S. 87, 122 L.Ed. 2d 445, 113 S.Ct. 1111 (1993) the Court, in a unanimous opinion by Kennedy, held

United States Sentencing Commission Guidelines, which permit imposition of an enhanced sentence if the Court finds the defendant committed perjury at trial, do not violate the Fifth Amendment right to give testimony on one's own behalf.

Doe v. United States 487 U.S. 201, 101 L.Ed. 2d 184, 108 S.Ct. 2341 (1988) the Court, in an opinion by Blackmun for 8 justices, held that the Fifth Amendment was not violated by a court order compelling a target of a grand jury investigation to authorize foreign banks to disclose records of his accounts. The Court found that the consent directive, which the target was required to sign in order for the banks to release records, was not testimonial in nature.

Allen v. Illinois 478 U.S. 364, 92 L.Ed. 2d 296, 106 S.Ct. 2988 (1986) the Court, in an opinion by Rehnquist for 5 justices, held that the Fifth Amendment guarantee against compulsory self-incrimination does not apply to proceedings under the Illinois Sexually Dangerous Person Act because the enabling legislation declares them to be civil proceedings.

United States v. Doe 465 U.S. 605, 79 L.Ed. 2d 552, 104 S.Ct. 1237 (1984) the Court, in an opinion by Powell for 6 members of the Court, held that the contents of documents subpoenaed by a grand jury were not privileged under the self-incrimination clause because they were not prepared involuntarily and the person subpoenaed was not forced to restate, repeat, or affirm the truth of the documents. However, the act of producing the documents, if compelled of the person who made them, is privileged because it involves testimonial self-incrimination.

South Dakota v. Neville 459 U.S. 553, 74 L.Ed. 2d 748, 103 S.Ct. 916 (1983) the Court, 7–2, in an opinion by O'Connor, held that the admission into evidence of the fact that defendant refused to submit to a blood-alcohol test did not offend the privilege against self-incrimination.

Andresen v. Maryland 427 U.S. 463, 49 L.Ed. 2d 627, 96 S.Ct. 2737 (1976) the Court, 7–2, in an opinion by Blackmun, held that the privilege against self-incrimination was not violated by the admission into evidence of personal files of an attorney, seized during a search of his law office pursuant to a search warrant. Defendant voluntarily made the documents and they were authenticated by someone other than the defendant.

Fisher v. United States 425 U.S. 391, 48 L.Ed. 2d 39, 96 S.Ct. 1569 (1976) the Court, in an opinion by White expressing the views of 6 members of the Court, held the privilege against self-incrimination did not bar the enforcement of a summons for the production of records prepared by the defendant's accountant and held by the defendant's attorney.

United States v. Nobles 422 U.S. 225, 45 L.Ed. 2d 141, 95 S.Ct. 2160 (1975) the Court, 8–0 with Douglas not participating, in an opinion by Powell, held that the privilege against self-incrimination did not prevent disclosure of the reports of a defense investigator who had taken the stand.

B. Double Jeopardy

Monge v. California 524 U.S. ___, 141 L.Ed. 2d 615, 118 S.Ct. 2246 (1998) the Court, 5–4 in an opinion by O'Connor, held that the double jeopardy clause does not prohibit retrial of the recidivism issue under a "three strikes" law, where a bifurcated trial was held and the defendant was convicted of the substantive offense but an appellate court ruled that insufficient evidence of the prior offense was introduced at the sentencing hearing.

Hudson v. United States 522 U.S. 93, 139 L.Ed. 2d 450, 118 S.Ct. 488 (1997) the Court, in an opinion by Rehnquist with 4 concurring opinions and no dissents, held that the double jeopardy clause does not bar criminal prosecution of a defendant who has been previously subjected to civil administrative proceedings that resulted in monetary penalties and occupational debarment for violation of federal banking statutes. The Court relied upon the fact that the prior proceedings were civil rather than criminal and explicitly stated that this

ruling largely disavows method of analysis used in *United States v. Halper* 490 U.S. 435 (1989) and reaffirms the previously established rule exemplified in *United States v. Ward* 448 U.S. 242 (1980).

United States v. Watts 519 U.S. 148, 136 L.Ed. 2d 554, 117 S.Ct. 633 (1996) the Court, in a *per curiam* opinion for 7 justices with 1 dissenting opinion, held that a federal judge sentencing a convicted defendant could consider facts from cases that resulted in acquittals. Federal sentencing guidelines permit consideration of evidence established by a preponderance of the evidence.

Witte v. United States 515 U.S. 389, 132 L.Ed. 2d 351, 115 S.Ct. 2199 (1995) the Court, in an opinion by O'Connor for 6 justices with 2 additional justices concurring, held that double jeopardy was not violated by a federal cocaine conviction, even though the facts that gave rise to the prosecution had previously been considered when sentencing the defendant on a federal marijuana offense.

United States v. Dixon 509 U.S. 688, 125 L.Ed. 2d 556, 113 S.Ct. 2849 (1993) the Court, in an opinion by Scalia for 5 justices, held that double jeopardy bars prosecution on substantive criminal charges based on the same elements for which nonsummary criminal contempt was previously imposed. *Grady v. Corbin* 495 U.S. 508 (1990) was overruled. The Court reverts to the rule in *Blockburger v. United States* 220 U.S. 338 (1911), which bars the second prosecution if the second crime contains the same elements as the first.

United States v. Felix 503 U.S. 378, 118 L.Ed. 2d 25, 112 S.Ct. 1377 (1992) the Court, 7–2 but unanimous in parts, in an opinion by Rehnquist, held introduction of evidence as "prior acts evidence" at one trial does not bar the same acts from being the subject of criminal charges at a later trial. For double jeopardy purposes, charges of conspiracy are distinct from the underlying offense, and prosecution for the underlying offense does not bar later prosecution for the conspiracy.

United States v. Halper 490 U.S. 435, 104 L.Ed. 2d 487, 109 S.Ct. 1892 (1989) the Court, in a unanimous opinion by Blackmun, held that under the double jeopardy clause a defendant who already has been punished in a criminal prosecution may be subjected to an additional civil sanction to the extent that the second sanction may fairly be characterized as remedial, such as restitution, but not if it is for deterrence or retribution.

Ricketts v. Adamson 483 U.S. 1, 97 L.Ed. 2d 1, 107 S.Ct. 2860 (1987) the Court, in an opinion by White for 5 justices, held that double jeopardy was not violated by prosecution of the defendant for first-degree murder following his breach of a plea agreement under which he had pled guilty to a lesser offense, had been sentenced, and had begun serving a term of imprisonment.

Smalis v. Pennsylvania 476 U.S. 140, 90 L.Ed. 2d 116, 106 S.Ct. 1745 (1986) the Court, in a unanimous opinion by White, held that the trial judge's granting of a defense demurrer at the end of the prosecution's case was an acquittal under the double jeopardy clause. The state's appeal was barred because reversal would have led to further trial proceedings.

Morris v. Mathews 475 U.S. 237, 89 L.Ed. 2d 187, 106 S.Ct. 1032 (1986) the Court, in an opinion by White for 5 justices, held that the double jeopardy clause was not violated when a court modified a jeopardy-barred conviction and imposed a sentence for a lesser-included offense that was not jeopardy-barred. To show a violation of the double jeopardy clause under these circumstances, the defense has the burden of demonstrating there is a reasonable probability that the defendant would not have been convicted of the nonjeopardy-barred offense absent the presence of the jeopardy-barred offense.

Heath v. Alabama 474 U.S. 82, 88 L.Ed. 2d 387, 106 S.Ct. 433 (1985) the Court, in an opinion by O'Connor for 7 justices, held that under the "dual sovereignty" doctrine succes-sive prosecutions by two states for the same conduct are not barred by the double jeopardy clause.

Arizona v. Rumsey 467 U.S. 203, 81 L.Ed. 2d 164, 104 S.Ct. 2305 (1984) the Court, 7–2, in an opinion by O'Connor, held that when the judge, due to misconception of the state's law on aggravating circumstances, imposed a life sentence without possibility of parole instead of the death sentence, double jeopardy barred the state from seeking the death penalty when the case was remanded by the appellate court for resentencing.

Justices of Boston Municipal Court v. Lydon 466 U.S. 294, 80 L.Ed. 2d 311, 104 S.Ct. 1805 (1984) the Court, in an opinion by White joined in pertinent part by 5 members of the Court, held that double jeopardy did not prevent the state from retrying a defendant who had been convicted in a bench trial, where the retrial was a trial *de novo* before a jury.

Oregon v. Kennedy 456 U.S. 667, 72 L.Ed. 2d 416, 102 S.Ct. 2083 (1982) the Court, in an opinion by Rehnquist for 5 members of the Court, held that double jeopardy was not a bar to a retrial based on prosecutorial or judicial misconduct unless the conduct in question was intended to provoke the defendant into moving for a mistrial.

Bullington v. Missouri 451 U.S. 430, 68 L.Ed. 2d 270, 101 S.Ct. 1852 (1981) the Court, in an opinion by Blackmun for 5 justices, held that where the penalty phase of a capital case was tried before a jury, and the jury sentenced the defendant to life imprisonment, the prosecution was barred upon retrial from seeking the death penalty because the penalty phase jury had in effect acquitted the defendant on the death sentence issue.

Hudson v. Louisiana 450 U.S. 40, 67 L.Ed. 2d 30, 101 S.Ct. 970 (1981) the Court, in a unanimous opinion by Powell, held that retrial was barred by double jeopardy when the trial court had granted a new trial because the state had failed to prove its case as a matter of law.

United States v. Scott 437 U.S. 82, 57 L.Ed. 2d 65, 98 S.Ct. 2187 (1978) the Court, in an opinion by Rehnquist for 5 justices, held that double jeopardy did not apply in a case where the first trial was terminated at the request of the defendant.

Crist v. Bretz 437 U.S. 28, 57 L.Ed. 2d 24, 98 S.Ct. 2156 (1978) the Court, 6–3, in an opinion by Stewart, held that jeopardy attaches when the jury is impaneled and sworn.

Burks v. United States 437 U.S. 1, 57 L.Ed. 2d 1, 98 S.Ct. 2141 (1978) the Court, 8–0 (Blackmun did not participate), in an opinion by Burger, held that double jeopardy prohibits the retrial of a defendant who has had a conviction reversed solely for lack of sufficient evidence to sustain the jury's verdict. Defendant's motion for a new trial does not waive the double jeopardy defense.

United States v. Wheeler 435 U.S. 313, 55 L.Ed. 2d 303, 98 S.Ct. 1079 (1978) the Court, 8–0, in an opinion by Stewart, held that double jeopardy did not bar prosecutions by the United States and the Navajo Tribe for the same offense. Tribal court was acting as "independent sovereign" and not as an arm of the federal government, although it was enforcing a federal statute.

Arizona v. Washington 434 U.S. 497, 54 L.Ed. 2d 717, 98 S.Ct. 824 (1978) the Court, in an opinion by Stevens for 5 members of the Court, held that double jeopardy did not bar a retrial where the judge granted a motion for a mistrial. "Manifest necessity" was found based on misconduct by defense attorney during his opening statement.

Harris v. Oklahoma 433 U.S. 682, 53 L.Ed. 2d 1054, 97 S.Ct. 2912 (1977) the Court, in a unanimous *per curiam* opinion, held that when a conviction for a greater crime (felony murder) could not be had without a conviction for a lesser crime (robbery with a firearm), double jeopardy barred prosecution for the lesser crime after conviction for the greater.

Breed v. Jones 421 U.S. 519, 44 L.Ed. 2d 346, 95 S.Ct. 1779 (1975) the Court, unanimously in an opinion by Burger, held that the prosecution of a juvenile as an adult, after the adjudicatory hearing in Juvenile Court, was barred by double jeopardy.

Benton v. Maryland 395 U.S. 784, 23 L.Ed. 2d 707, 89 S.Ct. 2056 (1969) the Court, 6–2 in an opinion by Marshall, held that the double jeopardy clause of the Fifth Amendment is applicable to the states through the due process clause of the Fourteenth Amendment. The decision overruled *Palko v. Connecticut* (1937).

C. Indictment

Hurtado v. California 110 U.S. 516, 28 L.Ed. 232, 4 S.Ct. 292 (1884) the Court held that the protection of the life and liberty of the person afforded by the due process clause of the Fourteenth Amendment does not require a state to use an indictment or presentment of a grand jury in prosecution for murder or other offenses.

V SIXTH AMENDMENT ISSUES

A. Right to Counsel

Nichols v. United States 511 U.S. 738, 128 L.Ed. 2d 745, 114 S.Ct. 1921 (1994) the Court, 6–3 in an opinion by Rehnquist, held that the use of a prior misdemeanor conviction in order to impose a longer sentence for a new conviction was valid, even though the defendant was not represented by counsel in the case involving the misdemeanor conviction. Court explicitly overruled *Baldasar v. Illinois* 446 U.S. 222 (1980) and reaffirmed *Scott v. Illinois* 440 U.S. 367 (1979).

Austin v. United States 513 U.S. 5, 130 L.Ed. 2d 219, 115 S.Ct. 380 (1994) the Court, in a unanimous *per curiam* opinion, held that under the Criminal Justice Act of 1964 (18 U.S.C. §3006A), which applies to appointment of counsel for indigents on appeals in federal courts, and rules implemented by the various circuits, an appointed attorney is not required to file briefs in frivolous cases or seek *certiorari*.

Godinez v. Moran 509 U.S. 389, 125 L.Ed. 2d 321, 113 S.Ct. 2680 (1993) the Court, in an opinion by Thomas for 5 justices, held that the competency standard for pleading guilty and for waiver of the right to counsel is the same as the competency standard for standing trial. Seven justices agreed that in addition to being competent, the defendant needs to make the decision knowingly and voluntarily.

Powell v. Texas 492 U.S. 680, 106 L.Ed. 2d 551, 109 S.Ct. 3146 (1989) the Court, in a unanimous *per curiam* opinion, held that while a defendant's raising an insanity defense may waive some Fifth Amendment rights and give the prosecution the right to have the defendant examined by prosecution experts, conducting such evaluation without prior notice to defense counsel violates the Sixth Amendment.

Perry v. Leeke 488 U.S. 272, 102 L.Ed. 2d 624, 109 S.Ct. 594 (1989) the Court, in an opinion by Stevens for 5 justices, held that the trial judge's order directing the defendant not to consult with his attorney during a brief recess, called while the defendant was on the witness stand, did not violate the defendant's Sixth Amendment right to counsel.

Penson v. Ohio 488 U.S. 75, 102 L.Ed. 2d 300, 109 S.Ct. 346 (1988) the Court, in an opinion by Stevens for 8 justices, held that the state appellate court's action in permitting appellate counsel to withdraw after stating the conclusion that the case had no merit, violated the defendant's Sixth Amendment right to counsel even though the appellate court stated that it would independently review the record thoroughly to determine whether any error existed that required reversal.

Patterson v. Illinois 487 U.S. 285, 101 L.Ed. 2d 261, 108 S.Ct. 2389 (1988) the Court, in an opinion by White for 5 justices, held that giving Miranda admonitions and obtaining a valid waiver of these rights prior to post-arraignment interrogation is sufficient to apprise the defendant of the nature of his/her Sixth Amendment rights and of the consequences of abandoning those rights.

Wheat v. United States 486 U.S. 153, 100 L.Ed. 2d 140, 108 S.Ct. 1692 (1988) the Court, in an opinion by Rehnquist for 5 justices, held refusal to permit an attorney to represent two defendants despite defendant's waiver of the right to conflict-free counsel was within the discretion of the trial judge both in cases where the judge sees an actual conflict of interest and where a potential for such a conflict exists.

Pennsylvania v. Finley 481 U.S. 551, 95 L.Ed. 2d 539, 107 S.Ct. 1990 (1987) the Court, in an opinion by Rehnquist for 5 justices, held that there is no constitutional right to appointed counsel when mounting a collateral attack, such as *habeas corpus*, on a conviction.

Smith v. Murray 477 U.S. 527, 91 L.Ed. 2d 434, 106 S.Ct. 2661 (1986) the Court, in an opinion by O'Connor for 5 justices, held that a deliberate tactical decision not to raise an issue on direct appeal bars its introduction in a writ of *habeas corpus* absent a showing that there is a probability that counsel's procedural default resulted in the conviction of an innocent person.

Murray v. Carrier 477 U.S. 478, 91 L.Ed. 2d 397, 106 S.Ct. 2639 (1986) the Court, in an opinion by O'Connor for 5 justices, held that an inmate petitioning for a writ of *habeas corpus* on the grounds of ineffective assistance of counsel on appeal needs to establish that there was some external impediment that might have prevented counsel from raising the appropriate claims in the briefs on direct appeal. The federal courts retain the authority to consider cases in which there is a probability that the defendant was factually innocent.

Michigan v. Jackson 475 U.S. 625, 89 L.Ed. 2d 631, 106 S.Ct. 1404 (1986) the Court, in an opinion by Stevens for 5 justices, held that police interrogation after an arraignment at which defendants had requested appointed counsel, but prior to their having had an opportunity to consult with counsel, violated their Sixth Amendment right to counsel and statements made were inadmissible. A request for counsel at arraignment is presumed to be a request to be represented by counsel at all future proceedings, including interrogation.

Moran v. Burbine 475 U.S. 412, 89 L.Ed. 2d 410, 106 S.Ct. 1135 (1986) the Court, in an opinion by O'Connor for 6 justices, held that the failure of police to inform suspect of his attorney's telephone call did not affect validity of uncoerced waiver of Miranda rights; Sixth Amendment right to counsel and right to have counsel intercede does not attach until formal charging proceedings.

Nix v. Whiteside 475 U.S. 157, 89 L.Ed. 2d 123, 106 S.Ct. 988 (1986), the Court, in an opinion by Burger for 5 justices, held Sixth Amendment right to counsel was not violated by attorney who refused to cooperate with defendant's wishes to present perjured testimony.

Maine v. Moulton 474 U.S. 159, 88 L.Ed. 2d 481, 106 S.Ct. 477 (1985) the Court, in an opinion by Brennan for 5 justices, held that statements obtained by codefendant who had decided to cooperate with police after indictment and wear a concealed microphone during a conference with defense attorneys were inadmissible as a violation of the Sixth Amendment right to counsel.

Evitts v. Lucey 469 U.S. 387, 83 L.Ed. 2d 821, 105 S.Ct. 830 (1985) the Court, in an opinion by Brennan for 7 justices, held that defendant has due process right to effective assistance of counsel on first appeal.

Smith v. Illinois 469 U.S. 91, 83 L.Ed. 2d 488, 105 S.Ct. 490 (1984) in a *per curiam* opinion for 7 justices, held that when deciding whether a request for counsel during interrogation was ambiguous, an accused's post-request responses to further interrogation may not be used to cast retrospective doubt on the clarity of the initial request itself.

Strickland v. Washington 466 U.S. 668, 80 L.Ed. 2d 674, 104 S.Ct. 2052 (1984) the Court,

in an opinion by O'Connor for 7 justices, established a two-part test for ineffective assistance of trial counsel: (1) counsel was not functioning as the counsel guaranteed by the Sixth Amendment; and (2) defendant must be able to show that there is a reasonable probability that, except for counsel's errors, the outcome of the trial would have been different.

Jones v. Barnes 463 U.S. 745, 77 L.Ed. 2d 987, 103 S.Ct. 3308 (1983) the Court, in an opinion by Burger for 6 justices, held that counsel who is appointed to handle an appeal for a criminal defendant does not have a constitutional duty to raise every nonfrivolous issue requested by the defendant.

Lassiter v. Department of Social Services of Durham County, North Carolina 452 U.S. 18, 68 L.Ed. 2d 640, 101 S.Ct. 2153 (1981) the Court, in an opinion by Stewart for 5 justices, held that there is no absolute right, under Fourteenth Amendment due process clause, to appointed counsel at hearing to terminate parental status. The decision to appoint counsel was delegated to the trial courts for a case-by-case determination.

Estelle v. Smith 451 U.S. 454, 68 L.Ed. 2d 359, 101 S.Ct. 1866 (1981) the Court, in an opinion by Burger for 5 justices, held that the use of testimony, at the penalty phase of a capital case, of a psychiatrist who conducted a court-ordered pretrial evaluation of defendant for competency to stand trial, violated the defendant's Fifth and Sixth Amendment rights. The examination of defendant while in jail by court-appointed psychiatrist was a "critical stage" of the proceedings and the right to counsel attached.

United States v. Henry 447 U.S. 264, 65 L.Ed. 2d 115, 100 S.Ct. 2183 (1980) the Court, 6–3, in an opinion by Burger, held that statements obtained by an informant from a defendant while in jail were inadmissible. Although the informant had been cautioned not to initiate any conversations with the defendant, the informant was paid on a contingent fee basis. The Court found that this intentionally created a situation likely to induce the defendant to make incriminating statements in the absence of counsel.

Cuyler v. Sullivan 446 U.S. 335, 64 L.Ed. 2d 333, 100 S.Ct. 1708 (1980) the Court, in an opinion by Powell for 7 justices, held that joint representation of codefendants by one attorney does not require automatic reversal. The trial judge is not required to appoint separate attorneys unless there is reason to believe that a conflict exists. The judge is not required to initiate an inquiry into the propriety of joint representation unless a party to the case, or his/her attorney, raises an objection. Defendants have the burden of showing that joint representation adversely affected the performance of counsel.

Baldasar v. Illinois 446 U.S. 222, 64 L.Ed. 2d 169, 100 S.Ct. 1585 (1980) the Court, 5–4 in a *per curiam* opinion that relied on 3 concurring opinions, reversed a felony conviction for petty theft with a prior petty theft conviction. The prior petty theft conviction had been obtained in a proceeding in which the defendant was not represented by defense counsel. Overruled by *Nichols v. United States* (1994).

Scott v. Illinois 440 U.S. 367, 59 L.Ed. 2d 383, 99 S.Ct. 1158 (1979) the Court, 5–4, in an opinion by Rehnquist, held that the Sixth Amendment right to counsel requires that any defendant who is sentenced to imprisonment have been represented by counsel at trial. Counsel is not required so long as the defendant does not receive a sentence including imprisonment.

Holloway v. Arkansas 435 U.S. 475, 55 L.Ed. 2d 426, 98 S.Ct. 1173 (1978) the Court, 6–3, in an opinion by Burger, held that automatic reversal was required where the trial judge, over timely objection, improperly required codefendants to be represented by the same counsel.

Moore v. Illinois 434 U.S. 220, 54 L.Ed. 2d 424, 98 S.Ct. 458 (1977) the Court, in an opinion by Powell for 7 justices, held that evidence of the fact that the rape victim identified the defendant at his preliminary hearing

was inadmissible because he was not represented by counsel at that hearing. In this case the preliminary hearing marked the initiation of criminal proceedings.

Weatherford v. Bursey 429 U.S. 545, 51 L.Ed. 2d 30, 97 S.Ct. 837 (1977) the Court, 7–2, in an opinion by White, held that presence of an undercover agent at a pretrial conference between the accused and his attorney did not violate the accused's Sixth Amendment rights. The undercover agent only attended the meetings in order to maintain his cover and did not reveal anything learned at the meetings.

Geders v. United States 425 U.S. 80, 47 L.Ed. 2d 592, 96 S.Ct. 1330 (1976) a unanimous Court, in an opinion by Burger (with Stevens not participating in the case), held that a court order denying the defendant the right to consult with counsel during a 17-hour, overnight recess in the case violated the right to counsel.

Middendorf v. Henry 425 U.S. 25, 47 L.Ed. 2d 556, 96 S.Ct. 1281 (1975) the Court, 5–3 with Stevens not participating, in an opinion by Rehnquist, held that a summary court-martial was not a "criminal proceeding" for purposes of the right to counsel.

Faretta v. California 422 U.S. 806, 45 L.Ed. 2d 562, 95 S.Ct. 2525 (1975) the Court, in a 6–3 opinion by Stewart, held that the Sixth Amendment guarantees self-representation to a state criminal defendant who voluntarily and intelligently waives the right to the assistance of counsel and who insists on conducting his own defense.

Gerstein v. Pugh 420 U.S. 103, 43 L.Ed. 2d 541, 95 S.Ct. 854 (1975) the Court, in an opinion by Powell, held that the defendant does not have the right to be present or the right to be represented by counsel at a probable cause hearing.

Ross v. Moffitt (1974) 417 U.S. 600, 41 L.Ed. 2d 341, 94 S.Ct. 2437 (1974) the Court, 6–3 in an opinion by Rehnquist, held that states do not have to provide counsel for indigents wishing to make discretionary appeals to the state's highest court or to the United States Supreme Court.

Fuller v. Oregon 416 U.S. 40, 40 L.Ed. 2d 642, 94 S.Ct. 2116 (1974) the Court in a very narrow holding said that probation may be conditioned on repayment of the cost of prosecution so long as adequate protections exist to protect the truly indigent person from imprisonment for his/her inability to make payments.

Gagnon v. Scarpelli 411 U.S. 778, 36 L.Ed. 2d 656, 93 S.Ct. 1756 (1973) the Court through Justice Powell held, 8–1, that under some circumstances the state may be required to assign counsel at probation revocation hearings.

Argersinger v. Hamlin 407 U.S. 25, 32 L.Ed. 2d 530, 92 S.Ct. 2006 (1972) the Court, 6–3, in an opinion by Douglas, held that all defendants facing a possible jail sentence are entitled to be represented by legal counsel in their trial, and that the state must provide a lawyer if the defendant wants one and cannot afford the cost. See *Scott v. Illinois* (1979) and *Nichols v. United States* (1994).

Coleman v. Alabama 399 U.S. 1, 26 L.Ed. 2d 387, 90 S.Ct. 1999 (1970) the Court, in an opinion by Brennan, held that a preliminary hearing, if held, is a "critical stage" and an indigent defendant has a constitutional right to the appointment of counsel under the Sixth and Fourteenth Amendments.

Brady v. United States 397 U.S. 742, 25 L.Ed. 2d 747, 90 S.Ct. 1463 (1970) (together with *McMann v. Richardson*, 397 U.S. 759, 25 L.Ed. 2d 763, 90 S.Ct.1441, and *Parker v. North Carolina* 397 U.S. 790, 25 L.Ed. 2d 785, 90 S.Ct.1458) the decisions in these three cases attach paramount significance to the presence of counsel for the defendant during the plea-bargaining process.

Johnson v. Avery 393 U.S. 483, 21 L.Ed. 2d 718, 89 S.Ct. 747 (1969) this ruling held invalid a prison regulation that forbade the legal assistance of a "jailhouse lawyer" to other inmates. If no other legal assistance were available, such a regulation would result in a denial of access to the courts.

Mempha v. Rhay 389 U.S. 128, 19 L.Ed. 2d 336, 88 S.Ct. 254 (1967) the Court held that an indigent defendant who is to be sentenced as a part of probation revocation proceedings must have counsel provided for him/her.

Massiah v. United States 377 U.S. 201, 12 L.Ed. 2d 246, 84 S.Ct. 1199 (1964) the Court held, 6–3, that interrogation under any circumstances, in the absence of the defendant's attorney or a waiver thereof, after the defendant is indicted, violates his/her Sixth Amendment right to counsel. In *McLeod v. Ohio*, 381 U.S. 356 (1965) the Court made the *Massiah* doctrine binding on the states under the Fourteenth Amendment.

Douglas v. California 372 U.S. 353, 9 L.Ed. 2d 811, 83 S.Ct. 814 (1963) the Court held, 6–3, that there is an absolute right to the assistance of counsel during the first appeal under the equal protection clause of the Fourteenth Amendment.

Gideon v. Wainwright 372 U.S. 335, 9 L.Ed. 2d 799, 83 S.Ct. 792 (1963) the Supreme Court included among the fundamental rights of persons, guaranteed by the Fourteenth Amendment, the Sixth Amendment right to be represented by counsel when a person is being tried for a crime in a state court. This includes the right of an indigent defendant to have counsel assigned by the court.

Griffin v. Illinois 351 U.S. 12, 100 L.Ed. 891, 76 S.Ct. 585 (1956) the Court held 5–4, that the due process and equal protection clauses of the Fourteenth Amendment require that all indigent defendants be furnished a transcript, or a record of sufficient completeness, for an appeal.

B. Grand and Petit Juries

1. Trial Juries

Lewis v. United States 518 U.S. 322, 135 L.Ed. 2d 590, 116 S.Ct. 2163 (1996) the Court, 7–3 in an opinion by O'Connor, held that a defendant in a federal criminal prosecution has the right to a jury trial only if the sentence for a charge exceeds six months; sentences for lesser offenses cannot be aggregated in order to trigger the right to a jury trial.

Purkett v. Elem 514 U.S. 765, 131 L.Ed. 2d 834, 115 S.Ct. 1769 (1995) the Court, 7–2 in a *per curiam* opinion, reiterated the holding in *Batson v. Kentucky* (1986) that peremptory challenges could not be used for racially discriminatory purposes. Once the defense raises this issue during jury selection, the prosecution must state a "legitimate reason" for the challenges that have been used. In this context, "legitimate reason" means a reason that does not deny equal protection; it does not have to be a reason that makes sense. The last step for the trial judge to take is consideration of whether the reason is real or a pretext.

J. E. B. ex rel. TB. 511 U.S. 127, 128 L.Ed. 2d 89, 114 S.Ct. 1419 (1994) the Court, 6–3 in an opinion by Blackmun, held that the Fourteenth Amendment equal protection clause prohibits the use of peremptory challenges by state actors on the basis of gender. Case arose from a civil paternity suit filed by the State of Alabama. The equal protection clause prohibits discrimination in jury selection on the basis of gender, or on the assumption that an individual will be biased in a particular case for no reason other than the fact that the person happens to be a woman or happens to be a man.

Sullivan v. Louisiana 508 U.S. 275, 124 L.Ed. 2d 182, 113 S.Ct. 2078 (1993) the Court, in a unanimous decision by Scalia, held that failure to give the jury an adequate instruction on "proof beyond a reasonable doubt" violates the defendant's right to a jury trial and is a fundamental error requiring reversal. Harmless-error analysis is not appropriate in this type of case.

Georgia v. McCollum 505 U.S. 42, 120 L.Ed. 2d 33, 112 S.Ct. 2348 (1992) the Court, 6–3 in an opinion by Blackmun, held that the Constitution prohibits a criminal defendant from engaging in purposeful discrimination on the grounds of race in the exercise of peremptory challenges. If the state demonstrates a *prima facie* case of racial discrimination by the defendant, the defendant must articulate a racially neutral explanation for peremptory challenges.

Morgan v. Illinois 504 U.S. 719, 119 L. Ed. 2d 492, 112 S.Ct. 2222 (1992) the Court, 6–3 in an opinion by White, held that due process was violated when a trial judge refused to ask potential jurors in a capital case if they would automatically impose the death penalty upon conviction.

Mu'Min v. Virginia 500 U.S. 415, 114 L.Ed. 2d 493, 111 S.Ct. 1899 (1991) the Court, 5–4 in an opinion by Rehnquist, held that questioning during *voir dire* in a capital murder case, which asked jurors if they had heard something about the case and formed an opinion, but did not ask specifics regarding what prospective jurors had heard, did not violate the Sixth and Fourteenth Amendments.

Powers v. Ohio 499 U.S. 400, 113 L.Ed. 2d 411, 111 S.Ct. 1364 (1991) the Court, 7–2 in an opinion by Kennedy, held that a white defendant had standing to have a conviction reversed due to violation of the equal protection clause if the prosecutor used peremptory challenges to exclude prospective black jurors.

Blanton v. City of North Las Vegas, Nevada 489 U.S. 538, 103 L.Ed. 2d 550, 109 S.Ct. 1289 (1989) the Court, in a unanimous opinion by Marshall, held that for offenses with a maximum sentence of six months or less, the defendant is entitled to a jury trial only if he/she can demonstrate that any additional statutory penalties, viewed in conjunction with the maximum authorized period of incarceration, are so severe that they clearly reflect a legislative determination that the offense in question is a "serious" one. The Court also stated that the fact that increased penalties are imposed for repeat offenses is not to be considered.

Ross v. Oklahoma 487 U.S. 81, 101 L.Ed. 2d 80, 108 S.Ct. 2273 (1988) the Court, in an opinion by Rehnquist for 5 justices, held that failure of the trial judge to remove a prospective juror under *Witherspoon v. Illinois* does not require reversal of the conviction under the Sixth and Fourteenth Amendments. Reversal is mandated only if the defendant exhausts all peremptory challenges and an incompetent juror is forced upon him/her.

Lockhart v. McCree 476 U.S. 162, 90 L.Ed. 2d 137, 106 S.Ct. 1758 (1986) the Court, in an opinion by Rehnquist for 5 justices, held the Constitution does not prohibit the removal for cause, prior to the guilt phase of a bifurcated capital trial, of prospective jurors whose opposition to the death penalty is so strong that it would prevent or substantially impair the performance of their duties as jurors at the sentencing phase of the trial.

Batson v. Kentucky 476 U.S. 79, 90 L.Ed. 2d 69, 106 S.Ct. 1712 (1986) the Court, in an opinion by Powell for 7 justices, held the equal protection clause forbids prosecutorial use of peremptory challenges to exclude potential jurors solely on account of their race or on the assumption that black jurors as a group will be unable to impartially consider the state's case against a black defendant. To establish a *prima facie* case the defendant must show: he/she is a member of a cognizable racial group; and the prosecutor has exercised peremptory challenges to remove members of defendant's race from the jury. Once the defense makes a *prima facie* showing, the burden shifts to the State to come forward with a neutral explanation for challenging jurors.

Turner v. Murray 476 U.S. 28, 90 L.Ed. 2d 27, 106 S.Ct. 1683 (1986) the Court, in an opinion by White for 5 justices, held that a defendant in a capital case who is accused of an interracial crime is entitled to have prospective jurors informed of the race of the victim and questioned on the issue of racial bias. A defendant cannot complain that the trial judge did not question prospective jurors on racial prejudice unless the defendant specifically requested such an inquiry during jury selection.

Wainwright v. Witt 469 U.S. 412, 83 L.Ed. 2d 841, 105 S.Ct. 844 (1985) the Court, in a opinion by Rehnquist for 6 justices, held a juror may be excluded in a death penalty case if his/her personal views on capital punishment would prevent or substantially impair the performance of his/her duties as a juror in accordance with the instructions and his/her oath.

Burch v. Louisiana 441 U.S. 130, 60 L.Ed. 2d 96, 99 S.Ct. 1623 (1979) the Court, in an opinion by Rehnquist for 6 justices, held that conviction by a non-unanimous six-person jury in a state criminal trial for a nonpetty offense violated the Sixth and Fourteenth Amendments.

Duren v. Missouri 439 U.S. 357, 58 L.Ed. 2d 579, 99 S.Ct. 664 (1979) the Court, 8–1, in an opinion by White, held that a state statute that exempted women but not men from jury service upon request violated the male defendant's Sixth and Fourteenth Amendment rights to a jury drawn from a fair cross-section of the community.

Ballew v. Georgia 435 U.S. 223, 55 L.Ed. 2d 234, 98 S.Ct. 1029 (1978) the Court, although unable to agree upon an opinion, unanimously agreed that a jury of less than six persons in a criminal trial violated the Sixth and Fourteenth Amendments.

Ristaino v. Ross 424 U.S. 589, 47 L.Ed. 2d 258, 96 S.Ct. 1017 (1976) the Court, in an opinion by Powell for 5 members of the Court, held that the defendant had the right to have prospective jurors questioned regarding their racial prejudices only if the facts of the case suggested a significant likelihood that racial prejudice might infect the black defendant's trial.

Taylor v. Louisiana 419 U.S. 522, 42 L.Ed. 2d 690, 95 S.Ct. 692 (1975) the Court, in an opinion by White for 7 members of the Court, held that the exclusion of women from jury service unless they volunteered violated the Sixth and Fourteenth Amendments. A male defendant has standing to object to this type of unconstitutional procedure.

Johnson v. Louisiana 406 U.S. 356, 32 L.Ed. 2d 152, 92 S.Ct. 1620 (1972) the Court, 6–3, in an opinion by White, held that a state law allowing non-unanimous jury verdicts in criminal trials utilizing a 12–person jury panel did not violate the Sixth Amendment. A minimum of 9 out of 12 votes were needed to convict.

McKiever v. Pennsylvania (In *re Barbara Burrus et al.*), 403 U.S. 528, 29 L.Ed. 2d 647, 91 S.Ct. 1976 (1971) the Court, 6–3 in an opinion by Blackmun, held that the Sixth Amendment does not require trial by jury in state juvenile delinquency proceedings.

Williams v. Florida 399 U.S. 78, 26 L.Ed. 2d 446, 90 S.Ct. 1893 (1970) the Court, in an opinion by White, held that the traditional 12-person jury was the result of historical accident and that smaller juries are permissible under the Sixth Amendment.

Witherspoon v. Illinois 391 U.S. 510, 20 L.Ed. 2d 776, 88 S.Ct. 1770 (1968) the majority opinion held that a sentence of death cannot be carried out if the jury that imposed or recommended it was chosen by excluding prospective jurors for cause simply because they voiced general objections to the death penalty, or expressed conscientious or religious scruples against its infliction. *Bloom v. Illinois* 391 U.S. 194, 20 L.Ed. 2d 522, 88 S.Ct. 1477 (1968) held that the right to trial by jury in serious criminal contempt cases in state courts is constitutionally guaranteed.

Singer v. United States 380 U.S. 24, 13 L.Ed. 2d 630, 85 S.Ct. 783 (1965) the Court, in a unanimous opinion by Warren, held that a criminal defendant does not have the right to be tried without a jury if the prosecution requests a jury.

2. Grand Juries

Campbell v. Louisiana 523 U.S. ___, 140 L.Ed. 2d 551, 118 S.Ct. 1419 (1998) the Court, in an opinion by Kennedy pertinent portions of which represented the unanimous opinion of the Court, held that a white criminal defendant had standing to raise equal protection and due process objections to discrimination against black persons in the selection of grand jurors.

United States v. Williams 504 U.S. 36, 118 L.Ed. 2d 352, 112 S.Ct. 1735 (1992) the Court, 5 in an opinion by Scalia, held that the government has no duty to disclose "substantially exculpatory evidence" in its possession to the grand jury when seeking an indictment.

Butterworth v. Smith 494 U.S. 624, 108 L.Ed. 2d 572, 110 S.Ct. 1376 (1990) the Court, in a unanimous opinion by Rehnquist, held that a Florida law that prohibited a grand jury witness from disclosing his/her own testimony after the term of the grand jury had ended violated the First Amendment.

Hobby v. United States 468 U.S. 339, 82 L.Ed. 2d 260, 104 S.Ct. 3093 (1984) the Court, 6–3, in an opinion by Burger, held that racial or sexual discrimination in the selection of a federal grand jury foreman does not require reversal of a white male defendant's conviction because the role of foreman of a federal grand jury is not so significant that discrimination in his/her selection undermines the integrity of an indictment.

Rose v. Mitchell 443 U.S. 545, 61 L.Ed. 2d 739, 99 S.Ct. 2993 (1979) the Court, in an opinion by Blackmun joined in pertinent parts by 5 members of the Court, held that discrimination in the selection of members of a grand jury is valid ground for setting aside a criminal conviction, even though a guilty verdict had been rendered by a properly selected trial jury.

United States v. Wong 431 U.S. 174, 52 L.Ed. 2d 231, 97 S.Ct. 1823 (1977) the Court, in a unanimous opinion by Burger, held that failure to advise a witness before a grand jury of the privilege against self-incrimination, in addition to the oath to tell the truth, did not require suppression of the testimony given before the grand jury when the defendant was on trial for perjury arising from false testimony before a grand jury.

C. Trial

1. Public Access to Trial

Press-Enterprise Company v. Superior Court of California for the County of Riverside 478 U.S. 1, 92 L.Ed. 2d 1, 106 S.Ct. 2735 (1986) the Court, in an opinion by Burger for 7 justices, held that the qualified First Amendment right of access to criminal proceedings applies to preliminary hearings as they are conducted in California. The judge may not close the preliminary hearing based on a cursory assertion that publicity might deprive the defendant of the right to a fair trial. Any limitation on access to the preliminary hearing must be narrowly tailored to serve First Amendment interests.

Waller v. Georgia 467 U.S. 39, 81 L.Ed. 2d 31, 104 S.Ct. 2210 (1984) the Court, in a unanimous opinion by Powell, held that the right to a public trial under the Sixth and Fourteenth Amendments applies to pretrial hearings held to determine whether evidence should be suppressed.

Press-Enterprise Company v. Superior Court of California, Riverside County 464 U.S. 501, 78 L.Ed. 2d 629, 104 S.Ct. 819 (1984) the Court, in an opinion by Burger signed by 8 justices, held that the guarantees of open public proceedings in criminal trials included the right of the press to cover *voir dire* examination of potential jurors. Closure of *voir dire* proceedings may be allowed rarely and only on a showing of cause that outweighs the value of openness.

Globe Newspaper Company v. Superior Court for the County of Norfolk 457 U.S. 596, 73 L.Ed. 2d 248, 102 S.Ct. 2613 (1982) the Court, in an opinion by Brennan for 5 justices, held that a Massachusetts statute providing for exclusion of the general public from the trials of specified sexual offenses involving a victim under the age of 18 was unconstitutional. Neither the state's interest in protecting minor victims of sex crimes from further trauma and embarrassment, nor its interest in encouraging such victims to come

forward and testify, justified this wholesale exclusion.

Richmond Newspapers, Inc. v. Virginia 448 U.S. 555, 65 L.Ed. 2d 973, 100 S.Ct. 2814 (1980) 7 members of the Court, although unable to agree upon an opinion, held that the trial judge's order, at request of defendant and without objection by the prosecution, that the defendant's murder trial be closed to the public and press violated the First and Fourteenth Amendments.

Gannett Co., Inc. v. DePasquale 443 U.S. 368, 61 L.Ed. 2d 608, 99 S.Ct. 2898 (1979) the Court, in an opinion by Stewart for 5 justices, held that where the trial judge had adequately considered the balance of the right of the defendant to a fair trial against the right of the press and public to attend a suppression hearing, the order closing the suppression hearing to the press and public was constitutional.

2. Publicity

Florida Star v. B. J. F. 491 U.S. 524, 105 L.Ed. 2d 443, 109 S.Ct. 2603 (1989) the Court, in an opinion by Marshall for 5 justices, held that imposing civil penalties for publication of the name of the victim of a sex crime in violation of Florida law violated the First Amendment. The Court held that truthful publication was not automatically protected but set out a three-point test: whether the newspaper lawfully obtained truthful information about a matter of public significance; whether the sanctions protected a need to further a state interest of the highest order; and whether the statute was overbroad or underinclusive.

Chandler v. Florida 449 U.S. 560, 66 L.Ed. 2d 740, 101 S.Ct. 802 (1981) the Court, in an opinion by Burger for 6 justices, held that states could experiment with the use of electronic media and still-photographic coverage of public judicial proceedings without violating the constitutional rights of the defendant.

Oklahoma Publishing Company v. District Court in and for Oklahoma County, Oklahoma, 430 U.S. 308, 51 L.Ed. 2d 355, 97 S.Ct. 1045 (1977) the Court, in a unanimous *per curiam* opinion, held that a pretrial order that enjoined members of the news media from publishing, broadcasting, or disseminating in any manner the name or picture of a 11-year-old defendant in a juvenile court case violated the free press guarantee of the First and Fourteenth Amendments.

Nebraska Press Association v. Stuart 427 U.S. 539, 49 L.Ed. 2d 683, 96 S.Ct. 2791 (1976) the Court, in an opinion by Burger for 5 justices, held that a court order prohibiting the publication or broadcasting of accounts of confessions, admissions made by the accused, or facts strongly implicating him was unconstitutional. The record did not show an adequate consideration of alternatives to prior restraint that might have mitigated the adverse effect of pretrial publicity. Prohibition of reporting and commenting on court proceedings that were held in public clearly is invalid.

Murphy v. Florida 421 U.S. 794, 44 L.Ed. 2d 589, 95 S.Ct. 2031 (1975) the Court, in an opinion by Marshall for 7 justices, held that denial of a motion for change of venue on grounds of pretrial publicity did not violate the defendant's constitutional rights. Defendant had failed to show that the setting of the trial was inherently prejudicial or that the jury selection process permitted an inference of actual prejudice.

Sheppard v. Maxwell 384 U.S. 333, 16 L.Ed. 2d 600, 86 S.Ct. 1507 (1966) the Court, 8–1 in an opinion by Clark, held that prejudicial publicity made it impossible for the defendant to have a fair trial. This decision contains an extensive discussion of the effect of unfairly distorted publicity upon the jurors at the time of trial. The decision notes that neither prosecutors, counsel for defense, the accused, witness, court staff, nor enforcement officers coming under the jurisdiction of the trial court should be permitted to frustrate its

function by actions or statements threatening the fair trial of the defendant.

Rideau v. Louisiana 373 U.S. 723, 10 L.Ed. 2d 663, 83 S.Ct. 1417 (1963) the Court, 7–2 in an opinion by Stewart, held that the defendant was denied a fair trial because of publicity, including locally televised interviews of the sheriff discussing the defendant's confession. This decision contains a good discussion of the right of a defendant in a criminal action to a fair trial by unbiased jurors.

3. Plea Bargaining

Godinez v. Moran 509 U.S. 389, 125 L.Ed. 2d 321, 113 S.Ct. 2680 (1993) the Court, in an opinion by Thomas for 5 justices, held that the competency standard for pleading guilty and for waiver of the right to counsel is the same as the competency standard for standing trial. Seven justices agreed that in addition to being competent, the defendant needs to make the decision knowingly and voluntarily.

United States v. Broce 488 U.S. 563, 102 L.Ed. 2d 927, 109 S.Ct. 757 (1989) the Court, in an opinion by Kennedy for 6 justices, held that the entry of guilty pleas foreclosed the defendant's right to challenge those pleas by collateral attack on double jeopardy grounds.

Ricketts v. Adamson 483 U.S. 1, 97 L.Ed. 2d 1, 107 S.Ct. 2860 (1987) the Court, in an opinion by White for 5 justices, held that double jeopardy was not violated by prosecution of the defendant for first-degree murder following his breach of a plea agreement under which he had pled guilty to a lesser offense, had been sentenced, and had begun serving a term of imprisonment.

Mabry v. Johnson 467 U.S. 504, 81 L.Ed. 2d 437, 104 S.Ct. 2543 (1984) the Court, in a unanimous opinion by Stevens, held that the defendant's acceptance of a proposed plea bargain the prosecutor erroneously made does not create a constitutional right to have the bargain enforced by the trial court.

Corbitt v. New Jersey 439 U.S. 212, 58 L.Ed. 2d 466, 99 S.Ct. 492 (1978) the Court, in an opinion by White for 5 justices, upheld a New Jersey law that made a sentence of life imprisonment mandatory upon jury conviction for first-degree murder, but allowed lesser sentences if the defendant entered a plea of *non vult* or *nolo contendere.*

Hutto v. Ross 429 U.S. 28, 50 L.Ed. 2d 194, 97 S.Ct. 202 (1976) the Court, in a *per curiam* opinion expressing the views of 8 justices, held that a confession was not *per se* inadmissible in a criminal trial merely because it was made as the result of a plea-bargain agreement.

Henderson v. Morgan 426 U.S. 637, 49 L.Ed. 2d 108, 96 S.Ct. 2253 (1976) the Court, 7–2, in an opinion by Stevens, held that defendant's plea of guilty was involuntary because he had not received adequate notice of the charges and the elements of the crimes charged.

4. Filing Additional Charges and Imposing Greater Sentences

Alabama v. Smith 490 U.S. 794, 104 L.Ed. 2d 865, 109 S.Ct. 2201 (1989) the Court, in an opinion by Rehnquist for 8 justices, held that even when the original trial judge presides over the retrial and sentencing for the same crime, the difference in sentences cannot be presumed to be the result of vindictiveness, because the facts available when making the sentencing decision after a trial will usually give him/her a fuller appreciation of the nature of the crimes.

Texas v. McCullough 475 U.S. 134, 89 L.Ed. 2d 104, 106 S.Ct. 976 (1986) the Court, in an opinion by Burger for 5 justices, held that due process was not violated when the defendant received a longer sentence after a retrial than at the original trial. The Court repudiated language in *North Carolina v. Pearce* that had been interpreted by the lower courts as only permitting a harsher sentence if there had been relevant conduct of the defendant occurring subsequent to the original sentencing.

Thigpen v. Roberts 468 U.S. 27, 82 L.Ed. 2d 23, 104 S.Ct. 2916 (1984) the Court, 6–3, in an opinion by White, held that the prosecution of the driver for felony manslaughter,

after he had exercised his right to appeal a misdemeanor conviction based upon the same criminal acts, was an unconstitutional violation of due process.

United States v. Goodwin 457 U.S. 368, 73 L.Ed. 2d 74, 102 S.Ct. 2485 (1982) the Court, in an opinion by Stevens for 6 justices, held that the fact that the prosecutor filed additional felony charges, based on conduct already the subject of a misdemeanor complaint, immediately after the defendant refused to plea bargain, did not trigger a presumption that the prosecutor's conduct was vindictive.

Bordenkircher v. Hayes 434 U.S. 357, 54 L.Ed. 2d 604, 98 S.Ct. 663 (1978) the Court, 5–4, in an opinion by Stewart, held that due process was not violated when a prosecutor carried out a threat, made during plea bargaining, to reindict the defendant on more serious charges if the defendant refused to plead guilty to the offense originally charged.

5. Speedy Trial

Doggett v. United States 505 U.S. 647, 120 L.Ed. 2d 520, 112 S.Ct. 2686 (1992) the Court, 5–4 in an opinion by Souter, held that an 8-year delay between indictment and trial could be used to show denial of speedy trial even though there was no showing of actual prejudice. In cases with extraordinary delays, the longer the delay the less other evidence of prejudice is needed.

United States v. Loud Hawk 474 U.S. 302, 88 L.Ed. 2d 640, 106 S.Ct. 648 (1986) the Court, in an opinion by Powell for 5 justices, held that the time that no indictment was outstanding against the defendants does not violate their Sixth Amendment right to a speedy trial. Time expended on interlocutory appeals by the government should not be considered when determining if the right to a speedy trial has been violated.

United States v. Lovasco 431 U.S. 783, 52 L.Ed. 2d 752, 97 S.Ct. 2044 (1977) the Court, 8–1, in an opinion by Marshall, held that the right to a speedy trial based on due process was not denied where the delay between the commission of the crime and the initiation of prosecution was for the purpose of investigating the offense. The fact that defendant might have been somewhat prejudiced by the lapse of time was not determinative.

Dillingham v. United States 423 U.S. 64, 46 L.Ed. 2d 205, 96 S.Ct. 303 (1975) the Court, 7–1, in a *per curiam* opinion, held that a showing of actual prejudice was not necessary in order for preindictment delay to violate the Sixth Amendment right to a speedy trial. In this case 22 months had elapsed between arrest and indictment, and an additional 12 months between indictment and trial.

Barker v. Wingo 407 U.S. 514, 33 L.Ed. 2d 101, 92 S.Ct. 2182 (1972) the Court, in an opinion by Powell, held that violation of the Sixth Amendment right to a speedy trial is judged by weighing four factors, no one of which is conclusive: length of delay, reason for delay, defendant's assertion of his right, and prejudice to the defendant.

6. Confrontation and Cross-Examination

United States v. Scheffer 523 U.S. 303, 140 L.Ed. 2d 413, 118 S.Ct. 1261 (1998) the Court, in an opinion by Thomas pertinent parts of which represented the views of 8 justices, held that Military Rule of Evidence 707, which prohibits the introduction of testimony regarding polygraph examinations, does not violate the defendant's right to present a defense. The rule was a rational response to the disarray of opinion on the scientific validity of the polygraph.

Gray v. Maryland 523 U.S. 185, 140 L.Ed. 2d 294, 118 S.Ct. 1151 (1998) the Court, 5–4 in an opinion by Breyer, held that redactions that replace a proper name with an obvious blank, the word *delete*, a symbol, or similarly notify the jury that a name has been deleted violate the rights of the codefendant because they do not protect those rights any better than unredacted confessions.

White v. Illinois 502 U.S. 346, 116 L.Ed. 2d 848, 112 S.Ct. 736 (1992) the Court, 7–2 in an opinion by Rehnquist, held that the confrontation clause is not violated by admitting hearsay without showing that the declarant is unavailable under the spontaneous declaration or statements made in the course of securing medical treatment exceptions to the hearsay rule.

Michigan v. Lucas 500 U.S. 145, 114 L.Ed. 2d 205, 111 S.Ct. 1743 (1991) the Court, 6–3 in an opinion by O'Connor, held the Sixth Amendment was not violated when the trial court refused to allow evidence of prior sexual conduct between a defendant in a rape case and the victim. The Court rejected a *per se* rule that preclusion is unconstitutional in all cases but did not elaborate on when exclusion of evidence of prior sexual conduct would violate the Sixth Amendment.

Maryland v. Craig 497 U.S. 836, 111 L.Ed. 2d 666, 110 S.Ct. 3157 (1990) the Court, in an opinion by O'Connor for 5 justices, held that the confrontation clause of the Sixth Amendment did not categorically prohibit a child witness in a child abuse case from testifying against a defendant at trial, outside the defendant's physical presence, by one-way closed circuit television. The Court found it significant that while Maryland prevented the child witness from seeing the defendant as he/she testified, all other elements of confrontation were preserved. The requisite finding of necessity to deny face-to-face confrontation must be made on a case-specific basis.

Idaho v. Wright 497 U.S. 805, 111 L.Ed. 2d 638, 110 S.Ct. 3139 (1990) the Court, in an opinion by O'Connor for 5 justices, rejected use of Idaho's "residual hearsay exception" to admit statements of a 2-year-old girl who was allegedly molested by her father. The "residual hearsay exception" was not a firmly rooted hearsay exception for confrontation clause purposes. To be admissible under the confrontation clause, hearsay evidence used to convict a defendant must possess indicia of reliability by virtue of its inherent trustworthiness, not by reference to other evidence at trial. Corroboration of a child's statement by use of medical evidence of abuse sheds no light on the reliability of the allegations regarding the identity of the abuser.

James v. Illinois 493 U.S. 307, 107 L.Ed. 2d 676, 110 S.Ct. 648 (1990) the Court, in an opinion by Brennan for 5 justices, held that statements that were the product of an illegal arrest could not be used to impeach a defense witness who is not the defendant in the case.

Olden v. Kentucky 488 U.S. 227, 102 L.Ed. 2d 513, 109 S.Ct. 480 (1988) the Court, in a *per curiam* opinion for 8 justices, held that in a case involving rape, the trial court's refusal to allow cross-examination of the victim on possible motive to lie deprived the defendant of his Sixth Amendment rights. The Court stated that speculation as to the effect of jurors' racial biases cannot justify exclusion of cross-examination that has a strong potential to demonstrate the falsity of the witness's testimony.

Coy v. Iowa 487 U.S. 1012, 101 L.Ed. 2d 857, 108 S.Ct. 2798 (1988) the Court, in an opinion by Scalia for 6 justices, held that placing a screen between the defendant and the complaining witnesses, to block the defendant from the sight of the witnesses, violated the defendant's Sixth Amendment right to face-to-face confrontation of the witnesses against him/her.

United States v. Owens 484 U.S. 554, 98 L.Ed. 2d 951, 108 S.Ct. 838 (1988) the Court, in an opinion by Scalia for 6 justices, held that the confrontation clause does not bar testimony concerning a prior, out-of-court identification when at trial the identifying witness is unable, because of memory loss, to explain the basis for the identification.

Bourjaily v. United States 483 U.S. 171, 97 L.Ed. 2d 144, 107 S.Ct. 2775 (1987) the Court, in an opinion by Rehnquist for 6 justices, held that Federal Rule of Evidence 801 (d)(2)(E), which declares that coconspirator statements made during the course of and in furtherance of the conspiracy is not hearsay, does not violate the confrontation clause of the Sixth Amendment.

Rock v. Arkansas 483 U.S. 44, 97 L.Ed. 2d 37, 107 S.Ct. 2704 (1987) the Court, in an opinion by Blackmun for 5 justices, held that a state's *per se* evidentiary rule prohibiting the admission of hypnotically refreshed testimony violated the defendant's constitutional right to testify on his/her own behalf.

Kentucky v. Stincer 482 U.S. 730, 96 L.Ed. 2d 631, 107 S.Ct. 2658 (1987) the Court, in an opinion by Blackmun for 6 justices, held that exclusion of the defendant, but not defense counsel, from proceedings held to determine the competency of child witnesses to testify did not violate either the defendant's rights under the confrontation clause of the Sixth Amendment or the due process clause of the Fourteenth Amendment.

Richardson v. Marsh 481 U.S. 200, 95 L.Ed. 2d 176, 107 S.Ct. 1702 (1987) the Court, in an opinion by Scalia for 6 justices, held that the confrontation clause is not violated by the admission of a nontestifying codefendant's confession with a proper limiting instruction when the confession was redacted to eliminate not only the defendant's name, but any reference to his/her existence.

Cruz v. New York 481 U.S. 186, 95 L.Ed. 2d 162, 107 S.Ct. 1714 (1987) the Court, in an opinion by Scalia for 5 justices, held that, where a nontestifying codefendant's confession incriminating the defendant is not directly admissible against the defendant, the confrontation clause bars its admission at their joint trial even if the jury is instructed not to consider it against the defendant, and even if the defendant's own confession is admitted against him/her.

Pennsylvania v. Ritchie 480 U.S. 39, 94 L. Ed. 2d 40, 107 S.Ct. 989 (1987) the Court, in an opinion by Powell pertinent parts of which were signed by 5 justices, held that in a child molestation case the due process clause gives the defendant the right to have the court conduct an *in camera* review of records of the agency handling child abuse. Due process does not require that the defense be given full access to confidential materials.

Crane v. Kentucky 476 U.S. 683, 90 L.Ed. 2d 636, 106 S.Ct. 2142 (1986) the Court, in a unanimous opinion by O'Connor, held that a defendant may introduce evidence about the physical and psychological circumstances under which a confession was obtained in order to show lack of trustworthiness of the confession; this is independent of ruling on Miranda issues.

Lee v. Illinois 476 U.S. 530, 90 L.Ed. 2d 514, 106 S.Ct. 2056 (1986) the Court, in an opinion by Brennan for 5 justices, held that a confession of a codefendant and alleged accomplice inculpating the accused is viewed with suspicion and presumptively unreliable; use of such confession against an accused at trial without benefit of cross-examination violates Sixth Amendment right of confrontation if the presumption of unreliability is not overcome by a showing of sufficient independent indicia of reliability. The harmless error rule is used in these types of cases.

Delaware v. Van Arsdall 475 U.S. 673, 89 L.Ed. 2d 674, 106 S.Ct. 1431 (1986) the Court, in an opinion by Rehnquist for 6 justices, held that the Sixth Amendment was violated by cutting off all questioning about an event, which the prosecution conceded occurred, that the jury might reasonably have found furnished the witness with a motive for favoring the prosecution in his testimony.

United States v. Inadi 475 U.S. 387, 89 L. Ed. 2d 390, 106 S.Ct. 1121 (1986) the Court, in an opinion by Powell for 7 justices, held that the confrontation clause of the Sixth Amendment does not require the prosecution to show that a nontestifying coconspirator is unavailable to testify as a condition for admission of that coconspirator's out-of-court statements that were made in furtherance of the conspiracy.

Delaware v. Fensterer 474 U.S. 15, 88 L.Ed. 2d 15, 106 S.Ct. 292 (1985) the Court, in an opinion by Burger for 7 justices, held that the confrontation clause contains no guarantee that prosecution witnesses will refrain from giving testimony marred by forgetfulness, confusion, or evasion.

United States v. Valenzuela-Bernal 458 U.S. 858, 73 L.Ed. 2d 1193, 102 S.Ct. 3440 (1982) the Court, in an opinion by Rehnquist for 5 justices, held that absent a showing that the testimony of the witness in question was both material and favorable to the defense, the deportation of a witness did not deprive the defendant of the Sixth Amendment right to confront his/her accusers or the Fifth Amendment right to fundamental fairness.

Ohio v. Roberts 448 U.S. 56, 65 L.Ed. 2d 597, 100 S.Ct. 2531 (1980) the Court, 6–3, in an opinion by Blackmun, held that use of the transcript of the testimony of a witness at the preliminary hearing did not violate the defendant's Sixth Amendment right to confrontation. The witness was unavailable for trial and the testimony at the preliminary hearing bore sufficient indicia of reliability; counsel at the preliminary hearing had conducted a full examination of the witness.

Davis v. Alaska 415 U.S. 308, 39 L.Ed. 2d 347, 94 S.Ct. 1105 (1974) the Court, 6–3 in an opinion by Burger, held that a defendant in a criminal case had the right to cross-examine a witness for impeachment purposes regarding a conviction that occurred while the witness was a juvenile.

Bruton v. United States 391 U.S. 123, 20 L.Ed. 2d 476, 88 S.Ct. 1620 (1968) overruling *Delli Paoli v. United States*, 352 U.S. 232, the Court, with Brennan writing for the majority, held that a confession of one defendant cannot be used at a joint trial in which it might prejudice a codefendant because of the substantial risk that the jury, despite instructions to the contrary, looked to the incriminating extrajudicial statements in determining the nonconfessing codefendant's guilt.

7. Prosecutor's Misconduct

United States v. Robinson 485 U.S. 25, 99 L.Ed. 2d 23, 108 S.Ct. 864 (1988) the Court, in an opinion by Rehnquist for 5 justices, held that the prosecutor's comment during closing arguments that the defendant "could have taken the stand and explained it to you," was a valid response to the defense attorney's argument that the government had not allowed the defendant to explain his side of the story and did not violate the privilege to be free from compulsory self-incrimination.

Darden v. Wainwright 477 U.S. 168, 91 L.Ed. 2d 144, 106 S.Ct. 2464 (1986) the Court, in an opinion by Powell for 5 justices, held that the relevant question when evaluating the prosecutor's comments in closing arguments is whether the prosecutor's comments "so infected the trial with unfairness as to make the resulting conviction a denial of due process." When reviewed by writ of *habeas corpus*, the court must restrict itself to the narrow standard of due process and not the broad exercise of supervisory power. The fact the comments were undesirable or even universally condemned is insufficient grounds for reversal of a state court conviction in federal court.

Fletcher v. Weir 455 U.S. 603, 71 L.Ed. 2d 490, 102 S.Ct. 1309 (1982) the Court, in a *per curiam* opinion for 7 justices, held that cross-examination of a defendant regarding his/her post-arrest silence did not violate due process when the silence was not attributable to invocation of Miranda rights.

Carter v. Kentucky 450 U.S. 288, 67 L.Ed. 2d 241, 101 S.Ct. 1112 (1981) the Court, 8–1, in an opinion by Stewart, held that a defendant has the right to have a cautionary instruction given to the jury explaining that an inference of guilt cannot be drawn from the defendant's failure to testify at trial.

Jenkins v. Anderson 447 U.S. 23, 65 L.Ed. 2d 86, 100 S.Ct. 2124 (1980) the Court, in an opinion by Powell for 5 justices, held that use of pre-arrest silence to impeach a defendant who testified at his/her own trial did not violate either the Fifth Amendment right to remain silent or the Fourteenth Amendment right to fundamental fairness.

Lakeside v. Oregon 435 U.S. 333, 55 L.Ed. 2d 319, 98 S.Ct. 1091 (1978) the Court, in an opinion by Stewart for 6 justices, held that giving the cautionary instruction regarding not drawing inferences of guilt from the defendant's failure to testify, over the defendant's objection, did not violate either the constitutional guarantees against compulsory self-incrimination or the right to counsel.

Doyle v. Ohio 426 U.S. 610, 49 L.Ed. 2d 91, 96 S.Ct. 2240 (1976) the Court, 6–3, in an opinion by Powell, held that impeachment based on the failure of the defendants to make a timely allegation, during custodial interrogation after having been apprised of their Miranda rights, that they had been framed violated due process.

Malloy v. Hogan 378 U.S. 1, 12 L.Ed. 2d 653, 84 S.Ct. 1489 (1964) the Court held, 7–2, that the states, like the federal government, cannot compel incriminating testimony—thus overruling *Adamson v. California*, 353 U.S. 46 (1947).

8. Role of Judge and Jury

Taylor v. Illinois 484 U.S. 400, 98 L.Ed. 2d 798, 108 S.Ct. 646 (1988) the Court, in an opinion by Stevens for 5 justices, rejected a rule giving trial judges complete authority to exclude testimony of material witnesses due to discovery violations. The Court stated that the trial judge may insist on an explanation for a party's failure to comply with a request to identify his/her witnesses in advance of trial. If that explanation reveals that the omission was willful and motivated by a desire to obtain a tactical advantage that would minimize the effectiveness of cross-examination and the ability to adduce rebuttal evidence, it would be entirely consistent with the purpose of the confrontation clause simply to exclude the witnesses' testimony.

California v. Brown 479 U.S. 538, 93 L. Ed. 2d 934, 107 S.Ct. 837 (1987) the Court, in an opinion by Rehnquist for 5 justices, held that an instruction given during the penalty phase of a capital murder trial informing jurors that they "must not be swayed by mere sentiment, conjecture, sympathy, passion, prejudice, public opinion or public feeling" did not violate the Eighth and Fourteenth Amendments.

North v. Russell 427 U.S. 328, 49 L.Ed. 2d 534, 96 S.Ct. 2709 (1976) the Court, in an opinion by Burger for 5 justices, held that the use of lay judges did not violate due process where a trial *de novo* before a lawyer-judge was available if the defendant was convicted.

9. Other Issues

a. Insanity and Competency to Stand Trial

Medina v. California 505 U.S. 437, 120 L.Ed. 2d 353, 112 S.Ct. 2572 (1992) the Court, 5–4 in an opinion by Kennedy, held that a statute that required the party raising the issue of competency to stand trial to prove the issue by a preponderance of the evidence was constitutional.

Foucha v. Louisiana 504 U.S. 71, 118 L.Ed. 2d 437, 112 S.Ct. 1780 (1992) the Court, 5–4 in an opinion by White part of which was the opinion of the Court, held that defendants accquitted on a plea of not guilty by reason of insanity could be held in a mental hospital only so long as they were dangerous to themselves or others.

Powell v. Texas 492 U.S. 680, 106 L.Ed. 2d 551, 109 S.Ct. 3146 (1989) the Court, in a unanimous *per curiam* opinion, held that while a defendant raising an insanity defense may waive some Fifth Amendment rights and give the prosecution the right to have the defendant examined by prosecution experts, conducting such evaluation without prior notice to defense counsel violates the Sixth Amendment. The Court reiterated that the prosecution does not have the right to subject the defendant to psychiatric examination in order to show future dangerousness without first informing him/her of the right to remain silent and that anything said can be used against him/her at a sentencing proceeding.

b. Immunity

United States v. Apfelbaum 445 U.S. 115 63 L.Ed. 2d 250, 100 S.Ct. 948 (1980) the Court, in an opinion by Rehnquist for 6 justices, held that neither the Fifth Amendment privilege against compulsory self-incrimination nor federal statutes preclude the use of immunized grand jury testimony in a trial for the charge of false swearing before a grand jury.

New Jersey v. Portash 440 U.S. 450, 59 L.Ed. 2d 501, 99 S.Ct. 1292 (1979) the Court, 7–2, in an opinion by Stewart, held that the Fifth and Fourteenth Amendments prohibit a prosecutor from using a person's legislatively immunized grand jury testimony to impeach that person's credibility if he/she is a defendant in a subsequent criminal trial and takes the witness stand.

c. Security in the Courtroom

Holbrook v. Flynn 475 U.S. 560, 89 L.Ed. 2d 525, 106 S.Ct. 1340 (1986) the Court, in a unanimous opinion by Marshall, held that the defendant's right to a fair trial was not violated when court security was supplemented by four uniformed officers seated in the front row of the spectator section. The Court required a case-by-case analysis of security measures.

Illinois v. Allen (1970) 397 U.S. 337, 25 L.Ed. 2d 353, 90 S.Ct. 1Q57 (1970) the Court, in an opinion by Black, held that an extremely disruptive defendant has no Sixth Amendment right to remain in the courtroom during his/her trial.

VI EIGHTH AMENDMENT ISSUES

A. Death Penalty

Calderon v. Coleman 525 U.S. ___ 142 L.Ed. 2d 521, 119 S.Ct. 500 (1998) the Court, 5–4 in a *per curiam* opinion, held that in a death penalty case the Court will intervene only if it finds that an error, in the whole context of the particular case, had a substantial and injurious effect or influence on the jury's verdict.

Hopkins v. Reeves 524 U.S. ___, 141 L.Ed. 2d 76, 118 S.Ct. 1895 (1998) the Court, 7–2 in an opinion by Thomas, reaffirmed the duty to give jury instructions on lesser included offenses but held that in a capital murder case the trial judge did not violate the defendant's rights by declining to give jury instructions on second-degree murder and manslaughter when these crimes were not lesser included offenses.

Ohio Adult Parole Authority v. Woodard 523 U.S. 272, 140 L.Ed. 2d 387, 118 S.Ct. 1244 (1998) the Court, in an opinion by Rehnquist pertinent parts of which were unanimous, held that there were no violations of the Fifth Amendment when death-row inmates seeking clemency were given the choice of testifying at a voluntary clemency hearing or allowing adverse inferences to be drawn from failure to testify.

Buchanan v. Angelone 522 U.S. 269, 139 L.Ed. 2d 702, 118 S.Ct. 757 (1998) the Court, 6–3 in an opinion by Rehnquist, held that in a death penalty trial it was not mandatory to give the jury specific instructions on the concept of mitigation or statutorily defined mitigating factors when the jury was informed that it must consider "all of the evidence" and if it found the aggravating factors were established beyond a reasonable doubt then it "may fix" the penalty at death; the jury was also directed that if it believed that all the evidence justified a lesser sentence then it "shall" impose a life sentence.

Gray v. Netherland 518 U.S. 152, 135 L.Ed. 2d 457, 116 S.Ct. 2074 (1996) the Court, 5–4 in an opinion by Rehnquist, held that a defendant in a capital case does not have a special right to notice of the evidence that will be used against him at the penalty phase of the hearing.

Loving v. United States 517 U.S. 748, 135 L.Ed. 2d 36, 116 S.Ct. 1737 (1996) the Court, in an opinion by Rehnquist for 6 justices and concurring opinions for the remaining justices, held that Congress' delegation to the president, as commander in chief, of the authority to prescribe aggravating factors for use in determining if military personnel should receive the death penalty for a killing committed in the

United States in peacetime, was consistent with the separation-of-powers principles.

Lonchar v. Thomas 517 U.S. 314, 134 L.Ed. 2d 440, 116 S.Ct. 1293 (1996) the Court, in an opinion by Breyer for 5 members of the court with 4 other justices concurring, held that a death-row defendant's first federal *habeas corpus* petition, even though filed in the "eleventh hour," must be reviewed within the framework of the *habeas corpus* rules and settled precedents and cannot be dismissed due to the fact that a stay of execution must be granted.

Tuggle v. Netherland 516 U.S. 10, 133 L.Ed. 2d 251, 116 S.Ct. 283 (1995) the Court, 9–0 in a *per curiam* opinion, held that failure to provide an indigent defendant with assistance of an independent psychiatrist in a death penalty case where the prosecution used psychiatric evidence to show the defendant's future dangerousness was reversible error that could not be outweighed by the fact that there was at least one valid aggravating circumstance presented at the penalty phase of the trial.

Netherland v. Tuggle 516 U.S. 951, 132 L.Ed. 2d 879, 116 S.Ct. 4 (1995) the Court, 5 in a *per curiam* opinion, vacated a stay of execution granted by the federal Court of Appeals in a death penalty case. The Court emphasized that when granting a stay of execution the Court of Appeals must find a "significant possibility of reversal" or believe that four Supreme Court Justices would find the underlying issue sufficiently meritorious to grant *certiorari*.

Harris v. Alabama 513 U.S. 504, 130 L.Ed. 2d 1004, 115 S.Ct. 1031 (1995) the Court, 8–1 in an opinion by O'Connor, upheld an Alabama law that vests capital sentencing authority in the trial judge but required the judge to consider an advisory jury verdict without specifying the weight that the judge must give the advisory verdict.

Schiro v. Farley 510 U.S. 222, 127 L.Ed. 2d 47, 114 S.Ct. 783 (1994) the Court, 7–2 in an opinion by O'Connor, held that the sentencing phase of a bifurcated death penalty trial is not a successive prosecution for the purposes of double jeopardy. The jury's failure to return a verdict is tantamount to an acquittal for double jeopardy purposes only if the record establishes that the issue was actually and necessarily decided in the defendant's favor. This is determined by an examination of the entire record.

Tuilaepa v. California 512 U.S. 967, 129 L.Ed. 2d 750, 114 S.Ct. 2630 (1994) the Court, in an opinion by Kennedy for 6 justices, held that three of California's special circumstances in death penalty cases were not unconstitutionally vague; juries can be required to consider a relevant, open-ended factor, such as the circumstances of the crime, without being required to answer a factual question; and it was not a flaw to fail to instruct jurors how to weigh any of the facts.

Romano v. Oklahoma 512 U.S. 1, 129 L.Ed. 2d 1 114 S.Ct. 2004 (1994) the Court, 5–4 in an opinion by Rehnquist, held that under the circumstances of the case, the use of a prior murder conviction as a special circumstance at the penalty phase of the current capital murder trial did not violate the defendant's rights, even though an appellate court reversed the first case after the jury returned the death penalty verdict. The jury found four aggravating circumstances had been established.

Simmons v. South Carolina 512 U.S. 154, 129 L.Ed. 2d 133, 114 S.Ct. 2187 (1994) the Court, without a majority opinion, held the trial court violated due process by refusing the defense's request to inform the jury that a life imprisonment verdict in a death penalty case meant that the defendant would not be eligible for parole.

Johnson v. Texas 509 U.S. 350, 125 L.Ed. 2d 290, 113 S.Ct. 2658 (1993) the Court, 5–4 in an opinion by Kennedy, held that in the penalty phase of a capital murder case the defendant must be allowed to introduce evidence that his/her youth contributed to the crime, but the judge is not required to give a specific instruction telling the jury to consider this as a mitigating circumstance.

Arave v. Creech 507 U.S. 463, 123 L.Ed. 2d 188, 113 S.Ct. 1534 (1993) the Court, 7–2 in an opinion by O'Connor, held that an aggravating circumstance of "utter disregard for human life" was valid in light of the consistent narrowing definition given to the term by the Idaho Supreme Court. The limiting instructions included descriptive phrases such as "acts or circumstances surrounding the crime which exhibit the highest, the utmost, callous disregard for human life, i.e., the cold-blooded, pitiless slayer."

Delo v. Lashley 507 U.S. 272, 122 L.Ed. 2d 620, 113 S.Ct. 1222 (1993) the Court, in a *per curiam* opinion for 6 justices, held that in a capital case there is no constitutional requirement that the judge give a jury instruction on mitigating circumstances when the defendant has not introduced any evidence in mitigation.

Lockhart v. Fretwell 506 U.S. 364, 122 L.Ed. 2d 180, 113 S.Ct. 838 (1993) the Court, 7–2 in an opinion by Rehnquist, held that counsel's failure to make an objection in the penalty phase of death penalty case to the improper use of an aggravating circumstance did not constitute ineffective assistance of counsel. The court found that the result of the sentencing proceeding in the case was not rendered unreliable or fundamentally unfair as a result of counsel's failure to make the objection.

Espinosa v. Florida 505 U.S. 1079, 120 L.Ed. 2d 854, 112 S.Ct. 2926 (1992) the Court, 6–3 in a *per curiam* opinion, held that in a capital case a jury instruction on an unconstitutionally vague aggravating factor ("especially wicked, evil, atrocious or cruel") produced reversible error where the jury rendered an advisory verdict to the judge and the judge was required by state case law to give "great weight" to the jury finding.

Morgan v. Illinois 504 U.S. 719, 119 L. Ed. 2d 492, 112 S.Ct. 2222 (1992) the Court, 6–3 in an opinion by White, held that due process was violated when a trial judge in a capital case refused to ask potential jurors during *voir dire* if they would automatically impose the death penalty upon conviction.

Sochor v. Florida 504 U.S. 527, 119 L.Ed. 2d 326, 112 S.Ct. 2114 (1992) the Court, 7–2 in an opinion by Souter, held that failure to make a timely objection to a jury instruction on an invalid aggravating circumstance in a capital sentencing hearing waives the right to appeal that jury instruction.

Dawson v. Delaware 503 U.S. 159, 117 L.Ed. 2d 309, 112 S.Ct. 1093 (1992) the Court, 8–1 in an opinion by Rehnquist, held that admission of evidence at a penalty phase of a capital trial of defendant's membership in the Aryan Brotherhood did not violate his First Amendment rights.

Gomez v. United States District Court 503 U.S. 653, 118 L.Ed. 2d 293, 112 S.Ct. 1652 (1992) the Court, 7–2 in a *per curiam* opinion, held that a court may consider the last-minute nature of an application for a stay of execution and that there was no good reason for the abusive delay, which was compounded by last-minute attempts to manipulate the judicial process, as negating the right to equitable relief.

Payne v. Tennessee 501 U.S. 808, 115 L.Ed. 2d 720, 111 S.Ct. 2597 (1991) the Court, 6–3 in an opinion by Rehnquist, held that the Eighth Amendment does not bar the introduction of victim-impact evidence during the penalty phase of a capital case.

Lankford v. Idaho 500 U.S. 110, 114 L.Ed. 2d 173, 111 S.Ct. 1723 (1991) the Court, 5–4 in an opinion by Stevens, held that imposition of the death penalty violated due process where the prosecutor had notified the trial judge and defendant that the state would not recommend the death penalty but the judge sentenced the defendant to death.

Lewis v. Jeffers 497 U.S. 764, 111 L.Ed. 2d 606, 110 S.Ct. 3092 (1990) the Court, in an opinion by O'Connor for 5 justices, held that if a state has adopted a constitutionally narrow construction of a facially vague aggravating circumstance, and if the state has applied that construction to the facts of the particular case, then the "fundamental constitutional requirement" of "channeling and limiting... the sentencer's discretion in imposing the death penalty" has been met.

Walton v. Arizona 497 U.S. 639, 111 L.Ed. 2d 511, 110 S.Ct. 3047 (1990) the Court, in an opinion by White relevant parts of which represented the opinion of 5 justices, held: (1) Arizona's capital sentencing law, which allowed the judge rather than the jury to decide what aggravating and mitigating circumstances are present, was not unconstitutional; and (2) an aggravating circumstance of "especially heinous, cruel or depraved" was not unconstitutional for failure to provide adequate guidelines, because the Arizona Supreme Court had defined these terms sufficiently by stating "a crime is committed in an especially cruel manner when the perpetrator inflicts mental anguish or physical abuse before the victim's death"... and "mental anguish includes a victim's uncertainty as to his ultimate fate."

Whitmore v. Arkansas 495 U.S. 149, 109 L.Ed. 2d 135, 110 S.Ct. 1717 (1990) the Court, in an opinion by Rehnquist for 7 justices, held that in order to proceed as "next friend" and appeal a death sentence for a defendant who has refused to seek an appeal, there must be showing that the party in interest is not capable of litigating his/her own case due to mental incapacity, lack of access to court, or other similar disability.

Clemons v. Mississippi 494 U.S. 738, 108 L.Ed. 2d 725, 110 S.Ct. 1441 (1990) the Court, in an opinion by White for 5 justices, held that a state appellate court may uphold a death sentence that was based in part on an invalid or improperly defined aggravating circumstance if it does one of the following: (1) reweighs the aggravating and mitigating evidence utilizing the appropriate standards; or (2) finds that the harmless error rule applies.

McKoy v. North Carolina 494 U.S. 433, 108 L.Ed. 2d 369, 110 S.Ct. 1227 (1990) the

Court, in an opinion by Marshall for 5 justices, held that North Carolina's requirement that jurors only consider mitigating circumstances on which the jury unanimously agreed violated the defendant's right to have mitigating evidence considered.

Boyde v. California 494 U.S. 370, 108 L.Ed. 2d 316, 110 S.Ct. 1190 (1990) the Court, in an opinion by Rehnquist for 5 justices, held that California jury instruction that required jurors to vote for the death penalty if the aggravating circumstances outweighed the mitigating circumstances was constitutional. The defendant's argument that the jury must have the freedom to decline to impose the death penalty was rejected.

Blystone v. Pennsylvania 494 U.S. 299, 108 L.Ed. 2d 255, 110 S.Ct. 1078 (1990) the Court, in an opinion by Rehnquist for 5 justices, held that Pennsylvania law that required the jury to impose the sentence of death if it finds at least one aggravating circumstance and no mitigating circumstances is constitutional.

Stanford v. Kentucky 492 U.S. 361, 106 L.Ed. 2d 306, 109 S.Ct. 2969 (1989) the Court, in an opinion by Scalia for 5 justices, held that there was no national consensus that execution of 16- and 17-year-olds for capital crimes was cruel and unusual.

Penry v. Lynaugh 492 U.S. 302, 106 L.Ed. 2d 256, 109 S.Ct. 2934 (1989) the Court, in an opinion by O'Connor for 5 justices, found that, at the present time, there is insufficient evidence of a national consensus against executing mentally retarded people convicted of capital offenses for the Court to conclude that it is categorically prohibited by the Eighth Amendment. Case involved man with IQ between 50 and 63 and mental age of 6 years.

Hildwin v. Florida 490 U.S. 638, 104 L.Ed. 2d 728, 109 S.Ct. 2055 (1989) the Court, in a *per curiam* opinion for 6 justices, held that a Florida statute that required that the findings of aggravating and mitigating circumstances be made by the judge in a capital case after the jury recommends the death sentence did not violate the Sixth Amendment, because there is no constitutional right to be sentenced by a jury.

Johnson v. Mississippi 486 U.S. 578, 100 L.Ed. 2d 575, 108 S.Ct. 1981 (1988) the Court, in an opinion by Stevens for 8 justices, held that the fact that the felony conviction relied upon by the trial court as an aggravating circumstance was subsequently reversed on appeal requires that the defendant's death sentence be reexamined.

Mills v. Maryland 486 U.S. 367, 100 L.Ed. 2d 384, 108 S.Ct. 1860 (1988) the Court, in an opinion by Blackmun for 5 justices, held Maryland's capital punishment statute unconstitutional because it required unanimous agreement on mitigating circumstances by jurors before the balance of aggravating and mitigating circumstances could be considered.

Maynard v. Cartwright 486 U.S. 356, 100 L.Ed. 2d 372, 108 S.Ct. 1853 (1988) the Court, in a unanimous opinion by White, held that an Oklahoma statute that listed "especially heinous, atrocious or cruel" as an aggravating circumstance that could be considered in capital murder cases fails to adequately inform juries what they must find to impose the death penalty.

Lawenfield v. Phelps 484 U.S. 231, 98 L.Ed. 2d 568, 108 S.Ct. 546 (1988) the Court, in an opinion by Rehnquist for 5 justices, held that the fact that an aggravating circumstance used to determine eligibility for the death penalty duplicated one of the elements of the crime does not violate any constitutional rights.

Sumner v. Shuman 483 U.S. 66, 97 L.Ed. 2d 56, 107 S.Ct. 2716 (1987) the Court, in an opinion by Blackmun for 6 justices, held that a state statute that made the death penalty mandatory for prison inmates who are convicted of murder while serving a life sentence without possibility of parole violates the Eighth and Fourteenth Amendments.

Booth v. Maryland 482 U.S. 496, 96 L.Ed. 2d 440, 107 S.Ct. 2529 (1987) the Court, in an opinion by Powell for 5 justices, held that introducing a victim-impact statement, which described the personal characteristics of the victim and emotional impact of the crimes on the victim's family as well as the family's opinions of the defendant and characterization of the crimes, during the penalty phase of a capital case, introduced irrelevant information and created a constitutionally unacceptable risk that the jury might impose the death penalty in an arbitrary and capricious manner.

Gray v. Mississippi 481 U.S. 648, 95 L.Ed. 2d 622, 107 S.Ct. 2045 (1987) the Court, in an opinion by Blackmun pertinent parts of which were signed by 5 justices, refused to apply the harmless error rule to a conviction in a capital case where a prospective juror had been improperly excluded from the jury panel under *Witherspoon v. Illinois*.

Hitchcock v. Dugger 481 U.S. 393, 95 L.Ed. 2d 347, 107 S.Ct. 1821 (1987) the Court, in a unanimous opinion by Scalia, held that instructing the sentencing jury that they could only consider statutory mitigating circumstances clearly violated the defendant's Eighth Amendment rights.

McCleskey v. Kemp 481 U.S. 279, 95 L.Ed. 2d 262, 107 S.Ct. 1756 (1987) the Court, in an opinion by Powell for 5 justices, held a complex statistical study that indicated that black defendants received the death penalty more often than whites, especially when the victim was white, was not sufficient to demonstrate that racial considerations enter into capital sentencing determinations. The Court found that the defendant did not show a violation of equal protection because he had not shown that there was purposeful discrimination in his own case.

Tison v. Arizona 481 U.S. 137, 95 L.Ed. 2d 127, 107 S.Ct. 1676 (1987) the Court, in an opinion by O'Connor for 5 justices, held the death penalty can be constitutionally imposed in felony-murder cases, even though the defendant did not have the intent to kill, if there

was major participation in the felony combined with reckless indifference to human life.

California v. Brown 479 U.S. 538, 93 L. Ed. 2d 934, 107 S.Ct. 837 (1987) the Court, in an opinion by Rehnquist for 5 justices, held that an instruction given during the penalty phase of a capital murder trial informing jurors that they "must not be swayed by mere sentiment, conjecture, sympathy, passion, prejudice, public opinion or public feeling" did not violate the Eighth and Fourteenth Amendments.

Ford v. Wainwright 477 U.S. 399, 91 L.Ed. 2d 335, 106 S.Ct. 2595 (1986) the Court, in an opinion by Marshall for 5 justices, held the Eighth Amendment prohibits a state from carrying out a sentence of death upon a prisoner who is insane.

Lockhart v. McCree 476 U.S. 162, 90 L.Ed. 2d 137, 106 S.Ct. 1758 (1986) the Court, in an opinion by Rehnquist for 5 justices, held the Constitution does not prohibit the removal for cause, prior to the guilt phase of a bifurcated capital trial, of prospective jurors whose opposition to the death penalty is so strong that it would prevent or substantially impair the performance of their duties as jurors at the sentencing phase of the trial.

Poland v. Arizona 476 U.S. 147, 90 L.Ed. 2d 123, 106 S.Ct. 1749 (1986) the Court, in an opinion by White for 6 justices, held the double jeopardy clause does not bar a second capital sentencing proceeding when, on appeal from a sentence of death, the reviewing court finds the evidence insufficient to support the only aggravating factor on which the sentencing judge relied, but does not find the evidence insufficient to support the death penalty.

Turner v. Murray 476 U.S. 28, 90 L.Ed. 2d 27, 106 S.Ct. 1683 (1986) the Court, in an opinion by White for 5 justices, held that a defendant in a capital case who is accused of an interracial crime is entitled to have prospective jurors informed of the race of the victim and questioned on the issue of racial bias. A defendant cannot complain that the trial judge did not question prospective jurors on racial prejudice unless the defendant specifically requested such an inquiry during jury selection.

Skipper v. South Carolina 476 U.S. 1, 90 L.Ed. 2d 1, 106 S.Ct. 1669 (1986) the Court, in an opinion by White for 6 justices, held that the state unconstitutionally denied the defendant the right to introduce mitigating evidence at the penalty phase of a capital case when the judge refused to allow testimony regarding defendant's good behavior in jail during the seven months that he awaited trial.

Cabana v. Bullock 474 U.S. 376, 88 L.Ed. 2d 704, 106 S.Ct. 689 (1986) the Court, in an opinion by White for 5 justices, held that as long as the state court determines that a person in fact killed, attempted to kill, or intended to kill, the Eighth Amendment is satisfied regardless of whether it was the trial jury, trial judge or an appellate judge that made the required determination of culpability.

Caldwell v. Mississippi 472 U.S. 320, 86 L.Ed. 2d 231, 105 S.Ct. 2633 (1985) the Court, in an opinion by Marshall for 5 members, held that it is constitutionally impermissible to rest a death sentence on a determination made by a sentencer who has been led to believe that the responsibility for determining the appropriateness of the defendant's execution rests on the state's Supreme Court.

Ake v. Oklahoma 470 U.S. 68, 84 L.Ed. 2d 53, 105 S.Ct. 1087 (1985) the Court, in an opinion by Marshall for 8 justices, held: (1) where defense makes preliminary showing that sanity may be significant factor in case, indigent is entitled to assistance of psychiatrist if defendant cannot afford to hire one; (2) in capital case, indigent's defense is entitled to appointed psychiatrist if prosecution intends to use psychiatric evidence of defendant's future dangerousness.

Wainwright v. Witt 469 U.S. 412, 83 L.Ed. 2d 841, 105 S.Ct. 844 (1985) the Court, in a opinion by Rehnquist for 6 justices, held a juror may be excluded in a death penalty case if his/her personal views on capital punishment would prevent or substantially impair the performance of his/her duties as a juror in accordance with the instructions and his/her oath.

Spaziano v. Florida 468 U.S. 447, 82 L.Ed. 2d 340, 104 S.Ct. 3154 (1984) the Court, in an opinion by Blackmun, held the Florida system of allowing the judge to impose the death penalty after the jury recommended life imprisonment was not unconstitutional.

Pulley v. Harris 465 U.S. 37, 79 L.Ed. 2d 29, 104 S.Ct. 871 (1984) the Court, in an opinion by White for 6 members of the Court, held that appellate courts in death penalty cases are not required to compare the sentence in the case before them with sentences imposed in similar cases.

Wainwright v. Goode 464 U.S. 78, 78 L.Ed. 2d 187, 104 S.Ct. 378 (1983) the Court, 7–2 in a *per curiam* opinion, held that the act of the trial court in considering aggravating circumstances not authorized by state statute did not require reversal because the state procedures did not produce an arbitrary or freakish sentence. Similar results were reached in *Barclay v. Florida* 463 U.S. 939, 77 L.Ed. 2d 1134, 103 S.Ct. 3418 (1983); and *Zant v. Stephens* 462 U.S. 862, 77 L.Ed. 2d 235, 103 S.Ct. 2733 (1983).

California v. Ramos 463 U.S. 992, 77 L.Ed. 2d 1171, 103 S.Ct. 3446 (1983) the Court, in an opinion by O'Connor for 5 members of the Court, held that in death penalty cases instructing the jury that a sentence of life imprisonment without parole could be commuted by the governor to a sentence allowing parole did not violate the Constitution.

Marshall v. Lonberger 459 U.S. 422, 74 L.Ed. 2d 646, 103 S.Ct. 843 (1983) the Court, 5–4, in an opinion by Rehnquist, held that the use of a guilty plea, knowingly and voluntarily made in a prior case, to establish an aggravating circumstance in the current murder case was constitutional.

Enmund v. Florida 458 U.S. 782, 73 L.Ed. 2d 1140, 102 S.Ct. 3368 (1982) the Court, 5–4, in an opinion by White, held that the death penalty was unconstitutionally imposed in a felony murder case where the defendant had aided and abetted the felony but had not killed, attempted to kill, intended to kill, or contemplated that life would be taken during the commission of the felony.

Eddings v. Oklahoma 455 U.S. 104, 71 L.Ed. 2d 1, 102 S.Ct. 869 (1982) the Court, 5–4, in an opinion by Powell, held that the death sentence was unconstitutional because the state court found, as a matter of law, that it could not consider the defendant's unhappy childhood and emotional disturbance as mitigating circumstances.

Bullington v. Missouri 451 U.S. 430, 68 L.Ed. 2d 270, 101 S.Ct. 70 (1981) the Court, 5–4, in an opinion by Blackmun, held that the imposition of the death penalty at the retrial of a defendant, who had successfully sought a new trial after a conviction for murder with a sentence of life imprisonment, was barred by double jeopardy.

Hammett v. Texas 448 U.S. 725, 65 L.Ed. 2d 1086, 100 S.Ct. 2905 (1980) the Court, 6–3, in a *per curiam* opinion, allowed a prisoner sentenced to death to withdraw petition for hearing by the Supreme Court, which the prisoner's counsel had filed without his consent.

Beck v. Alabama 447 U.S. 625, 65 L.Ed. 2d 392, 100 S.Ct. 2382 (1980) the Court, in an opinion by Stevens for 6 members of the Court, held that in a capital case it was reversible error to fail to give a jury instruction on a lesser included noncapital offense when the evidence would support a conviction for such offense.

Coker v. Georgia 433 U.S. 584, 53 L.Ed. 2d 982, 97 S.Ct. 2861 (1977) the Court, 7–2, in an opinion by White for 4 members of the Court, held that the imposition of the death penalty for the rape of an adult female was unconstitutional.

Dobbert v. Florida 432 U.S. 282, 53 L.Ed. 2d 344, 97 S.Ct. 2290 (1977) the Court, in an opinion by Rehnquist for 6 members of the Court, held that imposition of the death penalty did not violate the prohibition of *ex post facto* laws where the state had changed some of the procedures and now allows the judge to impose the death penalty despite a jury recommendation of life imprisonment, where judges previously lacked this authority.

Roberts (Harry) v. Louisiana 431 U.S. 633, 52 L.Ed. 2d 637, 97 S.Ct. 1993 (1977) the Court, 5–4, in a *per curiam* opinion, held that a statute violated the Eighth Amendment by mandating a death sentence for killing a peace officer without consideration of particularized mitigating factors.

Gardner v. Florida 430 U.S. 349, 51 L.Ed. 2d 393, 97 S.Ct. 1197 (1977) the Court reversed a death penalty but was unable to agree on an opinion. It held that the failure to disclose confidential portions of the presentence report to the defendant in a capital case was unconstitutional.

Gregg v. Georgia 428 U.S. 153, 49 L.Ed. 2d 859, 96 S.Ct. 2909 (1976) the Court, 7–2, affirmed a death penalty but was unable to agree on an opinion. An opinion by Stewart, for 3 members of the Court, found the Georgia statutes constitutionally adequate because: they specified aggravating circumstances with clarity; they required the jury to consider the circumstances of the crime and the character of the defendant; required the state supreme court to determine whether the death sentence was the result of passion or prejudice, if it was supported by evidence establishing a statutory aggravating circumstance, and was not disproportionate in comparison with sentences imposed in similar crimes. The vesting of unfettered discretion in the prosecutor to file charges and accept plea bargains, in juries to convict for lesser included offenses, and in the executive branch to commute death sentences did not invalidate the statutory scheme. An opinion by White, for 3 members of the Court, found: the statutes adequately guided the jury in its exercise of discretion to impose the death penalty; the state supreme court had the authority, and there was no evidence that it was incapable of performing the task, to review death penalty cases and determine if the death penalty was being administered in a discriminatory, standardless, or rare fashion; and it was not error to vest total discretion in the prosecutor for the filing of capital charges and accepting of pleas in capital cases.

Furman v. Georgia 408 U.S. 238, 33 L.Ed. 2d 346, 92 S.Ct. 2726 (1972) the Court, in 9 separate opinions, held that the manner in which the death penalty was imposed and carried out under the laws of Georgia and Texas was cruel and unusual punishment, in violation of the Eighth and Fourteenth Amendments.

Witherspoon v. Illinois 391 U.S. 510, 20 L.Ed. 2d 776, 88 S.Ct. 1770 (1968) the majority opinion held that a sentence of death cannot be carried out if the jury that imposed or recommended it was chosen by excluding prospective jurors for cause simply because they voiced general objections to the death penalty or expressed conscientious or religious scruples against its infliction.

Louisiana ex rel. Francis v. Resweber 329 U.S. 459, 91 L.Ed. 422, 67 S.Ct. 374 (1947) the Court, 5–4, held that a second attempt to execute a defendant after he escaped death the first time due to mechanical failure of the electric chair did not violate the Eighth Amendment.

B. Other Eighth Amendment Issues

United States v. Bajakajian 524 U.S. ___, 141 L.Ed. 2d 314, 118 S.Ct. 2028 (1998) the Court, 5–4 in an opinion by Thomas, held that forfeiture of $357,144, which defendant attempted to transport out of the United States, as a penalty for violation of the federal law for which the maximum fine under the Federal Sentencing Guidelines was $5,000, violated the Eighth Amendment excessive fines clause.

Farmer v. Brennan 511 U.S. 825, 128 L.Ed. 2d 811, 114 S.Ct. 1970 (1994), the Court, 8–1 in an opinion by Souter, clarified the "deliberate indifference" standard under which prison officials violate the Eighth Amendment by failing to protect an inmate from injuries by other inmates. The Court held a prison official may be liable under the Eighth Amendment for denying humane conditions of confinement only if he knows that inmates face a substantial risk of serious harm and disregards that risk by failing to take reasonable measures to abate it.

Wilson v. Seiter 501 U.S. 294, 115 L.Ed. 2d 271, 111 S.Ct. 2321 (1991) the Court, in 5–4 opinion by Scalia, held that claims that the conditions of confinement constitute cruel and unusual punishment in violation of the Eighth Amendment should be judged by the "deliberate indifference" standard.

Harmelin v. Michigan 501 U.S. 957, 115 L.Ed. 2d 836, 111 S.Ct. 2680 (1991) the Court, 5–4 in an opinion by Scalia, held that the Eighth Amendment is not violated in noncapital cases by severe mandatory sentences.

Hunter v. Underwood 471 U.S. 222, 85 L.Ed. 2d 222, 105 S.Ct. 1916 (1985) the Court, in an opinion by Rehnquist unanimously declared an Alabama statute unconstitutional that disenfranchised a person convicted of a misdemeanor involving moral turpitude.

Solem v. Helm 463 U.S. 277, 77 L.Ed. 2d 637, 103 S.Ct. 3001 (1983) the Court, 5–4, in an opinion by Powell, held that a sentence of life imprisonment without possibility of parole, given under a habitual criminal statute, for the crime of passing a "no account" check for $100 by a person with 7 prior nonviolent felony convictions, violated the Eighth Amendment. The Court noted that the defendant, who had committed a relatively minor crime, was treated much more harshly than other criminals in the same state who had committed much more serious crimes, and that the defendant received a harsher sentence than he would have in 48 other states. *Rummel v. Estelle* was distinguished on fact that sentence in that case held possibility of parole while the sentence here did not.

Hutto v. Davis 454 U.S. 370, 70 L.Ed. 2d 556, 102 S.Ct. 703 (1982) the Court, in a *per curiam* opinion for 5 justices, held a sentence of two consecutive 20-year prison terms and two fines of $10,000 for conviction of possession and distribution of 9 ounces of marijuana did not violate the cruel and unusual punishment clause. The Court refused to note disparity in sentencing schemes between this and other crimes in the state, or disparity between sentences for similar crimes in other states.

Rummel v. Estelle 445 U.S. 263, 63 L.Ed. 2d 382, 100 S.Ct. 1133 (1980) the Court, 5–4, in an opinion by Rehnquist, held that a life sentence imposed pursuant to a recidivist statute did not violate the cruel and unusual punishment clause.

Robinson v. California 370 U.S. 660, 8 L.Ed. 758, 82 S.Ct. 1417 (1962) the Court held that addiction to drugs is a disease and cannot be criminally punished where there is no evidence of possession of drugs or violation of any other law.

VII DUE PROCESS ISSUES

A. General Standard

Reno v. Flores 507 U.S. 292, 123 L.Ed. 2d 1, 113 S.Ct. 1439 (1993) the Court, 7–2 in an opinion by Scalia, held that an Immigration and Naturalization Service rule that permits the release of alien juveniles only to their parents or other related adults does not violate substantive due process.

Griffin v. United States 502 U.S. 46, 116 L.Ed. 2d 371, 112 S.Ct. 466 (1991) the Court, in a 7–2 opinion by Scalia, held that the Fifth Amendment due process clause does not require a general guilty verdict on a multiple-object conspiracy charge to be reversed if the evidence is inadequate to support conviction as to one of the objects.

Arizona v. Fulminante 499 U.S. 279, 113 L.Ed. 2d 302, 111 S.Ct. 1246 (1991) the Court, 5–4 in an opinion by White, held that

a confession obtained by a prison informant under circumstances where there was a credible threat of physical harm by other inmates unless the informant intervened was coerced and violated due process. The Court also held, 5–4 (a different majority) in an opinion by Rehnquist, that convictions from trials in which coerced confessions were introduced are subject to the harmless error rule.

Washington v. Harper 494 U.S. 210, 108 L.Ed. 2d 178, 110 S.Ct. 1028 (1990) the Court, in an opinion by Kennedy for 6 justices, held that the due process clause permits the state to administer antipsychotic drugs against an inmate's will if the inmate has a serious mental illness and the inmate is dangerous to him/herself or others and the treatment is in the inmate's medical interest. Procedural due process was satisfied by a policy that provided for a hearing by a committee composed of one psychiatrist, one psychologist, and the prison superintendent. Adversarial hearing before this committee gave inmate the right to be present and cross-examine witnesses. Inmate had right to lay advisor but no constitutional requirement that he/she be represented by counsel. The fact that the committee met with staff prior to hearing did not violate due process as long as committee did not form final decision prior to hearing. Hearing does not need to be conducted in accordance with rules of evidence; case does not need to be established by "clear, cogent, and convincing" standard of proof.

De Shaney v. Winnebago County Department of Social Services 489 U.S. 189, 103 L.Ed. 2d 249, 109 S.Ct. 998 (1989) the Court, in an opinion by Rehnquist for 6 justices, held that while the state has a duty to protect a person from harm when it restrains that individual's freedom to act on his own behalf (through incarceration, institutionalization, or other similar restraint of personal liberty), it has no due process duty to protect a person's liberty interest against harm inflicted under other circumstances. The county was found to have no liability under 42 U.S.C. §1983 for injuries inflicted on a baby by its natural father after a social worker from children's protective services failed to heed signs of abuse and remove the child from the home.

Bowers v. Hardwick 478 U.S. 186, 92 L.Ed. 2d 140, 106 S.Ct. 2841 (1986) the Court, in an opinion by White for 5 justices, held that the due process clause does not confer a fundamental right upon homosexuals to engage in sodomy; therefore state laws that make such conduct illegal are valid provided they meet other constitutional standards.

Rochin v. California 342 U.S. 165, 96 L.Ed. 183, 72 S.Ct. 205 (1952) the Court held that evidence obtained by tactics that shock the conscience or offend the sense of justice must be excluded on due process grounds. The Court in this pre-*Mapp* case refused to exclude the evidence solely on the grounds that the defendant's Fourth Amendment rights were violated when his stomach was pumped in order to obtain evidence that he had swallowed to foil police attempts to seize it.

B. Parole and Probation

Young v. Harper 520 U.S. 143, 137 L.Ed. 2d 270, 117 S.Ct. 1148 (1997) the Court, in a unanimous opinion by Thomas, held that a program operated by the State of Oklahoma to release prison inmates early on "preparole" in order to alleviate overcrowding was functionally similar to parole; therefore the procedural protections set forth in *Morrissey v. Brewer* (1972) apply to revocation proceedings.

Griffin v. Wisconsin 483 U.S. 868, 97 L.Ed. 2d 709, 107 S.Ct. 3164 (1987) the Court, in an opinion by Scalia for 5 justices, held that the warrantless search of a probationer's home by probation officers was "reasonable" within the meaning of the Fourth Amendment because it was conducted pursuant to a valid regulation governing probationers. It is reasonable to permit information provided by a police officer, whether or not on the basis of firsthand knowledge, to support the search of a probationer.

Board of Pardons v. Allen 482 U.S. 369, 96 L.Ed. 2d 303, 107 S.Ct. 2415 (1987) the Court, in an opinion by Brennan for 6 justices, held that Montana statutes which state that, subject to specified restrictions, the Board of Pardons "shall release on parole... any person... when in its opinion there is reasonable probability that the prisoner can be released without detriment to the prisoner or the community" created a liberty interest in parole release that is protected under the due process clause of the Fourteenth Amendment. Any statute that mandates parole creates a presumption that the parole release will be granted.

Kelly v. Robinson 479 U.S. 36, 93 L.Ed. 2d 216, 107 S.Ct. 353 (1986) the Court, in an opinion by Powell for 7 justices, held that any condition a state criminal court imposed as part of a criminal sentence, including restitution, cannot be discharged in bankruptcy.

Gagnon v. Scarpelli 411 U.S. 778, 36 L.Ed. 2d 656, 93 S.Ct. 1756 (1973) the Court, 8–1 in an opinion by Powell, held that "a probationer, like a parolee, is entitled to a preliminary and a final revocation hearing, under the conditions specified in *Morrissey*." Where "special circumstances" exist the state authority may be required to assign counsel at the hearing.

Morrissey v. Brewer 408 U.S. 471, 33 L.Ed. 2d 484, 92 S.Ct. 2593 (1972) the Court in an opinion by Burger, held that due process establishes the right of a parolee to a preliminary and final hearing before his/her parole can be revoked.

C. Detention

County of Riverside v. McLaughlin 500 U.S. 44, 114 L.Ed. 2d 49, 111 S.Ct. 1661 (1991) the Court, 5–4 in an opinion by O'Connor, held that arraignments, which are also used as probable cause hearings to satisfy *Gerstein v. Pugh*, satisfied the Fourth Amendment if they were held within 48 hours of the arrests. Local practice of interpreting 48 hours to mean 48 hours plus Saturdays, Sundays, and court holidays was not constitutionally permissible.

Schall v. Martin 467 U.S. 253, 81 L.Ed. 2d 207, 104 S.Ct. 2403 (1984) the Court, in an opinion by Rehnquist for 5 members of the Court, held that a New York law authorizing pretrial detention of accused juvenile delinquents did not violate due process. The law in question also required that probable cause be established to show that the juvenile committed the offense and provided other procedural safeguards during the confinement, which was for a maximum of 17 days.

Gerstein v. Pugh 420 U.S. 103, 43 L.Ed. 2d 54, 95 S.Ct. 854 (1975) the Court, in an opinion by Powell for a unanimous Court, held persons arrested without a warrant and charged by information are entitled to a timely hearing before a neutral judge to determine probable cause for detention prior to trial. Five members of the Court held that the hearing involved did not have to include the full panoply of adversary safeguards and that it was not a "critical stage" at which the defendant had a right to have counsel present. Confrontation and cross-examination are not constitutionally required.

D. Standard of Proof

Victor v. Nebraska 511 U.S. 1, 127 L.Ed. 2d 583, 114 S.Ct. 1239 (1994) the Court, in an opinion by O'Connor part of which was unanimous, held that states can word their jury instructions on proof beyond a reasonable doubt any way they wish as long as there is no reasonable likelihood that the jury understands the instruction to allow conviction based on proof insufficient to meet the due process standard. California's instruction, which uses the phrases "moral certainty" and "abiding conviction" and "not a mere possible doubt," was upheld because other instructions sufficiently defined these key terms. Nebraska's instruction that required "substantial doubt" was found to comply with due process because "substantial" was defined as "not seeming or imaginary" rather

than referring to the magnitude of the doubt; a phrase "strong probabilities" did not understate the prosecution's burden, given the ensuing statement that such probabilities had to be strong enough to exclude a reasonable doubt.

Sullivan v. Louisiana 508 U.S. 275, 124 L.Ed. 2d 182, 113 S.Ct. 2078 (1993) the Court, in a unanimous decision by Scalia, held that failure to give the jury an adequate instruction on "proof beyond a reasonable doubt" violates the defendant's right to a jury trial and is a fundamental error requiring reversal. Harmless-error analysis is not appropriate in this type of case.

Parke v. Raley 506 U.S. 20, 121 L.Ed. 2d 391, 113 S.Ct. 517 (1992) the Court, in an opinion by O'Connor for 8 justices, held that there was no violation of due process in a Kentucky rule that required defendants charged under recidivist statutes to bear the burden of proof when challenging the use of prior guilty pleas.

Martin v. Ohio 480 U.S. 228, 94 L.Ed. 2d 267, 107 S.Ct. 1098 (1987) the Court, in an opinion by White for 5 justices, held that a state law that declares that self-defense is an affirmative defense on which the defendant has the burden of proof does not violate the due process clause.

McMillan v. Pennsylvania 477 U.S. 79, 91 L.Ed. 2d 67, 106 S.Ct. 2411 (1986) the Court, in an opinion by Rehnquist for 5 justices, upheld the constitutionality of a Pennsylvania law that provided that anyone convicted of certain enumerated felonies was subject to a mandatory minimum sentence of five years' imprisonment if the sentencing judge found, by a preponderance of the evidence, that the person "visibly possessed a firearm" during the commission of the offense. There is no right to jury sentencing, even where the sentence turns on specific findings of fact.

Cooper v. Mitchell Brothers' Santa Ana Theater 454 U.S. 90, 70 L.Ed. 2d 262, 102 S.Ct. 172 (1981) the Court, 6–3, in a *per curiam* opinion, held that states were free to decide whether or not to use the beyond-a-reasonable-doubt standard of proof in civil obscenity cases. The case involved a state civil statute for public nuisance abatement of theaters showing obscene movies.

Patterson v. New York 432 U.S. 197, 53 L.Ed. 2d 281, 97 S.Ct. 2319 (1977) the Court, 5–3 in an opinion by White, held that a state law requiring the defendant to bear the burden of persuasion for an affirmative defense did not violate due process where the affirmative defense was a separate issue and did not serve to negate any facts of the crime that the state had the burden of proving.

Mullaney v. Wilbur 421 U.S. 684, 44 L.Ed. 2d 508, 95 S.Ct. 1881 (1975) the Court, in a unanimous opinion by Powell, held that due process requires that the prosecution prove beyond a reasonable doubt every fact necessary to constitute the crime charged. A rule requiring the defendant to establish heat of passion on sudden provocation by a preponderance of the evidence violated due process.

E. Vagueness

Kolender v. Lawson 461 U.S. 352, 75 L.Ed. 2d 903, 103 S.Ct. 1855 (1983) the Court, 7–2, in an opinion by O'Connor, held that a loitering statute requiring "credible and reliable" identification upon request by the police was unconstitutionally vague. Such failure to specify the type of identification required was found to encourage arbitrary enforcement of the law.

City of Mesquite v. Aladdin's Castle, Inc. 455 U.S. 283, 71 L.Ed. 2d 152, 102 S.Ct. 1070 (1982) the Court, in an opinion by Stevens for 7 members of the Court, held a city licensing ordinance permitting the denial of a license for the operation of coin-operated amusement establishments if the applicant had any "connection with criminal elements" was not unconstitutionally vague.

F. Discovery

Bracy v. Gramley 520 U.S. 899, 138 L.Ed. 2d 97, 117 S.Ct. 1793 (1997) the Court, in a unanimous opinion by Rehnquist, held that

district court judges should fashion appropriate discovery orders in federal *habeas corpus* suits when "good cause" was shown.

Wood v. Bartholomew 516 U.S. 1, 133 L.Ed. 2d 1, 116 S.Ct. 7 (1995) the Court, 5–4 in a *per curiam* opinion, held that the prosecution's failure to turn over the results of a polygraph examination of a key witness that would have been inadmissible at trial did not violate the defendant's due process right to discovery under *Brady v. Maryland*. The Court noted that granting relief on a *habeas corpus* appeal was not justified because the case against the defendant was overwhelming and there was no likelihood that disclosure of the test results would have altered the outcome of the trial.

Kyles v. Whitley 514 U.S. 419, 131 L.Ed. 2d 490, 115 S.Ct. 1555 (1995) the Court, 5–4 in an opinion by Souter, held that an inmate was entitled to a new trial because the prosecutor failed to disclose evidence. The Court reaffirmed that the government's duty to disclose evidence favorable to the defense turns on the cumulative effect of all such evidence that was suppressed by the government. The prosecutor remains responsible for gauging the effect regardless of any failure by the police to bring favorable evidence to the prosecutor's attention.

Arizona v. Youngblood 488 U.S. 51, 102 L.Ed. 2d 281, 109 S.Ct. 333 (1988) the Court, in an opinion by Rehnquist for 5 justices, held that unless a criminal defendant can show bad faith on the part of the police, failure to preserve potentially useful evidence does not constitute a denial of due process of law.

Taylor v. Illinois 484 U.S. 400, 98 L.Ed. 2d 798, 108 S.Ct. 646 (1988) the Court, in an opinion by Stevens for 5 justices, rejected a rule giving trial judges complete authority to exclude testimony of material witnesses due to discovery violations. The trial judge may insist on an explanation for a party's failure to comply with a request to identify his/her witnesses in advance of trial. If that explanation reveals that the omission was willful and motivated by a desire to obtain a tactical advantage that would minimize the effectiveness of cross-examination and the ability to adduce rebuttal evidence, it would be entirely consistent with the purpose of the confrontation clause simply to exclude the witnesses' testimony.

Pennsylvania v. Ritchie 480 U.S. 39, 94 L. Ed. 2d 40, 107 S.Ct. 989 (1987) the Court, in an opinion by Powell, pertinent parts of which were signed by 5 justices, held that in a child molestation case, the due process clause gives the court the right to conduct an *in camera* review of pertinent records of the agency handling child abuse prior to releasing them to the defense attorney. Due process does not require full access to confidential materials.

United States v. Bagley 473 U.S. 667, 87 L.Ed. 2d 481, 105 S.Ct. 3375 (1985) the Court, in an opinion by Blackmun, pertinent parts of which represented the views of 5 justices, held that a conviction would be reversed for failure to provide the defense with items during discovery in compliance with *Brady v. Maryland* only if the withheld evidence was material in the sense that its suppression undermined confidence in the outcome of the trial.

California v. Trombetta 467 U.S. 479, 81 L.Ed. 2d 413, 104 S.Ct. 2528 (1984) the Court, in a unanimous opinion by Marshall, held that due process does not require law enforcement agencies to preserve breath samples of suspected drunk drivers.

United States v. Agurs 427 U.S. 97, 49 L.Ed. 2d 342, 96 S.Ct. 2392 (1976) the Court, 7–2, in an opinion by Stevens, held that the due process right to a fair trial required a prosecutor to volunteer exculpatory matter to the defense.

Brady v. Maryland 373 U.S. 83, 10 L.Ed. 2d 215, 83 S.Ct. 1194 (1962) the Court, in an opinion by Douglas for 6 justices, held the failure of the prosecutor to give the defense a copy of an accomplice's confession violated the defendant's due process rights. Defense had made a timely request for the confession.

G. Presumptions

Carella v. California 491 U.S. 623, 105 L.Ed. 2d 218, 109 S.Ct. 2419 (1989) the Court, in a *per curiam* opinion for 5 justices, held that a jury instruction which said a person "shall be presumed to have embezzled" a rental car if it was not returned within five days of the expiration of the rental agreement, and that "intent to commit theft by fraud is presumed" from failure to return rented property within 20 days of demand, created mandatory presumptions that violate due process. These mandatory jury instructions directly foreclosed independent jury consideration of whether the facts proved established certain elements of the offense and relieved the state of its burden of proof.

Francis v. Franklin 471 U.S. 307, 85 L.Ed. 2d 344, 105 S.Ct. 1965 (1985) the Court, in an opinion by Brennan for 5 justices, held that a jury instruction was unconstitutional if a reasonable juror, in the context of the jury charge as a whole, could have concluded that there was a mandatory presumption that shifted the burden of persuasion on the crucial element of intent to the defendant.

Sandstrom v. Montana 442 U.S. 510, 61 L.Ed. 2d 39, 99 S.Ct. 2450 (1979) the Court, in a unanimous opinion by Brennan, held that in a trial for deliberate homicide, a jury instruction that "[t]he law presumes that a person intends the ordinary consequences of his voluntary acts" violated due process. The instruction could be assumed to state a conclusive presumption and thus modify the prosecution's burden of proof and shift the burden of persuasion to the defendant to prove that he lacked the requisite mental state.

County Court of Ulster County, New York v. Allen 442 U.S. 142, 60 L.Ed. 2d 777, 99 S.Ct. 2213 (1979) the Court, in an opinion by Stevens for 5 members of the Court, held that a permissive presumption that a firearm in an automobile is in the illegal possession of all persons then occupying the vehicle does not violate due process. The presumption comports with the constitutional standard that permissive presumptions are allowed if there is a rational connection between the basic fact that the prosecution proved and the ultimate fact presumed and that the latter is more likely than not to flow from the former.

Kentucky v. Whorton 441 U.S. 786, 60 L.Ed. 2d 640, 99 S.Ct. 2088 (1979) the Court, 6–3, in a *per curiam* opinion, held failure to give a jury instruction on the presumption of innocence did not *per se* require reversal. Due process requires a review of the totality of the circumstances including the jury instructions given, arguments of counsel, and the weight of the evidence of guilty.

Taylor v. Kentucky 436 U.S. 478, 56 L.Ed. 2d 468, 98 S.Ct. 1930 (1978) the Court, 7–2, in an opinion by Powell, held that due process was violated by refusal to give a jury instruction on the presumption of innocence. Factors in the decision included: reasonable doubt instruction was weak, harmful inferences could be drawn from prosecutor's misconduct, and that the decision rested on the victim's word against that of the defendant.

H. Insanity and Competence to Stand Trial

Cooper v. Oklahoma 517 U.S. 348, 134 L.Ed. 2d 498, 116 S.Ct. 1373 (1996) the Court, in a unanimous opinion by Stevens, held that an Oklahoma law establishing a presumption that a defendant in a criminal case is competent unless incompetence is established by clear and convincing evidence violates due process under the Fourteenth Amendment because the defendant could be put on trial even though it is more likely than not that he/she is incompetent.

Shannon v. United States 512 U.S. 573, 129 L.Ed. 2d 459, 114 S.Ct. 2419 (1994) the Court, 7–2 in an opinion by Thomas, reviewed the federal Insanity Defense Reform Act of 1984 and held that the statute does not require the judge to give an instruction as to the consequences of a verdict of not guilty by reason of insanity unless there is a specific need for it, such as a witness or prosecutor

stating that the defendant will go free if found not guilty by reason of insanity.

Medina v. California 505 U.S. 437, 120 L.Ed. 2d 353, 112 S.Ct. 2572 (1992) the Court, 5–4 in an opinion by Kennedy, held that a statute that required the party raising the issue of competency to stand trial to prove the issue by a preponderance of the evidence was constitutional.

Foucha v. Louisiana 504 U.S. 71, 118 L.Ed. 2d 437, 112 S.Ct. 1780 (1992) the Court, 5–4 in an opinion by White, part of which was the opinion of the Court, held that defendants acquitted on a plea of not guilty by reason of insanity could be held in a mental hospital only so long as they were dangerous to themselves or others.

Riggins v. Nevada 504 U.S. 127, 118 L.Ed. 2d 479, 112 S.Ct. 1810 (1992) the Court, 6–3 in an opinion by O'Connor, held that a criminal defendant could be forced to take antipsychotic drugs only so long as medically necessary. Administration of such drugs violates the right to counsel where the drugs interfere with the defendant's ability to communicate with counsel and assist with the defense.

Ake v. Oklahoma 470 U.S. 68, 84 L.Ed. 2d 53, 105 S.Ct. 1087 (1985) the Court, in an opinion by Marshall for 8 justices, held: (1) where defense makes preliminary showing that sanity may be significant factor in case, an indigent defendant is entitled to assistance of psychiatrist if defendant cannot afford to hire one; (2) in capital case, indigent's defense is entitled to appointed psychiatrist if prosecution intends to use psychiatric evidence of defendant's future dangerousness.

Jones v. United States 463 U.S. 354, 77 L.Ed. 2d 694, 103 S.Ct. 3043 (1983) the Court, 5–4, in an opinion by Powell, held that a finding of insanity by a preponderance of the evidence at a criminal trial was sufficient to commit a defendant to a mental institution indefinitely until the person regains sanity or is no longer a danger. The length of the detention is not tied to the sentence that the person could have received had he/she been convicted of the offense charged.

Drope v. Missouri 420 U.S. 162, 43 L.Ed. 2d 103, 95 S.Ct. 896 (1975) the Court, in a unanimous opinion by Burger, held that a defendant's due process right to a fair trial was violated by the trial judge's failure to hold a hearing on competency to stand trial. There was sufficient evidence of incompetence on the record to require that the judge order such an examination.

I. Forfeiture Proceedings

United States v. Bajakajian 524 U.S. ___, 141 L.Ed. 2d 314, 118 S.Ct. 2028 (1998) the Court, 5–4 in an opinion by Thomas, held that forfeiture of $357,144, which defendant attempted to transport out of the United States, as a penalty for violation of the federal law for which the maximum fine under the Federal Sentencing Guidelines was $5,000, violated the Eighth Amendment excessive fines clause.

United States v. Ursery 518 U.S. 267, 135 L.Ed. 2d 549, 116 S.Ct. 2135 (1996) the Court, in an opinion by Rehnquist for 5 justices and concurring opinions by 3 other justices, held that civil forfeiture proceedings that are separate from the criminal charges relating to the same transaction do not constitute "punishment," and therefore do not violate the double jeopardy clause.

Bennis v. Michigan 516 U.S. 442, 134 L.Ed. 2d 68, 116 S.Ct. 1560 (1996) the Court, 5–4 in an opinion by Rehnquist, held that a Michigan court did not offend due process clause of the Fourteenth Amendment or the taking clause of the Fifth Amendment when it ordered the forfeiture of an automobile in which the husband engaged in sexual activity with a prostitute. Forfeiture was based on a public nuisance law with no offset for the wife's interest in the car notwithstanding her lack of knowledge of her husband's activity.

United States v. James Daniel Good Real Property 510 U.S. 43, 126 L.Ed. 2d 490, 114 S.Ct. 492 (1993) the Court held, 5–4 in an opinion by Kennedy, that in civil forfeiture proceedings against real property, a party has the right to notice and a hearing before the property is seized. Property may be seized before notice is given in exigent circumstances. The Court approved *Calero-Toledo v. Pearson Yacht Leasing Co.* 416 U.S. 663 (1974), which permitted seizure of personal property prior to giving notice if the property was of a type that could be removed to another jurisdiction, destroyed, or concealed, if advance warning of confiscation were given.

United States v. One Assortment of 89 Firearms 465 U.S. 354, 79 L.Ed. 2d 361, 104 S.Ct. 1099 (1984) the Court, in a unanimous opinion by Burger, held that the acquittal of a gun owner on charges involving firearms does not preclude a later forfeiture proceeding against the same firearms.

J. Sexually Violent Predators

Kansas v. Hendricks 521 U.S. 346, 138 L.Ed. 2d 501, 117 S.Ct. 2072 (1997) the Court, 5–4 in an opinion by Thomas, held that Kansas's Sexually Violent Predator law did not violate due process. The law permitted confinement of sexually violent predators in a mental health facility based on proof beyond a reasonable doubt that the person had past sexually violent behavior and a present mental condition that creates a likelihood of such conduct in the future if the person is not incapacitated. Conviction and/or serving a sentence for a sex crime is not a prerequisite to proceedings under the act; if the person was serving time for a prior felony sex offense, a separate hearing under the Sexually Violent Predator Act must be instituted at the end of the prison term. Confinement is permitted until the person's "abnormality or personality disorder has so changed that the person is safe to be at large," but yearly reviews are mandated.

K. Intoxication Defense

Montana v. Egelhoff 518 U.S. 37, 135 L.Ed. 2d 361, 116 S.Ct. 2013 (1996) the Court, 5–4 in an opinion by Scalia, held that a Montana law that provided that voluntary intoxication "may not be taken into consideration in determining the existence of mental state which is an element of a criminal offense" did not violate due process. Doctrines such as *actus reus*, *mens rea*, insanity, mistake, justification, and duress are within the province of the states.

L. Other Issues

City of West Covina v. Perkins 525 U.S. ___, 142 L.Ed. 2d 636, 119 S.Ct. 678 (1999) the Court, in an opinion by Kennedy for 7 justices with two justices concurring, held that the due process clause does not require state or local agencies to give detailed and specific instructions or advice to owners who seek return of property that was lawfully seized but is no longer needed for the police investigation or criminal prosecution.

County of Sacramento v. Lewis 523 U.S. 833, 140 L.Ed. 2d 1043, 118 S.Ct. 1708 (1998) the Court, in an opinion by Souter for 6 justices, held that an officer does not violate the Fourteenth Amendment's guarantee of substantive due process by causing death through deliberate or reckless indifference to life during a high-speed automobile chase aimed at apprehending a suspected offender. Only a purpose to cause harm unrelated to the legitimate object of arrest will establish a violation of due process based on arbitrary conduct that shocks the conscience.

Lachance v. Erikson 522 U.S. 262, 139 L.Ed. 2d 695, 118 S.Ct. 753 (1998) the Court, in a unanimous opinion by Rehnquist, held that the due process clause does not prohibit sanctioning a federal employee for making false statements to a federal agency regarding his/her alleged employment-related misconduct.

Washington v. Glucksberg 521 U.S. 702, 138 L.Ed. 2d 772, 117 S.Ct. 2258 (1997) the Court, in an opinion by Rehnquist for 5 justices with the remaining justices concurring, held that Washington's law prohibiting "causing" or "aiding" a suicide did not offend the Fourteenth Amendment due process clause. See also, *Vacco v. Quill* (1997).

Pounders v. Watson 521 U.S. 982, 138 L.Ed. 2d 976, 117 S.Ct. 2359 (1997) the Court, 7–2 in a *per curiam* opinion, held that a state court judge was justified in holding an attorney in summary contempt for asking questions of a witness after being admonished that the line of questioning was not permitted. The acts occurred in the presence of the court, and the fact that they had prejudicial impact on the jury was sufficient to show the need for summary contempt to vindicate the court's authority. Issuing summary contempt order by the original judge and without a trial did not violate due process under these circumstances.

Goeke v. Branch 514 U.S. 115, 131 L.Ed. 2d 152, 115 S.Ct. 1275 (1995) the Court, in a unanimous *per curiam* opinion, held that Missouri had not violated the defendant's constitutional rights when it dismissed a direct appeal because the defendant was a fugitive at the time the appeal was scheduled to be heard.

VIII EQUAL PROTECTION ISSUES

Vacco v. Quill 521 U.S. 793, 138 L.Ed. 2d 834, 117 S.Ct. 2293 (1997) the Court, in an opinion by Rehnquist for 5 justices with the remaining justices concurring, held that laws enacted by the state making assisted suicide a crime do not violate equal protection. Court distinguished the right of dying patient to refuse "heroic means" from laws making it a crime for doctors to help terminally ill patients who wished to commit suicide. See also, *Washington v. Glucksberg* (1997)

M. L. B. v. S. L. J. 519 U.S. 102, 136 L.Ed. 2d 473, 117 S.Ct. 555 (1996) the Court, 6–3 in an opinion by Ginsburg, held that a state may not withhold a "record of sufficient completeness" to permit proper appellate consideration of a decision to terminate paternal rights where the parent who wishes to appeal the termination decision cannot afford to pay for the court record.

Romer v. Evans 517 U.S. 620, 134 L.Ed. 2d 855, 116 S.Ct. 1620 (1996) the Court, 6–3 in an opinion by Kennedy, held that "Amendment 2" of the Colorado constitution, which repealed all local ordinances which prohibited discrimination on the basis of sexual orientation violated the equal protection clause of the Fourteenth Amendment. It concluded that the classification of homosexuals in "Amendment 2" did not further a proper legislative end but made them unequal to everyone else.

United States v. Armstrong 517 U.S. 456, 134 L.Ed. 2d 687, 116 S.Ct. 1480 (1996) the Court, 8–1 in an opinion by Rehnquist, held that an African American defendant who sought discovery on his claim that the U.S. Attorney singled him out for prosecution on the basis of race failed to satisfy the threshold showing that the government declined to prosecute similarly situated suspects of other races. The Court restricted the analysis to persons prosecuted for crack cocaine. Although the defense showed that more than 90 percent of persons sentenced in 1994 for crack cocaine trafficking were black, it failed to identify individuals who were not black, could have been prosecuted for the offense for which respondents were charged, but were not so prosecuted. The Court found it irrelevant that powdered cocaine cases, which had predominantly Caucasian defendants, received much lighter sentences.

J. E. B. ex rel. T. B. v. Alabama 511 U.S. 127, 128 L.Ed. 2d 89, 114 S.Ct. 1419 (1994) the Court, 6–3 in an opinion by Blackmun, held that the Fourteenth Amendment equal protection clause prohibits the use of peremptory challenges by state actors on the basis of gender. The equal protection clause prohibits discrimination in jury selection on the basis of gender, or on the assumption that an individual will be biased in a particular case for no reason other than the fact that the person happens to be a woman or happens to be a man.

Georgia v. McCollum 505 U.S. 42, 120 L.Ed. 2d 33, 112 S.Ct. 2348 (1992) the Court, 6–3 in an opinion by Blackmun, held that the Constitution prohibits a criminal defendant from engaging in purposeful discrimination on the grounds of race in the exercise of peremptory challenges if the state demonstrates a *prima facie* case of racial discrimination by the defendant, the defendant must articulate a racially neutral explanation for peremptory challenges.

Hernandez v. New York 500 U.S. 352, 114 L.Ed. 2d 395, 111 S.Ct. 1859 (1991) the Court, 6–3 although unable to agree on a majority opinion, held the equal protection clause was not violated by the exclusion of Hispanic jurors due to fear that they would rely on their own knowledge of Spanish rather than the translation of the court's interpreter.

Powers v. Ohio 499 U.S. 400, 113 L.Ed. 2d 411, 111 S.Ct. 1364 (1991) the Court, 7–2 in an opinion by Kennedy, held that a white defendant had standing to have a conviction reversed due to violation of the equal protection clause if the prosecutor used peremptory challenges to exclude prospective black jurors.

Batson v. Kentucky 476 U.S. 79, 90 L.Ed. 2d 69, 106 S.Ct. 1712 (1986) the Court, in an opinion by Powell for 7 justices, held that the equal protection clause forbids prosecutorial use of peremptory challenges to exclude potential jurors solely on account of their race or on the assumption that black jurors as a group will be unable impartially to consider the state's case against a black defendant.

Bearden v. Georgia 461 U.S. 660, 76 L.Ed. 2d 221, 103 S.Ct. 2064 (1983) the Court, in an opinion by O'Connor for 5 members of the Court, held that automatic revocation of probation for failure to pay a fine, without first determining that the probationer had not made sufficient bona fide efforts to pay the amount due or that adequate alternative forms of punishment existed, was a violation of equal protection.

Jones v. Helms 452 U.S. 412, 69 L.Ed. 2d 118, 101 S.Ct. 2434 (1981) the Court, in an opinion by Stevens for 8 members of the Court, held that a Georgia law that transformed the crime of abandonment of a child from a misdemeanor to a felony if the parent leaves the state after abandoning the child did not violate equal protection.

Michael M. v. Superior Court of Sonoma County 450 U.S. 464, 67 L.Ed. 2d 437, 101 S.Ct. 1200 (1981) the Court, in an opinion by Rehnquist for 4 members of the Court with concurring opinions by Stewart and Blackmun, found that statutory rape laws that punish only males do not violate equal protection. A sufficient state interest in preventing teenage pregnancies was found to support the laws.

Mayer v. City of Chicago (1971) 404 U.S. 189, 30 L.Ed. 2d 372, 92 S.Ct. 410 (1971) the Court, 7–2 in an opinion by Brennan, held that a rule that provided trial transcripts for defendants on appeal of felony but not misdemeanor cases was unconstitutional.

Douglas v. California 372 U.S. 353, 9 L.Ed. 2d 811, 83 S.Ct. 814 (1963) the Court held, 6–3, that there is an absolute right to the assistance of counsel during the first appeal under the equal protection clause of the Fourteenth Amendment.

Grifin v. Illinois 351 U.S. 12, 100 L.Ed. 891, 76 S.Ct. 585 (1956) the Court held, 5–4, that the due process and equal protection clauses of the Fourteenth Amendment require that all indigent defendants be furnished a transcript, or a record of sufficient completeness, for an appeal.

IX RIGHTS OF THE INCARCERATED

Edwards v. Balisok 520 U.S. 641, 137 L.Ed. 2d 906, 117 S.Ct. 1584 (1997) the Court, in a unanimous opinion by Scalia, held that the inmate's claim for declaratory relief and money damages based on allegations of deceit and bias on the part of the decision maker at a prison disciplinary hearing, that necessarily imply the invalidity of the punishment imposed but not the insufficiency of the facts establishing the violation of prison rules, is not cognizable under §1983.

Young v. Harper 520 U.S. 143, 137 L.Ed. 2d 270, 117 S.Ct. 1148 (1997) the Court, in a unanimous opinion by Thomas, held that a program operated by the State of Oklahoma to release prison inmates early on "preparole" in order to alleviate overcrowding was functionally similar to parole; therefore the procedural protections set forth in *Morrissey v. Brewer* (1972) apply to revocation proceedings.

Lewis v. Casey 518 U.S. 343, 135 L.Ed. 2d 606, 116 S.Ct. 47 (1996) the Court, in an opinion by Scalia for 5 justices which was joined in part by 3 additional justices, held that prison inmates who claim that they have been denied access to the courts and that the prisons failed to comply with *Bounds v. Smith* must show that their rights were prejudiced as a result of the denial of these rights in order to recover in a Section 1983 suit.

Sandin v. Conner 515 U.S. 472, 132 L.Ed. 2d 418, 115 S.Ct. 2293 (1995) the Court, 5–4 in an opinion by Rehnquist, held that the defendant's confinement in disciplinary segregation did not present the type of atypical, significant deprivation that affords inmates the right to a disciplinary hearing under the due process clause. The Court found no significant difference between conditions in disciplinary segregation and housing areas where prison authorities had the discretion of transferring inmates. The opinion calls for case-by-case review of prison conditions; no general conclusion that disciplinary segregation does not warrant a disciplinary hearing can be drawn.

Helling v. McKinney 509 U.S. 25, 125 L.Ed. 2d 22, 113 S.Ct. 2475 (1993) the Court, 7–2 in an opinion by White, held that an inmate stated a cause of action under the Eighth Amendment by alleging that prison officials had, with deliberate indifference, exposed him to levels of environmental tobacco smoke that pose an unreasonable risk of serious damage to his future health. The inmate must be given an opportunity to prove both the subjective and objective elements necessary to establish the Eighth Amendment violation. The prison's adoption of a smoking policy bears heavily on the inquiry into deliberate indifference.

Rufo v. Inmates of the Suffolk County Jail 502 U.S. 367, 116 L.Ed. 2d 867, 112 S.Ct. 748 (1992) the Court, 5–3 in an opinion by White, held that in a jail-overcrowding case, a party seeking modification of a consent decree must establish that a significant change in facts or law warrants revision of the decree and that the proposed modification is suitably tailored to the changed circumstances. It is not necessary to show that a "grievous wrong" will occur if the consent decree is not changed.

Thornburgh v. Abbot 490 U.S. 401, 104 L.Ed. 2d 459, 109 S.Ct. 1874 (1989) the Court, in an opinion by Blackmun for 6 justices, held that regulations that permit the Federal Bureau of Prisons to reject incoming publications found to be detrimental to institutional security are valid if they are "reasonably related to a legitimate penological interest." The rules were facially valid, but the court remanded the case for an individual determination of their application to each of 46 publications.

Bennett v. Arkansas 485 U.S. 395, 99 L.Ed. 2d 455, 108 S.Ct. 1204 (1988) the Court, in a unanimous *per curiam* opinion, held that 42 U.S.C. §407 (a), which bars attempts to attach Social Security benefits, preempted the state's attempt to seize inmates' Social Security benefits under the Arkansas State Prison Inmate Care and Custody Reimbursement Act.

O'Lone v. Shabazz 482 U.S. 342, 96 L.Ed. 2d 282, 107 S.Ct. 2400 (1987) the Court, in an opinion by Rehnquist for 5 justices, held that a prison regulation that prohibited inmates on outside work details from returning to the main prison building during the day, and thereby prevented them from attending Muslim religious services that the Koran dictated be held during the early afternoon on Fridays, did not violate their First Amendment rights. Prison officials need only show that the regulation was reasonably related to the security interest of the prison and do not have to show that there is no other reasonable alternative that would not infringe on the right to practice religion.

Turner v. Safley 482 U.S. 78, 96 L.Ed. 2d 64, 107 S.Ct. 2254 (1987) the Court, in an opinion by O'Connor for 5 justices, held that the test of reasonable relationship to legitimate penological objectives, not strict scrutiny, is used to determine if prison rules that affect only inmates are constitutional. A rule prohibiting inmate-to-inmate correspondence was upheld because it was content-neutral, logically advanced the goals of institutional security and safety, and was not an exaggerated response to these objectives. The Court held that a prison regulation that amounted to an almost complete ban on the decision to marry was not reasonably related to legitimate penological objectives.

Whitley v. Albers 475 U.S. 312, 89 L.Ed. 2d 251, 106 S.Ct. 1078 (1986) the Court, in an opinion by O'Connor for 5 justices, held that where a prison security measure that indisputably poses significant risks to the safety of inmates and prison staff was undertaken to resolve a disturbance, the inquiry must focus on whether the actions were taken in a good-faith effort to maintain or restore discipline or maliciously and sadistically for the purpose of causing harm.

Davidson v. Cannon 474 U.S. 344, 88 L.Ed. 2d 677, 106 S.Ct. 668 (1986) the Court, in an opinion by Rehnquist for 5 justices, held that neither procedural nor substantive due process is violated by a lack of due care (simple negligence) by prison officials.

Daniels v. Williams 474 U.S. 327, 88 L.Ed. 2d 662, 106 S.Ct. 662 (1986) the Court, in an opinion by Rehnquist for 6 justices, held that negligent acts of correctional officers that lead to unintended loss of property or injury do not violate inmates' due process rights.

Cleavinger v. Saxner 474 U.S. 193, 88 L.Ed. 2d 507, 106 S.Ct. 496 (1985) the Court, in an opinion by Blackmun for 6 justices, held that members of a federal prison's Institutional Discipline Committee who hear cases in which inmates are charged with rules infractions are entitled to qualified immunity from personal damages liability for actions that violate the U.S. Constitution as long as they follow the clear constitutional requirements of *Wolff v. McDonnell.*

Superintendent v. Hill 472 U.S. 445, 86 L.Ed. 2d 356, 105 S.Ct. 2768 (1985) the Court, in an opinion by O'Connor, relevant parts of which were signed by all 9 justices, held that due process is satisfied if the record relied on by a prison disciplinary board to revoke goodtime credits contains some evidence that supports that decision. The relevant question is whether there is any evidence in the record that could support the conclusion reached by the disciplinary board.

Ponte v. Real 471 U.S. 491, 85 L.Ed. 2d 553, 105 S.Ct. 2192 (1985) the Court, in an opinion by Rehnquist for 6 justices, held that when prison officials deny an inmate the right to call witnesses at a disciplinary hearing, their reason for denying the request need not be made a part of the administrative record of that disciplinary hearing. If an inmate brings suit to challenge the denial of a request to call witnesses, the prison officials may be required to state in court their reasons for denying the request.

Block v. Rutheiford 468 U.S. 576, 82 L.Ed. 2d 438, 104 S.Ct. 3227 (1984) the Court, in an opinion by Burger for 5 members of the Court, held that a total prohibition on contact visits by pretrial detainees at a jail is a reasonable response to legitimate security interests and does not violate the Fourteenth Amendment.

Hudson v. Palmer 468 U.S. 517, 82 L.Ed. 2d 393, 104 S.Ct. 3194 (1984) the Court, in an opinion by Burger for 5 members of the Court, held that an inmate did not have a reasonable expectation of privacy in his/her cell entitling him/her to Fourth Amendment protections against unreasonable searches and seizures. The Court also refused to find a due process violation where the inmate had been deprived of property by a state employee, because state law provided for a meaningful post-deprivation remedy for the loss.

United States v. Gouveia 467 U.S. 180, 81 L.Ed. 2d 146, 104 S.Ct. 2292 (1984) the Court, in an opinion by Rehnquist for 6 members of the Court, held that inmates were not constitutionally entitled to appointment of counsel while the inmates were in administrative segregation prior to initiation of adversary judicial proceedings against them.

Ohm v. Wakinekona 461 U.S. 238, 75 L.Ed. 2d 813, 103 S.Ct. 1741 (1983) the Court, in an opinion by Blackmun for 6 members of the Court, held that an inmate was not denied due process by a transfer to an out-of-state prison without a hearing. The Court found that the Hawaii statutes involved did not sufficiently limit official discretion in the placement of prisoners to create a liberty interest subject to protection under the due process clause.

Hewitt v. Helms 459 U.S. 460, 74 L.Ed. 2d 675, 103 S.Ct. 864 (1983) the Court, in an opinion by Rehnquist for 5 members of the Court, held that an informal, nonadversary, evidentiary review was sufficient for the transfer of an inmate to administrative segregation pending a complete investigation of the alleged misconduct.

Jago v. Van Curen 454 U.S. 14, 70 L.Ed. 2d 13, 102 S.Ct. 31 (1981) the Court, in a *per curiam* opinion for 5 members of the Court, held that the revocation of a parole date, prior to release of the inmate on parole, did not require a hearing.

Connecticut Board of Pardons v. Dumschat 452 U.S. 458, 69 L.Ed. 2d 158, 101 S.Ct. 2460 (1981) the Court, 7–2, in an opinion by Burger, held that the fact that the Board of Pardons granted approximately three-quarters of the applications for commutation of life sentences did not create a liberty interest for inmates that required the Board to explain its reasons for denial of the application for commutation.

Rhodes v. Chapman 452 U.S. 337, 69 L.Ed. 2d 59, 101 S.Ct. 2392 (1981) the Court, in an opinion by Powell for 5 members of the Court, held that double celling at a prison does not constitute cruel and unusual punishment where there is no evidence that the conditions in question inflict unnecessary or wanton pain, or are disproportionate to the severity of crimes warranting imprisonment.

Cuyler v. Adams 449 U.S. 433, 66 L.Ed. 2d 641, 101 S.Ct. 703 (1981) the Court, 6–3, in an opinion by Brennan, held that prisoners transferred pursuant to Article IV of the Interstate Agreement on Detainers (18 U.S.C. Appx.) are not required to forfeit any pre-existing rights under state or federal law in order to challenge their transfer. Prisoners incarcerated in states that have adopted the Uniform Criminal Extradition Act are entitled to a hearing before transfer pursuant to Article IV of the detainer agreement.

Hughes v. Rowe .449 U.S. 5, 66 L.Ed. 2d 163, 101 S.Ct. 173 (1980) the Court, in a *per curiam* opinion for 5 members of the Court, held that an inmate's proper allegation that he had been unnecessarily confined to segregation was adequate to require a response by the defendant rather than a dismissal outright. The Court also held that attorney fees should not have been awarded to the defendant-state without a finding that the prisoner's action was groundless or without foundation.

Viteck v. Jones 445 U.S. 480, 63 L.Ed. 2d 552, 100 S.Ct. 1254 (1980) the Court, in an opinion by White, joined in pertinent parts by 4 other members of the Court, held that an involuntary transfer of a prisoner to a mental hospital required a hearing that included written notice of the transfer, an adversary hearing before an independent decision maker, written findings, and effective and timely notice of these rights. The Court relied upon both the state statute that created a liberty interest in remaining at the prison and upon the stigmatizing consequences of a transfer to a mental hospital as reasons that due process required a hearing.

Greenholtz v. Inmates of the Nebraska Penal and Correctional Complex 442 U.S. 1, 60 L.Ed. 2d 668, 99 S.Ct. 2100 (1979) the Court, in an opinion by Burger for 5 members of the Court, upheld Nebraska's procedures for granting parole. The procedures included a preliminary hearing where the inmate is permitted to appear before the board and present letters and statements on his/her own behalf, and a final hearing for those who passed the first hearing. At this final hearing the inmate is allowed to call witnesses, present evidence, and be represented by private counsel of his choice. Inmates are notified in advance of the month of the hearing, but the exact day is not released until the morning of the hearing. The Court also found that due process does not mandate that the parole board specify the particular evidence on which it relied in ruling against parole.

Bell v. Wolfish 441 U.S. 520, 60 L.Ed. 2d 447, 99 S.Ct. 1861 (1979) the Court, in an opinion by Rehnquist for 5 members of the Court, held: double bunking of pretrial inmates did not violate their constitutional rights under the circumstances (length of confinement, length of time in cell per day, physical conditions in jail); a publisher-only rule (books could be received by inmates only if they were mailed directly from the publisher) was a rational response by prison administrators to security risks; restrictions on receipt of packages to one package per year were not unreasonable based on security and sanitation requirements; cell searches did not violate the rights of inmates; visual body cavity searches conducted after visits and without probable cause were legal. The case stressed reliance on the prison administration for determining a rational reason for a given prison rule.

Houchins v. KQED, Inc. 438 U.S. 1, 57 L.Ed. 2d 553, 98 S.Ct. 2588 (1978) the Court, although unable to agree upon a decision, agreed that the press did not have a right to access jails superior to that of the general public.

Procunier v. Navarette 434 U.S. 555, 55 L.Ed. 2d 24, 98 S.Ct. 855 (1978) the Court, in an opinion by White for 7 members of the Court, held that in suits under 42 U.S.C. § 1983, prison officials were entitled to qualified, rather than absolute, immunity.

Jones v. North Carolina Prisoners' Labor Union, Inc. 433 U.S. 119, 53 L.Ed. 2d 629, 97 S.Ct. 2532 (1977) the Court, in an opinion by Rehnquist for 6 members of the Court, held that prison rules prohibiting the solicitation of members for the prisoners' union, barring meetings of the union, and refusing to deliver packets of union publications that were sent to the prison in bulk mailings did not violate First Amendment freedom of speech and association or equal protection rights.

Bounds v. Smith 430 U.S. 817, 52 L.Ed. 2d 72, 97 S.Ct. 1491 (1977) the Court, in an opinion by Marshall for 6 members of the Court, held that prisoners must have access to an adequate law library if no adequate form of legal assistance was provided for them.

Estelle v. Gamble 429 U.S. 97, 50 L.Ed. 2d 251, 97 S.Ct. 285 (1976) the Court, in an opinion by Marshall for 7 members of the Court, held that deliberate indifference to a prisoner's serious medical needs constituted cruel and unusual punishment in violation of the Eighth Amendment.

Montanye v. Haymes 427 U.S. 236, 49 L.Ed. 2d 466, 96 S.Ct. 2543 (1976) the Court, in an opinion by White for 6 members of the Court, held that there was no due process right to a hearing prior to the transfer of an inmate from one prison facility to another, absent some right or justifiable expectation, rooted in state law, that the inmate would not be transferred except for misbehavior or some other specific event.

Meachum v. Fano 427 U.S. 215, 49 L.Ed. 2d 451, 96 S.Ct. 2532 (1976) the Court, in an opinion by White for 6 members of the Court, held that there was no due process requirement of a hearing prior to transferring an in-

mate from a medium-security institution to a maximum-security facility. It was noted that no pertinent state law conditioned such transfers on proof of serious misconduct or the occurrence of any other event.

Baxter v. Palmigiano 425 U.S. 308, 47 L.Ed. 2d 810, 96 S.Ct. 1551 (1976) the Court, in an opinion by White for 6 members of the Court, held that during a prison disciplinary hearing: an inmate has no due process right to retained or appointed counsel regardless of the charges; the Fifth Amendment does not prohibit the drawing of adverse inferences from the inmate's failure to testify at the hearing; inmates do not have a right to confront and cross-examine the witnesses against them. Authorities do not have to state reasons for denying these rights.

Estelle v. Dorrough 420 U.S. 534, 43 L.Ed. 2d 377, 95 S.Ct. 1173 (1975) the Court, in a *per curiam* opinion expressing the views of 5 members of the Court, held that a Texas statute that provided for automatic dismissal of pending appeals if the defendant felon escaped from prison for more than ten days while the appeal was pending did not violate equal protection.

Wolff v. McDonnell 418 U.S. 539, 41 L.Ed. 2d 935, 94 S.Ct. 2963 (1974) the Court, in an opinion by White for 6 members of the Court, held that in major prison disciplinary proceedings, due process requires that written notice of the charges be given to the inmate; the fact-finder make written statements of the evidence relied upon and reasons for the disciplinary action taken; the inmate be allowed to call witnesses and present documentary evidence except when doing so would be unduly hazardous to institutional security or correctional goals. Due process does not require confrontation and cross-examination of adverse witnesses or the right to counsel. The Court upheld a regulation allowing guards to open incoming mail from an attorney if done in the presence of the inmate.

Pell v. Procunier 417 U.S. 817, 41 L.Ed. 2d 495, 94 S.Ct. 2800 (1974) the Court, 6–3 in an opinion by Stewart, held that a prison regulation prohibiting face-to-face press interviews did not violate the First Amendment because other avenues were available to the media.

Johnson v. Avery 393 U.S. 483, 21 L.Ed. 2d 718, 89 S.Ct.747 (1969) the Court held a prison regulation invalid that forbade an inmate to provide legal assistance ("jailhouse lawyer") to other inmates if no other legal assistance was available.

X JUVENILE COURT PROCEEDINGS

Schall v. Martin 467 U.S. 253, 81 L.Ed. 2d 207, 104 S.Ct. 2403 (1984) the Court, in an opinion by Rehnquist for 5 members of the Court, held that a New York law authorizing pretrial detention of accused juvenile delinquents did not violate due process. To justify detention under this statute, a court must find that there was a serious risk that the juvenile might commit a crime before the return date.

Smith v. Daily Mail Publishing Co. 443 U.S. 97, 61 L.Ed. 2d 399, 99 S.Ct. 2667 (1979) the Court, in an opinion by Burger for 7 members of the Court, held that a West Virginia law that made it a crime to truthfully publish legally obtained names of alleged juvenile delinquents violated the First Amendment.

Breed v. Jones 421 U.S. 519, 44 L.Ed. 2d 346, 95 S.Ct. 1779 (1975) the Court, in a unanimous opinion by Burger held that double jeopardy can be invoked after a transfer hearing (waiver of jurisdiction) to prevent a subsequent criminal trial in adult court. The Court's ruling in effect requires that the transfer hearing be held prior to the adjudicatory hearing.

McKiever v. Pennsylvania (In re Barbara Burrus et al.), 403 U.S. 528, 29 L.Ed. 2d 647, 91 S.Ct. 1976 (1971) the Court, 6–3 in an opinion by Blackmun, held that the Sixth Amendment does not require trial by jury in state juvenile delinquency proceedings.

In re Winship 397 U.S. 358, 25 L.Ed. 2d 368, 90 S.Ct. 1068 (1970) the Court held, 5–3, through Brennan, that the due process clause requires that a criminal conviction be based upon proof of guilt beyond a reasonable doubt; the same standard applies to the adjudicatory stage of a juvenile delinquency proceeding in which a youth is charged with an act that would constitute a crime if committed by an adult.

In re Gault 387 U.S. 1, 18 L.Ed. 2d 527, 87 S.Ct. 1428 (1967) the Court held that the due process clause of the Fourteenth Amendment applies to proceedings in state juvenile courts to adjudicate a juvenile a delinquent. At the adjudicatory stage of a juvenile court proceeding, a juvenile is entitled to substantially the same rights that are accorded to an adult in a criminal court.

Kent v. United States 383 U.S. 541, 16 L.Ed. 2d 84, 86 S.Ct. 1045 (1966) the Court, dividing 5–4, held that a juvenile court must conduct a hearing prior to the entry of a waiver order transferring jurisdiction to a criminal court. (The opinion is decided on statutory grounds as an interpretation of the District of Columbia Juvenile Court Act).

XI USE OF ILLEGALLY OBTAINED EVIDENCE

A. Exclusionary Rule

Pennsylvania Board of Probation and Parole v. Scott 524 US ___ 141 L.Ed. 2d 344, 118 S.Ct. 2014 (1998) the Court, 5–4 in an opinion by Thomas, held that the exclusionary rule that prohibits introduction of evidence obtained in violation of a defendant's Fourth Amendment rights does not apply to parole revocation hearings.

Arizona v. Evans 514 U.S. 1, 131 L.Ed. 2d 34, 115 S.Ct. 1185 (1995) the Court, 7–2 in an opinion by Rehnquist, held that the "good faith" exception to the exclusionary rule applies to evidence seized incident to an arrest resulting from an inaccurate computer record indicating that there was an outstanding arrest warrant for the suspect, regardless of whether police or court personnel were responsible for the record's continued presence in the police computer.

New York v. Harris 495 U.S. 14, 109 L.Ed. 2d 13, 110 S.Ct. 1640 (1990) the Court, in an opinion by White for 5 justices, held that the exclusionary rule does not bar statements obtained outside the suspect's home after a probable cause arrest was made inside the residence in violation of *Payton v. New York*. This rule would not apply if statement was coerced, if Miranda had been violated, or if counsel had been denied under *Edwards v. Arizona*.

James v. Illinois 493 U.S. 307, 107 L.Ed. 2d 676, 110 S.Ct. 648 (1990) the Court, in an opinion by Brennan for 5 justices, held that statements that were the product of an illegal arrest could not be used to impeach a defense witness other than the defendant.

Murray v. United States 487 U.S. 533, 101 L.Ed. 2d 472, 108 S.Ct. 2529 (1988) the Court, in an opinion by Scalia for 4 justices (2 justices did not participate in the decision), held that evidence seen during an illegal entry but seized during the execution of a search warrant at a later time was admissible if the search pursuant to the warrant was in fact a genuinely independent source of the evidence seized.

Illinois v. Krull 480 U.S. 340, 94 L.Ed. 2d 364, 107 S.Ct. 1160 (1987) the Court, in an opinion by Blackmun for 5 justices, held that the "good faith" exception to the exclusionary rule applies to searches conducted by police officers acting in objectively reasonable reliance upon a statute authorizing warrantless administrative searches even though the statute was later found to violate the Fourth Amendment.

Rose v. Clark 478 U.S. 570, 92 L.Ed. 2d 460, 106 S.Ct. 3101 (1986) the Court, in an opinion by Powell for 5 justices, held that the harmless-error rule should be applied in a case where the jury was instructed that "all homicides are presumed to be malicious in the absence of evidence which would rebut the implied presumption." This case gives a good listing of which constitutional errors are governed by the harmless-error rule and which are grounds for automatic reversal.

Immigration and Naturalization Service v. Lopez-Mendoza 468 U.S. 1032, 82 L.Ed. 2d 778, 104 S.Ct. 3479 (1984) the Court, 5–4, in an opinion by O'Connor for 4 members of the Court and joined in pertinent part by Burger, held that the exclusionary rule need not be applied in civil deportation proceedings.

Massachusetts v. Sheppard 468 U.S. 981, 82 L.Ed. 2d 737, 104 S.Ct. 3424 (1984) the Court, in an opinion by White for 6 members of the Court, held that the exclusionary rule should not be applied to evidence obtained during the execution of a defective search warrant where the officers acted in objectively reasonable reliance on a warrant issued by a detached and neutral magistrate.

United States v. Leon 468 U.S. 897, 82 L.Ed. 2d 677, 104 S.Ct. 3405 (1984) the Court, 6–3, in an opinion by White, held that evidence seized under a facially valid warrant executed in good faith should only be suppressed in the unusual cases in which exclusion will further the purposes of the exclusionary rule. This has been called the "good faith" exception to the exclusionary rule.

Segura v. United States 468 U.S. 796, 82 L.Ed. 2d 599, 104 S.Ct. 3380 (1984) the Court, in an opinion by Burger relevant parts of which were joined by 5 justices, held that notwithstanding an earlier illegal entry, the Fourth Amendment did not require suppression of evidence later from a private residence pursuant to a valid search warrant because the warrant was issued on information obtained by police before the illegal entry was made. This decision is based on the independent source rule.

New York v. Quarles 467 U.S. 649, 81 L.Ed. 2d 550, 104 S.Ct. 2626 (1984) the Court, in an opinion by Rehnquist for 5 members of the

Court, held that an overriding consideration of public safety justified the officer's failure to provide Miranda warnings before asking questions regarding the location of a weapon the defendant had apparently abandoned immediately prior to arrest.

Nix v. Williams 467 U.S. 431, 81 L.Ed. 2d 377, 104 S.Ct. 2501 (1984) the Court, in an opinion by Burger for 6 justices, held that the body of a murder victim, which was found after the defendant was illegally interrogated, was admissible on the grounds it would inevitably have been discovered even if no violation of any constitutional or statutory provisions had taken place. Prosecutor must show inevitability of discovery by preponderance of evidence and need not show absence of bad faith in originally securing the evidence. This decision is the basis for the inevitable discovery exception to the exclusionary rule.

Wainwright v. Sykes 433 U.S. 72, 53 L.Ed. 2d 594, 97 S.Ct. 2497 (1977) the Court, in an opinion by Rehnquist for 6 members of the Court, held that the state may utilize a contemporaneous objection rule whereby the defendant waives the right to challenge the voluntariness of a confession unless a timely objection to its voluntariness is made. This waiver will preclude review on federal *habeas corpus* unless the defendant can establish "cause" or "prejudice" and show a miscarriage of justice.

United States v. Janis 428 U.S. 433, 49 L.Ed. 2d 1046, 96 S.Ct. 3021 (1976) the Court, 5–3 with Stevens not participating, in an opinion by Blackmun, held that the exclusionary rule did not make evidence illegally seized by the Los Angeles Police Department inadmissible in a civil tax case brought against the defendant by the Internal Revenue Service.

Oregon v. Haas 419 U.S. 823, 43 L.Ed. 2d 570, 95 S.Ct. 1215 (1975) Justice Blackmun, speaking for the Court, allowed voluntary statements obtained in violation of Miranda to be used for impeachment.

Mapp v. Ohio 367 U.S. 643, 6 L.Ed. 2d 1081, 81 S.Ct. 1684 (1961) expressly overruling its 1949 *Wolf* decision, the Court dividing 5–4, held that the Fourth Amendment exclusionary rule is applicable to the states through the due process clause of the Fourteenth Amendment.

Elkins v. United States 364 U.S. 206, 4 L.Ed. 2d 1169, 80 S.Ct. 1437 (1960) the 5–4 decision overturned the so-called silver platter doctrine, which had permitted evidence of a federal crime that state police came upon in the course of an illegal search while investigating a state crime to be turned over to federal authorities so long as federal agents did not participate in the illegal search.

Wolf v. Colorado 338 U.S. 25, 93 L.Ed. 1782, 69 S.Ct. 1359 (1949) the Court, 5–4 in an opinion by Frankfurter, stated that the Fourth Amendment applied to the states, but the majority declined to take the step of enforcing this constitutional protection by banning use of the illegally seized evidence in court. Case was later overruled by *Mapp v. Ohio* (1961).

Weeks v. United States 232 U.S. 383, 58 L.Ed. 652, 34 S.Ct. 341 (1914) the Court, in a unanimous opinion by Day, held that in a federal prosecution the Fourth Amendment barred the use of evidence secured through an illegal search and seizure by federal officers.

Boyd v. United States 116 U.S. 616, 39 L.Ed. 746, 6 S.Ct. 524 (1886) is the first case where the Court excluded evidence seized by federal officers in violation of the Fourth Amendment.

B. Fruit of the Poisonous Tree and Related Doctrines

Lanier v. South Carolina 474 U.S. 25, 88 L.Ed. 2d 23, 106 S.Ct. 297 (1985) the Court, in a *per curiam* opinion for 8 justices, held that a finding that a confession was voluntary is merely a threshold requirement for Fourth Amendment analysis of confessions made after an illegal arrest. The fact Miranda warnings have been given is not enough, in and of itself, to purge taint of illegal arrest.

Taylor v. Alabama 457 U.S. 687, 73 L.Ed. 2d 314, 102 S.Ct. 2664 (1982) the Court, in an opinion by Marshall for 5 members of the Court, held a confession obtained through custodial interrogation, after an illegal arrest, should be inadmissible unless the confession is sufficiently an act of free will to purge the taint of the illegal arrest.

United States v. Havens 446 U.S. 620, 64 L.Ed. 2d 559, 100 S.Ct. 1912 (1980) the Court, in an opinion by White for 5 members of the Court, held that illegally seized evidence could be used to impeach the defendant's statements made on direct examination during a criminal trial.

United States v. Crews 445 U.S. 463, 63 L.Ed. 2d 537, 100 S.Ct. 1244 (1980) the Court held, in an opinion by Brennan joined in pertinent parts by 4 other members of the Court, that an in-court identification is not made inadmissible solely because the defendant's original arrest was illegal.

United States v. Ceccolini 435 U.S. 268, 55 L.Ed. 2d 268, 98 S.Ct. 1054 (1978) the Court, in an opinion by Rehnquist for 5 members of the Court, held that statements made by an eye witness were sufficiently removed from the illegal search to dissipate the taint. The opinion emphasized the role of the witness's free will in dissipating the taint.

Brown v. Illinois 422 U.S. 590, 45 L.Ed. 2d 416, 95 S.Ct. 2254 (1975) the Court held, through Justice Blackmun, that the mere giving of the warnings required by *Miranda v. Arizona* does not dissipate the taint of a defendant's illegal arrest and render admissible statements given after the arrest.

Michigan v. Tucker 417 U.S. 433, 41 L.Ed. 2d 182, 94 S.Ct. 2357 (1974) in an opinion by Justice Rehnquist, the Court held, 8–1, a witness's testimony against defendant's interest is admissible even though a statement made

by the defendant, without full Miranda warnings, led the police to the witness.

Wong Sun v. United States 371 U.S. 471, 9 L.Ed. 2d 441, 83 S.Ct. 407 (1963) the Court, in an opinion by Brennan for 5 members of the Court, held that the defendant's statements were admissible because the connection between an illegal arrest and the statements had "become so attenuated as to dissipate the taint."

C. Standing

Minnesota v. Carter 525 U.S. ___, 142 L.Ed. 2d 373, 119 S.Ct. 469 (1998) the Court, in an opinion by Rehnquist for 5 justices with 2 justices concurring, held that a person who visits a residence for a brief period for business-related purposes lacks the expectation of privacy needed to challenge an illegal entry and search by the police. The Court reaffirmed the holding in *Minnesota v. Olson* which recognized that overnight guests in a residence have a legitimate privacy interest while there.

United States v. Padilla 508 U.S. 77, 123 L.Ed. 2d 635, 113 S.Ct. 1936 (1993) the Court, in a unanimous *per curiam* opinion, held that co-conspirators have standing if their personal expectation of privacy is invaded but refused to give a co-conspirator standing based on his/her supervisory role in the conspiracy or joint control over the place or property involved in the search or seizure.

Minnesota v. Olson 495 U.S. 91 (1990) the Court, 7–2 in an opinion by White, held that overnight guests in a house have an expectation of privacy protected by the Fourth Amendment.

Rawlings v. Kentucky 448 U.S. 98, 65 L.Ed. 2d 633, 100 S.Ct. 2556 (1980) the Court, in an opinion by Rehnquist for 5 justices, held that Fourth Amendment standing issues should be analyzed in terms of the defendant's reasonable expectation of privacy.

United States v. Salvucci 448 U.S. 83, 65 L.Ed. 2d 619, 100 S.Ct. 2547 (1980) the Court, 7–2, in an opinion by Rehnquist, held that defendants charged with crimes of possession do not have "automatic standing" to challenge the legality of the search. Standing must rest on reasonable expectation of privacy. Court explicitly overruled *Jones v. United States* 362 U.S. 257, 4 L.Ed. 2d 697, 80 S.Ct. 725 (1960).

Rakas v. Illinois 439 U.S. 128, 58 L.Ed. 2d 387, 99 S.Ct. 421 (1978) the Court, 5–4, in an opinion by Rehnquist, held the defendants lacked standing to challenge the illegal search of the car they had been occupying immediately before the search. The fact that they were in the car with the permission of the owner was not determinative of their reasonable expectation of privacy in particular areas of the car, namely under the front seat and in the glove compartment.

XII CIVIL RIGHTS ACT AND CONSTITUTIONAL TORTS

Kalina v. Fletcher 522 U.S. 118, 139 L.Ed. 2d 471, 118 S.Ct. 502 (1997) the Court, in a unanimous opinion by Stevens, held that when a state prosecutor assumes the role of complaining witness and signs an affidavit supporting the application for an arrest warrant, he/she does not have absolute prosecutorial immunity in §1983 suits for false statements in those affidavits.

Richardson v. McKnight 521 U.S. 399, 138 L.Ed. 2d 540, 117 S.Ct. 2100 (1997) the Court, 5–4 in an opinion by Breyer, held that guards employed by a private firm operating the state's prisons were not entitled to qualified immunity in Civil Rights Act cases. Court did not address issue of when guards employed by private corporations are liable to suit under the act.

McMillan v. Monroe County 520 U.S. 781, 138 L.Ed. 2d 1, 117 S.Ct. 1734 (1997) the Court, 5–4 in an opinion by Rehnquist, held that when Alabama sheriffs execute law enforcement duties, they are state officials and therefore not subject to suit under the Civil Rights Act. Opinion stressed that this con-clu sion is

based on the law of the State of Alabama and is not a blanket rule for all states.

Edwards v. Balisok 520 U.S. 641, 137 L.Ed. 2d 906, 117 S.Ct. 1584 (1997) the Court, in a unanimous opinion by Scalia, held that the inmate's claim for declaratory relief and money damages was not cognizable under §1983 because the inmate did not deny there were sufficient facts presented at the prison disciplinary hearing to support the charged violation of prison rules. Allegations of deceit and bias on the part of the decision maker that resulted in the imposition of an invalid punishment did not state a cause of action where the facts demonstrated guilt for the alleged violation.

Board of the County Commissioners of Bryan County, Oklahoma v. Brown 520 U.S. 397, 137 L.Ed. 2d 626, 117 S.Ct. 1382 (1997) the Court, 5–4 in an opinion by O'Connor, held that a person seeking to recover from a municipality under the Civil Rights Act (42 U.S.C. § 1983) for actions of employees must demonstrate that a municipality's decision reflects deliberate indifference to the risk that a violation of a particular constitutional or statutory right will follow the decision. The official's failure to adequately scrutinize the applicant's background constitutes "deliberate indifference" only where adequate scrutiny would lead a reasonable policy maker to conclude that the plainly obvious consequence of the decision to hire the applicant would be the deprivation of a third party's federally protected rights.

United States v. Lanier 520 U.S. 259, 137 L.Ed. 2d 432, 117 S.Ct. 1219 (1997) the Court, in a unanimous opinion by Souter, held that the defendant, who was convicted for violation of civil rights, had the right to fair notice that the actions involved violated the victim's constitutional rights. A conviction can be entered only if, "in the light of pre-existing law the unlawfulness [under the Constitution is] apparent." It is not necessary to show other cases that were "fundamentally similar" in that sexual assault by a state court judge was used as grounds for a prosecution under the Civil Rights Act.

Elder v. Holloway 510 U.S. 510, 127 L.Ed. 2d 344, 114 S.Ct. 1019 (1994) the Court, in a unanimous opinion by Ginsburg, held that when a federal appellate court reviews District Court rulings on qualified immunity for police officers making a warrantless arrest, the appellate court must review all relevant precedents, not just those cited by the parties or discovered by the District Court.

Heck v. Humphrey 512 U.S. 477, 129 L.Ed. 2d 383, 114 S.Ct. 2364 (1994) the Court, in an opinion by Scalia for 5 justices, held that in a Civil Rights Act case under 42 U.S.C. §1983 that alleged malicious prosecution, the plaintiff must show that his/her case ended in his/her favor (acquittal, reversed on direct appeal, conviction expunged by executive order, declared invalid by a state or federal court on *habeas corpus*).

Buckley v. Fitzsimmons 509 U.S. 259, 125 L.Ed. 2d 209, 113 S.Ct. 2606 (1993) the Court, in an opinion by White for 5 justices, held that prosecutors have qualified immunity for acts performed during the investigative phase of a case and for statements made to the press.

Bray v. Alexandria Women's Health Clinic 506 U.S. 263, 122 L.Ed. 2d 34, 113 S.Ct. 753 (1993) the Court, in an opinion by Scalia for 5 justices, held prior case law requires that in private conspiracy cases under 42 U.S.C. §1985(3), the plaintiff must show "some racial, or perhaps otherwise class-based, invidiously discriminatory animus [lay] behind the conspirators' action," and the conspiracy "aimed at interfering with rights" that are "protected against private, as well as official, encroachment."

Farrar v. Hobby 506 U.S. 103, 121 L.Ed. 2d 494, 113 S.Ct. 566 (1992) the Court, in an opinion by Thomas for 5 justices, held that in a case filed under 42 U.S.C. §1983, a plaintiff who receives nominal damages is a prevailing party and eligible to receive attorney's fees

under 42 U.S.C. §1988, but awarding attorney fees is not appropriate when there is only a "technical" victory.

Denton v. Hernandez 504 U.S. 25, 118 L.Ed. 2d 340, 112 S.Ct. 1728 (1992) the Court, 7–2 in an opinion by O'Connor, held that in *forma pauperis* suits under 42 U.S.C. §1983 could be dismissed as frivolous, without requiring the defendant to answer, when the facts alleged rise to the level of the irrational or the wholly incredible, whether or not there are judicially noticeable facts available to contradict them; they may not be dismissed simply because the court finds the plaintiff's allegations unlikely.

McCarthy v. Madigan 503 U.S. 140, 117 L.Ed. 2d 291, 112 S.Ct. 1081 (1992) the Court, 6–3 in an opinion by Blackmun, held that a federal prisoner does not have to exhaust administrative remedies before filing a *Bivens* suit for monetary damages, because neither Congress nor the federal Bureau of Prisons has made an adequate administrative remedy available.

Hudson v. McMillian 503 U.S. 1, 117 L.Ed. 2d 156, 112 S.Ct. 995 (1992) the Court, 6–3 in an opinion by O'Connor, held that use of excessive physical force against a prisoner may constitute cruel and unusual punishment even though the inmate does not suffer serious injury. Whenever prison officials stand accused of using excessive physical force in violation of the cruel and unusual punishments clause, the core judicial inquiry is that set out in *Whitley v. Albers* (1986): whether force was applied in a good-faith effort to maintain or restore discipline, or maliciously and sadistically to cause harm.

Hunter v. Bryant 502 U.S. 224, 116 L.Ed. 2d 589, 112 S.Ct. 534 (1991) the Court, 5–3 in a *per curiam* opinion, held Secret Service agents were entitled to immunity from *Bivens* suits when making an arrest if a reasonable officer would have believed that probable cause existed for the arrest, even if their evaluation of probable cause to arrest was in error.

Hafer v. Melo 502 U.S. 21, 116 L.Ed. 2d 301, 112 S.Ct. 358 (1991) the Court, in a unanimous opinion by O'Connor, held that a state official could be held personally liable under 42 U.S.C. §1983 if constitutional rights were violated when firing employees.

Mireles v. Waco 502 U.S. 9, 116 L.Ed. 2d 9, 112 S.Ct. 286 (1991) the Court, 5–4 in a *per curiam* opinion, held that a judge has absolute immunity under 42 U.S.C. §1983 for actions performed in his/her judicial capacity even if he/she authorized or condoned excessive force by police officers to carry out the judge's orders.

Burns v. Reed 500 U.S. 478, 114 L.Ed. 2d 547, 111 S.Ct. 1934 (1991) the Court, 6–3 in an opinion by White, held that a prosecutor has absolute immunity for actions at a probable cause hearing to determine if a warrant should be issued but only qualified immunity for advice given to police regarding the investigation.

West Virginia University Hospitals, Inc. v. Casey 499 U.S. 83, 113 L.Ed. 2d 68, 111 S.Ct. 1138 (1991) the Court, 6–3 in an opinion by Scalia, held that 42 U.S.C. § 1988, which permits the prevailing party to collect attorney fees from the opposing side, does not allow recovery of fees for services rendered by expert witnesses and consultants on handling the case. Experts appearing at trial are entitled to fees set by Congress in 28 U.S.C. §1920 and 1921.

Ngiraingas v. Sanchez 495 U.S. 182, 109 L.Ed. 2d 163, 110 S.Ct. 1737 (1990) the Court, in an opinion by Blackmun for 6 justices, held that the Territory of Guam and Guam's territorial officers acting in their official capacity are not "persons" subject to liability under 42 U.S.C. §1983.

Venegas v. Mitchell 495 U.S. 82, 109 L.Ed. 2d 74, 110 S.Ct. 1679 (1990) the Court, in a unanimous opinion by White, held that contingent fee contracts for the representation of a plaintiff filing a civil rights action under 42 U.S.C. §1983 are valid even if they exceed the "reasonable attorney's fee" awarded in 42

U.S.C. §1988. Section 1988 limits what a defendant can be ordered to pay but has no bearing on what the plaintiff may contract to pay.

Will v. Michigan Department of State Police 491 U.S. 58, 105 L.Ed. 2d 45, 109 S.Ct. 2304 (1989) the Court, in an opinion by White for 5 justices, held that a state is not a "person" within the meaning of 42 U.S.C. §1983. Suits against state officials in their official capacity are not suits against them personally but against the state. Such suits are barred by the Eleventh Amendment unless the state waived its immunity or Congress has exercised its power under Section 5 of the Fourteenth Amendment to override that immunity. The Court found no congressional intent to do so.

Graham v. Connor 490 U.S. 386, 104 L.Ed. 2d 443, 109 S.Ct. 1865 (1989) the Court, in an opinion by Rehnquist for 6 justices, held that in suits under 42 U.S.C. §1983, allegations of excessive force in a nonprison setting should be analyzed under the Fourth Amendment's "objective reasonableness" standard, rather than under a substantive due process standard.

Brower v. County of Inyo 489 U.S. 593, 103 L.Ed. 2d 628, 109 S.Ct. 1378 (1989) the Court, in an opinion by Scalia for 5 justices, held that the act of placing a roadblock across all lanes of traffic in order to stop a fleeing suspect was sufficient to establish a seizure under the Fourth Amendment. If such a seizure was unreasonable, it would establish liability under 42 U.S.C. §1983.

City of Canton, Ohio v. Harris 489 U.S. 378, 103 L.Ed. 2d 412, 109 S.Ct. 1197 (1989) the Court, in an opinion by White for 6 justices, held that a municipality has liability under 42 U.S.C. §1983 for constitutional violations resulting from its failure to train municipal employees only where its failure to train evidences deliberate indifference to the constitutional rights of its inhabitants.

De Shaney v. Winnebago County Department of Social Services 489 U.S. 189, 103 L.Ed. 2d 249, 109 S.Ct. 998 (1989) the Court, in an opinion by Rehnquist for 6 justices, held that while the state has a duty to protect individuals from harm when it restrains their freedom to act on their own behalf (through incarceration, institutionalization or other similar restraint of personal liberty), it has no due process duty to protect a person's liberty interest against harm inflicted by other means. The county had no liability under 42 U.S.C. §1983 for injuries inflicted on a baby by its natural father after a social worker from children's protective services failed to heed signs of abuse and remove the child from the home.

Felder v. Casey 487 U.S. 131, 101 L.Ed. 2d 123, 108 S.Ct. 2302 (1988) the Court, in an opinion by Brennan for 7 justices, held that 42 U.S.C. §1983 preempts a Wisconsin statute that provides that before any suit may be brought in state court against a state or local governmental entity or officer, the plaintiff must notify the governmental defendant of the circumstances giving rise to the claim, the amount of the claim, and his/her intent to hold the named defendant liable.

West v. Atkins 487 U.S. 42, 101 L.Ed. 2d 40, 108 S.Ct. 2250 (1988) the Court, in an opinion by Blackmun for 8 justices, held that a physician who is under contract with the state to provide medical services to inmates at a state prison hospital on a part-time basis acts "under color of state law" and is liable under 42 U.S.C. §1983 for his/her actions.

Anderson v. Creighton 483 U.S. 635, 97 L.Ed. 2d 523, 107 S.Ct. 3034 (1987) the Court, in an opinion by Scalia for 6 justices, held that a federal law enforcement officer who participates in a search that violates the Fourth Amendment may not be held personally liable for money damages if a reasonable officer could have believed that the search comported with the Fourth Amendment.

Hewitt v. Helms 482 U.S. 755, 96 L.Ed. 2d 654, 107 S.Ct. 2672 (1987) the Court, in an opinion by Scalia for 5 justices, held that in order to be entitled to attorney fees in an action under 18 U.S.C. §1983, a litigant must be a "prevailing party." This means that the litigant must receive at least some relief on the merits of his/her claim. A court's conclusion that the inmate's constitutional rights were violated by prison officials who are immune from suit does not justify the awarding of attorney's fees. Neither does the fact that prison officials decided to change their regulations as a result of the lawsuit even though the court did not order them to do so.

Newton v. Rummery 480 U.S. 386, 94 L.Ed. 2d 405, 107 S.Ct. 1187 (1987) the Court, in an opinion by Powell, relevant portions of which were signed by 5 justices, held that in most cases a court properly may enforce an agreement in which a criminal defendant voluntarily released his/her right to file an action under 42 U.S.C. §1983 in return for a prosecutor's dismissal of pending criminal charges.

City of Riverside v. Rivera 477 U.S. 561, 91 L.Ed. 2d 466, 106 S.Ct. 2686 (1986) the Court, without a majority opinion, held that attorneys' fees under 42 U.S.C. §1988 do not have to be proportionate to the size of the monetary recovery in the case.

City of Los Angeles v. Heller 475 U.S. 796, 89 L.Ed. 806, 106 S.Ct. 1571 (1986) the Court, in a *per curiam* opinion for 6 justices, held that there is no authorization for an award of damages against a municipality based on the actions of one of its officers when in fact the jury has concluded that the officer inflicted no constitutional harm.

Pembaur v. City of Cincinnati 475 U.S. 469, 89 L.Ed. 2d 452, 106 S.Ct. 1292 (1986) the Court, in an opinion by Brennan for 6 justices, held that a municipality could be liable under §1983 based on a policy decision if, and only if, a deliberate choice to follow a course of action was made from among various alternatives by the official or officials responsible for establishing final policy with respect to the subject matter in question.

Malley v. Briggs 475 U.S. 335, 89 L.Ed. 2d 271, 106 S.Ct. 1092 (1986) the Court, in an opinion by White for 7 justices, held that an officer who obtained an arrest warrant has immunity from suits under 42 U.S.C. §1983 for an unconstitutional arrest made pursuant to that arrest warrant except where the warrant application is so lacking in indicia of probable cause as to render the officer's belief in its existence unreasonable.

City of Oklahoma City v. Tuttle 471 U.S. 808, 85 L.Ed. 2d 791, 105 S.Ct. 2427 (1985) the Court, without a majority opinion, held that a single isolated incident of excessive force by a police officer cannot establish an official policy of inadequate training that is sufficient to render a municipality liable for damages under 42 U.S.C. §1983.

Tower v. Glover 467 U.S. 914, 81 L.Ed. 2d 758, 104 S.Ct. 2820 (1984) the Court, O'Connor writing for a majority of 5 and in pertinent part for all 9 justices, held that public defenders do not have absolute immunity from liability in suits under 42 U.S.C. §1983.

Pulliam v. Allen 466 U.S. 522, 80 L.Ed. 2d 565, 104 S.Ct. 1970 (1984) the Court, 5–4 in an opinion by Blackmun, held that judicial immunity under 42 U.S.C. §1988 does not bar an award of attorney's fees.

Smith v. Wade 461 U.S. 30, 75 L.Ed. 2d 632, 103 S.Ct. 1625 (1983) the Court, 5–4 in an opinion by Brennan, held that punitive damages could be awarded in a Civil Rights Act suit when the defendant was shown to have an evil motive or intent, or when it was demonstrated that the defendant was reckless or had callous indifference to federally protected rights.

Briscoe v. Lahue 460 U.S. 325, 75 L.Ed. 2d 96, 103 S.Ct. 1108 (1983) the Court, in a 6–3 opinion by Stevens, held that a person convicted in state court based on perjured testimony by a police officer may not bring suit under 42 U.S.C. §1983 against the police officer for damages.

Polk County v. Dodson 454 U.S. 312, 70 L.Ed. 2d 509, 102 S.Ct. 445 (1981) the Court, 8–1, in an opinion by Powell, held that for purposes of a civil rights action under 42 U.S.C. §1983, the public defender does not act "under color of state law."

City of Newport v. Fact Concerts 453 U.S. 247, 69 L.Ed. 2d 616, 101 S.Ct. 2748 (1981) the Court, 6–3 in an opinion by Blackmun, held that cities are immune from punitive damage awards under 42 U.S.C. §1983.

Carlson v. Green 446 U.S. 14, 64 L.Ed. 2d 15, 100 S.Ct. 1468 (1980) the Court, in an opinion by Brennan for 5 justices, held that the mother of a deceased inmate could maintain a *Bivens* suit against federal prison officials even though an action under the Federal Tort Claims Act [28 U.S.C. §2680(h)] was also available.

Moore v. Sims 442 U.S. 415, 60 L.Ed. 2d 994, 99 S.Ct. (1979) the Court, 5–4 in an opinion by Rehnquist, held that it was improper for a federal court to issue an injunction in a Civil Rights Act suit when proceedings to take custody of allegedly abused children had been filed and action was pending in state court.

Imbler v. Pachtman 424 U.S. 409, 47 L.Ed. 2d 128, 96 S.Ct. 984 (1976) the Court, in an opinion by Powell for 5 justices, held that a state prosecutor has absolute immunity from civil rights actions under 42 U.S.C. §1983 for actions taken while initiating and pursuing criminal prosecutions. This immunity applies even though the prosecutor knowingly used perjured testimony, deliberately withheld exculpatory information, or failed to make full disclosure of all facts that cast doubt on the testimony of prosecution witnesses.

Rizzo v. Goode 423 U.S. 362, 46 L.Ed. 2d 561, 96 S.Ct. 598 (1976) the Court, 5–3 with Stevens not participating, in an opinion by Rehnquist, held that a District Court order requiring the City of Philadelphia to develop an improved system for handling citizen complaints against police officers was improvidently entered. Factors considered in determining that no order should be made include: no pattern of violations of citizens' constitutional rights was shown; only a few officers appeared to be involved in these violations; no link between the misconduct and official department policy was shown; the total number of incidents involved (20 in 12 months) was small in comparison with the size of the city and the police department (city of 3,000,000 with 7,500 officers).

Hicks v. Miranda 422 U.S. 332, 45 L.Ed. 2d 223, 95 S.Ct. 2281 (1975) the Court, 5–4 in an opinion by White, held that a federal court must not interfere with pending state criminal prosecutions unless there are exceptional circumstances creating a threat of irreparable great and immediate injury.

Wood v. Strickland 420 U.S. 308, 43 L.Ed. 2d 214, 95 S.Ct. 992 (1975) the Court, 5–4, in an opinion by White, held that in civil rights actions under 42 U.S.C. §1983, a public official is liable for violations of civil rights if he/she knew, or should have known, that the actions taken violated constitutional rights, or if the violation was done with malicious intent to cause deprivation of constitutional rights or injury. This case has been generalized to actions of anyone acting "under color of state law." It allows for qualified immunity (also called a "good faith" defense) if the defendant can show both objective and subjective good faith in the performance of his/her duties.

Allee v. Medrano 416 U.S. 802, 40 L.Ed. 2d 566, 94 S.Ct. 2191 (1974) the Court held that a federal court had the authority to issue an injunction in a Civil Rights Act case when there was no interference with a pending state prosecution, if the plaintiff had demonstrated a pattern of police misconduct and irreparable injury would result if an injunction was not issued.

Bivens v. Six Unknown Named Agents of Federal Bureau of Narcotics 403 U.S. 388, 29 L.Ed. 2d 619, 91 S.Ct. 1999 (1971) the Court, 6–3, in an opinion by Brennan, held that a civil remedy could be based directly on the Fourth Amendment. These types of civil suits to recover damages for violation of constitutional rights by federal officers who are not covered by the Civil Rights Act have become known as "*Bivens*" cases or constitutional torts.

Younger v. Harris 401 U.S. 37, 27 L.Ed. 2d 699, 91 S.Ct. 746 (1971) the Court, 5–4 in an opinion by Black, held that issuing an injunction was improper in a case of goodfaith enforcement of a possibly unconstitutional statute.

Pierson v. Ray 386 U.S. 547, 18 L.Ed. 2d 288, 87 S.Ct. 1213 (1967) the Court, 8–1 in an opinion by Warren, held that judges have absolute immunity for their judicial acts; police have conditional immunity for acts done in good faith based on probable cause.

XIII *HABEAS CORPUS* IN FEDERAL COURTS

TO REMEDY CONSTITUTIONAL WRONGS

Hohn v. United States 524 U.S. ___,141 L.Ed. 2d 242, 118 S.Ct. 1969 (1998) the Court, 5–4 in an opinion by Kennedy, held that the Antiterrorism and Effective Death Penalty Act of 1996 did not restrict the Supreme Court's jurisdiction to review decisions of the federal courts of appeals denying applications for certificates of appealability.

Spencer v. Kemna 523 U.S. 1, 140 L.Ed. 2d 43, 118 S.Ct. 978 (1998) the Court, 8–1 in an opinion by Scalia, held that the fact that an inmate is in custody due to parole revocation is sufficient to satisfy the requirements to file *habeas corpus* under 28 U.S.C. §2254, but release from custody prior to the hearing makes the petition moot because it no longer presents a case or controversy under Title III Section 2 of the Constitution.

Bracy v. Gramley 520 U.S. 899, 138 L.Ed. 2d 97, 117 S.Ct. 1793 (1997) the Court, in a unanimous opinion by Rehnquist, held that District Court judges should fashion appropriate discovery orders in federal *habeas corpus* suits when good cause was shown.

Felker v. Turpin 518 U.S. 651, 135 L.Ed. 2d 827, 116 S.Ct. 2333 (1996) the Court, in a unanimous opinion by Rehnquist, held that restrictions on filing *habeas corpus* contained in Title I of the Antiterrorism and Effective Death Penalty Act of 1996 did not preclude the Supreme Court from entertaining an application for *habeas corpus* relief, although it does affect the standards governing the granting of such relief.

Gray v. Netherland 518 U.S. 152, 135 L.Ed. 2d 457, 116 S.Ct. 2074 (1996) the Court, 5–4 in an opinion by Rehnquist, held that a defendant in a capital case does not have a right to prior notice of the evidence that will be used against him at the penalty phase of the hearing.

Calderon v. Moore 518 U.S. 149, 135 L.Ed. 2d 453, 116 S.Ct. 2066 (1996) the Court, in a unanimous *per curiam* opinion, held the State was not precluded from appealing a *habeas corpus* ruling that the defendant was entitled to a new trial if the appeal was filed prior to the start of the new trial. Merely setting a date for the new trial did not preclude the appeal.

Bowersox v. Williams 517 U.S. 345, 134 L.Ed. 2d 494, 116 S.Ct. 1312 (1996) the Court, 5–4 in a *per curiam* opinion, held that the Court of Appeals acted improperly when it entered a summary order staying execution after the District Court denied the defendant's third federal *habeas corpus* petition. On a second or third *habeas* petition, entry of a stay is a drastic measure that should be done only if there are substantial grounds for relief.

Lonchar v. Thomas 517 U.S. 314, 134 L.Ed. 2d 440, 116 S.Ct. 1293 (1996) the Court, in an opinion by Breyer for 5 members of the court with 4 other justices concurring, held that a death-row defendant's first federal *habeas corpus* petition, even though filed in the "eleventh-hour" must be reviewed within the framework of the *habeas corpus* rules and settled precedents. The defendant's first *habeas corpus* petition cannot be dismissed solely due to the fact that a stay of execution would have to be granted.

Thompson v. Keohane 516 U.S. 99, 133 L.Ed. 2d 383, 116 S.Ct. 457 (1995) the Court, 7–2 in an opinion by Ginsburg, held that when a defendant files federal *habeas corpus* to challenge the failure to give Miranda rights, federal judges should conduct an independent review of the question of whether the defendant was "in custody" when interrogated.

Wood v. Bartholomew 516 U.S. 1, 133 L.Ed. 2d 1, 116 S.Ct. 7 (1995) the Court, 5–4 in a *per curiam* opinion, held that the granting of relief on a *habeas corpus* on appeal was improper even though the prosecution failed to turn over the results of a polygraph examination of a key witness. The test results would have been inadmissible at trial and the case against the defendant was overwhelming; there was no likelihood that disclosure of the test results would have altered the outcome of the trial.

Garlotte v. Fordice 515 U.S. 65, 132 L.Ed. 2d 36, 115 S.Ct. 1948 (1995) the Court, 7–2 in an opinion by Ginsburg, held a prisoner is "in custody" and thus eligible to file a petition for federal *habeas corpus*, when serving consecutive sentences even though the sentence for the case being considered has already been completed. The case is mirror image of *Peyton v. Rowe* 391 U.S. 54 (1968), where the Court held an inmate was "in custody" while serving consecutive sentences when petitioning for relief from the sentence that had not yet begun.

Duncan v. Henry 513 U.S. 364, 130 L.Ed. 2d 865, 115 S.Ct. 887 (1995) the Court, in a *per curiam* opinion for 5 justices, held that a state inmate may not file for federal *habeas corpus* relief unless the federal issue involved was raised on direct appeal in state courts.

Schlup v. Delo 513 U.S. 298, 130 L.Ed. 2d 808, 115 S.Ct. 851 (1995) the Court, in an opinion by Stevens for 5 justices, held that when a death-row inmate files a *habeas corpus* petition based on actual innocence in order to avoid the procedural bar to consideration of the merits of his constitutional claim, the inmate must show a constitutional violation has probably resulted in the conviction of a petitioner who is actually innocent.

O'Neal v. McAninch 513 U.S. 432, 130 L.Ed. 2d 947, 115 S.Ct. 992 (1995) the Court, 6–3 in an opinion by Breyer, held that when a federal judge considers a *habeas corpus* petition applying the harmless-error rule to constitutional issues, the case should be decided in the inmate's favor if there is grave doubt about whether the error had a "substantial and injurious effect or influence in determining the jury's verdict." By "grave doubt" the court means that, in the judge's mind, the matter is so evenly balanced that he/she feels him/ herself in virtual equipoise as to the harmlessness of the error.

Reed v. Farley 512 U.S. 339, 129 L.Ed. 2d 277, 114 S.Ct. 2291 (1994) the Court, 5–4 in an opinion by Ginsburg, held that a federal prisoner with a detainer filed by a state could not use federal *habeas corpus* to challenge violation of the 120-day limit on the starting of a trial under the Interstate Agreement on Detainers. The Court ruled that the violation did not amount to a violation of the Sixth Amendment right to a speedy trial; therefore the action was statutory and the necessary "fundamental defect" had not been shown.

McFarland v. Scott 512 U.S. 849, 129 L.Ed. 2d 666, 114 S.Ct. 2568 (1994) the Court, in an opinion by Blackmun signed by 5 justices, held under 21 U.S.C. §848(q)(4)(B), an indigent inmate who has been sentenced to death may apply to federal court and have an attorney appointed to handle federal *habeas corpus* proceedings under 28 U.S.C. §2254 or 2255. While federal *habeas corpus* petitioners do not have the right to an automatic stay of execution, a District Court can order a stay of execution in order to give effect to the right to have counsel appointed.

Withrow v. Williams 507 U.S. 680, 123 L.Ed. 2d 407, 113 S.Ct. 1745 (1993) the Court, in an opinion for 5 justices, held that *Stone v. Powell*, which denied federal *habeas corpus* relief to prisoners making Fourth Amendment claims if the state courts pro-

vided a full and fair chance to litigate the issues, cannot be used to deny federal *habeas corpus* relief to a state prisoner's claims that a conviction rests on statements obtained in violation of Miranda.

Brecht v. Abrahmson 507 U.S. 619, 123 L.Ed. 2d 353, 113 S.Ct. 1710 (1993) the Court, in an opinion by Rehnquist for 5 justices, held that no federal *habeas corpus* relief should be granted where post-Miranda silence was used for impeachment but the error was found to be harmless. The standard for determining whether *habeas corpus* should be granted in this type of case is whether the violation of the right to remain silent had substantial and injurious effect or influence in determining the jury's verdict.

Herrera v. Collins 506 U.S. 390, 122 L.Ed. 2d 203, 113 S.Ct. 853 (1993) the Court, in an opinion by Rehnquist for 5 justices, held that in a death-penalty case, affidavits alleging factual innocence of the defendant are not grounds for granting federal *habeas corpus* relief. A claim of innocence must be evaluated in light of all the previous proceedings in the case, particularly evidence produced at the trial and the fact the issue was raised for the first time eight years after the trial. The Court points to executive clemency as an appropriate recourse in this type of case.

Dobbs v. Zant 506 U.S. 357, 122 L.Ed. 2d 103, 113 S.Ct. 835 (1993) the Court, in a *per curiam* opinion for 5 justices, held that in a state *habeas corpus* proceeding involving a defendant who had been sentenced to death, the appellate court erred when it refused to consider the transcript of the sentencing hearing when evaluating a claim of ineffectiveness of trial counsel.

Sawyer v. Whitley 505 U.S. 333, 120 L.Ed. 2d 269, 112 S.Ct. 2514 (1992) the Court, 6–3 in an opinion by Rehnquist, held that the defendant filing federal *habeas corpus* must show "actual innocence" by clear and convincing evidence when he/she has previously filed successive, abusive federal *habeas* claims or defaulted in such suits. In a capital case, petitioner must show that "but for constitutional error," no reasonable juror would have found him/her eligible for the death penalty.

Keeney v. Tamayo-Reyes 504 U.S. 1, 118 L.Ed. 2d318, 112 S.Ct. 1715 (1992) the Court, 5–4 in an opinion by White, held a defendant filing federal *habeas corpus* to challenge a state court conviction was entitled to an evidentiary hearing if he/she could show cause for his/her failure to develop the facts in state court proceedings and that actual prejudice resulted from that failure. A *habeas* petitioner's failure to develop a claim in state court proceedings will be excused and a hearing mandated if he/she can show that a fundamental miscarriage of justice would result from failure to hold a federal evidentiary hearing.

In re Blodgett 502 U.S. 236, 116 L.Ed. 2d 669, 112 S.Ct. 674 (1992) the Court, 7–2 in a *per curiam* opinion, held that in a death-penalty case the grant of a stay of execution directed to a state by a federal court imposes on that court the concomitant duty to take all steps necessary to ensure a prompt resolution of the matter, consistent with its duty to give full and fair consideration to all of the issues presented in the case.

Ylst v. Nunnemaker 501 U.S. 797, 115 L.Ed. 2d 706, 111 S.Ct. 2590 (1991) the Court, 6–3 in an opinion by Scalia, held that when a state inmate files for federal *habeas corpus* relief and the last decision(s) in the case states no reason for its holding, it is presumed that the decision affirms the most recent decision in the case that stated a reason for its holding. If the last such decision shows that there is a procedural default that would bar *habeas corpus*, the federal courts should dismiss the petition for federal relief.

McCleskey v. Zant 499 U.S. 467, 113 L.Ed. 2d 517, 111 S.Ct. 1454 (1991) the Court, 6–3 in an opinion by Kennedy, held that raising issue(s) in a second or subsequent petition for federal *habeas corpus*, when the issue(s) were not raised in the first petition, is an abuse of the writ and merits dismissal of the case.

Lozada v. Deeds 498 U.S. 430, 112 L.Ed. 2d 956, 111 S.Ct. 860 (1991) the Court, 7–2 in a *per curiam* opinion, held that a defendant who made a substantial showing that no appeal was filed in state court due to ineffective assistance of counsel was entitled to a certificate of probable cause so that federal *habeas corpus* could be pursued.

Delo v. Stokes 495 U.S. 320, 109 L.Ed. 2d 325, 110 S.Ct. 1880 (1990) the Court, in a *per curiam* opinion expressing the views of 5 members, held that a stay of execution pending disposition of a second or successive federal *habeas* petition should be granted only when there are "substantial grounds upon which relief might be granted."

Maleng v. Cook 490 U.S. 488, 104 L.Ed. 2d 540, 109 S.Ct. 1923 (1989) the Court, in a unanimous *per curiam* opinion, held that for the purpose of federal *habeas corpus*, a person does not remain "in custody" after the sentence imposed has fully expired merely because of the possibility that the prior conviction will be used to enhance the sentence imposed for any subsequent crimes. Defendant was found to be "in custody" on a conviction that ran consecutive to the one he was currently serving even though he would not actually start serving it for several years.

Smith v. Murray 477 U.S. 527, 91 L.Ed. 2d 434, 106 S.Ct. 2661 (1986) the Court, in an opinion by O'Connor for 5 justices, held that a deliberate tactical decision not to raise an issue on direct appeal bars its introduction in a writ of *habeas corpus* absent a showing that there is a probability that counsel's procedural default resulted in the conviction of an innocent person.

Murray v. Carrier 477 U.S. 478, 91 L.Ed. 2d 397, 106 S.Ct. 2639 (1986) the Court, in an opinion by O'Connor for 5 justices, held that an inmate petitioning for a writ of *habeas corpus* on the grounds of ineffective assistance of appellate counsel needs to establish that there was some external impediment that might have prevented counsel from raising the appropriate claims in the appellate briefs.

The federal courts retain the authority to consider cases in which there is a probability that the defendant was factually innocent.

Cardwell v. Taylor 461 U.S. 571, 76 L.Ed. 2d 333, 103 S.Ct. 2015 (1983) the Court, in a *per curiam* opinion for 7 members of the Court, held that a claim that a confession was inadmissible as the product of an illegal arrest could not be raised in federal court if the petitioner had had an opportunity for a full and fair hearing on that claim in state court.

Anderson v. Harless 459 U.S. 4, 74 L.Ed. 2d 3, 103 S.Ct. 276 (1982) the Court, 6–3, in a *per curiam* opinion, held the petitioner had not exhausted his state court remedies where the due process claim presented in state court was not self-evident from the arguments made there, and the claim raised in federal court was different and broader than that raised in state court.

Engle v. Isaac 456 U.S. 107, 71 L.Ed. 2d 783, 102 S.Ct. 1558 (1982) the Court, in an opinion by O'Connor for 5 members of the Court, held that the petitioners had forfeited their constitutional claims by not complying with the state's contemporaneous objection rule.

Rose v. Lundy 455 U.S. 509, 71 L.Ed. 2d 379, 102 S.Ct. 1198 (1982) the Court, in an opinion by O'Connor joined in pertinent parts by 5 other members of the Court, held federal district courts must dismiss *habeas corpus* petitions that contain any claims for relief that have not been exhausted in state courts. Petitioner has the option of returning to state court to seek relief for previously unexhausted claims or amending federal petition to eliminated unexhausted state claims.

Duckworth v. Serrano 454 U.S. 1, 70 L.Ed. 2d 1, 102 S.Ct. 18 (1981) the Court, 8–1, in a *per curiam* opinion, held that a claim of ineffective assistance of counsel was not an exception to the requirement that a petitioner must exhaust state court relief prior to filing in federal court.

Jackson v. Virginia 443 U.S. 307, 61 L.Ed. Zd 560, 99 S.Ct. 2781 (1979) the Court, in an opinion by Stewart for 5 members of the Court, held that when the petitioner, who has met the exhaustion requirement, alleges that a state court conviction rests upon insufficient evidence, the federal court must consider whether there is sufficient evidence to justify a rational trier of the facts finding guilt beyond a reasonable doubt.

Wainwright v. Sykes 433 U.S. 72, 53 L.Ed. 2d 594, 97 S.Ct. 2497 (1977) the Court, in an opinion by Rehnquist for 6 members of the Court, held that a state may utilize a contemporaneous objection rule whereby the defendant waives the right to challenge the voluntariness of a confession unless a timely objection to its voluntariness is made. This waiver will preclude review on federal *habeas corpus* unless the defendant can establish "cause" or "prejudice" and show a miscarriage of justice.

Stone v. Powell 428 U.S. 465, 49 L.Ed. 2d 1067, 96 S.Ct. 3037 (1976) the Court, 6–3, in an opinion by Powell, held that where a state has provided an opportunity for full and fair litigation of a Fourth Amendment claim, state prisoner may not be granted federal *habeas corpus* relief on the ground that the evidence was obtained in violation of the Fourth Amendment.

Leflcowitz v. Newsome 420 U.S. 283, 43 L.Ed. 2d 196, 95 S.Ct. 886 (1975) the Court, 5–4, in an opinion by Stewart, held that where state law allows a defendant to plead guilty without forfeiting a right to appeal specified constitutional issues, the defendant is also not foreclosed from pursuing those constitutional claims in federal *habeas corpus* proceedings.

XIV OTHER CONSTITUTIONAL ISSUES

A. Ex Post Facto Laws

Lynce v. Mathis 519 U.S.433, 137 L.Ed. 2d 63, 117 S.Ct. 891 (1997) the Court, in an opinion by Stevens for 7 justices with the remaining 2 justices concurring in part, held that a Florida law that retroactively canceled release credits for prison inmates violated the *ex post facto* clause.

California Department of Corrections v. Morales 514 U.S. 499, 131 L.Ed. 2d 588, 115 S.Ct. 1597 (1995) the Court, 7–2 in an opinion by Thomas, held that amended rules that permitted the Board of Prison terms to decrease the frequency of parole suitability hearings were not *ex post facto* laws when applied to inmates who were sentenced prior to the date the amendments went into effect.

Collins v. Youngblood 497 U.S. 37, 111 L.Ed. 2d 30, 110 S.Ct. 2715 (1990) the Court, in an opinion by Rehnquist for 6 justices, held that a Texas statute, passed after defendant's crime, that allowed the reformation of an improper jury verdict did not violate the *ex post facto* clause. The statute did not: punish as a crime an act previously committed, which was innocent when done; nor make more burdensome the punishment for a crime, after its commission; nor deprive one charged with a crime of any defense available according to law at the time when the act was committed.

Miller v. Florida 482 U.S. 423, 96 L.Ed. 2d 351, 107 S.Ct. 2446 (1987) the Court, in a unanimous opinion by O'Connor, held that the application of Florida's sentencing guidelines, which had been revised in a manner that increased the defendant's presumptive sentence between the time he committed the crime and the date of sentencing, violated the *ex post facto* clause.

B. Jurisdiction over the Military

Solorio v. United States 483 U.S. 435, 97 L.Ed. 2d 364, 107 S.Ct. 2924 (1987) the Court, in an opinion by Rehnquist for 5 justices, expressly overruled *O'Callahan v.*

Parker and held that the jurisdiction of a court-martial convened pursuant to the Uniform Code of Military Justice to try a member of the armed forces is not limited to cases where there is a "service connection" with the offense. The offenses must be committed while the service person was on active duty but the acts do not need to occur on post.

C. Other Issues

New Mexico ex rel. Ortiz v. Reed 524 U.S. ___ 141 L.Ed. 2d 131, 118 S.Ct. 1860 (1998) the Court, in a unanimous *per curiam* opinion, held that under the extradition clause, the asylum state is not permitted to litigate issues regarding the legality of the penal system (including parole revocation) of the demanding state.

Printz v. United States 521 U.S. 898, 138 L.Ed. 2d 914, 117 S.Ct. 2365 (1997) the Court, 5–4 in an opinion by Scalia, held that Congress had no authority to mandate that local law enforcement officials conduct background checks before a person could purchase firearms as mandated by the Brady Bill. Congress does not have the authority to order states to enforce federal regulations; neither may it conscript local officials to do so.

United States v. Lopez 514 U.S. 549, 131 L.Ed. 2d 626, 115 S.Ct. 1624 (1995) the Court, 5–4 in an opinion by Rehnquist, held that provisions of the Gun-Free School Zones Act of 1990 that made it a federal offense "for any individual knowingly to possess a firearm at a place that the individual knows, or has reasonable cause to believe, is a school zone" were invalid because Congress exceeded its authority under the commerce clause; the act neither regulates a commercial activity nor contains a requirement that the possession be connected in any way to interstate commerce.

INDEX OF CASES

E

F

G

Gagnon v. Scarpelli 411, 432
Gamble, Estelle v. 444
Gannett Co. v. DePasquale 382, 415
Gardner v. Broderick 403
Gardner v. Florida 429
Garlotte v. Fordice 455
Garner, Tennessee v. 398
Gates, Illinois v. 394
Gault, In re 445
Geders v. United States 410
Gentile v. State Bar of Nevada 381
Georgia v. McCollum 412, 439
Gerstein v. Pugh 410, 433
Gilbert v. California 399
Gitlow v. New York 381
Globe Newspaper Co. v. Superior Court 382, 415
Godinez v. Moran 408, 416
Goeke v. Branch 438
Gomez v. United States District Court 425
Goode, Wainwright v. 428
Gooding v. Wilson 381
Goodwin, United States v. 417
Gouveia, United States v. 442
Graham v. Connor 398, 451
Gray v. Maryland 418
Gray v. Mississippi 427
Gray v. Netherland 423, 455
Greenfield, Wainwright v. 401
Greenholtz v. Inmates of Nebraska Penal and Corr. Complex 443
Greenwood, California v. 391. 398
Greer v. Spock 381
Gregg v. Georgia 429
Gregory v. City of Chicago 381
Griffin v. California 404
Griffin v. Illinois 411, 440
Griffin v. United States 431
Griffin v. Wisconsin 394, 432
Gustafson v. Florida 387

H

Hafer v. Melo 451
Halper, United States v. 406
Hammett v. Texas 429
Harmelin v. Michigan 430
Harper, Washington v. 431
Harris, City of Canton, Ohio v. 452

Harris, New York v. 403
Harris v. Alabama 423
Harris v. New York 402
Harris v. Oklahoma 407
Harvey, Michigan v. 400
Havens, United States v. 448
Hayden, Warden v. 388
Hayes v. Florida 393
Heath v. Alabama 406
Heck v. Humphrey 450
Heller, City of Los Angeles v. 453
Helling v. McKinney 440
Helms, Jones v. 439
Henderson v. Morgan 417
Henry, United States v. 409
Hensley, United States v. 394
Hernandez v. New York 439
Herrera v. Collins 456
Hewitt v. Helms 442, 452
Hialeah (City of), Church of the Lukumi Babalu Aye v. 384
Hicks, Arizona v. 391
Hicks v. Miranda 454
Hildwin v. Florida 426
Hill, Houston v. 380
Hill, Superintendent v. 442
Hitchcock v. Dugger 427
Hobby v. United States 414
Hodari D., California v. 391
Hoffa v. United States 397
Hoffman Estates v. Flipside 380
Hohn v. United States 454
Holbrook v. Flynn 422
Holloway v. Arkansas 410
Hopkins v. Reeves 422
Horton v. California 391
Houchins v. KQED 443
Houston v. Hill 380
Hudson v. Louisiana 406
Hudson v. McMillian 450
Hudson v. Palmer 442
Hudson v. United States 405
Hughes v. Rowe 443
Hunter v. Bryant 450
Hunter v. Underwood 430
Hurley v. Irish-American Gay, Lesbian, and Bisexual Group of Boston 378
Hurtado v. California 407
Hutto v. Davis 431
Hutto v. Ross 417
Hynes v. Borough of Oradell 381

T

U

V

W

Y

Z

APPENDIX A

DOCTORAL PROGRAMS IN CRIMINAL JUSTICE

The American University
School of Public Affairs
4400 Massachusetts Avenue, NW
Washington, DC
(Ph.D. programs with concentration in justice,
law, and society available in departments of
Political Science, Public Administration, and
Sociology

Arizona State University
School of Justice Studies
Tempe, AZ 85287

Bowling Green State University
Sociology Department
Bowling Green, OH 43403

Claremont Graduate School
Center for Politics and Policy
Claremont, CA 91711

Florida State University
School of Criminology
Tallahassee, FL 32306

Indiana University of Pennsylvania
Criminology Department
Indiana, PA 15705

John Jay College of Criminal Justice
Criminal Justice Program
New York, NY 10019

Michigan State University
School of Criminal Justice
East Lansing, MI 48824

Pennsylvania State University
Administration of Justice
University Park, PA 16802

Portland State University
Administration of Justice Department
P.O. Box 751
Portland, OR 97207

Rutgers University
School of Criminal Justice
Newark, NJ 07102

Sam Houston State University
College of Criminal Justice
Huntsville, TX 77341

State University of New York at Albany
School of Criminal Justice
Albany, NY 12222

Temple University
Department of Criminal Justice
Philadelphia, PA 19122

University of California at Berkeley
Jurisprudence and Social Policy
Berkeley, CA 94720

University of California at Irvine
Program in Social Ecology
Irvine, CA 92717

University of Delaware
Sociology and Criminal Justice
Newark, DE 19716

University of Illinois at Chicago
Criminal Justice Department
1007 West Harrison Street
Chicago, IL 60607

University of Maryland
Institute of Criminal Justice and Criminology
College Park, MD 20742-8235

University of Missouri–St. Louis
Department of Criminology and Criminal Justice
8001 Natural Bridge Road
St. Louis, MO 63121

University of Nebraska at Omaha
Director of Graduate Studies
Department of Criminal Justice
Omaha, NE 68182

University of New Haven
Public Safety & Professional Studies
300 Orange Avenue
West Haven, CT 06516

Western Michigan University
Sociology and Criminology
Kalamazoo, MI 49008

School of Criminology
University of Montreal
C.P. 6128, Montreal, Quebec H3C 3J7 Canada

APPENDIX B

FORENSIC AGENCIES AND ORGANIZATIONS

American Academy of Forensic Sciences
225 South Academy Boulevard
Colorado Springs, CO 80910

American Board of Forensic Entomology
University of Missouri–Columbia
Columbia, MO 65211

American Board of Forensic Psychiatry
c/o Medical and Chirurgical Faculty of Maryland
1211 Cathedral Street, Baltimore, MD 21201

American Board of Odontology
c/o Homer R. Campbell, D.D.S.
6800 C Montgomery, NE
Albuquerque, NM 87109

American Board of Pathology
c/o 112 Lincoln Center
5401 West Kennedy Boulevard
Box 24695, Tampa, FL 33623

American Society of Crime Laboratory Directors
c/o Jerry Chisum
California Department of Justice
2213 Blue Gum Avenue
Modesto, CA 95351

American Society of Forensic Odontology
c/o Dr. James D. Woodward
School of Dentistry, University of Louisville
Louisville, KY 40292

American Society of Questioned Document
Examiners
1415 Esperson Building
Houston, TX 77002

Armed Forces Institute of Pathology
Washington, DC 20306

Center for Human Toxicology
University of Utah
Salt Lake City, UT 84112

Drug Enforcement Administration
Forensic Science Section

1405 I Street, NW
Washington, DC 20537

FBI Laboratory Division
10th Street and Pennsylvania Avenue, NW
Washington, DC 20535

Federal Bureau of Investigation
Training Academy
Forensic Science Research Training Center
Quantico, VA 22135

Forensic Sciences Foundation
Suite 201, 225 South Academy Boulevard
Colorado Springs, CO 80910

Independent Association of Questioned
Document Examiners
518 Guaranty Bank Building
Cedar Rapids, IA 52401

International Association for Identification
Box 139
Utica, NY 13503

International Association of Coroners and
Medical Examiners
2121 Adelbert Road
Cleveland, OH 44106

International Reference Organization in
Forensic Medicine and Sciences
c/o Dr. William G. Eckert Laboratory
St. Francis Hospital
Wichita, KS 67214

Milton Helpern Institute of Forensic Medicine
520 First Avenue
New York, NY 10016

National Association of Medical Examiners
1402 S. Grand Boulevard
St. Louis, MO 63104

U.S. Department of the Treasury
Bureau of Alcohol, Tobacco, and Firearms
Forensic Science Laboratory
1401 Research Boulevard
Rockville, MD 20850

World Association of Document Examiners
111 North Canal Street
Chicago, IL 60606

APPENDIX C

CRIMINAL JUSTICE WEB SITES

This compilation is a sampling rather than a comprehensive guide to Web sites that may be of interest to students, instructors, and professionals in law enforcement and related fields. They can be sources for news, trends, statistics, research, and people with specialized knowledge and experience. Note that some URLs may have changed since the listing was compiled and that new sites are created frequently.

U.S. GOVERNMENT
Department of Justice:

http://www.icpsr.umich.edu/NACJD/home. html (National Archive of Criminal Justice Data)

http://www.ojp.usdoj.gov/bjs (Office of Justice Programs, Bureau of Justice Statistics)

http://www.ojp.usdoj.gov/nij (Office of Justice Programs, National Institute of Justice)

http://www.ojp.usdoj.gov/ovc (Office for Victims of Crime)

http://www.nlectc.org (Justice Technology Information Network)

http://www.usdoj.gov/marshals (United States Marshals)

http://www.usdoj.gov/dea/index.htm (Drug Enforcement Administration)

http://www.usdoj.gov/cops (Community Oriented Policing Services)

Other federal organizations:

http://www.fbi.gov/ucr (FBI's Uniform Crime Reports)

http://www.fbi.gov/vicap (FBI's Violent Criminal Apprehension Program)

http://www.nida.nih.gov (National Institute on Drug Abuse)

www.atf.treas.gov (Treasury Department's Bureau of Alcohol, Tobacco and Firearms)

http://www.bop.gov (Bureau of Prisons)

http://www.ncjrs.org (National Criminal Justice Reference Service)

http://www.lab.fws.gov (Fish and Wildlife Service's forensic science site)

http://www.albany.edu/sourcebook (Criminal Justice Statistics)

LAW AND JUSTICE ORGANIZATIONS

http://www.law.cornell.edu (Legal Information Institute)

http:oicj.acsp.uic.edu/spearmint (Office of International Criminal Justice)

http://www.splcenter.org/splc.html (Southern Poverty Law Center)

http://193.123.144.14/interpol.com (Interpol)

http://www.fire-investigators.org (International Association of Arson Investigators)

http://www.ict.org.il/inter_ter/attacksearch.cfm (The Interdisciplinary Center's guide to terrorist attacks) http:www.bsos.umd.edu/asc/four.htm (American Society of Criminology)

http://aclu.org/issues/criminal/hmcj.html (ACLU's criminal justice home page)

PRIVATE ORGANIZATIONS

http://www.coplink.com/HOME.htm (news of and for the law enforcement community)

http://www.noblenatl.org (National Organization of Black Law Enforcement Executives)

http://www.corrections.com/aja (American Jail Association)

http://www.criminaljusticepress.com (publisher)

http://www.apai.org (American Police Association)

http://www.terrorism.com

http://www.crime-times.org/titles.htm (sponsored by the Wacker Foundation)

www.crime-free.org

LINKS TO OTHER CRIMINAL JUSTICE AND RELATED SITES

http://www.staff.uiuc.edu/~royw/row_ho10. HTM#links (compiled by Roy A. Walker, Ph.D, University of Illinois Police Training Institute)

http://www.apbonline.com (police and crime news)

http://faculty.ncwc.edu/toconnor (compiled by Tom O'Connor, Ph.D., at North Carolina Wesleyan College)

http://www.policeforum.org/index (sponsored by the Police Executive Research Forum)

http://www.appstate.edu/~robinsnmb/crime. htm (links compiled by Matt B. Robinson, Ph.D.)

APPENDIX D

JURIED/REFEREED JOURNALS

(Journals that have outside experts judge submitted manuscripts on merit alone, without knowledge of the author's identity.)

ADVANCES IN CRIMINOLOGICAL THEORY (annually). Affiliation: School of Criminal Justice, Rutgers University, 15 Washington St., Newark, NJ 07102. (201) 648-5073.

AMERICAN JOURNAL OF CRIMINAL JUSTICE (Spring/Fall). Affiliation: The Southern Criminal Justice Association. Published by the School of Justice Administration, College of Urban and Public Affairs, University of Louisville, Louisville, KY 40292. (502) 588-6567.

AMERICAN JOURNAL OF CRIMINAL LAW (3 times a year). Managing Editor, 727 E. 26th St., Austin, TX 78705. (512) 471-9200.

AMERICAN JOURNAL OF POLICE (quarterly). Affiliation: Police Executive Research Forum (PERF) and Police Section of the Academy of Criminal Justice Sciences. Published by AMP, the University of Nebraska–Omaha, Department of Criminal Justice, Omaha, NE 68182-0149.

CRIME AND DELINQUENCY Published by Sage (quarterly). Submit manuscripts to Don Gibbons, Ph.D., 1100 S.W. Hillcroft, Portland, OR 97225.

CRIMINAL JUSTICE AND BEHAVIOR Published by Sage (quarterly). Submit manuscripts to CJB, Curt R. Bartol, Ph.D., Dept. of Psychology, Castleton State College, Castleton, VT 05735.

CRIMINAL JUSTICE ETHICS (semiannually). Affiliation: John Jay College of Criminal Justice, 899 Tenth Ave., New York, NY 10019 (212) 237-8415.

CRIMINAL JUSTICE JOURNAL (semiannually). Affiliation: Western State University College of Law, 2121 San Diego Ave., San Diego, CA (619) 298-3111.

CRIMINAL JUSTICE POLICY REVIEW (quarterly). Affiliation: Department of Criminology, Indiana University of Pennsylvania, Indiana, PA 15701. (412) 357-2471.

CRIMINAL JUSTICE REVIEW (Spring/Fall). Affiliation: American Society for Public Administration. Published by the College of Public and Urban Affairs, Georgia State University, Atlanta, GA 30303-3091. (404) 651-3515.

CRIMINOLOGY (quarterly). Affiliation: American Society of Criminology. Published by ASC, 1314 Kinnear Road, Columbus, OH 43212. (614) 292-9207.

GANG JOURNAL: AN INTERDISCIPLINARY RESEARCH QUARTERLY Affiliation: Department of Criminal Justice, Chicago State University, 95th St. at King Drive, HWH 329, Chicago, IL 60628. (312) 995-2108.

HOMICIDE STUDIES Published by Sage (quarterly). Submit manuscripts to HSIIJ, M. Dwayne Smith, Ph.D., Dept. of Sociology, University of North Carolina at Charlotte, Charlotte, NC 28223.

INTERNATIONAL JOURNAL OF LAW AND PSYCHIATRY (quarterly). Affiliation: International Academy of Law and Mental Health. Published by Pergamon Press, c/o Osgoode Hall Law School, York University, 4700 Keele St., Downsview, Ontario M3J 2R5, Canada.

INTERNATIONAL JOURNAL OF OFFENDER THERAPY AND COMPARATIVE CRIMINOLOGY Published by Sage (quarterly). Submit manuscripts to IJOTCC, George B. Palermo, M.D., 925 East Wells St., Milwaukee, WI 53202

JOURNAL FOR JUVENILE JUSTICE AND DETENTION SERVICES (biannually). Affiliation: National Juvenile Detention Association. Contact JJJDS, Dept. of Correctional and Juvenile Justice Studies, Eastern Kentucky University, 105 Stratton Bldg., Richmond, KY 40475-3102. (606) 622-1155.

JOURNAL OF CONTEMPORARY CRIMINAL JUSTICE Published by Sage (quarterly). Affiliation: Department of Criminal Justice, California State University, Long Beach. For themes and guest editors, contact George E. Rush, Ph.D., Dept. of Criminal Justice, 1250 Bellflower Boulevard, Long Beach, CA 90840.

JOURNAL OF CORRECTIONAL EDU-CATION (quarterly). Published by Karez, McGing, and Associates. 26 E. Exchange St., St. Paul, MN 55101 (612) 224-3340.

JOURNAL OF CRIME AND JUSTICE (biannually). Affiliation: Midwestern Criminal Justice Association. Published by JCJ, Bowling Green State University, Criminal Justice Program, Bowling Green, OH 43403.

JOURNAL OF CRIMINAL JUSTICE ED-UCATION (Spring/Fall). Affiliation: Academy of Criminal Justice Sciences. Published by the School of Criminal Justice, State University of New York at Albany, Albany, NY 12222. (518) 455-6322.

JOURNAL OF INTERPERSONAL VIO-LENCE Published by Sage (monthly). Submit manuscripts to JIV, Jon R. Conte, Ph.D., School of Social Work, University of Washington, 4101 15th Ave., NE, Mailstop 354900, Seattle, WA 98195.

JOURNAL OF OFFENDER REHABILI-TATION (quarterly). Affiliation: Newhouse Center for Law and Justice, Rutgers State University, 15 Washington St., Newark, NJ 07102 (908) 753-4030.

JOURNAL OF POLICE AND CRIMI-NAL PSYCHOLOGY (semiannually). Affiliation: Department of Criminal Justice, Southwest Texas State University, San Marcos, TX 78666 (512) 245-2174.

JOURNAL OF PRISON AND JAIL HEALTH (semiannually). Affiliation: Department of Social Medicine, Montefiore Hospital and Medical Center, 111 E. 210th St., Bronx, NY 10467 (212) 920-6226.

JOURNAL OF QUANTITATIVE CRIM-INOLOGY (quarterly). Printed by Plenum Publishing Corporation. Published by JQC, College of Criminal Justice, Northeastern University, 360 Huntington Ave., Boston, MA 02115.

JOURNAL OF RESEARCH ON CRIME AND DELINQUENCY (quarterly). Published by Sage. Send manuscripts to JRCD, Mercer Sullivan, Ph.D., School of Criminal Justice, 15 Washington Street, Rutgers Campus at Newark, Newark, NJ 07102.

JUDICATURE: THE JOURNAL OF THE AMERICAN JUDICATURE SOCIETY (bimonthly). Published by AJS, 25 East Washington Street, Chicago, IL 60602. (312) 558-6900.

JUSTICE QUARTERLY (quarterly). Affiliation: Academy of Criminal Justice Sciences (ACJS). Published by ACJS, 402 Nunn Hall, Northern Kentucky University, Highland Heights, KY 41076-1448. (606) 572-5634.

POLICE PRACTICE AND RESEARCH (quarterly). Affiliation: International Police Executive Symposium. Submit manuscripts to PPR, Arvind Verma, Dept. of Criminal Justice, Indiana University, Bloomington, IN 47405.

POLICE STUDIES: THE INTERNA-TIONAL REVIEW OF POLICE DEVEL-OPMENT (quarterly). Affiliation: Police Section of the Academy of Criminal Justice Sciences. Published by Police Studies, John Jay College of Criminal Justice, Office of Publications, 899 10th Ave., New York, NY 10019.

POLICING (quarterly). Published by Police Review Publishing Company, 14 St. Cross Street, London E1N 8FE, England.

PRISON JOURNAL: AN INTERNATION-AL FORUM ON INCARCERATION AND ALTERNATIVE SANCTIONS (quarterly). Published by Sage. Send manuscripts to TPPJI-FIAS, Alan Harlan, Ph.D., Dept. of Criminal Justice, Gladfelter Hall, 5th Floor, Temple University, Philadelphia, PA 19122.

SOCIOLOGY AND SOCIAL RESEARCH JOURNAL (quarterly). No affiliation. Published by the Department of Sociology, University of Southern California, University Park, Los Angeles, CA 90089-2539. (213) 743-2658.

THE JUSTICE PROFESSIONAL (Spring/Fall). No affiliation. Printed by Wyndham Hall Press. Published by Department of Sociology and

Social Work, Pembroke State University, Pembroke, NC 28372. (919) 521-4214.

THEORETICAL CRIMINOLOGY (quarterly). Affiliation: Department of Criminology, University of Southern Maine, 1 Chamberlain Ave., Portland, ME 04103.

TRAUMA, VIOLENCE, & ABUSE: A REVIEW JOURNAL (TVAR) (quarterly). Published by Sage. Submit manuscripts to TVAR, Jon R. Conte, Ph.D., School of Social Work, University of Washington, 4101 15th Ave., NE, Mailstop 354900, Seattle, WA 98195.

VIOLENCE AGAINST WOMEN: AN INTERNATIONAL AND INTERDISCIPLINARY JOURNAL (monthly). Published by Sage. Submit manuscripts to VAWIIJ, Claire M. Renzetti, Ph.D., Dept. of Sociology, St. Joseph's University, Philadelphia, PA 19131.

WOMEN IN CRIMINAL JUSTICE (bi-annual). Published by The Haworth Press, Inc., 10 Alice Street, Binghamton, NY 13904-1580. (800) 342-9678.